Readings in the International Relations of Africa

IAI International African Institute

Readings in African Studies

Series Editors
Jocelyn Alexander, University of Oxford
David Pratten, University of Oxford

Readings in African Popular Culture
Edited by Karin Barber

Readings in African Popular Fiction
Edited by Stephanie Newell

Readings in African Politics
Edited by Tom Young

Readings in Gender in Africa
Edited by Andrea Cornwall

Readings in Modernity in Africa
Edited by Peter Geschiere, Birgit Meyer, and Peter Pels

This series makes available to students a representative selection of the best and most exciting work in fields where standard textbooks have hitherto been lacking. Such fields may be located anywhere across the full range of Africanist humanities and social sciences. The emphasis is on newly emerging fields or fields that cross older disciplinary boundaries. The aim is to bring together central, key works—that help define the field—with other significant pieces that cut across established or conventional positions. As far as possible, all the subregions of sub-Saharan Africa are covered in each volume.

Each reader aims to include materials from journal and books, work published in Africa, and newly commissioned texts to cover significant gaps and recent developments. The significance of the readings is discussed in the introductory sections, which aim to make significant contributions in their own right. The overall level is for postgraduate and late stage undergraduate courses, and the emphasis is on assembling titles that can be used as textbooks.

Readings in the International Relations of Africa

EDITED BY TOM YOUNG

Indiana University Press • *Bloomington and Indianapolis*

This book is a publication of

Indiana University Press
Office of Scholarly Publishing
Herman B Wells Library 350
1320 East 10th Street
Bloomington, Indiana 47405 USA

iupress.indiana.edu

The paper used in this publication meets the minimum requirements of the American National Standard for Information Sciences—Permanence of Paper for Printed Library Materials, ANSI Z39.48-1992.

MANUFACTURED IN THE
UNITED STATES OF AMERICA

Library of Congress
Cataloging-in-Publication Data

Names: Young, Tom, editor.
Title: Readings in the international relations of Africa / edited by Tom Young.
Other titles: Readings in African studies.
Description: Bloomington : Indiana University Press, 2016. | Series: Readings in African studies | Includes index.
Identifiers: LCCN 2015022399| ISBN 9780253018809 (cloth : alk. paper) | ISBN 9780253018885 (pbk. : alk. paper) | ISBN 9780253018946
Subjects: LCSH: Africa—Foreign relations. | Africa—Politics and government—21st century.
Classification: LCC DT30.5 .R435 2016 | DDC 960.33—dc23 LC record available at http://lccn.loc.gov/2015022399

1 2 3 4 5 20 19 18 17 16 15

CONTENTS

ACKNOWLEDGMENTS

This volume complements an earlier one on politics. The intentions are much the same, to provide the reader with both a large collection of material from which to learn and on which to reflect, as well as a guide through the development of the field of enquiry. A number of readers of the previous volume have suggested that I craft an introduction that was more helpful, at least less interpretative, to the reader, and this advice I have tried to follow.

I am grateful to the Publications Committee of the International African Institute for its painstakingly meticulous examination of many versions of the volume's design and contents as well as to the support of the editors of the series in which it appears. I am grateful also to Richard Al-Qaq for permission to reprint his work and to Richard for helpful suggestions on how the volume might be organized. Two of the texts reproduced here are by former PhD students of mine (Al-Qaq and Kelsall). A fact I mention to acknowledge not only how much I learned from them, but also to pay tribute to their dogged determination to pursue enquiry in directions not always congenial to received wisdom, a virtue with which British academia at least is not self-evidently oversupplied. Another former student David Williams and I have continued a modest collaboration over the years around some of the themes raised in this book. In the introduction I have almost certainly borrowed ideas and formulations from him, and this also I would like to acknowledge. Finally, I must express my gratitude to Stephanie Kitchen, managing editor of the International African Institute for guiding this volume through some considerable technical difficulties and problems.

NOTE ON ORIGINAL SOURCES

While some of the content has been written specially for this Reader, most of the material included here has been extracted from published sources and selectively edited or abridged. References, bibliographies, and notes have for the most part been omitted to render the texts as self-contained and coherent as possible. A full reference to the original publication or source is given in the List of Original Sources at the end of the Reader. Readers are encouraged to pursue their interests by consulting the full versions.

Readings in the International Relations of Africa

INTRODUCTION

Tom Young

THE DISCIPLINE OF INTERNATIONAL RELATIONS AND AFRICA

Academic literature on Africa and international relations is still relatively rare, and what there is often consists of little more than lengthy complaints about the lack of consideration of Africa, or the non-Western world more generally, within the discipline of International Relations (IR). More often than not, such complaints go on to hint at some nefarious motive for this neglect, either, at worst, "racism," or, almost as bad, lack of ethical concern, or, and perhaps more usually, conceptual and/or empirical irrelevance or blindness.[1] Tempting though it would be to suggest that the endless repetition of the word *racism* is rarely illuminating in theory or in life (Hobson), that IR scholars might legitimately feel that there is little they can usefully say about volcanoes or mud slides (Thomas and Wilkin), and that it is not ethnocentric to suggest that the notion of "human rights" is of Western provenance (Kayaoglu), space precludes picking apart these arguments here. Rather, I will limit myself to the observation that much of this complaint is somewhat overdone, and we can see that there are a number of reasons for the relative lack of interest of IR in Africa, some to do with the state of the world and some to do with the way in which IR has tried to understand that world.

The first reason is that the object of IR theory, the world of states and their relations, is both relatively modern and of essentially Western origin. Many of its structures, practices, and norms were in place by the early nineteenth century. African polities did not participate in creating this conceptualization, indeed in some ways, they were victims of it. To make this point is not to commit the sin of "Eurocentrism," but to assert simple fact. Second, IR theory also tended to concentrate its attention not merely on states, but even among them on the Great Powers, and this also tended to reflect the reality of international politics in the nineteenth and twentieth centuries. Although African states have now been independent for some fifty years or so, none of them has yet become a Great Power, or even a medium-sized power. On any of the criteria normally used by scholars, and indeed other observers, to measure the strength of states—for example, population, economic output, size of armed forces, weapons manufacturing, and so on—all African states remain weak, with little capacity to project force. These two reasons for the relative neglect of Africa by IR were reinforced by a third: not only have no African states become Great Powers, in many ways, they do not seem to function like states at all. That is to say, they were and still are characterized by very limited degrees of social cohesion and very limited state capacities in general. African polities, and later African states, were unlikely to attract much attention from an academic discipline that developed in a world dominated by Great Powers—in the nineteenth century, the major European states, and in the twentieth century, the superpowers—an academic discipline that took pride in emphasizing the centrality of states, an intellectual position that came to be known as "realism."[2]

But even if we reject some of the more exaggerated accusations thrown at IR theory, we can still acknowledge that, however understandable it might have been in certain historical contexts, there was always a degree of intellectual myopia about realism's tendency to ignore certain plainly international phenomena even in the nineteenth-century heyday of the Great Powers. How, for example, could one explain the campaigns against the Atlantic (and other) slave trades on the basis of realist assumptions, ignoring the role of changes in beliefs, a Christian sense of mission, and so on?[3] Or how could one account for the attitudes of the European powers toward the American Civil War without taking note of notions about freedom and equality as well as calculations of power and interest?[4] This purely intellectual myopia was and is not so much a function of the historical context in which the IR discipline emerged, but is better explained in terms of certain peculiar cognitive features of that discipline, particularly in its American variants. Two of these features are critical here. First, IR operated with rather simple-minded notions of "interests" (particularly of states but to some extent beyond them) as though they were simply given facts in the world. Second, thinking of interests in this manner seemed to offer a way to connect with notions of science and system in the fond (but foolish) belief that eventually knowledge of international relations would acquire a genuinely "scientific" status.[5]

Whatever the rights and wrongs of these debates (and these are weighty issues which cannot be pursued here) in the early twenty-first century, it is clear that all of these reasons for the disconnect between Africa and International Relations are becoming less plausible.[6] The international order may be of Western origin, but it is now participated in by many, indeed virtually all, states. African states may be weak, but some of them are becoming regionally dominant, and many possess resources that the world increasingly wants. We live in an age when power politics of the old-fashioned kind is frowned on in many circles and the conduct of international politics is articulated in a different vocabulary. Even though "globalization" may have become a cliché, it is clear that the sovereignty of states is increasingly challenged by new forms of international order. Finally, we might note that IR as a discipline, partly for all these reasons, having once been a model of realist and positivist rectitude, has exploded into a thousand fragments, all engaged in vigorous (some might say chaotic) dispute, but certainly all the more interesting for that![7]

SOVEREIGNTY AND STATEHOOD

How then are we to make sense of Africa's relations with the world? Even if states have become, or appear to have become, less important in recent times, we cannot ignore them. The central political fact here is that between 1957 and 1980 some forty-five or so independent, or sovereign, states emerged in sub-Saharan Africa. Although sovereignty is often said to be a muddled or incoherent idea, the contrast between colonialism and independence makes its core meaning very clear.[8]

Colonial rule is precisely the denial of sovereignty. During the nineteenth century, the European Great Powers conquered virtually the whole of sub-Saharan Africa and imposed their rule on the new territories that they divided between them.[9] It is true that this rule was modified by all sorts of practical limitations (shortage of resources and manpower, intermittent resistance by indigenous populations, the sheer size of some territories), but the principle of alien rule was clear. Equally clear was that barely a few decades later, African nationalists began to demand independence and sovereignty. They knew exactly what they meant: sovereignty was the right to throw off alien rule and acquire independent statehood. What *sovereignty* means then is that a people and their state cannot legitimately be ruled by another people and state. Or to put it another way, no other state can legislate for, say, the United States. It is important to acknowledge the normative aspect of this. The idea of sovereignty does not say that other states cannot put pressure on or threaten the United States, simply that they cannot legislate for it. Sovereignty, in other words, is something that very weak states (such as Tuvalu) have, but much bigger political organizations (such as California) or capitalist enterprises (such as Shell Oil) do not have. In this rather narrow sense, we might say that sovereignty is an either/or concept: either you have it or you do not.

So far so good. The difficulty, however, is that the notion of sovereignty, or self-rule, is linked to a set of other political ideas and concepts that are much more ambiguous and contested. A moment's reflection on the term *self-rule,* for example, raises questions about "the self" (in a political sense), the answers to which are not obvious. Are Americans a people? Are Zambians? How is "a people" to be defined? In practice, the way in which these terms are used together is informed by the process of state formation in earlier historical periods. Clearly this process had involved virtually endless conflict, the maintenance and vigilant guarding of borders, and the mobilization of resources to sustain a capacity for self-defense (consider all the implications of this: taxation, universal conscription into military service, the creation of national symbols, and so on).[10] The term *state* then gradually came to denote two linked features: internally, states were entities that had consolidated control over a territory and a population; externally, they could defend themselves, either on their own or in alliance with others. But these features are clearly much more a question of degree: one can imagine more or less control of territory and population and so on. So in this broader sense, sovereignty is at least more open to interpretation. There is a further complication. Because sovereign states need to maintain relationships with each other, the sovereignty of any one state is partly a matter of its "recognition" by other states. Just as in life, we can sometimes pretend that a situation is so (when it is not) or that it is not so (when it is), so states can, and do, sometimes pretend that entities that look like states are not, and that entities that do not look like states, are.[11]

These conceptual issues notwithstanding, African states certainly did not come into the world as a result of long-term historical changes of the European type. Although there is much to argue about as to the causes of decolonization, what is indisputable is that it was a much more rapid process than had been anticipated and was shaped by a new set of norms.[12] The first normative change was that no status short of full sovereignty was acceptable to territories and political movements claiming independence. Whereas in earlier historical periods, for example after both world wars, all kinds of trusteeship-type arrangements had been conceivable, by the 1950s, the either/or understanding of sovereignty was unchallenged. The second change was that no conceivable set of circumstances could be allowed as grounds for withholding independence from a territory claiming it.[13] These two changes were connected. Whereas historically it had been assumed that there were preconditions for statehood (for example, a certain degree of development, or a contiguous territory, or a degree of political unity), and it was therefore possible to conceive of limited degrees of statehood, all such preconditions were now swept away. Independence was available to any people or territory demanding it. Finally, and quite crucially in the African case, the "self" in the idea of "self-determination" came to be understood as applying not to *peoples,* as that term had been understood—that is, an organized group with some sense of identity and historical place—but rather to the territory itself. It was for that reason, among others, that African nationalists insisted that colonial boundaries remain sacrosanct.

This particular combination of historical and conceptual circumstances led to the emergence of a class of states that had not had the historical experience of gradual formation but were recognized, overnight as it were, as states by other states. It was this dramatic change in world politics after the Second World War that led some scholars to coin the term *quasi-states.* The idea was that these new states were in some ways state-like (they were treated as states by other states and in terms of international law), so they possessed what Jackson calls "juridical" sovereignty, but in other ways they lacked certain features of statehood. For example, they did not necessarily fully control their own territory or have monopoly control of the use of force within it. In Jackson's terms, they lacked "empirical" sovereignty.[14] While it is true that the term *quasi-state,* and the analysis behind it, remains contested by some scholars, many others have found it useful in making sense of the location of African states in the international order.[15]

AFRICA AND THE INTERNATIONAL ORDER

As African states became independent, they faced the issues that all states face: consolidating their internal social and political institutions and practices, and learning to conduct their relations with other states and international institutions. The first of these is not our primary concern, though we will see that it is impossible to avoid some reflection on the nature of African statehood.[16] As regards the second, however, it can be suggested that newly independent African states faced three different kinds of problem in negotiating their place in world politics. First, they had to engage with an international order not of their making, which had shifted in quite substantial ways after the Second World War. Second, they had to manage relations with their old colonial masters, who had left many marks on the colonies and whose legacy and influence, African nationalist rhetoric notwithstanding, could not easily be set aside. Third, they had to deal with the increasingly fundamental issue of international relations in the post–Second World War period, namely the confrontation between the United States and its allies and the Soviet Union and its allies, the confrontation known as the Cold War.

The discussion of the idea of quasi-states has already suggested that one of the most dramatic changes in the international order was decolonization, indeed that decolonization was the extension on a global scale of the arrangements that the European Great Powers had constructed for themselves perhaps as far back as the Treaty of Westphalia (1648), which had first registered the idea of states as sovereign. With decolonization, for the first time in international history, all entities carrying the label *state* were conceived of as sovereign, and their sovereignty was of the same value.[17] Not only were African states a product of decolonization, but the shifts in understanding of sovereignty proved very advantageous for these states, as their implications were developed and became clearer. As Clapham puts it, "if there was ever a moment for poor, divided and defenceless states to take their bow on the international stage, the fifteen years or so after 1956 provided it."[18] There were at least three aspects to this. First, the postwar order consolidated strong normative sanctions (for example, in the Charter of the United Nations) against the use of armed force between states except on grounds of self-defense. Second, it increasingly asserted the absolute illegitimacy of colonial rule. Third, it increasingly maintained the inviolability of inherited frontiers and the impermissibility of external interference in the internal affairs of states. The significance of this was considerable. Weak states, which in the historical past would have certainly been dominated—if not annexed—by stronger ones, did not have to provide in any serious sense for their own defense because conquest and annexation were no longer acceptable.

But the postwar order provided a second advantage to African states: a substantial aid regime. There are all sorts of arguments about aid (its motives, effects, and so on), some of which will be touched on in this volume, but the crucial point is that this was a historically unprecedented commitment by one group of states (primarily Western) to effect large-scale transfers of resources to another group of states.[19] Though it was on nothing like the same scale, this state aid was supplemented by an increasing volume of aid provided by what are now called nongovernmental organizations. The significance of this was also considerable, in that, for many African states, relatively plentiful resources were available to supplement meagre national budgets. During this period, neither donor states nor nongovernmental organizations considered that the aid they provided justified interference in the internal affairs of the receiving states. Finally, we should note that it took some time before the illegitimacy of colonial rule had effects on those parts of Africa where colonial powers or white rulers refused to cede power peacefully, namely the Portuguese Empire (now Angola, Mozambique, Guinea-Bissau, Cape Verde, and São Tomé and Príncipe), Rhodesia (now Zimbabwe), and South Africa. By the early 1970s, however, anticolonialism had become a global cause. Whatever the justice of that cause, it must be acknowledged that the enormous political capital generated by the illegitimacy of colonialism could be used to direct attention against white settler rule in the southern part of the continent, while obscuring developments elsewhere. To be blunt, massacres in Rwanda or Burundi were ignored; massacres in Mozambique or South Africa grabbed the attention of the world.

AN AFRICAN ORDER

In the immediate aftermath of independence, African states had to adapt to the world order, but part of that adaptation over which they had more control was to shape relations among themselves. As with relations between states anywhere else, such relations had elements of "order" and elements of interest and power. Because of a common bond of racial oppression in the past (of which the remaining white regimes were a constant reminder) and a fear of domination in the future (they knew how weak they were), the newly independent African states fashioned for themselves both a continental organization and regional organizations that aspired to rid the continent of racial oppression, to at least place an obstacle in the way of balkanization and outside interference (a fear that seemed all the more plausible during the Congo crisis of the early 1960s), and that would also help to overcome the legacy of underdevelopment that was in part a result of colonial rule. The detailed politics of the Organisation of African Unity (OAU) is involved, but the basic points are clear.[20] Ghana's independence in 1957 under President Kwame Nkrumah, a radical who was committed to Pan-Africanism, intensified at least the rhetorical pace. But Nkrumah's radicalism elicited a conservative response from many states, notably Nigeria and Ethiopia. The OAU as it finally emerged was a compromise between the various viewpoints, and the charter that stabilized this compromise contained elements on which all African states could agree. These included the inviolability of inherited frontiers, noninterference in domestic affairs, peaceful settlement of disputes, and general opposition to colonialism and white-minority rule (institutionalized in a Liberation Committee based in Dar es Salaam). Although the institutional architecture replicated the familiar forms of other international organizations (an Assembly of Heads of State, a Council of Ministers, a General Secretariat), the ensemble was structured in such a way as to hamstring any limitations on states; in particular, there was no provision for sanctions against them. Generally speaking, decisions were to be made by consensus. These principles more or less held firm. With the exceptions of Morocco and Somalia, existing boundaries were accepted. Formally, at least, noninterference in domestic affairs also prevailed, though there were exceptions: for example, the Tanzanian intervention in Uganda in 1979 and a certain amount of covert activity. All African states maintained a highly vociferous denunciation of remaining white rule in Africa. This was something on which they could all agree, though many failed to make much contribution to overthrowing it, and some, especially Malawi and Côte d'Ivoire, even seemed prepared, at times, to compromise with it.

In addition to the OAU, African states, again like states elsewhere, set up regional organizations. Some of these were by no means novel but had been attempted in some form by the colonial powers. They included the Economic Community of West African States (1975) and the East African Community (1967). As their titles imply, these organizations (at least at this stage) had largely economic aspirations. The new African leaders were acutely aware of both their economic dependency (their economies were still largely linked to the old colonial power) and their general economic "backwardness" (small modern sectors, low productivity, and so on), and they had come into office in part on the basis of (often quite extravagant) promises of rapid economic improvement in the lives of their citizens. Individual states, even if they were relatively large, had very small markets and relatively little scope for economies of scale. In these circumstances, it seemed sensible to try to create larger economic spaces that would produce dynamic effects and enhance economic growth.

But precisely because African states themselves were weak, these projects were bound to be vitiated almost from the beginning, so that what emerged was a weak continental organization and notoriously feeble regional organizations (some of which even collapsed). The OAU rarely secured any political consensus among African leaders, while the results of the regional organizations were uniformly disappointing and they failed to do the one thing they were supposed to do: increase intraregional trade. While the weak-state factor is the largest part of the explanation, there were a number of other factors in play. It was perhaps unrealistic to expect leaders who had just attained sovereignty (however constrained in fact) to surrender substantial elements of that sovereignty the day after. Political, ideological, and even personality differences between leaders (for example, between Idi Amin of Uganda and Julius Nyerere of Tanzania) played a role. Regional structures often polarize the benefits of regional organizations and produce unequal gains (Kenya, for example, gained much more than Uganda or Tanzania in the East African Community) and the tensions over such matters were difficult to manage. Such organizations faced severe structural obstacles anyway in the nature of African economies, because African countries tend to have rather similar endowments (exporting and importing similar goods), so there is little trade potential between them.

AFRICA AND THE GREAT (AND NOT SO GREAT) POWERS

Although the international order was relatively supportive of newly independent African states, and they designed a regional architecture that would further buttress their still fragile independence, they could not avoid relations with other states. One group of countries that would remain central to the international relations of African states, decades of anticolonial rhetoric notwithstanding, were the old colonial powers. Britain and France had possessed the lion's share of African colonies. Both decolonized at around the same time, both retained considerable influence, and both sought to create associations of states within which they could retain some prestige (the British Commonwealth and *Francophonie*). Generally speaking, relations between African states and the old colonial powers remained cordial, even warm. The ex-colonial masters tended to favor their ex-colonies, although they were not of high priority, through trading and other arrangements. Unavoidably, as African states struggled to master the arts of independence and government, they remained dependent on metropolitan models, in administration, welfare, education, and much else. Quite a number of colonial officials stayed on to advise and work for the new governments, which also helped to ensure a degree of continuity.[21]

Yet the differences between France and Britain, or rather the French and British governments, were striking and important. In the British case, it was almost as if Africa fell off the map. Although much attention was devoted to the unfinished business of decolonization (notably Rhodesia/Zimbabwe, and in a rather different way South Africa), it was precisely that—unfinished business—and not part of an ongoing commitment to or interest in Africa. The British political class almost entirely abandoned any interest in Africa; Tony Blair (U.K. Prime Minister 1997–2007) was the first political figure of any stature since decolonization to take an interest in the continent. France, by contrast, continued to be heavily involved with its ex-colonies. It maintained defensive alliances with and stationed troops in a number of them. The interaction between the French political elite and francophone African elites remained substantial (and they were and are culturally much closer).[22] Perhaps most importantly, virtually every French president has taken a close interest in African issues, and France's Africa policy has remained very much a presidential matter, run from the Elysée Palace and entirely distinct from the supervision of the Ministry of Foreign Affairs.[23] It should be noted, however, that in the wider societies of France and Britain, the roles were almost entirely reversed. There was little popular concern about Africa in France until quite recently, whereas significant sections of British society were concerned with opposition to apartheid and the issues of poverty and "development" more generally.

Unlike Britain and France, neither of the superpowers that so rapidly came to dominate the world after 1945 had any great interest (or interests) in Africa, though they had some marginal historical involvement (the United States with Liberia and the Union of Soviet Socialist Republics with Ethiopia). Certainly neither had a colonial history (in Africa at least), and both could plausibly claim (this was perhaps the one area of agreement, if tacit, between them) that they were hostile to European colonialism. Nor, with the partial exception of the Horn, did Africa's regions form part of either superpower's hinterland or an area of confrontation. Both superpowers came to Africa through their wider confrontation. In the Soviet case, it was not until after Stalin's death (1953) that the USSR began vigorously to support the call for colonial independence; indeed such a position became an increasingly useful part of the Soviet stance toward the West, as supporting liberation movements gained it widespread sympathy in the Third World. The emerging logic of the Cold War pushed the decolonization process forward, but also inclined the United States not to pressure its junior allies, either because of fears about communism or, in the case of Portugal, as a result of the overriding need for access to the North Atlantic Treaty Organization base in the Azores (mid-Atlantic islands that form part of metropolitan Portugal). The United Nations became an important arena in which the superpowers tried to solicit the support of smaller states, or at least head off disapproval. We should note the interesting and special case of South Africa, which raised almost all these issues in an acute form. It was a long-standing ally of the West, which maintained an internal racial order of white domination that was increasingly unpalatable to Western opinion. The Cold War logic of supporting regimes that were resolutely anti-Soviet stumbled here, because South Africa was an anti-Soviet regime that could not be supported.

The period sometimes called the Second Cold War (roughly between the U.S. withdrawal from Vietnam in 1975 and the mid-1980s) saw a greater degree of Soviet global activism. It is important to remember that for much of the Cold War period, the United States was by far the more powerful country. It was only by the 1970s that the USSR had to some extent caught up with its rival, particularly in the capacity to project force globally, and in a greater degree of political boldness and willingness to intervene in distant parts of the world. Proxy confrontations intensified; in Africa, these changes showed themselves in the flashpoints of southern Africa, with the collapse of the Portuguese Empire, and in the revolution in Ethiopia in 1974. In both of these places, we saw the complexities of relations both between the superpowers and their allies (notably the USSR and Cuba) and in relation to regional dynamics. Analysts disagree as to the extent to which the superpowers imposed themselves on Africa or were drawn into African conflicts in which local actors played the lead role, but certainly an excessively simply picture of superpower domination is not plausible: junior allies always have some room to maneuver.

AFTER THE COLD WAR: CONFLICT, WAR, AND INTERVENTION

Many observers had hoped, and expected, that with the end of the Cold War, and especially with the end of apartheid in South Africa, a new era for the world and Africa would dawn. There were, it is true, some gains. Southern African states were no longer destabilized and the Western powers no longer thought they needed to bolster unsavory regimes simply because they had been "anti-Communist." Despite these gains, however, other developments brought much greater misery for Africa than most observers had expected. There were three main reasons for this. The first, and arguably the most important, was the weakening of many African states. The task of nation-building, the hard business of welding together disparate groups into something like a coherent political entity, has proved much more difficult in Africa than (almost) anyone had foreseen. Difficult enough in itself, the task of building nation-states proved even more intractable in the economic circumstances of the late 1980s and early 1990s, when many African economies suffered a precipitous economic decline, which encouraged violent social protest and political opposition. Second, the end of the Cold War removed two constraints on African insurgents. Small arms became much easier to obtain (particularly from certain countries once part of, or allies of, the USSR), and a much more globalized world made it easier for armed movements to sell valuable natural resources (diamonds, tropical hardwoods, coltan—a substance used in the manufacture of mobile phones) to fund their activities. At least as important, the end of the Cold War removed an ideological constraint: the superpowers and their allies had demanded a certain degree of conformity to their own ideological viewpoints, or insurgent movements thought such conformity necessary to secure continuing support. But a new generation of African insurgencies began to abandon such ideological compliance and turned to local meanings and expressions that were more difficult for outsiders to make sense of.[24] Third, we can point to an increasing tendency on the part of African states to ignore the norms of noninterference that they had put in place in the OAU Charter. African states became increasingly prepared to intervene with force in their neighbors' affairs, if they judged it to be in their own interests.

The outside world might well have washed its hands of these matters, but increasingly it did not, for a number of reasons.[25] First, not the least of the effects of the end of apartheid in South Africa was that attention could not be so easily distracted from problems elsewhere in Africa and, given the desperate poverty of most African people, increasing levels of conflict came to be seen by the outside world as unacceptable. Second, the end of the Cold War made the whole idea of supporting unsavory regimes, just because they were (or claimed to be) anti-Soviet or anti-Communist, redundant. The most obvious casualty of this development was President Mobutu of Congo/Zaire, who had been consistently supported by both the United States and the World Bank while presiding over one of the most venal and incompetent regimes Africa has ever experienced. Third, the United Nations, which, for its supporters at least, had always been hamstrung by the superpower confrontation, was now free to perform the roles that many had once hoped it would, of bringing about peace, and also development, in the world. Finally, there were important changes in the world of ideas, particularly in the idea of sovereignty. Here we can see an interesting effect of the ambiguities around state recognition. Western states, at least, increasingly espoused the idea that sovereignty was more than something possessed by states, but rather inheres in the relation between states and their citizens. The details of these arguments are often quite complex, but the basic thrust is very clear: to distinguish "proper" states, whose sovereignty must be respected, from others, whose sovereignty can, at least in certain circumstances, be overruled.

It was the conjunction of these developments, inside and outside Africa, that brought about what might be called a "new humanitarianism." There were (and are) many aspects to this, but the crucial one was a much greater willingness to intervene to prevent conflict. Whereas earlier, during the Cold War, ferocious conflicts in Rwanda, Burundi, and Zaire, and a great deal of smaller-scale political violence all over Africa, had attracted relatively little outside interest, now they were at the center of global attention. Such interventions have taken many forms, and it is by no means clear even now that such variety will not continue. Some interventions have been full-blown U.N. ("blue helmet") operations (Somalia and Mozambique in 1992); some have been carried out by one power under U.N. auspices (France in Rwanda in 1994); and some have been unilateral interventions subsequently legitimated by international agreement (Britain in Sierra Leone in 2002). But beneath this variety, one clear trend is unmistakable, namely an increasing willingness to intervene in African conflicts on a particular side.

GLOBALIZATION AND A NEW WORLD ORDER?

This tendency to intervene in support of one set of combatants rather than another points to a second dimension of outside engagement with Africa going beyond mere conflict-prevention. Such conflicts as that in Somalia—but many others in Africa (Sudan, Sierra Leone, Liberia, Rwanda, Burundi, Uganda, Côte d'Ivoire)—the dynamics of which seem largely internal, have fuelled calls for different kinds of intervention, not as a form of prevention but rather to ensure that they do not happen again. So it is not merely that in the post–Cold War world conflict in Africa has become a matter of global concern, but that the factors that apparently cause such conflicts have also come under the microscope and led to demands for political and social change within African states. It could be argued that this process began before the end of the Cold War. By the 1980s, the Bretton Woods institutions (the International Monetary Fund and the World Bank) were demanding that African states make fundamental changes to their economic policies. But at this point, sovereignty was still deeply ingrained in the working norms of international organizations, and African states, although deemed to be pursuing "mistaken" policies, were still considered to be committed to "development." Constrained by sovereignty, the international financial institutions limited themselves to imposing certain "conditionalities"—that is, demanding changes in economic policy linked to access to financial and other resources.[26]

Gradually, however, and certainly after the end of the Cold War, this gave way to a view that African states were not merely incompetent but malign, not part of the solution, but part, indeed most, of the problem. Not only did they seem unable to resolve conflict, but they also often seemed actively to promote it; not only did they seem uncommitted to development, but they also seemed positively uninterested in it. This shift in understanding generated a whole new vocabulary of "failed states" (and many synonyms), and, along with the gradual erosion of the notion of sovereignty, it became possible to think and act along two possible lines of engagement. The first is best understood as an extension of the idea of conditionality, initially imposed within the narrow field of economic policy-making. It was obviously possible to extend the scope of such conditionalities to virtually any field of policy, so by the 1990s, the Bretton Woods institutions were indeed interfering freely, indeed virtually no policy area remained outside their purview. But beyond that process these and other international agencies now sought to change not merely particular policies but the form of the African state. This led in the direction of what came to be known as "governance," that is to say not just the capacities of the state to carry out certain functions, but more generally the relationship between the state and the wider society (so encompassing such matters as the legal system).[27] Elaborate programs were designed both to increase the capacity of African states and to greatly restructure them.

These programs did not necessarily meet with great success, but the increasing tendency to treat African states and societies as problems to be operated on encouraged yet more engagement with their internal social and political structures. Indeed the relative failure of governance structures opened up a second line of engagement that focused not on African states but on the social forces within them. Here the argument suggested that changes in African states could be brought about only by local social forces, but these needed to be mobilized and encouraged from outside. This led to calls not merely for electoral democracy, but also for major processes of social change along the lines of Western liberal society. The historical parallels are fascinating. Although the demands for social change are no longer articulated in the aggressive accents of nineteenth-century colonialism, with its talk of "evolution" and "civilisation," the two periods, the colonial and the post–Cold War, exhibit remarkable similarities. Where the nineteenth century said "civilisation," the twenty-first says "human rights," but the substance is identical. Western forms of social organization are not merely superior forms, but the only thinkable ones, and African societies must emulate them as rapidly as possible.

AN AFRICAN RENAISSANCE?

These developments could hardly go unnoticed in Africa itself. By the late 1990s, the feeling was growing, at least among some African leaders, that it was necessary for the continent to change direction. This mood was driven forward by a group of larger African countries, which were inclined to keep the peace in their own "backyards" partly in their own interests and partly out of a concern for regional stability. These same countries were, by virtue of their size and importance, more active on the diplomatic stage and more aware of Africa's plummeting reputation in the wider world.[28] The key players here were South Africa and Nigeria, medium-sized countries by world standards and big powers in Africa. During the 1990s, both emerged from authoritarian regimes (of rather different kinds), with new leaders recognizing that they had to adjust to new global realities. South Africa, in particular, capitalizing on the successful transition from apartheid and the universal popularity of Nelson Mandela, spoke of an "African Renaissance," a grand vision of continental renewal.[29] But this rhetoric had to be cashed out in firm proposals, which took some years of discussion with other African states. The two big issues of conflict and security on the one hand and development on the other were seen as linked. The outcome of the discussions was a two-track process of change at continental level.

One track, concerning questions of development, which came to be known as the New Economic Partnership for Africa's Development, was finally launched in Abuja, Nigeria, in 2001. The New Economic Partnership for Africa's Development documents essentially signaled two things. First, the idea that globalization, and integration into the global economy, was a necessity for Africa, indeed that it was the only way to ensure economic growth and relieve the continent's poverty. Second, that for Africa to benefit from globalization it must commit itself to major reforms in *governance,* understood, in the sense already discussed, to mean not only the capacities of states, especially those involved in the management of the economy, but also the broader notion of electoral democracy and civil society. Put simply, Africa would put its own house in order with the West's support. A number of initiatives were proposed to deliver this promise, probably the most novel being the African Peer Review Mechanism. This is a framework in which African states volunteer to be reviewed by a small group of experts who assess their general standards of governance in terms of recognized "international" and African standards. The report is made public and suggestions are made as to how the country might improve. There are, however, no sanctions attached to compliance, and it is at least questionable whether this device will make much difference to the behavior of African states.[30]

The more dramatic of the two tracks, and certainly the one with greater implications for conflict and security, was the reform of the OAU, which began in September 1999, when the organization adopted a resolution to transform itself into the African Union, a process which was completed by 2002. This process also was pushed by Nigeria and South Africa, though Libya also played a role. Although the AU Constitutive Act continued to assert the importance of African sovereignty, it added two new elements. One was a more elaborate model and a more detailed timetable for continental integration. So the African Union has equipped itself with a raft of institutions (some yet to come into operation), including a Parliament, a Court of Justice, and continent-wide economic structures. The second new principle reserved the right of the African Union to intervene in the internal affairs of member states in "grave circumstances" (crimes against humanity, human rights abuses, and so on), which also included unconstitutional changes of government. There had been some precedents for this. In 1997, the OAU had condemned the coup that removed President Kabbah of Sierra Leone and had requested African states not to cooperate with or recognize the military regime that supplanted him. But these precedents became principles only with the new AU Act. All such matters come under the purview of a Peace and Security Council (which looks much like the Security Council of the United Nations, though without permanent members).[31]

THE RETURN OF GEOPOLITICS?

For twenty years or so after the end of the Cold War, virtually all the policy debate, and much of the academic debate, about Africa, in the face of persistent poverty and continued political instability, turned largely on questions of development, governance, and ultimately the nature of African societies. But there have always been some scholars and analysts for whom this kind of emphasis misses a crucial point: in fact, it positively obscures the degree to which outside forces, both political and commercial, are really concerned with power and advantage in Africa. This kind of argument has always seemed more plausible at certain historical junctures, for example, in explanations of colonialism, and it should not be lightly dismissed.[32] What makes it plausible now? The two obvious new factors in the international relations of Africa are China's engagement with the continent, and oil. Indeed, these two phenomena are linked. Of the greatly enhanced role of China in Africa, there can be no doubt, but it comprises a number of different dimensions.[33] China's earlier engagement with Africa was largely shaped by the context of both the Cold War and, more particularly, the Sino-Soviet conflict (when the Chinese slogan was "against hegemonism"). The more recent phase began after the incidents around Tiananmen Square in 1989 (when the Chinese government ruthlessly suppressed domestic dissent), as a result of which China found itself widely condemned and internationally isolated. African states showed some sympathy for China's position and, partly as a response, China embarked on a much more active diplomacy aimed at, and stressing solidarity with, the underdeveloped world, especially the African countries. China no longer talks the language of revolution, but rather of the solidarity of all developing countries. A second, though not new, aspect of this diplomacy is the campaign to persuade the world that Taiwan is a part of China, not an independent state. Only four African states now recognize Taiwan. The final obvious, and perhaps most important, factor is the rapid expansion of the Chinese economy, now the third largest in the world after the United States and Japan. This astonishing growth has meant a rapid rise in its consumption of fossil fuels. It is projected that its oil consumption will more than double by 2025. China is the world's second-largest oil importer, after the United States, importing some 30 percent of its oil from Africa. Its largest presence is in Sudan, where it owns 40 percent of the biggest oil-producing company in the country, but it has also been acquiring stakes in Nigeria and Angola, Africa's two leading oil producers.

Although China's economic relations with Africa are by no means limited to oil, or even to trade, it is the connection between China and the world's oil production that has excited so much interest. The bulk of the world's oil reserves remain in the Middle East (a notoriously volatile region), so China is not the only oil consumer looking to Africa. Both China and the United States have small, declining, levels of domestic oil production. Both are seeking to diversify their sources of supply. There are many advantages to African oil. African countries are heavily dependent on the export of raw materials and therefore cannot afford to leave the oil in the ground. Their oil is often of high quality, and therefore needs less refining, and is often located offshore (Angola, Nigeria, Equatorial Guinea) and so less likely to be affected by political disruption. Finally, Africa is geologically the least well-mapped region on earth, and if there are to be major finds, they may well be on the continent, as recent prospecting and discoveries in Uganda and Ghana suggest. For all these reasons, there has been intense interest and involvement in the oil sector in Africa.[34]

At the moment it is very difficult to assess these trends, but two lines of development seem likely. All sorts of factors can change—China may experience internal upheavals, oil prices can fall as well as rise, new technologies are becoming available—which makes prediction hazardous, if not foolhardy. It seems likely that the combination of the global distribution of oil, political militancy in at least parts of the Muslim world, continued if not increased Western hostility to any challenges to its hegemony, the determination of China to become a global power, and the emergence of "middle rank powers"—India, Brazil, possibly Indonesia—will all ensure a continued interest in the world's last great mineral treasure-house, Africa. It is inevitable also that even if outside powers claim not to be interfering in Africa, given the unstable nature of much of the continent, they will in fact be dragged into greater involvement. This is clearly the case with China already. As it extends its economic activity, it will incur greater scrutiny and greater criticisms about working conditions, as recent experience in Zambia shows.[35] Despite its claims of noninterference, China has already become involved in Sudan, providing troops as part of a U.N. mission and exerting pressure on the Khartoum government to listen to the United Nations with respect to Darfur. The other line of development, which also appears likely to continue, is that the combined effect of these factors is to give African states more room to maneuver than they have had since the end of the Cold War. The advantages for African oil producers are self-evident. They can avoid the burden of debt, which hugely reduces the leverage held over them by international financial institutions, and they can exploit rivalries between different oil companies and their "parent" governments. Even the non–oil producers in Africa have more choices—for development aid, trade, and political support—with China active on the continent. The very presence of China in Africa may strengthen those voices in the West that suggest (at the moment very quietly) that we must deal with Africa as it is, not as we would like it to be. This would mean abandoning some twenty-five years of lecturing Africa and attempting to change its behavior from outside, to which many agencies have been committed. So the least that can be said is that there is rising tension between an improving agenda (promoted by Western civil society and its domestic African allies and more or less supported by Western states and the international organizations they control) and a more "realist" one based on calculations of advantage and interest.

This survey must conclude on an open-ended note. Africa's international relations, indeed its prospects more broadly, remain difficult to assess, much less predict. But some things are clear. The continent is growing at a remarkable speed. Population rates remain the highest in the world, and so Africans will constitute a much larger proportion of the world's population by 2050. The continent is urbanizing fast and will become a more and more important market, even amid widespread poverty. It is also beyond question that the continent remains extremely diverse, as do individual African states, and that many deep-seated problems remain unresolved and may well precipitate new waves of conflict both within and between states. But all history shows that conflict, tension, and violence, however regrettable they may be, are not incompatible with growth and change. While in earlier historical periods it may have made sense to regard Africa as a relatively marginal part of the world, those times have gone. In all sorts of ways, some of which we may not like, Africa is going to have effects on the world. There has never been a more interesting time to study its international relations.

NOTES

1. See, respectively, J. M. Hobson, "Is Critical Theory Always for the White West and for Western Imperialism? Beyond Westphilian towards a Post-racist Critical IR," special issue, *Review of International Studies* 33, no. S1 (2007): 91–116; C. Thomas and P. Wilkin, "Still Waiting after All These Years: The Third World on the Periphery of International Relations," *British Journal of Politics and International Relations* 6, no. 2 (2004): 241–58; T. Kayaoglu, "Westphalian Eurocentrism in International Relations Theory," *International Studies Review* 12, no. 2 (2010): 193–217. The attentive reader will note that all these articles, like the vast majority of the literature they form part of, advocate explicitly political goals.

2. There is a mountain of literature on this topic. A good, clear introduction is J. Donnelly, *Realism and International Relations* (Cambridge: Cambridge University Press, 2000).

3. For a balanced survey see Herbert S. Klein, *The Atlantic Slave Trade* (Cambridge: Cambridge University Press, 2010).

4. For an illuminating account, see A. Foreman, *A World on Fire: An Epic History of Two Nations Divided* (London: Penguin Books, 2011).

5. Even for many of the critics this aspiration remains. Cf. S. Neumann, ed., *International Relations and the Third World* (Basingstoke, Macmillan, 1998), 17.

6. For a more careful, nuanced discussion of these issues, see William Brown, "Africa and International Relations: A Comment on IR Theory, Anarchy and Statehood," *Review of International Studies* 32, no. 1 (2006): 119–43.

7. As a glance at C. Reus-Smit and D. Snidal, eds., *The Oxford Handbook of International Relations* (Oxford: Oxford University Press, 2010) would suggest. But this book merits more than a glance!

8. The literature on sovereignty is enormous. A good place to start is George Lawson and Robbie Shilliam, "Beyond Hypocrisy? Debating the 'Fact' and 'Value' of Sovereignty in Contemporary World Politics," *International Politics* 46, no. 6 (2009): 657–70.

9. For rather different approaches to this, see Niall Ferguson, *Empire: How Britain Made the Modern World* (London: Allen Lane, 2003), and T. Pakenham, *The Scramble for Africa 1876–1912* (London: Weidenfeld & Nicolson, 1991).

10. C. Tilly, "War Making and State Making as Organised Crime," in *Bringing the State Back In,* ed. P. Evans, D. Rueschemeyer, and T. Skocpol (Cambridge: Cambridge University Press, 1985). The late Charles Tilly pioneered this kind of analysis in modern scholarship.

11. As is usually the case in life, the trick is not to figure out what something "really" means but to figure out what people are doing with it.

12. For the best recent survey, see M. Shipway, *Decolonisation and Its Impact* (Oxford: Wiley-Blackwell, 2008).

13. This is the burden of the famous U.N. General Assembly resolution 1514, Declaration on the Granting of Independence to Colonial Countries and Peoples, adopted December 14, 1960.

14. R. H. Jackson, *Quasi-States: Sovereignty, International Relations & the Third World* (Cambridge: Cambridge University Press, 1990) is the classic argument.

15. The readings in Part I give the flavor of some of the debate. See also Christian Reus-Smit, "Human Rights and the Social Construction of Sovereignty," *Review of International Studies* 27, no. 4 (2001): 519–38.

16. These topics are covered in the companion volume to this one, T. Young, ed., *Readings in African Politics* (Oxford: James Currey; Indianapolis: Indiana University Press; London: International African Institute, 2004).

17. David Chandler makes these points very clearly in "International Justice," *New Left Review,* 2nd ser., 6, no. 6 (2000): 55–66.

18. C. Clapham, *Africa and the International System* (Cambridge: Cambridge University Press, 1996), 43.

19. A good place to start is D. H. Lumsdaine, *Moral Vision in International Politics* (Princeton: Princeton University Press, 1993).

20. The most comprehensive study is K. van Walraven, *Dreams of Power: The Role of the Organisation of African Unity in the Politics of Africa 1963–1993* (Aldershot: Ashgate, 1999).

21. For an interesting, detailed study of this phenomenon, see Kate Skinner, "Who Knew the Minds of the People? Specialist Knowledge and Developmentalist Authoritarianism in Postcolonial Ghana," *Journal of Imperial and Commonwealth History* 39, no. 2 (2011): 297–323.

22. So, for example, almost every political scandal in France has had an African dimension. See J. Garrard and James L. Newell, eds., *Scandals in Past and Contemporary Politics* (Manchester: Manchester University Press, 2006), chap. 10.

23. J. Chipman, *French Power in Africa* (Oxford: Basil Blackwell, 1989) remains a classic study.

24. It was these developments that helped produce the not very useful notion of "new wars." See Mary Kaldor, *New and Old Wars: Organised Violence in a Global Era* (Cambridge: Polity Press, 1999); for a critique, see Helen Dexter, "New War, Good War and the War on Terror: Explaining, Excusing and Creating Western Neo-interventionism," *Development and Change* 38, no. 6 (2007): 1055–71. For more nuanced accounts of the African scene, see C. Clapham, ed., *African Guerrillas* (Oxford: James Currey, 1998), and M. Bøås and K. Dunn, eds., *African Guerrillas Raging against the Machine* (Boulder, CO: Lynne Rienner, 2007).

25. It is still worth reading Edward N. Luttwak, "Give War a Chance," *Foreign Affairs* 78, no. 4 (1999): 36–44.

26. G. Harrison, *Issues in the Contemporary Politics of Sub-Saharan Africa* (New York: Palgrave Macmillan, 2002) gives a very clear account of the "structural adjustment" controversy.

27. For background on governance, see D. Williams and T. Young, "The World Bank and the Liberal Project," in *The World Bank: Development, Poverty, Hegemony,* ed. D. Moore (Scottsville, South Africa: University of KwaZulu-Natal Press, 2007). For more extensive treatments, see G. Harrison, *The World Bank and Africa: The Construction of Governance States* (London: Routledge, 2004), and D. Williams, *The World Bank and Social Transformation in International Politics* (London: Routledge, 2008).

28. For example, the notorious cover of *The Economist,* May 13–19, 2000, which dubbed Africa "the hopeless continent." To be fair, we should note that *The Economist* has shifted its ground: see the issue of June 10, 2010.

29. The use of the term *renaissance,* almost always associated with a crucial period in Europe's historical and cultural development, seems odd.

30. For a detailed, if perhaps overly sympathetic, account, see *The African Peer Review Mechanism: A Compilation of Studies of the Process in Nine African Countries* (Johannesburg: Open Society Initiative for Southern Africa, 2010).

31. For an assessment of this body, see Paul D. Williams, "The Peace and Security Council of the African Union: Evaluating an Embryonic International Institution," *Journal of Modern African Studies* 47, no. 4 (2009): 603–26. On the AU, see U. Engel and J. Porto, eds., *Africa's New Peace and Security Architecture* (Farnham: Ashgate, 2010), and J. Akokpari, A. Ndinga-Muvumba, and T. Murithi, eds., *The African Union and its Institutions* (Auckland Park, South Africa: Fanele, 2008). For a recent assessment, see Alex Vines, "Decade of the African Union," *International Affairs* 89, no. 1 (2013): 89–109.

32. See the contribution by Warner in this volume for the historical dimension of this debate. For a modern version, see P. Bond, *Looting Africa: The Economics of Exploitation* (London: Zed Books, 2006).

33. For excellent background and guide to further reading, see D. Large, "Beyond 'Dragon in the Bush': The Study of China–Africa Relations," *African Affairs* 426 (2008): 45–61.

34. On oil see Ricardo Soares de Oliveira, *Oil and Politics in the Gulf of Guinea* (London: Hurst and Co., 2007), and N. Shaxson, *Poisoned Wells: The Dirty Politics of African Oil* (New York: Palgrave, 2007).

35. See Padraig Carmody and Ian Taylor, "Flexigemony and Force in China's Resource Diplomacy in Africa: Sudan and Zambia Compared," *Geopolitics* 15, no. 3 (2010): 496–515.

Part One
Sovereignty and Statehood

INTRODUCTION

These texts provide some historical background to the period of African decolonization. They also raise, and discuss, some key questions about sovereignty and statehood, and in so doing, point to some of the theoretical debates about these matters. Jackson tells the story of the decolonization of Africa in terms of the idea of "quasi-states," suggesting that decolonization was driven by an international normative shift that rendered anything less than full sovereignty illegitimate. The effect of this was that African states were treated as states but in fact lacked many of the key characteristics of states. Grovogui approaches things from a different theoretical angle, bringing together an argument about the African state and the international order to make a critique of the idea of the quasi-state. He suggests (and there are some similarities with Warner's arguments here) that Jackson's account neglects both the colonial impact on Africa's states and the unequal structure of the postwar international order. As a result, he also raises important questions about later ideas, such as "failed states." Warner reviews a huge amount of evidence about precolonial African polities and links her discussion to controversies concerning the meaning of the term *state*.

1
Independence by Right

ROBERT H. JACKSON

THE REVOLT AGAINST THE WEST

The historical change from positive to negative sovereignty is most specifically and concretely evident in European political disengagement from Asia, Africa, and Oceania. As indicated in the last chapter, the right to independence and the corresponding duty to decolonize was installed as an international categorical imperative following the second world war and by 1960 it was the unchallenged and unchallengeable declaration of the United Nations. There is no better place to look for changing norms and assumptions about sovereign statehood, therefore, than in the sphere of decolonization. It is one of the momentous international reversals of the twentieth century whose consequences—material and moral, intended and unintended—continue to reverberate and will for decades to come. We live in a post-colonial world which has undoubted significance for international relations.

Decolonization is often understood as a successful revolt against the West and there is evidence to recommend this positive sovereignty view. The usual image is of a decline of European primacy by the devastation and demoralization of two global wars and the rise of powers on the peripheries of Europe (United States, Russia) and beyond (Japan) which 'ultimately displaced the European system'. It is indicated by vigorous anti-colonialism during and following the second world war which made it impossible to re-establish Dutch rule in the East Indies and French colonialism in Indochina. British decolonization in the subcontinent in reaction to credible nationalist movements, such as the long-established Indian Congress, is a further instance. The successful anti-colonial war of liberation against the French in Algeria is yet another. These episodes are consistent with positive sovereignty: new statehood is primarily a question of fact.

In many other parts of the Third World, however, forceful and credible anti-colonial nationalism capable of inheriting sovereignty in rough conformity with positive international law usually did not develop. This is evident from British revisionist colonial historiography based on the post-1945 imperial archives. And in government discussion papers of the day 'there was little sense . . . of Britain being too impoverished for the task of colonial rule, or of her retreating in the face of nationalist hostility'. Nor was there any conviction that Africans were now adequately trained and equipped for self-government.

The pressures for transferring sovereignty were to an increasing extent international and principled. The post-war era witnessed an anti-colonial ideology expressed with growing conviction by the annually enlarging number of newly enfranchised states. Anti-colonialism in retrospect looks more and more like a sea change in international legitimacy. Their claims of domestic jurisdiction in the colonies and of the lack of indigenous capacity for self-government fell increasingly on deaf ears—especially at the UN. By the late 1950s international opinion had turned fundamentally against colonialism.

The image of a massive and violent revolt against the West is most apt as regards the break-up of the Dutch East Indies and French Indochina. The successful invasions of these territories and others by Japan during the second world war are unambiguous instances of the decline of European power in that part of the world. At the time, however, it was far from certain that colonialism would not be restored when Japan was defeated. In 1942, according to Lord Hailey, the Netherlands government contemplated granting 'autonomy' to the East Indies but within the framework of a continuing union with Holland.

European decolonization in these parts of Asia signaled 'the end of empire-as-power'. In most places after the mid-1950s the revolt against the West ceased to be a credible rebellion against colonial power and became instead a worldwide moral campaign against the ideology and institutions of colonialism. The doctrine of negative sovereignty in post-war decolonization is therefore seen most clearly in the international emergence of Black Africa and Oceania. Before this sea change of international legitimacy the complete independence of these areas was rarely contemplated.

Although there is wide agreement about the significance of the episode, the underlying causes of decolonization continue to be debated and no consensus among scholars has yet emerged. What is important from the perspective of this study, however, is not only its significance but also its character. Independence became an unqualified right of all colonial peoples: self-determination. Colonialism likewise became an absolute wrong: an injury to the dignity and autonomy of those peoples and of course a vehicle for their economic exploitation and political oppression. This is a noteworthy historical shift in moral reasoning because European overseas colonialism was originally and for a long time justified on legal positivist and paternalist grounds which postulated the unpreparedness of such peoples for self-government and the responsibility of 'civilized' states to govern them until they were prepared. It is difficult to make this point today without seeming to be a colonial apologist. But the fact is that until the second world war and even for some time afterwards this was the predominant doctrine of international legitimacy and law. Decolonization amounted to nothing less than an international revolution on this question in which traditional assumptions about the right to sovereign statehood were turned upside down.

EVOLUTIONARY DECOLONIZATION

British colonialism operated with the idea of trusteeship: colonies were held in trust by Great Britain until such time as they were able to govern themselves in accordance with 'modern ideas of civilized rule', as Lord Hailey once put it. In British political thought this idea was at least as old as Burke. Not every people were yet able to stand alone under the arduous conditions of the modern world. Nor were all indigenous rulers capable of civil government. Just as it was a dereliction of duty for a British colonial ruler to act unconstitutionally so also would it be a dereliction of duty if, for example, northern Nigeria were restored 'to the uncontrolled rule of the emirs, or Malay to that of its sultans'. Indeed, the policy of indirect rule or what Lord Lugard called

'The Dual Mandate'—which pursued the goal of transforming traditional authorities into modern local governments—was intended to avoid this.

Moreover, it would be premature to assume that every unit within the British Empire would eventually attain complete sovereignty. Many had populations which were still almost entirely illiterate not only in the strict linguistic sense but also—and perhaps more importantly—in the institutional sense of having little or no understanding of the workings of a modern state and the responsibilities of citizenship. Many were plagued by divisions among their population which were so deeply rooted in religion, language, or custom that democratic self-government without an impartial external referee seemed impossible. Many were too small for independence regardless of their level of development. And furthermore it could not be assumed that every colony would necessarily seek self-government: a policy of categorical independence for all would abandon many against their will. The only practical and responsible course of action was the continuation of colonial development following the distinctive lines of each particular colony under the overall protection, freedom, and justice afforded by the imperial system.

The British had long operated with the apparently contradictory concept of 'colonial self-government'. Since Lord Durham's Report of 1839 which launched responsible government in Canada, decolonization meant achieving self-government within the empire. Britain, according to John Stuart Mill, had 'always felt under a certain degree of obligation to bestow on such of her outlying populations as were of her own blood and language, and on some who were not, representative institutions formed in imitation of her own'. Britain could not transfer sovereignty to non-constitutional governments and remain faithful to her ideology of developing the civil and political as well as the social and economic conditions of colonies.

The British Empire and Commonwealth was likened to a grand political procession whose members were positioned according to their degree of self-government with Britain and the independent dominions in the vanguard and the least developed African and Pacific colonies bringing up the rear. This Whiggish metaphor of colonial development contrasted sharply with the static image of the old British Empire in which dependencies revolved around the mother country in perpetuity like the solar system and could never develop to equality with it. The constitutional shape of the new empire was constantly evolving, therefore, and the position of each colonial unit was only a temporary stopping place along the road to eventual self-government.

For those many backward territories at the rear of the procession, however, the road ahead was still long and difficult. The British were operating within a familiar tradition of colonial development which had already led to dominion status for white colonies and, according to Margery Perham, 'there was no reason why it should cease to operate for brown or black ones'. Constitutional development was a far more formidable assignment in Asia, Africa, and Oceania than it had been in the dominions, however, where it occurred more or less naturally within predominant European communities. New Zealanders were as capable of self-government as their first cousins in the British Isles. The same could not be said of Nigerians or Fijians who sprang from entirely different stocks.

After the 1941 entry of the United States into the second world war, however, significant new demands were placed on the colonial powers to make plans for decolonization. It was now necessary to explain the practices and institutions of colonialism which were no longer self-justifying as they previously had been—at least within the Eurocentric international community. The British in particular were faced with justifying their long-standing conception of evolutionary decolonization to suspicious if not outright anti-colonial American allies who were now in the driver's seat. The American view of decolonization was almost exactly the opposite: idealist and revolutionary.

This questioning of the European empires by the superpower at the moment of its ascendancy could not but undermine their international legitimacy to some degree. Although the United States' enthusiasm for universal decolonization declined following the advent of the cold war and its new realities and complexities, from this time the practices and institutions of colonialism had to be supported by an ideology which could communicate to states that were constitutionally unsympathetic to the enterprise and more likely to construe it as exploitation than benevolence and enlightenment. During the war when Britain was heavily dependent on the United States this required diplomacy and careful attention to terminology, as when Lord Hailey, the foremost colonial theorist of the time, noted to his British colleagues that any attempt to draw a distinction between 'self-government and independence suggests a refinement which will be viewed with a great deal of suspicion in the USA'. Hailey was commissioned by the British government during the war to report on prospects for political development in the colonies. He cautioned against premature and ill-considered changes.

In defending the empire against criticism, leading British spokesmen felt obliged to point out, repeatedly, that the conditions for granting independence were far from existing in many colonies which still required tutelage and would require it for some time to come. The British government frequently confronted critical opinion within parliament particularly from the Labour Party left wing. Colonial Secretaries or Under-Secretaries had to defend their policies in parliamentary statements. In 1943 the Colonial Secretary declared in the House of Commons that 'it is no part of our policy to confer political advances which are unjustified by circumstances, or to grant self-government to those who are not yet trained in its use'. A year later a British memorandum prepared for the Dumbarton Oaks Conference observed that 'the development of self-government within the British Commonwealth' must occur 'in forms appropriate to the varying circumstances of Colonial peoples'. And in an influential 1945 *Foreign Affairs* article written for a select American audience Marjory Perham revealed not only the official British mind but also uncanny foresight about the likely consequences of rapid universal decolonization: 'Were they [the colonies] thus cut loose, they would probably be set up as very weak units under an experimental world organization.' Here was the emergent imperial riposte to those who assumed that independence was a categorical good which required no further justification.

The British continued after the war to regard American attitudes to decolonization as a simplistic and an uninformed belief that colonialism was but a mask on simple 'exploitation'. The task was to counter these attitudes with facts about the reality of the colonial situation which varied greatly from one place to the next. However, the idealist outlook in favour of universal decolonization was also reflected by official pronouncements of Soviet bloc countries, many Latin American governments, and the UN General Assembly—whose anti-colonial voice strengthened with the admission of every new ex-colonial member. It was also expressed by articulate liberal and left-wing opinion in the imperial countries themselves.

In 1946 it was evident to Margery Perham that the gradual pace of constitutional development in British colonies had to be more rapid than was previously thought desirable or even possible in some cases. However, she felt obliged to identify 'four chief obstacles to the achievement of early and effective self-government': (1) the general populations of many colonies if not most were still 'too unaware' of the operations of modern, large-scale government to be capable of citizenship; (2) most colonies as yet lacked any basis of national unity; (3) a number of colonies were so insubstantial that 'anything more than a limited internal self-government' was impossible; and lastly (4) the level of economic development was still far too low to support a modern state.

British colonial policymakers were at one in assuming self-government to be generations distant. Although in public it was becoming impolitic to say so, in private memoranda colonial officials still spoke of political change in terms of generations or longer. Commentators took it for granted that some dependencies were so far removed from the conditions of a modern sovereign state that they would probably have to remain as colonies indefinitely.

There was also a moral issue: the concern that a premature transfer of power would leave many simple, rural folk in the colonies vulnerable to inefficiency, exploitation and even oppression by indigenous governments staffed by inexperienced or inadequately educated or self-serving elites. British commentaries on imperial subjects in the late 1940s therefore reveal a continuing assumption that indigenous peoples must achieve an acceptable level of competence and responsibility before self-government could be granted. In private the point was made with greater candour. The point was made with less restraint in a 1947 diary entry of Sir Philip Mitchell, then Governor of Kenya, who observed that as yet there was no reason 'to suppose that any African can be cashier of a village council for 3 weeks without stealing the cash'.

DECOLONIZATION AND DEVELOPMENT

Evolutionism was reflected in British decolonization policy by both Conservative and Labour governments, although the former were more inclined to believe that some colonies would never achieve independence whereas the latter felt that it was a question ultimately of colonial development. This idea eventually prevailed. Since 1929 the Labour Party had strongly supported the progressive policy reflected in Colonial Development and Welfare Acts which were renewed in 1940 and 1945. In 1944 the Colonial Office saw 'a dynamic programme of colonial development' as the most effective way of addressing critics who were demanding decolonization. Development would later become an international doctrine, except that independence would no longer depend on it and the international community—including particularly the rich countries—would then be responsible for assisting the development of poor countries.

Before the great depression of the 1930s, however, colonies were not usually conceived in terms of development planning. Instead, they were opportunities for private investment in agriculture or mines or infrastructure, and sometimes for European settlement. The earliest organized expressions of European colonialism were profit-seeking companies of private adventurers: the Hudson's Bay, Dutch East Indies, Royal Niger, and British South Africa Companies—among many others. Burke characterized the British East India Company as 'a state disguised as a merchant' but the reverse could equally be said of many colonies. They were commercial enterprises whose native inhabitants were treated as economic instruments: suppliers of cheap labour who could be exploited to enhance the profitability of foreign capital. The role of colonial government was limited to that of providing law, order, and perhaps education—if missionaries were not available to take on the latter task. This instrumental and inhumane orientation undoubtedly shaped the current image of colonialism as the institutionalization of exploitation or at least capitalist profit-seeking.

However, as with any significant institution there were other facets of colonialism, including, as indicated, a trusteeship idea that colonies were to be developed at least in part for the benefit of indigenous inhabitants. This was the doctrine which prevailed in international law. It is evident in Article 6 of the General Act of the Berlin Conference (1885), which bound all colonial powers in Africa 'to watch over the preservation of the native tribes, and to care for the improvement of the conditions of their moral and material well-being'. The idea was expanded in the League Mandates and UN Trusteeship Systems.

British Colonial Development and Welfare Acts also disclosed the ideology. The 1929 Act gave the Treasury and the Colonial Secretary concurrent authority to allocate funds for agricultural and industrial development in the colonies. The object, as Barbu Niculescu comments, was not 'to exploit' the natural resources of the colonies but 'to use' the capital and technology of Britain 'to enable' their development. Likewise, the aim of the 1940 Act was to establish 'the duty' of British taxpayers 'to contribute directly and for its own sake' to the development of colonial peoples. Of course, this did not exclude the desire that colonies be economically self-sustaining or that colonial development contribute to British power and prestige. But it did provide explicitly for the economic welfare of indigenous peoples.

Once the prospect of decolonization began to appear the British believed, as previously indicated, that substantial colonial economic development was necessary before sovereignty could be transferred. Until that time it was a colonial responsibility to promote development. Development was evidently the highest stage of colonialism.

In December 1948 the colonial theorist and then Labour Colonial Secretary, Arthur Creech-Jones, told the Commonwealth Affairs Committee that complete independence could be achieved only if a territory was 'economically viable and capable of defending its own interests' which also implied the capability of self-defence. He emphasized that while the policy of self-government was a general one, colonial withdrawal obviously depended on the circumstances of each colony at a given time. Empiricism continued to be evident in British policy well into the 1950s, although the egalitarian Labour Party view that every territory was a candidate for eventual self-government began by then to prevail.

But institutions are not impersonal machines which run by themselves. They are human arrangements which require knowledge, cooperation, good will, and above all leadership to work. It was for long widely assumed among colonial officials that responsible self-government in colonies therefore necessitated the formation of an indigenous ruling class with a solid political education. Colonial tutelage was necessary until a level of competence sufficient to manage an independent country had been achieved. Transferring power without providing instruction would—in the words of the Labour Deputy Leader, Herbert Morrison—be 'like giving a child of ten a latch-key, a bank account and a shot-gun'. The most essential element was education and training to enable indigenous people to occupy not only junior but also senior administrative posts in the bureaucracies of the various colonies. The length of time required to institutionalize self-government therefore depended on the creation of a competent and dedicated indigenous elite.

Circumstances were still a consideration as late as 1957. A paper prepared for the British Cabinet recommended that colonies should not be abandoned if they were not yet equipped for self-government or 'capable of sustaining independent status with a reasonable standard of government'. Another Cabinet report in the same year took pains to warn that 'any premature withdrawal of authority by the United Kingdom would seem bound to add to the areas of stress and discontent in the world'. It was now feared, however, that there might no longer be sufficient time to prevent it. In the case of Nigerian decolonization, for example, which still confronted enormous and potentially disintegrative problems of regionalism, it was believed that the accelerated independence of the Gold Coast (Ghana) had 'cost us some fifteen to twenty years'. Nevertheless, even at this date it was still officially assumed at the highest levels of the British government that not every colony could realistically expect to become fully self-governing. Consequently, some intermediate statuses between colonialism and sovereignty would probably be occupied indefinitely. Sierra Leone, for example, was only likely to achieve 'internal self-government'. The Gambia probably could not even 'aspire to independence'. But this traditional reasoning was definitely ending and Britain was about to embark on an acceleration of decolonization which would result in the independence of virtually every colony regardless of its circumstances. Under timetables being shaped increasingly by international politics, the time for evolutionary decolonization was running out. The world was becoming horizontal morally and legally if in no other ways.

Although seemingly reasonable and empirical, the theory of colonial development proved to be very vulnerable. Once it was confronted by practical questions and particular cases it was found wanting in the lack of precision of its answers. What level of development was necessary for independent statehood? What criteria were appropriate to make such a determination? And when and where in the past was independence granted on such a basis? The international system had never operated in such a deliberate way: politics, which is to say diplomacy or war, had always been the final arbiter. It was of course impossible to point to any uncontestable criteria of empirical statehood for determining independence that would satisfy those for whom colonialism was becoming unnecessary and illegitimate. Neither Lord Hailey nor Margery Perham nor anyone else was able to do it. Politicians recognized this reality. In his now famous 1960 speech in Cape Town, British Prime Minister Harold Macmillan, who once spoke of political change in terms of centuries, now declared categorically: 'The wind of change is blowing through this continent. Whether we like it or not, this growth of national consciousness is a political fact. We must all accept it as a fact. Our national policies must take account of it.'

If nobody could say what amount or type of development was necessary for self-government, then development could not be a justification for granting or denying independence. Nor could small or even micro-states be refused if that was what their indigenous inhabitants desired. Independence was a matter of political choice and not of empirical condition. New Third World heads of government at the 1964 Commonwealth Conference made what by then was already the standard moral argument: the conference should not be discussing decolonization but rather the 'development of all former colonies and the material aid the Commonwealth could provide'. The issue, as the new Prime Minister of Trinidad and Tobago (Dr Eric Williams) put it, was no longer independence but 'development needs'. Decolonization would contribute to development by giving governments control over their economies which colonialism denied them. This was the argument of the first UN Conference on Trade and Development (1964). Independence was now necessary for development. But it was an independence without precedent supported by novel international organizations which inherited many responsibilities from colonialism but no powers.

ACCELERATED DECOLONIZATION

When it initially became conceivable that some British colonies would probably move towards self-government more rapidly than was previously thought possible the hitherto unquestioned assumption that the transfer of sovereignty must be contingent on empirical conditions began to be undermined. Decolonization was divorced from the capacity for both self-government and political development in the plans of the Colonial Office. The traditional requirement that independence follow development started to erode and the progressive assumption that it could prepare the way for development began to prevail. A younger generation of colonial officials was coming to the fore—men such as Sir Andrew Cohen—who did not share Hailey's conservatism and came to believe that colonial governments should be working themselves out of business by transferring power to indigenous peoples as rapidly as possible even at the risk of inviting post-independence problems. By the late 1950s this was the new orthodoxy.

In numerous British colonies, therefore, plans were stepped up to engineer the institutional framework of a modern constitutional democracy, complete with legislative, electoral, and judicial institutions which were grafted to what had been primarily although not exclusively a colonial administrative state. In British constitutional logic a colony overseas was the equivalent of a county in Britain: it was subordinate to parliament at Westminster. The principle had to be reversed to achieve responsible self-government. Independence was a graded process, and political education was like any other: one had to pass through the various grades in order to graduate. The following stages of constitutional development were necessary for this to happen: (1) formation of a legislature if one was not already in existence; (2) creation or expansion of an electorate; (3) electoral control of the legislature; (4) legislative control of the executive; and (5) independence from the British government. These stages reflected the constitutional development of Britain, which was a history of evolving independence of parliament from the crown and of increasing dependence of the House of Commons on an electorate eventually based on universal suffrage.

What was distinctively democratic about British decolonization was the requirement that all previous stages be passed before the last stage was completed. Every colony that achieved independence proceeded through all these grades, although at the end of empire after 1960 the passage was made with increasing and even unseemly haste. The British stuck with the process often in difficult circumstances where it was not at all certain that effective legislative and electoral institutions had been formed, not only because this was their traditional approach to decolonization but also to demonstrate their long-standing claim that the empire existed ultimately to prepare colonial peoples for constitutional self-government. Any act of decolonization which bypassed these stages would be not only irresponsible but an admission of failure also.

The year of Ghanaian independence, 1957, is perhaps the date which marks the time from which British decolonization accelerated. The British Cabinet became more directly involved and the responsibilities of the Colonial Office were reduced to organizing conferences for the transfer of power. In 1957 the Labour Party claimed that all the smaller territories had a right to the constitutional status of a dominion within the British Commonwealth. But as late as 1959, according to J.M. Lee, the British Conservative Colonial Secretary reportedly contemplated self-government for Tanganyika by 1970 and for Kenya by 1975. Independence for each country and also Uganda arrived in the early 1960s. Britain was now prepared to grant independence to very marginal African dependencies, such as the Gambia, Zanzibar, and the High Commission territories (Lesotho, Botswana, Swaziland). In 1965 the Labour Colonial Secretary, Anthony Greenwood, declared categorically that Britain's main task was 'to liquidate Colonialism either by granting independence to a number of territories or by evolving for the others forms of government which secure basic democratic rights for the people but which involve some degree of association with this country without any stigma of colonialism'. The latter alternative—the last whisper of positive sovereignty—proved to be impossible in all but very few cases and title to independence was duly transferred to virtually every remaining dependency regardless of its capacities or circumstances.

Decolonization had ceased being a substantive enterprise aimed at state-building and had become a formal activity to transfer negative sovereignty. Apart from Southern Rhodesia, all of the remaining British colonies in Central and Southern Africa, whatever their substance, achieved independence by 1968. Most of the numerous and tiny British island territories in the Caribbean, Pacific, and Indian oceans acquired sovereignty in the later 1960s and 1970s. Decolonization in its final stages was separated not only from considerations of development and leadership but from almost any empirical considerations whatsoever. Of the Commonwealth's 49 members in 1985, 27 had populations under 1 million and 14 occupied land areas of less than 1,000 square kilometres.

The hierarchical procession of miscellaneous British dependencies of the past had turned into an egalitarian vanguard of uniformly emerging states with almost every remaining dependency now in the front rank impatiently demanding equal independence and receiving it in fairly short order.

Rapid and general decolonization also had to be accommodated by a reshaped Commonwealth. Most ex-British colonies altered or abandoned their Westminster constitution as rapidly as they acquired it. Many became presidential republics in theory but personal dictatorships in practice. If they were to remain members of the Commonwealth, political expediency stipulated that its received institutional assumptions would have to be given up. Instead of an association of states sharing not only the English language and an affection for the royal family but also an inheritance of British political arrangements and legal practices, by the mid-1960s it was a new orthodoxy to regard the Commonwealth as a convenient and very loose and constitutionally undemanding association: a club of rulers who succeeded the British. The effect was to enhance the liberties of ex-colonial sovereigns who felt under no obligation or pressure to conduct their governments in terms of constitutional democracy and the rule of law as historically understood by older Commonwealth members.

In a prophetic essay on 'The Colonial Dilemma' published in the *Listener* in 1949, which was intended to respond to colonial leaders and new members of the United Nations who were demanding or expecting 'quick results' from colonial development, Margery Perham observed that the colonial peoples least equipped to operate a modern sovereign state were likely to have the shortest apprenticeship in modern statecraft: 'This is because they are reaching it, not as with the older dependencies because of internal growth, but mainly as a result of external influences and pressures which accelerate the movement to self-government.' This was in fact what happened.

PRECIPITOUS DECOLONIZATION

The policy of preparing colonies for self-government so that the colonial mission would be vindicated was most clearly evident in the British Empire. The other colonial powers lacked this tradition and consequently had difficulty seeing and responding to international changes which were beginning to expect decolonization. France, in particular, had long operated with the contrary idea that colonialism was preparation not for independence but for assimilation in the metropolitan community. The British conception was the key to the fate of the European empires, however. If the largest and most significant empire was to embark on constitutional decolonization it would establish a precedent which other democratic imperial powers could not ignore. A small example is the French trust territory of Togoland which in 1955 was made into an autonomous republic within the French Union as the result of British decolonization in adjoining Gold Coast. But French and Belgian decolonizations were more precipitous and were undertaken with minimal conviction that successor constitutional governments could be established. They also assumed that after independence some form of close association with their ex-colonies could be maintained, which proved to be the case in regard to many former French dependencies. Authoritarian Portugal was the only colonial power that completely ignored international condemnation of colonialism and never became reconciled to decolonization, which took place only after the Caetano regime in Lisbon was overthrown by a military coup in 1974.

The historical policy of France, like that of Portugal, was integrative. The French did not officially refer to their 'empire' but instead used the expression *La France d'outre-mer.* Until 1956 the French could scarcely conceive of colonies in the British manner as schools for self-government. On the contrary, French colonialism involved 'assimilation' rather than 'autonomy': the development of overseas France as a whole rather than constituent units within it. Uniformity and not diversity was the French way. The idea was the education of individuals in the language and culture of France and the creation of elites consisting of such individuals who could serve in the colonial administration at the highest level. They could also become citizens of France and even members of the French government—as a few did. French policy, as is frequently pointed out at least by Anglo-Saxon commentators, reflected the Francophone proclivity for universalism. Although he could not foresee the policy of assimilation reaching its logical conclusion by the incorporation of the colonies in the metropole, in 1943 Lord Hailey saw 'no indications' of any definite developments toward self-government in French colonies.

In 1946, as a direct result of the war, France was reconstituted as the Fourth Republic which at the same time changed its relationship to the colonies. The French Union was formed which united metropolitan France and the overseas departments and territories. The distinction between *citoyens* and *sujets* in overseas France as well as other legal disabilities of colonial subjects, such as forced labour (*indigenat*), were abolished. Elected assemblies were also established overseas. However, the franchise was based on criteria of civic competence, such as French literacy, and therefore stopped well short of one-person-one-vote. Colonial citizens nevertheless did elect representatives not only to their own territorial assemblies but also to the French National Assembly—although representation was limited and there was obviously no intention of allowing overseas deputies 'to become so numerous as to make France a colony of her colonies'.

In the African territories of overseas France in 1956 the *Loi-Cadre* (Reform Act) was instituted which significantly extended representative government. Black African leaders were involved in writing the *Loi-Cadre*, and one-person-one-vote was instituted for the first time. Although the *Loi-Cadre* was a turning point which gave French overseas territories many powers comparable to those granted to British colonies during the terminal colonial period, there was still no clear intention that it would lead inexorably to independence. In 1958 the Fifth French Republic was formed and, as in 1946, the new constitution extended to overseas France. The French Union was replaced by the French Community: a looser framework which gave increased autonomy to overseas territories but not independence. Foreign, defence, and economic policy was still controlled by Paris. The changes therefore built upon the *Loi-Cadre* reforms by differentiating between France and the French overseas African territories which were reconstituted as states within the Community. This equivocal arrangement did not last, however. In a referendum on the proposed Community held throughout overseas France, the West African territory of Guinea, under the leadership of the radical Sékou Touré, voted *non* and became independent almost immediately. In 1959 President Charles de Gaulle acknowledged the right of Franco-African states to become sovereign, and in 1960 every dependency of France in sub-Saharan Africa acquired constitutional independence. Within four years French colonial policy had been completely overturned.

In Dakar, Senegal in 1959 at a meeting of the executive council of the French Community, President de Gaulle acknowledged the independence of Mali formed earlier that year by the union of Senegal and the former French Sudan. As if to avoid the stark reality of negative sovereignty, significant ties providing for military, economic, and cultural cooperation were retained between Paris and every new Francophone African state—except Guinea. French financial aid in particular was made available and this continuing external dependency was later reinforced by the close association of the Franco-African states and other former French colonies with the European Economic Community under the Lomé Convention. They also became associated in *La Francophonie*—a French-speaking parallel to the Commonwealth—which included Canada as a major new source of foreign aid.

Decolonization of the Belgian Congo (Zaire) was compressed into what not only in retrospect but even at the time was an impossibly short period, with the major steps frantically taken between January 1959 and June 1960. 'It is hardly surprising that it was fraught with disaster', as one historian put it. The episode was completely unforeseen until almost the last moment not only by Europeans but also by Africans. Even the man who became the first Prime Minister and martyr of the new African state, Patrice Lumumba, wrote in 1956 that it was too early to say whether the

Congo would achieve 'the more advanced degree of civilization and the required political maturity' to enable it to be 'raised to the ranks of self-governing peoples'. These evolutionary assumptions were abruptly abandoned in the late 1950s.

A progressive coalition government which came into office in Belgium in 1954 initiated tentative political changes in the Congo. But it was planning, along the lines of British indirect rule, in terms of developing African local government. In 1957 the first municipal elections were held. Late in 1955 a leading Belgian professor of colonial law, A.A.J. van Bilsen, shocked his countrymen by proposing a plan of decolonization which anticipated Congolese self-government in thirty years upon successful completion of a 'positive' process of creating capable and responsible Congolese elites and gradually transferring control of government to them. He emphasized the changed international situation and the movements for independence elsewhere in Africa, and concluded that Belgium would not be able to ignore them. His prognosis was correct but the timetable proved utterly mistaken. In January 1959, only a year and a half before independence, a Belgian working group still 'considered that decolonization would be a long-term process. Van Bilsen's thirty years certainly seemed to them a minimum'. As late as December 1959, according to Crawford Young, the Belgians conceived of 'independence' as involving 'continued Belgian sovereignty in several key policy fields (defence, foreign affairs, currency, and telecommunications)'.

After the Belgians belatedly awakened to the revolution of international legitimacy which condemned colonialism categorically, they hastily fell in line with the British and the French. Belgium was a democracy and a staunch member of the NATO alliance. When it became clear that the United States and some other democratic NATO allies would not support a prolonged period of gradual decolonization and that Belgium would also be condemned loudly by the UN General Assembly, the government felt it had no alternative but to decolonize as quickly as possible. Events in British and French Africa, especially the independence of Ghana in 1957 and even more so the abrupt decision of France to decolonize undoubtedly provoked the Belgians to dramatically alter course. If France was going to accept international demands for immediate decolonization, how could Belgium reject them?

INTERNATIONALIZATION

Following the second world war no colonial power could escape the chorus of international questioning and criticism even if, like Portugal and South Africa, it chose not to listen. The UN General Assembly played a central role in internationalizing the issue of decolonization and removing it from the sphere of exclusively domestic jurisdiction of the colonial powers. Although the UN Charter was rather conservative on the issue of decolonization by making self-government subject to 'circumstances' and 'stages of advancement', the General Assembly read it differently and sought to legislate on colonial questions. At the first UN session in February 1946 it became clear that many non-colonial powers wished to extend UN supervision not merely over trust territories but over all colonies.

Initially the leading colonial powers held international meetings among themselves in the attempt to control international politics on colonial questions. But it was not easy for Britain and France—who had a large role in setting up the UN—to ignore international opinion. The democratic colonial powers were accustomed to conducting their own governments according to majority rule and found it difficult to repudiate that democratic practice at the UN concerning colonial issues. International pressure to decolonize increased until by 1960 the emerging Afro-Asian bloc and its supporters in Latin America and elsewhere ensured that anti-colonial resolutions could not be defeated in the General Assembly. The overwhelming passage of UN Resolution 1514 marked the victory of a far more expansive reading of the Charter and constituted in effect a major revision. From about this time arguments to delay independence on grounds of circumstance were considered morally inferior to universal claims to self-determination. Although in the past Britain had publicly voiced the empirical argument that many remaining territories were lacking in important requisites of independent statehood, most UN members ignored such arguments or dismissed them as self-serving attempts to delay granting independence which was an unequivocal good. Latter day Burkes could make no headway against the *philosophes* of contemporary international relations. Rationalism had triumphed over empiricism. Thereafter the British pragmatically sought 'to carry international opinion with us' as the Labour Colonial Secretary put it in 1965.

The Commonwealth also became an important vehicle of international pressure for decolonization. By the early 1960s British Colonial Secretaries were reporting on their decolonization plans and policies to the Commonwealth Prime Ministers. Australia and New Zealand, which administered UN Trust Territories in the South Pacific, also engaged in such reporting. At the 1961 Commonwealth Meeting, Prime Minister Nehru of India publicly reminded his colleagues that the 1960 UN Declaration 'was an indication of the weight of world opinion on the need to bring colonialism to a speedy end'. Three sessions of the 1964 meeting of Commonwealth leaders were devoted to decolonization. British Prime Minister Sir Alec Douglas-Home, although reminding his colleagues that decolonization was the constitutional responsibility solely of the British government, acknowledged that it was also a legitimate concern of the Commonwealth. Later that year the new Labour Secretary of State for Colonies said he had been appointed with 'the task of working himself out of a job as soon as possible'.

The egalitarian argument that independence should be granted categorically even if the territory in question was extremely marginal became morally impregnable. According to President Kwame Nkrumah of Ghana, it was now the responsibility not only of Britain but all rich countries to enable his country and all other poor ex-colonies to develop by providing foreign aid. Sovereignty was a right not only to political independence but also to development assistance afterwards because colonialism was not merely political but also social and economic. Decolonization would not be complete until the international economy was reformed to give less developed countries an equal opportunity to become developed. This became Third World orthodoxy on North–South issues. The political difficulty of arguing for the contrary view that a different juridical status should be held by marginal states until they were more developed is indicated by a message sent from Canadian Prime Minister Lester Pearson to British Prime Minister Harold Wilson in 1965. Pearson reportedly expressed 'uneasiness' at the unexpectedly rapid growth of the Commonwealth but 'realized' that to refuse, or suspend, such applications would have been 'difficult'. He suggested that the Commonwealth might reconsider its organization with a view to membership on a different basis for 'smaller dependent territories'. Even this very restrained proposal to consider empirical qualifications in determinations of membership could not get anywhere in the face of the postulated international equality of all peoples.

The Commonwealth felt it had to accommodate as a full member any ex-British Colony which was a UN member. The UN could deny membership to no former colony which asked for it and actually solicited such requests.

The internationalization of the decolonization issue is evident in the ultimately successful attack on the traditional right of domestic jurisdiction over colonial territories.

Geography was the fatal vulnerability of the first argument. Looking at a map it was difficult to believe that Angola was an ordinary province of Portugal despite its substantial number of Portuguese settlers. The same could even be said of Algeria which, although on a different continent, was in closer proximity to France and had a larger settler population. In 1960 the emergent anti-colonial majority in the UN secured a General Assembly resolution stating that Algeria had a right to self-determination and that the UN had a duty to advance that right. In subsequent resolutions the UN repudiated the legal ground of colonialism in domestic jurisdiction. This was simultaneously an affirmation of the current doctrine 'that colonial powers have no valid claim to sovereignty over non-self-governing territories beyond their metropolitan bounds, regardless of whether they call them colonies or provinces'. This legitimation of the international use of force for the liberation of colonized peoples was subsequently affirmed by a series of UN resolutions concerning Portuguese Africa and Rhodesia.

The Belgian thesis is more telling because it disclosed the ambiguities and hypocrisy in the decolonization argument. Numerous independent countries contain non-self-governing territorial groups which may or may not be permitted to participate constitutionally and equally in the political life of the ruling community. Domestic legal and administrative arrangements of a paternalist kind sometimes exist for dealing with them—such as the specialized laws, bureaucracies, and policies by which American, Canadian, and Australian governments have historically ruled aboriginal peoples. In some cases they are victims of political or economic oppression by the dominant community. Legitimate and indeed lawful international concern for the welfare of such groups was established under the Covenant of the League of Nations and some international organizations, including the International Labour Organization and the UN Educational, Scientific and Cultural Organization (UNESCO), regard them as 'within the same category as colonial inhabitants'. One is strongly tempted to conclude, therefore, that the Belgian thesis in particular had to be rejected because it probed the 'internal colonialism' of too many existing independent countries, developed and underdeveloped alike. This was of course the appeal of the argument from the Belgian viewpoint but it backfired because the numerous states to which it applied were determined to deny it. To have done otherwise would have opened a Pandora's box. Most new ex-colonial states in particular had to reject an argument which would expose them to demands for self-determination by the usually numerous ethno-nationalities they contained.

Internationalization was most dramatically evident in the decolonization of Portuguese African territories (Angola, Mozambique, Guinea-Bissau) and Southern Rhodesia (Rhodesia cum Zimbabwe). Portugal did not become a UN member until 1955. After the 1960 UN Declaration—which in effect passed censure on Portugal—this argument could no longer be sustained. Lisbon's NATO allies deserted her on the issue. During this period Portugal very nearly became another Rhodesia or South Africa in terms of international legitimacy: an outcast under UN censure. In a series of subsequent resolutions the world body mounted a normative assault on Portuguese colonialism which undoubtedly contributed to its eventual demise. Portuguese resistance to decolonization therefore served as a major opportunity for international society to repudiate colonialism totally and explicitly. From serving as an agency of civilization less than a century before, colonialism had become not only morally repugnant but also a crime against humanity.

The universal condemnation of the Ian Smith regime flowed directly and powerfully from this new doctrine of international legitimacy. Rhodesia after its white settlers' Unilateral Declaration of Independence (UDI) from Britain in 1965 is therefore a telling instance of the ascendancy of negative sovereignty in decolonization. Since 1923 it had been a 'self-governing colony' under the control of European settlers during which time British authority was minimal. It was never part of the dependent empire but was a sort of semi-dominion under the Dominions Office. The day after UDI, however, Britain abandoned its earlier argument that intervention was forbidden by Article 2 (7) of the Charter and called upon the UN to intervene on the grounds that an illegal government based on white minority rule was a matter of world concern. The Ian Smith regime was universally denied recognition—even by South Africa—despite the fact that it satisfied criteria of positive sovereignty in the determination of statehood for more than ten years. The Rhodesian courts accordingly held that since the United Kingdom had lost its efficacy the regime was the sovereign government. Even Britain's high court, the Judicial Committee of the Privy Council, ruled that it was impossible to predict with certainty whether or not Britain would regain its sovereign control. Despite the fact that Rhodesia disclosed traditional characteristics of a sovereign state at least for most of its existence, it was universally denied recognition. Instead, the principle of 'no independence before majority African rule' prevailed, strongly supported by Britain, the Commonwealth, and the UN. Rhodesia was morally repugnant to the international community of the late twentieth century and in the end that proved decisive in its downfall.

2

Regimes of Sovereignty: International Morality and the African Condition

SIBA N. GROVOGUI

Theorists of the 'African state' and its external relations have recently focused on the causes, consequences and repercussions of its failures. They are justified in their appreciation of 'failure' and in their concerns for African populations who bear the brunt of political dysfunction. Yet, their diagnoses are frequently erroneous, particularly in regard to the genesis of the African state and the modes of governance within which it has come to exist. One source of mis-diagnosis is the assumption that modern sovereignty is a derivation of the peace of Westphalia in 1648 and that it has led today to an international order of relatively autonomous states. This view is supported by the notion that, through the agency of European empires and decolonization, a Westphalia-derived morality of state sovereignty gradually became the basis for the international system or community of states.

This 'Westphalian commonsense' effects an economy of knowledge consisting of shared truths, premises, assumptions, structures of beliefs and stocks of findings on the nature and goals of global political existence and its participants. Consistently, it has allowed its adherents to orient their inquiries and research agendas toward particular perceptions of the world to effect specific understandings of 'international reality'. To the extent that it prevails, Westphalian commonsense translates into the perception of a normative lack when it comes to postcolonial Africa. Instead of treating the African condition as evidence that undermines the empirical thesis of a uniform international morality, theorists often construe deviations from the Western state model as a sign of the inability of African states to live up to the requirements of sovereignty.

The related theses of an African deviation have been frequently postulated without interrogating either the Westphalian model or the extent to which the model fits the European experience. However, the insufficiency of Westphalian commonsense becomes apparent when one considers the properties of institutional arrangements that have effected modern state sovereignty. As I show later, there has never been a uniform international system of sovereignty across space and time. In fact, the practice of sovereignty has been characterized by concurrent but parallel coordinates that prescribe and legitimize specific patterns of actions in each region of the world. The resulting institutional arrangements or international regimes gave form to international governance through different but complementary rules, norms and standards of behaviour for agents and actors situated in different regions of the world and held together by historic power relations.

To illustrate this point, I contrast the effects that the historical coordinates of sovereignty instituted by hegemonic powers have had in Europe and Africa during the modern era. My aim is to show that the resulting regimes of sovereignty converged to produce congruent modulations of power, interest and identity that continue to favour European entities at the expense of African ones. While one regime contributed to the 'resilience' of European 'quasi-states', another helped to undermine the sovereignty of African entities and, later, to assist in the 'failure' of a number of African states. Specifically, the regime of sovereignty applied by European powers to Belgium, from its inception in 1830 to the present, contrasted greatly with that applied to the Congo, from the Berlin Conference in 1884 to the end of Belgian colonial rule in Congo in 1960. The same is true of Switzerland and Zaire in the post-World War II era. These contrasts are significant because Westphalian commonsense has enabled many theorists to favourably compare Belgium, as a successful 'quasi-state', to such 'failed' 'quasi-states' as Congo. A similar contrast has been made between Switzerland, a centrally weak European state, and such weak African states as Congo, in order to posit differences between the Westphalian model and African deviation.

Specific historical regimes of sovereignty played a role in engendering differences between such European quasi-states as Belgium and Switzerland and the African ones to which they are often favourably compared: e.g. Congo. For instance, although European powers competed with each other for hegemony in the 19th century, they concurred across national competition to establish institutions of global governance that set 'Europe' apart from regions such as 'Africa'. In the 19th century, the Great Powers instituted parallel and concurrent practices of sovereignty that regulated intra-European relations and European access to the strategic resources of the emergent global political economy. These juridico-political regimes allowed the sovereign and economic agents of Belgium, one of the smallest European states, to conquer vast expanses of African lands to be known as Congo. Likewise, at Congo's independence, a group of Western states destroyed Patrice Lumumba's ruling coalition and supported Mobutu Sese Seko's subsequent despotism. These events were compounded later by an ethos of permissiveness that enabled graft and embezzlement of public Congolese funds and helped to bring Zaire to the brink of financial bankruptcy. Swiss banking institutions, which are shielded by state-enacted secrecy regulations, provided the channels for these transactions. The effect has been to allow a net transfer of power and wealth from places in Africa (Congo) to others in Europe (Belgium and Switzerland).

I do not seek to impute to Europe responsibility for the corruption of public life in postcolonial Africa and the resulting political violence. Nor do I seek to accuse Belgium or Switzerland of immoral practices and to hold them up as the principal agents of the colonial enterprise and the subsequent misery of Africans. Rather, my goal is to refute Westphalian commonsense and to highlight the instrumentalities of sovereignty as means to rethinking the postcolonial African condition and potential solutions to it. I wish to explore the variations between historical regimes of sovereignty in regard to their induced relationships among and within political entities in the different regions of the world. For while there are local practices of sovereignty in Africa that have alienated the citizenries of many states, these institutions are not the only instruments of power that bear on the postcolonial African condition. Africa is also subject to external institutional regimes that give form to trans-territorial expressions of power and shape the involvements of external powers, their agents and base corporations.

This article focuses, therefore, on the properties of institutional arrangements that characterized sovereignty. Such properties are to be investigated in all instances in their formulations and expressions and in regard to their objects; that is, they are not to be derived solely from proclaimed political ideals, cultural expectations and intellectual commonplaces. I am mainly interested here in the properties of the peculiar rules that governed the practices of sovereignty and, relatedly, their consequences for the participating entities.

COMMONSENSE AND NOT-SO COMMONPLACES

There are externalities to any discursive setting that betray even the most thorough research or theoretical agenda. These externalities include political loyalties and complex ideological, institutional and methodological pressures that shape the commonsense underlying research and theory. One is that the study of International Relations is subject to local exigencies that often exceed the best theoretical overviews. Similarly, Thomas Biersteker argues that distinctive cultural orientations and foreign policy pressures prevail in different states and regions, and linguistic and cultural groupings. This broader context carries implications for the 'content, epistemology, and ontology' of International Relations theory.

It seems that various theories which promised to elucidate the institutional arrangements that give stability and predictability to the behaviour of states and non-state actors capitulated to parochial cultural and intellectual traditions. Regime theories, for instance, once applied empirical inquiry and historical analyses to the study of institutional arrangements that included principles, norms, rules and decision-making procedures. In Anglo-Saxon approaches, these investigations of the origins and consequences of institutions quickly devolved to the preoccupations of three schools of thought—realism, neoliberal institutionalism, and cognitivism. As a result, the studies of international regimes reproduced idealized and formal interpretations of the nature of politics and the behaviour of their agents and actors. They contributed to the understandings of power, interest and identity; yet, they neglected the political passions, material interests and ethical perversions that give form to international regimes in the first place.

Once they accepted Westphalian commonsense unreflectively as self-evident and transcendental, regime theorists and others lost sight of the regional coordinates of sovereignty, or normative variables through which states, their agents and others have given form, substance and effect to sovereignty. They erroneously predicated their analyses of sovereignty upon three commonplace assumptions, all derived from Westphalian commonsense. The first, best articulated by Hedley Bull and others of the English School, postulates that the present order evolved from a multitude of loosely related but distinct international systems. These prior systems were situated in different regions of the world and therefore were subject to distinct political moralities. These regions are said to have competed with one another according to a singular political ethos of supremacy.

The presumed inevitability of cooperation, competition and conflict provides the key to the second commonplace, which justifies state-sponsored violence as a political instrument in defence of imperial or 'national' interest. Accordingly, Europe was justified in its use of violence against competing regional systems and states during colonialism. By advancing these commonplaces as objective standards of conduct, theorists exhibit *inter alia* their affinities for specific articulation of power, desire and interest. Nonetheless, as I indicate later, the related theoretical imputations do not represent the life experiences of all constituencies of the international order. Specifically, they are unappreciative of the textures and qualities of the relationships that preceded European hegemony. They are particularly neglectful of particularities of the political decisions leading to the transformations of those prior connections.

The third commonplace or Westphalian assumption holds that Europe provided the catalyst for the transformations that led to a singular international order of autonomous states. It did so, paradoxically, by undermining the autonomy of competing modes of rule—villages, federations, dynasties and other empires—through enslavement, conquest, colonialism and other forms of political violence. Bull and others are careful not to postulate a mere process of imposition. They argue that, despite inter-systemic competitions, the various regions of the world shared certain interests, purposes and institutions. These commonalities of interest and purpose converged toward the Westphalian ethos of political autonomy. Accordingly, the end of European empires through decolonization completed the transformation of the international system into one of fully autonomous states, dependent upon a Western-based political ethos which is encoded albeit imperfectly into a singular regime of sovereignty. The conclusion, therefore, is that European conquest and colonization facilitated the convergence in international morality that laid the groundwork for the international community of states and, later, international society.

Many Africanists uphold Westphalian commonsense in believing that the state is the principal unit of the international system and that Western states provide the paradigm for its organization. Among them, Robert H. Jackson and Christopher Clapham maintain that Western states possess an organic coherence that is generated by a purposeful fit between state and nation and a legitimate desire to maintain this relation. They also argue that these states are able to create and maintain a secure environment for the nation and its citizens. Accordingly, they embody the capacity of the state to defend its sovereignty against competing entities. In contrast, based on Westphalian commonsense, they have argued that traditional statehood and international morality do not apply to all regions. According to them, the postcolonial African state lacks the capacity and institutional requisites to exert sufficient hegemony over civil society. This truism is accompanied by the commonplace that African 'rulers' lack the institutional restraints of classical states and, relatedly, display a disregard for modern norms of governance, economic management and/or democracy. These views set up the thesis of the failed state according to which corruption in public life has caused an 'exit' from the civil order by the disenfranchised, the politically marginal and those worn down by the norms of politics.

Jackson makes the most compelling case about African 'quasi-statehood'. He seeks to bring a historically nuanced theory of African politics to correct the inadequacies of structural theories of imperialism, dependency and neocolonialism. He traces the existence of 'quasi-states' to a post-World War II juridical fiction that granted sovereignty to postcolonial entities that lacked the attributes for real or positive sovereignty—among them, the capability to deliver domestic security and welfare. In this sense, the 'sovereign status' granted by Western powers to postcolonial entities was a gift of 'negative sovereignty', or a mere protection against interference in the domestic affairs of the quasi-states. This gesture was supposedly an historical exception undertaken to 'cater' to the needs of colonial entities upon achieving political independence. Jackson finds the resulting situation troubling. He argues that while this 'negative sovereignty' sheltered African autocrats, it did not empower citizenries. Blaming 'international liberalism' for this state of affairs, he concludes that Western generosity paradoxically established a new international morality for states that did not meet classical standards of statehood. Jackson argues that this morality was misguided and that it supported illegitimate, disorganized, corrupt and even chaotic states. To reverse this state of affairs, he calls for 'subduing' African sovereignty to secure political stability, economic justice, human and property rights, and to meet the humanitarian needs of its populations.

Jackson is justified in highlighting the corruption and mismanagement that have eroded the legitimacy of the state and reduced local economies to informal networks of exchange. Yet, while he redresses the oversights of others, Jackson's understanding of the forms and functions of sovereignty in Africa is incomplete. First, he focuses on the domestic instantiations of sovereignty and thereby reduces the empirical portion of his study to a chronicle of the performance of the African state. He underplays the importance of the mechanisms of global governance that determined state capacity upon decolonization. These mechanisms originated from political and legal arrangements that shaped the activities of agents operating within colonial territories and structures, on the one hand, and the postcolonial state, on the other. Second, Jackson dispenses with two key elements of African claims to sovereignty. The first is that the vast majority of Africans had hoped that decolonization would eliminate the material structures of political and economic subordination in the postcolonial international order. In addition, the anti-colonialists expected effective participation in (and not continued exclusion from) the decision-making structures of global governance. Jackson and like-minded analysts ignore the structural inequities of the present international system in order to conjure up African agency after decolonization. Once they imputed African responsibility, these theorists ignored the role that Europe and the West played in developing colonial structures and laying the foundations for the postcolonial state in Africa. These theorists displaced Western accountability for Africa's power structures. They also impaired their ability to imagine alternative African modes of governance.

Jackson's work shows how the current theories of African sovereignty arise from legitimate concerns over the 'failure' of the state and the misery of its populations that are subjected to violence, wars and famine. This work also shows how descriptive and scientific categories depend upon discrete normative priorities. So far, so good. But Jackson's moral theory is built upon two disjointed contentions. One is that political intolerance and economic mismanagement are endemic to the postcolonial condition because these states deviate from Western traditions of constitutionalism, political toleration and democratic pluralism. The other commonplace is that the ability of Western states to live up to Westphalian norms endows them with the capacity and wisdom to know the standards of conduct to which others must conform. These two assumptions lead Jackson to propose that Western states should take an active role in rethinking the 'right' of postcolonial states to 'non-intervention'. The aim of Western intervention would be to protect the interests of the citizenries against tyrants, dictators and corrupt officials.

But good insights and motives can lead to misplaced self-confidence and deceptive pretenses. While Jackson and others have highlighted flaws in domestic African institutions, their thesis that Africa deviates from classical norms does not provide a complex picture of the practices of sovereignty. This mode of analysis brackets the effects of the international order on African states and treats the problems that arise in them as internally created. Projecting this perspective on to the past, Naomi Chazan and others have gone so far as to reject the idea that the slave trade had any consequences for Africa in the present. Such positions imply that African rulers alone control the general environment of political violence, corruption and financial embezzlement that cause the net outflow of resources from Africa to other regions. But this impression is founded upon the dubious notion of the sovereignty of African states, a notion that other parts of their own analysis calls into question.

THEORY AND PRACTICE OF SOVEREIGNTY

It would be misplaced therefore to expect any theory to exhaust all questions pertaining to interests and power or desire and will in International Relations. It would certainly be mistaken to expect regime theories in their present idealized formulations to elucidate the complex practices and processes that give form to sovereignty and international morality. Indeed, the connections between politics, power and interests cannot be inferred solely from singular points of view, methods or legacies. It is my contention that the ethos of order and the means to ensuring stability have remained the same in modern international relations whether in situations of conflict or cooperation. Both situations have been subject to hierarchy and policing, that is the enactment of rules and their enforcement by a limited number of participants. In either set of circumstances, international relations have resulted in the establishment of a hegemonic order without necessarily attaining stability. Thus, the conditions of order—hegemony and hierarchy—may be taken to transcend historical contexts, ideological dispositions and technologies of power, including the organization of international life.

The above assertions may be illustrated by the indisputable connections between modern domestic European contests, the advent of the state and the European balance of power, on the one hand, and the historical methods or systems of international governance on the other. For instance the 18th-century Anglo-Dutch wars did not merely spell the end of the Dutch Republic as a world power. The outcome propelled England to imperial hegemony. Great Britain used this position to impose the terms of international relations or *Pax Britannica* which structured all international regimes, whether they applied to special activities (e.g. communication) and objects (waterways), regulated conduct (through conventions) and delineated power (including in the colonial domains). A similar situation arose with the ascendance of the United States to hegemony when, during the Cold War and its aftermath, its allies and partners were given access to the resources of power and influence where others were excluded and subordinated to the aims of the few.

It is in this sense that it may be argued that the regimes of sovereignty instituted by various modern hegemons have been united by an ethos of hierarchy and privilege, on the one hand, and corresponding mechanisms of subordination and discrimination, on the other. Indeed, the modern imaginary of sovereignty has contained concurrent but dissimilar regional coordinates which have guided Western designs and conduct of foreign policies, including but not limited to those involving colonialism. From the 17th century onward, each hegemon and its inspired coalitions have prescribed standards of behaviour for each region in conjunction with their power differentials and their need to regulate access to strategic resources—raw materials for industry; market for manufactured products; and capital for investment. To these ends, the relevant powers applied sovereignty regimes to intra- and inter-European affairs that differed fundamentally from those applicable in Africa and other regions. To sustain their designs, modern hegemonic powers also sought to regulate the knowledge, production and circulation of the means of war and violence to their advantage. These differences contributed to distinct forms of sovereignty and performance of states in each region. As I will show later, European entities were unlikely to find themselves subjected to the kinds of interventions practiced in Africa.

These outcomes were not *entirely* happenstance. To be sure, the various regimes of sovereignty reflected historical dynamics of conflict and negotiation among unequal agents across geographic regions. However, discrepancies among states led simultaneously to toleration and assistance to one set of political entities, while they resulted in discrimination and domination for another. The contention that distinct regimes of sovereignty give different standings to actors is borne out in the observations of philosophers and political observers of the modern practice of sovereignty. Friedrich Hegel, for instance, provides a compelling explanation of the necessary concurrence of multiple regimes of sovereignty and their origin in the aspirations of the more powerful and politically significant actors of the international community. In Hegel's view, sovereignty reflects dynamics of conflict and negotiation among unequal agents across time and space. Specifically, the 19th-century intra-European regime originated in wars and social conflicts, but also negotiations and political settlements among dynastic rulers, princes and other rulers in competition and coalition with other politically significant actors—burghers, merchants, financiers and, later, industrialists and other capitalists. The wars reflected the conflicting wills and interests of presumptive sovereigns while political settlements echoed a common European desire to achieve an order ensuring its collective survival. This situation required a common understanding, a controlling ethos, of the mechanisms for reconciling conflicting wills and divergent interests. The result was a political ethos that uneasily accommodates autonomy and interdependence, antagonism and cooperation, exclusion and inclusion, freedom and subordination, and so on.

This is to say that the conditions of sovereignty are *not* entirely *in*dependent of the collective decisions of hegemonic powers to establish convenient and politically acceptable rules and norms, on the one hand, and mechanisms of resolution of competing interests, on the other. In other words, sovereignty cannot be envisioned without considering the subjective ends of pertinent regimes toward internal subjects and external objects of actions. The most elemental of these ends had been the determination of Western powers, beginning in the 16th century, to 'emancipate' themselves from the political chaos and anarchy generated by the antagonisms of the Reformation, Counter-Reformation and related political events. To achieve this goal, the peace treaties of *inter alia* Augsburg (1555), Westphalia (1648) and Vienna (1815) established consensual rules of mutual recognition and the principle of cooperation for the attainment of collective historical ends—cultural, ideological, economic, or otherwise.

These compacts created an ethical reality—a code of rules, norms, and principles that governed the actions of competing sovereigns towards one another. They created a juridical equality between states actually unequal in size, capacity and legitimacy. This fiction allowed European states to coalesce into the Concert of Europe, the Holy Alliance and later the North Atlantic Treaty Organization. In turn, these associations and organizations enacted structures and mechanisms that enabled the coexistence of powerful centralized states (like France) alongside 'quasi-states' (like Belgium), weak states (Switzerland) and micro-states (the Vatican, Andorra and Liechtenstein). The capacity of smaller states—like Belgium, Luxemburg, Denmark and Switzerland—to survive intact as national entities does owe something to the capacity of their citizens and leaders to maintain and reproduce the conditions for domestic development. Yet, it would be fanciful to imagine, first, that these microstates possess the capacity to defend themselves or wage war against more powerful neighbours and, second, that such a capability accounts for their international standing. Rather, their statehood was aided by the structures of the international political economy and by the normative regime of sovereignty in which they participated. Even today, their existence depends upon geopolitical considerations of adjoining powers and the applicable ethos of sovereignty. In short, the European regime of sovereignty did not depend solely upon domestic legitimacy and the capacity of sovereigns to ward off external intrusion. The participant states were given formal equal standing with respect to each other, despite significant variations in their capacities and resources.

Hegel makes another point of relevance to International Relations. This is that the material discrepancies among states can lead to two or more outcomes. In modern Europe, as shown above, it assisted in developing an ethos of toleration and reciprocity among those involved in regional treaties and associations. Alternatively, however, the distribution of power has served to promote mechanisms of hierarchy and domination. Consistently, in an era of empire building culminating in the 1884 Berlin Conference, European powers imposed a regime of sovereignty for weak political entities in Africa that differed markedly from that which was set up for weaker European states. They were influenced in this regard by international outcomes, that is the gains made by their own subjects abroad. Having implanted themselves in far corners of the world, involved European citizens and economic agents needed extra-territorial juridical arrangements that, first, afforded them protection and, later, granted them control of those foreign lands. These processes set the context for another political ethos consistent with a different international morality than applied in Europe. In Africa, European states and their agents translated the weakness of political institutions and political turmoil into a licence to conquer and colonize. To this end, European powers not only claimed sovereign rights over Africans, they bestowed the resulting authority upon their citizens and corporate entities operating in the concerned geographical spheres.

The regimes that governed the interactions among European communities within the boundaries of Western Christendom formed a particular body of law known as *jus gentilis.* By design, this law differed from the rules and procedures applicable to transactions among Christian merchants, settlers and adventurers abroad. These two sets of laws bore no resemblance to yet a third set, which governed the dynamics between Westerners and non-Europeans. Indeed, with the advent of the modern era, European formulations of rights to property, principles of reciprocity and justice increasingly had little application in large regions of Africa, Asia and the Americas. Settlers and theorists held that indigenous populations possessed inferior religion, social habits, moral sentiments and political structures. Either Europeans opined that the 'natives' of these regions did not 'own' their lands or they held that the latter lacked the sovereign capacity to enter into binding agreements. 'Natives' were also deemed to lack civil institutions and notions of rights. A related sentiment that prevailed until the beginning of the 20th century was that the natives had no physical, legal or emotional attachment to land or territory worthy of European respect.

Although the above reasoning enabled colonialism, the process of domination was neither straightforward, nor entirely coercive, nor even free of bargains and negotiations. Yet, one cannot understand colonialism without, first, illuminating its basic imaginary of sovereignty and the extant regime(s) that embodied it. In this imaginary, colonial governance depended upon a hierarchy of subjects based upon different degrees of moral solicitude. Europe imagined moral solicitation on the basis of racial, ethnic and religious affiliations as well as other subjective considerations of ideological affinities, political alliances and/or economic interests. Unlike Europe where an ethos of reciprocity and mutuality prevailed, Western powers extracted compliance from subordinated territories in Africa through negotiation and superior military power. Further, European powers instituted sovereignty regimes that treated small states in Europe and political entities in Africa very differently. Specifically, the hegemonic powers countenanced the wills and desires of the least powerful European states by giving a stamp of approval and legitimacy to the colonizing enterprise of weaker states and/or sovereigns. Overnight, therefore, quasi- and weak states like Belgium became colonial powers alongside powerful states such as France. In contrast, the conquered regions were treated as territories to be ceded either by the natives to European states or by colonial states to one another.

The significant point is that the Western imaginary of sovereignty ordered civilizations and human faculties such that European conceptions of community, religion, citizenship and property took precedence over all others. Hence, in the colonial context, the general condition of international governance was to effectively transfer sovereign authority and privileges to colonial powers at the expense of the colonized. The resulting ethical project limited the policy options of the colonizers and 'native' populations alike. In the first instance, the hegemonic powers required their subordinated populations to tailor their spiritual and ideological dispositions as well as their political and economic expectations in accordance with those of their colonial 'masters'. When this condition was attained, Europeans rewarded their African wards with treaties of protection and corresponding forms of political recognition. Where native populations and their rulers opposed this hegemonic project, the prospective colonial powers punished their insubordination through coercion, including war, resulting in punishing treaties of capitulation and concessions, or political liquidation.

In any case, the implementation of the colonial regime of sovereignty involved interfering with African processes and structures of legitimation. Hence, the flurry of questionable treaties and other kinds of political machinations by European powers prior to the 1885 partition of Africa at the conclusion of the Berlin Conference. These treaties and agreements were often extracted through force, negotiation and deceit by individual and corporate European profiteers. These accords transferred political authority, including the right to self-govern, away from Africans to colonial agents and powers. By imposing heavy burdens on the local populations, these colonial 'accords' exceeded the standards that governed intra-European conventions. They subordinated 'Africa' to the requirements of global political and moral economies. This scenario did change much after the eclipse of formal empires when, motivated by geopolitical aims, Western powers competed with the Soviet Union to establish alliances with less than legitimate African rulers.

REGIMES OF SOVEREIGNTY AND GLOBAL GOVERNANCE

The above arguments suggest that sovereignty gives different standings to actors within states and across them. It takes form through multiple and complex institutions that congeal into formal and informal regimes of authority and practices which delineate the various regions of the world for its key participants. The mechanisms of differentiation are recognizable norms, rules and ethical standards that guide collaborating, competing or mutually unintelligible geopolitical entities. Together the regional coordinates of sovereignty promote hierarchical systems among states and regions of the world. They modulate power trans-territorially and across geopolitical regions to give form to international governance. Thus, sovereignty regimes reflect historical distributions of power and subjectivity within the international order and corresponding symbolic and material economies. These allotments depend upon the complementary processes of imposition, subordination, negotiation and abjuration of interest and values by relevant actors. In short, sovereignty regimes define the place and role of each geopolitical region along with the range of sovereignty practices available to it.

International actors themselves may be states, but there are also non-state corporate agents who operate across national boundaries. Their modes of action may take the form of unilateralism, intervention and aggression but they may also comprise acts of solidarity, cooperation and humanitarianism. From the standpoint of actors and agents, modern international morality is founded upon multiple movements of the will in the spaces where their powers, interests and identity apply or are implicated. In one instance, agents and actors may enter a communion of wills, whether within the states or across them within international society. In another instance, they may privilege the autonomy of the will within the states in pursuit of self-determination or self-defined national interest. In either case, the corresponding ethos manifests the wills and capacities of the politically significant actors and agents within the state and across them.

Following the Berlin Conference, the politically significant actors in Congo, Belgium and Switzerland were not contained within their territorial boundaries. The colonial regimes of sovereignty gave priorities to these actors in conformity with the hierarchies of the global order. Consistently, the Great Powers subjected Congo to different regimes that favoured the weak European state to the detriment of Congo. Western powers effected this discrimination despite the fact that in the 19th century the political entities of Congo and Belgium were 'quasi-states' in their own ways. Significantly, the European 'Africa regime' was independent of the power, form or accomplishment of the African entities involved. This pattern of intervention continued in the post-World War II era. A transatlantic Western Alliance imposed different regimes in Europe and Africa whose outcomes for Switzerland and Congo, for instance, would vary greatly. Both Congo and Switzerland have approximated multi-ethnic states with weak central administration and, therefore, are in need of a favourable international environment for state consolidation. Yet, the intra-European regime of sovereignty worked to the advantage of the European entity while a permissive ethos in Africa undermined the consolidation of sovereign capacities in Congo. Related institutional variations have persisted to date in Congo, where they are implicated in the collapse of the state.

At the time of its inception in 1830, Belgium lacked all but a few features of the most established states. It was a prototypical artificial state. Much like many African countries today, it emerged primarily through a revolt by people united primarily by an aversion to incorporation into another country—the Netherlands. In an historical parallel to contemporary African cases, the creation of Belgium was precipitated by the urgent strategic realities of the moment. The Great Powers of the Concert of Europe deliberately nurtured the new state as an independent entity by prohibiting outside interference in its internal affairs. Further, these powers assured Belgium's survival through a system of neutrality guaranteed by a political structure of alliances backed by the threat of force. The regime of sovereignty applied to Switzerland also breaks with formal readings of the Westphalian model. As it remains in the present, it was never ethnically unified and its administration was a very loose amalgamation of cantons. Yet, European powers laboured to integrate the new state into the system of sovereign states.

In short, Belgium and Switzerland owed their survival partly to the 'Great Powers'. From 1815, these hegemons decided, in the interest of the balance of power and regional stability, to incorporate some of the weakest states into the continental structures of power. This collective European will to nurture weaker states was particularly evident during the era of imperial conquest, when Belgium was given access to the important *strategic resources* of a global power. Despite its intrinsic deficiencies, this small kingdom played a role during the 1884–85 scramble for Africa that far surpassed its size and strategic capability. It thus emerged from the Berlin Conference as a colonial contender, alongside the traditional and more powerful colonial powers—France, Germany, Great Britain and Portugal. European powers ensured Switzerland's survival by recognizing and enforcing its neutrality, which it maintains today, and by extending to it a regime of non-interference, cooperation and assistance. The assistance that Switzerland received in these respects prepared the way for its later participation in the European regime of sovereignty in Congo.

The Western regimes of sovereignty over Africa, in contrast, have not helped to consolidate Congo. Prior to the 19th century, the region now amalgamated as Congo consisted of loosely connected kingdoms and political entities, some of them confederated. The name of the region (now country) is derived from one of these old kingdoms, the Kongo. To be sure, the princely African entities differed in outlook from European ones in that they all emanated from historically specific cultural and political traditions. They also depended upon endogenous structures of legitimation. It is easy to surmise that these structures of legitimation—unaffected by the political culture that led to the Renaissance, the Reformation and the Counter-Reformation—differed profoundly from those of the monarchical and confederate systems of Belgium and Switzerland. Nonetheless, various European powers viewed African political entities as equivalent to European ones in that their modes of legitimation corresponded to the domestic political necessities of governance. Some African rulers in the region had maintained diplomatic relations with the papacy and a succession of Portuguese monarchs. Throughout the era preceding the slave trade and Western imperialism, the populations of the region maintained regular (if contentious) contacts with Sudanese, Arab and European officials, associations and individual traders, merchants, adventurers and others. Once again, the latter included Portuguese, Spanish, French, English and, later, Belgian ones. In short, it was not uncommon for Europeans to recognize non-Christian structures of legitimation as functionally equivalent to their own.

By the 19th century, however, European powers initiated a new approach that broke the centuries of diplomatic contact and mutual recognition between European and African political and religious entities. Beginning with the transatlantic slave trade and spanning the era of informal empire, the imperial powers no longer honoured their own traditions of state recognition, political toleration and religious coexistence in Africa. They no longer recognized domestic African structures of governance as functionally equivalent to their own. They effectively altered their orientation to the operative African structures of authority, power and legitimacy. The new pragmatism also banished African models of political authority from the sovereign imaginary.

The prevailing Western imaginary of sovereignty unified Africa under a single political economy subordinated to peculiar Western wills, desires and/or needs. This is the context in which the fate of Congo (or Zaire) became closely linked to that of Belgium and Switzerland. From 1885 to the present, both Belgium and Switzerland benefitted directly from privileges accorded to them by the major Western powers. By design, the corresponding regime of sovereignty undermined the viability of an independent and autonomous Congo and effected the transfer of strategically significant resources from Congo to Belgium (from 1884 to the political independence of the former in 1960), and Switzerland (from the time of the independence of the African country to the present). The nature of these resources varied depending upon the requirements of the global political economy and the self-perceived needs of the European states—commercial interests, empire, natural resources and financial resources.

In 1885, therefore, Western powers (including the United States) established the Congo Free State to serve the commercial interests of the participants. King Leopold of Belgium transformed the Free State into, first, a personal fiefdom and then bequeathed it to Belgium as a colony. At the time, Belgium lacked the political and military wherewithal to project power and influence in Europe or, significantly, to match the more established Portuguese, French, British and German interests in Africa. Indeed, the discrepancy between the face of the regime of sovereignty within Europe and toward Africa was dramatic. The regime imposed upon Congo enabled Leopold to establish a trading empire in central Africa through methods prohibited by the Vienna Congress. These included the establishment of state monopoly over trade to advance private interests; the systematic use of force; the recruitment of mercenaries; and the use of forced or 'slave' labour in developing rubber plantations for the purpose of export toward Europe.

Western attitudes towards Switzerland also varied greatly from those shown to the Congo and the difference allowed the European country to participate in undermining the postcolonial Congo state. Again, as with Belgium, this resource-poor country was aided in its ascendancy as an influential player in the global political economy by European regimes of sovereignty that produced different effects in Europe and elsewhere. As indicated earlier, European hegemons enforced Swiss neutrality conjointly with their design of the balance of power on their continent. These hegemons also assisted the Swiss state in the consolidation of its control over its diverse ethnic enclaves. This European disposition contrasted greatly with the attitude of Western powers toward the desire of Lumumba and other nationalist elites to consolidate Congo's ethnic diversity. At the time of Congo's independence, Belgium and its Western allies viewed in Congo's ethnic diversity an opportunity to weaken the authority of Lumumba's central government over its regional units, particularly the mineral-rich Katanga. When the secession of the mining region of Katanga failed to materialize, these powers turned to Mobutu, but not before the overthrow and assassination of Lumumba. Thereafter, the United States, Belgium, their allies and home-based corporations enlisted Mobutu's support for access to Congo's strategic assets and natural resources. Specifically, Western powers showed interest in Congo's rare minerals which offset Soviet advantages in raw materials. Mobutu was also eager to offer these powers valuable strategic military airbases, training grounds and logistical support to anti-communist guerrillas in Angola and elsewhere in Southern Africa. In exchange, Western powers fed Mobutu's appetite for power and wealth. He evolved into a ruthless and corrupt dictator.

Switzerland exploited the intra-European regime to successful ends, particularly in using its bank secrecy laws to draw capital and finance from the rest of the world. In effect, officials, non-governmental agencies and transnational corporations used Swiss banks to circumvent the domestic structures and processes of authority of the African states concerned. This is not to say that Swiss banks initiated these money laundering schemes or plotted to maintain African dictatorship. The principal actors in Congo were former colonial powers, Cold War antagonists and their agents, on the one hand, and the dictator Mobutu Sese Seko and his cronies, on the other. Yet, Mobutu was aided in his kleptomania by a discretionary regime of sovereignty that condoned a double standard in the monitoring of Swiss banking practices. Switzerland continued to lend its authority to the institution of secret bank accounts even as it became evident that relevant banking practices served illicit ends. The United States and other Western states had detailed knowledge that Mobutu diverted state funds to special foreign accounts. The embezzlement of public funds and the plunder of Congo's resources helped to bring that country to the brink of bankruptcy. This near bankruptcy also made Congo more dependent upon the uncertain largess of international financial institutions for its salvation. Nonetheless, Western powers maintained a calculated silence. They neither investigated the corporations that provided the incentives for corruption nor sanctioned the Swiss banking networks through which funds were siphoned out of Zaire.

Doubtless, the United States and its European allies were motivated by Cold War calculations in enabling Mobutu's corrupt rule. Nonetheless, these states, their representatives and corporations instituted an ethos of permissiveness that enabled political dictatorship and economic mismanagement to bring Zaire/Congo to the brink of financial bankruptcy. A similar ethos prevailed throughout most of Africa. The vast majority of the collapsed states—Angola, Liberia, Sierra Leone and Somalia among them—were central pawns in the unfolding of the Cold War drama in Africa. These countries, like Congo, lie in ruins—as failed states, again left to be picked apart by domestic and foreign actors—corporations, individual profiteers, thugs and the like. It remains puzzling that theorists of International Relations continue to ignore the political ethos projected by the various regimes of sovereignty in Africa.

KNOWLEDGE, OBJECTIVITY AND THE HUMAN INTEREST

Any international theorist with training and intuition can formulate questions bearing on the ethical commonplaces of justice, rights and human solidarity. This capacity is a blessing. It is significant that analysts commit themselves to the ethical commonplaces of securing stability, extending justice, restoring rights and/or meeting Africans' human(itarian) needs. But, generic ethical principles become ineffectual if they do not reflect an appreciation of the complex hierarchies of the international order. This is because the underlying model through which analysts simplify the complexity of the world exerts a significant effect on where injustice is identified, how responsibility is assessed, and what types of remedy are proposed.

According to Richard Falk, there exist formal commonplaces that remain rooted in 'forms of knowledge' dependent upon colonial relationships and their psychic, ideological and political dispositions. Mahmood Mamdani too deplores the fact that some theorists perpetuate the notion that Africa is chronically engulfed in chaos. While some attribute this condition to an inherent antagonism of opposing 'tribes', others view in it the absence of civil institutions that can temper the obsessive pursuit of self-interest by domestic groups at the expense of the majority. These two pieces of commonsense result in two divergent responses. One, backed by Stephen Krasner, is indifference. This is premised upon a perceived commonality of cultural deficiency in Africa between the oppressors and the oppressed. The other is grounded in abstract empathy with the oppressed and summons the African state—again encompassing the oppressor and the oppressed—to surrender large pieces of its sovereignty to external powers. This position is endorsed by Jackson who erroneously assumes that the intervening Western states are constitutively disposed to equitable solutions. Ironically, both camps tend to assume a uniformity in the dispositions of Africans toward the international order and its political economy. Both sides forget the broader context of economic collapse and political repression in Africa.

Regime theorists and other institutionalists particularly omit the political arrangements that hampered Africans from positively exercising self-determination. Upon decolonization, African and other so-called Third World states were inspired to reform by Western precedents at Bretton Woods (1944) and elsewhere. The Third World agenda for global restructuring included attempts to bring about a new international economic order; to maintain neutrality in the Cold War; to institute equitable international regimes of the sea, air and space; to reorient global resources from the arms race to human needs; to preserve the cultural heritage of humanity; to redefine the purpose of scientific and cultural activities in the human interest; etc. This agenda came to a halt in the late 1970s, as Western powers opposed it on account of their own sovereignty. Indeed, there is an eerie coincidence between the final defeat of the Third World reform agenda in the late 1970s, and the onset of the current African crisis. The policies put in place by Western powers in lieu of Third World ones promoted investment guarantees, financial deregulation, foreign aid conditionalities and other neoliberal orthodoxies subtended by the need for immediate aggregate economic growth—and not social and human development. These policies contributed to the marginalization of Africa. The growing intrusion of Western-dominated financial institutions in the domestic African policy arenas also gained momentum during this time. The active support of Western powers for globalized private capital and finance further entrenched the shift of power away from financially strapped states to global institutions.

This rough convergence of policy does not imply a total accord of interests between hegemonic states and their base-economic agents. It does demonstrate, however, that states are not the only agents enabled by the regimes of sovereignty and that regional coordinates of sovereignty do effect differences in state capacity. To return to our case, the agents of colonization of Congo were private entities led by the International Association of Congo. Assembled later under the flag of the Congo Free State, these companies were endowed with special rights of legation that enabled them to negotiate 'treaties' with the rulers of crumbling African domains and estates. That scenario is not unlike what now occurs in parts of Africa where states have collapsed. Note the haste with which mining companies shifted their allegiance from the Mobutu regime to Laurent Kabila prior to his advent to power. One may recall too that, due to the business of diamond dealers, the Dutch airline company, KLM, flew into Freetown half-empty throughout much of the civil war in Sierra Leone. KLM, diamond cartel, arms merchants and transnational mercenaries all capitalized on the money that accrued from illicit trades of minerals while contributing to the misery of the populations of Sierra Leone.

These events suggest that Westphalian commonsense and its model of statehood are not attuned to the circumstances upon which they are made to bear. And neither are the ethical commonplaces. Appeals to justice and the rule of law miss the mark if they are framed by understandings which ignore the role of the European regime of sovereignty in the region. In other words, it serves no legitimate purpose to hold on to ethical commonplaces if the commonsense upon which they are based is erroneous.

A change in perspective on the 'failure' of the African state is needed. A new understanding of the international order and the African experience has begun to emerge in a burgeoning international society of human rights activists, health care professionals, refugee advocates, socially conscious scientists and other activists throughout the world. The participants no longer assume the model of a world of sovereign states, but many have begun to recognize the importance of international regimes and to appreciate the practical consequences of their contrasting ethos. Therefore, their conviction that states and other corporate entities must be made to live up to 'common standards' is frequently connected to an invitation to rethink the imputation of the commonplace that some region or groups of states are better positioned than the rest to enact the norms to which all must conform.

This development is helpful in that it broadens the policy perspectives of practitioners. It could be aided by an analogous effort by International Relations theorists wishing to remedy the African condition and to restore justice, autonomy and dignity to those affected by the 'collapse' of the state. This effort requires an appreciation of the domestic institutions that corrupt public life but also of their broader context—the complex instantiations of power relations that manifest themselves temporally and spatially as international regimes. Such an approach would bring into focus the desires, wills and interests of the entities that analysts now wish to recognize and, by this token, sharpen policy prescriptions.

3
The Rise of the State System in Africa

CAROLYN M. WARNER

Africa's relation to the concept and practice of 'state' and 'states system' has been problematic since its first encounters with those who were armed with the concept. In observing the collapse of authority and governance in a number of African states, some scholars have suggested that Africa presented the states system with alternative political organisations. Others argue that so long as there is a kernel of armed authority in territorially demarcated areas, a state exists. Africa's polities have often responded unconventionally, yet strategically, to interaction with the sovereign state system first elaborated by the Europeans. To comprehend the novelty, or lack of it, in the 'state system' of contemporary Africa, we need to know something about its pre-colonial political structures and organisations and about the imprint of empires (the construct which effectively limited the 'international' system of sovereign states to the West) on Africa. Did colonialism and the Western system of sovereign states rule out alternative structures for the newly independent African states? What might alternative structures have looked like? What impact did colonial rule have on the development of states in Africa? Does contemporary Africa have a 'state system'?

This chapter begins by considering alternative, abstract conceptions of the political communities which constitute states. Attempting to use these definitions in the African context illustrates the difficulties of formulating a workable definition of the state, and also highlights the differences among various scholars about what constitutes a suitable definition. Realist, Institutionalist, Constructivist, and Comparativist criteria face a terminological jungle as well as incredible empirical diversity when studying African polities over the last 500 years.

DEFINING THE STATE

In an essay titled 'The Character of a Modern European State', Michael Oakeshott writes that in the sixteenth century the word 'state' 'stood for a somewhat new kind of human association which had been emerging, more rapidly and more clearly in some parts of Europe than in others, for over a century'. He adds that the word 'provided little to identify, and much less to specify, the character of the association thus named'. Four hundred years later, and with an added concern to understand the development of 'state systems' in non-European parts of the world, the problem is still with us.

To the question, 'what is a state?', numerous definitions have been offered by scholars from different subfields of political science. Most definitions convey the notion that the state is an entity which controls conflict between individuals within a bounded territory, or, conversely, calls upon individuals to participate in conflicts with other bounded territories. Another view is that the state is the allocative mechanism within a political system. Such a system is one in which humans continuously interact with one another as they seek to satisfy their individual desires. In a political system, there is some general agreement on the 'rules of the game', and support for the government in its role as the mediator of competing claims. A third view is of the state as a symbolic system, in which ritual and culture create and bind a political community.

The Realists present a forceful rebuttal to these views. Perhaps the most well-known challenge to the view of the state as an authoritative allocator of values is that of Carl Schmitt. He points out that humans may be organised into communities, but each community inhabits an anarchic international system. Therefore, the essence of the political is making a distinction between 'friend and enemy'. What matters is not the character of the state, but whether there exists a community willing and able to define itself against a 'non-self'. This is strictly a public act. The political entity understands itself as such only because of 'the real existence of an enemy'. Only after this political entity is protected can other values and projects be pursued. The state is that entity which is capable of imposing 'its own unqualified right to existence in the face of all other vital forces'. The definition of a political entity is one-dimensional: 'that grouping is always political which orients itself toward this most extreme possibility', that is, making and acting upon a friend–enemy distinction. The locus of sovereignty is in that which makes the decision for the group, and the state is that which holds power over the physical lives of men.

Other theorists have argued that, fundamentally, the state is 'organised violence'. Alexandro Passerin D'Entreves makes the argument that the development of the notion of the state as a sovereign, legal entity grew out of the historical necessities confronting medieval political theory. There was a need to characterise the 'greater complexity of human intercourse', and a need to 'assess the proper seat of power' in such a way as 'to differentiate the State from other social institutions'. D'Entreves notes that the concept is indebted to Roman law, for it is Roman law which posits that 'there is somewhere in the community . . . a *summa potestas,* a power which is the very essence of the State'.

By restricting the 'political' to the capacity of a community to make and act on such a distinction, Schmitt misses the politics and process inhering in the act of constituting the collectivity. How do members of what appears to be a political community come to recognise themselves as being a community, distinct from other individuals and other entities, and as being a community worthy of self-defence? Is the threat of elimination *the* one element which 'forges' the 'decisive entity which transcends the mere societal-associational groupings'? Africa provides some interesting perspectives on this view.

The state, then, is the supreme political entity; it represents the '*institutionalisation* of power' the nature of which is nevertheless dependent upon the manner in which people order their self-interested interactions with one another. This concentration of power, this bid for state sovereignty, whether by an individual or group, entails a struggle not just over power but over the rules which are to control its legitimate expression. The state's recognition of itself as a distinct entity is dependent upon the outcome of internal allocative struggles and upon the generation of values held in common. The values and culture can transform the very nature of the actors within the state, leading to a transformation in the character of that state. Implicit in this is the notion that the character of a state is being perpetually redefined. How it comes into being, even whether it will, can never be taken for granted.

Territoriality has come to be a key feature in several definitions of the state. In Weber's famous formulation, '[t]he term "political community" shall apply to a community whose social action is aimed at subordinating to orderly domination by the participants a "territory" and the conduct of the persons within it, through readiness to resort to physical force, including normally force of arms'. For scholars and the international legal community, sovereign control over a specific territorially-bounded population has continued to be a defining feature of a state. When pressing beyond the Realist assumption that takes the existence of states for granted, to ask why states and not some other type of entity are the main units in the international arena, some scholars of IR have distilled the state's features to three key institutions: (1) a hierarchical authority structure which accepts no extra-territorial jurisdiction, that is, it has sovereign authority; (2) territorial demarcation with formal boundaries; and (3) a public judicial authority with codified laws. The latter criterion implies that there is a division between public office and the person who occupies the office. The argument is that, given extant political and economic conditions during a particular era of European history, these traits proved themselves to be more functional, in an evolutionary sense, than those of the state's rivals (city-states and city-leagues). These traits are in line with a definition generally accepted by Comparativists who consider the state to be a set of organisations invested with the authority to make binding decisions for people and organisations juridically located in a particular territory and to implement these decisions using, if necessary, force.

Constructivists and some legal scholars argue that this is a thin definition of a state. It ignores the community which constitutes the state, and since not all entities called or recognised as being 'states' meet those criteria, it is a deceptive definition. Statehood, according to Christopher Clapham, had as its central concept a '*public* character', in which states claim 'to act collectively on behalf of their citizens'. Presumably, those political communities which did or do not do so are not states. Yet the extent to which any sovereign state acts for the common good of its citizens and not the private interests of certain powerful groups and individuals is a much debated topic.

As Robert Jackson has argued, numerous political communities which do not meet Clapham's criterion are now accorded sovereign status, and others, which would seem to meet it, are not. The response of the Constructivist school is that states exist because we say that they do.

While Weber is most remembered for defining the state as 'a human community that (successfully) claims the monopoly of the legitimate use of physical force within a given territory', it is worth noting, as Constructivists have, that Weber suggested that a state exists when 'the action of various individuals is oriented to the belief that it exists or should exist'. That the state is territorial and sovereign over a territory depends on us defining it as such, and on others acting as if it were. This gives entry to the Constructivist definition of a state, that it is a 'corporate agency', which is also more than the sum of its individual parts; it is a set of rules and an organisation that acts (or claims to act) on behalf of a collectivity—a community. It also depends on a 'story of origins' which sees the Peace of Westphalia as having instituted the sovereign territoriality of state-like polities, inaugurating the international system of states. The Constructivist view implies that the development of the state system in Africa has been dependent on 'actors' defining, while using the terms and concepts of sovereign statehood, 'who they are and what they want'.

In practice, scholars of different traditions, such as the Institutionalists and Constructivists, borrow from each other. One noted Institutionalist stipulates that the spread of sovereign territorial states partly depended upon states recognising, anointing, certain other political entities as being like them. Constructivists stress that the state has bureaucratic (and not just symbolic, discursive) structures of control and of collective decision-making.

While mainstream IR and its critics have been preoccupied by the idea that, as of about 1600, the international system became one of sovereign territorial states—the 'Westphalian' system—other political forms simultaneously existed in the world, and other political forms with considerable international reach and influence were developed by the same 'sovereign, territorial' states, namely, empires. Yet the point of departure is still the existence of some semblance of a sovereign territorial state—a state which decides to act towards, or which is acted upon by, other states.

THE PRE-COLONIAL SYSTEM OF POLITICAL ENTITIES IN AFRICA

In the pre-colonial era, some political entities began to approximate the Westphalian state, others had different organisation structures and operating principles. In the postcolonial era, the Westphalian model is violated as much by the states' failure to generate an authority which could, by contract or convention, alienate its own sovereignty, as by coercion or imposition of a rival power base *from within*. This section surveys the varieties of polities present in Africa at the time that states were consolidating in Europe. The differences are quite enlightening. In fact, the various types of political communities which existed in Africa before colonialism present problems for our use of the term 'state'. The easiest solution is to assign them other labels, reserving 'state' for those entities which are sovereign, territorial, and bureaucratised, with a legal system separate from any specific rulers. There is an inevitable Western bias in doing so: states as so defined first emerged in the West. The purpose of the following section is to review some of the pre-colonial African polities, their authority structures, and to discuss the problem of the definition of the state through an analysis of Islam-based polities.

To read the history of fifteenth to nineteenth century Africa is to be struck by the wealth of organisational forms taken by its polities, not to mention the plethora of terminology which European scholars have applied to them. It is hard to know whether the variety of fifteenth–nineteenth century political entities named by scholars really were distinctly different categories, or whether scholars are merely trying to vary their vocabulary. In one region, Senegambia, the same scholar discusses 'states', 'kingdoms', 'autocracies', 'vice-royalties', 'confederations', coastal and island 'peoples', and 'theocracies'. Another scholar refers to 'city states', 'empires', 'sultanates', 'states', 'dynasties', and 'nomadic confederations' in North Africa and Central Sudan. Others note 'pastoral societies', 'clans', 'tribes', 'war lords' and 'semi-autonomous vassal states', and still others, 'cities' and 'houses'. East Africa was apparently populated by 'dynasties', 'tribes', 'states', 'kingdoms', 'tributary states', 'sub-dynasties', 'clans' and 'sub-kingdoms'. A state might encompass several kingdoms. More recently, the terms 'decentralised' or 'stateless' societies have been used to refer to very small polities with personalised rule, in which no one had the power or authority to coerce anyone else.

How were these polities structured? In the area now known as Uganda, some polities were based on the 'free association of men in clientelist relations'. The fifteenth and sixteenth centuries saw the formation of 'confederacies' of small communities based on 'kinship or clan ties'. Other structures were more complicated. The 'Houses' of polities in the Eastern Niger Delta were structured much like small city-states of medieval and early modern Europe. Based on wealth acquired through trade, entrepreneurs 'began to build up their personal households'. Marriages also enabled an entrepreneur to increase his personal control over individuals, and thus increase his power in the community. Stripped of its cultural and ethnic content, this could describe a form of political organisation in medieval Europe. Polities sometimes consolidated for protection against pirates, head hunters, slave raiders or other attackers, or were linked in vertical ties to one authority when one, in taking over a trade route, obtained *de facto* control over the villages along the route.

Scholars who have developed classification schemes for pre-colonial African polities have noted extensive diversity within very broad categories. There is extensive debate about the extent to which sovereign state concepts of public authority, that were distinct from the specific individual who held authority, existed. As with the formative years of the European sovereign territorial states, the physical boundaries of these kingdoms are not clear to scholars and seem not to have been always clear to the populations concerned.

Islamic States/polities

In fact, for Islamic-based polities, territoriality was a secondary consideration. Membership in the polity (and community) was tied to allegiance to a belief and not to a clan, class or territory. Because Islam had a substantial impact on the shape and destiny of many African polities, and because of the challenges which Islamic-based polities pose for definitions of the state, it is instructive to consider how Islamic polities were governed.

In the basic formulation of Islam, there is indeed no distinction between 'the state' and 'religion'. The clearest evidence for the validity of this claim is that the life and career of Muhammad are the ideal, the perfect model of politico-religious leadership for Muslims. However, after Muhammad's death (and the resulting conflict over leadership of the Islamic community—the *ummah*), and the responsibilities associated with governing the vast expanses of territory and the array of peoples which had come under the Islamic empire's sway, a very clear distinction between the two realms emerges, best illustrated by the two 'offices' which develop:

- the '*caliph*' (from the Arabic '*khalifah*', the 'successor'), who is the 'successor' of Muhammad as the leader of the *ummah;*
- the '*sultan*' (from the Arabic 'salata', which means 'power', 'might', 'strength', and most importantly, 'authority'), who is the individual who exercises power and authority—in other words, what Western political thought would recognise as the 'head of government', that is, the individual who controls the administrative machinery and personnel of the 'state' and is the primary policymaker in temporal affairs.

This distinction enables us to say that, indeed, a state exists (since there is a separation of functions). Note that the distinction of 'state' which is being used here is that there is a piece of territory under the exclusive domain of the ruler, there is a population which recognises and/or accepts the individual as ruler, and there is a bureaucracy which administers the law, collects taxes, and so on. While that conclusion may therefore be warranted, there are additional considerations.

First, nearly every ruler of an Islamic polity (whether Sunni or Shi'a) was inclined to term himself 'amir al-mu'minin' ('commander of the faithful'), the *political equivalent* of 'caliph'. In other words, he laid claim to being Muhammad's successor as the head of the 'true' community of Islam, the real ummah. The rather clear implication is that there is no distinction between the 'state' and the 'religion' at this level of analysis.

Second, all such rulers essentially carried out the secular function of 'kingship', that is, they were the primary policymaker within their polity; they controlled the machinery of the 'state' (such as it was), the military, were recognised by others in their leadership position, and also carried out the 'religious function' of being the leader of an, if not the only, Islamic community.

Third, after the fall of Baghdad to the Mongols and the 'death' of the Abbasid 'state'

(1258 ad), no Muslim ruler was willing to arrogate to himself the title of caliph; the term went into desuetude (which is not to say that some Muslim rulers did not think of themselves as legitimate successors to leadership of an Islamic community).

Fourth, not one of these rulers ever arrogated to himself the right to make laws or policy for the non-Muslim inhabitants; indeed, in modern terminology, they were autonomous entities within the confines of the Islamic polity. In that sense, it is important to remember that the Islamic polity did not see itself as a territorial enterprise.

Fifth, these rulers typically made no distinction between a 'public' and a 'private' sphere of activities, policies, and spheres of control. In fact, traditional Islam provides no basis for making a distinction between these two spheres, and in reality the vast majority of Islamic rulers made no such distinction.

This characteristic continues into modern times: the Islamic rulers of polities in various places throughout the Islamic world had no reason to implement any such distinction: the private 'purse' of the ruler is the same thing as the 'public purse'.

At the next level of analysis, once again we are faced with the lack of any clear distinction between the state and religion, between public and private spheres—they are all part of a seamless web of relationships and responsibilities.

Modern Islamic reformers have sought, and generally found, citations in Islamic texts, including the Qu'ran, which can be used to support their call for reform and modernisation of these traditional institutions and practices; but it is important to remember that the average Muslim finds nothing particularly offensive or unusual when a Muslim ruler makes no distinctions between his religious function/leadership, his political, economic and social responsibilities, and his private life.

In those West African polities which came under the influence of Islam prior to their confrontations with the West and its (nation-)states, a number of these ideas and conceptions were an integral part of their views of the nature of government, politics and religion. It would appear that among these were (in no particular order):

(1) The view that a leader who carries out what we might term 'secular' functions, such as controlling the military, ineluctably also carries out religious functions, and *vice-versa.*
(2) The community, the *ummah,* consists of individuals (and groups) who have accepted membership and the responsibilities and rights associated with such membership; those who have not elected to join are not considered 'citizens' or subject to the decisions (military, political, social, economic, and so on) made by the *ummah.*
(3) Legal requirements, that is, the Law (the *Shari'ah*), applies only to members of the community; non-members are not bound by its moral, ethical, economic and social prescriptions and rules. Non-Muslims may live under their own code of laws as long as they do not try to impose them on Muslims.
(4) Muslims are bound by the requirements of their legal and religious systems even if living under the temporal control of non-Muslims. It was always believed that Muslims should attempt to bring non-Muslim areas into the Dar al-Islam (the House of Islam, that is, where Islam is numerically and politically dominant).
(5) The 'realm' of the ruler (no matter the indigenous term used, such as caliph or Amir) extends to all of the adherents of the faith, no matter where they may be at any given time; it is *not* territorially bound, defined or delimited.

It should not, therefore, be terribly surprising that the political interaction between the very differing conceptions of community, the 'state', and the role of religion held by Catholic and Protestant Europeans and Muslim

Africans, would lead to friction, misunderstandings, and conflicting claims in the realm of economics, politics, and social *mores*. It was probably inevitable that without any structural mechanism to facilitate compromise, much less any organised effort to reconcile differing views on such matters, who emerged as the 'victor' would be the result of conflicts carried out using economic and military measures. With fewer resources, a far less centralised administration, and a decentralised relationship between the pieces of the realm, the Islamic states of West Africa stood very little chance against the economic and military might of the European empires.

One such case is the Sokoto Caliphate. While often referred to by Africanists as a 'state', the Sokoto Caliphate was a congeries of 'emirates', or local governments, which were united 'by common membership of one Umma [community of believers] dedicated to the upholding of Islam and of Dār-al-Islām', who agreed that the Caliph was the supreme temporal and spiritual authority. It was not a set of people brought into a contiguous territory with a marked separation of private from public power. This was also the case for the nascent states/large kingdoms of West Africa in their dealings with the Europeans. Islam-based polities also signed treaties with other states or polities (an accepted practice, even with non-Muslim polities), and attempted to enforce their control over territories. When Umar Tal, the prominent leader of what most historians refer to as the *jihad* in West Africa which formed the basis of the Tukulor empire, entered a rival polity's vassal city, the latter's leader wrote to Umar, saying 'It has come to our attention that you entered Sinsani without our knowledge or permission'. Even if the polity's territory was non-contiguous, it would claim that its treaties were binding on those who were members of the *ummah*.

Even though the Caliph was considered sovereign for those communities which swore allegiance to him, and though he claimed the right to establish treaties, the leaders (emirs) of those communities often had separate enemies. The Caliph became involved in trying to co-ordinate defence efforts. Such a system makes a hash of Schmitt's view that the central criterion of a political community or state is that which distinguishes itself from all the enemies—all in the community have the same enemy. It also contravenes the accepted social science view of a state as being that which represents all its inhabitants uniformly in dealings with an identifiable 'external' realm—that is, with other states and international actors.

The structure of the African Islamic polities also poses a problem for our idea of a state to the extent that each emirate was composed of multiple villages, and while the emirate claimed a central authority structure, most of what passed for politics occurred at the village level as a result of decisions and actions taken at the local level.

If we choose not to call the Sokoto Caliphate a state, and instead call it an empire, we must be careful to recognise that it had structures of governance which succeeded in making the 'authoritative allocations of values' which are held to be a key activity of a state. In addition, the Sokoto Caliphate rulers used patronage to secure their support bases; disputes between sub-units (the emirates) were mediated by the Caliph who also chose, from a list of suggested 'candidates', the emirs, and 'had a coherent machinery of government'. That said, social scientists might be more comfortable calling the Caliphate an empire—an entity claiming 'military and spiritual' sovereignty without territorial limits. The Sokoto Caliphate was not the only type of Islamic polity in Africa. Others, such as the Tukulor empire, known for its 'national unity and political centralisation', appear to have more closely approximated a 'traditional' state structure. Its authority structures evolved over time: the Islamic-based Tukulor empire at first was heterocephalous, with multiple authorities laying claim to the population. These Islamic polities point to the insufficiency of the term 'state' in describing many pre-colonial African societies (and contemporary political systems). This descriptive inadequacy is not due to the fact that their sovereignty as states was breached but that they do not meet the basic criteria set for them by the Western sovereign state model.

PRE-COLONIAL AFRICA IN THE INTERNATIONAL POLITICAL ECONOMY

If, in the West, trade was a major factor in the development of sovereign territorial states, what was its impact in Africa? In particular, what effects did the international political economy have on emerging African political structures? Were there patterns to its effects? A study aimed at answering these questions has yet to be written, perhaps because it appears there was no consistent pattern.

It has generally been thought that the slave trade, and then other forms of trade, began to favour the coastal polities. Several of the polities that were slave hunters or producers of gold became powerful kingdoms. This thesis, as summarised by Martin Klein, 'links the formation of highly militarised states in West Africa to the increase in demand for slaves after the development of sugar plantations in the West Indies and sees slave production and the slave trade as crucial to the functioning and reproduction of such states as Oyo, Asante, Futa Jallon and Segu'. Recently, several historians have convincingly argued that 'slave production and trade' could flourish even in the absence of militarised kingdoms such as Asante. Slave traders were not restricted to suppliers from the large militarised states such as Asante, but were also able to create networks which took advantage of inter- and intra-village disputes to generate a supply of slaves. While the market may have prompted notable adjustments in social and political structures within and across African polities, it did not inexorably distil African polities into two types: powerful, militarised states and weak, defenceless, acephalous societies.

Scholars disagree on whether Islam provided the impetus or the excuse for political organisation in parts of Africa, but it is clear that Islam conditioned large parts of Africa's pre-colonial politics. The Arab historian of the fourteenth century, Ibn Khaldūn, wrote of the Islamic conquest in the Sudan that the Muslims 'triumphed over the Sudanese, destroyed their dwellings and country, levied tribute, forced many of them to join Islam, and subjugated them'. That Islam had a role in the destruction and subjugation may be irrelevant: humans always find ways to dominate and kill each other. What is more important was the influence Islam had on the type of political structures put in place after conquest. The reforming zeal of a certain leader 'can be seen, on the one hand, as having led to the creation of the Sokoto Caliphate, with the captives and the slave trade as a side effect, or, on the other, as the political reorganisation of a society that was becoming increasingly dependent on slave labour for production'. Manning gives an economic interpretation to an apparently religious movement, the Mahdist of the [Nilotic] Sudan, noting it coincided with an 'anti-slave-trade' agreement between the ruler of the Sudan and the British: 'Those who then joined with the Mahdi to proclaim a rightly guided, theocratic state included slave merchants and planters, whose slave villages produced grains and manufactures for domestic sale and export'. The Sokoto Caliphate had no scruples about slavery or about providing male slaves with female slaves in order to make control easier, yet treated slaves according to Islamic principles.

Changes in the slave trade (with demand from Europe and the Americas having fallen) ended the population drain, (the demographics are themselves a heavily disputed subject), and also prompted some traders to invest in (local slave) plantations. This, in turn, led to 'rapid population growth and disputes over land ownership'. This could have been expected to have led to a demand, on the part of quarrelling land owners, for a sovereign authority to adjudicate conflicts and to guarantee contracts—in other words, a state. Instead, as Europeans became involved in disputes, sometimes deliberately exacerbating them and thus artificially heightening the 'demand' for authority, their actions and the European political responses prevented a local, autonomous 'supply' of authority from reorganising and emerging.

In West Africa, several powerful kingdoms emerged with the slave trade and Africa's incorporation into the international economy: Asante, Fante, Denkyira, Akwamu, Dahomey. At the same time, several Islamic empires established themselves. Both political forms, kingdoms and empires, appear to have profited from the slave trade and other kinds of business, rendering it difficult to argue that, in Africa, trade was a force for establishing the Westphalian style of sovereign state. Non-contiguous, and hence non-territorially fixed, organisations (such as Tukulor, Sokoto) seem to have been able to profit from international trade, and, after the British banned slavery, to have been able to shift to other forms of commerce. Co-existing with, at times conquered by, these powerful polities were a variety of other types of polities. Some scholars argue that, at least for the slave trade, effects 'varied sharply from polity to polity'. By the mid-nineteenth century, after 250 years of international trade, largely in primary products (if one can also call a human being such), the natural selection effects expected by the IR Institutionalists appear not to have occurred. Trade in Africa appeared to have allowed a variety of forms to flourish.

The European powers preferred this multiplicity of political communities, as it prevented any one or two powerful African states from emerging and dominating international trade, setting mercantilist prices and terms of trade. The alleged advantages of sovereign statehood were not recognised by the Europeans: any efficiencies the Europeans would have derived from one African sovereign representing and guaranteeing the behaviour of a set of people within a specific territory were, apparently, considered negligible in comparison to the profits to be had by preventing African trade monopolies.

To the extent that mutual recognition of state sovereignty was necessary to grant African polities statehood, it is clear that the Europeans were unwilling, perhaps unable, to recognise 'stateness' or similarities in the organisational structure of various African polities. There was a change over the centuries in the labels given to African rulers. Those offices which had previously been called 'kingships' were later labelled 'chieftancies'. Racism may have been a factor, so too the European perception of great contrasts in infrastructures, population, military power, influence over the hinterland, and so on: Kumasi was not London, and Masina was not Paris.

The Europeans sought to thoroughly dominate the area and monopolise its trade; their method was, at first, to prevent further consolidation of African kingdoms, then, second, to colonise them. The Realist response, logically enough, would be that this was the inevitable result of an extraordinary imbalance of power between industrialising European states and agricultural African polities.

Amidst this patchwork quilt of political entities, several were apparently moving in the direction of sovereign statehood, consolidating rule with territorial boundaries, developing notions of a supreme authority, and of at least some public law not dependent on the persona of the ruler (but see the above discussion of Islamic entities). Whether they would have become what Western scholars recognise as modern sovereign states is not knowable. We can only conjecture that since a number seemed to be developing the requisite attributes prior to colonisation, they may have.

I have argued that the failure of African polities to become what Westerners recognise as sovereign territorial states was not due to an incapacity to participate in international trade, or withstand the changes in social structure brought by changes in trade commodities. Rival arguments suggest the opposite. No matter how one constructs the argument, and what evidence one brings to bear on the hypotheses, it is clear that the myriad historical structures of pre-colonial Africa were eclipsed by the Westphalian state model. Yet that political structure was not imposed on the African polities *until decolonisation*. If, following the logic of the political economists, sovereign territorial statehood met the material interests of European traders and monarchs in Europe, it appears that empire met their interests elsewhere. Alternatively, one would have to postulate the argument that empire, rather than sovereign territorial statehood, was a more 'efficient' form in general, for the international system.

Decolonisation also depended upon the will of the more powerful states, and it is to the post-colonial era that I now turn.

WHAT IMPACT DID THE EMPIRES HAVE ON THE CURRENT AFRICAN STATE SYSTEM?

The imprint of empire on the African state system was undoubtedly substantial. I will not try to evaluate the extent of it, but rather raise points about several major effects. At one extreme is the argument that colonial rule had an enormous, deleterious and completely transformative effect on Africa. Crawford Young puts it most forcefully: 'one consequential factor in the crisis faced by most African states by the late 1970s—and intensifying since—was the singularly difficult legacy bequeathed by the institutions of rule devised to establish and maintain alien hegemony'. Africa faced the brunt of the developed sovereign territorial state competing not with one or two other powers, but with several all at once. In addition, the imperial powers insisted that the colonies pay for themselves and pay immediately. According to Young, this led to repressive and brutal extractive mechanisms. These imperatives were backed by an ideology of racism which was at its 'historical zenith', and by advanced military technologies.

Colonial rule infantilised African politics, stunting its growth. Imposing colonial authority over local authority inevitably undermined the latter. The French were particularly insistent that 'the native chief must be our instrument'. One could argue that had colonial rulers established complete hegemony and totally reorganised African society in the manner which they desired, it is quite possible that the African states would have started with a much more stable and extensive political and economic infrastructure, and that these states would be better able to cope in the modern world.

There is a revisionist current which argues that African polities only partly absorbed European notions of 'stateness' and political behaviours. Just as a number of scholars have argued that the sources of pre-colonial demise were largely rooted in the African polities themselves, recent works take issue with Young's claim that the colonial state 'totally reordered political space, societal hierarchies and cleavages, and modes of economic production'. These revisionists emphasise continuities in structures and practices, adaptations but not submission to European concepts of politics and state. For instance, in Buganda, the English only grafted their ideas and practices of individual land ownership on to pre-colonial practices, turning peasants and chiefs into tenants and landlords, thus continuing the original hierarchies.

Yet the revisionists, to make their point, must downplay the extent to which the interests of the colonised were shaped by the new colonial structures. For instance, private property created a new set of interests and strategies for attaining them. Goals changed, self-definitions altered, and the colonised Africans incorporated new concepts into their politics. As A.F. Robertson's work on the deposition of Asante chiefs shows, British 'over-rule added a further level of authority to the Ashanti chiefly hierarchy'.

The colonial powers' efforts to dramatically alter African societies also have their source in the ideology of scientific planning which became prevalent in the West (and the Soviet Union) in the 1920s and 1930s and lasted through the 1950s. With domination as the effective result, the British undertook large-scale agricultural transformations, all of which failed (for example, Shire Valley in Malawi, groundnut production in Tanganyika). As James C. Scott says, '[t]he point of departure for colonial policy was a complete faith in what officials took for "scientific agriculture" on the one hand and a nearly total scepticism about the actual agricultural practices of Africans on the other'. British experts were brought in to plan the colonies' agricultural development. They 'were inclined to propose elaborate projects—"a total development scheme," a "comprehensive land usage scheme"'. The planners dismissed the local knowledge of the peasants, since it hadn't been arrived at by 'scientific' analysis.

Oddly, the failures of these large-scale planned 'rural settlement and production schemes' did not dissuade post-colonial states from attempting some of their own. It is not clear that this was, as Young might expect, because the colonial states had inculcated the new elite with the colonials' way of thinking and governing, or whether it was because the new leaders were attracted by the communist ideology, which was inherently optimistic about the possibilities (and exigent about the need) for large-scale planning involving extensive resettlement and massive agricultural production. It's also plausible that the new elites, bequeathed political structures, societies and economies woefully behind the Western world and needing development in order to profit from international trade, saw large-scale transformations as the only means of catching up to the West.

In Tanzania, Julius Nyerere tried a version of collectivisation, with rural populations forced to move into government built, standardised villages, and to work on large, single-crop farms. His justification: 'if you ask me why the government wants us to live in villages, the answer is just as simple: unless we do we shall not be able to provide ourselves with the things we need to develop our land and to raise our standard of living'. While state involvement in development may have been the solution, the specific strategy, given the conditions, doomed the project to failure. But the concern here is what connection the strategy had with the imprint of empire. While the idea of massive development and transformation may have been internalised and used by the new elite, Nyerere did try to give his strategy a non-Western stamp: 'we should gradually become a nation of *ujamaa* villages where the people co-operate directly in small groups and where these small groups co-operate together for joint enterprises'. To the extent one can say that empires bequeathed underdeveloped state institutions and a faith in planning to the independent African rulers, the empires had a definite long-term impact on the character of states in Africa, and on their *non*-development.

The impact is also seen in the state-building efforts of early post-independence leaders, and here, it seems, colonial rule was not the juggernaut Young depicts it as: if it had been, the African elite would not have needed to build up their bureaucracies. The colonial state apparatus had, if at all, built only weak administrative and infrastructure links to much of the state's territory. Independence leaders had to build the state and establish an administrative presence in areas the colonial powers had left untouched. Unfortunately, they replicated both the colonial states' use of large-scale planning and homogenised housing and agriculture, and their use of force when incentives did not work.

An additional effect is conceptual: the impact came from the beliefs, or, as Benedict Anderson put it, the 'imaginings', of Europeans. Indigenous political thought, concepts of authority and government, and so on, of African polities were largely superseded by or subordinated to European versions. If one accepts the constitutive force of ideas, this is of no small consequence. Young argues that the newly independent states were 'successors to the colonial regime, inheriting its structures, its quotidian routines and practices, and its more hidden normative theories of governance. Thus, everyday reason of state, as it imposed its logic on the new rulers, incorporated subliminal codes of operation bearing the imprint of their colonial predecessors' (and, of course, most of the post-colonial elites were Western-educated).

One might also consider that the new African political elite may have chosen to adopt the programmes and policies which were associated with, and promoted by, the clearest, most obvious, most powerful opponent of the former colonial powers in the international arena, that is, the Soviet Union. In many quarters, there was the widespread view of the USSR of a state and government which, through massive programmes of industrialisation had succeeded in moving from being a third-rate agricultural state into the status of a world power, challenging the United States and its (former colonialist) allies for control, leadership, and power in the modern world, and even beating the US in the 'space race'.

The fact that Ethiopia, which was never colonised, also, but later (in the 1970s and 1980s) tried forced resettlement and large-scale agricultural production suggests that the colonial state had less to do with these post-colonial states' activities than did elites' interests in making their entities into Western-style sovereign states and in 'modernising' the economy. Mengistu 'decried Ethiopia's reputation as "a symbol of backwardness and a valley of ignorance"'. In the end, the dislocations, the starvation, and brutality which the forced resettlements and new agricultural techniques produced in turn contributed to political instability and to the growing economic problems. Farmers went from producing surpluses on their own plots, thanks to their intimate knowledge of local conditions and their initiative, to being unskilled workers on 'foreign' terrain. Efforts to achieve rapid development, which were simultaneously efforts to seem like a state, had devastating results.

PAN-AFRICANISM

Upon gaining independence, was it inevitable that the former colonies would become sovereign states? Why did the pan-African movement not provide an alternative conception and structure for political organisation and authority in Africa? To answer these questions we must first address the questions of what the pan-African movement was and what a pan-African polity would have looked like.

The history of the pan-African movement has been well documented, as has the fact that it took a variety of forms: in addition to being a political movement, it was also a literary and cultural movement. Yet to speak of 'it' in the singular implies unity in a movement that was characterised by myriad interpretations of 'pan-Africanism' and its goals, and promoted by multiple and diverse organisations and leaders. Contemporary observers used the plural when writing of the unity movements, and there, perhaps, lies the crux of 'its' downfall: a multiplicity of material interests, some with significant structural bases, and of ideological leanings and goals. At the broadest level, there were disagreements within the so-called 'Black Triangle' of the United States, the West Indies, and Black Africa, and there were divisions within each of these. A case in point is the fact that the man whose name is most closely linked with the movement, W.E.B. Du Bois, thought continental Africans needed civilising, and were not ready for self-governance. That view was rebuked by many continental Africans.

The death-knell to the cross-continents and regions movement was sounded in 1958 by Kwame Nkrumah. Concerns in Africa had, logically, turned towards a specific goal which set continental Africans apart from those in the US and the West Indies: that of attaining independence from colonial rule.

Following the pan-African movement was the Organisation of African Unity (OAU). The OAU, however, had entered a world already peppered with a plethora of regional and rival 'unity' groups. Like the pan-African movement, the OAU foundered on the incentives political leaders had to promote the specific interests of their states and themselves, and on competing definitions of goals.

The Failure of Pan-Africanism

As with the failure of the pan-European movement after World War II, the failure of the pan-African movement may have been overdetermined. Constructivists would emphasise the hegemony of the idea of the sovereign state: the international system would not have recognised any political structure other than a sovereign state as the basis for political organisation in Africa; Institutionalists would emphasise the incentives which borders and existing political structures created. The quasi-statehood school, incorporating aspects of both perspectives, would note that pan-Africanism was not an alternative because independence leaders got sovereignty 'on the cheap'. To have superseded the sovereign state structure, they would have had to expend enormous resources. With ordinary state sovereignty, politicians did not even have to demonstrate that they had the full institutional structures of modern states, nor demonstrate that they had full authority. According to Robert Jackson, sovereign statehood was seen as 'egalitarian' and arguments for it being 'granted categorically even if the territory in question was extremely marginal became morally impregnable'. Institutionalists note that sovereign territorial statehood is convenient as an information economiser. As Jeffrey Herbst suggests, recognising boundaries and control of the capital city obviates other states' needs to see if a 'state' really has effective control of a territory, really does act for the collectivity, really has a public administrative and judicial system, and so on.

The Institutionalist arguments take two forms. One argues largely from the basis of colonial institutions, the other on the logic of boundaries. There is extensive debate about the extent to which colonial institutions 'froze' pre-existing political arrangements. If the 'freezing' argument is correct, then pan-Africanism was doomed to failure because it had neither the material resources nor the ideological means to bring together in a coherent governing structure the myriad polities and ethnicities that marked the colonial states. If colonial rule did not 'freeze' pre-colonial structures and alignments, it nevertheless deliberately discouraged unity within each colonial state in order to reduce the likelihood of successful challenges to colonial rule. An alternative argument would say that pre-colonial polities were not frozen in place under colonial rule; rather, the colonial states did not implement any significant changes for the simple reason of cost considerations. Thus, the colonial powers only discouraged unity as a side-effect of trying to rule on the cheap—trying to rearrange African political structures, and trying to bring some uniformity to the societies within the territorial boundaries, would have been an enormously expensive undertaking for which the colonial governors had not the resources. Ruling through local political structures was the rational response to the conditions. Whatever the exact character of transformation effected by the colonial powers on the pre-existing African polities, the pan-African movement faced enormous obstacles to unity.

Herbst's boundaries argument, while more directed at accounting for why, despite their lack of correspondence to ethnic, national, and political organisations, the sovereign state boundaries drawn up at the partition of Africa have remained largely unchallenged, provides a concise answer to the question of why the pan-African movement failed. Herbst reasons that Africa poses particular problems to creating a boundary system, and that once any boundaries are in place, the risks of disaster to each state in trying to alter them are far greater than any problems created (for the actors in control) by the boundaries themselves. Applied to the failure of pan-Africanism, Herbst's view would say that African elites had a very strong incentive to adhere to their states' status as sovereign territorial entities, rather than to renounce territoriality as a key organising principle.

The Rationalist argument, posited by Hendrik Spruyt, views boundaries and sovereignty from a different angle, which suggests a slightly different account of why pan-Africanism failed. This argument stresses that sovereign territoriality reduced 'transaction and information costs' between economic actors. States became the dominant 'unit' in the international system because, first, they were more effective at mobilising their societies' resources, were able to make credible commitments about future actions between their populations and other international actors, and because states had 'spatial limits to authority' thus avoiding confusing and costly jurisdictional overlap. As Spruyt notes, this type of unit, the sovereign territorial state, arose at a particular time and in response to a convergence of socio-economic and political developments, and so we might expect that at some time in the future, the state will give way to something else.

In the context of the contemporary African system of states, what is striking about Spruyt's analysis is the fact that many African states are not similar to sovereign territorial states, yet they remain considered so. The fact that they are may lend further support to the claim in Spruyt's argument that sovereign states prefer, as a matter of efficiency and reduced transaction costs, dealing with what they are willing to consider sovereign states, so will continue to act as if such entities exist even where they do not (Zaire/the Congo, Rwanda, Sierra Leone). As William Reno states, 'Stronger state reluctance to permit disorder ensures nominal support for territorial integrity.' Thus, pan-Africanism failed because the other units in the international system valued sovereign states.

SOME REFLECTIONS ON THE CONTEMPORARY AFRICAN STATE SYSTEM

According to international law, and as recognised by other states, Africa is home to a multitude of sovereign states. While for the most part current boundaries are accepted as legitimate, many states themselves may lack a central locus of authority, and there are significant areas where boundaries are in dispute. In numerous places states do not seem to be 'sovereign' even if they are territorial. Crawford Young bluntly notes that African states are characterised by '[f]ragments of state authority [which have] become instruments of predation among dispersed structural segments and individual actors'. Robert Jackson and Carl Rosberg have called these 'quasi-states'—states with the internationally recognised juridical trappings of sovereign statehood, but which lack the features expected elsewhere in a state. A greater proportion of Africans than in the past are now experiencing political life with no minimally viable state presence.

Some observers are not so pessimistic, but they seem contradicted by the perspective and evidence to which they point. Catherine Boone suggests that Africa does have cases of relatively successful state-building efforts, and that these have usually occurred 'in the Africa of peasant commodity production' rather than 'in the extractive and plantation enclaves'.

State collapse in Africa has been fuelled by the efforts of competing elites to control the state or to create one of their own. The internal conflicts are still over issues which seem to be core questions of state: who controls what territory and which institutions for the benefit of whom, who has the authority to make friend/enemy distinctions, and what is the political community's identity and what are its constitutive elements? Yet the modern state is not adequate to meeting the demands placed on it. What is striking is that even when the state was apparently at its zenith, it constructed other organisational forms: the empire, and, after two world wars raised questions about the severe costs of the world being defined by sovereign territorial states, the regional economic or political union. And as African states began to attain independence, they immediately created numerous cross-national organisations.

The current 'state system' in Africa is marked by numerous 'states' in which rule based upon violent accumulation creates archipelagos of control rather than hegemony over a contiguous territory. As the warlord polities of Zaire/the Congo, and of Liberia have shown, new political organisations have emerged in Africa that are not states, yet are capable of 'sovereign' diplomacy in the international state system. A number of militarised elites have violated sovereign state boundaries, have engaged in deliberate state destruction, and otherwise appear to be ignoring the alleged advantages of boundaries and sovereign statehood. They have been able to control the distribution of resources, and have appropriated for themselves the right to identify enemies. This, unfortunately, is the world as Schmitt saw it: raw force defining 'international' relations and relations between 'communities'. There is no agreement on the 'authoritative allocation of values', on the rules governing resource access and distribution. What matters is not the character or structure of the state, but whether there exists a community willing and able to define itself against a 'non-self'. The political entity is a political entity only because of 'the real existence of an enemy'. The essence of a political community is its willingness and ability to differentiate itself, to assert its existence. Applied to the African context, whether warlords and rebel groups, or the existing 'state', can succeed may not depend so much on their attaining the structure of a sovereign territorial state but on their ability to crush rivals. Their capacity to do so may, in turn, depend on their control of resources valued in the international economy, and on their links to public and private international economic actors. Perhaps the problem for Africa is that, given international norms and the current structure of the international system of states, it is constrained to force its politics into the 'state' format, even while it seems unable to do so.

Part Two

Africa and the International Order

INTRODUCTION

Some texts in this section may appear rather distant from international relations as traditionally understood, but they provide considerable evidence as to how such relations began to change after the Second World War. At a general level, Killick gives us a nuanced and judicious discussion of British aid to Africa in terms of both its scope and extent and the factors influencing it. At a more detailed level, Jennings discusses a fascinating example of how aid was shaped by certain ideological assumptions and how, as a result, a major Western nongovernmental organization subordinated itself to an African state. Another key novelty of the post–Second World War order was the United Nations, and in particular its growing role in relation to South Africa. Stultz outlines these developments against the background of some International Relations theory and shows the beginnings of the emergence of a human rights "regime." Part of such an emergence may be "moral shock," specifically the incidents at Sharpeville in March 1960 in which some seventy Africans were killed. In 1972, when at least 100,000 Africans were killed in Burundi, there was no moral shock, as Lemarchand's account (written not long after the events themselves) makes clear. There are important, if uncomfortable, questions to be asked about the difference between the two situations.

4

Policy Autonomy and the History of British Aid to Africa

TONY KILLICK

ELEMENTS OF POLICY

Aid Volumes and Concessionality

The volume of direct British aid to Africa is constrained by the substantial level of its contributions to multilateral programmes (including those of the European Union). The multilateral agencies, of course, also provide large volumes of aid to sub-Saharan Africa, of which the UK finances its share, but the following discussion is restricted to the bilateral element in British aid to Africa.

How did Africa fare in this context? The position today remains, as it has always been, that in relative terms Africa is strongly favoured over Asia.

Moreover, British assistance to Africa has always been highly concessional. For most of the last 20 years virtually all assistance to African (and other least developed) countries has been in the form of grants, as against loans, but even as early as the mid-1970s UK aid to the least developed countries was recorded as having a 99 per cent grant element. The UK has also implemented an active programme of bilateral debt forgiveness, in effect converting past loans into grants, as well as supporting the international HIPC scheme of debt relief, from which African countries have been among the largest beneficiaries.

Modalities and End-use Composition

The dominant form of financial assistance in the earlier years of British aid was to finance discrete development projects, to which was commonly linked the provision of technical assistance. The dominance of the project mode in Africa began to diminish during the 1980s, with the emergence of various forms of programme assistance, generally in support of the 'structural adjustment' programmes of the IMF and World Bank (the International Financial Institutions, or IFIs). The structural adjustment agenda gathered force in the 1980s and continued strongly into the 1990s. However, during the latter part of that decade there was a growing acceptance among donors, including the UK, that in Africa conditionality-based structural adjustment was bringing few of the intended benefits.

This realisation fed into a major re-think of aid priorities and modalities, in a landmark report by the OECD-Development Assistance Committee (DAC) in 1996. Among other things, this report greatly enhanced the priority accorded to the objective of reducing poverty and related variables—a thrust which eventually evolved into today's Millennium Development Goals (MDGs). The OECD-DAC report also placed issues of aid effectiveness more firmly on the agenda, and this latter thrust helped to sustain the trend towards programme assistance, even though structural adjustment was running out of steam. Since the late 1990s, the Department for International Development (DFID) has been among the leading advocates of programme modalities (largely direct budget support but also sectoral, through the modality of sector-wide programmes or SWAPs), as against projects.

How does the actual composition of British aid to Africa marry up with this description of global trends? First, a rather sharp upward trend is revealed in the share of projects in total bilateral aid to Africa since the beginning of the 1990s. However, interpretation of this is made more difficult by the lumping together into this category of project and sector assistance, even though some of the latter would be better regarded as programme assistance, via SWAPs and similar schemes. In any case, even at its peak, project/sector aid is shown as making up less than a fifth of the total.

Another noteworthy feature has been the persistently large scale of technical co-operation, again somewhat contrary to DFID intentions, although there has been a downward trend since the late 1990s. Technical assistance has throughout been by far the largest category of spending: even in 2003/4 over £250 million (British pounds sterling) was spent on this. Many people do not realise the large scale of technical assistance to Africa. Perhaps the biggest surprise is the rather constant share, at around 30 per cent, of programme aid—despite DFID's vigorous espousal of this aid form in recent years. It appears that DFID has been having difficulty in implementing its preferred shift from projects to budget support.

If the above trends suggest inertia in the composition of UK aid, DFID can certainly show that the sectoral allocation of its present-day support is strongly consistent with its chosen concentration on the direct reduction of poverty and promotion of the MDGs.

An even more dramatic demonstration of change is given by the following data showing aid to Africa for what can broadly be described as investment in 'directly productive' activities (economic plus rural livelihoods) as a percentage of 'social' spending (education plus health plus social plus governance): 1988/9–1989/90 371%; 1993/4–1994/5 208%; 1998/9–1999/00 49%; and 2003/4 45%.

The Evolution of Policy Priorities

An important feature of the administration of British aid is that, from the creation in 1964 of a Ministry of Overseas Development, execution of the great preponderance of the country's total overseas assistance has been concentrated in a single department of government. However, this does not mean that the disinterested promotion of social and economic development has always dominated the policy priorities of successive administrations. Aid has also, of course, been used to promote Britain's national interest. One obvious issue here is the standing of developmental considerations *vis-à-vis* foreign policy, security, immigration and commercial objectives. An important clue is provided by the fluctuating status of the government department responsible for aid.

The points of substance beneath this apparent game of ping-pong were the signals the changes sent about the relative importance attached by successive governments to developmental and foreign policy objectives. Developmental considerations were more likely to be subordinated when the department came formally under the responsibility of the Foreign Secretary, although the contrasts between the two situations were not in practice as dramatic as might have been expected. Even when part of the FCO, the department had considerable latitude in pursuing developmental goals, just as, when independent, it has been far from immune to the influence of foreign policy considerations. Party politics has been a strong influence in these matters, as will be described below.

Just as the influence of foreign-policy-*cum*-security considerations has waxed and waned, so too has the influence of commercial motives. Of considerable importance was the common practice of procurement tying. This meant that imports financed by British aid were restricted to goods and services originating in the UK, a form of protectionism which often greatly cut the real value of the 'assistance' provided and effectively reduced its concessionality. In the 1980s, nearly half of total UK bilateral aid (to all countries) was tied in this way, although this fell in the 1990s and was applied to only about a seventh of total bilateral aid by 1996. It was abolished altogether in 2001.

Lessons from experience also led to changes. This was particularly the case with project-based and technical assistance modes of aid delivery, with neither of these now viewed as having been very effective, partly because of the high transaction costs they generate. Along with other donors, the UK has therefore turned towards programmatic forms, as mentioned earlier.

British aid policies to Africa have changed in other major ways. Among the most obvious in recent years is the extent to which DFID's agenda has shifted from a project-led promotion of economic growth to concentration on the goal of poverty reduction and achievement of the MDGs. The Public Service Agreement which it has with the Treasury is defined almost exclusively in terms of progress towards the MDGs and the reduction of poverty. Although it was the 1975 White Paper which first gave prominence to the poverty-reduction objective, this was then a less dominant theme and was viewed more in terms of rural development.

The nature of the relationships which the UK as a donor has sought to establish with recipient governments has also undergone substantial change. This has been partly the result of the waxing and waning of non-developmental foreign policy and commercial motivations. It has also resulted from the move from project to programmatic modalities. This shift first achieved prominence in the 'structural adjustment' era of the 1980s and earlier 1990s, when the IFIs were highly active in the placing of adjustment credits, especially in Africa, and when an increasing share of British aid was used in support of these. As this developed, relationships became increasingly based on donors' desires to improve economic and institutional policies within recipient countries, attempting to use financial leverage through the application of extensive policy conditionality. During the 1980s, the UK was largely content to piggy-back on the conditionality of the IFIs (especially the IMF), generally making access to its own programme assistance conditional upon a country's continued satisfactory implementation of IFI adjustment programmes.

An extension of conditionality-based assistance occurred in the early 1990s, with a sharply increased use by the UK and other bilateral donors (and with the IFIs this time trailing behind) of political and governance-related conditionality.

In practice, neither the policy conditionality of the IFIs nor the political conditionality of the bilaterals was pursued with consistent rigour, and recipient governments quickly learned how to play the conditionality game without prejudicing continued inflows of assistance. It is perhaps not surprising, therefore, that a major feature of the 1997 White Paper was an announced move away from relationships based on conditionality in favour of more even-handed 'partnerships' involving mutual recipient-donor responsibilities. Policy and governance issues were still regarded as of central importance but these were henceforth to be based on local ownership, policy dialogue and mutual agreements among parties. An implication of this shift was also that the UK would henceforth be more selective in the African (and other) governments it supported, cutting its aid to those which did not meet minimum conditions of trustworthiness and commitment to promote poverty reduction. However, it is not clear that there has since been any decisive move towards greater selectivity. It is probably also true to say that it has proved quite difficult to draw and maintain the line between a relationship based on conditionality and one rooted in ownership and partnership. It is likely that only in a few British-aided African countries has there been a clear and generally recognised change in relationships, although DFID's intentions are undoubted.

Lastly, and related to the moves towards programme aid and policy dialogue, the substantial decentralisation that has occurred in DFID's operational structure has been another important development. In virtually all major African recipients, substantial financial and policy authority is vested in the local DFID representatives, with reference back to London restricted to the most major or sensitive issues. A possible down-side of this is that DFID headquarters may now find it harder to secure uniform implementation of its policy objectives.

To sum up, it is evident from the above account that there has been quite a lot of fluidity in British aid policies towards Africa over the last four decades. Major movements have occurred in almost every dimension, although inevitably the reality of change on the ground has often been less dramatic than the observable shifts in headquarters policies. The main task of the remainder of this chapter is to try to identify the principal determining influences on the evolution of policy described above.

DETERMINING INFLUENCES

The long-term course of the policies of any institution is the result of interplay between inertial forces tending to perpetuate the *status quo*, and active forces for change. Policy-makers are constrained by history, by special interests which benefit from existing policies, by settled ways of viewing problems and by the perceived dangers or uncertainties of changing course. The extent to which they are free of inertial forces—especially the restraining hands of interest groups—shows the extent of their *autonomy*, a concept which became popular in the literature explaining the relative success of the East Asian 'miracle' economies, where policy-makers were seen to have enjoyed substantial autonomy from special interest groups.

In what follows, both inertial and proactive forces are described, but what is already suggested by the policy fluidity is that British aid administrators have enjoyed quite a high degree of autonomy, although more so at some times than others. The following account identifies three broad influences: historical; ideological and intellectual; and what is termed the global politics of aid.

The Influence of History

British imperialism—and post-colonial guilt—offer an obvious starting point. A direct line can be traced back from the creation of the Ministry of Overseas Development in 1964 to grants in aid provided to colonies from the 1870s. Such assistance was more formally organised under the 1929 Colonial Development Act and the Colonial Development and Welfare Acts of 1940 and 1945. The provision of this support was intended to come to an end as colonies became independent, with what would now be called development assistance then to be restricted to the provision of some technical assistance and contributions to multilateral institutions like the World Bank. The strength of the British anti-colonial movement, the adoption elsewhere of bilateral aid programmes and a change of government altered this, however, and led to the creation of the Ministry in 1964.

Forty years later the influence of the UK's colonial history is still evident, even if it is gradually being eroded. As recently as 1999/2000 no less than 72 per cent of DFID's total bilateral aid (excluding humanitarian assistance) went to Commonwealth countries, about the same amount as ten years earlier. This share has since diminished but was still as high as 60 per cent in 2003/4, when 15 of the top 20 recipients were Commonwealth countries. Former British colonies in Africa have benefited from this bias. Twelve of the top 20 were African countries, of which only one (Ethiopia) was not a Commonwealth member. The strength of the historical factor is illustrated by the continued enjoyment of substantial British assistance by Malawi and Zambia, neither being a country that would appear to merit priority in terms of the effectiveness of such aid.

The lingering influence of British imperialism, then, has acted as an inertial force. A more recent historical development, however, was a potential spur to change, namely, the end of the Cold War at the beginning of the 1990s. This undermined the raison d'être for supporting certain corrupt and anti-developmental regimes, which, however, had enjoyed geopolitical importance during the period of East-West stand-off. However, such considerations had not exerted a large influence on UK aid distributions, and the end of the Cold War actually had only limited impact on its aid to Africa.

More generally, the end of the Cold War did tend to reduce the weight attached to foreign policy considerations in British aid allocations. It was not a coincidence that the political conditionality referred to earlier did not begin to assume prominence until the 1990s. In principle, the collapse of communism as a possible threat could have brought a 'peace dividend' to the aid budget, but the priorities of the government of the time did not favour this. In fact, the decision of the incoming Labour government of 1997 to stick for two years with the announced spending allocations of its predecessor meant that it was not until the end of the 1990s that the aid budget was able to begin a period of rapid real growth that has continued through to today and is announced to be sustained for some years hereafter.

History enters the story in another way too, through its influence on the course of British domestic macroeconomic policies. There were long periods during the post-1945 period when, from today's perspective, successive administrations pursued inappropriate macro policies which, in turn, impacted on the scale of the country's aid budget. Thus, throughout much of the 1960s and 1970s governments sought to maintain relatively fixed ('adjustable peg') exchange rates which were inconsistent with their fiscal stances and the relative inflexibility of the economy, leading to sometimes acute balance-of-payments difficulties ('sterling crises'), which they sought to resolve through imperfectly executed policies of financial stringency. As an economist in the then Ministry of Overseas Development in the late 1960s, the present writer well remembers the balance-of-payments justifications offered for the squeeze on the aid budget of that time.

Of course, Britain's aid budget is a small part of total government spending (under 5 per cent), so it has always been possible to argue that it would not matter in macroeconomic terms if the government of the day chose to give priority to maintaining the aid budget even during periods of general financial stringency. It is certainly the case that the administrations in power in the periods when aid was in decline—the second half of the 1960s and the 1980s and much of the 1990s—demonstrated a relatively low regard for aid (Mrs Thatcher, who was premier for most of the latter period, famously dismissed it as 'hand-outs'), but even with good will it could be electorally difficult to justify special treatment when the domestic provision of state services was being squeezed. As it is, although the existence of an aid budget enjoys considerable public support, questions about the level and composition of aid have had little influence on general election results.

Ideological and Intellectual Influences

The last paragraph brings us naturally to consideration of ideology and party politics. The design of aid strategies and the specifics of policy have, by and large, not been the subject of any deep disagreement between the two main political parties, although differences have arisen on the extent to which aid should be used explicitly to promote British interests and on the desirable scale of the aid budget.

As regards the pursuit of British interests, the main contrast that is often drawn is between the views of successive Conservative administrations from 1979 to 1997 and their Labour predecessors and successors. In fact, one of the ways in which party politics has played out over the years has been over the status enjoyed by the aid administration. One of the main points at issue being the extent of independence which the department should enjoy from the foreign policy establishment. In essence, Labour has stood for a relatively strong and independent aid ministry, the Conservatives for a weaker department formally located within the FCO.

Within the UK since 1997 the primacy of developmental considerations has been powerfully reasserted, not least through the publication of two White Papers and supporting legislation. In fact, the 2002 International Development Act made it unlawful for British aid to be used for any purpose other than the furtherance of sustainable development or improving the welfare of the populations of assisted territories. Interestingly, these changes were not the subject of much party-political controversy. The Conservative response to the seminal 1997 White Paper was muted but essentially supportive. More recently, the Conservative Party has formally pledged to match Labour's commitment to achieving the UN target of an aid programme equivalent to 0.7 per cent of GDP by 2013 (although with more of it going through bilateral programmes). Indeed, in the specifics of aid policy, there has throughout been a degree of consensus between most interested members of both parties. In the design of aid policies towards Africa, it is not clear that inter-party differences have made much difference.

Changes in the intellectual climate have had more impact. Evolving perceptions of the meaning and nature of 'development', and of how aid can best contribute to this, have certainly fed into the redesign of aid policies. In the 1960s and beyond, an economistic view predominated, in which development was largely seen in terms of economic growth, with the pace of growth largely viewed as a function of the rate of investment. Poor countries were seen as having limited saving capacities, resulting in major gaps between domestic investable resources and the volume of investment required to raise per capita incomes at an acceptable pace. Aid, then, was to help fill this financing gap (and also a foreign-exchange gap). One way of ensuring that aid was indeed used for investment (it was then believed, before the subversive notion of fungibility took hold) was to devote it to the financing of development projects, hence the dominance in this earlier period of the project mode in aid delivery.

In this period the UK, like others, was concerned to get out of budgetary aid and to use projects to boost official development expenditure—on education and agriculture as well as infrastructure. There was heavy emphasis on technical and administrative assistance, to permit substituting African cadres for British technical assistance personnel. Faithfully reflecting the dominant view of the time, aid administrators believed in the efficacy of a state-led 'big push'.

Thinking about development has since moved on in many ways that have had a bearing on aid policies. A more multi-dimensional view is now taken, with social, quality-of-life and 'governance' variables now also seen as central, alongside economic ones. While poverty has always been a concern of development economists, there is now much less willingness to take for granted that economic growth will provide a sufficient solution, not least because poverty is now viewed as involving more than material deprivation and as having important non-economic dimensions. Even in the economic sphere, experience has taught that there is more to achieving growth than simply maximising the rate of investment: the quality of investment decisions, the productivity of past investment and associated rates of technological progress are all important. In turn, these variables came to be seen as crucially determined by the policy environment, and a more sceptical view was taken of the efficacy of the state as an economic agent.

Amongst students and practitioners of development, there has also been a growing awareness of the limitations of what can be achieved by external assistance, and of the centrality of domestic sources of change within poor countries (although the most recent developments imply a return to the aid optimism of an earlier time—see below). It is this realisation, partly fuelled by the perceived ineffectiveness of conditionality and financial leverage, which lies behind the present-day emphasis on the salience of domestic ownership of policies and institutional development.

Mention should also be made of the existence within the UK of a strong and increasingly sophisticated group of civil society organisations which have been supportive by raising public awareness of the problems of Africa and other poor countries (for example, by mobilising the public during the Ethiopian famine of 1984 and in favour of a better deal for Africa through the 'Live 8' campaign of 2005). Although these bodies have not always enjoyed the influence to which they aspired, they have undoubtedly been a strong influence on specific UK policies relating to the quality of aid (for which the Independent Group on British Aid was an effective lobby during the 1980s and into the 1990s). The umbrella NGO group Jubilee 2000 was highly effective in campaigning for debt forgiveness at the turn of the century, while well resourced and organised NGOs like Oxfam and Christian Aid exert an on-going influence through their research-based campaigning.

The Global Politics of Aid

It is sufficiently well-known to need no elaboration that, by comparison with other developing regions, Africa has emerged as the most problematical and the biggest challenge to all who aspire to end poverty in the world (although this is subject to the usual caveat against over-generalising about a continent that actually contains a wide range of experiences). The long-term lagging pace of growth and development in much of the continent, the tendency for poverty to increase overall rather than decline, the record of failed states, of international and internal conflicts and associated mass movements of refugees, are well known. Recurrent famines and other disasters, for example, in Ethiopia in 1974 and 1984, have received much media attention and aroused public sympathy, making it impossible for aid administrations not to respond. It is this failure of economic development within the continent which explains the extent to which international aid efforts have become concentrated on Africa during the last two decades or more. The UK, as shown earlier, has shared in this concentration.

Conditions in many African countries also help explain other aspects of the changing policies recorded above, such as the extremely high levels of concessionality and the (albeit lagging) provisions of debt relief, the retreat from project assistance, the intense focus on structural adjustment in the 1980s and beyond, the growing interest in issues of 'governance' and institution-building, and the rise in the scale of humanitarian assistance. To a substantial extent, then, UK policy changes have been in response to conditions in Africa and the slow progress on much of the continent.

British policies have also been shaped by other agencies working in the aid field. The IFIs have been particularly important, not least through their influence on the changes in attitudes towards development sketched earlier. The direct influence of the IFIs on British policy during the structural adjustment phase of the 1980s–90s has already been noted, formalised by cross-conditionality between country execution of IFI (especially IMF) adjustment conditionality and access to British programme aid. It is similarly said that the theme of the 1975 White Paper on meeting basic needs was a result of work by the World

Bank's staff. More generally, the IMF has been important in changing developing country attitudes towards the importance of sound macroeconomic management, while the Bank's research and publications have influenced thinking about many aspects of development.

In parallel with this, the Development Assistance Committee (DAC) of the OECD has been working quietly, trying to persuade bilateral donors to co-ordinate better and to reform practices, like tying, which reduce the value and effectiveness of aid. For long an ineffectual talking shop, the DAC has become somewhat more influential over the past decade, as concerns about aid effectiveness and transaction costs have grown, and with its initiation of a process culminating in the formulation of the MDGs and the March 2005 *Paris Declaration* on aid effectiveness. The work of the DAC and the views of its members have undoubtedly fed into the evolution of British policies, which are nowadays focused on achievement of the MDGs and are strong on the desirability of donors working collectively to harmonise their efforts and to become more cost-effective. There have been other external influences too: various United Nations conferences, the work of the UNDP on country-level aid co-ordination and other UN agencies, the Development Committee of the IMF and World Bank, the Strategic Partnership with Africa, and others. Like-minded aid ministers and their agencies—a shifting body of alliances—have also been influential at different times.

However, while these various donor-based activities have doubtless fed into UK policies, it is probably accurate to say that DFID and its predecessors, as among the most professional of the bilateral aid agencies, have acted more as leader than as follower. Even since as long ago as the 1970s, the UK, under successive Chancellors of the Exchequer from both main parties, has been in the lead in pressing for debt relief for poor countries. However, leadership has been at its strongest in the most recent period, when, working with 'like-minded' donors, DFID has somewhat self-consciously sought a leadership role, in the vanguard in advocacy of harmonisation around the MDGs, in favour of debt relief, direct budget support and other measures to lower aid's transactions costs, working towards collective donor decisions to increase their aid budgets, and promoting the creation of an International Financing Facility (IFF). In other words, participation in the various collective forums has more often represented a platform than an external input into policy change.

CONCLUSION AND IMPLICATIONS FOR THE FUTURE

We have shown that there have been many influences on British aid policies, both generally and towards Africa. There have been some important forces making for continuity: the influence of the country's imperial past; the influence of commercial interests intent upon preserving trading and investment advantages; and delays in turnaround leading to discrepancies between what headquarters says its policies are and what actually happens in the field.

Overall, however, it is change, not inertia, which marks the record of British aid policies towards Africa. On election to power, political parties have been relatively unconstrained in pursuing desired policies in a top-down manner—what we earlier called policy autonomy. What governments have wanted to do was, in turn, influenced by the evolving intellectual climate, by what the IFIs and other bilateral donors were doing, and by the campaigns of civil society organisations. Parliament has rarely been much of an influence, because of the degree of cross-party agreement, because of the general weakness of parliamentary scrutiny in the UK, and because the specifics of aid policies have largely been seen as technocratic matters in which Parliament has little expertise or interest.

It is possible to go further, to point out that, by and large, policy autonomy has been used for the pursuit of long-term development goals, as against the promotion of the UK's national interest. There are, of course, specific exceptions to this, but it would be difficult to interpret the history of UK aid to Africa as a cynical and exploitative promotion of national commercial or foreign policy objectives. Developmental goals have been particularly dominant in the most recent years.

To those who are sceptical about the wisdom of such acceleration of aid flows as seen for example during Tony Blair's premiership, this represents a reversal of the greater realism that emerged during the previous two decades about what can be achieved by external assistance, and an implicit rejection of the primacy of domestic ownership. The intended scale of the expansion and the enormous pressures to spend which it would create would, critics argue, undermine the efforts of the recent past to enter into partnership-based relationships. On this view, by going beyond countries' absorptive capacities, the expansion would also undermine efforts to improve the cost-effectiveness of aid.

Whether or not these fears are justified, the changes now planned by the government represent a prime example of top-down policy autonomy. Of course, the change is not unconstrained. The government wants to carry other donors with it and a good few of them are reluctant, although the government has made it clear that it will go ahead unilaterally, if necessary. The lead time between announcement of a major change and its implementation is bound to be substantial, just as DFID has found it difficult to shift further towards direct budgetary support as fast as it wished. Moreover, there is likely to remain a strong Anglophone bias in UK aid to Africa, albeit one which is diminished by the emergence as substantial recipients of such countries as Ethiopia and Mozambique. There will be constraints, then, but nothing powerful enough to frustrate a governmental exercise of political free will in favour of much more aid to Africa.

AID VOLUMES AND AFRICA'S SHARE[1]

The dominating story of the years since the early-2000s is one of an extraordinary expansion in the UK's total provision of development assistance, from £5.2bn in 2004 to £8.6bn in 2012 and a budgeted £11.2bn in 2013. This doubling in less than a decade is admittedly in nominal terms but deflating this by a suitable price index still leaves a roughly 70 per cent real terms rise in 2004–13. The focus of policy-makers was on the rate of Overseas Development Assistance (ODA) as a proportion of national income, with a cross-party commitment to attain the UN target of 0.7 per cent of Gross National Income (GNI) by 2013. This target was duly achieved.

The UK was thus able to boast that it was the first G8 country (but far from the first European country) to hit this target, although statistically it was helped to do so by an economic recession after 2007 resulting in below-trend values for the GNI denominator.

As can be seen from the figures above, bilateral aid flows to Africa fully participated in this expansion. Taking the period as a whole, UK multilateral aid contributions expanded rather faster than bilateral flows but within the declining bilateral proportion Africa's share rose. Bilateral aid to Africa grew even more rapidly than the total aid spend. Twelve of the top 20 recipients of UK aid were African countries; were the aid spending to be presented in per capita terms, the skew would be even more marked.

THE UNDERLYING POLITICS

The increases just recorded look all the more remarkable when set in the context, after the general election of 2010, of the UK government determined above all to bring down the budget deficit, primarily through reduced spending. Most departments of state were faced with budget cuts. Only a few escaped: the aid budget joined domestic education and health as the only departments whose budgets were ring-fenced from spending cuts. Moreover, Prime Minister David Cameron and other members of his government repeated their commitment to the UN 0.7% target that had been adopted by the preceding Labour government, despite every sign that this was unpopular with many Conservative Party members and evidence also of declining public support for the aid programme. There is no reason to doubt the sincerity of the Prime Minister's support for the UK's aid effort. Equally, however, there seems little doubt that it was symbolic of his efforts to 'modernise' his party and to give it a more benign public image, in response to a perception that the party was seen by the electorate as 'the nasty party'. As we have just shown, Africa fully benefitted from the aid expansion, although DFID's policies were not expressed in regional terms and there was little public discussion of the regional distribution of the increases.

The outcome of the 2010 election also interrupted 'the game of ping-pong' determining the formal status of DFID reported above. Historical precedents suggested that DFID would again have been demoted to a more junior, non-Cabinet status, formally attached to the Foreign and Commonwealth Office. In the event, DFID retained the full status it had enjoyed under the previous Labour administration. The fact that the government formed in 2010 was a parliamentary coalition of the Conservative and Liberal-Democrat parties probably guaranteed that DFID would retain its status but there is no reason to believe the Conservatives would have demoted it even if they had alone been able to form a government.

AID DELIVERY POLICIES

In the original article above I noted the retreat from what could broadly be described as aid for 'economic' sectors in favour of social services and 'governance'. The figures in Table 4.1 below bring this story up to 2012 and broadly consolidate the trends noted for the earlier years.

The small share of aid allocated to 'economic' sectors relative to the social services and governance categories remained striking for these years, although as shown below this situation may well be changing.

In terms of the modalities through which the aid was delivered, the data are not good enough to permit confident generalisations. It appears that 'project-type' assistance gained in relative importance during the years under review here and was substantially greater than programmatic aid (i.e. budget support and sector programme support), although the share of programmatic aid to Africa appears larger than for other recipients. Technical assistance—whose continuing large scale was highlighted in the original article—appears to have declined in importance in the more recent years to less than 10 per cent of total bilateral aid to the region. However, the data are not conclusive.

It is perhaps consistent with the relative decline of programmatic aid, and the stress that was placed in earlier years on the importance of recipient policies as determining aid effectiveness, that much less stress was placed on the language of conditionality in more recent years. In 2011 DFID published what was, in effect, the coalition government's White Paper on aid policy but it had little to say on this subject. The application of conditionality was not mentioned at all.

Table 4.1. UK aid to Africa by sector, %

	2007/08	2011/12
Economic	22.1	19.0
Social services	48.4	52.3
Environment	0.7	2.6
Governance	25.4	20.4
Water supply & sanitation	3.5	5.5

One of the features of the UK's aid programme noted in the original article was the extent to which it was spread over a large number of recipient countries. The 2011 policy statement stated a desire to achieve a greater concentration on a smaller number of recipients, identifying 27 countries of concentration (subsequently reduced to 25 after the subsequent dropping of India and South Africa, but then mysteriously increased to 28 in 2014). The choice of these recipients was justified in terms of their particularly severe concentrations of poverty, ill-health and insecurity. Of the original 27 countries, 17 were in Africa. The intention was also stated to raise the proportion of aid going to war-torn and unstable countries.

The choice of countries of concentration was also intended to 'Re-emphasise the importance of the Commonwealth'. Fourteen of the original 27 countries were Commonwealth countries, although only 12 were left after the dropping of India and South Africa. My original article noted the continuing influence of history on the allocation of aid, as represented by Commonwealth membership. About 55 per cent of the total was going to Commonwealth countries in 2002. By 2012, however, the figure was down to 30 per cent. Aid to Commonwealth African countries was more prominent, however, amounting in 2012 to 48 per cent of the UK's total bilateral aid to Africa.

POLICY AUTONOMY CONTINUES

The principal contention of the original article was that policy-makers have in the past been relatively unconstrained by external forces in setting aid policies generally and towards Africa in particular. Does more recent experience bear out this thesis? The period covered by this postscript straddles several years of a Labour government and then a few years of a Conservative-Liberal Democrat coalition, from May 2010. In the latter period there have been two Secretaries of State: Andrew Mitchell held office until September 2012 and was succeeded by Justine Greening.

Mitchell's period marked a high degree of continuity with the policies of his predecessors. Indeed, he is on record as saying that 'There is not a Conservative, Liberal-Democratic or Labour development policy but a British one.' His chief innovation, stemming from a conviction that DFID must justify the privilege of its ring-fenced budget by demonstrating value for money, was to greatly strengthen the results orientation of his department and independent scrutiny of its performance. A Results Framework was created to facilitate comparison of aspirations with actual results, and an Independent Commission for Aid Impact to provide an external view. But the previous administration's policies remained broadly in place, especially its emphasis on poverty reduction and on promoting the achievement of the Millennium Development Goals.

Although it is too early to assess her actual impact, the arrival of Justine Greening brought a marked change of approach. Relatively young, evidently ambitious and anxious to make her mark, a few months after taking office she delivered a speech stating as a priority 'ramping up the focus on DFID helping to drive economic growth', signalling a major policy change. In another speech a year later she elaborated at length. 'Economic development' was now to be a core priority—a 'fundamentally smarter' approach to aid—where she clearly equated 'development' with economic growth, albeit inclusive, labour-intensive growth. Between these two speeches, she asserted, DFID had been on a 'transformational journey' involving 'a radical shift in the way that [it] works'. The past welfare-oriented approach remained important but it was not enough. DFID had now adopted a 'frontier economy strategy'. A growth priority, she asserted, was the best long-term solution to poverty and, by helping to develop the next generation of rapidly-growing economies, it would be good for British trading and financial interests too. The amount of bilateral aid targeted on 'economic development' was to be more than doubled to £1.8bn between 2012/13 and 2015/16. Shortly afterwards DFID elaborated with a 'strategic framework' setting out the case for the new stress on growth. What this policy shift might mean for Africa was not spelled out. It is not obvious that Africa would benefit from adoption of a 'frontier economy strategy', although the strategy paper did confirm that DFID would continue to focus efforts on its chosen countries of concentration.

It appears, then, that in short order a new minister had thoroughly shaken up the previous cross-party consensus. Such a seemingly radical shift might have been expected to stir controversy, especially given Greening's reassertion of the use of aid to promote British interests, but the reality has been otherwise. A year on from Greening's 2013 speech the Labour opposition has been silent. There has been no Parliamentary debate on this policy change. The usually active House of Commons Committee on International Development has been similarly unforthcoming. Even the usually vocal international NGOs have been quiet. In short, policy autonomy has reigned supreme. The minister's 'transformational journey' has gone all but unnoticed, with unpredictable consequences for Britain's aid to Africa.

NOTE

1. Postscript, 2014–15: The original article was written in early 2005. Since then a good deal has happened with the UK's aid to Africa and the purpose of the remainder of the essay is to provide a brief update.

5

'Development Is Very Political in Tanzania': Oxfam and the Chunya Integrated Development Programme 1972–76

MICHAEL JENNINGS

During the 1960s and 1970s, the British charity Oxfam pursued a development programme in Tanzania that sought to help the Tanzanian government implement the policy of Ujamaa. Yet this policy was not an uncontroversial exercise in the remodelling of a nation: within the space of a decade, upwards of ten million people were shifted from their homes into new nucleated villages—95 per cent of the population were moved into these new rural centres of living and production. Nor was it a policy that was implemented without force: stories of burning huts and excessive coercion by soldiers and party officials were common currency. By 1976, it had become clear that villagisation and Ujamaa policy had effectively masked a massive extension in the authority of the central state machinery and a process of authoritarianism that sought to dominate all aspects of rural life. Tanzania by the end of the 1970s had moved from a position of advocating grass-roots democracy in development to a fully-fledged statist model of governance.

During the 1960s, Oxfam had formed an increasingly ideological attachment to Tanzania and to the needs of development in general. It made no pretence to be a neutral organisation promoting technical responses to the needs of poverty. Moreover, the NGO assumed that its supporters shared this position. Oxfam's agenda was situated in the liberal-left spectrum of politics, and was, in the main, distrustful of governments and the motives of those governments. The Oxfam 'worldview' regarded the process of development as something that could only occur through the empowerment of the poor, a concept that became formalised in policy with the adoption of 'conscientisation' in the 1970s. Paulo Freire enunciated the concept of conscientisation in Brazil in the early 1970s. It held that development could only occur when the poor were granted the political power to manage development themselves. Through such empowerment, by becoming responsible for their own development, the real needs of the peasantry could be met, and the ability to plan, organise and implement would be learnt. According to this discourse, the NGO was to be a partner in the process of development, not a remote donor or planner, intervening from on high and promoting its own sense of needs and priorities. For Oxfam, Ujamaa embodied this new philosophy: the new Ujamaa villages would create forums for grass-roots democracy and hence bring development planning to the people. Yet the fact is that the promises of the rhetoric of Ujamaa were not being met by the

1970s. The peasantry were being pushed ever further away from the arenas of power.

The central question, as concerns Oxfam's role in Tanzania in this period, is how such an organisation, with an openly anti-authoritarian agenda, came not only to support this system in word, but actually became part of the process of the extension of state authority. Oxfam had become, in effect, a surrogate of the state, bound by chains of its own forging. It sought to promote grass-roots democracy and an extension of power to the peasantry, but in effect supported the opposite. How did this NGO, with two field officers working in the country and excellent sources of information, fail to perceive the realities of Ujamaa as it was being implemented in the 1970s?

From a position in the late 1960s of convergence between the NGO and the state over definitions of Ujamaa, by 1969 these interpretations of Ujamaa and the official development policy had begun to diverge. For the state, it became a means of exerting control over peasant production. The primary purpose of development policy, for the state, was to increase the level of agricultural production and to secure greater state control over the results of that production. For Oxfam, the mode of production remained the key objective: communal production and ownership was of greater significance than the level of production achieved. Villagisation, for Oxfam, was about the promotion of democracy and greater popular participation in the decision-making process. For the state, villagisation had become a means of exerting increased authority over the rural sector. Villages, for the government, were centres of mechanisms of control, not of socialist living.

It is the assertion of this chapter that Oxfam was blinded to the realities of Ujamaa and Tanzanian development as a result of the politicisation of poverty it held as central to its charitable mission, and its ideology of development. Oxfam identified so completely with the socio-political agenda of Ujamaa that it geared its entire development programme in Tanzania to assisting in the implementation of this ideology. The realities and technical aspects of Ujamaa were ignored or downplayed in the pursuit of wider socio-political aims. In a seeming reversal of James Ferguson's 'anti-politics machine', Oxfam became a 'politics machine'.

BACKGROUND TO THE CHUNYA INTEGRATED DEVELOPMENT PROGRAMME

Oxfam and Ujamaa

Oxfam is currently the largest British NGO, and one of the largest worldwide development agencies. In the financial year 1958–59, its income was £500,000 (British pounds sterling). By 1997 its income reached £91.8 million, of which 82 per cent was spent on development and relief work, 6 per cent on education and information campaigns, 10 per cent on fund-raising costs, and the remainder on administration and other miscellaneous costs. Oxfam was created in 1942 as part of the response to widespread starvation in Greece resulting from the Allied blockade. It was the only regional Famine Relief Committee to continue after the war, and turned its attention to post-war reconstruction in Europe. Throughout the 1950s, it remained essentially a donor organisation, providing funds and materials for use in emergency relief to be distributed and managed by local agencies. During the 1960s, the 'Decade of Development', participation in the Freedom from Hunger Campaign and the 1960/61 Congo famine led to an understanding that the needs of poverty required action to prevent disaster, not just a palliative after disaster had struck. Development was to become the mainstay of the Oxfam mission. In 1961, with the appointment of the first Field Director to southern Africa—Jimmy Betts—Oxfam began the process of establishing a direct presence in the geographical areas where it funded projects. Throughout the 1960s and

1970s, Oxfam was in the process of defining and understanding its development mission and role. It was a fluid period, in which administrative structures were established as need arose and policy was formed to meet the new challenges.

Development policy in Tanzania, and Ujamaa in particular, thus arose at a crucial point in Oxfam's emergence as a development agency. During the 1960s, as Oxfam sought to shift the balance of its operations from emergency relief to development, Ujamaa emerged as a major ideological force in the development world. By the 1970s, as Oxfam underwent a period of redefinition in its development strategy with the impact of conscientisation, the example of Tanzania was again to prove crucial. The Chunya Integrated Development Programme, 1972–76, was central to this process.

Nyerere had begun outlining his vision of Ujamaa from the early 1960s. It placed an emphasis on the community and a vaguely defined concept of 'familyhood'. An emphasis on equality and the need to prevent exploitation lay at the roots of Ujamaa. For Nyerere, economic advancement and development could spring from social change. Ujamaa, as a radical policy of social change, could thus form the basis of development. It was an attempt to remodel Tanzanian society along socialist lines. Nyerere's vision was not based upon Western or Soviet models, but rather based on the peasants: rural socialism. The importance of China in the practical application of this 'African Socialism' (as it became known in the North) came in the form of the villagisation programme. The centres for rural socialism were to be the Ujamaa villages: nucleated settlements incorporating both communal living and communal production. Services would be more rationally provided through these villages, and the establishment of a system of village government would create the mechanisms for grass-roots participation in the development process. Communal production would not only bring economies of scale to the agricultural sector, but would allow for a more equitable distribution of the rewards of that production.

Ujamaa became the official policy of Tanzania in 1967, following the publication and acceptance by TANU of the Arusha Declaration. This document, with further elaboration in *Freedom and Development* and *Socialism and Rural Development*, set out the framework for Ujamaa theory and policy as a development tool. The Arusha Declaration outlined the theoretical position. It declared the intention to establish a society based on democracy, equality, dignity and respect. It announced a programme of nationalisation, shifted the focus from the industrial sector to the rural and outlined the position on foreign aid (Tanzania should accept foreign aid, but remain cautious as to the conditions accompanying it). *Socialism and Rural Development* applied Ujamaa to the rural sector. Resettlement policy became an instrument for achieving the establishment of rural socialism.

From 1967, the village unit became the central focus of Tanzanian development policy. It was the target for government aid and assistance; it was the focus for government and bank loans and finance, and subsequent development programmes, such as water-supply, agricultural improvement, service provision, marketing and training, used the Ujamaa village as the basic unit. Villages, based on communal production, were to provide the foundations for agricultural expansion and hence development. In theory at least, such communities differed radically from previous settlement policies. Tanzania post-1967 regarded resettlement in a social capacity in contrast to, in particular, the technical approach of the World Bank-sponsored schemes of the first half of the 1960s. It was designed to affect all peasants, not a select few, and to promote a form of social organisation that would lead to increased production, but on a socialist footing. It was to affect minds as much as bodies. Yet, for all the rhetoric couched in the language of tradition and the promotion of an African moral economy, the Ujamaa village programme remained entrenched in 'transformation' philosophy, but on a scale undreamed of by the World Bank. Over the course of the next decade, the very landscape of Tanzania was to be transformed, as literally thousands of new villages arose—and scattered huts and compounds were destroyed.

In 1967, then, the Ujamaa village policy became the official Tanzanian development policy. Such villages were to be established by encouragement and the voluntary initiative of the peasantry. By 1969, only 5 per cent of the population resided in Ujamaa villages. In March of that year, the government demanded an increased effort to quicken the pace of change: all government policies were henceforth to be geared to the implementation of communal living and production. The Second Five Year Plan (FYP) (1969–74) adopted the 'frontal approach'—government officials were to be more proactive in their attempts to establish villages. Moreover, the FYP declared that all rural projects were to be based in villages. Development funds were made available only to those residing, or intending to reside, in the new Ujamaa settlements. Large-scale, district-wide campaigns were organised in the creation of villages and resettlement of peasants: Dodoma, Kigoma and Chunya, for example, all underwent 'operations' between 1969 and 1973. By 1973, however, only 15 per cent of the national population had been resettled. Large-scale operations had failed to make a deep impact. A new emphasis on 'development villages' was announced, envisioned as a halfway house to Ujamaa villages, and operations were undertaken in low-population-density areas. In September 1973, a new policy of compulsory, national villagisation was announced. Henceforth, all Tanzanians were to reside in nucleated village settlements within three years. Rural socialism had become mass resettlement.

Oxfam had become involved at a deep level with the philosophy of Ujamaa through the Ruvuma Development Association (RDA) and the actions of the first Field Director, Jimmy Betts. The RDA was a self-governing collection of villages in Ruvuma Region, seeking to establish settlements run along communal lines: rural production, local industries, the provision of child care and even education were all to be established on a communal basis. It was Oxfam's first contact with Ujamaa philosophy in practice. However, by 1969, factional opposition to the RDA had spread from local government to the centre, and the association was disbanded, its assets seized by the state and its members persecuted. Oxfam, however, remained committed to the ideology that had formed the basis of this experiment in social and productive living. By 1972, it began to seek another project that would epitomise its commitment to Ujamaa. This project evolved as the Chunya Integrated Development Programme and, through participation in it, Oxfam became further enmeshed in the Tanzanian state objectives of development.

It is perhaps worth noting at this stage that Oxfam was not alone in its commitment to Ujamaa. It was a position shared with many radical analysts and academics, as well as other NGOs and church organisations throughout the world. Tanzania became for many during this period a real alternative to development strategies as practised elsewhere, a genuine attempt to base national growth upon the rural sector and (perhaps most significantly) to stress the social as much as the economic elements of development.

If Oxfam became indirectly implicated in some of the less savoury aspects of the implementation of Ujamaa, it was not alone. The power of the rhetoric seemingly drew in countless numbers of people searching for alternatives to the Western capitalist and Soviet state communism models of development.

Operation Chunya

Chunya District is part of Mbeya Region in south-western Tanzania. Although Mbeya was relatively wealthy, Chunya District was the poorest area within the region, subject as it was to regular famines. Approximately half of its population of 60,000 lived in the relatively fertile and well-watered strip down to Lake Kukwa. The population was not predominantly indigenous, many having migrated during the gold-rush in the 1930s and 1940s. A significant proportion of the population were, according to the official mind at least, honey-gatherers and did not reside in villages. The district was entirely rural—the main town had a population of just 1,000.

In 1969, with the abolition of the Ruvuma Development Association, a more 'frontal approach' to resettlement in Ujamaa villages was adopted. Voluntary villagisation was to be discouraged, and officials were to direct efforts to establish the new villages. A series of villagisation campaigns—operations—were launched in several districts, and Chunya District was part of this first stage in state-led villagisation. Operation Chunya provided the backdrop to Oxfam's involvement in the district. Village settlement projects in Chunya District began in 1971 when the World Bank financed a tobacco cultivation project with a loan of £65 million. The aim was to create 'tobacco complex' areas, each consisting of ten Ujamaa villages and an area of eighty square miles, with one hundred families per village. In Chunya, five areas were selected as 'complex' areas (i.e. fifty Ujamaa villages and 5,000 families)—Mtanila, Gua, Ifuma, Mafyeko and Luwalaje and Matwiga (the latter two counted as one area). It was planned to have settled fourteen villages with 1,400 families by June 1972. In January 1972, only 262 families had been settled in five villages. Operation Chunya, launched in May 1972, in the tobacco-growing areas, achieved modest successes in moving people into the 'complex' villages, where they were expected to cultivate tobacco. In July 1972, the second phase of Operation Chunya further increased the number of settlers. By August 1972, nine villages contained 502 households.

Ostensibly, Operation Chunya was a villagisation campaign designed to create Ujamaa villages for the eradication of famine and to raise living standards. The objectives, as stated by the regional administration, were: to intensify modern agricultural methods; to raise tobacco and cotton production in the Ujamaa villages; to make Ujamaa villages self-reliant in food production; to improve the bee-keeping industry; to introduce ranching; to promote a fishing industry; and to provide social and other infrastructural services. In other words, Operation Chunya officially aimed at the promotion of development within Ujamaa villages by raising production and living standards—a 'standard' villagisation campaign, then. However, the timing of the operation is significant. The World Bank settlements were failing to reach the targeted number of settlers, and therefore failing to produce the target tobacco production. In order to repay the £65 million, the settlements needed to succeed, hence the operation to resettle farmers into these areas. By 1976/77, the pressure to ensure that 'tobacco complexes' succeeded led to concentration on tobacco production over other village activities. Villagisation in Chunya was not driven by notions of introducing communal ownership and production (the Ujamaa ideology); it was driven by the external requirements of a major donor. Communal farms gave way to block-farming. Farmers were resettled to reach tobacco production targets, not to implement rural socialism.

The Ten-cell System

In 1973, a new Area Commissioner was appointed to Chunya District—K. Nsa Kaisi. Regarded by Oxfam as capable and committed to development, he began to experiment with the social organisation in his district. The ten-cell unit was the basic unit of social organisation within Tanzania, headed by a TANU ten-cell leader and consisting of ten households. In reality, it was little more than a mechanism for control, a means of stretching the tentacles of the governing party to every level of society. Kaisi intended to turn these units into something more meaningful. They were to become the basic units of production in the new villages. The basis for this new system was outlined at a conference at Kivukoni Ideological College in March 1975. The difficulties faced in implementing Operation Chunya had forced a strategic reappraisal. If people were unwilling to move, they had to be educated and involved in the process. The people due to be resettled were carefully prepared first; all plans were explained via the TANU leaders, starting at the ten-cell level. To avoid mistakes, committees of ten-cell leaders organised the people in their own areas. In adopting the village development plans, the village party leaders (and especially the ten-cell leaders) were used to implement them. In other words, the basic unit of Tanzanian social organisation—the ten-cell unit—was involved in the villagisation plans and resettlement operation. It was a strategy that seems to have worked. Between 1972 and 1974, 47,727 people were resettled, some 72 per cent of the Chunya population.

As a result of this experience, the role of the ten-cell unit was widened. In Chunya District, under Kaisi, the ten-cell unit became the basic unit of production in the new Ujamaa villages. Progress towards Ujamaa was based on a two-stage process. After resettlement, fields were divided into block-farms, and each ten-cell unit was given communal responsibility for its cultivation. Each ten-cell unit decided whether to cultivate its block-farm on an individual, communal or mixed pattern, although most cleared the land on a communal basis (as was traditional). The agricultural extension services were targeted on these units, using the ten-cell system for the teaching and control of agriculture. The ten-cell leader's role was to ensure that the members carried out their agricultural responsibilities in line with the detailed farming calendar drawn up by the extension workers. As this proved successful and as communal production became more widespread, it was envisaged that a second stage would be reached, whereby ten to fifteen ten-cell units would combine to form a brigade and cultivate a large communal field.

Of the thirty-two Ujamaa villages established in Operation Chunya, twenty-one had adopted the system, although, as a unit of production and organisation, it was confined to agriculture; other village activities such as village industries, bee-keeping, oxen, etc. were external to it. The system was not perfect, as Oxfam noted: ten-cell leaders, although in theory the mouthpieces of their unit, were not necessarily on the Village Committee. Thus rather than acting as spokesmen and decision-makers at grass-roots level, they could be 'messengers and policemen'. Moreover, the system faced criticism from some quarters outside the district, when it was regarded as a retreat from communalism and Ujamaa.

Oxfam was greatly in favour of the experimental system, and regarded it as a revolution in the lives of the people of Chunya. The promotion of the ten-cell system was to become an integral objective of the Integrated Development Programme (IDP). Just as participation with the Ruvuma Development Association had been based upon notions of involvement in a significant and radical departure from orthodoxy, so too was the Chunya programme. It seemed to tie up with the policies of Oxfam: community participation; village democracy; and communal living and production. It aimed at slowly building up to Ujamaa in the villages. Communalism was optional at this stage, but it was hoped that it would ultimately be adopted once deep-rooted individualism had been usurped.

Oxfam was determined to promote this system, where possible gearing projects to utilise it. An oxen project provided ten-cell units with a pair of oxen to be owned communally, funded with a grant of £2,199. Oxfam would contribute Tsh 400/– per ten-cell, and each household member of the ten-cell unit would add a further Tsh 20/– towards the purchase of the oxen. The stated objective was 'to encourage communal activity at the ten-cell level'. The comparison with the RDA was explicit for Oxfam. The Field Director wrote, '[t]o us it is in a direct line with the Ruvuma Development Association'. The RDA experience not only coloured the interpretation of the ten-cell experiment, it also brought a warning: experiments were controversial. Caution was advised by the Field Director in Oxfam's approach to publicising the system, especially in the light of criticisms already voiced about it. Oxfam had been burnt once and had learnt from its experience: 'memories of the Ruvuma Development Association are still around'.

For Oxfam the ten-cell element of the Chunya programme was the crucial part of its attraction, it was a real attempt to implement the formation of a new form of social organisation based on communal production. If it was successful, its example could be spread to other areas in Tanzania. This was the objective of the programme, and the various projects that formed the programme were fundamental to bringing about its success. Once more, Oxfam was involved in an experiment in social organisation and, again, another potentially controversial experiment.

THE CHUNYA INTEGRATED DEVELOPMENT PROGRAMME

The Chunya IDP was important to the Oxfam experience of Tanzania for three reasons: first, it was the first time that Oxfam had worked with regional government as the major partner; secondly, the programme was explicitly aimed at reinforcing the government's villagisation campaign that was in the process of being implemented at that time—Operation Chunya; and, thirdly, the ten-cell experiment element attracted Oxfam's predisposition for innovative and experimental schemes, whilst also serving to define for the NGO (in much the same way as Oxfam's work with the Ruvuma Development Association had) the nature and objectives of the Tanzanian government's Ujamaa policy, it was also of importance to Oxfam as an NGO in the global sense: the programme was part of an experiment in new ways of funding development that allowed for an increased participation of the peasant farmers. Oxfam was to be a partner, rather than a benefactor. The IDP represented the application of the conscientisation approach in practice, one of the first such schemes to be established by Oxfam outside Brazil. The increased scope of Oxfam's activities in Tanzania meant that the Chunya programme, in the scale of financial assistance, was small in comparison with others. However, despite this, it was invested with an importance by both field staff and Oxford staff that cannot be explained by the visible results of the programme.

Despite its title, the programme was not an 'integrated development programme' in the proper sense. Individual projects remained isolated, with no real attempt being made to establish links in any meaningful manner. The only common factor that bound the disparate elements together was the support each project gave to the wider villagisation campaign—Operation Chunya. This lack of cohesion was recognised by Oxfam, who nevertheless hoped it would eventually evolve into an integrated programme. Operation Chunya and the ten-cell experiment provided the backdrop to Oxfam's involvement in the district. The Chunya IDP was developed by district development staff as a programme to support the implementation of Operation Chunya. In other words, it was specifically designed to function as an integrated part of the villagisation campaign. It was based on the development of tobacco and cotton production, the improvement of food supplies, developing other sources of income, and the improvement of medical facilities and water supplies. It was to be a three-year programme, with estimated costs of approximately US$ 70,000. It was open for any donor support for all or part of the programme and aimed at being ultimately self-financing.

The first evaluation of the project was in April 1974 and, despite limited tangible results, this deemed the project to be on track. Accurate assessment of progress was hampered by conflicts between the reports on wider development in the district prepared by the district administration and those of the World Bank. Moreover, according to Oxfam's Field Director, the initial World Bank appraisal had not been realistic in its expectations: targets were too ambitious and problems related to the implementation of communal agriculture had been underestimated. The Oxfam grant, although made in June 1973, had not reached the CDTF until September, and the rains in December added to the delay in implementation of many of the projects. However, the Oxfam assessment was that good work was being undertaken in the villages. Lack of visible progress was not a major problem: according to the Field Director, 'more important than the speed with which people act is what they do when they act'. The emphasis on slow but steady progress was reflected in the Africa Committee's assessment of the situation. Commenting on the field director's report, a committee member wrote:

> I am not unduly worried about the slowness of the implementation of our Chunya project. It may be a blessing in disguise. The important aspect is that it has now been launched.

The projects were grouped into three main types: schemes to raise food production—small-scale and capable of being organised by the villagers themselves; village income- and employment-generating schemes; and the mobile health clinic. Progress in all three was limited. Sixteen oxen had been purchased, trained and disbursed to the villages, but had not yet been used in the fields. It was hoped that they would be in the coming agricultural season. The goats and chickens had not been purchased, and the chicken shed had been constructed poorly and collapsed in the rains. Of the 609 planned beehives, only 154 had arrived, but, despite a lower than forecast harvest, the project was popular. Neither of the two village industry projects—the pit-saws and carpentry workshops—were in operation. Finally, the Landrover was yet to arrive in the district. Oxfam remained unconcerned, and even recommended extending the project with the incorporation of four new production schemes.

By mid-1975, there was still little sign of significant advancement. The beehives project was the most successful, achieving 50 per cent higher yields with the new equipment; 642 of the planned 762 hives had now arrived. The pit-saws were also producing good results, with 640 planks sold for Tsh 13,500/–. The other schemes were less successful. The goat project was withdrawn: three goat sheds had been built, but no goats purchased. The poultry scheme had been delayed as, again, no poultry had been bought. Although some tools had been distributed to carpentry workshops, work had not begun. The expenditure of the allocated £20,000 attests to the slow progress of the programme: by November 1975, only £8,967 had been used.

However, again the overall evaluation was positive. The Oxfam projects were the only productive schemes in Chunya, according to the Field Director, that gave the villagers a choice on how to organise and on the subsequent use of the income. This freedom to make decisions was well-used: in the villages visited by Oxfam, 'there was heated and intelligent argument [on] how to organise the schemes'. This was the crux of the project, according to his assessment:

> I was struck by the value of the Oxfam projects in promoting this sort of practical discussion and decision . . . It seemed to me that our original aim that the projects would produce not only physical results but also help people to learn how to organise their own affairs, has been substantially achieved.

Oxfam should continue, the report adds, to support such small-scale productive programmes that gave real power over decision-making to the villagers. Another objective of the programme had been to give a boost to the Ujamaa villages and the communal production concept and this too should continue to be the aim.

The result of the two evaluations in 1974 and 1975 was to shift the terms of the evaluation away from material progress to a more nebulous concept of socio-political/socio-economic aims: the promotion of community participation in decision-making and communal production and ownership.

Oxfam had shifted from a functional view of development to one in which the social engineering element was pushed to the forefront. As the statement above makes clear, material progress was of secondary concern: as long as a change in social organisation of production and ownership was achieved, Oxfam's primary objective had been reached (regardless of whether that change brought about increased levels of production). Social organisation was regarded as the necessary precursor to material development. A project within the Chunya programme was not an end in itself (for example, an increase in the number of oxen), but a means to a wider end (the social organisation of how those oxen were used by the community). For Oxfam, community participation was the key to development: material progress was a secondary cause of village-level democracy, not vice versa. The lessons of the RDA had become imbued within the Oxfam ideology.

Whilst such an evaluation may be commonplace today, it is important to recognise the relatively innovative aspect that such an assessment held in the mid-1970s. 'Development' was still largely a technical and quantifiable process undertaken, in large part, by state actors and large multinational organisations, such as the World Bank. Oxfam was shifting into a new arena in its evaluations of the Chunya Integrated Development Programme. The Chunya programme was in large part a major impetus in the realignment of Oxfam in the 1970s, as it sought to create a role for itself as a 'partner' in the development process and as it identified 'empowerment' as a major tool of that development. Within the evaluation paradigm set up by Oxfam, the projects could be deemed successful, regardless of their actual achievement of stated objectives. The key objective was to begin a process within the villages: the physical results of that process were secondary. Thus the initial application for a project—for example to increase the number of eggs for consumption—was not matched by the evaluation criteria—what social organisation had managed the production. A twin-track approach had developed, the gap between them ever widening—project selection and project evaluation, even if carried out by the same person, pursued different agendas. The failure of a project could be overlooked in the evaluatory process, concentrating as it did on a new agenda: a project begun with the aim of achieving objective A was now judged on fulfilling objective B once it was up and running. Perhaps this accounts for Oxfam's continued failure to see the true nature of Ujamaa; it concentrated on the potential long-term success, rather than seeing the immediate failure—the ideology was paramount, not material progress.

After a visit in December 1976, the Field Director remained encouraged. However, after three years the results did not suggest good cause for such optimism. The chicken units were making a profit (albeit small); six pit-saws (out of fifteen) were in operation in Mafyeko village, providing a village income of Tsh 14,835/–; and the beehives were making considerable profits. However, other projects were not faring as well. The carpentry tools had still not been allocated, and the oxen were not a great success in agricultural terms. The intention to diversify income-generating activities had given way in face of pressure to produce tobacco and cotton. The optimism was based on the factors outlined above, however. The oxen were being used in a communal setting; and a major positive side to the beekeeping was the social organisation established by the villagers. If development was political in Tanzania, Oxfam's assessment was ideological.

In 1976, administrative changes in the district, part of the standard practice of shifting administrative personnel, led to Kaisi's departure. The incoming administrative officials regarded Oxfam as troublesome; Oxfam asked too many questions, argued too much and made too many demands for the small level of financial support it provided. It rejected the 'grandiose' ideas put forward by the new Regional Commissioner. Conflict emerged between the NGO and the regional administration: an increasingly bureaucratic approach to Oxfam was adopted, using the Prime Minister's Office ruling on foreign agencies late in 1976, that all activity was to be closely coordinated with government, as a tool for obstruction. Relations rapidly deteriorated, and the District Development Director was on the point of throwing Oxfam out of the district. The NGO was not invited to the region to oversee the projects in 1977. The following year, the

Regional Development Director failed to meet with an Oxfam representative on tour in the region to undertake an assessment of Oxfam's future there. It emerged that the Landrover for the mobile health clinic was being used improperly by the district administration. Finally, in an 'offhand letter' to Oxfam's local field staff, the District Development Director requested a grant for a road-building project that had already received backing from the Norwegian Agency for International Development (NORAD). In 1979, Oxfam withdrew from Mbeya Region.

OXFAM AND UJAMAA

The importance of the Chunya programme lay in the impact it had on Oxfam's operations in Tanzania, and in the impact on the development of the wider 'Oxfam vision' of development. The Chunya programme not only acted as a point of entry for Oxfam into the Ujamaa philosophy, it also acted as the prism through which that philosophy was defined. Oxfam already possessed a definition of Ujamaa, through its experiences with the Ruvuma Development Association. The Chunya IDP added to and to some extent modified this definition. Three main elements emerge from the experience of Chunya: Tanzania became increasingly identified as the 'ideal' nation with which to work; Oxfam increased its support for Ujamaa, or, rather, with the particular definition of Ujamaa it held; and the more negative aspects of villagisation were ignored or explained away.

'Almost an Oxfam in Itself'

In his 1972 report on Tanzania and the Chunya IDP, the Field Director linked the Tanzanian development vision with that of Oxfam:

> But there is another reason for Oxfam to help Tanzania. It is that, perhaps more than any other country in the world, Tanzania is aiming to produce the kind of development, the kind of society, that Oxfam supporters would like to see everywhere.

Nyerere aimed, according to the report, to create 'a country where all her citizens are equal'. Five sub-aims were particularly appealing to the Oxfam world-view: to prevent urban dwellers exploiting the peasantry (Oxfam's Tanzanian operations displayed a markedly rural bias); to prevent the establishment of a privileged elite class; to avoid the distortions of foreign aid; to develop along lines relevant to Tanzanian society (i.e. Ujamaa villages); and to involve people in their own development. Tanzania was, for the Field Director at least, 'very much the model Oxfam country'. Dr Walker of Oxfam's Medical Panel described Tanzania as 'almost an Oxfam in itself. The key to this identification was Ujamaa: 'Tanzanian philosophy is Oxfam philosophy.' The Information Department similarly saw Tanzania in a favourable light: 'If any country were to be labelled "ideal" for Oxfam's work in terms of basic philosophy, I suppose Tanzania would come closest.'

Tanzania's development programme aimed to establish precisely the type of society Oxfam wished to create. Having failed to achieve the creation of utopia in the West, the impetus and potential had shifted South. Tanzania, with Oxfam's assistance (the NGO believed), could perhaps act as an example to the rest of the developing world. Through participation in the formation and implementation of Ujamaa ideology in the 1960s, Tanzania came to hold for Oxfam a position of tremendous importance. Oxfam felt that it had a responsibility to provide support (both financial and moral) to the ideology of Ujamaa that the NGO felt was truly a radical programme of rural social reform. An indelible impression had been left on Oxfam through support for the RDA and Ujamaa, which had helped shape an emerging Oxfam development consciousness.

Seduced by the rhetoric of Ujamaa, and blinded by the continuing influence of the RDA and the Chunya programme, Oxfam failed to see the ruins of Ujamaa development in its utopian vision of a socialist future.

Oxfam and 'Ujamaa' Villages

Oxfam's participation in Chunya, as has been seen, was characterised by the shift in the evaluatory yardstick from physical and material progress to the social and political aspects of the programme. The main function of the Chunya programme, from its formation by the district officials, was to provide support for the implementation of Ujamaa and Ujamaa villages. The individual projects supported by Oxfam were chosen with these aims in mind. The bee-keeping project had a dual function: it was not only to provide opportunities for a village income, but was also part of an enticement strategy to encourage traditional honey-gatherers into the new villages. A proposed project to train village bookkeepers was driven by a fear that the mistrust and anger generated by mistakes (genuine or fraudulent) could threaten the Ujamaa programme:

> Even when a genuine mistake has been made, villagers often feel they have been cheated. This situation is quite serious; unless checked, it could undermine the whole basis of Tanzanian socialism.

The oxen project was similarly designed to hasten the adoption of communal production in the new Ujamaa villages. All oxen were to be held in common by the ten-cell units, and used for communal tasks.

The decision to support the Ujamaa system was a deliberate decision to do so, not by default. One Oxfam member wrote to another, after consideration of Oxfam's appropriate response to Ujamaa, and declared:

> I realise that one could argue very cogently in favour of a quite different strategy of development for rural Tanzania, but since this is the one they have chosen then I feel that if we are going to help we sshould [*sic*] try to do so in the spirit of Ujamaa socialism.

The Ujamaa system had several major advantages for development, the Field Director advised the Africa Committee: it facilitated extension work; it avoided creating a debt burden for villagers; and it provided an insurance policy for the village members against illness, old age and injury. It combined, therefore, two of Oxfam's major aims: the promotion of development; and help for the needy. The Chunya IDP was the perfect tool for supporting Ujamaa:

> The main way that Oxfam can help to strengthen the Ujamaa system of handling development is to use it. All the village-based projects do this both philosophically and practically. Philosophically because before Ujamaa, only the richer could afford a pit-saw, a plane or a plough. Now everyone can (even if they only own it communally) . . . And practically, all the village-based projects give rise to discussion on labour, marketing, investment etc.

By making use of the system, such projects also reinforced it. It was crucial to make Ujamaa villages attractive places to live in. If people did not want to live in the villages 'they will either leave for the towns or the countryside, or be forced to stay—and either way development will suffer'. The Ujamaa village was, for Oxfam, the key to development.

The Chunya project was not the sole attempt to gear an ostensibly 'development' project to the needs of the Ujamaa system. An Oxfam project in 1977 purchased twenty ox-carts for two villages. It hoped to promote communal ownership in 'a modest way'. The development application assessment form, designed to add a rationale to project selection included 'Helping Tanzanian Socialism' as one of the criteria. The Chunya programme became for Oxfam a point of reference in how to operate within Tanzania and the Ujamaa system. In refusing an application for a grant in 1973, the Africa Committee explained its decision:

> We have considerable experience of dealing with Ujamaa villages from the project at Chunya which [the Field Director] studied and was approved by the Africa and Overseas Aid Committees. It is suggested that in respect of Buhigwe and other Ujamaa villages our approach should be on the lines of the Chunya project.

The integrated approach was considered to be the correct mode of operation. It offered vital support to the state's efforts to effect Ujamaa in rural life.

Oxfam's Definition of Ujamaa

Just as Oxfam's participation with the RDA and policy debates in the 1960s had influenced Oxfam's understanding of what Ujamaa meant, so too did the Chunya experience add to that definition. However, Ujamaa in the 1970s meant something different from what it had in the late 1960s—it had become more strongly identified with the Ujamaa village as an entity. The Chunya programme had a key impact on shaping Oxfam's response to Ujamaa from 1972/73.

When Oxfam declared its intent to aid and support the Ujamaa programme, or the Tanzanian socialist experiment, what exactly did it mean? Whereas between 1967 and 1969 there had been a common understanding between the state and the NGO, from 1969 onwards there was a growing and significant disparity between what Oxfam sought to support and what was being effected by the state in the name of Ujamaa. How could Oxfam justify its support for a rural policy that seemed to imply little more than an extension of government control over all aspects of production? In what way was the Tanzanian system 'socialist'? Clearly Oxfam's interpretation of Ujamaa had diverged from that of the state. The paradigm within which Oxfam operated—both field staff and Oxford staff—was still dictated by the early experiences of the 1960s (especially the Ruvuma Development Association). Yet the Chunya programme added an extra dimension to the definition. It rested upon two fundamental elements: communalism and grass-roots participation. For the Field Director, 'the whole basis of Tanzanian socialism [is] the eventual communal ownership and operation of the village activities'. Citing a previous Field Director's assessment, he similarly asserted the primacy of popular participation for Ujamaa ideology:

> To many people in the developed countries, Tanzania's brand of socialism and its implementation through the Ujamaa programme appears as the real example of grassroots development . . . It has great appeal to those of us who are idealists . . . As a philosophy it is hard to beat.

These two aspects were the foundation-stone of the RDA experiment and the subsequent Chunya IDP, and for Oxfam came to define its response to the Ujamaa programme. Thus, in supporting Ujamaa, Oxfam meant it was supporting communalism and a concept of a village-level democracy.

It was a definition that had little in common with reality. The assertion in late that a farmers' training project would 'help boost communality very considerably' seems naive in its expectations after a TANU statement in 1973 in which the active promotion of communal production was dropped. The CDTF had followed the new official stress on the purposes of Ujamaa villages. In its application for the water-supplies project in 1974, the CDTF commented on the new Operation Vijijini. The establishment of Ujamaa villages was to create centres of production, to provide a viable social infrastructure for the rural population and to modernise and mechanise the social economic aspects of production (for example, with credit facilities). There was no mention of communal production or of boosting grass-roots decision-making. The period from 1969 was one of steady encroachment by the state over civil society. Democracy and avenues for popular expression were gradually eroded. The Ujamaa villages had become centres of control, not of grassroots development and rural socialism.

An Emerging Critique of Villagisation

What makes the Oxfam definition of Ujamaa all the more surprising perhaps, is its awareness of some of the negative aspects of the implementation. Moreover, this was an awareness held by both field staff and Oxford. Oxfam did not have its head stuck in the sand. The critique was based upon three main areas: violence in the resettlement campaigns; factional struggles and conflicts of interest; and failures of planning. In 1972, the Field Director noted the use of police and troops to enforce resettlement. Although he was assured that 'overt force is no longer used' in the Ujamaa village programme, those who did not join 'may not be eligible for water supplies, agricultural or medical extensions [*sic*] services'. Reports existed in 1975 that those who refused to resettle faced 'over-zealous' persuasion from officials:

> I have no evidence on the truth or otherwise of the stories of guns and fire being used to get people to move; but given the low calibre of some Party workers, and the power of ambition and fear, it sounds pretty likely that they were used in some places.

Chunya officials continued to assert that no force had been used, and the Field Director did not seek contrary evidence. He did, however, note:

> Those who refused to move were 'persuaded'; neighbours and party workers 'offered' to help moving their effects etc. The pressure must have been quite tough.

The Field Director found residual resentment over the resettlement of Lupatingatinga. The original settlement had been razed, and a new site established just a couple of miles away. There had been a significant degree of trouble over the thorough and forceful effort to move such a short distance. The Africa Committee received negative reports from other sources, as well as the reports from field staff, and asked the field staff to comment on such reports: one was asked to send further information 'in view of the criticisms which are being voiced about the implementation of the Ujamaa philosophy'. In particular, the Committee wished to know of ill-feeling and unrest, and the reaction of the authorities to potential trouble. Oxford was concerned over the level of criticism in the mid-1970s and requested as much information as possible. The Information Department also asked another NGO (Catholic Relief Services [CRS]) for its thoughts on the Ujamaa village programme and its effect on people's lives. Tanzania may have been the 'ideal' partner; nevertheless, Oxford noted, 'there are still a lot of questions'.

That Ujamaa was not an uncontroversial policy, supported by all Tanzanians, was also, noted. The opponents of Ujamaa, according to the Field Director's analysis, consisted of those who had done well under the 'old system', including businessmen, landowners and successful small farmers. The strength of opposition was such that a Regional Commissioner in Iringa had been murdered. The main problem for the implementation of Ujamaa was, according to the Field Director, that it depended on the support of an elite whose self-interest it went against. It also relied on the voluntary acceptance of Ujamaa by a population who understood little of what was being done and failed to see the benefits. In other words, it depended on everyone 'being good'. Experience with the RDA left Oxfam with no doubt that government was not a unified monolith, an impression reinforced by the different reactions of local officials to Ujamaa.

The planning of Ujamaa left a lot to be desired. There were few competent officials able effectively to plan Ujamaa villages. This lack of planning and advice, the shortage of a trained cadre to educate the people, and unmotivated officials offering conflicting advice, all added to problems in the new villages. One Oxfam fieldworker noted that: '[t]he programme has suffered very greatly from being started too hastily without adequate preparation and planning'. The Field Director was informed by the District Development Director of Mbulu District, Arusha, that '[t]here is a vacuum between the (Regional) office and the villages. Too much is superimposed. The villagers are told what to do, not why.' Operation Maduka, the nationalisation of village shops, was introduced at 'high political speed', which resulted in a lack of adequate preparation.

Despite such criticisms, however, Oxfam remained committed to the implementation of Ujamaa. Throughout this period, it sought to use its projects to strengthen the village structures. Despite no official encouragement towards communal production after 1973/74, Oxfam retained its belief that this was the ultimate goal. It instituted Village Council training projects to build up the capability of what it believed was the expression of the grass roots voice. Yet it was aware that progress on the way to achieving such objectives was painfully slow. Oxfam had already, however, instituted the analytical means for bypassing such problems. The overriding socio-political objectives meant short-term problems, or particular inconsistencies could be ignored. Evaluations of Tanzania's performance were based on what it was moving towards, not where it was currently at. Provided the government continued the rhetoric of communal production, village democracy and socialist equality, it could undertake the opposite without fear of censure. The shift in terms of evaluation, seen in the Chunya programme, locked Oxfam on to a path of almost unqualified support. The ends justified the means: even if 'Oxfam may not go as far as Tanzania in all-out support for Ujamaa villages', it did favour 'the development of appropriate social machinery based on traditional forms'. To achieve the type of society Oxfam believed it was helping to create, 'the only way to make a useful contribution to the development of the people is to work wholeheartedly within the Ujamaa system'.

This forms the crux of Oxfam's relationship with Ujamaa. It ultimately felt that the system, once working and accepted, was the ideal form of social and political organisation in which development could take place. All, ultimately, would be for the best.

The debates within Oxfam did not question Ujamaa as a philosophy. The issue was a more theoretical one of how Oxfam should participate in Tanzania. For Oxfam, Ujamaa meant communal production and grass roots decision-making and was unquestionably deserving of support. Nyerere's thoughts in the 1960s and the experience of working with the RDA had shaped not just Oxfam's operations in Tanzania, but its development philosophy worldwide. For all the detailed analyses of Tanzania produced by the NGO (which are, it must be noted, of significant quality), Oxfam was seduced by the rhetoric of Ujamaa. Long after it had ceased to have any real meaning in the Oxfam definition, the NGO failed to perceive this.

Oxfam never sought to adopt a neutral stance in its position in Tanzania. It was avowedly ideological and campaigning. Yet the reality is that Oxfam projects were supporting a system that was in many ways opposed to that ideology. Moreover, Oxfam seems, throughout the 1970s, to have failed to perceive that fact. James Ferguson has shown in Lesotho the extent to which development agencies undertake programmes of rural development that fail to incorporate a political dimension to their perception of the problems and needs of the poor. Within the project blueprint, poverty is reduced to a technical issue. The effect is to depoliticise the nature of poverty. In pushing the technical aspects to the forefront, as Ferguson showed in his study of a CIDA project in Lesotho, political operations can be performed, involving the entrenchment and extension of state power under the cover of a neutral and technical mission. He writes:

> In this perspective, the 'development' apparatus in Lesotho is not a machine

> for eliminating poverty that is incidentally involved with the state bureaucracy; it is a machine for reinforcing and expanding the exercise of bureaucratic state power which incidentally takes 'poverty' as its point of entry—launching an intervention that may have no effect on the poverty but does in fact have other concrete effects.

According to Ferguson, this process occurs so regularly within development agency projects that it must be judged as an integral (albeit unintentional) aspect of development discourse. Development agencies become an 'anti-politics machine'. The political aspects of a project are removed from the analysis of project aims and objectives and thus, under cover of a technical programme, such agencies achieve 'the suspension of politics from even the most sensitive political operations'. In the case of the CIDA projects in the Thaba-Tseka area, Lesotho, the concrete result was the extension of state power in an ostensibly technical development programme.

The analysis offered by Ferguson is important, and its logical consequence, for a development agency, is to recognise both the implicit and explicit political nature of poverty, and hence development. However, the example of Oxfam in Tanzania during the 1960s and 1970s reveals some of the weaknesses of the argument. For here was an NGO which envisaged development as explicitly and inherently political. Its programmes and projects consciously included a socio-political element in the project 'blueprint'. Moreover, Oxfam believed that the national government had a responsibility to play a central role in directing development. Nevertheless, the unintended, but instrumental, effect of the projects was to reinforce the emergent statism and a massive extension of centralised control. The NGO never failed to appreciate or sought to minimise the political aspects of development. Rather it embraced the belief that 'development is very political in Tanzania'. The paradox of Oxfam's policy in Tanzania is simple. It sought to create institutions for the articulation of peasant objectives and to implement a process of awareness amongst the poor. But by undertaking the very projects it believed could help achieve these aims, it was in effect undermining the very things it stood for. In providing support for Ujamaa and in identifying so completely with the Tanzanian state, it became part of a process that withdrew power and representation from the grass roots.

So why did Oxfam fail to recognise the contradictions inherent in Tanzanian development? It was the heavily ideological agenda—the political dominance of the development discourse—that constrained the NGO. In reducing the technical aspects of development to a secondary place, Oxfam failed to adequately analyse the material and physical impact of Oxfam and state development policy. The dominance of Ujamaa as a theory within Oxfam and the increasing dominance of 'conscientisation' and concepts such as 'empowerment' and 'popular participation' in project design led Oxfam to interpret Ujamaa implementation through the rhetorical prism erected by this discourse. The NGO became trapped within a discourse of development. The power of the symbolism of Ujamaa and the tangible image of that symbol, the Ujamaa village, exerted a tremendous force upon Oxfam, as well as other NGOs, analysts and academics. It served to disguise the contradictions as it became an end in itself.

From the mid-1960s and throughout the 1970s, Oxfam's Tanzanian 'programme' sought to assist in the remodelling of a nation. Projects such as the Chunya Integrated Development Project were designed with the intention of aiding the implementation of Ujamaa and its most visible ramification, the Ujamaa village. In concentrating on the ideological and the political philosophy of development rhetoric, Oxfam failed to perceive the reality. If Oxfam became a surrogate of the state during this period, it had done so willingly.

The politics of development in Tanzania during the 1960s and 1970s led several NGOs to become surrogates of the state—bound to the ideology of Ujamaa and implicitly involved in the extension of the power of the central government. During the following decade a new power dynamic emerged that placed both the Tanzanian state and the NGO under considerable pressure from the donor community. Tanzania's successful appropriation of the development discourse was ended as the Northern donors and their representatives, the World Bank and the International Monetary Fund (IMF), established their control over the prevailing paradigm. The era of structural adjustment was inaugurated in the early 1980s, and African governments were regarded with suspicion by the international donor community. They were held to be the main obstacles to development due to their supposedly inherent bureaucracy, mismanagement and corruption. The state was no longer to be the initiator and director of development policy: the free market and private sector were to be the key engines of growth in this new era. Development policy was externalised and the NGO community now had to deal with new potential masters.

The changes in the environment within which the NGO operated during this period were considerable. With the retreat of the state came a greater focus on service provision as part of the humanitarian mandate. In order to cope with the new demands made upon the sector, Northern NGOs assisted in the process of expansion of local NGOs and community-based organisations. The Tanzanian state came to an agreement with the World Bank in 1986, and accepted a structural adjustment programme that gradually withdrew many of the powers through which Ujamaa and 'African socialism' had been implemented. It no longer sought to identify and enforce its own development vision: the development discourse was now enunciated by the donor community. NGOs ceased to identify with a state offering something tangibly different and grew more distant. Poverty alleviation in the face of economic crisis, provision of social services and encouraging sustainability became the primary focus of the NGOs. The dominant socio-political strain of organisations such as Oxfam was tempered.

Towards the end of the 1980s and in the early 1990s, the international climate began to focus on the promotion of multi-party democracies in Africa. This had implications for the NGO sector and its operations within Tanzania. NGOs became concerned with building up a civil society that could support the emergent democracies. The programme of building up Southern NGOs and community-based organisations increased in pace. The governance agenda—in which democracy and development were inextricably linked—was made a central element in the mandate of the NGO sector. Community-based groups based on land-rights issues, environmental concerns, gender issues and so forth were supported and encouraged. The consequence was again to shift the nature of the NGO–state relationship, inviting a potential conflict between the two to emerge. NGOs were now attempting to build up the voices of opposition to government and government policy.

Development was to remain, for the NGOs, very political in Tanzania, but the focus of that political aspect was to be enacted in different directions.

6 Evolution of the United Nations Anti-Apartheid Regime

NEWELL M. STULTZ

CONCEPTUALIZATION

In recent decades 'regime analysis' has become commonplace within the study of international relations, perhaps even 'faddish'. Although there are a number of variations on what constitutes a regime, Stephen Krasner's 1982 definition remains the standard one. According to Krasner, an international regime consists of the 'principles, norms, rules, and decision-making procedures around which actor expectations converge in a given issue area'. In our case the 'issue area' is international opposition to South African apartheid.

Applying the regime concept to the field of international human rights, Jack Donnelly collapsed Krasner's four definitional elements into just two variables—regime norms (or normative principles), and decision-making procedures. Based on the decision-making activities sanctioned in particular cases, he identified four regime types—declaratory, promotional, implementing, and enforcement. For Donnelly, regimes gain strength as their relevant norms, or at least some of them, are transformed from non-binding international 'guidelines' into 'binding international standards' (or 'rules', as I shall call them), as the regime's decision-making activities move from the declaratory end of the spectrum towards the enforcement end. Presumably a regime is also stronger the larger the number of international actors that subscribe to it. In this paper I take regime evolution to be synonymous with the appreciable strengthening of a regime in any of these three respects—its norms, sanctioned activities, or membership. I will examine the types of UN anti-apartheid regimes: declaratory, promotional, implementation, and enforcement.

DECLARATORY REGIME

Declaratory regimes affirm international norms. These regimes require no collective action or joint decision-making other than that needed for the initial creation of their norms, or perhaps for their periodic reiteration thereafter. Wholly national decision-making is thus the pattern. As was implied earlier, the declaratory mode is the most elementary and weakest of international regime types.

The beginnings of the international regime under review here might thus be dated 8 December 1946. On this day the General Assembly first challenged the Union of South Africa, by a vote of thirty-two to fifteen with seven abstentions, to treat its 285,000 citizens of Indian origin 'in conformity with . . . relevant provisions of the UN Charter'. This was a reaction to proposed new legislation in South Africa that adversely affected the rights of the Union's Indians to acquire or dispose of real property, among other matters.

What were these 'relevant provisions' of the Charter? A subsequent resolution of the General Assembly in 1952 listed five, the most specific of which is probably Article 55. Here the members of the United Nations commit themselves to promote 'universal respect for, and observance of, human rights and fundamental freedoms for all without distinction as to race, sex, language, or religion.' However, the South African view, as first enunciated in New York by Prime Minister Smuts, who was himself the principal drafter of the preamble to the UN Charter, was that these words created no special obligations for UN members, including South Africa. Smuts based his view on the absence of a widely accepted definition of 'human rights and fundamental freedoms'. A substantial majority of the General Assembly disagreed with Smuts. As seen in retrospect, it seems that these members were in the process of creating a new international norm of worldwide racial equality to challenge and eventually replace the racist norms inherent in European colonialism.

The following section examines other examples that similarly illustrate the declaratory regime.

Universal Declaration of Human Rights

Two years later, this process of norm creation within the field of human rights was greatly advanced when, on 10 December 1948, the General Assembly adopted a 'universal declaration of human rights' by a vote of forty-eight to zero with eight abstentions. South Africa was among the abstainers. The text of the Universal Declaration of Human Rights covers a broad range of rights, from the right of an individual not to be held as a slave, to the right of parents to choose the kind of education their children should receive. The word 'race' appears in the Declaration just twice. The first of these references is in Article 2: 'Everyone is entitled to all the rights and freedoms set out in this Declaration, without distinction of any kind, such as race, colour, sex, language, religion, political or other opinion, national or social origin, property, birth or other status.' The relevance of the Declaration for race relations is thus both broad and specific. Significantly, however, the norm cited above is still only a 'guideline'. No enforcement of it is provided for or suggested.

The adoption of the Universal Declaration of Human Rights did not immediately enlarge the membership of the United Nations' declaratory regime on South African race policy, notwithstanding well-publicized press accounts of the expedited passage of new segregationist laws. In fact, in many cases the number of countries adhering to this declaratory regime diminished. The reason for this reduction was that a minority of mainly industrialized Western states in the United Nations questioned the competence of the organization to intervene in what on the face of it appeared to be a domestic affair of a member state. Indeed, Article 2 (7) of the Charter seems to expressly forbid such intervention. It was such a reading of Article 2 (7) that proved to be an obstacle to any sudden increase in the membership of the declaratory regime throughout the decade of the 1950s. In spite of this, anti-apartheid majorities in the General Assembly did gradually increase over time, as a result of growth in the number of third world states belonging to the United Nations.

Sharpeville

Scholars concerned with how international regimes arise and change share a similar understanding of how this process occurs. Two independent variables recur: change in the structure of international power, and change in the operative international political culture. For Donnelly the latter involves a change in perceptions of global moral interdependence. This can arise, Donnelly writes, from 'international moral shock' at some event or set of events. Here I want to argue that the shootings of African demonstrators at Sharpeville in March 1960 (together with the immediately ensuing events) produced such an international moral shock regarding apartheid and South Africa. At the same time, an increase in the African membership in the United Nations provided a change in the structure of international power, at least within the General Assembly itself. A transformation of the character of the UN anti-apartheid regime in the early 1960s can easily be traced to both these occurrences.

Sharpeville is an urban black township on the edge of the Transvaal industrial city of Vereeniging, fifty miles south of Johannesburg. Shortly after noon on 21 March 1960, a crowd of about 5,000 unarmed Africans protesting South Africa's pass laws was confronted by 300 armed policemen outside the township police station. A scuffle broke out and portions of the crowd surged forward. Though no order to fire was given, a few policemen panicked and began shooting directly into the crowd, many of whom turned and fled. In the confusion other policemen began firing, and minutes later sixty-seven Africans lay dead or dying, many shot in the back while apparently running away. Another 186 people, all of them black, were wounded.

That evening 6,000 Africans demonstrated at Langa township near Cape Town. Here too the police opened fire, killing two and injuring forty-nine. Rioting occurred in Langa that night and was followed in the next days by a general strike of African workers in Cape Town, which spread later to several other urban centres. On 30 March, Pretoria proclaimed a state of emergency in eighty-six of the country's 300 magisterial districts and immediately arrested hundreds under the new emergency regulations. In a spontaneous protest of these arrests, 30,000 Africans marched into the centre of downtown Cape Town. In response, the government hurried security legislation through parliament allowing it to ban the two foremost African liberation movements of the period, the African National Congress and the Pan Africanist Congress. A climax of sorts was reached on 9 April, when Prime Minister Verwoerd was shot twice in the head while attending the Union Exposition in Johannesburg. Though gravely injured, Verwoerd survived; his white assailant was found to be acting out of confused but apparently apolitical motives. The overall effect of these and other events shook white public confidence. In a five-month period, shares on the Johannesburg stock exchange had lost 23 per cent of their value.

Internationally, the onrush of events in South Africa could scarcely be ignored. Just seven weeks after British Prime Minister Harold Macmillan had spoken to white parliamentarians in Cape Town of 'winds of change' blowing through Africa, news stories from South Africa were seldom off the front pages of the world's great newspapers for almost a month. Apartheid and the conduct of the South African police were condemned officially and unofficially in many parts of the world.

At the United Nations, twenty-nine African and Asian states demanded that the Security Council take up the matter. In the end, the Council on 1 April 1960 passed a resolution deploring 'the policies and practices' of Pretoria by a vote of nine to zero with two abstentions (Britain and France).

Thus, only days after the 'international moral shock' produced by the Sharpeville shootings and the civil unrest that immediately followed within the Union, the UN Security Council became an additional arena for the consideration of apartheid.

Sanctions

South Africa's failure to heed earlier General Assembly resolutions on apartheid, together with the Sharpeville killings and an increase in African membership in the United Nations, eventually led to pressure within the United Nations for economic sanctions against Pretoria. In April 1961, one full year after Sharpeville, twenty-six members of the General Assembly, all of them African states and all but eight new members, introduced a motion calling for comprehensive sanctions against South Africa. This effort fell nine votes short of passage. An identical resolution which included a demand for South Africa's expulsion from the United Nations lost seven months later with the margin of defeat cut in half. Finally, one year later, this now familiar proposal for five specific sanctions came before the General Assembly, and passed easily, sixty-seven to sixteen, with twenty-three abstentions. The General Assembly was at last on record favouring certain specific sanctions against South Africa as a means of ending apartheid. Of course the Assembly lacked the authority to mandate such sanctions; the proposal was still technically only a recommendation. But the principle had been accepted in the Assembly that international opposition to apartheid ought to be enforced. For the General Assembly, at least, the relevant anti-apartheid norm was no longer a mere 'guideline'.

The changed normative context was evident when the Security Council conducted its second debate on apartheid in August 1963. Both Great Britain and France now changed their positions on the issue of jurisdiction, though for different reasons neither was able to support the motion concerning South Africa that the Security Council passed on 7 August. Thus, by the middle of 1963 the international community had reached virtual unanimity on the proposition that, 'South Africa's is the world's business'. The UN anti-apartheid regime had reached the outer limits of its declaratory mode.

PROMOTIONAL REGIME

'Once states accept norms stronger than guidelines', Donnelly writes, 'declaratory regimes readily evolve into promotional regimes'. Donnelly's hypothesis is relevant to the case we are considering. In the same November 1962 resolution in which the General Assembly accepted the principle that UN opposition ought to be enforced by the imposition of various sanctions, the members also agreed to establish a new 'special committee' in order to keep South Africa's racial policies under review between annual sessions of the Assembly. The next year this responsibility became continuous. The new 'Special Committee on Apartheid' assumed a decidedly activist role in what four years later the General Assembly would formally designate as the 'international campaign against apartheid'. The result was that in 1963 the United Nations' strong declaratory regime on apartheid evolved quickly into an energetic promotional one.

Intervention of the Secretary-General

The United Nations made a third attempt to provide promotional 'assistance' towards eliminating apartheid by the Security Council's adoption of the resolution on South Africa on 1 April 1960. The last paragraph of the resolution asked the secretary-general to consult with Pretoria and to make 'such arrangements as would adequately help in upholding the purposes and principles of the Charter [in South Africa]'. In other words, the resolution called on the secretary-general to intervene personally in the apartheid situation.

Responding to an invitation from the Union's government, Secretary-General Dag Hammarskjöld did in fact visit South Africa for six days in early January 1961. During this period he held extensive discussions with Prime Minister Verwoerd, members of his cabinet, and leaders from the several racial communities. Despite these openings, however, Hammarskjöld admitted in his report to the Security Council that no mutually acceptable arrangement for ending apartheid had been found 'so far'. The secretary-general did indicate that he expected to continue his discussions with the South African government and that he planned to return to South Africa for this purpose.

However, Hammarskjöld died soon after in a plane crash in Northern Rhodesia. With his untimely passing, the unprecedented diplomatic opening Hammarskjöld had created between his office and the Pretoria government on the apartheid issue lapsed for twenty-nine years. As these words are being written in June 1990, a high-level UN delegation representing Secretary-General Javier Perez de Cuellar has arrived in South Africa for a ten-day visit to hold discussions with the government on its newly announced plans for moving the country towards democracy. This mission was authorized by the General Assembly in December 1989 and would seem to contemplate UN 'assistance' of a promotional nature. Ominously, however, President de Klerk's office in Cape Town announced that de Klerk's schedule is too full to allow the president himself to meet the UN delegation.

The Special Committee

We now return to consideration of the Special Committee on Apartheid which in its very early years after 1962 was not an impressive enterprise, bureaucratically speaking.

From the outset the goals of the committee in practice were overwhelmingly promotional in the broadest sense of the word. In 1967, the committee took upon itself the job of appealing directly to governments and numerous non-governmental organizations to honour the General Assembly's designation of 21 March, the anniversary of the shootings at Sharpeville, as an 'international day for the elimination of racial discrimination'. In time the United Nations practice of designating commemorative days, weeks, years, and even decades for various aspects of the anti-apartheid struggle would become a familiar aspect of the organization's promotional agenda.

In its annual report for 1966, the special committee noted that its activities were already outstripping its initial mandate and accordingly asked that its charge be enlarged in several particulars, which the General Assembly did. The special committee was instructed in 1967 to promote the international campaign against apartheid, to consult broadly towards this end, and to suggest measures to broaden the dissemination of information on apartheid's 'evils'. To meet these new tasks, the last one in particular, a subcommittee of the special committee was created in 1969 on information on apartheid. Further elaborations of the committee's mandate came later, proposed by the special committee itself.

A reading of the annual reports of the special committee in light of ensuing resolutions of the General Assembly on apartheid suggests that even from the committee's beginnings, the General Assembly has always been exceptionally responsive to the committee's recommendations. A majority of the Assembly has been willing to authorize or endorse at first opportunity almost any new initiative the Committee has wished to undertake, or to see undertaken by others.

The problem from the perspective of the special committee has been that overwhelming majorities in the General Assembly in favour of its recommendations count for little when those members with the power to damage South Africa's material interests significantly—the country's principal trading partners—refuse to go along with enforcement strategies intended to take advantage of such leverage. This is particularly a problem when permanent members of the Security Council oppose sanctions, because these states, by virtue of Security Council membership, are in a position to veto any such decision. Yet early on it was clear that three permanent members—Britain, the United States, and usually France—were opposed to sanctions, joining (as late as 1980) other Western industrialized countries such as Belgium, Canada, West Germany, the Netherlands, Portugal, and Italy.

Thus, by the end of the special committee's first half-decade it was apparent that a stalemate existed within the United Nations regarding apartheid. Responding to this, the leadership of the special committee sought to enlarge its membership beyond its eleven member countries in the hopes of associating at least some Western states with future committee recommendations. It sought specifically to include some permanent members of the Security Council, some of South Africa's principal trading partners, and states from geographic regions not previously represented. The following year the General Assembly agreed and asked the Assembly's president to appoint six new members to the special committee according to the above criteria. In June 1966 the president reported to Secretary-General U. Thant that he had been unable to meet this assignment. Fourteen of the states the president had approached had refused to serve, while those who had agreed to join did not collectively meet the stipulated specifications.

Later, a single criterion, geographical representation, was relied upon, and the special committee was enlarged to fifteen members, and later to eighteen. But these changes did nothing to alter the fundamentally pro-sanctions political complexion of the committee. Thus, at the end of its first decade, the special committee's pre-eminent goal of sanctions against South Africa seemed scarcely closer than it had been in November 1962.

In the early 1970s, therefore, the special committee decided on a new tactic: to appeal to world public opinion directly, targeting those states that continued to maintain substantial trade with South Africa. To assist the special committee in this regard, a 'Trust Fund for Publicity Against Apartheid' was established in early 1975 to which governments were asked to make voluntary contributions. By the end of 1980, forty-one states had already contributed US$619,000.

Over the years, this promotional campaign has become quite sophisticated. In 1976, for example, the committee indicated it favoured targeting 'specialized groups' possessing 'high opinion-building potential' within their countries, such as student organizations, trade unionists, and media specialists. Earlier, the committee decided to promote the establishment of 'national committees' to assist in the global campaign against apartheid. And in 1982, the committee saw fit to openly endorse 'public actions' such as church and university divestment campaigns, especially in countries whose governments were thought to be resisting implementing the UN anti-apartheid resolutions. This last tactic prompted hostility and opposition towards the committee from many of the governments so targeted, in particular the US government.

During this time, the General Assembly's objections to apartheid were presented in greater detail. This eventually resulted in some elaboration of the norms of the UN anti-apartheid regime. Within a few years of the inception of the special committee, four anti-apartheid norms had become explicit in many UN pronouncements. Not all of these norms were supported unanimously or even supported by every organ of the United Nations. However, each norm did have substantial support in the General Assembly and in the Economic and Social Council, and several were supported (or at least not opposed) by the five permanent members of the Security Council as well. The norms were:

1. Apartheid is a crime against humanity, not just against persons of color within South Africa. Apartheid is moreover a threat to international peace and security.
2. The struggle of the oppressed people of South Africa to end apartheid is a legitimate one, deserving of international assistance. In particular the South African liberation movements recognized by the Organization of African Unity (the ANC and the PAC) merit all possible encouragement and support.
3. The United Nations itself has a vital role to play in promoting international action against apartheid.
4. International action against apartheid should focus upon isolating South Africa in all possible ways.

In spite of constant reiteration and elaboration of these anti-apartheid norms within the United Nations, support for resolutions embodying these norms did not increase. The average number of states supporting anti-apartheid resolutions in the General Assembly actually declined from 91.9 per cent in 1970 to 81.2 per cent in 1976, although this seemed to be in part due to inclusion of specific condemnation of Israeli contact with South Africa in certain resolutions from 1973 onwards. In 1986, however, the level of support had reached an average of 83.7 per cent.

IMPLEMENTATION REGIME

For Donnelly, an international regime's implementation activities can include certain kinds of monitoring, coordination of national policies and forms of information exchange. This is a pretty vague category in that the boundaries between implementation and promotional activities, and even regime enforcement, are none too clear. Here I shall take 'implementation' to mean the 'doing of something' beyond mere advocacy of regime norms by utilizing measures that fall short of effective coercion of states. The latter measures we shall shortly treat as regime enforcement.

Donnelly has written that the evolution of an international regime from a promotional mode to an implementation mode requires 'a major qualitative jump [in national commitment] that most states strongly resist'. To effectuate such a commitment, relative cultural homogeneity, in which people share widespread perceptions of moral interdependence, is important. Just as domestic political action and international 'moral shock' may be necessary to create even a declaratory international regime, similar discontinuities may be necessary if a regime is to move beyond a promotional mode.

This analysis does not appear to be very helpful in understanding the case at hand. Even if the United Nations had wanted to move from promoting to implementing or enforcing activities against apartheid, it was held back by Article 10 of the UN Charter, which limits the General Assembly to an essentially advisory role and delegates enforcement powers to the Security Council. Had the General Assembly possessed the authority to apply sanctions against South Africa at the time, it would more than likely have acted as early as November 1962. As it was, the UN anti-apartheid regime took on implementing functions gradually, beginning in the mid-1960s, always as supplements to, rather than substitutes for, its previous declaratory and promotional activities of the regime. The following gives examples of these implementing functions.

Material Assistance

If individual states are free to ignore decisions of the General Assembly, the secretary-general has no such freedom. Three years after the General Assembly first recommended that sanctions against South Africa be applied, the Assembly requested—that is to say, it directed—Secretary-General Hammarskjöld to establish a 'United Nations Trust Fund for South Africa'. Consisting of voluntary contributions from both public and private sources, the fund was to coordinate and centralize legal, educational, and humanitarian assistance to victims of apartheid and their dependents, including refugees. By March 1988 a total of US$31.2 million in voluntary contributions to the trust fund had been collected, supporting the awarding of 145 grants up to that point.

Even before the establishment of the UN trust fund for South Africa, the Security Council had 'invited' the secretary-general in June 1964 to establish a programme for educating and training black South Africans abroad. This effort later merged with a similar UN program for Namibians, creating the 'United Nations Educational and Training Programme for Southern Africa'. As of September 1987, a total of 20,436 awards had been granted under this programme (many of these are extensions of earlier awards). In 1985, 766 South Africans received assistance, at a total cost estimated at nearly US$2.7 million. These funds came from the voluntary contributions of organizations, individuals or states.

Criminalization of Apartheid

The General Assembly's first reference in December 1966 to apartheid as a 'crime against humanity' did not of course make apartheid illegal under international law. No organ of the United Nations has the power to create new international legal obligations for the organization's members. But under authority granted in Article 13 (1a) of the Charter to encourage 'the progressive development of international law', the General Assembly has from time to time prepared draft international conventions for submission to UN members for ratification.

In November 1973, the General Assembly approved the text of a proposed 'International Convention on the Suppression and Punishment of the Crime of Apartheid'. This document was introduced by Guinea, Nigeria, and the Soviet Union and had previously been considered by both the Human Rights Commission and the Economic and Social Council. The draft convention came into force in 1976 when the requisite twenty states had ratified it. As of the middle of 1985, a total of eighty-one states, slightly more than half of the membership of the United Nations, had become parties to the Convention.

The International Convention on Suppression and Punishment of the Crime of Apartheid makes individuals, organizations, and governments within states that are parties to the convention legally liable for 'inhuman acts' in which they may become involved 'resulting from the policies and practices of apartheid'. Persons charged under the convention may be tried in the courts of any signatory, but as of 1990 no such prosecutions have occurred. This suggests that the convention itself might better be seen as anti-apartheid regime promotion rather than as a part of regime implementation.

In a similar fashion, on 10 December 1985 the General Assembly adopted an 'International Convention Against Apartheid in Sports', which put into legal form the prohibition against sporting contact with South Africa that the General Assembly had endorsed in a lengthy 'declaration' on the subject in December 1977. By signing this convention, the forty-one states currently party to it have agreed that they will not permit sporting contact with South Africa and will take action against international athletes who compete in South Africa.

Similarly, since the early 1980s, the special committee has maintained and occasionally published a similar register of artists and entertainers who have ignored repeated General Assembly calls for a cultural boycott of South Africa. As of yet, however, there is no international convention prohibiting cultural contact with South Africa.

Expulsion

At the height of the Sharpeville crisis in 1960, Secretary-General Hammarskjöld was quoted in the *New York Times* as saying, '[i]n the human rights field, the United Nations law, so to say, has principles and purposes, but very weak procedures'.

An example of a weak procedure is the right of the United Nations under Article 6 of the Charter to expel a member deemed to have 'persistently violated the [Charter's] Principles.' The idea of expelling South Africa has long appealed to the African members of the United Nations. The General Assembly alluded to this option as early as November 1962, at the end of the same resolution recommending creation of the Special Committee on Apartheid. But Article 6 of the Charter stipulates that expulsion of a member can only be accomplished by a decision of the General Assembly following a Security Council recommendation for expulsion. Such a recommendation has always been regarded as improbable due to the opposition of the Western powers, opposition that is based on the principle that UN membership should be universal.

However, the General Assembly's own rules do give it the right to review the credentials of its members. Seizing upon this, Algeria, Liberia, and the Soviet Union made an effort as early as 1963 to have the credentials of the South African delegation declared invalid. This initial effort failed, but two years later the General Assembly did choose to withhold approval of the South Africans' credentials. This had no immediate practical effect, however, and for some years the tactic was allowed to lapse.

In 1970, the General Assembly once again declined to approve the credentials of the South African delegation, a decision it repeated in 1971, 1972, and 1973. A 1970 ruling of the Assembly's president, Norway's Edvard Hambro, allowed the South African delegation to continue to occupy its seats on the floor of the Assembly, effectively annulling the impact of the Assembly decision. In September 1974, after again rejecting the credentials of the South Africans, the Assembly asked the Security Council 'to review the relationship between the United Nations and South Africa in the light of the constant violation by South Africa of the principles of the Charter and the Universal Declaration of Human Rights'.

The proponents of expulsion later offered three reasons for this step: apartheid's violation of the principles and purposes of the United Nations; South Africa's assistance to the 'illegal' regime in Southern Rhodesia; and South Africa's refusal to withdraw from Namibia as repeatedly demanded by the United Nations. When it came to a vote within the Council, Britain, the United States, and France vetoed the expulsion proposal. This action led the Assembly's new President, Abdelaziz Bouteflika of Algeria, to reverse the so-called 'Hambro ruling' of 1970, and declare that the Assembly's repeated rejection of the South Africans' credentials warranted the Union's exclusion from participating in Assembly business. This unprecedented decision, which effectively circumvented Article 6 of the Charter as far as membership in the Assembly was concerned, was immediately upheld by a vote of the Assembly as a whole, ninety-one to twenty-two with nineteen abstentions. This vote has excluded official South Africans from the floor of the General Assembly ever since.

Following this decision, the General Assembly resolved in 1973 that the South African regime had 'no right to represent the people of South Africa' and, in 1974, that it should therefore be excluded from all 'international organizations and conferences under the auspices of the United Nations.' The following year the Assembly would characterize the Pretoria government as 'illegitimate'.

Also in 1973, the Assembly acknowledged the ANC and the PAC as 'the authentic representatives of the overwhelming majority of the South African people'. In 1975 and periodically thereafter, representatives of both groups were invited to participate in Assembly debates on South Africa, initially within the Special Political Committee and later in plenary sessions. Two years later, in 1977, the Security Council followed suit, even though it still allows South Africa's official representatives to appear when the Security Council considers South African issues.

ENFORCEMENT REGIME

Unlike the concept of an implementing regime, the idea of an enforcement regime is conceptually clear and straightforward. Enforcement activities, according to Donnelly, involve institutionalized international decision-making whose results are binding on members of the international community as well as 'the stronger forms of international monitoring.' As indicated earlier, within the UN system only the Security Council is competent under the Charter to issue binding decisions, and only then following a finding by the Security Council that the situation being addressed represents a 'threat to the peace, breach of the peace or act of aggression'. Absent such a determination, a decision by the Security Council is only advisory in nature, rather than obligatory or mandatory.

Over the next thirteen years the continuing threat of a veto from one or more of the Security Council's Western permanent members caused African and other sponsors of resolutions on apartheid to suppress their clear preference for mandatory measures in the interest of gaining consensus in the Council on these questions. However, in late 1977 this cautious attitude suddenly changed. Spurred by widespread international outrage at the recent death in South African police custody of Steve Biko and the banning by Pretoria of eighteen domestic anti-apartheid organizations, Benin, Libya, and Mauritius, acting on behalf of forty-nine African states, brought before the Security Council four motions that had been pending for more than six months.

One of these expressly declared that the policies and actions of the South African regime 'constitute a grave threat to international peace and security' and contemplated unspecified actions under Chapter VII of the Charter should Pretoria continue to ignore relevant Security Council resolutions as well as its obligations as a UN member. In an unprecedented step, the United States, the United Kingdom, and France (together with Canada and West Germany, who in 1977 were elected members of the Council) now announced their willingness to see a mandatory arms embargo applied against South Africa. On 4 November, a prior advisory endorsement of an arms embargo became compulsory.

Even though the five Western members declined to support the African group's other proposals for sweeping economic sanctions against South Africa, the legal barrier to the application of Chapter VII had at last been overcome. It was a somewhat circumspect process, though, given that it concerned the acquisition of arms by South Africa rather than apartheid itself, which the Western permanent members of the Council at last accepted as constituting a threat to international peace.

In retrospect, it appears that passage of this resolution by the Security Council in November 1977 opened the door—albeit slowly—to debate within the Security Council on the merits of mandatory sanctions against South Africa.

The foregoing account is far from comprehensive. The goal has been to describe the evolution of the UN anti-apartheid policy over time—a question of process—rather than the detailed substance of that policy.

From this perspective it is noticeable that not all major upheavals in South Africa over the period considered have been reflected in qualitative changes in the nature of the UN anti-apartheid regime. For example, civil unrest in South Africa in the mid-1980s attendant to the introduction of changes in the country's constitutional system produced no such result. On the other hand, most of the regime changes that did occur can be linked with some major happening within South Africa at the time. This is especially true of the Sharpeville massacre in 1960 together with the events that immediately followed it, as well as the urban civil unrest of the later 1976–77 period. Thus with the exception of the regime's movement from a promotional mode to an implementation mode, which seems to have occurred in a gradual way, the evolution of the UN anti-apartheid regime has been an essentially discontinuous process, seemingly highly responsive to happenings within South Africa itself.

Indeed, South Africa's principal adversaries at the United Nations have not been unmindful of this fact. It is clear that in the Security Council, African members in particular have perceived the tactical value of focusing the Council's attention on South Africa at precisely those moments when some well-reported event in the southern African region has incited widespread public excoriation of the Pretoria government. The African members' obvious hope has been to make it more difficult for the Security Council to oppose motions against apartheid proposed by the Africa group. On the other hand, without an immediate connection with a newsworthy event in the southern African region, debates on apartheid in the Security Council, when they have occurred, have tended to flounder.

To date the 1977 arms embargo has clearly provided the high water mark in the United Nations' on-going international campaign against apartheid. In spite of the undoubted symbolic value of this decision to the global anti-apartheid movement, however, its practical consequence—and therefore the tangible significance of the current enforcement features of the UN anti-apartheid regime—may actually have undermined the movement's goals. In response to this embargo, the Republic accelerated development of its domestic arms-making industry and has now become one of the foremost suppliers of military armaments in the world. Indeed, as early as 1984, the Security Council found it necessary to urge all states 'to refrain from importing arms, ammunition of all types and military vehicles produced in South Africa'.

As for implementing activities of the regime, these have certainly been more numerous than the single enforcement step that has been taken, and collectively they have probably been of more practical assistance to those persons actively working to overthrow apartheid. Still, these implementing activities have been limited in scope, and the funds dedicated to their support have also been limited, especially those funds that have been provided directly by the United Nations rather than through voluntary contributions from member states and private sources. On the whole, then, promotional activities of the UN anti-apartheid regime have overshadowed both its implementation and enforcement aspects. Of particular note is the work of the Special Committee on Apartheid, assisted of course by the Centre Against Apartheid.

The evolution of the promotional activities of the UN anti-apartheid regime after its early stimulus thus appears to have been relatively consistent, rather than step-like.

Finally, although it is doubtless true that the UN anti-apartheid regime has become somewhat stronger over the years along all of the three dimensions of regime strength cited earlier—norms, sanctioned procedures, and membership—the apparent growing effectiveness of this regime is probably due to a different aspect of this case. This is the persistent and intensifying reiteration of the anti-apartheid regime's core normative message: the international unacceptability of racial discrimination and the desirability of applying economic sanctions to South Africa.

7

What Next? Selective Genocide in Burundi

RENE LEMARCHAND

The annihilation of the Hutu elites has effectively eliminated all potential threats to Tutsi hegemony from the Hutu, at least for the next generation; but it has by no means eliminated all sources of conflict. One of the unintended consequences of the slaughter has been to create the conditions for further conflict within the dominant stratum. Now that Hutu threats are no longer perceived as significant by the Tutsi minority, the focus of inter-group conflict is likely to move back once again to intra-Tutsi divisions, pitting north against south, Banyabururi against Banyaruguru, radicals against moderates. So far the Bururi 'lobby' has proved remarkably adept at exploiting the Hutu–Tutsi conflict to its own advantage, using violence as a resource to consolidate its position vis-à-vis both Hutu and Banyaruguru; but the latter (unlike the Hutu living in Burundi) are unwilling to give up their claims to power. In these conditions the continued exclusion of Banyaruguru elements from positions of responsibility within the army and the government may well become a source of increasing tension in years ahead within the Tutsi stratum, possibly leading to new confrontations. Another source of tension lies in the mutual hatreds generated among Tutsi as a result of the excesses committed during the repression. Conscious as most Tutsi were of the threats posed to their collective interest, indeed to their survival, by an impending Hutu takeover, many have since come to realise the enormous disproportion between the nature of the threat on the one hand, and the scale and arbitrariness of the repression on the other. Many are the Tutsi who lost Hutu friends, domestic servants and clients at the hands of the army and the *jeunesses,* knowing full well they were innocent. This forceful and unnecessary severance of the few remaining bonds of personal friendship and loyalty between themselves and their Hutu neighbours is what a great many Tutsi in the rural areas are as yet unable to comprehend or forgive. Nor are they likely to forget the share of responsibility borne by the Bururi elites in this and other matters. Thus it would be grossly misleading to conceive of the dominant minority as being all one politically and otherwise. Beneath the monolithic surface of Tutsi hegemony one can discern a variety of potential sources of conflict—some rooted in cultural and regional antagonisms, others in basic disagreements over the scale of the brutalities committed during the repression, others still in the frustrations experienced by specific groups of individuals as a result of their differential access to the rewards of office.

Whether intra-Tutsi tensions can be effectively mitigated by their awareness of future Hutu threats to their security is difficult to say. Internally, the ruling elites have no reason to anticipate further challenges from the Hutu community: lacking all potential sources of leadership, decimated and deeply traumatised by the terrible vengeance visited upon them, the Hutu living in Burundi are neither willing nor able to instigate further revolts. Entirely different, however, is the attitude of the Hutu refugee community in exile. The slaughter of 1972 has generated a massive involuntary migration of Hutu populations into Rwanda, Zaire and Tanzania (approximately 150,000), creating in each state a kind of 'privileged sanctuary' for the launching of refugee-led guerrilla operations against the Burundi government. This situation is made all the more explosive by the occasional 'spill-over' of anti-Hutu raids into neighbouring territories—and the possibility that the raids might miss their intended targets, killing civilian populations. Judging by the extreme seriousness of the diplomatic incident triggered by the mistaken strafing of a Tanzanian village by helicopters of the Burundi National Army in the spring of 1973, one can see why these retaliatory moves might lead to unintended hostilities between Burundi and any of its neighbours. Yet another element of uncertainty concerns the attitude of the Rwanda government vis-à-vis both the Hutu refugees from Burundi and the Burundi government: can the Rwanda government exercise effective control over the refugees and prevent both guerrilla attacks and retaliatory raids? Can it prevent a tactical alliance between the Hutu refugees from Burundi and the Hutu opposition—an alliance presumably designed to create border conflicts which each partner might then seek to exploit to its advantage, the refugees to fight their way back into Burundi and the domestic Hutu opposition to recapture power? There are no precise answers to these questions. What does seem reasonably clear is that the capacity of the Bururi 'lobby' to maintain itself in power will depend to a large extent on its ability to cope with the conditions of chronic instability arising from the spread of anti-regime (i.e. Hutu) forces into neighbouring political arenas.

Even more fundamental in the long run are the amounts and kinds of assistance which the Micombero regime can expect from foreign powers within and outside Africa. Burundi's strongest allies, for the time being, are Zaire and France, each for very different reasons. In the light of the ominous threats faced by the Zairian authorities during the 1964 rebellion it is easy to see why the Mulelist component of the Hutu rebellion should have produced a quick and positive response from Kinshasa—in the form of military assistance. The rapprochement brought to light during the crisis is more than a conjunctural phenomenon. A crucial element militating in favour of continued close relationships between Kinshasa and Bujumbura is the presence of a substantial number of Tutsi elements (most of them refugees from Rwanda) in specific sectors of the Zairian civil service—primarily in Agriculture and Education—as well as in top decision-making positions. The second most powerful figure in Kinshasa is none other than a former Tutsi refugee from Rwanda. In a way ethnicity is part of the social cement that makes for potentially close relationships between the two states, above and beyond the convergence of short-term interests.

The case of France is more difficult to explain, involving as it does a mixture of ignorance and opportunism, and a fetish-like attachment to the presumed virtues of francophonie. That 100,000 francophones, or potential francophones, happen to be massacred in the name of Tutsi supremacy makes little difference as long as France's brand of francophonie—meaning in effect the promotion of French, as distinct from Belgian, cultural values stands to profit. Nor does it matter if in this case Tutsi supremacy should contradict the fundamental principles of 1789. What matters ultimately is the expansion of France's sphere of influence in black Africa, culturally and politically. And since the Tutsi as a group are being viewed as having a greater nimbleness of mind and greater expressional skills than the Hutu, and on the whole more willing to do business with the French, they are generally viewed as a better 'investment' by French diplomats. These considerations are essential to an understanding of the supporting role played by French military assistants during and after the rebellion. As one knowledgeable observer put it: 'French military assistants flew and are still flying the regime's helicopters. This airborne was crucial in routing out the rebels in the south . . . Frenchmen were holding the helicopters steady while Burundi soldiers were machine-gunning Hutu rebels out of the side windows, and Frenchmen were at the wheel of the same helicopters in the incursions into Tanzania, in the course of which numerous Tanzanians were killed.' Under the cover of a *Société de Transports Aériens du Burundi* (whose initials, STAB, convey a more realistic appraisal of its role) French pilots and helicopters supply the Micombero regime with minimum guarantees of security against further rebel attacks.

The prominence of the French presence in Burundi, not only at the military level but in cultural, educational and technical spheres, has meant a corresponding loss of influence for Belgium, thus removing all credibility from the threats of economic sanctions raised in Brussels during the 1972 events. While Belgium was making a last-ditch effort to make sure that the educational component of its aid programme would not be used for discriminatory purposes, the French promptly offered to make up for whatever aid Belgium might withdraw! Such being the case one wonders whether there is any point in laying blame on the United States for its failure to act in any decisive way during the crisis. In a recent sponsored report by the Carnegie Endowment the suggestion is made that since the US buys approximately 80 per cent of Burundi's coffee (representing 60 per cent of its foreign earnings), the State Department possessed sufficient economic leverage to induce a basic change of attitude on the part of the Tutsi authorities. This is extremely dubious, however. When ethnic hatreds reached the point where people slaughter each other by the thousands, how much do they really care about the long-range implications of a reduction of coffee exports? Nor is it a foregone conclusion that this form of economic sanctions would in the long run produce the expected results. The Hutu masses would probably suffer just as much as the Tutsi elites from the consequences of this policy. But perhaps the basic flaw in the argument advanced by the authors of the Carnegie report is that it assumes that the United States enjoys a position of economic omnipotence in Burundi. It would be very surprising indeed if, in the event of an American decision to bar coffee imports from Burundi, alternative buyers did not materialise.

To bring effective pressure to bear upon the Burundi authorities would have required a concerted action on the part of all Western powers accredited in Bujumbura. Only in these conditions and through pressures involving not only moral persuasion but continued threats of economic sanctions was there a chance of limiting the scale of the massacre, and perhaps initiating a more liberal trend in the sphere of Hutu–Tutsi relations. At the time of the crisis, however, there was little agreement among Western diplomats as to what should or could be done. In fact some of the key figures in the Western diplomatic corps were not even on speaking terms with each other. The rift was even more conspicuous in the case of Communist powers. Whereas North Korea and China were the only powers outside Africa to officially support the regime, the Soviets showed no compunctions about signing the Western note of protest, in part because differences of opinion among Western diplomats made the note sound platitudinous, if not downright hypocritical. With the exception of Belgium, the dominant impression one gains of Western diplomacy during the crisis is one of almost total indifference in the face of an unrelieved tragedy.

Just as astonishing is the silence of the UN and the OAU, and the total inability, or unwillingness, of either organisation to register any kind of effective protest. In the case of the OAU this passivity is sometimes justified by the argument that since the Burundi crisis was a purely domestic matter (which it most emphatically was not), it was clearly outside the jurisdiction of the OAU. Perhaps a more realistic explanation is that most African states are, to a greater or lesser extent, potential Burundis. No African state wishes to establish a precedent that might prevent it from dealing with such crises by means of its own choosing. Even so, the wording of the resolution adopted at the OAU Summit in Rabat in late June strikes one as little short of astounding, amounting in effect to a message of support for Micombero: 'The Council of Ministers is convinced that, thanks to your saving action, peace will be rapidly re-established, national unity consolidated and territorial integrity preserved.'

These considerations are equally relevant to an understanding of the striking indecision displayed by the UN. According to the Carnegie report, Washington had apparently banked on UN observers constituting what one official described as 'a foreign presence that would be likely to halt the massive killings'. But when the two missions (sent by the UN) were limited to only five persons, that expectation evaporated. 'We had no illusions about what the UN could accomplish', admitted a high US official later. The fact which emerges with striking clarity from the record of UN involvement, or non-involvement in Burundi is that the latter ranked far too low in the scale of international priorities to justify anything more than a pro forma intervention. To put the matter crudely: as long as the killings involved only Hutu and Tutsi the crisis could be regarded as lying essentially within the domestic jurisdiction of the state of Burundi; only inasmuch as Hutu and Tutsi could be identified as being respectively pro-Western and pro-Communist (which was no longer the case in 1972), could the matter conceivably be viewed as a 'threat to peace' by Western powers. Only then could a rationale be established for intervention, and a criterion made available for discriminating between 'friend' and 'foe'. In the spring of 1972 the UN clearly lacked a rationale for intervention; yet, judging from the use made by the Burundi authorities of UNICEF trucks during the repression, the field agencies of the UN were by no means at a loss for identifying 'friends' and 'foes'. As Greenland tersely puts it, 'the UN said little, even when their own vehicles were requisitioned and used to take Hutu to their deaths. It was ironic to see Landrovers marked UNICEF being used for this purpose . . .' This is perhaps the reason why, until his death in Geneva earlier this year, the Head of the UN Development Programme in Bujumbura, Marcel Latour, was one of the two most highly regarded Western officials in Bujumbura, the other being his long-time friend, war comrade and compatriot, Henri Bernard, the French Ambassador.

Reflecting on the appalling events of 1972 one journalist was prompted to ask: does an international conscience exist? The answer given by a Western diplomat sums up the dilemma: 'Nobody wants to start up another fuss in a faraway country if personal interests are not involved'. Insofar as it can be detected at all, what goes by the name of an 'international conscience' is the expression of convergent national interests, not of a global commitment to moral values. How else is one to explain the blissful indifference of world opinion to what must be regarded as one of the most brutal massacres in the history of any single state? How can one otherwise explain the commotion produced in Africa and Europe (and particularly in England) by the alleged massacre of 400 Africans in Mozambique by Portuguese security forces, and the fact that the far larger killings in Burundi went almost unnoticed? The sad truth is that Burundi is too 'far away', too 'exotic', too small, in short too marginal in terms of the priorities set by international diplomacy to elicit concern or compassion among Westerners. Thus the death of scores of Africans at the hands of the Portuguese colonialists is viewed as an intolerable scandal by white liberals (as it should); the Burundi killings, by contrast, are seen as a mere statistic.

The crux of the dilemma concerning Burundi's future is whether further periodic massacres can be instituted without triggering conflicting moves on the part of its neighbours, Rwanda, Tanzania and Zaire. The latter two in particular, by virtue of their geographical position and political weight, have a vital role to play, not only in influencing President Micombero towards more moderate policies, but in preventing the occurrence of a 'client war' in which Rwanda would side with Tanzania and Zaire with Burundi. The most one can hope for the time being is for the three states that once made up Belgian Africa to evolve a common framework of co-operative relations with a view to maximising their chances of economic viability while at the same time reducing the risks of confrontation and hostility at the domestic and international levels. If neither the UN nor the OAU were able to influence the course of events in 1972, one would hope that they might at least try to mobilise world opinion in support of initiatives aiming at preventing the recurrence of these events in the foreseeable future.

Part Three

New States and the Continental Order

INTRODUCTION

In earlier historical periods, weak states could expect to be absorbed by stronger ones. By the twentieth century, this had become almost impossible, and as a result weak states could be virtually certain to survive. African states are a perfect example of that development, and Griffiths provides a geographical perspective on the origins and stability of their boundaries. Beyond relying on the international order to maintain their boundaries, the new states of Africa tried to build institutions that would sustain both their sovereignty and their development. The main institution was the Organisation of African Unity. May and Massey, examining a particular episode, throw considerable light on the difficulties that the Organisation of African Unity encountered in its checkered history.

8

The Scramble for Africa: Inherited Political Boundaries

IEUAN GRIFFITHS

The inherited political geography of Africa is as great an impediment to independent development as her colonially based economies and political structures. The colonial political geography derives from the Berlin Conference of 1884–85, which laid down the rules for the European partition of the continent. What were drawn as colonial boundaries have survived the transition from colonies to independent states and, more surprisingly, 25 years of African independence.

The boundaries themselves are only one aspect of Africa's inherited political geography. African states are territorially identical to the European colonies they replaced, for all their grotesque shapes and varied sizes. European colonialism lumped together peoples of diverse cultures and traditions, sometimes leading to secessionist movements and civil war. The creation of long and narrow states such as The Gambia and Togo meant that development concentrated on the short sea coast remote from up-country regions. Many African states are too small to make viable economic markets and are below the threshold of any possible industrialisation. Others are so large and diverse that effective government becomes difficult. There are 14 landlocked states in Africa, more than in the rest of the world put together. They all face chronic problems of access varying according to local circumstance. Colonial capital cities located on coastal peripheries have become national capitals of independent states.

Despite the obvious drawbacks of such an anomalous and anachronistic geographical framework, opportunities to change it have largely been ignored in post-independence Africa. Financial cost, vested interests, inertia and lack of perception have been inhibiting factors. The political geography of colonial Africa had a rationale rooted in colonialism itself but each aspect of it now presents modern Africa with problems which, taken in conjunction with inherited economic and political difficulties, severely impede progress towards complete independence. This lecture concentrates on international boundaries, arguably the fundamental ingredient in Africa's political geography. Boundaries collectively divide the continent into its many states and individually divide people. They are a source of international conflict and affect the spatial pattern of economic development.

THE EVOLUTION OF AFRICA'S BOUNDARIES

The political boundaries of modern Africa emerged mainly in the 30 years after the Berlin Conference. They were drawn by Europeans, for Europeans and, apart from some localised detail, paid scant regard to Africa, let alone to Africans.

Prior to the Berlin Conference few of the present boundaries of Africa existed. Those that did were limited to settler territories, in the north between Algeria and Morocco, and in the south to protect Basutoland against Boer encroachment, around the South African Republic (Transvaal), and the enclave of Walvis Bay.

In the five years following Berlin the European powers made bilateral treaties with each other, covering all parts of Africa. Boundaries were drawn to define the different European spheres of influence, first as short lines made roughly at right angles to the coast. In East Africa the German sphere was distinguished from the British to the north and the Portuguese to the south. The same Luso-German Treaty separated South West Africa from Angola. In equatorial Africa the French sphere was defined between the Congo Free State and the Spanish sphere. In West Africa, French Ivory Coast was separated from British Gold Coast, Sierra Leone was defined in relation to Liberia and the two enclave colonies of The Gambia and Portuguese Guinea were defined from surrounding French territory.

By the turn of the century almost the whole of southern Africa was divided in precisely the way it is today. The sole exception was the Anglo-Portuguese boundary where the powers could not agree. In north-east Africa lines were drawn separating the British, French and Italian spheres. The extent of the last was exaggerated because the arrogant European assumption that they were the only players on the board proved false when, on 1 March 1896, the Ethiopians defeated the Italians at Adowa. Ethiopia then indulged in its own empire building, to the lasting discomfiture of its neighbours. In the 1890s the Congo took shape and in West Africa the French defined their boundaries with Liberia and Sierra Leone and spent some time arguing with themselves over Ivory Coast, Guinea and Senegal.

By 1914 the partition of Africa was virtually complete. The only lines which remained to be drawn were: 1) in the Sahara, 2) the outstanding sub-divisions of the French colonial Africa, and 3) adjustments arising from the First World War. The Saharan boundaries were eventually resolved largely by the use of straight lines. Internal sub-divisions of the French empire came and went. Upper Volta (Burkina Faso) appeared in 1922, disappeared in 1932, and reappeared in 1948. Some boundaries between French territories were never quite completed and left thorny problems to be solved after independence, notably between Algeria and Morocco.

Changes consequent upon the 1914–18 war were several. Jubaland was given to Italy in 1924 but originally by the secret Treaty of London in 1915. The Portuguese took the Kionga (Quionga) triangle south of the Ruvuma estuary, a territory of 215 square miles, previously confirmed as German only in 1909 after long dispute. When Belgian ambitions for Portuguese territory near the mouth of the Congo had been thwarted, Ruanda-Urundi was separated from Tanganyika and placed under Belgian administration. In West Africa the Togo and Cameroon boundaries changed as the former German colonies were shared between France and Britain.

Other minor adjustments were made to suit the colonial powers: for example, the exchange between Belgium and Portugal in 1927 of the 3,500 sq km 'Botte de Dilolo' to Angola for 3 sq km in the Duizi valley near Matadi, to allow a cheaper and more convenient realignment of the Leopoldville railway.

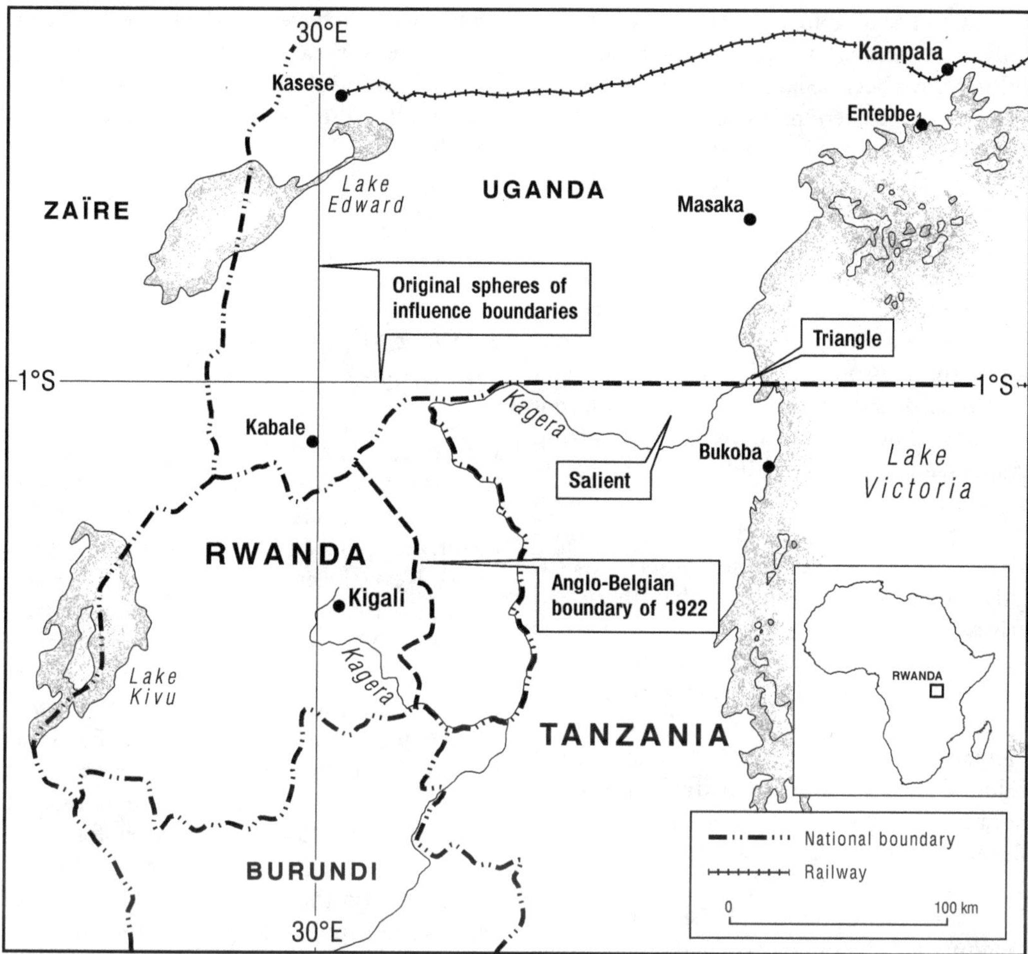

Map 8.1. Boundaries between Rwanda and Tanzania and between Tanzania and Uganda.

THE CHARACTERISTICS OF AFRICAN BOUNDARIES

The boundaries of Africa owe their special characteristics to the fact that the continent was partitioned by Europeans who at the time had limited knowledge of it. Physical features were used in boundary definition where known, or even known about, and failing them, lines of latitude and longitude (astronomical lines) or other straight lines.

BOUNDARIES AND ETHNICITY

At the continental scale the widespread use of physical features and astronomical lines largely de-humanised the boundaries of Africa. Although sometimes based on treaties between Europeans and local rulers, only rarely did colonial boundaries coincide with tribal or culture areas. Every land boundary in Africa cuts through at least one. The Nigeria–Cameroon boundary divides 14, while the boundaries of Burkina Faso cut 21 culture areas.

The problems caused by the imposition of boundaries in a manner so insensitive to African human geography would have been politically more serious had not the total number of culture areas been so large that most emergent states incorporated many complete culture areas as well as parts of others. In only a few states do divided peoples have sufficient influence to create international instability by attempting to re-unite themselves and in fewer still is there truly an irredentist movement.

The full impact of a divisive boundary is felt when it interferes with the daily routines of ordinary people. As long as people can obtain seed and implements, use traditional markets, choose spouses from neighbouring villages and send their children to the nearest school, irrespective of boundaries, all is well. It is when tribesmen are charged with smuggling, or of being illegal immigrants or are fugitives from one state's justice that discontent arises.

There were few attempts deliberately to draw African boundaries along traditional lines. One such was between Rwanda and Tanganyika (see map 8.1). It came late in the colonial period and demonstrated the ameliorating effect of the League of Nations on European imperialism. Both territories had been parts of German East Africa, given in 1919 as League of Nations Trust Territories to Belgium and Britain respectively. In 1922 the League approved the territorial division proposed by Belgium and Britain and separate administrations were set up. The agreed boundary line was influenced by a British notion to build a railway through the district to connect Uganda and Tanganyika. Almost immediately Belgian missionaries in Rwanda protested to the Permanent Mandates Commission of the League emphasising 'the social, political, and economic harm [to the Kingdom of Rwanda] caused by the imposition of this arbitrary division'. Belgium and Britain were persuaded to accept the Kagera river boundary in 1923 although problems of demarcation through the Kagera swamps delayed implementation until May 1938. Without the League of Nations to which to appeal, it is unlikely that the boundary adjustment would have taken place and a typically imperialist consideration of a tentative and anachronistic strategic railway route probably would have prevailed. The final irony is that the Kagera boundary, far from being a natural cultural divide, actually cuts across four small culture areas: Ha, Hangaza, Haya and Zinza.

AFRICAN INFLUENCE ON BOUNDARIES

It cannot be claimed that no attention was paid to Africans in the partition process because rival European claims to territory were frequently supported by treaties made with local rulers. Nevertheless, it was only when a European power concerned decided so, were treaties [with Africans] taken into consideration in connection with the territorial settlements. Sometimes local treaties became a currency for territorial bargaining between European powers. Even where tribal lands were agreed to lie within one sphere rather than another, boundary definition was a matter for Europeans who were quite capable of deciding, for example, that the boundary of Barotseland ran for 390 miles along astronomical lines. This arbitration by King Victor Emmanuel III of Italy in 1905 was perhaps the only occasion on which a traditional African kingdom was defined by astronomical lines. Although the arbitration favoured Britain rather than Portugal, the Foreign Office was later scathing about the 'arbitrary meridians and parallels adopted'.

LOCAL BOUNDARY ADJUSTMENTS

It would be likewise wrong to assume, though many do, that European-drawn boundaries invariably ignored local human geography. There was an agreement between Britain and

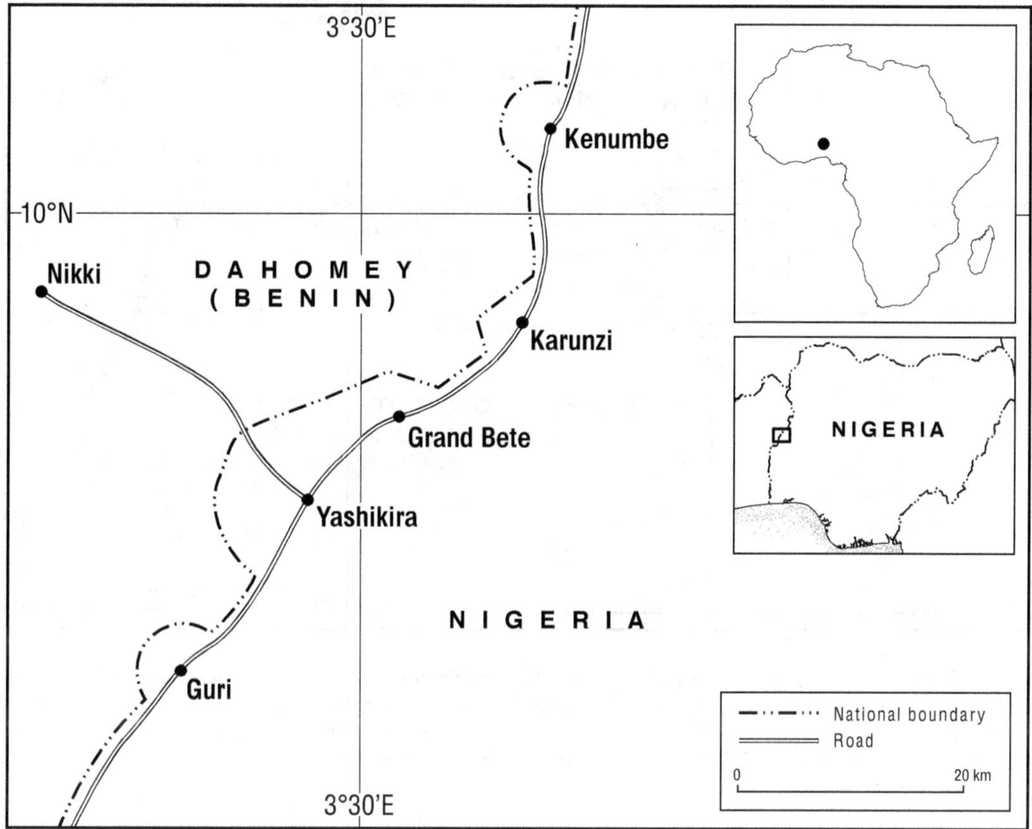

Map 8.2. Detail of boundary between Nigeria and Benin—place names rendered according to the Anglo-French agreement of October 19, 1906, and accompanying maps.

France which describes in detail what is now the Benin–Nigeria boundary (see map 8.2). Villages were allowed a 4 km semi-circular indentation into the boundary line which ran parallel to the road. Small towns warranted an 8 km indentation, an early practical recognition of an aspect of central place theory.

There was similar attention to local detail on the boundary between what are now Ghana and Burkina Faso (see map 8.3).

The detail of African boundaries is complex and often belies the simplification inherent in large-scale maps, let alone in attempts to classify boundaries on the basis of such maps. The astronomical line section of the boundary between modern Ghana and Burkina Faso shown in most atlases as a straight line is in fact only loosely based on the 11th parallel North. The arbitrariness of the original line was modified, in a stylised way, in response to local human factors. It is not a point to labour, rather one to counter the sweeping assertions so frequently made about the universal insensitivity to local conditions of European-drawn boundaries in Africa.

BOUNDARY PROBLEMS

The boundaries of Africa nevertheless do cause problems. Their arbitrariness divides people and in other ways results in absurd situations, their ambiguity and lack of definition make for differences of interpretation and opinion,

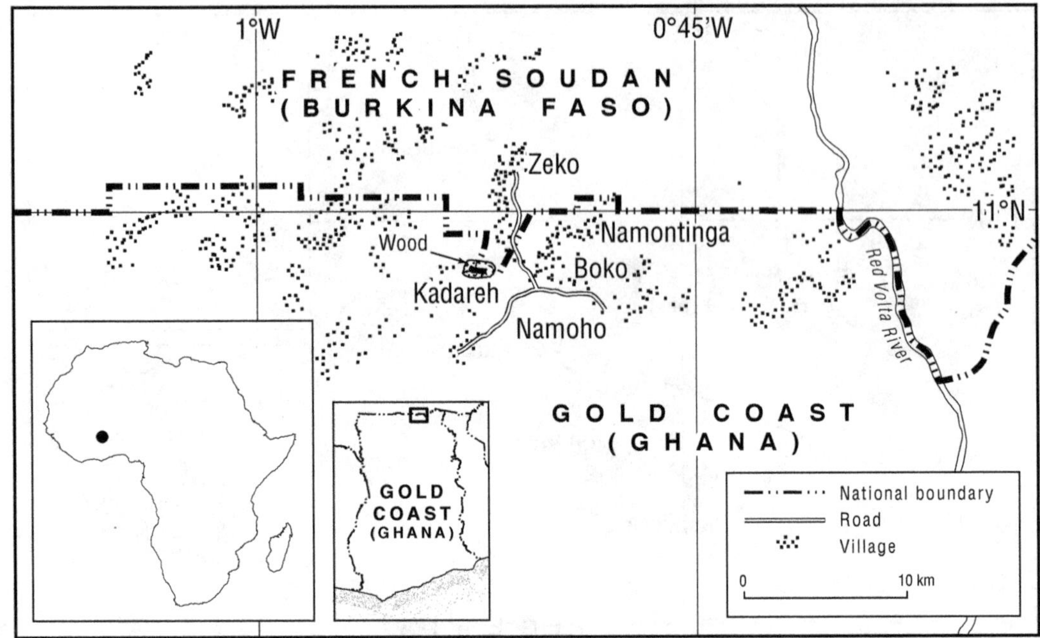

Map 8.3. Detail of boundary between Ghana and Burkina Faso—place names rendered according to the Anglo-French agreement of October 19, 1906, and accompanying maps. Modern country names have been added. The colony of "French Soudan" at times encompassed Senegal, Niger, Benin, Burkina Faso, and Mali. The location shown here is in contemporary Bukina Faso.

and their inconsistency in the use of physical features, taking for instance, the thalweg, either bank, or the median line where a river forms the boundary, creates further uncertainty. It all adds up to the fact that there are 'weak' boundaries throughout Africa. They do not represent perpetual problems but are time-bombs waiting for a change of political circumstance to ignite the fuse. Should the political context change, a point of weakness can become significant and provide a focal point for international antagonism, often leading to military conflict. The post-independence experience has been that, overall, few points of weakness have been eliminated and as a result many disputes involving boundaries have occurred. These disputes have weakened African states in general by diverting scarce resources to the military—sometimes merely in anticipation of frontier incidents.

THE MAURITANIA–WESTERN SAHARA BOUNDARY: THE RAILWAY TUNNEL TO NOWHERE

The boundary between Mauritania and Western Sahara (see map 8.4) consists of geometrical lines most of which are astronomical. From Cape Blanco the boundary runs along the 21° 20' North parallel for 260 miles into the Sahara to the intersection with the 13° West meridian. From this point, the boundary assumes a straight line approximately 6° west of north for 95 miles. Geometrical lines might be adequate means of defining desert boundaries but in this case the point where the boundary turns through 84° (Choum) is on the spur of a mountain range which otherwise lies entirely within Mauritania.

In the early 1960s French development of the Zouerate iron ore mines necessitated a

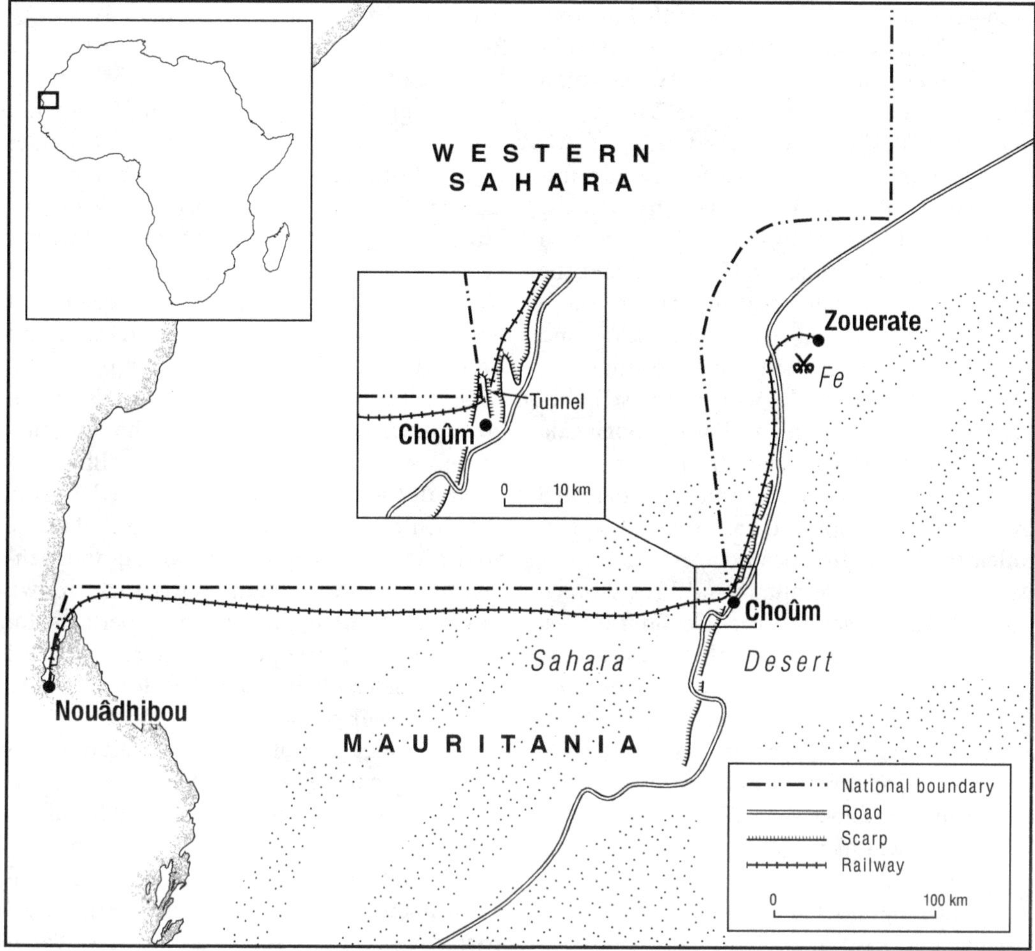

Map 8.4. The boundary between Mauritania and Western Sahara.

railway link with Port Étienne (Nouadhibou). It was built along the Cape Blanco peninsula but not directly towards the mines, because the Franco regime imposed unacceptable conditions for granting permission for the line to cross the Spanish Sahara boundary. The long deviation was tedious but the real problem was encountered at Choum where the railway engineers were left with no alternative but to tunnel for two kilometres through the granite spur, in effect into and out of the same side of the main mountain ridge, simply to keep inside French territory. The Choum tunnel is a monument to European stupidity in Africa and contrasts with the Botte de Dilolo deal between Belgium and Portugal.

THE BOUNDARIES OF NAMIBIA

Unless good sense prevails before independence, Namibia will inherit colonial boundaries more problematic than any others in Africa. Geographically the most obvious of these is the potential problem of the 187km long Caprivi Zipfel or strip. First agreed by Britain and Germany in 1890 it represents a German wish to have direct access to the Zambezi. It well illustrates European ignorance of African geography at the time, for a more difficult route to the Zambezi than through the Zipfel would be hard to find. It is cut by two major perennial rivers, the Okavango and the Cuando–Chobe, many seasonal rivers, and a large area of swamp between the Chobe and Zambezi. The Zipfel also cuts ethno-linguistic areas, the 16,000 people living in the strip being related to groups in Zambia and Botswana rather than to those in Namibia proper.

German forces in Caprivi were defeated by Rhodesian troops in 1915. The 6,722-square mile Zipfel then disappeared as it was administered as part of Bechuanaland Protectorate. But in 1929 it was returned to South West Africa, seven years after South Africa had assumed formal administration of that territory under League of Nations Mandate. The Bechuanaland connection was understandable because the Zipfel is remote and costly to administer from Windhoek.

The potential problem arising from the continued existence of the Caprivi Zipfel concerns the long-mooted development of northwestern Botswana by exploiting the juxtaposition of an area of water surplus, the Okavango swamp, and an area of water deficiency, the Kalahari desert. Namibia will be an additional interested party in the potential scheme and her concerns and priorities will have to be taken into account. Relations with Botswana could become strained should Namibia be seen to affect deleteriously Botswana's long-nurtured ambitions.

There are enough potential sources of friction between the two countries besides this example because the long astronomical line boundary between the two countries cuts across other culture areas. In particular, one small group of Tswana people live within the eastern boundary of Namibia (see map 8.5).

The urge to tidy up the map of Africa also prevails when considering the division of Ovamboland by the frontier with Angola. The parallel selected for the boundary is 17° 23' 23.73" South, its precision determined by the location of the Ruacana Falls on the Cunene River. Agreed in principle in 1886, but not demarcated until 1931, the boundary divides a large featureless plain which is home for a million Ovambo, the majority in Namibia. The idea of an independent Ovambo state has been mooted by those seeking alternatives to Namibian independence. Not surprisingly it has attracted no support from SWAPO (South West African People's Organisation) or from Angola, but a post-independence Namibian government may well regard the question of reuniting the Ovambo people differently. Their division has been emphasised during the Namibian conflict by a fence erected by the South African military. On gaining independence there will be a natural urge to tear down this symbol of oppression and perhaps for SWAPO, who have operated among Ovambos on both sides of the border, a desire to seek unity for their people.

The chief port of Namibia, Walvis Bay, is not legally part of Namibia but is a South African enclave which was annexed by Britain in 1878 and passed to the Cape Colony in 1884. When South West Africa became a South African mandate the South African Parliament passed an Act in 1922 to administer Walvis Bay as part of South West Africa. That Act was repealed in 1977 when Namibian independence seemed imminent and Walvis Bay reverted to South Africa. There the matter rests while the future of Namibia is decided. Namibia has no viable alternative port but OAU insistence on the integrity of colonial boundaries does extend to enclaves. However, Cabinda, an exclave attached to Angola, and likewise Ceuta and Melilla on the north Moroccan coast are not vital integral parts of the surrounding state as is Walvis Bay. Should good sense not prevail a Goa–India situation could develop with the important difference that the colonial power is adjacent and militarily powerful.

A similar colonial history accounts for the potential problem of Namibia's offshore islands. Possessed by Britain prior to German

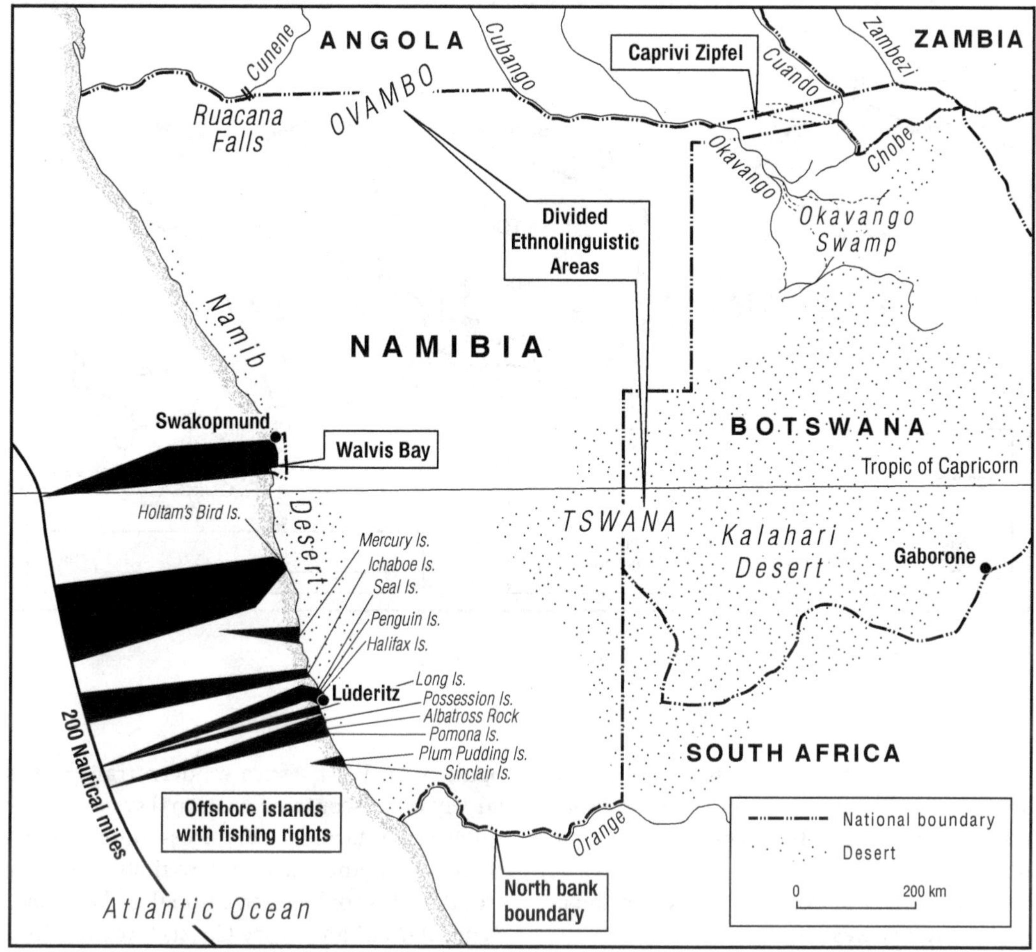

Map 8.5. The potential boundary problems of Namibia.

annexation of South West Africa and passed to the Cape in 1884, they are uninhabited islets, some within yards of a desert coast swept by the cold Benguela Current. The abundance of fish which first brought Europeans to Walvis Bay attracted millions of sea birds to the islands. In their wake came guano diggers, and initial British interest was based on this resource. Today the islands are significant because they give South Africa fishing rights off the Namibian coast. The twelve islands are carefully mapped and underlined in red on modern South African maps with the note: 'Islands with names underlined form part of the territory of the Republic of South Africa'. Elsewhere in Africa Spain holds small islands off the north Moroccan coast but fishing rights there are less important.

Namibia's fifth potential boundary problem is on its southern frontier with South Africa. The boundary is unambiguously the Orange River, but is the north (Namibian) bank, rather than the thalweg or median line. The potential problem relates to water rights which are of particular significance because the waters of the Orange are used extensively by South Africa, not just for irrigation in the Orange River valley, but for diversion through the tunnels of the Orange River Project to the Eastern Cape Province. As matters stand, Na-

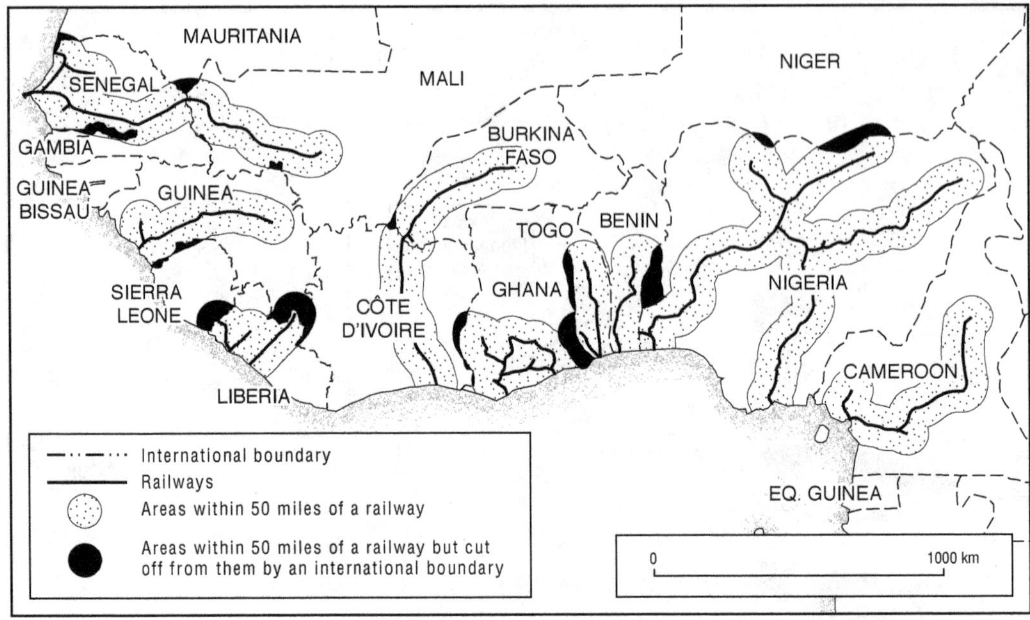

Map 8.6. Railways and international boundaries in West Africa.

mibia has no rights over the waters of the Orange River. The Liberia–Ivory Coast boundary is similar except that the chief issue concerned navigational rights, which made it easy for common sense to prevail even though the actual boundary was not changed.

BOUNDARIES REPEL ECONOMIC DEVELOPMENT

Boundary configurations of course strongly influence the distribution of economic activity. On a national scale, they largely determine what is core and what is periphery. A border region, by definition geographically marginal within a state, is also likely to be economically marginal unless it has some outstanding attribute, such as mineral wealth or a natural harbour, and the marginality of such areas is emphasised by poor infrastructural development. In West Africa modern transport is largely in self-contained national systems. Few railways or tarred roads cross international boundaries, and most end well short of any frontier. The only international railways are Senegal–Mali and Ivory Coast–Burkina Faso. The north-eastern two-thirds of Ghana and 85 per cent of Ghana's frontiers are more than fifty miles (eighty kilometres) from a railway. In Ivory Coast 60 per cent of the state but over 90 per cent of its boundaries are more than fifty miles distant from the single north-south railway which bisects the country. In West Africa as a whole, over 90 per cent of frontiers are more than fifty miles from a railway. On the other hand, because of the elongated shape of some states, several areas within fifty miles of a railway are denied access to it because of an international boundary (see map 8.6).

Another visible indication of the underdevelopment of frontier regions is the high proportion of game reserves to be found in such areas throughout Africa from the Kruger National Park along almost two hundred miles of the South Africa–Mozambique border to the Parcs Nationaux du 'W' which spread out from the tripoint boundary between Benin, Burkina Faso and Niger.

THE SURVIVAL OF AFRICA'S BOUNDARIES

As the European-drawn boundaries of Africa cause so many problems it is perhaps surprising that they have remained sacrosanct in the post-independence period. The answer lies with the OAU. By Paragraph 3 of Article III of the 1963 Charter of the OAU, all member states pledge 'respect for the sovereignty and territorial integrity of each state'. The OAU meeting in Cairo in July 1964 elaborated: 'Considering that border problems constitute a grave and permanent factor of dissension . . . all Member States pledge themselves to respect the borders existing on their achievement of national independence.'

The OAU did set up machinery for the peaceful settlement of boundary disputes, implying that solutions other than the status quo were acceptable. Actual OAU involvement has been rare and mainly to negotiate a cease-fire as in the Algeria–Morocco border war of 1963. The OAU called for a cease-fire in the Burkina Faso–Mali skirmishes of 1985 in the Agacher strip but it was actually negotiated by the regional defence organisation. Also the dispute had been put before the International Court of Justice at The Hague prior to the outbreak of hostilities and so was not being considered within the 'strictly African framework' called for by the OAU. No boundary change has ever emerged through OAU action, and no pair of member states has ever received OAU endorsement of mutually agreed change, although in 1982 the government of Swaziland apparently sought and obtained, from the then President of the OAU, approval for boundary changes inherent in the abortive 'land deal' with South Africa.

The net result is that, apart from one change agreed after independence but before the OAU Charter was signed, the colonial boundaries of Africa have survived intact. Boundaries in Africa are by no means a dead issue but the apparent hope of the OAU remains that if the line is held long enough the tendency to dispute boundaries will fade into universal acceptance of the status quo. That view could yet be right, but on the other hand the ostrich is indigenous to Africa.

The OAU position is ineffective. It has not prevented border disputes or frontier wars and has inhibited, if not obstructed, sensible pragmatic change such as that between Mali and Mauritania which pre-dated the 1964 resolution. The perceived blanket embargo on boundary changes interrupted a process of politically mature rationalisation of frontiers almost before it had begun.

SOLVING BOUNDARY DISPUTES

The practical suggestions that follow may be excessively optimistic, especially with regard to any meaningful role for the OAU. Success in any individual dispute is more likely from intervention by regional organisations but to gain acceptance for the view that positive steps should be taken to resolve the continent-wide boundary problems of Africa the OAU has to be involved.

SOLVING THE PROBLEMS OF DIVIDED CULTURE AREAS

The divided culture areas of Africa present continent-wide problems which rarely flare into armed conflict but none the less cause inconvenience for millions. One difficulty in coming to grips with this matter is to convince central governments of the need to ameliorate social and economic conditions in peripheral regions. Many national politicians would regard attempts to unite culture areas as pandering to tribalism and as being diametrically opposed to their central task of nation building.

Simple new-line solutions are not always possible because peoples are often intermingled and sometimes geographically spread over more than one boundary. Even where new-line solutions are appropriate central governments will be reluctant to surrender sovereignty. They will not want their action to be perceived as weakness. Above all, they will wish to avoid giving away something of value, for example, an undiscovered mineral source. With such considerations in mind a possible solution nevertheless does exist based on a precedent of over eighty years of success.

In 1899 the boundary between Egypt and the Sudan was fixed as the parallel 22° North. Inevitably, it cut across culture areas but unusually this was recognised and acted upon by local administrators. The use of administrative boundaries avoiding transfer of sovereignty would go some way towards easing Africa's problem of divided culture groups.

SOLVING THE PROBLEMS OF FRONTIER REGIONS

The problem of economic marginality of frontier regions requires other solutions: cooperation between states on a bilateral or, where necessary, trilateral basis; the allocation of resources from central governments; cooperation at local level between regional and local government authorities across any given international boundary. Organisations best placed to assist are those created for the purpose of international economic cooperation but on the limited scale of, for example, the Mano River Union. Specially created bi- or tri-lateral international authorities financed in the first instance by the member states might be most effective. The whole question of scale is vital to success which ultimately will depend on international cooperation at the local or regional level, whether it be in river valleys or culture areas. Investment in integrated frontier region schemes would compensate for the underdevelopment caused by the accident of colonial boundary alignment.

Africa's colonial boundaries set the basic political framework of the continent and in so doing create problems simply as boundaries. For 25 years post-independence Africa has chosen not to face these problems positively and has lost opportunities to eliminate potential and real points of conflict. A new approach is long overdue.

9
The OAU Interventions in Chad: Mission Impossible or Mission Evaded?

ROY MAY AND SIMON MASSEY

In 1967, Ali Mazrui declared that '*Pax Africana* asserts that the peace of *Africa* is to be assured by the exertions of *Africans* themselves.' This has remained an unfulfilled ambition. Yet, Mazrui contends that the goal of 'African solutions to African conflicts' is currently being discussed with more conviction than at any time since the independence period. The obstacles such a project would face are formidable. The Organisation of African Unity (OAU), the perceived motor for conflict resolution on the continent, need look no further than its ineffectual interventions in the Chadian civil war between 1980 and 1982 to enumerate the pitfalls.

BACKGROUND TO THE INTERVENTIONS

The narrative of Chad's post-independence history has become monotonous through repetition. A backdrop of unceasing civil strife has been interspersed with cyclical external interventions. By 1979, the main anti-government guerrilla movement, the *Front de Libération Nationale de Tchad* (FROLINAT) had splintered into numerous factions, while the country had been severed into effective fiefdoms under the control of warlords. Two major faction leaders enjoyed the support of external actors. Goukouni Oueddei was backed by Libya, while Hissène Habré's *Forces Armées du Nord* (FAN) was supported by France and the US. French troops occupied key installations in the capital, N'Djaména. For his part Colonel Qadafi was exercising leverage within Goukouni's forces to pursue his claim to a portion of land in northern Chad called the Aouzou Strip. Despite voicing concern over the extension and escalation of the conflict, the OAU remained passive. Inhibited by its own Charter and confined by the decrepitude of its conflict resolution mechanisms, the OAU resorted to offering ancillary support to the diplomatic efforts of the partial but powerful regional hegemon—Nigeria. A conference was held at Kano on 11 March 1979. The result was the formation of the first of a succession of stopgap transitional governments under the title *Gouvernement d'Union National Transitoire* (GUNT), together with an equally precarious ceasefire secured by the deployment of a Nigerian 'neutral force'. Nigeria's short-lived experience in N'Djaména proved to be a portent of the OAU's future peacekeeping efforts in Chad. Lacking any real mandate, other than vague plans to police the ceasefire, the Nigerian troops, both underfunded and undermanned, responded in a petty, heavy-handed fashion to the provocations of the factions in the capital. Nigeria learned during its brief mission that it would take more than troops—or more troops—to unravel Chad's factional quagmire.

In an effort to palliate Nigeria's growing exasperation with factional rivalry within the GUNT, the OAU determined to adopt a more robust approach to the conflict. The June 1979 summit meeting in Monrovia supported Nigeria's continuing efforts, including the initiative to force progress through the imposition of sanctions against the GUNT, while discussing the funding of a peacekeeping force under the auspices of the OAU. This shift in the onus for instigating mediation towards the OAU was a feature of the Lagos II meeting in August. The conference realised comprehensive participation by all major factions and neighbouring states. In an effort to 'Africanise' or 'de-Gallicise' the conflict, the OAU chose to place the abstraction of African unity over the pragmatic reality of Nigeria's unique position as the natural instrument for intervention in the region. Thus, a significant modification to the Kano Accords was the supersession of Nigeria by the OAU as the fulcrum for the independent monitoring of the ceasefire and as the organising body for a neutral force. In contrast to the unilateral intervention by the Nigerians, the new force would comprise troops from states that were non-contiguous with Chad—Guinea, Benin, and Congo. The GUNT was to be reconstituted with Goukouni as President and Habré as Minister of Defence. However, these were to prove essentially fictitious positions in a government which existed in name only. Further, the agreement called for those French troops still in Chad to withdraw. However, events on the ground emphasised the gulf between rhetoric and reality. The goodwill upon which Lagos II depended was absent. The intended demilitarisation of N'Djaména secured only token compliance from the factions. Moreover, despite the commencement of the French withdrawal, the construction of the replacement all-African force was becoming a painfully slow process. Henceforth, the impotence of the OAU would loom larger in the designs of the factions than its exhortations to make peace or its stated support for the transitional government. For the GUNT, as well as for FAN, the OAU would be seen as just another external actor among many others that might be played according to expedience.

Although deriving its mandate from Lagos II, rather than directly from the OAU, the troops that eventually arrived in January 1980 were recognised as the OAU Neutral Force. The hazards were the same as those facing the Nigerians a year before, writ large. Only the Congolese detachment of 550 men deployed. Finance, supposedly provided through a special OAU fund collected from all member states, amounted to less than US$250,000. When Algeria was not recompensed by the OAU for airlifting the Congolese to N'Djaména, they invoiced Brazzaville. Once more, the force on the ground faced immense problems of logistics and manpower. A working command structure was never properly established. One element of the monitoring commission, the GUNT, was irreconcilably split and another, Ethiopian Force Commander Major Gebre-Egziabher Dawit, was absent during most of the operation. Most significantly, the inadequate force was asked to fulfil a mandate that required them to uphold the ceasefire, keep the roads open for civilian traffic, disarm the population, restore order and bring the factions together into an integrated national army. Following the ignominious evacuation of the force on 26 March 1980, Secretary-General Kodjo travelled to N'Djaména to conduct a secret post-mortem. His report stressed the negative impact of the absence of Beninoise and Guinean contingents. However, the exasperated tone of the document only serves to stress the OAU's institutional and logistical inadequacies in the face of rapidly degenerating circumstances. While acknowledging the OAU's culpability in not pre-arranging a working budget for the operation, Kodjo placed most of the blame on the failure of the warring factions within the GUNT to fulfil the conditions of Lagos II. Kodjo's reasoning tended to be circuitous. The Congolese troops were unwilling to leave barracks in order to help with the demilitarisation of N'Djaména without the support of Benin and Guinea's forces. These were disinclined to deploy while the capital remained militarised. N'Djaména remained militarised since Habré's Ministry of Defence refused to convene the requisite committee charged with demilitarisation. For their part, the Congolese felt stung to react to the withering criticism of the force's performance. Habré had accommodated the force in deplorable conditions without running water or sanitation. They suffered casualties and lost a man in crossfire. The Congolese delegate at the UN denounced the 'slanderous campaign' of 'hate-filled and defamatory articles' by the West's 'blinkered press'. In the light of their unrewarding and unappreciated exertions, the decision of Congo (as well as other small country troop-contributors—Benin, Togo and Guinea) to withdraw from future interventions was understandable.

For the rest of 1980 the OAU always seemed to be a step behind events on the ground. Ironically, it was the successful Libyan incursion into Chad in late 1980 in response to a request from Goukouni for support against Habré's FAN, and the joint communiqué declaring a potential 'merger' between Chad and Libya, that galvanised the OAU into firmer action and created the strategic conditions for the IAF to deploy. Still more important, Qadafi's acceptance of Goukouni's demand for Libya's withdrawal in October 1981 left the OAU as the last, best repository of trust among the greatest number of players in the conflict.

ISSUES OF SOVEREIGNTY AND NON-INTERVENTION

The right to national sovereignty and the concomitant principle of non-interference in the internal affairs of another sovereign state were twin issues lodged in the back of the minds of those involved in the Chadian peace process. Yet, these most sacred of OAU tenets were rarely deliberated during the crisis. This studied indifference gives testament not only to an acceptance that the *locus* of Chadian sovereignty was uncertain, but also to a determination on the part of the Secretariat and the membership to avoid the dilemma in this case. Thus, Chad became the arena for OAU innovation. In a reversal of roles, the UN served as a forum during the crisis, while the OAU sought to free itself from its juridical fetters and expand its political capacity as an instrumental player in the conflict.

OAU orthodoxy on the question of non-intervention was forged in the aftermath of the debate that surrounded the organisation's formation. Post-war dominance of anti-imperial thought—'the dual legacy of Wilsonian and Marxist ideas and of the latent force of incipient decolonisation'—saw a melding of the contradictory elements of self-determination with state sovereignty, territorial integrity and non-intervention. African anti-colonial leaders grasped the assumed self-deterministic intent of the UN Charter and its supplements as an ineluctable opportunity to oust their imperial masters, despite the fact that by embracing 'the international rules of the game', Africa's new leaders were accepting potential brakes to future continental security. Political opinion was polarised. Pan-African radicals among the independence generation, notably Kwame Nkrumah in Ghana and Sekou Touré in Guinea, demanded to know whether Africa would acquiesce to the inviolability of the Berlin Conference boundaries or concertina history by circumventing the imposition of the Westphalian paradigm on the continent and accepting the intrinsic limitations to sovereignty of a supra-national authority.

Fear that a redrawing of boundaries along ethnic lines could lead to secessionist and irredentist chaos, together with an impulse to legitimise states that were not coterminous with their many nations proved potent stimuli. The conservatives triumphed. African unity was relegated from a putative, concrete institutional entity to a mere aspiration. Nkrumah was isolated. The grand pan-African project—political union based on defence, Foreign Affairs and Diplomacy . . . a Common Citizenship, an African Currency, an African Monetary Zone, an African Central Bank . . . or *Common Defence System with an African High Command*—was rejected. The exercise in self-emasculation was given standing in international law through Article III of the Charter of the OAU and subsequent resolutions of the organisation's Assembly of Heads of State and Government accepting that 'the borders of African states on independence constituted a *tangible reality*'.

Thus, prior to the onset of the Chadian crisis, with the partial exception of the Western Sahara case, the OAU conformed to the norm of non-intervention. A potential for *any* pan-African response to intra-African crises was derided by conservatives such as Felix Houphouët-Boigny as manifestly chimerical. Among the radicals the new organisation was 'a toothless, clawless lion in a decorated cage'. So, why did events in Chad provoke an effective sea change in OAU methodology and a redefinition of principles? The OAU lacked an institutional and legal structure for an armed intervention. Despite the long-standing presumption 'to try Africa first', the OAU's role in conflict resolution had not extended beyond facilitating mediation through their good offices and *ad hoc* committees. The civil war was a humanitarian disaster. Moreover, there was a clear potential for conflict to spread, either directly, or through contagion, to neighbouring countries or within the region. However, the OAU had assiduously avoided interference in the equally bloody and suffusive civil conflicts in Burundi and Sudan, or the secessionist struggle in Ethiopia. In lieu of positive grounds, the general absence of serious objections by the member states, and the temporary unity created by the Qadafi-factor, might be advanced as motives for the intervention. Certainly, from the OAU Secretariat's standpoint, there was a sense that Chad was placing the organisation's limitations in stark perspective. Secretary-General Kodjo recognised that its credibility was seriously threatened.

THE MANDATE

A successful peacekeeping operation is underpinned by an unambiguous and realisable mandate. Both the document signed by the OAU and the GUNT in Paris on 14 August 1981, and the subsequent review of the mandate in Nairobi two weeks later, failed to address these essential prerequisites. The IAF's commanders were presented with a set of mission aims that would have taxed a more experienced and better equipped force.

With a piece of characteristic circumlocution, the OAU appeared to both support the GUNT and maintain a neutral stance, while equivocating as to whether the IAF would act as a standard Chapter VI peacekeeping force or employ enforcement tactics to 'ensure the defence and security of the country'. Thus, the mandate begged two questions. Would the OAU support the GUNT as the sole responsible authority in Chad? If so, to what extent would the IAF act to uphold that authority?

Throughout the Paris and Nairobi talks, the OAU and French mediators needed a valid government in N'Djaména with which to negotiate the withdrawal of Libyan troops from Chad. Goukouni (and Gaddafi) obliged. In return there was an expectation that OAU recognition of the GUNT would become entrenched and irrevocable.

Goukouni was to be disappointed. As late as December, the upper echelons of the OAU in Addis Ababa were apparently willing to countenance a compromise scheme in which IAF units would substitute for GUNT forces in non-combat roles, thereby freeing government troops for front-line action. Nonetheless, by the New Year it had become clear to Goukouni that the IAF would not use force to protect the GUNT. His dismay was evident when he remarked, 'We do not need troops massing here increasing our difficulties, if they are not going to ensure the defence and security of the country . . . they should fight, otherwise their presence makes no sense'. The OAU's retrospective assessment of the IAF's mission emphasises its political role over any military dimension. The IAF had been deployed as an orthodox peacekeeping force, similar to UN Chapter VI operations in Cyprus and Lebanon. Without a truce to uphold, the IAF perforce adopted the role of *force d'interposition.* The rigidity of such a buffer depends on the availability of manpower and logistics, as well as political will on the part of its sponsors. However, it does not preclude a robust response if any party threatens a mandate to 'maintain peace and security'. Indeed, an intervention force is unlikely to retain respect and legitimacy, unless it shows itself willing to employ the judicious use of force at key moments during the deployment. While Goukouni was naive in expecting the IAF to act as a strident 'peace-enforcement' force, there was some justification in the accusation that the IAF neglected its mandate.

For the GUNT, the meeting of the OAU Standing Committee on Chad in Nairobi on 11 February 1982 shattered any vestigial illusion that the IAF might defend the government. Until that date the most charitable interpretation of the OAU's strategy was impotent procrastination. The final resolution cleared any ambiguity by stating: 'The Inter-African Force is a neutral force whose role is to maintain peace and ensure the formation of an integrated Chadian Army without favouring any political faction whatsoever.' The resolution went on to call for a series of wholly unattainable political objectives—a ceasefire by midnight 28 February, national reconstruction talks in March, the drafting of a new constitution and elections for May. It also set the deadline for the withdrawal of the IAF at 30 June 1982. The Standing Committee's political demands took the operation's abrogation of the sacrosanct principle of non-interference in the internal affairs of a member state a step further. The call for elections was egregiously hypocritical coming from a committee whose members exercised precious little democratic process themselves. It was also specious. Calls for an instant democratic solution to a profoundly undemocratic fratricidal conflict that had endured for 13 years went beyond wishful thinking. The response of the major protagonists was predictable. Goukouni quit Nairobi describing the meeting as an 'absurd scenario' and denouncing the OAU's treachery. For his part, Habré saw the *volte-face* as 'an enormous victory for the Chadian people and the OAU' (for which read 'for FAN'). Regardless of the OAU's protestations, the Nairobi meeting gave the impression that the OAU was shifting support away from the increasingly shrill Goukouni to the confident Habré. With Goukouni's legitimacy compromised, the GUNT collapsed. Following the rout of Goukouni's troops at Massaguet, Habré took N'Djaména in less than three hours on 7 June.

The Standing Committee's claims to have re-emphasised the political dimension of the peace process rewrote the operation's history. There had always been a military aspect to the force's deployment. FAN had only been prevented from taking the capital through the intervention of Libya. In Libya's absence, the deployment of the IAF clearly recognised the need for the balance of military strength within Chad to be redressed if the status quo was to be maintained. Diplomatic initiatives could have been made while Libyan troops maintained stability. Few outside the GUNT expected the IAF to take the battle to FAN. However, the total ineffectualness of the force, far from advancing a political solution, doomed the GUNT to defeat. The equation between 'force' and 'consent' was wrong. The

IAF, with negligible capacity for engagement and a lack of political will, needed a high level of consent from all combatants if a traditional peacekeeping methodology was to prove viable. It was asking for miracles for the actual scenario—low consent and low capacity for force—to prove anything other than unsustainable.

EXTERNAL INFLUENCES

The OAU's lack of salience or administrative wherewithal left it as just another actor in its own operation. The extra-continental protagonists, notably France and the United States, treated the OAU as a necessary evil, rather than as the instigator of the mission. Likewise, regional actors, including members of the IAF, worked to their own agenda. The layers of confusion and intrigue multiplied as the OAU acted as a conduit for self-interested international political realism played out on the Chadian stage.

France

By 1979, French economic interest in Chad was subordinate to French prestige. France perceived Africa as the cornerstone of its claim to be a great power. If France could not preserve leverage in one state, then its credibility in the others would be diminished.

French post-independence policy in Chad had been cautious to the point of vacillation. With few economic interests beyond the southern *Tchad utile,* the minds of the *Quai d'Orsay* and the *cellule africaine* of the Elysée Palace were occupied with stifling Libyan ambitions in the *chasse gardée* that was Francophone Africa. To this end France had not hesitated to use the blunt instrument of armed intervention. However, in 1981, transition from a Gaullist to a socialist government signalled a shift in French African policy. François Mitterrand had campaigned on a manifesto promise to end militarism on the continent. The new government was unwilling to reverse the Lagos II commitment to withdraw and embark on an illegal, uninvited intervention. In the absence of its accustomed military presence, the prospect of an OAU-sponsored intervention, potentially open to manipulation, offered a risk-free opportunity to maintain an interest in events.

The often delicate relationship between Nigeria and France was critical to the impetus to assemble the IAF. The sincerity, or otherwise, of the apparent *rapprochement* between the two rivals for regional supremacy was hidden beneath the usual veils of diplomatic verbal camouflage.

Expansive guarantees to underwrite the IAF operation's costs vanished with Gaddafi's rapid military withdrawal. The bulk of French military assistance was channelled through logistical support to the Senegalese contingent. A commitment made at the Franco-African summit to supply ODA and military supplies to the GUNT was neglected. A consignment of 25 tonnes of seized Kalashnikov rifles and ammunition proved to be a poor substitute for Goukouni's former shield—14,000 Libyan troops. Likewise, the GUNT's requests for an increase in French ODA to rebuild Chadian infrastructure in an effort to shore up the regime were largely rejected. French ODA to Chad as a proportion of overall French ODA declined between 1980 and 1982. In brief, France's rolling, but ultimately pragmatic, policy in Chad was always liable to forsake Goukouni's GUNT as being 'too divided, too weak and too incompetent'.

The United States

The escalation of the civil war, and Libya's involvement, coincided with the accession to the US Presidency of Ronald Reagan. Convinced that Libya was merely a surrogate for Soviet policy, the Reagan administration targeted Gaddafi's regime. When the CIA isolated Gaddafi's overextension in Chad as his weak link, the civil war became a focal point of Reagan's anti-Libyan offensive.

The State Department developed a two-pronged strategy. Officially, the State Department supported the French initiative with warm words that, nonetheless, honoured that policy more in the breach than the observance. Military aid for the Nigerian contingent (NICON) was loaded with conditions, while ODA to Chad amounted to only US$160,000 in 1981. The one element within the IAF that received consistent US support was the Zairean contingent (ZACON). Given the longstanding relationship between Zairean President Mobutu Sesi Seko and the new Director of the CIA, William Casey, there was a widespread assumption that ZACON was acting as a proxy for American interests in the conflict. With their premature deployment and unwillingness to leave N'Djaména, the Zaireans appeared to be ineffective and uncooperative. At a minimum ZACON, as a passive unit undermining the IAF's potential for a robust military presence, seemed to have supplied another facet of an American failsafe strategy. For Goukouni the plan was yet more sinister and extensive. He accused the United States of coordinating both the Zaireans and, more significantly, the Nigerians in a plan to 'gain the confidence of the GUNT and then to betray it'. He pointed to Nigerian and Zairean insistence, in the wake of Nairobi III in February, that GUNT troops withdraw from forward positions that were then yielded, without a fight, to advancing FAN troops.

There exists stronger evidence for the second strand of US Chadian policy. CIA files show that President Numeiri of Sudan had urged the CIA to support Habré. In response, covert supplies were sent to FAN camps in Sudan with Secretary of State Alexander Haig's stated purpose being to 'bloody Gaddafi's nose' and 'increase the flow of pine boxes back to Libya'. With an eye on possible human rights questions in Congressional oversight committees, the Directorate of Operations expressed qualms at the supply of lethal aid to FAN. America expended about US$10m on Habré. This relatively small amount of aid, nonetheless, was sufficient to sustain the FAN at a time of crisis. US$10m financed the FAN's push to N'Djaména and, in the process, undermined 'the one test that the French, Libyans, the OAU and Goukouni's government had agreed upon, the establishment of an OAU peacekeeping force'.

Regional Actors

Nigeria's motives for adopting a central role in the Chadian crisis were geopolitical and strategic, rather than economic. A need to counter rivals to Nigerian hegemony in the region, a vested interest in ensuring a stable government in Chad, together with a pan-African desire to aid a troubled sister state, dictated policy.

A natural rivalry existed between Nigeria and regional competitors, Libya and France. The former had been implicated in fostering internal unrest in Borno and Kano states. Moreover, Nigeria's regional hegemony was clearly challenged by Tripoli's expansionist policies in Chad. The prospect of an indefinite Libyan presence in Chad, still less the proposed 'merger' of the two countries, was unacceptable to Lagos. Likewise, as an Anglophone state surrounded by Francophone states, Nigeria had always felt compelled to fight its corner against persistent French influence. Clearly, if IAF troops, with Nigeria in the vanguard, could succeed in bringing stability to Chad it would enhance Nigerian prestige in the region.

As ever, the diplomacy was not cut and dried. Strong anti-colonial elements within Nigeria felt a degree of sympathy with Gaddafi's stance against 'Western imperialism'. At the same time there existed a constituency that favoured coordination with France to counter Gaddafi. The lack of a 'concrete national objective' left Nigerian foreign policy open to 'a certain vagueness and whimsicality'. While Nigerian involvement lent the IAF a credibility that the 1980 intervention lacked,

Presidents Olesegun and Shagari needed a quick and clear solution for which Lagos could take credit. Thus, Nigeria was never wedded to the GUNT or to any of the OAU's stated goals for the mission. As soon as the IAF's intrinsic institutional shortcomings became apparent, Nigeria began the process of pulling out.

A major complication for the OAU was the number of states that saw the Chadian conflict as an opportunity to exercise a measure of regional policy. For many neighbouring states, with comparably precarious legitimacy, the fear of the exportation of violence and instability by contagion was ever-present. Given the extent to which its material resources were stretched, the OAU was highly reliant on unity of political purpose from its members if the IAF was to succeed. However, two strategically vital states—Sudan and Egypt—far from supporting the operation, actively undermined it. The 'Sadat trail' that supplied FAN bases across the Sudanese border was an open secret. The willingness of Egypt and Sudan to arm and accommodate FAN subverted the OAU's salience as a body capable of preserving a true unity of purpose among its own members in the midst of a peacekeeping intervention undertaken under its auspices.

FINANCE

Chronic underfunding became an increasingly important determinant during the operation. The OAU, without any single state, or group of states, to underwrite peacekeeping initiatives, was the most populous, yet poorest, regional organisation in the world. In the fiscal year 1980–81 only US$3m out of US$17m was collected. In Chad, the simple arithmetic was devastating. The OAU costed the operation at US$162,900,000 per annum. In the first two months following the deployment of the Zairean battalion, they collected US$560,000 from member states.

Primarily, OAU penury threatened its ability to establish unconditional neutrality in a complex conflict like Chad. Unable to fund the IAF directly from Addis Ababa, the OAU were forced to allow the troop-supplying states to seek bilateral aid. This arrangement proved equally inadequate, while having the added disadvantage of further *extra*-African influence being brought to bear. Following a dispute between Lagos and Washington over the payment of wages for the Nigerian contingent, only US$6.6m of the US$12m passed by Congress for the IAF was sent. In contrast, the irresolute Zairean battalion was frequently resupplied by US planes. France concentrated its aid on Senegal. As well as funding transport and equipment, the French bolstered their own forces in the region to guarantee a rapid response in the event of a re-intervention by Libya. In fact, French and American interest in the project waned considerably once it became clear that Gaddafi would not defend the GUNT.

The OAU had predicted a need for UN funding for any peacekeeping intervention at the Freetown summit in 1980. However, several factors militated against such a rescue plan. UN Secretary-General Kurt Waldheim appeared unwilling to approve an unprecedented subvention for an operation not under UN control. Moreover, there was no support for funding from Western members of the Security Council. As ever, the OAU conspired to reach the worst solution. A voluntary fund organised by the UN was doomed to failure, while leaving the justifiable image of the OAU as impotent and dependent.

DEPLOYMENT AND 'COMMAND AND CONTROL'

Despite the protracted negotiating period between the withdrawal of the Congolese contingent in March 1980 and the arrival of Zairean troops in November 1981, the OAU failed to develop a workable system of command and control. The first sign that command of the IAF would lack cohesion was the premature deployment of the Zairean contingent. Detailed analysis of the mandate and the military response in terms of operational tactics and rules of engagement during the initial deployment remained vague. Additionally, Ejiga's original plan to assemble the full force at the Nigerian base at Maiduguri and enter Chad as a body was stymied from the outset. Tactical confusion was further aggravated by the non-arrival at the planning meeting in Kinshasa on 27 November of representatives from Togo, Benin and Guinea, imposing an immediate change in the proposed pattern of deployment. The backbone of the force, NICON, did not arrive until December. Commander Ejiga set up his headquarters in N'Djaména on 2 December. The force had, through financial necessity, been reduced from a proposed 11,500 troops to one of 3,275. The result was a logistical impasse. The IAF was expected to cover an area of 500,000 square miles or 100,000 square miles per battalion. The country had been split into seven zones. The GUNT reserved control of the front line in the east covering Abéché and Bilitine and the Kanem region in the west. The other zones were to be occupied by the five battalions of the IAF by 16 December. Only NICON 1 deployed on time. ZACON 2 did not materialise at all. Mobutu's paratroops in ZACON 1 refused their arranged deployment to BET, staying in N'Djaména until reluctantly moving to share Ati in central Chad with NICON 2. The Senegalese contingent were deployed in the south, although they never occupied the area around Am Timmam in Salamat province. This left some of the south, much of the east and all of the north beyond any intervention from the IAF.

Such large troop–territory ratios severely stretched supply lines and tested command and control capabilities. The harsh terrain, poor transport system, basic communication network and high temperatures would have strained a better-equipped force. The IAF entered Chad without any central supplies. Each contingent was dependent upon their own government and any bilateral support they could negotiate. Distances and terrain dictated a need for extensive air mobility. Each contingent relied on the relative capacities of their home air force, and such bilateral support as they could muster, to supply air transport. The force lacked sophisticated independent communications. The radios and transmitters they possessed frequently broke down in the heat and dust. Fuel was scarce owing to the high consumption rate and evaporation. As a serving officer in the force noted the, 'OAU peacekeeping effort in Chad suffered all the disadvantages of an ill-planned, ill-equipped and under-funded venture while enjoying none of the known advantages of a multi-national force of the United Nations.'

The IAF suffered from a severe credibility deficit. Without reinforcements and reorganisation there was no possibility of the force fulfilling the deterrent role vacated by the Libyans. Clearly the IAF would have been hard pushed to engage any of the battle-hardened factions. According to Ejiga's Operational Order No. 1, the principal directive of the mandate, 'to maintain peace and security', would be achieved using basic peacekeeping practice—patrols, road blocks, checkpoints, cordons and searches. Even these limited ambitions would be circumscribed by a tenuous chain of command and control. The structures in place were unfit to cope, either on a command or liaison basis, with the number of actors in theatre. For an operation, one of whose aims was to demonstrate unanimity of purpose on the part of the pan-African organisation, there was a propensity for each link to act as an independent entity. However, in so far as the various contingents and observer groups had cause to interact, there appears to have been a harmonious working relationship. The real problem lay with the inability of the Force Commander to maintain a common purpose and strategy against the interference of the contingents' home governments. The operation belonged to the OAU in name only; in reality it was a Nigerian, Zairean and Senegalese operation. Kupolati has castigated the system whereby direct communication between Secretary-General Kodjo and Force Commander Ejiga was replaced by an unorthodox connection between Force Headquarters and the current OAU Chairman, Daniel arap Moi, in Nairobi.

Despite an escalation in *intra*-state conflict in Africa since the IAF's withdrawal, a chastened OAU has not been tempted to employ intervention as a modality for the resolution of civil conflict. If the intervention had a virtue, it was that since there were shortcomings in every facet of the operation, the experience has been able to fully inform the debate over the future of African peacekeeping.

Although Goukouni's signature on the Paris Memorandum that set up the IAF superficially satisfied the OAU Charter's non-intervention principle, the stipulation persisted as a constraint on action throughout the mission. In an attempt to settle the contradiction between state sovereignty and non-intervention on one hand and humanitarianism and regional security on the other, the OAU adopted the Mechanism for Conflict Prevention, Management and Resolution in 1993. Yet, the Mechanism has been conspicuously inadequate in the recent series of catastrophes in the Great Lakes region of Central Africa. Plans for an all-African peacekeeping force were made outside the aegis of the OAU and were stymied from the onset by the same problems that befell the IAF—a lack of resources and potential troop-contributors following divergent agendas. In a further evocation of the Chadian operation, the Canadian-led multinational force proposed by the UN in November 1996 became the focus of power games between *extra*-African powers. The belief that the Mechanism could finally open an 'opportunity for the desensitisation of governments long obsessed with sovereignty and non interference' appears to be a victory of hope over experience.

Have other obstacles that beset the IAF been addressed with greater success? Finance became a critical stumbling block in Chad. The OAU's budget deficit is even more dire now than it was then. Few states meet their existing commitments, still less pay contributions to the Mechanism's Peace Fund. The OAU's persistent fiscal shortfall has thrown the potential for African conflict resolution capacity building into the mire of *extra*-continental financial and logistical assistance. Dependency on Western financial aid and logistical support seems as inevitable and as fraught with danger as it was in Chad. Mindful to wrap their proposals in suitable politically correct, anti-neo-imperialist rhetoric, both the US and France have come to the same solution—peacekeeping based upon all-African forces supplied and maintained by the West. The shades of Chad are apparent. As with Chad, the Western powers' input is firmly based on considerations of national interest. The specifics of the proposed force have barely been considered. Issues which were important in Chad such as the training of troops, supply of equipment and weapons and the formation of effective command and control, have been subsumed by general politicking. As with the IAF, *intra*-African tensions have influenced the debate. Lagos has stated that any standing force which sought to ignore Nigeria was doomed to failure.

The OAU's experience in Chad proved an inauspicious debut into the complex process of peacekeeping intervention. The IAF's failure led to a long period of self-contemplation which has obscured positive aspects of Africa's potential for conflict resolution. Africans possess good skills for reconciliation. Mazrui has alluded to a 'limited memory of animosity' as 'an important cultural resource, a valuable traditional *more*, for future conflict resolution'. The OAU must ameliorate its salience as the continent's conflict resolution body of first resort before it attempts intervention. Future IAFs must be wholly credible to all involved in the conflict if they are to succeed. A reoccurrence of the Chad intervention could demolish the possibility of a valid *Pax Africana.*

Part Four

Africa and the Great Powers

INTRODUCTION

Its African empire was always an important part of France's conception of itself as a great power, and even after independence, France's relations with Africa remained a central concern to the French political class. Chafer provides a rounded picture of that relationship and its importance both for France and for Africa's ruling elites. Africa's relationships with the then-superpowers were much more unstable and episodic, partly because neither the United States nor the Soviet Union, initially at least, had much knowledge or experience of sub-Saharan Africa. It is important not to lose sight of the more unsavory aspects of these relationships. There is little that is more unsavory in Africa than the Congo, long the site of battles between many different political forces, all of which have brought much suffering to the people living there. Stockwell gives an on-the-spot insider account that is still valuable, while Gleijeses, with impeccable scholarship, analyzes the broader context of U.S. policy in the Congo. There was an even wider context—namely the global confrontation between the United States and the Soviet Union—that for years was interpreted in a narrowly "realist" way. Westad's book *The Global Cold War* raised the intellectual level of the literature considerably, and the extract here gives a nuanced account of U.S. and Soviet involvement in the Horn of Africa.

10
French African Policy in Historical Perspective

TONY CHAFER

Two major themes underpin much of the literature published in recent years on French African policy. The first of these is the 'successful management' by France of the decolonisation process in French sub-Saharan Africa, both before and immediately after political independence, which laid the basis for the maintenance of close Franco-African relations in the post-colonial period. The prevailing view has been that sub-Saharan Africa was France's 'successful decolonisation': there was no war of decolonisation, the transition from colonial rule was not marked by large-scale violence or bloodshed, it was a largely smooth process, and the transfer of power was managed in such a way as to enable France to maintain its presence and a sphere of influence in Africa after political independence. According to this view, such an outcome was made possible by the actions of well-intentioned politicians and officials within France's governing elites and the enlightened leadership of a small number of African politicians who were deeply loyal to France. Their French education and political apprenticeship as *députés* (Members of Parliament) in the French National Assembly had prepared them admirably for their role as leaders of the new African nations that emerged from the federations of French West and French Equatorial Africa. This basic view has been carefully fostered by the French political establishment but finds expression in a variety of different forms. The Gaullist variant attaches central importance to the role played by De Gaulle at the Brazzaville Conference and in the immediate aftermath of the Second World War, downplays the role of Fourth Republic political parties and politicians, whose unstable parliamentary coalitions and governmental instability are held responsible for a series of disasters in French colonial policy: it highlights the speed with which De Gaulle moved to reform France's imperial relationship with Africa following his return to power in 1958. The view that sub-Saharan Africa was France's 'successful decolonisation' in which the enlightened actions of a small number of French politicians and officials played a determining role, is not, however, exclusively Gaullist and has been widely orchestrated by French political leaders from across the political spectrum.

The second theme which has emerged in recent commentaries on French African policy is that of French 'disengagement' and, linked to this, the 'normalisation' of Franco-African relations. The signs of French disengagement are not difficult to find: for example, the reduction in the number of French *coopérants* (e.g. technical advisors, teachers, administrators, doctors) working in Africa since the 1980s, notably but not only in the education field, the devaluation of the CFA franc (common currency used in Francophone Africa linked to the French franc) in 1994, the reductions in French military forces stationed in Africa in the 1990s, and the increased unwillingness to intervene militarily in Africa since the controversy over France's role in the Rwandan genocide of 1994. Whether these are actually signs of disengagement, or whether they represent, rather, an effort to reconfigure France's relationship with Africa, is a theme that we return to below. At the same time, some of the institutions and structures of French African policy have changed or been reformed. For instance, the Franco-African summits, instigated in 1973 as a gathering of French political leaders and the leaders of France's ex-colonies in Africa, have gradually been extended to include an increasing number of representatives of non-Francophone countries. France's commercial relations with Africa, traditionally centred on its former colonies, have changed in focus, so that Nigeria and South Africa are now France's major trading partners on the continent. And the Ministry for Co-operation, which has in effect traditionally been the Ministry for Francophone Africa, has been reformed and subsumed into the Ministry for Foreign Affairs. All these have been taken as signs that France has decided to 'normalise' its relations with sub-Saharan Africa by placing them on a footing more in keeping with the kind of relations that normally hold between sovereign, independent states.

In taking a longer, historical view of French African relations, the purpose of this article is not to deny that decolonisation in Africa was, from the French perspective, successful. On the contrary, French policy before and after political independence laid the basis for the maintenance of the French presence in sub-Saharan Africa and has, from a Realist perspective in international relations, been very successful in protecting and promoting French interests in the region. The intention here is, firstly, to suggest that this success has not been the product of some 'grand plan'. Rather, French policy-making towards sub-Saharan Africa in the modern period has, for the most part, been reactive and incremental. Yet, despite this lack of any over-arching strategy, France has been remarkably successful in projecting its power and defending its key strategic interests, and has actually done rather well at shoring up its position as it has gone along. Secondly, it will be suggested that analyses of Franco-African relations in terms of French 'disengagement' and 'normalisation' usually fail to take account of two key factors. On the one hand, from a French perspective, images, symbols and popular memory have historically played an important role in maintaining support for the French presence in Africa, both during and after the colonial period. While the emotional force and significance of these will tend to decline over time with the passing of generations, they remain nonetheless a key element in France's perception of itself as a world power. As a former major imperial power, the *besoin de rayonnement* (literally, need to shine) is an integral element of French national identity, and Africa has historically been a key arena for the projection of French power overseas. Indeed, since the 1950s, it has been *the* arena for the projection of such power. On the other hand, from an African perspective, those advocating the 'normalisation' thesis of Franco-African relations tend to take insufficient account of the dependent nature of these relations. In particular, Francophone Africa's governing elites are, with few exceptions, classic examples of post-colonial elites; they *need* France and have a great deal invested, politically, economically and often also emotionally, in this relationship. To be sure, their position has been complicated by the process of democratisation and the move towards multi-partyism since 1990, and there have been some changes in personnel at the highest echelons of the state. Nonetheless, these post-colonial elites have generally been fairly successful at maintaining their position. Moreover, it is difficult to see how any alternative government emerging from the democratisation process in most Francophone African countries could afford an abrupt break with France. The accession to power in 2000 of two of Francophone Africa's long-standing opposition leaders, Abdoulaye Wade in Senegal and Laurent Gbagbo in Côte d'Ivoire, both of whom immediately looked to France for endorsement, bears witness to this.

THE CONTEXT OF FRANCO-AFRICAN RELATIONS

The projection of French power beyond the metropole, through empire or, post-1962, neo-empire, has been a key element of French national identity in the twentieth century. After 1919 the possession of empire became a benchmark of the French claim to great power status. Since then the need to define, and redefine, the imperial relationship has been a constant preoccupation of French foreign policy, and indeed has emerged as one of the major themes in twentieth century French history. With the loss of empire just 40 years on, following two hugely destructive wars of decolonisation in Indochina and Algeria, the question of how to maintain France's world-power status became all the more acute and urgent. These wars put paid to any hope of a peaceful, negotiated redefinition of the imperial relationship. In these regions of the world, decolonisation, because of the form it had taken, represented a real watershed and marked the end of an era. In French Africa, in contrast, the decolonisation process was very different. Here, the transition to political independence was largely peaceful. Decolonisation did not mark an end, but rather a restructuring of the imperial relationship. French attention therefore naturally turned to sub-Saharan Africa as the chosen arena for the projection of French power.

This was done at a number of different levels. Politically, it was achieved through the cultivation of regional friends. Since the post-colonial leaders of the newly independent states of Francophone Africa were friends of France and many had been *députés* (members of parliament) in the National Assembly in Paris under the Fourth Republic, and since in most cases their countries were economically and politically weak, they for the most part favoured the maintenance of close links with France. Indeed, the initiative for the institution of the annual Franco-African summits came from an African political leader, the then President of Niger, Hamani Diori, in 1973. Networks of personal relationships, the most notorious of which were the *réseaux Foccart*, and regular French presidential visits to Africa further helped to maintain such links. The sending of large numbers of *coopérants*, notably as teachers, university lecturers and educational advisers, to former French Africa served to maintain, and indeed reinforce, the French cultural presence. Sub-Saharan Africa has also been the chosen zone for the projection of French military power beyond the metropole. Examples of this are the signature of a series of defence and military assistance accords with its former colonies, the stationing of French troops in several of these countries, and a series of military interventions, which took place at an average rate of one a year in the first 35 years after independence. At an economic level, the deployment of French public development aid, the great majority of which has gone to France's former African colonies, has served to underpin French strategic interests in the region. Finally, somewhat less tangibly but no less importantly, at an ideological level France has cultivated a sense of association and common heritage between France and Africa which has served to cement the links between them. Both during and after the colonial period, the projection of the 'universal' French republican values of liberty, equality and fraternity offered generations of French-educated Africans the hope of progress and the prospect of a partnership with France to bring it about. At the same time, the idea that, thanks to their shared history and experience, France has a special understanding of Africa and Africans, has had a powerful influence in shaping the attitudes and mind-set of governing elites in both France and Africa.

CONTINUITY AND CHANGE

One of the recurring themes in twentieth century French history is the need to rework the imperial relationship in the light of changing circumstances. In order to highlight the ongoing process of reconfiguration of this relationship, together with its underlying continuities, three key moments in this relationship will be examined here: the Popular Front government from 1936 to 1937, the Loi-cadre (Reform Act) of 1956 to 1957, and the Rwanda debacle of 1994. Each of these were significant moments in the evolving Franco-African relationship, demonstrating the way in which, under pressure from external circumstances, France has been forced to rethink its African links.

The Popular Front marked the first official recognition by France that old-style imperialism, based on exploitation, was unsustainable in the long term, and that there was a need for a new type of relationship. This notion of imperial renewal was encapsulated in the discourse of 'la colonisation altruiste' ('altruistic colonisation') of France's first socialist minister for the colonies, Marius Moutet. It proclaimed the need for a new form of 'disinterested' colonialism, based on the best values of republican France, whereby France and Africa would work together for the development of Africa, for the mutual benefit of both partners. The project to build a 'modern' Africa within the colonial system was expressed in the new discourse of modernisation and progress.

As a project, it confronted a number of major difficulties. The first of these was economic. Given the development gap between France and Africa, the plan was likely to be hugely expensive and it was not at all clear from where such resources might come, given the lack of a political will to invest public funds in overseas development projects and the traditional lack of enthusiasm of French private capital for investment in sub-Saharan Africa. Moreover, it was not at all clear what would be the basis for such a development plan, given the resistance at government level and in French business and trade union circles to industrial development in the empire, which would be likely to result in the emergence of colonial industries competing directly with metropolitan industry and the consequent loss of metropolitan jobs. The idea of a peasant-based development model, centred on the modernisation of the rural sector, was put forward, notably by Marius Moutet, but without being fully thought through, notably in terms of its implications for forced labour, which the Popular Front opposed in principle but without which its economic development programme risked being undermined, at least in the short to medium term.

The second major obstacle confronting the Popular Front's reform programme was political. French attitudes to empire in the inter-war period were fundamentally conditioned by the experience of the First World War, when 180,000 African soldiers had fought for France. As a result, popular attachment to empire had increased greatly, so that the 1930s may be seen as the high point of empire in France: the eight million visitors to the 1931 Paris Colonial Exhibition are one sign of this. Against this background, opponents of reform were able to accuse those who advocated imperial reform of threatening France's national interest and image in the world by putting the imperial link in jeopardy. Within the colonies, there was also resistance to reform from *colons* and from colonial officials, who feared the effect of reform on their authority. Such opposition was especially vocal from French settlers in Algeria.

In the end, the Popular Front, which was preoccupied by the implementation of its ambitious domestic reform programme, did not have either the political will or the time to see through its colonial reform project. In the empire, expectations were raised, only to be dashed by the fall of the Popular Front government in 1938 and then the outbreak of war a year later. The imperial reform project was, for the time being, shelved. Only after the Second World War, from which France emerged seriously weakened, was the project for imperial reform resurrected and, under pressure both internationally, notably from the United States, and from anti-colonial movements within the empire, a reform programme began to be implemented.

Despite its failure to carry out its reform plans, the Popular Front was none the less of major significance for two reasons. Firstly, it revealed the depth of the implication of the mainstream left in France's colonial project. The point about the Popular Front's reform plan was that it was a programme to build a 'modern' Africa *within* the colonial system and as such was intended to perpetuate French colonial rule in Africa. It represented a recognition that old-style imperialism was dead and that a different approach was necessary if French authority was to be maintained. There was absolutely no question of seeking to prepare the empire for self-government. This was to have profound implications, since it meant that, among France's governing elites of both right and left, there was support for, or in the case of the communists, acquiescence in, France's imperial project. After the War, these elites would do everything in their power to resist any move towards decolonisation, in the sense of political independence, for the colonies. Secondly, the Popular Front's reform project revealed clearly the contradictions inherent within the colonial project itself. As France's first socialist-led government, the Popular Front was committed, at least in principle, to reforming the imperial link. As a result, it was confronted, more starkly than previous administrations, with key questions about the nature of colonial rule itself. Could colonial rule, predicated as it necessarily is on authoritarianism and repression, ever be reconciled with the French republican values of liberty, equality and fraternity? Could it, in practice, ever be 'altruistic', progressive and modernising? The Popular Front did not remain in power long enough for it to be obliged to follow through and confront the implications of these questions. This was not to happen until the mid-1950s.

This brings us to our second major watershed in Franco-African relations: the Loi-cadre of 1956–57. By this time, the project to build a 'modern' Africa within the colonial system had begun to bear fruit. The First Loi Lamine Guèye had abolished the status of subject in 1946 and made all those living under French colonialism citizens of the French Union, as the empire was now to be called; four years later, the Second Loi Lamine Guèye had established the principle of 'equal pay for equal work' between Africans and Europeans. The Fides (investment funds for economic and social development of overseas territories), which had been proposed at Brazzaville and was set up in 1946, had begun to channel significant metropolitan funding to overseas development projects. And major investment had taken place in education and health, although it remained far from sufficient to satisfy African demands. At the same time, pressure from African political and social movements had led to increased wages and to the extension of various metropolitan economic and social benefits, such as family allowances and a metropolitan-style labour code, to certain categories of Africans, notably those employed by the colonial administration or working for European firms.

By the mid-1950s and against the background of colonial war, the cost to France of this project in both economic and political terms was beginning to frighten some of France's governing elites. By 1956, France had lost Indochina, it was implicated in an increasingly bloody war in Algeria, and it was under growing pressure from the nationalist movement in sub-Saharan Africa, where the policy of assimilation was proving financially unsustainable. Seeking to avoid opening a 'second front' in sub-Saharan Africa which it would not be in a position to face, the government decided to make a number of concessions to African demands, and it was only the timely introduction of the Loi-cadre, via a procedure that was strictly unconstitutional, that enabled France to regain control of the colonial agenda in Francophone Africa at the eleventh hour. By devolving certain powers to elected assemblies at territorial level which were dominated by African political leaders loyal to France, while at the same time maintaining French control over certain key areas of policy, the Loi-cadre finally succeeded in breaking the colonial logjam and opened the way to the maintenance of a French presence in sub-Saharan Africa after independence.

There were two strands to the Loi-cadre. On the one hand, it devolved to African elected assemblies power over expensive areas of policy, such as the funding of the civil service, which included the politically 'difficult' area of civil servants' pay, education, health and economic development, while on the other, it repatriated to Paris from the governments-general of French West Africa and French Equatorial Africa, which were situated respectively in Dakar and Brazzaville, responsibility for certain key, strategic areas of policy such as foreign affairs, defence, the currency, higher education, international communications and the media. In this way, the Loi-cadre enabled France to pursue its own national interest by retaining certain highly strategic powers, while at the same time giving an element of reality to the language of partnership between France and the overseas territories, on which the French Union was theoretically based but which had actually accorded only very restricted powers to the local elected assemblies. Moreover, it was this new relationship, for which the Loi-cadre laid the foundation, which enabled France to detach its 'civilising mission' from its 'colonial vocation' and thus facilitated the maintenance of the French presence in Africa after 1960. Freed from its colonial 'baggage', the civilising mission was able to find new expression, and gain increased acceptance, in the shared language of cooperation and partnership for the promotion of African development, even if the partnership remained an unequal one.

The Loi-cadre represented a belated and reluctant recognition by the French government of the increasing lack of acceptance of empire. Internationally, the tide of anti-colonial opinion was growing within the United Nations, especially following the 1955 Bandung conference. Within France, the government's colonial policy was increasingly under attack from a movement of anti-colonial, third-worldist opinion, which brought together intellectuals, students, elements of the extra-parliamentary left, and liberal Catholics in a growing movement of opposition to colonialism. Most importantly, nationalist movements were becoming increasingly intolerant of the colonial straitjacket. In Africa, political leaders, under pressure from an increasingly radical and effective nationalist movement, were demanding a greater say over their own affairs. Despite its rhetoric of assimilation, the French Union remained in practice a far cry from the equal partnership with Europeans for which many Africans had hoped at the end of the war. Political power still lay with colonial officials, from the Governor-General at the top down to the *commandant de cercle,* colonial officer at local level, and although Africans were consulted and the locally elected assemblies put in place after the war had a theoretical power of veto over the annual budget prepared by the government, they had no power to amend the budget and their decision-making powers remained severely circumscribed.

However, even at this late stage, there was no question of preparing the African colonies for self-government. Rather, it was a question of modernising the imperial link so as to make it more sustainable for France and more acceptable to Africans. The very fact that the procedure to get the Loi-cadre adopted was strictly unconstitutional is indicative of the difficulties facing any government in getting colonial reform measures accepted by the National Assembly. Since the provisions governing the French Union were established by the 1946 constitution, any major reform of the imperial link required that the constitution be amended. Such proposals immediately met with charges from opponents of reform that France was seeking to abandon its empire. In getting the Loi-cadre adopted, the government therefore had to convince the Assembly that it was not seeking to prepare for withdrawal from Africa, but rather that it was pursuing France's national interest by seeking to redefine the colonial relationship so as to allow France better to remain.

This was in fact the main significance of the Loi-cadre, in that it set the shape for Franco-African relations in the post-colonial period by ensuring that French decolonisation in sub-Saharan Africa did not mean, as it had in Indochina and Algeria, French departure. It laid the ground for the largely smooth transition from colonialism to post-colonialism. Symbolically, the Ministry for Overseas France (the former Ministry for the Colonies) was renamed the Ministry for Co-operation, and an array of bilateral accords between France and its former African colonies, together with the personal relations forged between French governing elites and African political leaders under the Fourth Republic, laid the foundations for the maintenance of a strong French presence in Africa after independence. Thus, although it was largely reacting to events outside its control, France was successful in pursuing its national interest, but in an incremental way and without any grand design.

The cost-effectiveness and desirability of such a policy was regularly challenged in official reports, but no significant changes were introduced during the Cold War period. The Cold War had opened a 'space' on the international stage in which France was able to present itself as the guarantor of Western interests in Africa, preserving it for the West and keeping it out of Soviet hands. However, France's motives in pursuing this policy were in practice fundamentally different from those of the United States: whereas US policy was driven by primarily Cold War concerns, France was motivated by the *besoin de rayonnement* and, linked to this, the strategic need to maintain a privileged sphere of influence in sub-Saharan Africa. The space for France to pursue this policy disappeared with the end of the Cold War, which leads us to the third watershed in Franco-African relations in the modern period.

France still needed Africa just as much for the projection of French power and prestige, for French *rayonnement* on the global stage, but the political opportunity to do this, to the extent that it meant justifying support for often unsavoury regimes in Africa with poor human rights records and even poorer records in the fields of economic and social development, was now greatly reduced. Under the pressure of circumstances, France was therefore obliged to undertake a further reconfiguration of the Franco-African relationship.

A series of measures was introduced to this effect. In the economic sphere, the devaluation of the CFA franc by 50 per cent in 1994 and the introduction of economic conditionality, the so-called 'Balladur doctrine', which made the granting of French public development aid conditional upon the prior signature of an accord with the International Monetary Fund (IMF) and World Bank, aimed at reducing the cost to France of its African policy and thus making it more financially sustainable. Mitterrand's announcement to African leaders at the 1990 La Baule Franco-African summit that France intended in future to reward those regimes which undertook political reform signalled a significant break with past French practice. Political conditionality in this form had traditionally never been part of French African policy. Also, a number of initiatives were undertaken with a view to burden-sharing. This was done at several levels. Within the European Union, France emerged as the most enthusiastic advocate of renewal of the Lomé Convention and the largest contributor of funds. It also sought, as already indicated, to co-ordinate its public development aid policy with the IMF and World Bank, which channel the majority of aid flows to Africa. At the same time, France sought to play a key role by maintaining a high profile within each of these different bodies.

These initiatives were interpreted by some commentators at the time as indicating a growing lack of enthusiasm for Africa among France's governing elites. 'Afro-pessimism' became fashionable and French African policy was subjected to unprecedented criticism. It was criticised on political and moral grounds as neo-colonial and for its failure, after over 30 years and despite the injection of billions of francs, to achieve its key objective of African development. It was also attacked on pragmatic grounds as a waste of money and for its failure to serve France's real national interests. Critics from this perspective pointed to the fact that Africa represented a declining proportion of French trade, and that other regions of the world were increasingly important markets for French goods and services. They questioned the wisdom of pursuing a policy which was increasingly coming under attack both from within Africa and internationally. Their message was essentially that, if aid policy was genuinely to serve French national interests, it should be refocused towards Eastern Europe and South-East Asia, where French economic interests were greater than in Africa.

In the end, however, talk of French withdrawal and the 'normalisation' of Franco-African relations turned out at this stage to be somewhat premature, and several of the changes outlined above proved to be more rhetorical than real. The devaluation of the CFA franc by 50 per cent was real enough. However, this need not be interpreted as indicating a lack of commitment to the franc zone, or even presaging an eventual French withdrawal of support for the zone. On the contrary, it can be explained as a long-overdue attempt to reduce the cost of its African commitments so as to make it more possible for France to remain in Africa. As for political conditionality, the discourse of change was belied by a political practice that appeared to continue the old ways. France's African networks continued to operate and even proliferated. The original Gaullist network, headed by Jacques Foccart until his death and subsequently taken over by Fernand Wibaux, continued to operate, alongside parallel networks operated by Mitterrand's son, Jean-Christophe, and a rival Gaullist network under Charles Pasqua. At the same time, Jacques Chirac has, since his election as president, retained Michel Dupuch, who was for many years France's ambassador in Côte d'Ivoire, as his personal adviser on African affairs, and the pattern of presidential visits to Africa has continued to favour France's traditional allies in the region. Chirac's first official overseas visit after his election as president in 1995 was to Francophone Africa, and his official visit to Africa in 1999 took in Cameroon and Togo, the political leaders of which are widely regarded as two of the leading 'dinosaurs' of Franco-African relations, whose poor records on human rights, corruption and poverty reduction in their countries are well documented. Finally, the suggestion that France is undertaking a process of 'normalisation' of its African relations, for example by extending its African links beyond the traditional *pré carré* (backyard) to encompass both Anglophone and Lusophone Africa and by distributing its aid more widely, is belied by the reality that two-thirds of French bilateral public development aid continues to go to France's traditional friends in sub-Saharan Africa. Thus, as the key strategic pillars in France's African relationship, Côte d'Ivoire, Senegal, Cameroon and Gabon have remained the principal beneficiaries of such aid.

The genocide in Rwanda also marked a real turning-point for Franco-African relations. Following the shooting down of President Habyarimana's plane, which resulted in his death, in April 1994, his supporters were responsible for the killing of some 800,000 Rwandan Tutsis and moderate Hutus in the space of two months. At the time France was widely criticised for its role in the country, as it had, from 1990–94, been the main external backer of the Habyarimana regime that prepared the genocide. Because of its previous support for the government which had masterminded the genocide, the French government took the decision to seek United Nations support for a humanitarian mission to the country, Opération Turquoise, in the summer of 1994. Indeed, successive French governments have, since 1994, been careful to seek UN Security Council (UNSC) approval for French military missions on the continent. It was also in the aftermath of the Rwanda debacle that the idea of creating an African peace-keeping force emerged, driven on the one hand by the need to gain increased international acceptance and consolidate domestic support for France's military effort on the continent, and on the other by the desire to share the burden, both militarily and politically, of this effort. Indeed, after Opération Turquoise, France initially showed far less willingness to intervene militarily on the continent, and substantial reductions were made in the number of French troops stationed in Africa, with two bases, in the Central African Republic, being closed in 1999.

Thus, under pressure from external forces which it did not control, France has been forced to undertake a further reconfiguration of its African policy. The military dimension is a key pillar of Franco-African relations. Military interventions, and indeed the possibility of intervention even if one does not actually take place, have consistently underpinned the French presence in Africa since political independence in 1960. The developments that have taken place since the events of 1994 in Rwanda thus represent a major change in policy. In reacting to these events, France has, as in the past, sought to protect its key strategic interests and maximise its position. But there has, once again, been no 'grand plan'.

AFRICAN ROLE IN THIS RELATIONSHIP

The perspective adopted here has been essentially Franco-centric insofar as it has focused on France's role and on French policy. However, it is important not to conclude from this that Africans have been simply passive 'recipients' of this relationship. Although it has undoubtedly been an unequal one, Africans have nonetheless played a key role in determining the pace and nature of change. In particular, they have been astute in exploiting France's 'need' for Africa in order to extract concessions from France. For example, at the socio-economic level, African political and social movements successfully exploited the French dream of creating a 'modern' Africa within the colonial system to obtain major improvements in African wage levels between 1936 and 1956, and in their campaigns for the extension of French metropolitan economic and social benefits such as family allowances and labour legislation, to Africans. Indeed, it was precisely this success that played a crucial role in rendering the French dream of a 'modern' Africa within the colonial system financially unviable and thus in obliging France to adopt a different approach to its relations with Africa. In this way, African intervention ensured that political independence was granted when it was, well before French policy-makers—and indeed some African political leaders such as Houphouët-Boigny and Senghor—had envisaged, and just 16 years after the very possibility of self-government had specifically been ruled out by the 1944 Brazzaville Conference. And African governing elites have played a key role in ensuring that France has not withdrawn from Africa in the post-colonial period.

Côte d'Ivoire has been chosen here to illustrate the way in which this has happened, although the recent history of almost any one of France's former African colonies could be used to illustrate the point that Africans were not simply passive recipients of French policy. Côte d'Ivoire is a particularly interesting case, as it is one of the small number of France's ex-colonies in Africa which had the economic potential to go it alone, but the leaders of which decided instead to maintain close links with France as the colonial period drew to a close.

Houphouët-Boigny, who was its political leader from 1945 to 1993, was a *député* in the French National Assembly until 1958.

This gave him access to the corridors of power in Paris, which he used to good effect to obtain concessions from France. One example of this was the Houphouët-Boigny Law abolishing forced labour, which was passed by the French parliament in 1946. It was this law that established his popularity in Côte d'Ivoire and laid the foundation for his political career. In 1950, he was instrumental in breaking the links between the Communist Party and the Parti Démocratique de la Côte d'Ivoire, which was the territory's main political party and of which he was leader, having made the calculation that there was more to be gained from a policy of co-operation with the colonial administration than from confrontation. Instead, he decided to affiliate to the centre-left party of the then Minister for Overseas France, François Mitterrand. He repudiated the term 'assimilation', which was no doubt too closely associated with his main rival in French West African politics, the Senegalese leader Senghor, and chose instead to promote 'the African personality', 'dialogue' and the idea of partnership with France. He was subsequently appointed a minister in successive French governments in the mid-1950s and used this position to influence the shape of the decolonisation process, notably by helping to scupper efforts to maintain the unity of the federations of French West and French Equatorial Africa in the run-up to the Loi-cadre of 1956–57. As a result, the federal governments-general in Dakar and Brazzaville were stripped of most of their powers, and Houphouët-Boigny achieved his objective of ensuring that in future Côte d'Ivoire would enjoy direct relations with Paris rather than having them mediated by a federal body based in Dakar. This ensured that, when independence came to Francophone Africa just four years later, it was granted to 12 separate states rather than to two federations. Most of these new states were small and, thanks to their state of underdevelopment, were necessarily heavily dependent upon France. They therefore signed a range of accords with France in the areas of defence, military, technical, economic and cultural co-operation. In the case of Côte d'Ivoire, this actually resulted in many ways in closer links with the former metropole than had been the case under colonialism, since a vast array of French specialists, far more than before 1960, now arrived in Côte d'Ivoire to take part in the new government's development effort. Teachers, economists, engineers, military and security advisers, health professionals and technicians all came to Côte d'Ivoire, representing what has sometimes been termed the 'second colonial occupation'. Moreover, in the early post-1960 governments of the newly independent state, there was usually at least one French minister and a plethora of French specialists acting as government advisers.

However, as has already been indicated, such dependency did not mean that Africans were mere spectators, the 'recipients' in a one-way relationship. On the contrary, Francophone Africa's governing elites have often been active agents, playing a key role in determining both the pace and nature of change. While they 'needed' France, they knew that France also 'needed' them, and they were often able to exploit this fact, for example by threatening to turn to another country, such as the US, for support, if France did not do what they wanted. Indeed, so strong was Houphouët-Boigny's influence that it was only after his death in December 1993 that the Balladur government felt able finally to devalue the CFA franc on January 11, 1994, a measure which Houphouët-Boigny had consistently opposed during his lifetime. These are highly significant elements, both for the way in which they call into question the notion of France's 'successful management' of Franco-African relations, and for the way in which they suggest that talk of France's long-predicted 'disengagement' from Africa and the 'normalisation' of Franco-African relations may be premature. The 'successful management' thesis implies some 'grand plan', as if France has enjoyed largely unchallenged control over a strategy for which it has been solely or mainly responsible. In the light of the foregoing, this needs to be substantially qualified. And those predicting French 'disengagement' and the 'normalisation' of Franco-

African relations all too often have a one-sided view of the dynamics of the relationship. Their focus is Franco-centric, which leads them to forget that it is not only France that has a great deal invested in this relationship and that African political leaders have their own expectations of the relationship and needs for diplomatic support in the international arena. For 'normalisation' to happen, both sides have to want it.

A historical perspective shows that the view of Franco-African relations as a relationship successfully managed by France so as to protect its key strategic interests in the region needs to be substantially qualified. Rather, it appears that French African policy has been characterised by a series of crises, brought on by factors beyond France's control, which have led to a succession of tactical retreats by France that are subsequently dressed up as strategy. Thus France has, to date, been relatively successful in the incremental pursuit of its national interest in a changing environment: there has been no 'grand plan', but rather, a tenacious holding operation.

The background to this has been that France has had so much invested in the relationship—not only in political, geopolitical and economic terms, but also in symbolic and emotional terms—that it has in practice always been difficult to get agreement on reform. The notion of France's 'successful management' of its African policy is thus somewhat misleading, insofar as it suggests that some kind of 'grand plan' has been successfully executed. In fact, French African policy has, like many other areas of public policy, been a battleground, which in this case has consistently opposed 'modernisers' ('les modernes') seeking to update French African policy, to 'conservatives' ('les anciens') seeking as far as possible to prolong the status quo. Over the years, the modernisers have persistently argued the need, on a combination of moral and political grounds, for French African policy to be made compatible with French republican values of liberty, equality and fraternity and for policy-makers to take account of changed circumstances by updating France's African policy before they are forced to do so under pressure from outside. Opponents of change, on the other hand, who have consistently had the upper hand in this debate, have invariably raised the spectre of French withdrawal. During the colonial period, reformers were accused of putting the imperial link in jeopardy and even of wanting to abandon the empire, while since independence it has been more a question of France letting down its loyal friends and reneging on its obligations. Both during the colonial period and since, the modernisers have been accused by the conservatives of diminishing France.

The key problem is that France has invested so much in its '*rayonnement*', in the projection of French power and prestige overseas, that it cannot afford to withdraw from Francophone Africa. This perception remains relevant to understanding Franco-African relations today. Since the First World War, and even more so since 1945, '*rayonnement*' has become an integral element of French national identity, and Africa is of crucial importance to France in this respect. The Popular Front's period in government from 1936 to 1938 revealed that this was as true for France's governing elites of the left as it was for the right. Its imperial reform project for the modernisation of Africa within the colonial system, the subsequent process of decolonisation leading to political independence, and recent changes in French African policy; all of these therefore need to be seen as part of an ongoing process of reconfiguration of France's relations with Africa. This process has been characterised as one of modernisation without reform. It is as yet far from clear whether the recent changes in French African policy will enable France to maintain this special relationship with, and privileged sphere of influence in, Africa into the twenty-first century.

Finally, it has been suggested here that those commentators predicting French 'disengagement' and the 'normalisation' of Franco-African relations need to bear in mind the wider context of these relations. Against the background of economic and political globalisation, in which Africa increasingly risks marginalisation, the continent needs economic and diplomatic support, political allies and trading partners. Given that France is one of the world's major economic powers and aid donors, that it has a strong diplomatic presence in Africa and a long history of involvement in the continent, it is difficult to see how it would be in the interest of the governing elites of Francophone Africa, of whatever political complexion, to refuse the offer of ties with, and support from, France. Moreover, analyses of Franco-African relations that focus on French policy while neglecting the broader context in which that policy is made often do not take sufficient account of the way in which France is involved in an intensifying international competition with other Western countries, and also with new players such as Japan, China and India, for influence on the continent. It is hardly in France's national interest to withdraw from this competition.

11
Propaganda and Politics

JOHN STOCKWELL

Politically the war was complicated, with a strange conglomeration of bedfellows. The FNLA and UNITA were supported at one time by the United States, China, Rumania, North Korea, France, Israel, West Germany, Senegal, Uganda, Zaire, Zambia, Tanzania, and South Africa. The MPLA was supported by the Soviet Union, Cuba, East Germany, Algeria, Guinea, and several Eastern European countries. Throughout the war there was a constant sorting out and dozens of countries eventually shifted their support to the MPLA. On October 24, the Chinese withdrew from the Angola war, their advisers packing and leaving, holding a press conference at Ndjili Airport as they left.

France was intrigued by the smell of Angolan oil and Zairian minerals, and predisposed to involvement in Angola by its long history of meddling in the affairs of young African countries. Like the United States, France saw the Angolan war as a chance to ingratiate itself with Mobutu. In August French intelligence directors had met with the CIA's deputy director, Vernon Walters, and obtained his promise that the CIA would give them $250,000 as proof of the United States' good faith in Angola. The money was delivered, although it was clear to no one, possibly not even to General Walters, why the United States had to prove its good faith in Angola to the French. A liaison evolved in which the CIA briefed the French intelligence service in detail about its Angola program, while the French listened carefully but told the CIA nothing about their own activities in Angola and Cabinda. France did provide ENTAC anti-tank missiles, 120mm mortar rounds, and ammunition for Mobutu's Panhard armored cars, which it asked the CIA to haul from Istres, France, to Kinshasa. In December, France donated four missile-firing helicopters, which were delivered to Kinshasa by the CIA without pilots or ground crews.

African leaders watched the birthing of the new nation in their midst with sympathy and jealous interest. By 1975 they had learned painful lessons about the competition of West and East in Africa. Almost to a country they had been exploited in civil wars, coups, arms races, and competitive aid programs by the Soviet Union, United States, and various European, Asian, and Latin American countries. They had of course encouraged the Angolan liberation movements in their struggles against Portuguese colonialism, and when civil war erupted in July 1975, most had supported an embargo on the delivery of additional arms to the Angolan factions. Most were predisposed to resent outside interference in what they regarded as a purely African matter. The flagrant Soviet arms program was at first greeted with noisy indignation. All but the staunchest Soviet allies protested the Soviet interference in Angola. The new government of Nigeria expressed its concern. President Nyerere of Tanzania made public speeches criticizing the Soviet arms program. Idi Amin of Uganda castigated the Soviet Union and stormily threatened to sever relations. Egypt and the Sudan denied them overflight clearances for their arms flights to the MPLA.

The United States launched a major political effort to embroil and entrap as many countries as it could into opposition of the MPLA. Secret agents were sent to third world conferences, including the Non-Aligned Nations summit in Sri Lanka, and the Organization of African Unity in Addis Ababa. United States ambassadors throughout Africa were 'brought onboard' in varying degrees, receiving carefully tailored messages which were formulated by the CIA and delivered to the State Department through the working group, ordering them to use whatever leverage they could manage with their host governments to prejudice them against the MPLA.

Savimbi caused the United States a minor embarrassment in September, when he sent feelers to the MPLA for a negotiated solution. The CIA learned of this move through an article in the world press, and a Kinshasa station officer promptly interrogated Savimbi. We wanted no 'soft' allies in our war against the MPLA. Similarly, on October 22, when an MPLA delegation arrived in Washington to plead the MPLA's potential friendliness towards the United States, it was received by a low-level State Department officer who reported perfunctorily to the working group.

President Kaunda was a potential problem. While he sympathized with Savimbi, he was primarily concerned with getting his copper to the sea, and with the Benguela railroad closed his only alternative was the expensive and humiliating route through Rhodesia and South Africa. On September 10 he gave Savimbi sixty days, until Angolan independence, to get the Benguela railroad open. Otherwise he could not guarantee continued support.

To the CIA, Kaunda's ultimatum was a challenge. How could we get him so involved he could never defect? The key seemed to be the transshipment of arms through Zambia. Kaunda had publicly supported the international embargo against the shipment of arms to Angola, and it was felt that if one planeload of arms could be introduced through Zambia, with Kaunda's permission, he would be irreversibly committed to UNITA's support—'pregnant', we said in CIA headquarters.

At first the African leaders did not know about the United States arms program thanks to our ruse of working through Kinshasa. Similarly, the Soviets tried to hide their shipments through the Congo (Brazzaville), but the size of their program made it impossible to conceal. And of course, the CIA launched a major propaganda effort to expose the Soviet arms shipments.

Propaganda experts in the CIA station in Kinshasa busily planted articles in the Kinshasa newspapers, *Elimo* and *Salongo*. These were recopied into agency cables and sent on to European, Asian, and South American stations, where they were secretly passed to recruited journalists representing major news services who saw to it that many were replayed in the world press. Similarly, the Lusaka station placed a steady flow of stories in Zambian newspapers and then relayed them to major European newspapers.

In Kinshasa, Ray Chiles's prolific pen and fertile imagination produced a stream of punchy articles and clever operations to spearhead the agency's propaganda effort. For example, he procured a mimeograph machine for FNLA headquarters in Kinshasa and produced leaflets, which were dropped from airplanes over Luanda itself. The first such leaflet was unaccountably read verbatim over the MPLA's Radio Luanda the next morning, provoking a ripple of laughter in CIA stations throughout Europe and Africa, when they heard of it.

The propaganda output from Lusaka was voluminous and imaginative, if occasionally beyond credibility. In late September, Lusaka news stories began to charge that Soviets were advising MPLA forces inside Angola. This was at first a plausible line and Lusaka kept it going. Certainly Soviet advisers might have been inside Angola, although we had no evidence to that effect. The world press dutifully picked up Lusaka's stories of Soviet advisers, while we at headquarters watched nervously, preferring that propaganda ploys have at least some basis in fact. Then, two months later, Lusaka reported that twenty Soviet advisers and thirty-five Cubans had been captured when UNITA took Malanje. UNITA spokesmen gave this information to David Ottoway, who was visiting Lusaka, and it as published in the November 22 edition of the *Washington Post.* The *Post* also printed the TASS denial the same day, carrying stories from the world's two largest intelligence services in the same issue; unwitting that the first story came from the CIA and that it was false; aware that TASS was the Soviet's propaganda arm, but not sure that this time it was telling the truth.

UNITA had captured no Soviet advisers nor had it taken Malanje. World interest in the story put UNITA under uncomfortable pressure and the CIA Lusaka station abashedly let the story die a quiet death.

Another Lusaka fabrication accused Cuban soldiers of committing atrocities in Angola. It mentioned rape and pillage. Then its stories became more specific, 'reporting' a (totally fictitious) incident in which Cuban soldiers had raped some Ovimbundu girls. Subsequently it wrote that some of those same soldiers had been captured and tried before a tribunal of Ovimbundu women. Lusaka kept this story going endlessly throughout the program.

Later, Caryle Murphy, a *Washington Post* stringer who had covered Luanda, told me the Cuban soldiers had universally fallen in love with Angola and were singularly well behaved. The only atrocity we were able to document had Cubans as victims rather than criminals. Sixteen Cuban soldiers captured in October were executed by UNITA soldiers at the end of the war.

Bubba Sanders returned to headquarters shortly after I did and began to work on a 'white paper' which the FNLA could present to the United Nations General Assembly. A white paper is one in which the source and therefore the potential bias is not concealed; the FNLA would readily admit their sponsorship of the document. The CIA's role would be concealed. Bubba collected information from agency intelligence reports about Soviet arms shipments and included photographs of Russian ships and weapons taken by journalists who were on the CIA payroll and had visited Luanda on the basis of their press credentials. One of Africa Division's translators put the text of Bubba's message into African-sounding French, i.e., with idioms and expressions which would be used by a literate man in Kinshasa but not in Paris.

Potts enjoyed this sort of thing. He supervised Bubba closely, questioning him in detail during each staff meeting, stubbornly insisting that no corners be cut, that the document meet rigorous standards. The two of them argued about paper and type, as well as text and layout. The end product was assembled in a small folder, printed on rough paper identical to that used by one of the Kinshasa printing offices and even printed with machines similar to those used in Kinshasa. The cover bore the picture of a dead soldier on the Caxito battlefield.

The white paper was barely off the press when FNLA representatives arrived in New York in late September to lobby at the United Nations General Assembly. They were broke. Bubba Sanders set up a small task force in a Manhattan hotel room to direct our United Nations propaganda operation. In daily meetings the New York officers secretly funded the FNLA delegation and plotted strategy as they made contacts at the United Nations and with the New York newspapers. They distributed the white paper in the UN and to the US press. They also toured Africa with it, and distributed copies to the Chinese.

The UNITA representatives also arrived broke, and although we did not have a paper for them to distribute, the New York officers provided funds and guidance. Far more capable than the FNLA, UNITA representatives began to establish useful contacts. Both delegations were supplied with up-to-date intelligence. News and propaganda releases were cabled directly from the African stations to the permanent CIA offices in the Pan Am building and two nearby skyscrapers on Third Avenue, and East Forty-second Street. The MPLA and Soviets were active too, but defensively so. Although they managed to prevent an open debate on Angola on the floor of the General Assembly, they could not check the momentum of sympathy which UNITA and the FNLA began to enjoy. Secretary General Waldheim expressed his concern, and announced that the United Nations would send a fact-finding mission into Angola.

During a staff meeting I voiced my concern to Potts—were we on safe ground, paying agents to propagandize the New York press? The agency had recently been warned against running operations inside the United States and propagandizing the American public. Potts seemed unconcerned. We were safe enough, he said, as long as we could plausibly claim that our intent was to propagandize foreigners at the United Nations.

I wasn't satisfied with Potts's attitude toward the situation in New York. It seemed to me that our propaganda operation was leading us on to explosively dangerous ground.

On October 2 the New York base telephoned headquarters, advising us that it was sending the two UNITA representatives down to Washington for the weekend for some medical treatment and to talk to members of the black caucus in Washington, seeking introductions to key senators and administration officials. The New York base requested that I meet them and give them whatever support they needed. I refused. After the call I went in to see Carl, then Potts. They both agreed that the UNITA representatives had to be reined in. We sent a cable to the New York base reminding them that lobbying in the United States by CIA agents was not permitted.

On Monday, an officer from New York arrived at headquarters, and I learned with a jolt that it was I who was out of step. To begin with, the two UNITA reps had spent the weekend in Washington after all. The officer cheerfully admitted that he had given them money for the trip because, he claimed, they were coming anyway, with or without his approval, and besides, they were damned effective. He described their progress in New York with infectious enthusiasm.

Potts bought the whole show. He and the officer devised a neat solution to our little CIA charter problem. In order to keep the two delegations doing their 'good work' in New York and in Washington and still protect the CIA from any blow-back, funds would be channeled to them via overseas banks. The officer at first resisted, on the grounds that this was cumbersome, that he or one of his assistants could just slip them some money when they needed it, say $500 every few days. But Potts insisted, and after the officer went back to New York the task force worked out the details by cabling New York, Lusaka, Kinshasa, and key European stations. Each delegation opened a bank account in Europe to which European-based CIA finance officers could make regular deposits. Thereafter the CIA could plausibly deny that it had funded anyone's propagandists in the United States. It would be extremely difficult for any investigators to prove differently.

This arrangement continued throughout the duration of the program, long after the UN General Assembly closed. The UNITA delegates in New York and Washington were increasingly effective. They managed to see State Department officials, White House representatives, and congressmen, as well as American journalists. Care was taken by their CIA case officers not to record their visits to Washington, although some visits were reported in official memos written by unwitting State Department officers and White House staffers, who did not know they had been visited by CIA agents. UNITA's 'news' from Angola continued to be drawn from CIA propaganda, fed to them by their case officers in New York.

In January 1976 Director Colby testified before the House Select Committee on Intelligence, saying: 'We have taken particular caution to ensure that our operations are focused abroad and not at the United States to influence the opinion of the American people about things from the CIA point of view.' A remarkable statement in view of what we had been doing in the task force.

It was impossible to measure the full impact in America of the FNLA and UNITA propagandists, except perhaps by the response of American citizens who were inspired to enlist to fight communists in Angola. The news services reported that Roy Ennis of the Congress on Racial Equality was seeking one thousand volunteers to join the FNLA in Angola. Another group began training in jungle tactics on a farm in North Carolina. Adventurers, self-styled mercenaries, and restless American citizens began to contact the FNLA, and eventually a few made it to the FNLA fighting front in northern Angola, where several met tragic deaths.

We had other lines into the American media. For example, a European film crew was sent to Silva Porto to make a film about the war. Featuring Cuban soldiers Savimbi had captured, the documentary it produced was quite successful on European television. It came to the attention of the Voice of America, which proposed to show it in the United States. After discussing the pros and cons, the working group decided to let it happen—subsequently parts of the film appeared on an American television show.

Another time, a European CIA station cabled headquarters, advising that a journalist was en route to Washington with an FNLA story. When he arrived, the task force deputy chief, Paul Foster, met him secretly in Washington, then brought an article he had written back to CIA headquarters, where a task-force linguist translated it into passable English. The next day Foster returned it to the reporter, who sold it to the *Washington Post,* which printed it.

The article covered several columns, reading in part:

> A stern countenance, mustachioed and goateed, a stocky frame in a Mao tunic, a sternness in his bearing and in his remarks, often belied by great bursts of truly African laughter—Holden Roberto is a strange blend of war chief and Alabama Baptist preacher, but a man who obviously inspires a quasi-mystical fervor in his men . . .
>
> Question: But you have South Africans on your side?
>
> Roberto strikes the table in his Headquarters violently and sends the general staff maps flying. He seems gripped by a cold rage and starts to walk back and forth across the room, his hands behind his back. 'You saw the South Africans, did you see them? I say, in the zones which we control, we, the FNLA? Go and see at Savimbi's headquarters . . . I am telling you that we have no South Africans or Rhodesians among us!

At first we were successful in keeping our hand in the war hidden, while exposing the Soviet arms program. However, cracks began to appear in our cover facade in early September and the working group discussed ploys to cope. When State Department representatives reported the department was receiving inquiries from the press about Angola, the CIA presented them with working group paper #18 which suggested lines to be used in formal press statements: We could refuse to comment. We could categorically deny US involvement. Or we could state that the United States had supported the Alvor Accord, which permitted the three liberation movements to participate equally in preparing Angola for independence, but the Soviet Union had delivered arms to the MPLA, producing heavy fighting. Angola's neighbors were concerned that the Soviet Union was attempting to carve out a dominant position in Angola. We would add that we were sympathetic but we had not supplied US arms to any of the liberation movements. Whichever, we should emphasize the Soviet Union, so it would not look as though we were attacking a minor liberation movement.

The State Department a few days later reported it had issued a statement refusing to substantiate press inquiries and denying United States involvement:

> We have not been in the business of providing arms to the Angolan movements. However, we have received reports that one of the movements, the MPLA, has for some time been receiving large shipments of weapons from the Soviet Union. It is understandable if African governments are concerned about this development and we are sympathetic to those concerns.

In the field our security was fairly good. We and our allies had control over the only transportation into the fighting areas, especially into Silva Porto, and could restrict those areas from all but a few selected reporters or the extremely hardy individuals who were willing to go in overland. However, one European reporter, whom we knew only as Germani, began focusing on Kinshasa itself and was scurrying about town with a good instinct for where we were hiding the stories. The Kinshasa station reported his presence and the working group discussed the threat he posed. It would be easy to have Mobutu throw him out of the country. Could we get by with asking Mobutu to do it? Germani wasn't American. Did we dare have cables on record ordering the station to pull strings and have a legitimate European reporter thrown out of Kinshasa? The press would be extremely angry if it ever found out. The working group stalled, wondering why the field hadn't thought of this solution without headquarters' guidance. They were in daily contact with Roberto and his deputies and could easily plant the idea. They could see Mobutu. There would be no record. Chiefs of station are supposed to have an instinct for such things.

Like magic, Germani was expelled from Kinshasa on November 22. Without any cables or memoranda being written at headquarters, the string was pulled, the problem solved, and there was nothing in CIA records prove how it had happened.

Increasingly, the propaganda war became uphill work. On September 10, when the FNLA retreated from Caxito the second time, it left behind crates of munitions which bore fresh US Air Force shipping labels. The MPLA displayed these trophies to western journalists and the press picked up our scent. Nor were the newspapers idle. In Washington and New York IAFEATURE was increasingly exposed with accurate reports of our program, our budget, even the amounts of money in our budget. The *New York Times* seemed to have a particularly direct line to the working group, and the thought that we might have a 'Deep Throat' in our midst added some desperately needed excitement to the working group sessions.

While IAFEATURE was being described in the *New York Times*, the presence of South African soldiers in Angola became known. On November 22, a journalist, Ken Bridgefield, filed a story in the *Washington Post*, from Lusaka, reporting that South African soldiers were fighting in Angola. The propaganda and political war was lost in that stroke. There was nothing the Lusaka station could invent that would be as damaging to the other side as our alliance with the hated South Africans was to our cause.

Nigeria, the economic giant of black Africa and the United States' second most important source of petroleum, emphatically shifted its support to the MPLA, providing it with $20 million in aid. A crowd of Nigerians demonstrated before the American embassy in Lagos. Tanzania announced plans to train MPLA soldiers in Tanzania in a joint program with the Soviets. Idi Amin reversed his decision to expel the Soviets from Uganda, and when the Soviets publicly defended their program in late December, Amin supported them. Other countries began to recognize the MPLA as the legitimate rulers of Angola.

12
'Flee! The White Giants Are Coming!': The United States, the Mercenaries and the Congo 1964–65

PIERO GLEIJESES

On 14 August 1964, Carl Rowan, the prominent black journalist who was then the director of the United States Information Agency, wrote President Lyndon B. Johnson that he sensed 'a real danger that in saving the present situation in the Congo we . . . could lose the longer range struggle for all of Africa. I am particularly concerned about the damaging implications of possible press reports that United States' planes are hauling in Belgian guns to be used by South African and Southern Rhodesian mercenaries to kill Africans and to protect "Tshombe and European financial interests"'. Rowan was writing in the midst of a crisis: on 5 August 1964, Stanleyville, the Congo's third largest city, had fallen to the rebels, while in Washington a National Intelligence Estimate on the Congo had predicted 'a total breakdown in governmental authority'.

How had the 'real danger' that worried Rowan arisen? Why had the Johnson administration decided to rely on mercenaries to 'save' the Congo, and what were the repercussions of this decision in Africa and at home? Mercenaries had been active in Africa before, but this was the first time they had been used as an instrument of US foreign policy. An analysis based on documents from the Johnson Library, the Mennen Williams Papers, and the Freedom of Information Act, and supported by a survey of the press and interviews with several protagonists, reveals that the costs of the policy were lower than Rowan had feared. This was due not to the genius of the public relations men but to the rapid and overwhelming success of the mercenaries, the inattentiveness of the US press, and the weakness of the African states.

Until the late 1950s, Africa had barely surfaced in US foreign policy. It had been ruled by clients and friends of the United States, and decolonization had appeared a distant prospect. When independence came, it took Washington by surprise. 'The withdrawal of Western political controls has produced potentially unstable situations in the emergent states', noted a National Intelligence Estimate in 1961, adding that the new countries' immaturity, and the resentment many of their leaders bore toward the West, offered unexpected opportunities to Moscow and Beijing. 'Communist Bloc influence has grown from negligible levels in 1958–1959 to substantial proportions today', warned the same report. 'The Communists probably will enjoy a number of advantages in the competition with the West'.

Though of unequal intensity, US fears about Africa and Latin America were born roughly at the same time, as the 1950s gave way to the next decade, and they subsided at roughly the same time, in the late 1960s. In Latin America, the failure of guerrilla effort after guerrilla effort had convinced the United States that there would be no second Cuba. In Africa, the signposts of success were the overthrow of the 'radical' leaders, communism's Trojan horses (Algeria's Ahmed Ben Bella, Ghana's Kwame Nkrumah, and Mali's Modibo Keita), and the failure of the guerrillas in Angola, Mozambique, and Rhodesia. In October 1967 the CIA observed that the Soviet Union had been 'burned by several misadventures' in Africa and that the Chinese had suffered 'humiliating setbacks' there.

Of all the signposts of victory, none seemed more important than the Congo because of its size, its central location, its mineral riches, and the apparent gravity of the challenge it had posed. 'For the last five years the Congo has been the principal insurgent theater in Africa, and second only to Vietnam', the US ambassador in Leopoldville, G. McMurtrie Godley, stated in late 1965.

The Congo had become independent on 30 June 1960. Unprepared for self-government, it had fallen into anarchy a few days later and been sucked into the whirlwind of the Cold War. Over the next two years the Communist bloc sent money and weapons to the Congo, but its interference there was very limited compared to that of the United States. In the summer of 1960 the Eisenhower administration had concluded that Patrice Lumumba, the country's first prime minister, was an African Castro, a Soviet instrument. (Scholars now agree that he was in fact 'a genuine nationalist, fanatical in his opposition to foreign control of the Congo'.) For the Americans, he was an enemy of the most dangerous type—charismatic and popular. It would not be enough to bring him down: he would have to be eliminated. But the CIA was beaten to the gate. On 17 January 1961 Lumumba was killed by his Congolese enemies.

President John F. Kennedy inherited a raging crisis as Lumumba's followers prepared to wage war to avenge their leader's death. Kennedy said that he wanted the Congolese to chart their own course and, moving beyond Eisenhower's narrow intransigence, expressed his preference for a coalition government that would include even Lumumbists. But when the Congolese parliament seemed ready to elect a Lumumbist as premier, Kennedy's response was not very different from what Eisenhower's would have been: US officials bribed the parliamentarians, plotted a military coup, and succeeded in having their candidate, the lackluster Cyril Adoula, elected premier in a contest that would otherwise have been won by the Lumumbist. In time, Washington would forget this and would come to consider Adoula the true and legal expression of the parliament's will.

Adoula's election did not resolve the Congo crisis. A few days after independence had been declared, the dynamic, brave, and corrupt Moise Tshombe had led the country's richest province, Katanga, into a war of secession. As the Congo's self-proclaimed arch anti-Communist, Tshombe enjoyed the sympathy of many Americans, including members of Congress. The Kennedy administration, however, thought that Katangan independence would lead to the fragmentation of the Congo and offer opportunities to the Soviet bloc. Therefore, Washington supported sending a UN peacekeeping force to the Congo. That force finally quashed the Katangan rebellion in January 1963.

With the defeat of Lumumba's followers and the reintegration of Katanga, the Congo settled into corrupt, oppressive, pro-American stability that rested on two pillars: the UN troops, numbering in the thousands, and the Congolese Army, led by General Joseph Mobutu. Therefore, in early 1964 when the UN troops prepared to leave, rebellion flared up again. Leading the revolt were the fractious followers of Lumumba, whose vague ideology was couched in Marxist jargon. 'It's definitely an African and a Congolese movement but all very confused', explained the US consul in Stanleyville, who had had frequent contacts with rebel leaders. Ethnic rivalries, old feuds, and the fear of witchcraft added to the brew that bubbled up through the thin crust of the Pax Americana.

The revolt spread with a rapidity that took the Johnson administration by surprise. But a few weeks later the Congolese army had virtually collapsed. The rebels, who had practically no weapons, were considered invincible because they were protected by witchcraft.

On 6 August, in a move that testified 'to the extent of the desperation felt by President Joseph Kasavubu and General Mobutu', Tshombe was appointed prime minister. 'It all happened so fast', observed the embassy's deputy chief of mission. 'Before we knew it the decision had been made. It was very much a Congolese decision'. Reserved at first, the US reaction soon turned into warm endorsement. 'Prime Minister Tshombe has brought zest and dynamism to his job', said Assistant Secretary Williams.

African leaders were less enthusiastic about Tshombe. Despised by many of them as 'a walking museum of colonialism' because of his ties with South Africans, Portuguese, and Belgians and his attempt to divide the Congo, Tshombe was also known to have been the moving force behind Lumumba's murder.

In the weeks that followed the appointment of Tshombe as prime minister, the United States increased its military aid to the Congo. But neither increased aid nor Tshombe's leadership could stem the revolt. By late July frantic cables were reaching Washington from Leopoldville: The rebels were winning, the army was collapsing, outside assistance—soldiers, not just material—was necessary.

Washington turned to Europe. Just as US officials had urged the British to send in troops to 'frustrate a Communist takeover' in Zanzibar a few months earlier, so now they turned to the Belgians. The most effective measure, Ambassador Godley informed Washington, would be the 'use of Belgian paratroop battalions to come in rapidly, clean up [the] situation and then withdraw as soon as possible'.

But the Belgians balked: They agreed to increase the number of their military advisers in the Congo, but 'no Belgian would be authorized to engage directly or indirectly in combat'.

The Americans were also rebuffed on a second proposal: that Belgium 'take the lead in the organization . . . of a joint military force of the Six, or some of its member nations'.

Not only did the 'gutless Belgians' fail to respond with the proper zest but they also seemed ready to collude with the enemy. Washington worried about the 'apparent Belgian preference to try to do business with the rebels, even if Communist, rather than facing up to putting down the rebellion'. In fact, the Belgians were simply being practical. They had no intention of sending in troops, they did not believe that anyone else would, and they had no confidence in the Congolese army's ability to do the job. Moreover, they did not consider the rebels to be Communists and thought they could achieve a modus vivendi with them should they win.

Washington was not interested in a modus vivendi with the rebels. US officials knew that the rebels were receiving very little outside assistance, and there was no indication that they were Communist.

A rebel victory would have ended the pro-American stance of the Congo that had taken four years and two US administrations to establish. As the 1964 presidential campaign gathered momentum in the United States, the loss of the Congo ('the richest country and the richest prize in Africa') could have become a major political issue.

On 11 August, Johnson and his key advisers met in a hastily called session of the, National Security Council (NSC). The discussion had an air of unreality. No European or African government was willing to send its troops, and Washington knew it. In addition to the Europeans, the administration had already approached Ethiopia, Nigeria, and Senegal and had been rebuffed. Moreover, had African troops landed in the Congo, they would not have been welcomed: Mobutu and Tshombe trusted neither black soldiers nor their governments.

The option that was not discussed at the 11 August NSC meeting was the use of mercenaries. The word was not mentioned. And yet the idea of using 'special volunteers' (the 'new euphemism for mercenaries') had by then become the most compelling solution to the Congo problem.

It represented no sudden shift. It was part of a two-track approach that had been under consideration from the outset. The United States preferred a 'clean solution' (European or African troops), but it would fall back on mercenaries if necessary. Washington concurred. 'Tshombe and the GOC should proceed soonest to establish an effective gendarmerie-mercenary unit.' Tshombe was an old hand at the mercenary game: They had helped him when he had been the leader of secessionist Katanga. He was happy to use them again.

In Brussels, on 7 August, Spaak told Harriman unequivocally that neither Belgium nor any other European country would send troops. That same day Rusk approved a proposal by Mennen Williams for an 'immediate effort . . . to concert with the Belgians to help Tshombe to raise a mercenary force', and he cabled Harriman urging 'Belgian help on the mercenary problem including recruitment of Belgians'. Washington and Brussels would supply the money to pay the mercenaries and the weapons to arm them; Washington alone would supply the planes to fly them. Bowing to US pressure, the Belgians jettisoned the idea of letting events in the Congo follow their own course and embraced the mercenary option. 'In fact, mercenaries were the only possible solution', writes Colonel Frederic Vandewalle, who would head the Belgian military mission in the Congo and who was briefed by Spaak on the talks with Harriman. 'In private, both Washington and Brussels admitted it'. And so the United States embarked on a dual policy in the Congo. It openly provided military aid to Tshombe while it covertly financed, armed, and oversaw the mercenaries.

The mercenaries flowed into the Congo. Within a few days, well over a hundred had arrived from South Africa and Rhodesia. 'At Johannesburg', wrote the weekly *Jeune Afrique*, 'they are lining up in front of the recruitment center. All you need to be is white, able to shoot, and ready to help Mr. Tshombe, "the good friend of Whites and foe of the Red Chinese." . . . *Air Congo* planes fly the South African mercenaries to Leopoldville. There, they are met by instructors who hand them machine guns (American), and then they are flown in planes (American) toward Stanleyville or Bukavu to crush the rebels.' By October their number would reach 'over a thousand'.

The US embassy kept the mercenaries at arm's length—in public. Close contact was maintained through the CIA, the military attachés, and the military mission.

Why did men volunteer? 'For money, first of all', five freshly arrived French mercenaries told a journalist over drinks in Leopoldville. But there were other, loftier reasons: 'Because we're ashamed of France. . . . We've lost Indochina; *le grand Charles* has tossed Algeria aside. *The fellouzes* will not get the Congo.'

The year 1963, mused a philosophical mercenary, 'was the heyday of African Unity, of the dream of African grandeur and of the expulsion of the white man from the continent'. The year 1964 would be the year of the White Giants—'tall, vigorous Boers from South Africa; long-legged, slim and muscular Englishmen from Rhodesia'—who would come to the Congo and restore the white man to his proper place. 'How often was I to hear the muffled drumming in the night, through forests and savannahs, "Flee! The White Giants are coming!"'

The mercenaries were thugs, and they were effective. They advanced along the paths of the Congo in mobile columns. When they met resistance, the mercenaries called on the Congolese air force, which included not one Congolese.

Throughout the war, US officials railed against the fact that the rebels were receiving outside military assistance. But the rebels got only small amounts of military aid from African countries, the Soviet Union, and China, and the weapons were of little value, for they did not know how to use them.

Only Cuba sent men—under Che Guevara. The Cubans arrived in late April 1965 and departed, as quietly as they had come, seven months later. CIA reports occasionally—and always calmly—mentioned them. According to the agency, 'over 100 Cuban military advisers trained and assisted—and some actually fought alongside—the Congolese rebels in the 1964–65 Congo rebellion'. But the Cubans 'looked as confused as everybody else'.

Thus, one by one, the rebel towns were recaptured, the rebel strongholds in the rural areas dispersed, and the borders across which the rebels might receive help secured until, by late 1965, the revolt had been brought under control. CIA reports, by far the best source on the campaign, are unequivocal: The mercenaries were indispensable, the army's victories were due to them, and the 'regular Congo army troops, with a few exceptions, are no better than they ever were'.

No US official questioned the necessity of using the mercenaries; not one expression of dissent emerges from thousands of pages of documents on the Congo. Nor did any official doubt that victory in the Congo would be Pyrrhic if it caused a backlash in Africa or at home. American officials were painfully aware that the United States was vulnerable to African charges of racism despite the sincere efforts of the Johnson administration to strengthen civil rights legislation. In the summer of 1964, as the Congo operation began, intermarriage was a crime in nineteen states, segregation rampant, and violence against blacks apparent to anyone who opened a paper or turned on a television. On 22 July, the second summit meeting of the Organization of African Unity unanimously approved a resolution condemning 'continuing manifestations of bigotry and oppression against Negroes in the United States', while race riots in New York reminded Africans that racial hatred was not limited to 'the ever-explosive Deep South'.

US officials went to work. 'I believe that there are some things that we can do to make our actions in the Congo more palatable internationally and to make ourselves less vulnerable to Communist propaganda', USIA director Rowan told Johnson. This meant polishing Tshombe's image. And it meant making the mercenary issue as anodyne as possible, while transforming the United States from the mercenaries' patron into a concerned onlooker. It was a painful exercise, at times successful, usually frustrating.

Through reams of documents, we see senior US officials trying to get Tshombe to utter the right noises and make the right gestures; they worked directly with him, and they worked through his advisers and public relations people. It was a thankless task, Ambassador Godley and his Belgian and British colleagues concluded, as they swapped stories of Tshombe's stubbornness. The man's survival depended on the United States, but he knew that his patrons also needed him.

Mindful of Tshombe's well-deserved reputation as the friend of Portuguese colonialism, US officials sought to drape him in anti-colonialist veils. 'I indicated [to him that] there are many rumors around Leo[poldville] that he is giving [rebel leader] Holden Roberto and his Angolans a rough time', Godley cabled in March 1965. 'He again referred to [the] fact that from his limited resources he gave Holden $800. . . . I suggested he let this be known to African leaders and that he not conceal his pro-Holden tendencies.' A few days later the US ambassador in Dar es Salaam chimed in: The Congo should make a 'special financial contribution' to Holden Roberto at the next meeting of the Liberation Committee of the Organization of African Unity. The contribution would be 'more symbolic than substantial and explicable to the Portuguese in these terms if the closed session leaked'.

The suggestions fell on deaf ears. 'Holden complains bitterly', *Jeune Afrique* reported two months later. 'Tshombe is making his life tough'. Tshombe, US officials groused, has an 'incredibly poor sense of public relations'.

The previous August, US efforts at image making had faced a far deadlier threat than Holden Roberto and the Portuguese. Unbeknown to Washington, Tshombe had asked Pretoria for weapons, 'white officers and white enlisted men'. While sympathetic to Tshombe ('whom they regard as the least of the black evils', explained the CIA), the South Africans were hesitant. They immediately told US officials that they were worried that evidence of their military involvement might be 'grist for the mill' of Tshombe's enemies and would complicate American efforts to aid the Congo.

Washington agreed heartily: The South African connection would be a 'continuing magnet for the cold war in the form of greater soviet bloc, chinese communist, and radical African interest'. Pretoria held back. It sent Tshombe a few military supplies—the arrival on 22 August 1964 of a South African C-130 'with what is obviously military equipment' was immediately reported in the press and proved embarrassing. And it sent, according to the CIA, some military personnel under cover: 'Many of the mercenaries arriving at the Congolese base of Kamina are actually South African Army regulars placed on leave status for six months.' There were a few dozen such soldiers, sent to perform specialized tasks and 'probably . . . to gather intelligence', observed a CIA official. Fortunately, for Washington, this operation remained a secret.

US officials would have preferred that both the South African government and the South African mercenaries stay out of the Congo, a point that Undersecretary Ball expressed forcefully. 'If Senator Thomas Dodd could get the following points across to Tshombe it would be immensely beneficial', he wrote. The 'Congo cannot expect its friends, such as Nigeria, Senegal, the Ivory Coast and others, to be effective in promoting its interests against [the] strong opposition of radical African states if the Congo does not take parallel actions which will make it more acceptable to Africa'. Among such actions, Ball stressed, was the 'replacement of at least the South Africans and Rhodesians among the mercenary contingents in the Congo ASAP'. In their stead should be Europeans. 'Such a shift', Harriman and Spaak concluded during a three-hour lunch in New York, 'would not in itself overcome African opposition to Tshombe but would make it easier for moderate African countries to support the Government of Congo'.

Although Spaak had refused to let Belgians serve as mercenaries in August, his reservations had soon been overcome. Honored as one of the fathers of European unity, Spaak appears here in less distinguished garb. Under his aegis, 'a recruitment center, shielded by diplomatic immunity, operated in rue Marie de Bourgogne in Brussels. There, the Congolese military attaché, Babia, was assisted by a Belgian adviser. A Belgian police doctor examined the candidates. . . . All this was public knowledge', remarks Colonel Vandewalle.

And yet, fewer than two hundred Belgians enlisted and even fewer Frenchmen; the number of Italians and Germans could be counted on the fingers of one hand; forty-six Spaniards (under an active duty officer on unpaid leave from the Spanish army) arrived in late 1965. The Americans were realistic: As long as so few Europeans volunteered, the southern Africans would have to stay. Godley was philosophical: Although a shift to Europeans might 'alleviate the political unacceptability of the mercenaries . . . none of us the Belgian and British ambassadors and Godley believe this would appreciably modify the situation'. Moreover, he added, 'the English-speaking mercenaries . . . have proven themselves more able than the Belgian and other heterogeneous French-speaking mercenaries'.

Since little could be done to change the mercenaries' mores or nationality, US officials did what they could to package the unsavory product better. Why not call the mercenaries 'military technical assistance volunteers', the US ambassador in Belgium asked. (Others preferred 'special volunteers'.) Well-meaning, repetitive suggestions rained on Godley. Rusk told him to 'play down to whatever extent possible the role of the mercenaries'. Rowan urged 'more emphasis on the Congolese and less on the mercenaries', and Ball insisted that Godley take 'measures to avoid publicity such as keeping mercenaries out of Leopoldville and impressing upon Hoare the necessity of keeping quiet'. Not an easy task: As the *Christian Science Monitor* noted, Hoare had already sold his story 'to British and South African newspapers. In the first article he bluntly states that he and his men "bore the brunt of all the fighting."' Hoare also told *Le Figaro Littéraire* that 'the Congo will need white troops for many years to come. . . . The work we have started has to be completed, and the only way to complete it is to kill all the rebels.'

Wary of being associated with the mercenaries, the United States stayed in the background. It built 'a few fires under the Belgians'; as the former colonizers, they could dirty their hands. 'We had to press them, cajole, yell at them', recalled a US official. The Belgians were 'small in resources and small in imagination', observed another. The Americans wanted the Belgians to take the lead in the Congo—the lead, that is, in executing Washington's policy. Belgium cooperated: It increased the number of its military advisers in the Congo, and it was these military advisers who openly maintained the daily contact with the mercenaries. 'Overtly at least', Godley recommended, 'US representatives should keep as far away from the mercenaries as possible'. The United States wanted the mercenaries to be seen as the responsibility of the Congolese government and of Brussels. To make this unequivocally clear, 'in accordance with the wishes of the American government', the mercenaries did not accept US citizens.

It is unlikely that US public diplomacy swayed many Africans. The governments of Algeria, Egypt, the Sudan, Guinea, Ghana, Congo Brazzaville, and Burundi lambasted US support for Tshombe ('Lumumba's murderer') and the mercenaries, as did the governments of Tanzania, Kenya, and Uganda, which usually had cordial relations with the United States. Moreover, many of these governments provided money or weapons to the rebels or allowed aid to pass through their territory.

Support for the rebels and anger at the United States were soon tempered, however, by pragmatic considerations. With the exception of Congo Brazzaville, these governments relied on US economic aid (or, in the case of Burundi, Belgian aid)—a fact that US officials did not let them forget. Moreover, from the outset England used its clout with African governments to rally support for US policy in the Congo, and in the spring of 1965 the French somewhat grudgingly joined in. Finally, the mercenaries' victories could not be overlooked. 'My personal relations with [President Jomo] Kenyatta healed slowly', writes the US ambassador in Kenya. 'But on May 5 1965 he called me over to the State House, held out his hand and said, "The Congo is finished. Now we can be friends again."'

The Sudan, which had allowed aid for the rebels to pass through its territory, was subjected to more direct pressure. In April 1965, Hoare's men reached the Sudanese border. On the 28th, the CIA reported that 'South African mercenaries sallied across the frontier'. Or, as one mercenary recalled more poetically, 'in the heart of Africa, at Aba on the border between the Congo and Sudan, South African soldiers sang the Boers' folksong in the tropical night'. It was an ominous humiliation for the Sudanese; they ended their support for the rebels and toned down their criticism of the United States. Congo Brazzaville, also fearful of a 'US-backed attack' by Tshombe's mercenaries, did 'little to aid the insurgents'.

At times, sheer luck helped the Americans. Algeria had been providing some matériel to the rebels ever since Belgian paratroopers, transported in US planes, had raided Stanleyville on 24 November 1964. 'We help the rebels. It is our duty', President Ben Bella proclaimed defiantly. US officials strongly objected to Ben Bella's 'fanatical emotions' about the Congo and his vehemence 'in attacking our support of Tshombe'. Relations between Algeria and the United States were strained, and Dean Rusk told the Algerian ambassador that 'bilateral relations could not usefully be discussed as long as Algerian policies on Vietnam and the Congo were at such variance with those of the US'. It was Ben Bella's overthrow at Houari Boumedienne's hands in June 1965 that broke the impasse. Algeria promised that no further aid would be given to the rebels. Boumedienne, the CIA noted, 'has been warm, open, and attentive with US officials'.

The storm was subsiding. Ghana's hostility was unchanged, but in material terms 'Nkrumah did not play a role in the Congo in 1964–65, or a very limited one at most'. Egypt, Burundi, Kenya, Uganda, and Guinea were 'adopting a more pro-Western stance'. Only one of the Congo's neighbors remained firm in its support for the rebels—Tanzania, defiant in its revulsion for the 'traitor' Tshombe and his mercenaries. 'The key place for the opposition was Brazzaville for the political meetings, and Tanzania for the action', observed a CIA official.

The military impact of Tanzania's stand was negated, however, by one of the CIA's most successful operations: the establishment, in the spring of 1965, or a naval patrol on Lake Tanganyika, which intercepted boat traffic to the beleaguered rebels. The trend line is going our way', the NSC specialist on Africa observed drily in June 1965.

The trend was going in the right direction at home as well. In August 1964, when the president sent four C-130s with American crews to the Congo and fifty-six US paratroopers to guard them, many Americans were reminded, with deep uneasiness, of Vietnam. 'The United States is getting itself militarily involved in still another conflict', warned the *New York Times.* It 'is starting with only enough arms, men and *matériel* to put out a little bonfire. . . . But as Southeast Asia showed, bonfires can grow into great conflagrations.' These fears were echoed, in the days that followed, by several members of Congress. 'Today we are providing transport service', remarked Senator John Stennis (D-MS). 'I cannot but wonder whether the next step will be the function of advising and training the Government forces, in the style followed in South Vietnam, so that ultimately our men will be fighting and dying in combat'.

The administration was eager to dispel these fears. The C-130s were 'mostly for evacuation purposes', George Ball assured Walter Lippmann. 'We have no intention of getting . . . bogged down in the African swamp.' And upon learning that the *New York Times* was 'thinking of writing some editorial on the Congo situation', Ball called editorial page editor John Ochs and volunteered to send Deputy Assistant Secretary Wayne Fredericks 'to NY and have him talk to Ochs and [his] colleagues'.

It was not Ball's or Fredericks's eloquence but the mercenaries' successes that quelled the fear that the United States might be 'drawn ever deeper into the Congolese jungle'. By using the mercenaries, C. L. Sulzberger noted in mid-September, 'Tshombe has already made inroads into rebel pockets'. Through the months that followed, the US press reported the obvious: 'It has been the white mercenary force . . . that has contained and rolled back the insurgents'. Led by the 'intelligent, poetry-reading Colonel Mike Hoare', the mercenaries squared the circle: The Congo would be saved, and American soldiers would not die.

Nor were the mercenaries such bad chaps either, according to the US press. 'They resemble rough-hewn college boys', one *Life* reporter wrote. The *New York Times,* which provided more intensive coverage of the Congo crisis than any other US newspaper, made only one attempt to show the American people who the mercenaries were. It did so by devoting two articles to Lieutenant Gary Wilson, 'a lean, 25-year-old South African' who had enlisted, he confided, 'because he believed Premier Moise Tshombe was sincerely trying to establish a multiracial society in the Congo. "I thought that if I could help in this creation, the Congo might offer some hope, some symbol in contrast to the segregation in my own country."' We hear Wilson's distress at what he witnesses in the Congo. 'It's a weird war', he muses, 'frightening, brutal, sometimes comic, utterly unreal'. We hear him talk about performing acts of great bravery. 'He recalled the time two weeks ago when he captured the town of Lisala with 15 men white mercenaries against more than 400. . . .'The rebs have one thing in common with our own Congolese', he adds. 'They don't take aim. They think that noise kills.' We hear his reaction to the cruelty of the Congolese—on both sides. 'It's mass murder, it's mass murder', he mutters. Moreover, we hear that 'his words summed up the feelings of most of his compatriots here'.

Perhaps Wilson was indeed the sensitive, idealistic man described by the *New York Times.* If so, he was the exception. More typical was Wally Harper, a fellow South African also fighting in the Congo. When asked, 'How do you feel when you're out there fighting? How do you feel about killing anyone?' Harper replied, 'Well, I've done a lot of cattle farming, you know, and killing a lot of beasts; it's just like, you know, cattle farming, and just seeing dead beasts all over the place. It didn't worry me at all.' Harper's words appeared in *Africa Today,* a scholarly magazine that very few Americans read, but not in the *New York Times.*

In its eighteen-month coverage of the war the *New York Times* reported the mercenaries' successes time and again; only rarely did it mention—and then ever so briefly—their transgressions. On 2 December 1964, Sulzberger abruptly referred to 'atrocities committed by white mercenaries in the Congo', but he provided no details; three weeks later he called them 'unsavory'. On 6 December, the *Times* wrote that the mercenaries 'stalked through' the African section of Stanleyville, 'looting and shooting. There seemed to be no end to the killing; any African man or woman was considered a rebel and shot on sight.' In January, the *Times* quoted a UN official in the Congo as saying that the mercenaries 'loot everywhere they can', and it noted in passing that 'the mercenaries habitually loot the towns they take'. This was the extent of the indictment. No photos like those published in the *Observer* appeared in the *Times.* Its readers learned instead of the mercenaries' efforts to protect the Congolese from both the rebels and the army.

The *Christian Science Monitor* mentioned the mercenaries' crimes once. 'The Western world has heard a lot about the vicious tactics of the rebels against their enemies and white captives', Robert Hallett wrote. 'At the same time', he added with uncommon sensitivity, 'the African nations have been similarly appalled by the cruelties of the white mercenaries toward Africans'. *Newsweek* regularly referred to black atrocities and to the mercenaries' revulsion at them. (After witnessing an atrocity by a government soldier, one mercenary, 'his face wrinkled in disgust, snapped out: "They are all the same. Take the uniform off that one [pointing to the soldier] and put it on that one [pointing to a dead rebel] and what's the difference?"') Only once did *Newsweek* mention a crime perpetrated by the mercenaries: In Stanleyville they 'divided their time between mopping up the remnants of rebel resistance and pillaging'. *Life, Time,* and *US News & World Report* constantly assailed the rebels' atrocities and the latter two occasionally mentioned those of the army, but none of them uttered a single word of criticism of the mercenaries. They stressed instead how the mercenaries were saving the Congo from communism. The closest the *Washington Post* came to mentioning mercenaries' crimes was an isolated reference to 'the wholesale looting, killing and burning of villages . . . in areas captured by mercenary-led forces in the northwest Congo'. There were no such references in the *Wall Street Journal.*

Looking back three decades later, one wonders why the American press was so silent about the atrocities the mercenaries committed. Perhaps it was because the American journalists who went to the Congo were dependent on the US embassy for information and transportation. Perhaps it was because the mercenaries were doing America's work. Perhaps it was because the mercenaries, like the journalists, were white (*Time* called them 'tough white fighters') and they killed only blacks, while they saved the lives of white hostages (including some Americans). *Le Monde* put it well: 'Western public opinion is more sensitive, one must acknowledge, to the death of one European than to the deaths of twenty blacks'.

Given the press's selective reporting, it is not surprising that very few white Americans expressed any qualms about the use of the mercenaries. African Americans were less placid. Malcolm X and Elijah Muhammad lashed out at President Johnson, at his 'hireling Tshombe' and his 'hordes of white Nazi-type mercenaries'. Pointing to the connection between the United States and the mercenaries, the Black Muslims' paper, *Muhammad Speaks,* asked: 'If it is wrong for a rich individual to hire a thug to kill his enemy, does it become right for a rich country to hire killers to slaughter people of another country? . . . Or is it forgiven because the killers we hire are just "killing niggers"?' Stressing the bonds of race over citizenship, Malcolm X called on African Americans and Africans to join together against their common enemy—in Mississippi and in the Congo alike.

Martin Luther King's wing of the civil rights movement was more cautious. The Call Committee of the American Negro Leadership Conference on Africa repeatedly expressed its unhappiness with US policy in the Congo, called for a withdrawal of 'mercenaries and other external forces', and asked that the problem be solved by negotiations. But these leaders and their constituencies were absorbed in the civil rights struggle that was raging in the United States. They had no desire to quarrel with a president whose help they needed. Insofar as they paid attention to foreign policy, they focused on issues that directly affected black Americans—Vietnam, above all, where black soldiers were dying. 'To them, Africa was distant, far off', remarked Congressman Charles Diggs (D–MI), one of the founders of the Black Caucus. Their energy for the Congolese drama was limited; their complaints, somewhat perfunctory. Nevertheless, even their mild criticism provoked hostile comment. 'Insofar as the civil rights leaders allow their movements to become hostage to the uncertain and confused events in Africa, they can provide heedless comfort to their enemies', lectured the *Washington Post* in an editorial. 'There ought to be the utmost caution in statements that can enable bigots to assert that race is a stronger bond than citizenship.'

In January 1965, National Security Adviser McGeorge Bundy informed Secretary Rusk that Johnson wanted him to meet with the leaders of the American Negro Leadership Conference on Africa. 'What the President hopes is that you might find a way of making the point that we do not think it is a good thing at all to encourage a separate Negro view of foreign policy', Bundy explained. 'I get loud and clear that the President wants to discourage emergence of any special Negro pressure group (*à la* the Zionists) which might limit his freedom of maneuver', noted a NSC official. In March 1965, Rusk met with King and other representatives of the Negro Leadership Conference. The meeting 'was quiet and friendly. Concerning the Congo, the Secretary and the Negro Leadership group agreed on the necessity . . . for Tshombe to get rid of the white mercenaries. . . . The meeting was given minimal press coverage and is not likely to give rise to any undesirable repercussions.'

Even the black press gave the meeting short shrift. With the notable exceptions of *Muhammad Speaks* and the *Afro-American*, it paid very little attention to Africa, and even less to the Congo. During the eighteen months that the crisis raged, the influential *Amsterdam News* published only four articles that mentioned it, and *The Crisis*, the monthly organ of the NAACP, printed not one word on the subject.

Throughout 1965 the political situation in the Congo worsened even as the military situation improved. Relations between President Kasavubu and Prime Minister Tshombe became increasingly strained. 'We've turned ourselves inside out to keep Kasavubu from firing Tshombe and to keep Tshombe from trying to take the presidency from Kasavubu', Bundy wrote Johnson in August. Nevertheless, in October, Kasavubu did indeed fire Tshombe, and a frustrated White House aide lamented: 'So, just when the mercenaries are mopping up the last organized rebel remnants, we have a real political mess on our hands.'

Tshombe and Kasavubu 'are moving toward a showdown', warned the NSC's Africa expert on 22 November. 'If [the] Belgians and we can't help patch up a compromise we face a painful choice.' Three days later the United States was spared the pain of making a decision as General Mobutu shoved both Kasavubu and Tshombe aside to take over as the Congo's strongman. Mobutu had worked with the CIA since 1960. The agency agreed with Spaak: Mobutu's coup was 'the best thing that could possibly have happened'.

The decision to rely on white mercenaries to win the civil war in the Congo did not stem from a belief that the rebels were Communists or that a major Soviet or Chinese offensive was under way in the Congo, but from the fact that the rebels were unfriendly to the United

States. At best, their victory would have meant an unpleasant neutralist regime in a country where both the Eisenhower and Kennedy administrations had labored mightily to impose a pro-American government. It came down, in the end, to a question of costs. If the cost of defeating the rebels could be kept low, then there was no incentive to explore alternative solutions, to run any risks, to accept any compromises. Had the only way to prevent a rebel victory been to dispatch US troops—with its high cost at home and abroad—then US officials might have allowed events in the Congo to run their course. As it was, there was very little debate among US policymakers about the proper course to take, and if the administration's 'doves'—Assistant Secretary Williams and his deputy, Wayne Fredericks—were uneasy, they kept their counsel.

'With Cyprus and Viet-Nam bubbling ominously, and the election two months away, the Administration is eager to keep the lid on the Congo pot', the *Washington Post* remarked in September 1964. It succeeded admirably. The costs for Washington of using the mercenaries were remarkably low. At home, after some initial hesitation, neither Congress nor the press questioned the administration's policy. Any doubts were dispelled by the mercenaries' victories.

Only two newspapers, both African American, roundly denounced the United States' role 'in the raising and paying of white mercenaries'. The *Afro-American* wrote: 'We hire the hated anti-Castro mercenary pilots. . . . If we must fight the Congolese people, why don't we openly send in our army, our navy and our airforce instead of hiring thugs to do our dirty work for us?'

The white press was more discreet. It mentioned that Cuban exiles were piloting the T-28s and B-26s provided by the United States, but it did not ask how these Miami Cubans had found their way to Leopoldville. In fact, the only references to any connection between the United States and the mercenaries were a phrase in *Life* about 'Cuban exiles' having been 'recruited by the United States' to fly the planes and three short sentences buried in a full-page article in the *Washington Post:* 'The United States is flying mercenaries to the front. Better still, the United States is in effect underwriting the cost of the entire force of 'operational technicians', as they are known in official circles. The monthly payroll: $300,000.' One might have expected other newspapers to pick up the story, or for *Life* and the *Washington Post* to elaborate on it. In fact, nothing happened. 'In those days there was not the adversarial relationship between the press and the government that now exists', explained the CIA station chief in Leopoldville. 'Most of them [the US journalists in the Congo] knew very well or guessed if they didn't know; but they didn't want to embarrass the US government the way they would now.'

This reticence was not new. It had been present in 1954, at the time of the CIA covert operation in Guatemala, and in 1961, in the weeks before the Bay of Pigs. 'If the leaders of the US government decide that all the risks and perils of a major covert operation are required . . . it is not the business of individual newspapermen to put professional gain over that of country', explains Joseph Alsop. This 'journalistic discretion' would survive the tumult of Vietnam and characterize the press's treatment of the 1975 Angolan civil war. Although aware of the US covert operation there, the press maintained its silence until the failure of US policy became too obvious to ignore. In the Congo, however, the mercenaries were successful, and the press applauded.

The US press did report on the Africans' outrage at the use of the white mercenaries, at times uneasily, at times contentiously. The *Washington Post* adopted a condescending tone: 'Dislike of Premier Tshombe has impelled other African leaders to withhold help to his regime—and then to condemn him for accepting aid elsewhere. It might be useful if the new African states reconsidered their own responsibility for the worsening Congolese debacle.' According to the press, the mercenaries were decent chaps and, in any case, they were Tshombe's responsibility, not Washington's.

Those African countries that felt humiliated and threatened by US policy in the Congo accepted the inevitable because, as one US official said, 'they had their own problems to worry about and because we were successful'. The rebels' disarray and lack of charismatic leaders, along with Tshombe's removal and the eventual departure of the white mercenaries, made it easier for the Africans to turn a blind eye to what happened in the Congo. The overthrow of President Ben Bella of Algeria in 1965 and Kwame Nkrumah of Ghana a year later removed the two leaders who would have been more troublesome, and in any event Africa would soon face new dramas and new humiliations, new reminders of its weakness and dependence on the Western powers, beginning with Rhodesia's Unilateral Declaration of Independence in 1965.

It was in the Congo, in 1964 and 1965, that the United States used mercenaries in Africa for the first time, and the policy was successful at a very low cost. In late 1975, during the Angolan civil war, the Ford administration found itself in a tight spot, and again the Americans turned to mercenaries. This time, history did not smile on them. This time, thousands of well-trained Cubans greeted the 'White Giants'. This time, the mercenaries fled. The White Giants—'who had sown death and despair in African countries in return for pay'—were finally defeated.

13
The Prospects of Socialism: Ethiopia and the Horn

ODD ARNE WESTAD

The Ethiopian revolution was the most important Marxist-inspired transformation in Africa during the Cold War. Because it took place in the only major African country that had defeated the European colonialists, many people on the continent saw the new regime in Addis Ababa as embodying the leftward trend in African nationalism. While the 1960s had belonged to African socialists such as Tanzanian president Julius Nyerere, the 1970s, many argued, belonged to Marxist-Leninists such as Ethiopia's leader Mengistu Haile Mariam. Only through the science of society and the state, tested out in the Soviet Union, could a socialism with foundations strong enough to withstand internal decay and future imperialist offensives be constructed. And, as the Angolan war had shown, if imperialism attempted to strangle a homegrown revolution in its cradle, then only an alliance with Moscow would be strong enough to withstand the attack.

For the Soviet Union, the alliance with Ethiopia became by far its most important intervention in Africa. The air bridge that supplied Mengistu's forces during the war against Somalia showed that Moscow could project its military power in a direct rivalry with the United States thousands of miles from its own shores, and come out victorious. The alliance also meant that in a strategic sense the Soviet Union had become a direct influence both in the Indian Ocean and in the Red Sea area, through its access to Eritrean ports such as Massawa and Assab. Just as during the Ogaden War, from March 1977 to May 1978, it is estimated that the Soviet Union delivered weapons to the value of roughly US$1 billion to Ethiopia.

But the Soviets and their Cuban and East European allies not only supplied and trained Mengistu's armies. They also set the ideological direction for the development of the Ethiopian state, joining the new leadership in a massive attempt at fundamental social and economic reforms that promised to turn the country toward modernity. Before collapsing in 1991, in the wake of ecological disaster, mass starvation, and ethnic rebellion, the Ethiopian regime was an experiment that on a gigantic scale attempted to prove the validity of the Soviet experience for Africa, in a manner similar to the US civilian effort in Vietnam.

Soviet leaders, after initial doubts, decided to ally themselves closely with Addis Ababa in 1976 for three main reasons. First, they were influenced by the local Soviet representatives in Ethiopia, who took an increasingly favourable view of the new regime. Second, the Soviet–Cuban victory in Angola in the spring of 1976 encouraged Moscow to intervene further in Africa. Third, the language and symbols of the Ethiopian revolution matched the ideology of the Kremlin leadership, creating the belief that Moscow's Ethiopian alliance would be a viable long-term investment. For the aging Soviet Politburo, the Ethiopian revolution was further proof that the Third World was turning toward socialism and that their experience would be crucial in securing and fostering that world-historical turn.

THE ETHIOPIAN REVOLUTION AND ITS OPPONENTS

Ethiopia in 1974 was an old Christian state with a regime that under two remarkable rulers (Menelik II, who set himself up as emperor in 1889, and Haile Selassie, in power since 1930) had not only avoided European colonisation, but had expanded its power and territories in the Horn of Africa. Traditionally led by Christian Amharas—about 25 per cent of the population living in the northern and central highlands—by the 1970s the other main groups in the motley Ethiopian empire were the mostly Muslim Oromos and Somalis in the south, 40 per cent and 8 per cent respectively; the northern Tigrinya, 12 per cent; and the Eritreans—inhabitants of the former Italian coastal colony—around 8 per cent. In the early twentieth century the imperial elite became dominated by a group that proposed defensive assimilation to Western technology and organisational methods. In Ethiopia this group was called the Japanisers—the example Japan had set from the 1860s onwards in staving off European expansion, improving skills and education, and while keeping its imperial form of government had made a profound impression among the elite in Addis Ababa. Haile Selassie brought in European and American experts to train the army and to begin developing the country's industries. Still, Ethiopia remained predominantly agricultural—by the time of the revolution there were only around 50,000 workers in a population of more than 35 million.

The end of the World War II Italian occupation and the return of Haile Selassie from exile in Britain increased the prestige of the emperor and made him intensify his attempts at modern development. Hundreds of new schools and academies were set up after 1945, and, although they trained only a minuscule portion of the population, the Ethiopian elite was transformed from the aristocracy of the past to a segment that sought its legitimacy in education and skills. An increasing number of the younger members of that elite went abroad to seek further education. Many educated Ethiopians served with international organisations and, after its creation in 1963, with the Organisation of African Unity (OAU), which had permanent headquarters in Addis Ababa. But while the aging emperor in the 1960s sought to be portrayed as the father of African independence, an increasing number of Ethiopians began to regret the lack of opportunities in their own country, the backwardness of its rural areas, and the corruption and inefficiency in Haile Selassie's administration. For many, the famine that hit parts of Ethiopia in 1972–73, and the lack of a coordinated response from the government, symbolised the collapse of the emperor's attempts at modernisation.

During the 1960s Haile Selassie had increasingly looked to the United States for assistance in developing his state and society. While never completely giving up his principle of seeking help from many sources—India, Israel, Scandinavia, and the Netherlands all gave both civilian and military assistance—it was the Americans who could make a difference both in terms of security and economic development. With regard to his country's international position, it was the conflict with the Arab world—especially since the independence of neighbouring Somalia in 1960 and the simultaneous outbreak of a rebellion in Eritrea, both supported by radical Arab regimes—that topped the emperor's agenda. Meanwhile, the emperor was pushing for increased US assistance for what the CIA called his 'program of painfully gradual economic and social reform.'

Ironically, the main ideological influence on young Ethiopian radicals in the early 1970s came neither from the Soviet Bloc nor from China, but from inside the United States and Western Europe. The many students who went abroad during the 1960s often returned home profoundly impressed by the radical student movement in the West, which not only showed that the intelligentsia and students had a role to play in politics, but that they could provide an alternative focus of power to that of the government. For a significant minority of Ethiopian students Marxism came to symbolise the alternative focus, both for future development plans and for theory explaining why the current regime could not fulfil the people's aspirations. The correctness of radical views among the intelligentsia in Ethiopia was confirmed through young Westerners—often sponsored by the US Peace Corps or European variants thereof—who brought their own radical thinking to the country and who were sincerely shocked by the government neglect and mass poverty they found in Ethiopia around 1970.

There were two main reasons why Haile Selassie's rule began to crumble in early 1974. As a result of the global oil crisis, the Ethiopian state was experiencing severe difficulties with its balance of payments, and, as a result, tried to cut down on its expenditure at home. While prices, especially for imported goods, went up, salaries in the public sector declined, and fewer graduates were hired for government jobs. Added to the economic problems, the emperor's age was preventing him from the kind of resolute action he had shown to overcome crises in the past; it became easy to accuse him and his government of a lack of response to people's concerns. As unrest increased, students, teachers, and other groups began taking to the streets to protest against the emperor's policies.

Civilian opposition to the regime could by itself probably have been overcome rather easily by the imperial government. The activism that by the beginning of 1974 was spreading among junior officers in the military was much more difficult to handle.

With the government on the wane in the military and with soldiers refusing to obey orders in many areas, by April 1974 the situation in the cities was getting out of hand for the Ethiopian state. Strikes spread to the ministries and key public services, such as transport and telecommunications, and the government was afraid to call on the army to intervene, since key units might disobey orders, even if they came from the emperor himself. With power hanging in the balance, the NCOs of the armed forces in and around the capital set up a coordinating committee in June that for the first time, on behalf of the soldiers, publicly linked demands for democracy with support for the civilian anti-government opposition. Soldiers proclaiming their support for the coordinating committee began randomly arresting ranking officers, government ministers, and members of the aristocracy. By the end of June the committee (or Derg in Amharic) was in control of the capital and had assembled a national meeting of soldiers' delegations. Gradually, up to its formal emergence as a government in September, the Derg took over the functions of the emperor's various ministries and agencies. With all communications in the hands of the rebels, there was little resistance to their orders.

The first national meeting of the Derg in mid-1974 showed that while the soldiers could agree on the need for reform, they disagreed on most matters more specific. The policy they declared, under the slogan 'Ethiopia First,' was a mixture of loyalty to the empire, punishment of corrupt officials, and general improvement of people's living conditions. But under the influence of Marxist advisers whom they brought into government, the majority of the Derg moved to the Left during the fall of 1974. Those who could not, or would not, follow them on that road were dealt with harshly; the emperor was deposed in September and later strangled in prison, while the first chairman of the Derg, Lieutenant-General Aman Andom, was killed together with sixty others in November. By the end of the year the Derg was arresting both members of the old elite and those within the former opposition who challenged its authority to rule, including a few leaders of the Left mainly associated with the Marxist Ethiopian People's Revolutionary Party (EPRP).

While the way in which the old regime had died showed that it had lost the confidence of most urban Ethiopians, the new military regime at the beginning had very few adherents of its own outside the barracks. With a vague programme and obvious inability to understand some of the critical issues facing the country, the junior officers' coup could be said to raise more questions than it solved. What the fall of the imperial government did do, however, was to open Ethiopian urban society to a new climate of debate and fervent, almost frenzied, political activity. Almost all observers agree that most of this activity came from below. 'Addis Ababa became a permanent seminar,' recalls Réné Lefort.

The sense of everything being under debate was true for the political conditions within the Derg as well, although—with the future of the country at stake—the consequences were often severe for those who lost the debates. The man who more than anyone else drove the Derg toward the Left and who gradually emerged as leader of the radical wing of the new regime by late 1974 was Major Mengistu Haile Mariam, who had arrived in Addis that summer as a delegate from the Third Army Division stationed in the south. Born in 1937, Mengistu was an Amharic-speaking servant's son, whose dark skin indicated to the northern elite that he had his family origins in the colonised south. He was a graduate of Holeta Military Academy, whose only criteria for admission had been the skill to read and write the official language and basic arithmetic, and his only visit abroad was an artillery course he had attended in the United States in 1971. It was first and foremost Mengistu's ability to think about the future of the Ethiopian revolution that made it possible for him to turn these disadvantages into strengths. His humble background appealed to those among the officers who wanted profound change, but also to the urban poor and the formerly disenfranchised national minorities. At the same time, his fervent Ethiopian nationalism gave legitimacy to his increasingly radical socialist thinking.

While the majority in the Derg in the first months after the revolution was satisfied with vague declarations of 'Ethiopian socialism'—patterned roughly on Nyerere's Tanzania—Mengistu by early 1975 had adopted at least some of the thinking of his Marxist student advisers about 'scientific socialism.' His greatest political success in the first year of the revolution was pushing through a set of comprehensive socio-economic reforms, by far the most important of which was a land reform campaign that regularised the land-holding patterns in what had been a complex, localised, and mostly feudal system. The Derg declared all rural land 'the property of the Ethiopian people', while dividing it up for cultivation by those who were willing to join in cooperatives or peasants' associations. Alongside land reform went a massive campaign for social equality and literacy in the Ethiopian countryside, and especially in the south. Thousands of students in the cities joined the 'brigades' that the government sent to rural areas to improve conditions. Their enthusiasm gave the Derg its first mass following.

But, as they penetrated deeper into the lowland regions in which the Ethiopian state earlier had had little influence, radical activists from the cities began running into trouble. Promoting land reform as a principle was not particularly difficult. Breaking up local patterns of power and social customs placed the students at great risk, mostly provoked by their own behaviour. In Maale, in the south, they met with disaster.

By late 1975 local power holders in areas all over the country had declared war on the regime, and it was only by using the army that the Derg gradually began to regain control over the situation. In the cities, at the same time, the government came under pressure from leftist organisations that criticised it for not going far enough in reform or for not having legitimacy from the working class. After unsuccessful attempts at incorporating all the leftist movements into a Provisional Office for Mass Organisational Affairs (POMOA), the Derg in April 1976 lost patience with its leftist critics. Declaring those who were not willing to join POMOA enemies of the revolution, the head of the Derg, Teferi Bante, and his deputy, Mengistu, started an intense persecution of leftist critics, most of whom were arrested, executed, or driven into exile.

While splitting the Left and maximising its number of enemies among the moderates and in traditional Ethiopian society, the Derg continued on its radical trajectory. Taking up many of the ideas of the Marxist-Leninists, in 1976 it replaced 'Ethiopian socialism' with what the leaders called the National Democratic Revolution Programme of Ethiopia. The Derg now declared that its aim was the complete elimination of feudalism, bureaucratic capitalism and imperialism from the country, to pave the way for transition towards socialism. It was a programme based on the Soviet experience, couched in a language that was immediately recognisable in Marxist terms, but which had little resonance with most Ethiopians.

The move to the Left did nothing to help the Derg with the nationalities issue, which fast became a key problem in 1976–77. Foremost among the many separatist movements that challenged the Ethiopian regime was the Eritrean People's Liberation Front (EPLF), a Marxist group that had received substantial support from South Yemen, the GDR, Cuba, and the Soviet Union. With the left wing within the Derg steadfastly refusing to compromise on 'one inch of national territory', as they called it, the EPLF gradually took control of most of rural Eritrea, leaving only the main cities in the hands of the Ethiopians. For Mengistu, especially, no negotiations with the Eritreans or other national movements were possible until they had recognised the 'leading role of the national government'. When the foreign affairs spokesman for the Derg, Sisay Habte, had the courage to suggest otherwise, Mengistu had him purged and shot.

After the execution of Sisay in July 1976, the regime seemed to be dissolving from within. Because of his willingness to sacrifice others for the cause of socialism, Mengistu began losing the confidence of some of his long-time associates within the Derg. At the same time armed attacks against the government by separatists, left-wing dissenters, and by representatives of the old regime intensified. By the end of the year few observers in Addis believed that the Derg could stay in charge much longer. Mengistu's response was to take complete power within the committee. In a firefight at government headquarters in early February 1977 Teferi Bante, the head of state, was killed with five of his key supporters. Thereafter Mengistu unleashed what he unabashedly called the 'Red Terror'—an attempt to kill as many as possible of the regime's real or imagined enemies, and thereby to force the population in the areas held by the Derg to obedience.

Although Mengistu would never have believed it, it was the Red Terror that led the United States to its final break with his regime. In the words of Paul Henze, who served in the US embassy in Addis and later on President Carter's National Security Council staff, the United States in the early 1970s had 'stood aside as Haile Selassie's authority eroded'.

To the Carter administration, with its emphasis on human rights as a guiding principle in foreign policy, the Ethiopian regime stood out as a sore spot from the moment the new president entered the White House. Receiving plentiful CIA information about the intensification of the Red Terror, the president immediately ordered a review of US links with Mengistu's regime, including Kagnew, the sensitive US-operated communications base at Asmara, Eritrea.

According to Washington, time had run out for the revolutionary experiment in Ethiopia, and it wanted to be in on picking up the pieces, at least if that could help driving the Soviets out.

THE EMERGENCE OF THE SOVIET–ETHIOPIAN ALLIANCE

Back in 1974, the Soviet embassy in Addis Ababa had had little sympathy for the Ethiopian radicals. The overthrow of Haile Selassie did not do much to change the embassy's perspective.

The Kremlin had few positive reports from its representatives in Addis Ababa to build on when the Provisional Military Administrative Council (PMAC) in January 1975 approached the Soviet Union in search of military assistance. The key problem for the new Ethiopian leaders was military assistance.

Why did the new Ethiopian regime decide to push so hard for an alliance with the Soviet Union? One reason was the wish to lessen the dependence on the United States in terms of military supplies. In the eyes of the radical wing of the Derg the relationship with the United States was closely associated with the policies of the old regime, and they suspected Washington of supporting counter-revolutionary groups. Mengistu and the radicals also identified the United States with Western imperialism, which they viewed as a threat to socialist movements across the African continent. This view became particularly pronounced as US criticism of the Ethiopian government mounted in the wake of the first purges within the Derg in late 1974.

Achieving an alliance with the Soviet Union would also provide the Derg with much-needed legitimacy among its potential domestic supporters. By signing agreements with Moscow, the Derg leaders hoped to get an external confirmation of the correctness of their statist development strategy, and thereby the means to deflect criticism of the ruling elite. Being seen as having Moscow on its side could help Derg radicals stave off other left-wing movements, which challenged the socialist credentials of the young army officers.

While the Soviet alliance did not materialise, however, the Derg was happy to work out new plans for military support from the United States, as long as the Americans did not try to block its plans for social transformation. To the extent that the Ethiopian relationship to the Soviets 'does not lead to systematic opposition to the United States, it still leaves ample opportunity for continued cooperation', the State Department argued as late as mid-1976.

But the other side to the Derg's alliance policies was its leaders' conviction that the Soviet Union would offer the kind of assistance they were seeking. The Soviet embassy understood this attitude—and the kind of leverage it gave Moscow over the new Ethiopian regime.

Based on the embassy's recommendations, Moscow decided to send a military delegation to Addis. The secret mission, which arrived on 20 March 1975, was met with far-ranging demands from the Ethiopian side. The Addis regime aimed at no less than a complete reorganisation of the armed forces within a five-year plan, primarily with the help of Soviet military advisers and Soviet and East European shipments of arms and equipment. The purpose of the plan, according to the Ethiopians, was to free Addis Ababa of its dependency on the United States.

The Ethiopian delegation that left for Moscow in April brought with them a top-level message from the Derg for the Soviet leadership. In this message the Ethiopian leaders presented their concrete suggestions for military cooperation. Some needs, they said, were urgent, because of their wish to reduce Ethiopia's military dependence on the United States and to change the positive views junior officers had of America. The amount of weapons needed in the initial period was 'comparatively modest'. A total revolution in the army was necessary, however, in the longer term, the more long-term goal was the socialist transformation of the army. While opting for socialism, the Derg, in other words, foresaw a short-term coexistence of Soviet and American military aid for their regime.

Even after the Moscow negotiations, which the Ethiopians characterised as a breakthrough in their relations with the Soviets, military aid was not immediately forthcoming. The Soviet leadership remained hesitant. Although the prospect of a development toward socialism in both countries on the Horn of Africa was attractive, the uncertainties as to the political situation in Ethiopia outweighed the possible dividends. Besides, Moscow found the PMAC's request for military assistance excessive. Ambassador Ratanov made it known that the Soviet Union normally reached such high levels of military cooperation with other countries only after the development of a fifteen-year relationship—or more. But Teferi again pressed the ambassador, saying that the modernisation of Ethiopia depended on having a modern army with which to defend the revolution.

Moscow, however, could not make up its mind on whether to supply weapons to Ethiopia. The summer and fall of 1975 were disappointing for the Ethiopian leaders in terms of foreign relations. They did not understand why the Soviet Union did not respond to their requests, and on several occasions went to see the Soviet ambassador with their complaints and misgivings. On at least one occasion, the chairman of the Derg's Political Committee, Sisay Habte, pointed out to Ratanov that there were 'alternative' ways to reorganise the Ethiopian Army.

The Derg's impatience in getting Soviet support was understandable in terms of the situation in Ethiopia. The Eritrean insurgents viewed the fall of General Andom as a sign of weakness in the regime, and started new offensives against government troops. In Ogaden, the predominantly Somali region in the east, there was also new unrest. Relations with Washington seemed to be souring, in part because of US reactions against the socialist proclamations of the new regime and against its human rights record. Under these circumstances the Ethiopian regime risked finding itself 'between two chairs', as an Ethiopian official put it—to lose US support and to fail to obtain new ties with the Soviets.

When Addis finally got a response from Moscow, on 15 November 1975, the Derg deemed the proposed plans for cooperation much too limited. The new regime had gambled much of its foreign policy—and a certain portion of its domestic legitimacy—on a Soviet alliance. What Moscow offered was a trifle: assistance with military training and the delivery of communications equipment both for military and civilian use. The Derg's leaders concluded that the Soviet Union was too focused on its alliance with Somalia to deliver military equipment that really mattered to the Ethiopians. The PMAC formally rejected the agreement. Its representative Addis Tedla noted icily that the Ethiopian side understood that the difficulties of the Soviet Union stemmed from its obligations toward 'the other country of this region' (i.e., Somalia) and suggested that the negotiations be broken off for the time being. Relations between Addis and Moscow had been put in the deep freezer.

The Soviet reluctance to deliver arms to Ethiopia made the PMAC continue to honour the agreements it had already signed with the United States. But the Soviet embassy knowingly or unknowingly read the wrong message out of the continued American arms sales. The embassy also reported on increased Ethiopian contacts with Israel and China.

While warning about the effects of a Soviet refusal to sell advanced arms, Ratanov had continued to push the credits of left-wing leaders of the Ethiopian regime. It noted that Major Mengistu Haile Mariam was the most influential member of the PMAC and that he was supported by the majority of the Derg. This majority was striving for progressive reforms in Ethiopia and was seeking close relations with the socialist countries. At the same time it was ready 'to fight seriously [against] its political enemies'. The embassy emphasised that it was Mengistu who had insisted on the execution of fifty-nine 'reactionaries' in November 1974, thus showing himself to be a leader not inclined to compromises or half-measures. The aim of the ambassador was clearly to prove to Moscow that the regime in Ethiopia was becoming more reliable and manageable.

By early 1976 Ambassador Ratanov and his military attaché also underlined to Moscow the strategic use of Ethiopia for Soviet military purposes. Ratanov stressed the opportunity for the Soviet Union to increase its influence in the whole region (Ethiopia, Somalia, and Sudan) and the operational possibilities for the Red Navy in the Red Sea. He also held up the spectre of greater influence of the United States and China, if Moscow did not respond positively to the Ethiopian leaders' overtures. Building solely on relations with Somalia would be dangerous, Ratanov felt—if the other powers got into the 'vacuum' Moscow could risk losing its positions in Somalia as well.

Ratanov suggested presenting a much broader proposal for Soviet military assistance by arming the Ethiopian Navy, its anti-aircraft defence forces, and the new militia. Moscow accepted this suggestion and put it forward during the visit of an Ethiopian delegation in June 1976. But to the Soviets' surprise the PMAC rejected this offer too.

It seems very likely that the visible stubbornness of the PMAC in the negotiations was due to their confidence in a favourable outcome. The Soviet embassy suspected that both Cuban and East European representatives had hinted to Mengistu that Moscow would eventually come round.

The left wing of the Derg, led by Mengistu Haile Mariam, wanted to use their links with the Soviets both to get political assistance and to convince Moscow of their trustworthiness. They stressed their wish to learn from the Soviet practice in 'building socialism' and organising society. From his very first conversations with the Soviet ambassador, Mengistu had asked for programmes for sending young Ethiopians to Moscow for education and political training. The candidates should study the theory of CPSU activities as well as the activities of trade unions and youth and womens' associations. They should also study Marxism.

In its annual report for 1976 the Soviet embassy told Moscow that 'the important practical results of the programme has been the introduction, on the orders of the PMAC, of obligatory study of the theory of scientific socialism in the army, police, governmental institutions, factories, and large farms'. In addition, discussions and publications in the press on the questions of socialism became a usual practice. 'All this,' the embassy proudly declared, 'has led to a considerable growth of interest in the theory of Marxism–Leninism and in its practical realisation in the Soviet Union and other socialist countries, which [again] has created the bases for a strengthening of our ideological influence.' The Ethiopian regime, in the Soviet embassy's view, had all the hallmarks of wanting to develop a state of socialist orientation.

The Soviet ambassador also found Mengistu Haile Mariam's ruthless removal of political rivals to be to his liking. In mid-July 1976, on the eve of the visit of the Ethiopian delegation to Moscow, Mengistu's most prominent opponent in the Derg, Sisay Habte, was purged and executed with eighteen of his supporters. By eliminating his enemies Mengistu became a 'resolute and uncompromising leader', in ambassador Ratanov's view. Watching the activities of Mengistu's supporters within the Derg with approval, local Soviet representatives noted the similarity with the early revolutionary experience in Russia with rooting out enemies of the people. And although they noted that Mengistu's enemies still had a foothold within the Derg, they now expected the 'Ethiopian revolutionary forces' and their agenda of social justice to gain the upper hand. By the end of 1976 the Soviet embassy no longer had any words of approval for the regime's left-wing critics.

Based on the embassy's reports, Moscow during 1976 gradually became convinced that extensive aid for the Ethiopian regime could not be put off any longer. On 14 December the two sides signed the first 'basic' agreement on military cooperation between the Soviet Union and Ethiopia. This agreement was a breakthrough not only for the PMAC but also for the Soviet leaders in their views of the region. They must have seen the possible consequences the signing might have for Soviet relations with Somalia and for the regional situation as a whole. But by 1976 the Soviets had already started to doubt the reliability of the regime of Siad Barre in Somalia. Already the previous summer, when commenting on the situation in Eritrea, the Addis embassy had observed that some Arab countries were trying to make the Red Sea an 'Arabian lake', something which would be 'a loss for other countries' [read the Soviet Union]. The embassy had argued that the influence of oil-rich 'reactionary' Arab countries such as Saudi Arabia and Kuwait on the positions of other Arab countries and on Somalia was on the increase.

However, even after the signing of the Soviet–Ethiopian agreement on military assistance the Moscow leaders were not ready to sacrifice their alliance with Mogadishu. Under the 1974 treaty of friendship and cooperation with Somalia the Soviets had sent US$30 million worth of arms, equipping the Somali Army with hundreds of tanks and dozens of modern fighter aircraft. On its side, the Soviet Union had built some of its largest naval facilities abroad at Berbera and Mogadishu. In the winter of 1976/77 Moscow focused its energies on finding ways of preserving its relations with its old ally, while beginning to build a stronger and ideologically based connection with Addis Ababa. At the end of January 1977 Leonid Brezhnev sent a personal and urgent request to Siad Barre that he reconsider the Somali position on Ethiopia and refrain from exacerbating the conflict.

The International Department and the Foreign Ministry held several crisis meetings on the situation in the Horn in early spring 1977. The reports coming in from both Addis and Mogadishu that regular Somali units had joined the Western Somali Liberation Front and other rebel groups fighting in the Ogaden made Moscow fearful that it would not be able—even in the short term—to balance its old and new alliances in the region. The Soviets had initially been sceptical of a December 1976 joint Cuban–South Yemeni mediation initiative, because of the outspoken Ethiopian resistance to it during the signing of the Soviet–Ethiopian agreement. But by February 1977 the situation in the Ogaden had deteriorated to such an extent that Moscow saw no other way out than to join Fidel Castro's initiative.

The real turning point in Moscow's approach to the region was Mengistu's coup on 3 February 1977, during which he assassinated most of his remaining rivals within the Derg. Although not informed in advance, the Soviets viewed the coup as a giant step forward in its relations with Ethiopia. On the morning of 4 February a representative of Mengistu contacted the Soviet ambassador and requested an urgent meeting. They met that evening. Mengistu set forward his version of the events in the Derg headquarters the previous day and assured Ratanov that his actions would strengthen the Ethiopian revolution. He asked for the support of the Soviet Union and socialist countries. Ratanov promised such support, without mentioning the killings and the reign of terror in the capital. Just a few days later the Soviet government issued an appeal to Arab countries and Somalia with the blessing of the Ethiopian leadership. Mengistu's putsch had reinforced Soviet confidence in the regime.

Right after taking power, Mengistu also appealed to other socialist powers for urgent assistance. In a letter to the GDR's Erich Honecker on 9 March 1977, Mengistu tried to portray events in Ethiopia as a counter-offensive by imperialism:

> During the past ten years, the oppressed peoples of Latin America, Indochina and Africa have succeeded in overcom-

> ing imperialism. . . . Now, [imperialism is] making a final but desperate assault in order to reverse the revolution of the oppressed people of Ethiopia and liquidate progressive revolutionaries. . . . We hope that you will respond urgently to our call for assistance in arming the Ethiopian masses, so that this young revolution on the African soil can forge ahead.

While keeping up its attempts at mediation, the Soviet government in early spring 1977 began to pour arms and military equipment into Ethiopia. According to Western estimates, by mid-April more than one hundred tanks and armoured personnel carriers were delivered from the Soviet Union. During his May visit to Moscow Mengistu obtained from the Soviets a commitment for between US$350 million and US$450 million of arms. In the spring of 1977, Moscow had overcome its former hesitancy with regard to the Ethiopian regime, in spite of continued advice from its other friends in the region—such as Iraq's Saddam Hussein—that the Ethiopians were not to be trusted.

The Mengistu regime, now confident of its own power, acted immediately to bring Ethiopian foreign relations in line with Soviet wishes. On 23 April the PMAC announced that five American organisations in Ethiopia—the Asmara base, the American consulate in Asmara, USIS offices throughout the country, the US Military Assistance Advisory Group office and the US Navy's medical research centre—should be closed forthwith. In its report to Moscow the Soviet embassy noted with satisfaction that 'these steps of the PMAC are its most important political action directed against US interests in Ethiopia . . . [which shows] the deepening of the revolutionary processes in Ethiopia . . . and the intensification of the struggle against internal reaction supported by imperialism as well as the beginning of a broad cooperation of Ethiopia with the Soviet Union, Cuba, GDR and other socialist countries, particularly in the area of military affairs'.

SOVIET INTERVENTIONISM AND THE COLLAPSE OF *DÉTENTE*

From the fall of 1977 onwards the number of civilian Soviet advisers in Ethiopia increased dramatically. By early 1979 the combined number of experts—civilian and military—from the socialist countries had reached more than seven thousand; the single largest foreign assistance programme the Soviets ever undertook after China in the 1950s. In a process coordinated by chief advisers working in part out of the Soviet embassy, foreign experts were in place in all ministries and departments, attempting to oversee and influence the direction that the building of socialism in Ethiopia would take. In some parts of the government bureaucracy, such as water supplies, energy, and transport, Soviets, East Germans, Bulgarians, and Cubans were carrying out most of the work with the help of interpreters (mostly from English), while suitable Ethiopian personnel were being trained in Eastern Europe or the Soviet Union. In Moscow the International Department was working overtime to supply the kinds of experts the Ethiopians needed—one official remembers sending off half the workers from a chocolate factory in Armenia to satisfy the needs of the Ethiopian revolution for the immediate construction of a confectionery industry.

The chief priority for the Soviet political advisers in Addis Ababa was the construction of a Marxist-Leninist party that could take charge of the Ethiopian revolution. While soldiers could set the country on the road toward socialist transformation, Mengistu was told, there needed to be a party to complete it. Mengistu heartily agreed. 'A shortcoming of the Ethiopian revolution is that it has no political organisation which, either in secret or openly, has been tested in struggle and which, equipped with working-class ideology, would give it direction', Mengistu declared when announcing the setting up of a Commission for the Organising of the Workers' Party of Ethiopia in 1979. But the problem with setting up a party, as the Soviet advisers well knew, was that the Derg had already executed, purged, or driven into exile most Ethiopian Marxists. The Soviets and the Cubans wanted Mengistu to make peace with some of the surviving leaders and to allow them to return to help set up the party. Mengistu understandably refused. By the end of 1979 Soviet advisers were telling the Derg that the foundations for constructing a Marxist-Leninist vanguard party simply did not yet exist in Ethiopia, and that much effort was needed to raise the consciousness of the workers to the point that such a party could be brought into existence. As a result of the stalemate that ensued, it took another five years—up to 1984, when Soviet influence was on the wane—before the Workers' Party of Ethiopia was founded. Until then, the Organising Committee was run as a government department.

The other big headache for the Soviet advisers in Addis Ababa was the Derg's ongoing war against the separatist movements in the northern coastal province of Eritrea. This conflict, which had lasted ever since imperial Ethiopia took control of the former Italian colony in the 1950s, was particularly troublesome to the Soviets because the leaderships of both the Eritrean People's Liberation Front (EPLF) and the Eritrean Liberation Front (ELF) were avowedly Marxist. Furthermore, the EPLF had received Soviet funding and been trained by the Cubans up to 1975. But piling pressure on Mengistu and the EPLF to find a peaceful solution simply did not help. The Soviet position—that Eritrea should remain a part of Ethiopia with extensive autonomy—was unacceptable to both sides. The Eritreans claimed that their former friends were pressing them to give up their fundamental goal of independence. Mengistu privately told Moscow that any deal on Eritrea 'would throw him to the nationalist wolves', making a formal request that his allies also send forces to Eritrea.

The two sides met several times, unsuccessfully, in East Berlin in the spring of 1978 to find a solution. Honecker attempted to get Soviet support in dictating a compromise to the Eritreans and the Ethiopians, but the Moscow International Department refused. Instead the East Germans learnt in early April that Soviet advisers had begun participating in the offensives against Eritrea and that advanced Soviet weapons had been supplied to the northern front.

Already by summer 1978, a few months after the decisive victory in the Ogaden, Soviet enthusiasm for Mengistu's regime had begun to deteriorate. The continuous infighting among the Ethiopian left infuriated Moscow's local representatives, who were reduced to writing extensive reports on conflicts such as the one between the 'Ethiopian Marxist-Leninist Revolutionary Organisation' and a group calling itself 'The Revolutionary Flame'.

While the Soviet leaders had been agonising over their options in the Horn of Africa, Moscow's intervention in the region had further antagonised the Carter administration. Coming at the same time as the president realised that there would be no quick breakthrough in the negotiations over nuclear arms limitation, Carter was increasingly sensitive to political pressure from the right, which claimed that he was making too many concessions to the Soviets in order to rescue *détente*. During a tense meeting with Soviet Foreign Minister Andrei Gromyko in May 1978, after the Ethiopian victory, Carter told him that the United States was strongly concerned 'over Soviet efforts to increase Soviet influence in Africa by supply of weapons and by encouragement of Cuban involvement'. For the US right wing, Carter's measures were too little, too late.

In 1978 most policy makers in Moscow were unaware of the profound effects their Third World policies were having on American perceptions of the future of the *détente* process. To Leonid Brezhnev and to the majority of his colleagues, the principle of superpower equality that they felt had been established in their negotiations with the Nixon administration not only entitled them to intervene in areas where local revolutions were coming under threat, but also to keep their Third World policies separate from the bilateral relationship to the United States. The Americans, after all, had not asked Moscow before they intervened against Allende's government in Chile or against other leftist movements elsewhere in the world. What had changed in the early and mid-1970s, the majority in the Politburo felt, was that the overall political trends in the South had turned toward the left, and that the Soviet Union had been able to protect, assist, and guide some of the Third World radical movements through the crucial stages of erecting revolutionary institutions and beginning to form new states. The Americans may protest these developments, the Soviets felt, but in the end Washington would not risk wrecking the overall process of *détente* because of developments in poor countries far away from the key strategic areas of the world.

It would take several years before the Soviet leadership began understanding how determined the US political elite was to resist the Soviet Union competing globally as an equal. But well before Moscow began realising the damage its Third World policies had done to its most cherished international aim—*détente* with the United States—opinions started to diverge within the Kremlin on the merits of Soviet involvement in the South in terms of Marxist-Leninist political theory. Spurred by the inability of Soviet advisers to influence the course of the Ethiopian revolution after military victory had been won, a few senior experts in 1978 began questioning the character of some of the national-democratic revolutions in the Third World. The burning issue was the degree to which a military regime such as Mengistu's could initiate the transition to socialism without itself being transformed through class-based action from below. In other words, did the Soviet Union and its allies through their support for such regimes risk standing in the way of the next stage in the revolution?

Among a small group of influential academics—mostly centred around the Institute of the Economy of the World Socialist System (IEMSS), headed by Oleg Bogomolov, and the Institute of Oriental Studies (IOS), headed by Evgenii Primakov—these questions were taken even further. Did some 'progressive' regimes in the Third World, through their inability to form united fronts with the local bourgeoisie, represent a 'Bonapartist' road away from the economic and social change that was needed to develop the working class? If that was the case, the Soviet Union might not only be risking its own position in these countries by supporting regimes that were by their very nature fickle and untrustworthy, but it might also be hindering the natural social development that at some stage in the future could begin to move these countries toward socialism. While these more radical Marxist perspectives were limited to small groups of intellectuals, there is no doubt that by the end of 1978 the broader disenchantment with Soviet Third World interventionism had spilled over to the key institutions of the government, such as the International Department and the KGB.

Within the institutions, it is striking how many in the mid-1970s had been enthusiastic supporters of further Soviet involvement in the Third World—and especially of the Angolan and Ethiopian interventions—yet by the end of the decade found themselves among the sceptics.

Much of the bitterness and disillusionment among some Soviet policy advisers undoubtedly came out of their personal encounters with the Third World. Up to the mid-1970s very few Soviet party leaders had had much personal experience with longer stays in Third World countries. The exceptions, of course, were Cuba and Vietnam, but the difficulties they encountered there could easily be brushed under the carpet in view of the front-line position these countries held in the battle against imperialism. The unwillingness to take Soviet advice among its new allies—Angola, Mozambique, Somalia, Ethiopia, South Yemen, Afghanistan—was quite another challenge. Soviets who served in these countries invariably reported back on the inefficiency, superstition, and dirt that were everywhere in society, and which only a methodical and theoretically correct transition to socialism could overcome. In light of the urgency with which a 'Soviet' solution was needed, the obstinacy and bad will with which local leaders often met the proposals of their foreign advisers appeared disheartening, and made some of the visitors lose taste for the whole project or at least want to curtail it. Rarely stopping to consider why their plans met local resistance, or contemplating the fact that local leaders may have understood the political complexities of their own countries better than the Soviets, the chief advisers tended to veer between recommendations of retrenchment or solidification of Soviet control as remedies for their troubles. For more junior experts, analysts, and agents in the field, the best course was simply to avoid difficulties by filing reports showing the fulfilment of the plan, just as they had been used to doing when living in the Soviet Union.

For the peoples of the Horn of Africa the war and the interventions of the late 1970s would beget apocalyptic consequences. On the losing side, the very existence of the Somalian state came under threat as Siad Barre's regime declined. By defecting from Marxism, Siad had gambled on receiving Arab and Western aid after the war. When very little was forthcoming, he tried to increase the government's income by introducing levies and taxes in the provinces, thereby reigniting much of the clan sentiment that the government had outlawed in 1973. With Ethiopia fomenting resistance against the government, and Siad's legitimacy in free fall—this was the man, after all, whom all Somalians had first been taught to revere as part of the socialist trinity of Comrade Marx, Comrade Lenin, and Comrade Siad—the whole Somalian state structure began to shake. When, in 1988, Siad tried one final desperate twist by allying himself with Mengistu's regime, all the Somali clans had had enough of him. Since Siad had effectively undermined any positive need that any Somali might see in a centralised state, the result of his fall was not regime change but civil war and clan rule. Any attempt—including that of the United States in the 1990s—of putting the Somalian state back together again has so far ended in utter failure.

In Ethiopia the victory and the Soviet support led Mengistu to intensify his attempts at transforming state and society. The nationalisation of land and the setting up of collective farming, which initially had increased productivity somewhat, provided fewer and fewer returns after 1979. The Derg's answer—with the help of its international allies—was to impose more intensive farming methods to increase short-term output. Together with the nationalisation of forest areas—which led to a free-for-all by peasants in need of firewood—the introduction of intensive farming led to massive soil erosion in the early 1980s. When the regime tried to push production to the limit in order to feed the army and the cities—and, hubristically, to begin exporting agricultural products—a crisis was in the making. With a difficult harvest and peasants in some areas keeping their products away from the market in order to prevent government confiscation, agricultural supplies collapsed. In 1984, in Wollo province alone, 500,000–750,000 people died of hunger. It was, in the words of the regime's own chief relief commissioner, Dawit Wolde Giorgis, a famine that never needed to have happened. It devastated Ethiopia and, with it, the dreams the regime had for the introduction of socialism in the Horn of Africa.

Part Five

Conflict, War, and Intervention

INTRODUCTION

In the aftermath of the end of the Cold War, there was much optimism about resolving outstanding conflicts around the world. Africa unfortunately belied that trend; indeed, conflict intensified in the 1990s, both within and between states, and brought forth new interventions. Prunier in his discussion, expertly weaves together the different levels and aspects of such conflicts, which is needed for a deep understanding of them. As conflict changed, so did demands for intervention. Much of the mainstream literature tended initially to assume that such intervention in African conflicts, for example in Somalia, was practically and normatively straightforward. Al-Qaq suggests reasons to doubt this: illustrating how the United Nations, and its modes of intervention, have changed since its foundation. Such critics, even if controversial, add their weight to the reflection on the growing experience of intervention itself, helping to spark a much more sustained debate about what has come to be called "peacebuilding." Eriksen provides a useful summary of that debate in the context of the Congo.

14
Rebel Movements and Proxy Warfare: Uganda, Sudan, and the Congo (1986–99)

GÉRARD PRUNIER

SUDANESE AND UGANDANS: SITTING ON THE ISLAMIC FAULT LINE

In spite of being neighbours and of both having been colonised by the British, it is difficult to imagine two countries more dissimilar than Uganda and the Sudan. Uganda is a medium-sized African country, with a relatively cohesive climate and landscape, while the Sudan is a multi-ecological giant whose identity is hopelessly split between an Arab North, a Black Christian South and an often overlooked African Muslim West, closely related to the Central African sultanates of Kanem, Bornu and Sokoto. Sudan's independence process was mainly an Arab affair. Until the 1980s, in spite of the long-drawn-out conflict between northern and southern Sudan and the Ugandan civil violence of the Idi Amin and Obote II regimes, there had been a limited amount of cross-border interference. Sudanese refugees had crossed into Uganda in the 1960s and Ugandan refugees had moved to the Sudan after the overthrow of Idi Amin in 1979. But none of these movements had entailed more than extremely temporary political interferences in each other's affairs.

Things were to change drastically with the advent of Yoweri Museveni to power in Kampala in 1986. One of the main problems came from a (wrong) personal inference. In the 1960s both Yoweri Museveni and Colonel John Garang, the then SPLA leader, had briefly been students at the University of Dar-es-Salaam, then the Mecca of young African left-wingers. When Museveni came to power the Sudanese regime was immediately persuaded that Uganda would become a rear base for the Sudanese rebel movement, although there were no signs of that. The whole 'radical student theory' was based on a mistake in the first place, since Museveni and Garang had attended Dar-es-Salaam University in different years and had hardly known each other during the two or three months when they had been there together. Fantasies notwithstanding, there was no 'Dar-es-Salaam left-wing old boys' network'. As for Ugandan support for the SPLA, it was non-existent till 1993 and there were times when a simple appointment with the Kampala SPLA representative (who did not even have an office) could cause him to be questioned and temporarily detained by the Ugandan police for 'unauthorised political activities'. Museveni was extremely careful not to antagonise Khartoum and when he finally resorted to helping the SPLA, it was only because his earlier policy of non-interference had ultimately failed to produce results.

THE MAKING OF ANTI-MUSEVENI GUERRILLAS

Khartoum's first efforts at helping the anti-Museveni forces had started very early on in 1986, when the new Ugandan regime had had to face resistance from the defeated Acholi in the North. The former chief of the Ugandan Military Council army, Acholi Brigadier Basilio Okello, had crossed into Sudan after being defeated by the National Resistance Army (NRA), and the Sudanese army had given him help. This first attempt at interfering with the new Ugandan regime did not work out very well, because the political guerrilla movement launched by Okello and his friends was soon bled dry of its men and equipment by a strange millenarian cult led by a young prophetess, Alice Auma nicknamed 'Lakwena', 'the messenger'. Alice's mystic leadership was more attractive to the bitter and disoriented young Acholi soldiers who had just lost power than the conventional political manifestos of Brigadier Okello and his former government associates. Alice and her bands of *dawa*-smeared combatants fought their way down to the south and were only stopped by superior firepower as they were nearing Jinja in October 1987. Alice, who was wounded, took refuge in Kenya and the movement almost collapsed. But Joseph Kony, a nephew or a cousin of Alice, also declared that he had had visions and laid claim to the rebellious prophet's mantle, creating the Lord's Salvation Army (LSA). Between 1988 and 1993 he kept a small guerrilla war going in north Acholi, in almost impenetrable terrain close to the Sudanese border. Up to late 1991 his position remained extremely difficult because the SPLA was on the other side of the border and was very hostile to the LSA. Although the Sudanese rebels were not getting any help from Museveni at the time, they were careful to stay on good terms with him, because Uganda was a major conduit for humanitarian aid channelled by lorry from Kenya to SPLA-occupied Equatoria.

The fall in 1991 of Colonel Mengistu's regime in neighbouring Ethiopia was to prove a boon for Joseph Kony and his men. The SPLA, which had been close to the former communist regime, suddenly lost its main source of support, and soon afterwards (August 1991) it split into two mutually hostile wings when its Nuer and Dinka units started fighting each other after the loss of their Ethiopian support had heightened their internal contradictions. The Sudanese government, which had already taken an interest in the Kony rebellion but had not been able to access it geographically, began to make contact with the LRA, following two successful LRA offensives in early 1992 and late 1993. The Sudanese army had acquired control of several stretches of the Sudan-Uganda border and Sudanese military security invited Kony to Juba where, in exchange for a symbolic smattering of Islam (some of the fighters took Muslim names and pretended to convert), he obtained serious military aid. The LRA, which had been down to about 300 fighters in mid-1993, was suddenly up to over 2,000 well-equipped troops by March 1994, and was in a position to raid the whole of northern Uganda.

It was then that the situation began to be seriously internationalised and that Zaire became involved. During the late 1960s and throughout the 1970s, Mobutu had followed policies on foreign intervention which he was relatively able to enforce, the clearest ones being the support he gave the FNLA and later UNITA in the Angolan civil war. But after the 1977 and 1978 Shaba invasions, and later when the democratisation process began in 1990, his capacity to control territory shrank radically. Contraband goods and, what was more serious, military equipment began to transit freely through Zairian territory, since there were only bribes to pay to the border guards. From then on, whatever political projections beyond Zaire's borders still occurred were carried out passively. An example of this 'passive action' was the right of passage through Zairian territory which President Mobutu secretly granted to the Sudanese government. Khartoum had approached Mobutu some time during mid-1994 and obtained his approval to run supply convoys from Wau in Bahr-el-Ghazal down to northern Uganda through the Central African Republic and the Uele Province of Zaire, allowing it to bypass SPLA positions in Western Equatoria and/or to attack Ugandan territory. Not only did the LRA now get some of its supplies through Zaire but Sudanese army security was able to contact the Kakwa and the Aringa, former Idi Amin soldiers who had been living in the area since 1979, and reorganise them into a fighting front. The West Nile Bank Liberation Front (WNBLF) was born in November 1994 in Faradje and, with Sudanese help, immediately started harassing Ugandan forces in West Nile from the Zairian side of the border.

This was bound to attract some kind of Ugandan reaction, and it did, but not immediately in the 'triple border' zone. There was another region further to the south, around the Ruwenzori and Virunga volcanic chain, where trouble between Uganda and Zaire had long been endemic, and in which Sudan was later to become embroiled. On the Ugandan side, this was an area of long-running conflict between the central government and the Bakonjo and Baamba tribes who live astride the Uganda–Congo border. In the early 1900s the Bakonjo had arbitrarily been made subjects of the Tooro kingdom, because the Tooro monarchy had rallied to the colonial occupation and the British wanted to reinforce it vis-à-vis its anti-British neighbour, Bunyoro. The Bakonjo and their Baamba neighbours accepted their subject status with patience, but ended up asking the colonial authorities for their own district in the 1950s. They were refused this, and launched a low-intensity guerrilla struggle against the British, which they continued throughout all the independent governments following decolonisation. This movement was called *Rwenzururu* and became famous as a kind of local folk epic.

After years of struggle the *Rwenzururu* leadership finally signed an armistice with the Obote II government in August 1982. The man who had been instrumental in this reconciliation was himself a Mukonjo called Amon Bazira, who had understood that the movement was by then largely middle-class and that it was possible to co-opt it with some commercial advantages. But Bazira, who was a staunch UPC supporter, left Uganda in 1985, after the fall of Obote. He later approached President Mobutu and President Daniel arap Moi of Kenya, both of whom had their own reasons to dislike the new Ugandan regime. They both supported a revival of the Bakonjo rebellion under the new label of the National Army for the Liberation of Uganda (NALU), a grander-sounding name than *Rwenzururu.* In fact, NALU was only a cut-rate version of *Rwenzururu,* without the popular appeal. But money could do wonders in an impoverished peasant milieu in a marginal region of Uganda. NALU soon grew sufficiently to become an irritant, and in 1992 Bazira was shot dead in a Nairobi street, most probably by Ugandan agents.

Museveni, who had always seen Mobutu as the African stooge of imperialism incarnate, was even further angered by the NALU episode and started looking for ways of getting back at the Zairian dictator. He was able to find them on the other side of the Virunga Mountains, across from the Ugandan town of Kasese, where the waning of the Congolese rebellion in 1965 had left lingering guerrilla remnants around Beni. Later, in 1986, groups of young Batembo, Bahunde and Banande who resented Mobutu's protection for local Banyarwanda land-grabbing, initiated a new low-intensity anti-government guerrilla army here under the leadership of Joseph Marandura's son. They had called their movement the Parti de la Libération Congolais (PLC), but their activity was mostly limited to raiding Ugandan border villages to steal goats and chickens. In 1988–89 they were severely mauled by the *Forces Armées Zaïroises* (FAZ) and forced to withdraw either north, all the way into the Garamba National Park, or deeper into the Beni Forest.

In November 1994 President Museveni had discussed the possibility of overthrowing Mobutu with a number of Congolese opponents. Although they had decided not to act at the time, this had not prevented the Ugandan External Service Organisation (ESO) from helping the Parti de la Libération Congolais. Colonel Kahinda Otafiire, one of the key Ugandan secret service operatives and a personal friend of Museveni, had recruited into the PLC an idealistic and dynamic young Mutetela named André Kisase Ngandu. Over the next two years Kisase was to become 'Uganda's man' in eastern Zaire, looking for ways of eventually transforming the PLC from a micro-guerrilla into a more serious military force. In the meantime, in spite of its limited size, the PLC could be used to retaliate in case of Zairian offences. On 17 June 1994 a group of uncontrolled Zairian soldiers had crossed the Ugandan border near Arua in West Nile and looted everything they could find, taking two Ugandan prisoners back with them. As this came in the wake of WNBLF cross-border actions, the ESO sent the PLC boys across from Bundibungyo to attack the FAZ in reprisal. They were allowed to retreat back into Uganda after their hit-and-run raid, and the Ugandan Ministry of Foreign Affairs denied the whole thing.

At the same time as Uganda sought to undermine President Mobutu, Kampala was pressuring the UN High Commission for Refugees to repatriate the so-called 'Amin's refugees' from Zaire's Province Orientale, since they provided the ready pond where Sudanese agents were fishing for WNBLF recruits. Meanwhile, arms trafficking continued to grow between Zaire, Sudan and northern Uganda, with disastrous consequences for the civilians. But soon a new dimension was to be added to this already strained situation.

In January 1995 a Muslim group calling itself the Uganda Muslim Liberation Army (UMLA) formally 'declared war' on the NRM government. The reasons it gave in its communiqué were somewhat hazy: the UMLA accused Museveni of having killed Muslims in 1979 at Nyamitaga, near Mbarara and later in 1983 at Butambala, near Mpigi. But there were two interesting points in the document: first, there was an obvious effort at presenting Museveni as an enemy of the whole Ugandan Muslim community by using somewhat contorted 'historical' arguments; second, most of the document's signatories were Muslim Baganda—a completely new development since, in the past, and notably during the 1981–86 bush war against Obote, the Baganda Muslims had given the NRA discreet but significant support. Historically, it is not even exaggerated to say that in early 1981 it was the timely financial and political support of Prince Badru Kakungulu which had enabled Museveni to turn his small band of outlaws—he had started his anti-Obote revolt with 26 men—into an efficient armed organisation.

But it was soon apparent that the puzzle of this role switch had more to do with Baganda factional politics than with Islam. During the bush war of 1981–86 and its immediate aftermath, the Baganda, who had been the main target of Obote's repression, had supported the NRA. However, soon after the end of the war the old and well-known ultra-monarchist tendencies, which had triggered the whole Ugandan catastrophe back in the 1960s, began to resurface. The monarchists, in an effort to resuscitate their movement, had targeted Museveni for a number of imagined ills, designed to mobilise Baganda opinion against the central government. It was partly to appease these neo-monarchists that Museveni had restored the kingdom of Buganda in 1993, albeit in a diminished and non-political form. But this 'clipped restoration' was precisely what the neo-monarchists could not accept. A number of them secretly created the Allied Democratic Movement (ADM) in London in January 1995. Later ADM documents are politically very crude, but can be understood if seen as in the direct tradition of the men who had pushed *Kabaka* Mutesa II into his ill-conceived confrontational politics of the 1960s. In the 1990s, even though he enjoyed full support from the US, and the Soviet Union had disappeared, these same people still called Museveni a communist. Talking with them could give one a feeling of being a time traveller, since their argumentation in the late 1990s was still pure 1965 *Kabaka Yekka* vintage, complete with its right-wing Cold War rhetoric. These were upper-class Protestant Baganda, but political opportunism was soon to bring them into a most unnatural alliance with the radical Muslim UMLA lumpen proletariat.

In fact, both the ADM and the UMLA had been born at the same time and both were led by Baganda. But there was a clear sharing of responsibilities: the ADM could recruit among ordinary Baganda (who are mostly Christians), while the UMLA could recruit both among the small Baganda Muslim community and among non-Baganda Muslims who tend to be at the bottom of Ugandan society. The two rebel movements complemented each other and cleverly exploited the complex interweaving of ethnic and class politics typical of most of today's Africa: the core leadership of the two organisations was the same (radical Baganda neo-monarchists in search of troops to fight Museveni), but the rank-and-file was anything they could pick up, mostly very poor people from a variety of tribes. The movement soon grew impressively. Later it was interesting to talk with UPDF officers who seemed puzzled as to what the guerrilla war was all about. There were two things which seemed to disturb them deeply: one, that the guerrilla war was not an ethnic one; two, that the prisoners they captured in Bundibungyo told them that they had been promised money to fight. The going rate was about USh500,000 for an ordinary fighter (enough to buy a kiosk from which to sell cigarettes and sodas at the bus park) and USh5 million for an officer (enough to buy a taxi). The UPDF officers were NRA veterans who would say: 'we fought for an ideal; how can these people fight for money, especially so little money?'. It was hard to get them to admit that, if their 'ideal' had brought them a certain modicum of prosperity, they were now facing the very people whom the so-called 'Ugandan economic miracle' had passed by; the notion that this social marginalisation was not attached to any given tribe, as had been the case in the past, seemed even stranger.

Since the 1987 monetary reform Uganda has enjoyed on average a five per cent yearly rate of economic growth, which puts it in the very limited group of IMF African success stories of the last fifteen years. But the product of that growth has been extremely unevenly distributed. NRM cadres and their political cronies creamed off the top and only a little was left for ordinary Ugandans. The Baganda conservatives who hated Museveni knew that they could play on the differential growth-induced social marginality. They were bourgeois but they knew that there was a lumpen proletariat which they could use, either from the young rural unemployed or among the city street youth. And since the Muslim community represented a very large proportion of that lumpen proletariat for historical reasons going back to the place of Muslims in Uganda's colonial society, a satellite Muslim organisation was an essential tool both in recruiting and in obtaining outside support from Sudan. This was a strange alliance and the good Protestant Anglo-Baganda bourgeois leadership which prided itself on its monarchical extremism (including die-hard Anglican high church credentials) felt somewhat ill at ease about this tactical alliance with Khartoum's radical Islam.

The first UMLA military efforts proved abortive and its forces were defeated in a series of encounters at Buseruka, near Lake Albert in Bunyoro (20–28 February 1995). Importantly, the survivors fled to Zaire, where they settled near Bunia. The reasons for their defeat were simple: they were city boys (and girls: there was an approximate 20 per cent female membership among them), without much knowledge of the terrain; in addition, they were a multi-ethnic group which had almost no local sympathisers. Finally, their armament was limited.

In Bunia, however, they soon made interesting new contacts. The Sudanese Army Security Services were at the time using the Bunia airfield to bring supplies both to the Rwandese *Interahamwe* and to the WBNLF, the group founded in 1994 by former Idi Amin commander, Juma Oris. Although based in Zaire, this was a Sudan-driven operation because Mobutu was far too weak to provide anything but the physical ground from which to operate. But in Bunia the Sudanese found the vanquished UMLA fighters licking their wounds, and took them in hand. Khartoum already knew about UMLA, but it had so far worked more with the radical Ugandan Muslim movement known as Tabliq. The *Tablighi Jama'at,* set up in India in the 1920s, had initially been a pietist and revivalist Muslim sect which started to spread worldwide in the 1950s and eventually reached Uganda. Tabliq 'missionaries' had penetrated the Uganda Muslim Youth Association (UMYA) in the early 1980s, at a time when the Ugandan Muslim community was still trying to recover from its embarrassing association with the Idi Amin dictatorship. By the 1990s the result of this initially rather mild faith renewal movement was the birth of a native Ugandan militant fundamentalism with strong connections to the Sudan. In 1991 the Tabliq had occupied by force the Kampala Central Mosque; four people had been killed, many had been wounded, and hundreds jailed and later tried in massive public trials. Whatever help Khartoum had channelled to the nascent UMLA before 1995 had gone through the Tabliq movement of Sheikh Jamir Mukulu, which had strong connections with the international fundamentalist networks and with Sudan.

It was from the Khartoum-sponsored fusion between the Allied Democratic Movement and the Uganda Muslim Liberation Army in Zaire that the Allied Democratic Forces was born. But the key element in that union was the realisation by the Sudanese operators that, without a good peasant grounding in local realities, the guerrillas would be defeated again. This is why they worked at incorporating within it the remnants of NALU, the old Bakonjo *Rwenzururu* movement of the Ruwenzori Mountains.

In August 1995 the Sudanese army, operating inside Zaire with WNBLF support, took the small strategic towns of Kaya and Oraba from the SPLA, a way of securing their supply lines and disrupting those of the SPLA. They celebrated their victory by shelling the Sudanese refugee camp at Koboko on Ugandan territory, from the Zairian side of the border. The Sudanese government was then at its most militant, having tried to assassinate President Mubarak of Egypt in June in Addis Ababa during an OAU meeting, and President Museveni felt there was enough international leeway to allow him to retaliate strongly. So the UPDF attacked the Lord's Resistance Army *inside* Sudan, pushing all the way to Owinyi-Kibul in a common operation with the SPLA (September–October 1995).

On the Zaire front, Crispus Kiyonga, who was President Museveni's Bakonjo representative, felt obliged to deny Ugandan support for the PLC; but this had become common knowledge in Bundibungyo on Uganda's western border, since PLC fighters were taking part in the local coffee-smuggling operations from Zaire which partially financed their movement. During the early months of 1996 both the old NALU and Tabliq networks continued to recruit young men in their different social environments; but the Sudanese had not yet managed to bring them together and an early UMLA/Tabliq attack on Kisoro ended in failure. The Muslim community was torn apart according to its pro-Museveni or pro-Khartoum choices, and in June 1996 the Tabliq tried to murder Suleiman Kakeeto, a moderate Uganda Supreme Muslim Council (USMC) leader who had publicly disavowed the guerrillas; as for Sheikh Jamir Mukulu, he fled to Khartoum just before Uganda's internal secret service, the Internal Security Organisation (ISO), could arrest him. Meanwhile, fighting was spreading in the north and in West Nile. The result of this escalation of military operations was to force Uganda to renege on the demobilisation programme it had started with World Bank support in 1994, with a target of cutting down the UPDF from 90,000 to 40,000 men. In June 1996 the Ministry of Defence had to review its budget and reinvest the US$29m it had so far saved through the demobilisation exercise, after letting go about 12,000 men. But the multi-nation attack on Mobutu's Zaire was soon to globalise the Ugandan–Sudanese problem and bring it into a continent-wide framework.

AS UGANDA FOLLOWS RWANDA IN ZAIRE, SUDAN SIDES WITH MOBUTU

When the Rwandese army began its operations against the refugee camps in South Kivu in September 1996, it was immediately obvious that, given the degree of Sudanese support for the Zaire-based Ugandan guerrillas, Kampala was going to take advantage of the general conflagration to do its own bit of cross-border cleaning up. The question was: how far and with what political agenda? The answers to this would become clearer only progressively, during the following months, after the refugee problem had been taken care of in the most radical fashion by the Rwandese Patriotic Army (RPA) and after Kigali had sponsored the birth of a 'Zairian rebel organisation', the *Alliance des Forces Démocratiques de Libération* (AFDL).

But the initiative to attack the Ugandan forces in Bundibugyo came from the guerrilla side. The ADF, which the Sudanese secret service had been preparing for months, went into emergency action on 13 November 1996 because, after the taking of Ishasha by the AFDL and their Rwandese allies, they had felt that their rear base at Kasindi in Zaire had now come under threat. Museveni telephoned Mobutu (who seemed genuinely surprised) and informed him that he would enter Zaire in hot pursuit in case of renewed attack. Meanwhile, trying to turn necessity into opportunity, ADM/ADF leader Ssentamu Kayiira issued a communiqué stating that his men were fighting 'to reintroduce multi-party politics in Uganda, stop Museveni's nepotism giving all the juicy jobs to Westerners [meaning people from Ankole and Kigezi, not Europeans] and re-establish cordial relations with Uganda's neighbours'. Since the Tabliq component of the ADF was at the same time preaching through its mosque circuit that it was fighting for an Islamic state with Jamir Mukulu as its president, while Bakonjo prisoners told UPDF interrogators that they were fighting because they had been promised that they would finally get their autonomous kingdom, there seemed to be a radical problem of political coherence among the rebel group. In any case, Museveni was now decided: he would have to go into Zaire to get the ADF and since the rebels were moving north it seemed to be a good time. This decision was a major step in the internationalisation of the Zaire war.

Meanwhile, the ADFL/RPA forces had started their general offensive into Zaire, and Kisangani was their first main target. So, in support of that movement, thirty Ugandan soldiers took Mahagi, just across the Uganda West Nile border, on 29 January 1997. The move was denied two days later by President Museveni himself in a radio interview, when he declared: 'We are not in Zaire . . . dissident groups have been present there for thirty years, Lumumbists, the Tshombe group, Mulele groups and others. They are the ones who have taken up arms.' On the day Museveni was making this disingenuous claim, his troops had reached Watsa in the north, forcing the white mercenaries, whom the French had recruited to try to bolster the crumbling FAZ, to flee back to Kisangani. Watsa had been taken to be the stepping-stone for Uganda's coming attack against the Sudanese army, the WNBLF and some Rwandan ex-FAR, in southern Sudan. By then AFDL forces were moving in many directions at once, and it had become obvious that their ultimate aim was the toppling of Mobutu. This did not interfere with the Ugandans fulfilling their 'Sudanese agenda' at the same time, as President Museveni had declared: 'We have run out of solutions with the Sudan. We are now seeking a solution on the battlefield.'

With the globalisation of the war, the Ugandan army had taken prisoner some former FAZ soldiers among the ADF guerrillas operating in the Kasese area, while the Sudanese were air-dropping supplies to the Lord's Resistance Army (LRA) in northern Uganda in the hope that it could hit the UPDF hard enough to stop it from joining the battle in Zaire. But the LRA was more of a terrorist outfit than a regular guerrilla army, and in the midst of the war it simply continued attacking villages in Acholi and murdering civilians, which only reinforced Museveni's decision to cut off support in Zaire. In early February 1997 the UNRF II guerrilla group led by Ali Bamuze had attacked the village of Midigo (Aringa County) in West Nile. This move had been organised by the Sudanese secret service which was anxious because the main body of West Nile guerrillas (the WNBLF) was at the time crossing over from its bases in Zaire and surrendering in large numbers to the Ugandan army. By then the Sudanese were desperately trying to co-ordinate with the white mercenaries and the FAZ remnants in Upper Zaire, but these were crumbling so fast that the Sudan border now lay open. On the other side, Museveni was working with the SPLA to try and squeeze the Ugandan rebels in northeastern Zaire in a three-pronged assault coordinated with the AFDL/RPA forces which were then moving northwards. The next step would be to push them back into southern Sudan.

Soon the triple alliance of AFDL, RPA and UPDF had driven the last FAZ remnants to the Sudanese border. Inside Sudan, SPLA forces besieging the Sudanese army garrison at Yei, southwest of Juba, had captured the supplies airdropped by the Sudanese Air Force, and on 13 March the town fell. But the Ugandan rebels moving northwards to escape the trap in Zaire did not know this. They trekked on foot from Morobo towards Yei, together with the bedraggled remnants of the FAZ and some Sudanese regulars, a column of over 4,000 men, women and children. They all fell into a major SPLA ambush half way to Yei on 12 March and 2,000 of them were killed, with over 1,000 captured. The survivors, including wounded WNBLF Commander Juma Oris, fled in disarray towards the safety of the Sudanese army garrison in Juba.

This massive defeat marked the end of Sudan's intervention in Mobutu's Zaire, but not in Kabila's Congo. Khartoum had maintained a close relationship with Mobutu because of the anti-SPLA possibilities he had afforded its army. But it had, of course, no cultural or ideological ties to his regime and its collapse simply meant that a careful new diplomatic initiative had to be undertaken. This happened very quickly. Laurent-Désiré Kabila was made the new head of the renamed Congo in April 1997 and by August of that year the Sudanese were already burrowing their way into his chaotic new regime. Their first argument had been one of opening up a political and military alternative for the new Congolese head of state. They represented a strongly anti-US stance, which could even be exaggerated in order to appeal to the former Marxist guerrilla who still looked to Beijing, Pyongyang and Havana for support. Khartoum remained discreet on Islamism and emphasised rather its anti-American (and anti-Museveni) positions. At the time, Kabila was a near prisoner of the Rwandan–Ugandan system which had propelled him into power. But when he broke free from their embrace, the Sudan immediately became a natural ally.

Kabila's victory had not put an end to Sudanese military activity in Congo's Province Orientale. The March 1997 slaughter of WNBLF forces in the Yei ambush had, of course, diminished the proxy fighting capacity the Sudanese had been trying to build in the Congo against Uganda. But they had not given up re-supplying the remnants of both the WNBLF and UNRF II in Garamba National Park. In addition, they continued to welcome the hard-pressed Rwandese former *Interahamwe* to southern Sudan, and in March 1998 Colonel Tharcisse Renzaho, former *Préfet* of Kigali, and Colonel Ntimiragabo, former Rwandese *Garde Présidentielle* commander, arrived in Juba from Nairobi to reorganise them.

SUDAN AND UGANDA IN THE NEW MULTI-NATION WAR

With the outbreak of the new multi-lateral war in August the Rwandese in Juba were joined by Idi Amin's son Taban who came to recruit FUNA West Nilers, and both these and the WNBLF guerrillas were later sent to bolster the defence of the eastern Congolese town of Kindu in Maniema. When Kindu fell in October, Rwandese and Congolese rebel forces captured a number of Ugandan rebels who were often described in the press as 'Sudanese' because they had come from Juba. Isiro had been attacked in late August and Kabila, who did not have the means to defend the northeast, flew to Ndjamena and then on to Tripoli, in defiance of the UN embargo, in the hope of getting help from his allies. President Omar el-Beshir was reluctant to commit forces he needed in Southern Sudan to the Congo theatre of operations, but he had asked Gaddafi to do it for him. Gaddafi did not want to commit troops either, so both Khartoum and Tripoli used their influence on Chad (which did not have any interests of its own in the Congo but was heavily indebted to Sudan and somewhat fearful of Libya) to persuade President Déby to supply the necessary manpower. On 18 September the first Libyan planes began to ferry a 1,000-strong Chadian contingent to defend the embattled north-eastern Congo. The troops were flown first to Gbadolite, and reaching the east from there was to prove a slow and difficult business. Tripoli kept a rigorous news blackout on its role, leaving Ndjamena to declare openly that it had sent its expeditionary force to the DRC 'to support the legitimate government'.

Khartoum was denying any form of military presence and was simply invoking 'diplomatic and political support' for the Kabila regime. But in fact it was going even further in its support of Kinshasa: the Sudanese government had invited 700 young Congolese cadets for training at the Khartoum Military Academy and had decided to sell some of the products of its new arms manufacture to Kinshasa. Congolese planes started to fly regularly to Khartoum to fetch weapons and ammunition. The deliveries were paid for promptly with diamonds and with cash. This was combined with continued military support for the LRA, and the UPDF had had to enter Sudan itself on several occasions to strike back at the Acholi guerrillas. On the Congolese side, ADF forces, which got regular arms air drops from Juba, were causing havoc in Bundibugyo (there were 50,000 internally displaced persons by late January and 70,000 by July), and when an ADF agent was caught in Mbarara in March and gave the names of his friends, all were Muslims. Amama Mbabazi, Security Adviser to President Museveni, declared: 'Khartoum's plan is to destabilise the region to prepare the ground for the spread of Islamic fundamentalism and Arabism'.

In addition to the various guerrilla groups (ADF, UNRF II, FUNA, LRA) all supported by Sudan, there were another 3,000 hostile troops in Garamba National Park, 200 km west of Arua, who were also occasionally supplied from Juba. None of these forces had on their own the capacity to overthrow the Ugandan regime, but together they continued to harass it, costing an inordinate amount of money. This, in turn, created problems for Kampala with the donors, because Uganda was benefiting from the HIPC initiative which obliged it to keep its military expenditure at under 2 per cent of GNP, something it never managed to achieve. In 1991, when the UPDF was 100,000 strong, the cost of keeping these troops was US$42 million a year. In 1996, after the demobilisation exercise the cost of only 50,000 troops had climbed to US$88 million.

At this point we need to note the perennial corruption of the Ugandan military, which has inflated the cost of the war and been a critical factor in its prolongation. During 1996–97 the estimate of James Kahooza, the Government's Inspector General, was that over US$400,000 a month was being stolen from the anti-LRA operational budget. In the Congo, where the UPDF was pressing hard on the ADF, General Kazini had admitted that he had only 6,000 men under his command and not 10,000, as shown in his books. Since late 1996, UPDF officers had found ways of quickly enriching themselves in the Congo and it was this new war pattern which eventually replaced the Khartoum-related security concerns which had initially motivated the intervention.

On occasions, the UPDF operated together with the SPLA inside Congo. On 25 September 1998 a combined UPDF/SPLA force had occupied Dungu, on the Sudan border, and the Sudanese rebels had immediately started looting the town. They even dismantled the local power station and took it to Yambio in the Sudan. They also corralled 46,000 Sudanese refugees from the local camps and pushed them back roughly into Western Equatoria. From Dungu they moved into Garamba National Park to scatter the Ugandan guerrillas hiding there, and then went on to take Isiro on 4 October. The Chadian contingent had not managed to transport itself all the way from Western Equatoria, but it soon became involved in the fighting anyway, because even if it did not succeed in moving eastwards the enemy was now coming westwards. With Ugandan support, Jean-Pierre Bemba had created the *Mouvement de Libération du Congo* (MLC), which immediately started to recruit among the tribes of the Bangala cluster which had been Mobutu's base of tribal support during his days in power. Kabila had no troops, money or transport to hold Equateur Province, which was now wide open to the coming MLC/Ugandan offensive. The Chadian contingent, which had finally reached the frontline, was mauled at Aketi and then at Bondo, where it lost over 70 men and 120 prisoners of war. A Ugandan helicopter immediately flew Bemba into Aketi as soon as it was taken, so that he could show himself and rally tribal supporters. He received a rousing welcome and a few days later, in the company of the Ugandans, his fledgling forces ambushed the Chadians again near Buta, killing 122 and capturing 148. As Bemba was driving deeper into Equateur, the SPLA was finishing its cleaning up in the northeast, bringing ever greater numbers of former Sudanese refugees back into Yambio. The Chadians were frustrated at their poor showing, and denied losing more than 250 casualties and over 400 POWs in a few weeks.

Bemba captured Gemena on 30 December, causing panic in Kinshasa since the capital itself now seemed to be within reach of the MLC-Ugandan forces. In the first days of January 1999 Namibian Boeings and Angolan Tupolev transport planes brought 1,000 *Forces Armées Congolaises* (FAC) soldiers to Bangui in the hope of mounting a counter-offensive in Equateur. The Sudanese joined in with daily bombings by Antonov An-12s from Juba, and the MLC/UPDF forces were unable to withstand the pressure. They withdrew to Lisala after losing Gemena, Businga and Libenge. Bemba disgustedly remarked: 'We are fighting a mixture of Sudanese, Chadians, Interahamwe and Central Africans; there are only very few Congolese among the FAC.' He conveniently forgot to mention that many of his own men had been recruited in the Central African Republic, and that the Ugandan army made up most of his battle corps. But the alliance Khartoum had managed to cobble together was slowly withering away, as its members increasingly failed to see the point of fighting Khartoum's battles in its place. On 17 April 1999 Kabila met with Museveni in Sirte (Libya) and signed a 'peace agreement' in the presence of Idriss Déby and Issayas Afeworki. Colonel Gaddafi, who wanted to disengage himself and his Chadian allies from what he increasingly saw as a useless conflict, had brokered the meeting. The 'agreement' was limited to the northern front of the Congo war (for Museveni its main purpose was to give the MLC a free hand in the hope that it could march all the way to Kinshasa), and it only achieved the Chadians' withdrawal from the conflict. Khartoum had lost its proxies and would now have to fall back directly on its own resources to keep its running war with Uganda going.

SUDAN AND UGANDA: THE MODALITIES OF AN ONGOING CONFRONTATION

There are a number of conclusions which can be drawn from the Khartoum–Kampala proxy wars in the Congo:

- First, Islam is only one of the motivating factors which explain Khartoum's anti-Ugandan policies.

- When Islam was indeed a component of these movements, it was more a case of social and economic marginalisation leading people to convert to Islam in order to benefit from Khartoum's support than of Muslims revolting to promote a Sharia-based government.
- If militant Islam played a somewhat minor role in this conflict, the racial and cultural factors were a major cause of Khartoum's confrontational politics.
- All the various efforts made, both in Kampala and in Khartoum, depend on the ethno-political networks available.
- As a final remark, we must remember that borders mean very little in such a situation. Not only are they often porous (the case of the Zaire/Congo being an extreme one), but ethnic solidarities existing across them are much more powerful than the formal citizenships people happen to carry.

15
The United Nations in Africa: The Rise of Peacekeeping and the Case of Somalia

RICHARD K. AL-QAQ

A distinctive characteristic of the international politics of contemporary Africa is the regular deployment by the United Nations Security Council of peacekeeping operations. Over the last two decades the UN has authorised more than 20 peace operations on the continent. The great majority of these have been deployed within sub-Saharan states in the context of overseeing some form of domestic peace settlement and, more generally, as part of some wider political and economic liberalisation of the subject society. For better or worse, United Nations peace operations today form an intrinsic part of the African political landscape, playing a considerable role in the external management of African affairs—be it in the Democratic Republic of the Congo, the Ivory Coast or Sudan. This chapter seeks to shed light on the origins, development and politics of UN peace operations in Africa by examining one of the first and arguably one of most revealing post-Cold War operations, the United Nations Operation in Somalia (UNOSOM), deployed between 1992 and 1995. This is because an examination of the UN–Somalia encounter helps to unwrap the astonishing process of ideological and political change that the UN itself has undergone since the collapse of the Soviet Union in 1991, and how this change has dramatically affected its programme of work. It is also more simply because the UN–Somalia encounter sheds light on the politicised nature of the organisation's involvement in the contemporary African context. Looking behind the facade of UN peace operations in today's Africa, we can see the frequent bolstering of internationally favoured domestic groups, the standardised political liberalisation of the state as well as the recent targeting and shaping of a subject state's civil society. In some African contexts, we see the UN not only as a significant political force in these societies, but also increasingly a military one. Before moving on to examine some of these dynamics in the specific case of Somalia, however, it is important to first set the scene by reviewing the various political epochs and transformations that the UN has gone through since its establishment in the 1940s.

THE POLITICAL AND IDEOLOGICAL CONTEXT OF THE UN DURING AND AFTER THE COLD WAR

Up until the collapse of the Soviet Union in 1991, the UN had been dominated by two distinct political periods. The first from 1945 to 1960 was an unabashed era of US domination and dictate, where on occasions the organisation was used as blunt instrument of the State Department's foreign policy. Among other infamous episodes, there was the case of Korea and that of the Congo, the question of who held the China seat in the Security Council, mainland Communist China or Republican controlled Formosa, and the embarrassing matter of an FBI 'field office', established with Trygve Lie's blessing, *within* the UN Secretariat building. Such a state of affairs was a consequence of the unfortunate Soviet boycotting of the Security Council, the 'majority' that the US could rely upon in the conspicuously white General Assembly, and the balance of staffing within the UN Secretariat, which was in the early years largely constituted by the ex-civil servants of wartime administrations in Western Europe and the United States. It is hardly surprising that the result was a UN whose programme of activities closely mirrored the agenda of the Western Bloc in general and the US in particular.

The second era began in 1960—the Year of Africa—with a wave of decolonisation and quickly grew into a radicalisation of the UN's agenda of work, especially in the area of political economy. With the rapid expansion in UN membership during this period, the balance of power increasingly rested with the General Assembly, as opposed to the Security Council, whose activism and output had halted altogether with the onset of superpower confrontation in the Council chamber. Indeed, from the early 1960s the General Assembly became the defining voice of the UN where its podium served as a world stage for denouncing 'Yankee Imperialism' in the Middle East, Latin America and South-East Asia, and European 'neo-colonialism' in Africa. More substantively, the overwhelming political current of period was that of the G-77 and the Non-Aligned Movement (NAM), with their fundamental rejection of the prevailing organisation of international order, particularly the separation of the political sphere from the economic sphere in world politics. It was precisely the goal of the G-77 and NAM to remake the UN into a world political body responsible for regulating the world economy. Obviously this agenda was at odds with the liberal–capitalist ideological currents, whatever the variations, which dominated the chancelleries of the First World at the time. Indeed, US policymakers still unhappily remember this period as the nadir of Washington's relations with, and influence in, the organisation.

The collapse of the Soviet Union, however, marked the end of this 'tyranny of the majority', as a former US ambassador to the UN labelled it, and heralded the start of an overhaul of the UN's political orientation and 'programme of work'. It was not simply a matter of the reactivation of the Security Council as consequence of the end of Soviet opposition from within the Council, though this was indeed vital. It was also due to the changed internal dynamics within the General Assembly as well. On the one hand, the formal admission to the UN of former USSR satellite states in Eastern Europe, which were now ideologically and politically aligned to the US, changed the balance of numbers in Assembly. On the other, and perhaps more profoundly, the 1980s' 'debt crisis' had forced many African and Latin American states to abandon any pretence of radical political economy policies and embrace a liberal-market democracy model and sensibility pushed by a resurgent World Bank. The political upshot was that the UN was again a much more pliable organisation, one in which US diplomacy could once more work its magic. The First Gulf War, the repeal of the Zionism 'equals racism' resolution, and the ability of the US to corral the UN's political organs in each of these instances served as a bellwether of the coming ideological dispensation of the UN.

THE REFOCUSING OF INTERNATIONAL INSTITUTIONS

The collapse of the USSR was a seminal moment in twentieth-century world politics and had considerable consequences for existing international organisations. The triumph of the US and the liberal capitalist system, in common with previous social and political victories in world history, provided the victors the opportunity to impose their vision of international order anew. Unlike 1919 or 1945, however, new institutions were not in this instance created to administer this vision; rather the existing canopy of post-1945 institutions—the World Bank, IMF, GATT, and the UN itself—were refashioned to oversee and promote a revised international social order. For the US in particular the establishment of new institutions was not necessary as the internal governing structure of each existing organisation already favoured their control; the IMF and World Bank are essentially run as private corporations, with weighted voting power that has historically favoured G-7 nations; and the UN's most powerful political organ, the Security Council, when stripped of the hyperbole is an institutionalised great-power forum where the victors of the Second World War and their allies *still* yield overwhelming legal, political and military prerogatives.

Rather than establish new organisations the US concentrated on priming their specific activities and political orientation. In the policy language of US diplomats at the time this was framed as creating a new 'international division of labour' among international organisations, which was to see each of them re-focus on discrete specialist activities. In the realm of political economy, the World Bank was to concentrate on the economic liberalisation of less developed countries, the WTO on extending and deepening the inter-state body of rules governing free trade, and the IMF on the swift economic deregulation of the Second World of Eastern Europe. In the political realm, the UN would refocus its resources and its attention on the question of peace and security in its less fortunate member-states. This involved a multiple transformation. First, it required the purge of all those political-economy programmes conducted by the UN and which US diplomats had long ago marked out for removal as 'politicised', 'inefficient' and 'duplicative'. Second, it entailed a rapid expansion of UN peacekeeping operations deployed *within* states to monitor ceasefires and enforce externally imposed peace-agreements. Finally, it saw the creation of a whole raft of new political activities in the areas of democratisation, human rights and good governance within states. Taken as a whole, it heralded the transformation of the UN into a specialist organisation focused on conducting political activities on the periphery of the world system.

THE UN AND THE NEW SECURITY AGENDA

Within the UN the framework of the organisation's new peace activities was set by the Security Council and then fleshed out by top UN officials. Specifically, the occasion for the public launch of the campaign to remodel the UN around peace operations was the January 1992 Security Council Heads of State Summit. Through a Presidential Statement, the Security Council formally tasked the new secretary-general, Boutros Boutros-Ghali, with thrashing out the parameters of the UN's revised political activities and accordingly updating the Secretariat's internal structure. Within only a month, Boutros-Ghali expanded the UN's political capacities by creating three new mega-departments: the Department of Peacekeeping Operations (DPKO), the Department of Political Affairs (DPA), and the Department of Humanitarian Affairs (DHA). The creation of the DPA was significant because it was established to conduct a range of new

UN political activities within Southern states such as oversee national elections, practice 'preventative' diplomacy, and coordinate post-conflict peace building. The latter activity has proved to be particularly consequential, as it has provided the basis for the imposition of the 'transitional administration' by UN officials of entire states such as in Kosovo and East Timor. Just under a year after this 'first-step' of internal reorganisation, in December 1992, Boutros-Ghali carried-out a second key round of restructuring of the Secretariat by relocating to the World Bank and UNCTAD or 'eliminating' altogether those awkward political economy programmes and units that were still, despite everything, running against the prevailing liberal market philosophy.

In relation to the setting-out of the UN's new terms of reference for peace activities the most important moment by far was the publication of Boutros-Ghali's *An Agenda for Peace* in September 1992. On the one hand, this was because the report formally introduced a number of new political activities for the UN to conduct, essentially all of them *within* states. On the other, and more importantly perhaps, the report challenged the traditional post-1945 basis of juridical state-sovereignty in Africa and Asia by linking this international norm to certain governance-related standards. States were only entitled to sovereignty if they met these standards.

The report goes on to firmly affix the stamp of 'good internal governance' with a very particular form of contemporary polity, liberal market democracy. It is therefore against this standard, the liberal-democratic one, that states were to be assessed. The initial reasoning here related to the belief that liberal polities are best suited for promoting peace, security and development. In other words, a somewhat uncomplicated version of the 'democratic peace theory' in international relations theory is applied to the complex question of social and political violence in post-colonial societies.

The logical and rather convenient inference of such a linkage was that the UN must now promote or support this preferred type of liberal polity within states in order to better further the cause of world peace. Indeed, this normative belief in the superiority of the liberal democratic model now informs a great deal of the UN's political activities on the periphery. Over the 1990s and into the 2000s, this liberalisation has moved far beyond simply installing the formal institutions of a liberal market democracy to conducting activities calibrated to foster appropriate political cultures and practices. Civil society is now an explicit target of reform and liberalisation.

This then is the overall political and ideological framework in which the current UN predilection towards peace operations needs to be situated. In the first place, as we have seen, the particular constellation of political power *within* the organisation impacts hugely on its 'programme of work' and ideological orientation. In the 1990s the UN dramatically expanded its peace operations and this largely reflected the political prerogatives of the US and its vision of what the UN should do. This was no less than the campaign for a New International Economic Order epitomised by the political preponderance of the G-77 in the UN in the 1970s. Rather than a normal set of activities for an international organisation to conduct, therefore, peacekeeping operations are in fact illustrative of a very specific political programme. Moreover, these peace activities are themselves not value-free; they reflect a clear normative bias towards the liberal market state and they signal a new institutionalised regime of international intervention in Southern states. Simply in terms of quantity, the UN has deployed no less than 45 peace operations since 1991. The overwhelming majority of these have been deployed within the Southern Hemisphere, largely in Africa. Today, UN peace operations are a rather unique aspect of the continent's political landscape.

THE UN IN SOMALIA

The UN intervention in Somalia between 1992 and 1995 is revealing precisely because the operation was played out during the initial transition to this new UN security order and, in many key respects, functioned as a test case for pushing the boundaries of peace activities in Africa. At the time this related to the objective of creating a working example of the new UN policy category of a peace enforcement operation—that is a mission forcibly deployed by the UN under Chapter VII of the Charter in order to impose order and conduct Security Council-mandated tasks. In fact, the UN–Somalia saga graphically illustrates the politics of the transition from a more conventional format of peacekeeping—relying on the principles of local consent and formal neutrality—to forced intervention under first US leadership (UNITAF) and then ostensibly UN 'command and control' (UNOSOM II). In the latter respect the UN–Somalia adventure is equally notable for underlining the method in which the UN intercedes in African polities, and how the organisation routinely serves to bolster favoured domestic factions. This was plainly the case in Somalia, where from the outset of its engagement, the UN was structured to favour one faction in the conflict—Ali Mahdi and the Somali Salvation Alliance (SSA) at the expense of General Mohammad Aideed and the Somali National Alliance (SNA). We are all broadly aware of some of the violent consequences of this UNOSOM military episode; the most infamous being the death of 18 US Army Rangers and more than 200 Somalis during a failed UNOSOM helicopter gunship attack on a meeting of SNA leaders in October 1993. This event was simply one moment in a vicious summer-long UN campaign to impose its authority on the country and rid Mogadishu of General Mohammad Aideed.

THE CAMPAIGN TO INTERVENE IN SOMALIA

Somalia has endured more than two decades of armed conflict, making it one of the world's longest ongoing wars. The UN's political engagement in the conflict spans the entirety of this period but was particularly intense in the early 1990s—when at its height in 1993 the UN was quite literally running the country and waging war on the SNA. The road to this military involvement in the Horn of Africa was profoundly political, revealing much about the early implementation of the UN's new security agenda. In this section the focus is on one distinctive aspect of these politics, the diplomatic campaign of UN officials for a military intervention in Somalia. Without doubt, other factors were important in fashioning this interventionary moment, including the politicised lobbying conducted by humanitarian forces such as CARE, and the preferences of the US Pentagon, which wanted to avoid a counterinsurgency quagmire in Bosnia in favour of a militarily 'doable' operation in Somalia. But perhaps most significant was the impulse of the George H. Bush Presidency to extend the UN's new centrality in the post-First Gulf War international security regime. This vision of a proactive UN Security Council led by the US fed directly into the work of UN officials—most obviously through the 1992 Security Council Summit—who were restructuring UN departments and activities around questions of peace and security. Somalia, for these officials, was the perfect occasion to crystallise their new security roles on the ground. And in fact their influence was second to none in the drive to intervene. In the first instance, UN officials were central in placing Somalia on the UN agenda and keeping it up there in the context of the war in the Balkans, which was surely one of the most significant geo-political crises in post-1945 Europe. Shortly thereafter UN diplomats were instrumental in setting the scene for intervention on the ground by systematically sidelining more consensual approaches to the crisis and instituting, in their stead, a rather bellicose attitude towards local political and military factions. And last but certainly not least there was the centrality of Boutros-Ghali in constructing the discourse and political framework for intervention, particularly in the Security Council.

By way of a brief background to this UN diplomacy, the origins of the Somali conflict lay in the disintegration of the post-independence regime of Siyad Barre in the 1980s, and the subsequent war that erupted *within* the armed movement, the United Somalia Congress, established to overthrow the dictatorship. The years 1990–93 were particularly violent and desperate: fighting between remnants of the Barre regime and the USC in southern Somalia halted food production in the 'bread basket' of the country, which in turn resulted in a severe famine for most of 1992; and, within the USC, a vicious conflict broke out in and around Mogadishu between its two main constitutive factions, the SSA and SNA. To get a basic idea of the scale of the crisis, it is worth citing some approximate figures: one million refugees and four and a half million people suffering severe malnutrition in the first six months of 1992; and up to five hundred thousand excess deaths by the end of the same year.

Nonetheless, up until early 1992 the UN was hardly engaged in the Somali crisis. Even specialised UN agencies such as UNDP, UNHCR, and the WFP had halted whatever operations they were carrying out in January 1991 due to the 'security situation'. The UN secretary-general at the time, Javier Perez de Cuellar, issued only one report on the situation during the entirety of 1991. However, right from the beginning of Boutros-Ghali's term as secretary-general, the UN directed an increasing amount of attention to the crisis. In fact as soon as he took up office in January 1992 no time was wasted—a trusted envoy, James Jonah, was immediately dispatched to discuss with Mahdi and Aideed the potential for a peace deal. Jonah returned with the tentative ceasefire agreement and a request for some form of UN ' . . . monitoring mechanism.' Security Resolution 751 (24 April 1992) followed with the establishment of UNOSOM—mandated to deploy fifty observers to monitor a ceasefire—and the endorsement of a proposal by the secretary-general to negotiate with local parties the deployment a 'Security Force' that had 'military training' and were 'sufficiently strong' to facilitate the UN's proposed humanitarian work in Mogadishu. To further negotiations for the security force, Boutros-Ghali appointed Muhammad Sahnoun, a former Algerian diplomat, as his Special Representative (SRSG).

Some of the most striking UN diplomacy followed this initial Security Council resolution—especially given the fact that officials were able to extend and deepen international involvement in Somalia despite the preoccupation of European states with the Balkans. In order to achieve this, UN diplomats utilised a mixture of public advocacy and diplomatic bargaining in the Security Council. The public advocacy of the UN was particularly aggressive, with officials voicing criticism of European bias and 'double standards'. Boutros-Ghali went so far as to label the Security Council 'Eurocentric' and preoccupied by a 'Rich Man's War.'

The diplomatic component was equally proactive with Boutros-Ghali refusing to endorse further UN engagement in Bosnia without additional action on Somalia. In an open letter to the Security Council about the London Plan for the cantonment of heavy weapons in Bosnia, he wrote:

> My concern is that if the Security Council continues to concentrate its attention and resources to such an extent on Yugoslav problems, this will be at the expense of the organisation's ability to help resolve equally cruel and dangerous conflicts elsewhere, for example in Somalia.

The reluctance of the secretary-general to rubberstamp the London Plan and, moreover, to actually question the appropriateness of the scheme was a direct challenge to the European sponsors of the proposal. The British government took particular offence and hit back with press leaks about Boutros-Ghali's 'imperious style' and talk of his early retirement. However, despite 'le petit guerre', as labelled by French diplomats, the issue was quickly resolved through a US acceptance of Boutros-Ghali's simple linkage: further UN work in Bosnia in return for more resources in Somalia. Indeed a few days later, the Security Council passed Resolution 767 (26 July 1992) endorsing the secretary-general's report on Somalia, which included a call for an '. . . urgent airlift operation'.

Aside from the additional engagement, Resolution 767 also marked a shift in the way UN officials dealt with the major belligerents, and with Somali society as a whole. A policy of consultation with local factions was swiftly replaced with one of UN unilateralism and dictate. This changed attitude stemmed from the impatience of UN officials in New York with the protracted negotiations that Sahnoun was conducting with Aideed to deploy a UN 'security force'. Of course at the time this type of consultation with local forces was a rather standard UN prerequisite for the deployment of peacekeepers, such as with UNITA in Angola. Yet Boutros-Ghali in particular did not approve of such a laborious process carried out by Sahnoun with the SNA. In his memoirs, Boutros-Ghali reveals his displeasure:

> I was worried by his efforts to 'understand' the militia leaders, Aideed and Mahdi, and establish 'warm relations' with them. This . . . perpetuated the criminal establishment that had taken over the country, and lengthy negotiations between the warlords had to be carried out before food could be distributed within the various fiefdoms under their control.

The disapproval of the secretary-general with Sahnoun's negotiations became crystal clear after a further UN report detailing the proposed enlargement of UNOSOM from 500 to 3,500 'security personnel' was announced in August 1992 without the knowledge of Sahnoun or the consent of the SNA. Both became aware via the BBC World Service. The implication of the announcement was clear to both parties: the UN was unhappy with the slow process of local dialogue that Sahnoun was conducting with the SNA; and that the UN was now committed to implementing and deploying peace operations *without* local consent. This announcement mirrored the characterisation of peacekeeping in *An Agenda for Peace,* published about the same time, and indicated a shift in UN practice:

> Peace-keeping is the deployment of a United Nations presence in the field, *hitherto* with the consent of all parties concerned . . . (emphasis added)

This type of approach to the Somali operation was further institutionalised on the ground after Sahnoun resigned in October. His replacement, Ismit Kittani, ended his predecessor's practice of meeting faction leaders—during his tenure he met Mahdi and Aideed twice—and openly criticised them in the press. Mockingly called 'Governor Kittani' by Mogadishu residents, he also extended the practice of deploying UN forces without local consent; before his arrival in the country he authorised the deployment of Pakistani peacekeepers at Mogadishu airport without SNA knowledge or agreement. Kittani's arrival thus marked the end of any facade of dialogue with local groups and indicated the hardening of UN policy.

This new policy on the ground was part of a much wider drive to change the nature of UN involvement in the country. Indeed, from July 1992 a drumbeat for military intervention began to gather momentum, especially in the United States, with humanitarian lobby groups and various US government agencies conducting a vocal campaign in the press and on Capitol Hill. The secretary-general played a central role in this unfolding drama, especially in setting the rationale and thereafter the framework for a military intervention. In the first place, Boutros-Ghali helped create a rather negative and erroneous picture of the situation in Somalia and the prospects for grass-roots reconciliation. Particularly conspicuous were the repeated claims of anarchy and generalised famine in the country. In one early but formative report, the secretary-general informed the Security Council that:

> Somalia is today a country without central, regional, or local administration, and without services: no electricity, no communications, no transport, no schools and no health services. Throughout the country, there are incredible scenes of hunger, disease and dying children.

Yet this was a partial and politicised depiction of the situation. First, famines are rarely universal or countrywide but are rather regionally selective and differentiated. Somalia was no exception in that the famine predominated in southern parts of the country. The label of anarchy too was misleading—anarchy in the terms routinely described by the UN implied chaos whereas in Somalia, despite the lack of an effective centralised state, alternative sources of governance existed. Certainly the clan social system and regionalised rule, such as in Somaliland, provided an imperfect but practical alternative to the central state, especially outside Mogadishu.

The secretary-general was not only crucial in perpetuating a discourse on the conflict that made alternative solutions to the crisis irrelevant, but also in constructing the rationale for intervention. This was most strikingly evident in a letter that Boutros-Ghali sent to the Security Council on 24 November 1992, which set the scene for the deployment of a UN mandated military intervention. In it Boutros-Ghali claimed that the situation in Somalia had deteriorated to such an extent that the 'basic premises and principles' of UNOSOM needed revision. The letter focused on the diversion of international aid by armed groups claiming that the '... humanitarian assistance that reaches its intended beneficiaries is often barely more than a trickle.' This statement was based on a UN estimate (expressed to the Security Council) that 70–80 percent of all aid was looted. But this figure was the most extreme available and misleading, as it did not reflect differences over time and place. Other organisations with large operations in Somalia, such as ICRC, calculated that aid diverted was running between 5 and 10 percent. The logical upshot of such an extreme view was that the UN must urgently tackle the safe delivery of aid:

> The cycle of extortion and blackmail must be broken and security conditions established that will permit the distribution of relief supplies.

Only a few days after this letter, and after close consultations with the US Executive, the secretary-general told the Security Council that it now had '. . . no alternative but to decide to adopt more forceful measures to secure humanitarian operations.' To this end, Boutros-Ghali endorsed an offer by the US to lead a UN mandated military intervention. Hence the creation of the United Task Force (UNITAF), which was deployed under Chapter VII of the UN Charter to ensure the safe delivery of aid in pre-defined areas of the country.

What this brief discussion of the road to military intervention in Somalia has sought to underline is the changing basis of UN involvement in the conflict and the important role of UN officials in this process. Given the new international order of things—in effect the political and ideological collapse of the Second and Third Worlds—the UN was moving to the centre of a US-orchestrated international security regime. This was not only demonstrated by the political reactivation of the Security Council and First Gulf War, but also by the move into the new business of humanitarian interventions and peacekeeping. Somalia was very much a timely opportunity for the UN to translate into reality the organisation's new security functions in world politics. Yet this required proactive and robust UN diplomacy—not only towards local factions but also in the Security Council. Part of the new job description of the UN was to sell the case for political and military interventions to UN member-states and to a wider public audience. The impact of the UN was indeed significant in this regard; UN officials successfully kept Somalia on the agenda and delivered a plausible narrative, when called upon, for military intervention in the country.

THE UN GOES TO WAR

The UN's achievement in establishing UNITAF was in fact later surpassed by the subsequent creation in March 1993 of UNOSOM II. Principally, this was because UN officials successfully lobbied for UNOSOM II to have a much wider remit than UNITAF. Deployed under Chapter VII of the UN Charter, UNOSOM II's mandate covered the entirety of Somalia and included Boutros-Ghali's vocal appeal for proactive measures to disarm local factions. Most remarkable, UNOSOM II's military resources were formally under UN command and control; the first occasion that the organisation conducted a military operation within an already sovereign state, and under UN executive authority.

The actual performance and conduct of UNOSOM II, however, was much less of a success, particularly in the political management of this armed force. From April 1993 the UN operation descended into a bloody counter-insurgency campaign, which was single-mindedly obsessed with wiping out the SNA. In Mogadishu, the UN authorised a set of devastating military operations, resulting in many fatalities, and found itself rationalising its actions in a manner more associated with the public diplomacy of the Israeli Defence Force in the Occupied Territories. Among others, there was a 'surgical' helicopter gunship strike on a meeting of the SNA on 12 July 1993—a success according to UN command—that killed seventy-three prominent individuals. Then there were the anti-UN demonstrators mown down by Pakistani peacekeepers on 13 June—casualties, according to UN spokesmen, who had been used as 'human shields' by the SNA or, even more ingeniously, killed by local militiamen bent on portraying UN forces as ' . . . shooting unarmed civilians'. And this is not to mention the many Somalis unlucky enough to be detained by the multinational corps of UN peacekeepers for whatever petty offence, and subjected to their swift justice—whether it was a public humiliation and a beating or even torture and summary execution.

Here the violence unleashed by the UN during the summer months of 1993 needs to be understood in the context of the overarching political and ideological rationale of the operation, and the objection of local forces to its enforced deployment. Most obviously, the UN administration of Somalia was imposed on the territory, against the will of the population, and this led the UN to resort to force more quickly than otherwise to assert its authority. The intervention was quite simply seen by Somalis as the latest chapter of foreign intervention and occupation of the country and, as such, was resisted from the outset. As significant, perhaps, was that at the core of UNOSOM II was the vision of constructing a modern democratic nation state and this, by definition, necessitated the destruction of alternative sources of power and governance, and entailed the monopolisation of force by the 'international community'. Last but not least, there was the question of the local politics of this UN peace operation where, right from the outset, UN diplomacy favoured the SSA—at the time the more acceptable face of Somali politics whose members were in control of what was left of the formal government apparatus.

In many respects the militarisation of the UN operation was a necessary consequence of the strategic rationale of UNOSOM II, which was markedly different from those operations in the country that had preceded it. Substituting the policy of 'shoot-to-feed', the basis of UNITAF, UNOSOM II was rather to '. . .

assume responsibility for the consolidation, expansion, and maintenance of a secure environment throughout Somalia.' Not simply a matter of establishing order, UNOSOM II was also tasked with reconstructing national institutions, such as a police force. In essence it was about moving beyond the geographically and politically limited objectives of UNITAF—the rather prudent policy position of the Pentagon—to one of incorporating the 'anarchic' territory back into the world system of functioning states. The operation was about relaunching the liberal project of nation building in a post-Cold War Africa. The US Ambassador to the UN at the time, Madeleine Albright, expressed the spirit of the venture most lucidly to the *New York Times,* August 1993:

> The decision we must make is whether to pull up stakes and allow Somalia to fall back into the abyss or stay the course and help lift the country and its people from the category of failed state into that of an emerging democracy. For Somalia's sake, and for ours, we must persevere.

Of course, in order to achieve this objective the 'international community' was required to first assume effective control on the ground, which entailed the monopolisation of the means of coercion in the territory. And in no small measure the UN was given the resources and firepower to achieve this rule—28,000 personnel, a budget of US$1.5 billion, and the use of a US Army Quick Reaction Force (QRF). These were resources that the UN utilised freely.

The deployment of US military resources has of course been taken as a sign that the UN operation was, in reality, a US one. And there are some elements of truth in these claims: the QRF, while under UN chain of command, did have the authority to carry out missions independently; the head of UNOSOM II was an ex-Navy serviceman, Admiral Jonathon Howe; and senior political advisers were drafted in from the Department of State, such as Ambassador April Glaspie. It is also true that other Western states, notably France and Italy, were locked out of key positions of the operation and consequently unable to influence formal UN policy. In these regards, it is reasonable to say that the US had a special interest and privileged role in the operation. Though, having said this, it is the norm in other peacekeeping contexts for the lead contributors to be given senior leadership roles on the ground.

But it is rather at the deeper level of the experimental forms of international intervention built into UNOSOM II that the influence of the US is most pertinent, and indeed interesting. Here, the entire operation was part of a new framework of post-Cold War international order sponsored by the US in which the UN was to have an important role. All peace operations authorised after 1991 were, to a greater or lesser extent, part of this new framework. An essential dimension of this role was conferring on the UN some tactical autonomy in the conduct of its new security activities. In some ways, Somalia was about experimenting with the extent to which the US could subcontract, delegate, and devolve its foreign policy objectives in peripheral territories to the UN. The exact formula stumbled upon in UNOSOM II was one where UN and US officials were relatively integrated and fixed on pursuing the same overall strategy—the monopolisation of force in the country through, among other channels, the physical destruction of the SNA. These UN and US officials, in New York as well as in Mogadishu, were zealous in their pursuit of this mutual agenda. If anything, senior UN officials in New York were the most outspoken advocates of utilising more rather than less military muscle. A complementary corollary of this policy position was the firm opposition of UN managers to any initiation of political dialogue with the SNA. During one notable occasion, Kofi Annan (then head of DPKO) unilaterally sacked or, in UN speak, 'repatriated' the commander of the Italian contingent (General Loi) for the negotiations he concluded with General Aideed's aides for the peaceful redeployment of his troops in north Mogadishu.

The hostility of Boutros-Ghali and other UN officials towards the SNA was one which dated back to the beginning of UN involvement with the country, and which can be considered as part of the local politics of the intervention. Indeed, from the outset of UN engagement, in January 1992, the UN approach was prejudiced, albeit discreetly. For a start, the entire basis of UN conflict mediation was centred on the formal request of the Government of Somalia to place the crisis on the 'Agenda of the Security Council'. Routine as this manoeuvre may at first appear, it was a politicised decision on the UN's part to accept its legitimacy because the government apparatus of Somalia, including the network of overseas embassies, were in the gift of Ali Mahdi. In effect, Mahdi had requested and received UN intervention, arguably because his faction would benefit militarily and politically most from international involvement. This of course fed Aideed's suspicions of the UN, and explains his initial attempt at minimising UN involvement by dragging out negotiations with Sahnoun for the deployment of a UNOSOM I 'security force' in 1992. As we have seen, Boutros-Ghali quickly became impatient with these negotiations and thereafter sought to freeze Aideed out of the process of augmenting the UN presence; from September 1992 the SNA was simply not consulted about new peacekeeping deployments.

But it was only from the start of UNOSOM II that the UN was legally, politically and materially in a position to take on various aspects of Aideed's Mogadishu power base. Perhaps the seminal moment here was the UNOSOM inspection on 5 June 1993 of an authorised SNA heavy-weapons storage facility located in the grounds of Radio Mogadishu. Interpreting the action as a threat to the radio station, SNA fighters ambushed the UN peacekeepers conducting the inspection. Twenty-six Pakistani peacekeepers and many Somalis died in the course of the event, which led to a Security Council resolution authorising the secretary-general to 'take all measures against all those responsible'. To some extent the resolution confirms SNA suspicions about UN intentions with regard to the radio station when it took note of: 'the crucial importance of neutralising radio broadcasting systems that contribute to the violence and attacks directed against the Operation'. It was from this point on that UNOSOM conducted an extensive set of ground and air operations against General Aideed and his political assets. Radio Mogadishu was taken out by air strikes on 12 June, and his 'headquarters' were destroyed on 17 June. Various other military operations targeted the leaders of the SNA, such as the one cited earlier on a political meeting of the SNA that killed seventy-three. As in others, the explicit end goal of this mission was the physical elimination of Aideed.

UN PEACEKEEPING AND THE NEW INTERVENTIONISM

In sum, UNOSOM II was a remarkable venture. Not only was it pioneering in terms of the sheer range of nation-building tasks (and authority) but also in respect to the chain of military operations that the UN conducted over the summer of 1993. Indeed, at the time, one of the most striking aspects of the UNOSOM II episode was the violence freely utilised by peacekeeping troops and the public relations discourse deployed to rationalise this force. Part of the significance of the words and actions of the UN was perhaps that they generated all sorts of unfavourable historical associations with previous interventions in sub-Saharan Africa. Here the modalities may have changed—be it a colonial expeditionary force, a straightforward great-power incursion or a multinational peacekeeping mission—but the ideological rationale of these interventions has certainly not. All have been justified along the lines of helping African societies on the road to liberal modernity. To highlight an important and interesting historical continuity in Somalia, where in 1950 the UN Trusteeship Council (then the central institutional mechanism in UN for decolonisation and nation-building) assigned the ex-colonial power (Italy) with the 'trusteeship' of the country. The mission of the 'Administering Power' was no less than the complete modernisation of social relations—the abolition of slavery, the legal establishment of private property and the like—and the creation from scratch of the institutions of a nation state, such as a universal education system and police force. With UNOSOM II, as we have seen, the object was also the recreation of the central state through the destruction of alternative sources of authority and the reconstruction of national institutions.

The difference between the trusteeship of Somalia in the 1950s and UNOSOM II in the 1990s was much less the overarching rationale than the modalities of effecting the requisite social and political change. UNOSOM was essentially an experiment in international intervention where the boundaries of peacekeeping were being rapidly expanded. Among other notable components, there was the loosening of the necessity of 'local consent' for deployment, the hard sell by UN officials of the humanitarian crisis to a wider diplomatic and public audience and, finally, the untested and novel format of peace enforcement under UN executive control. The issue of peace enforcement, as we have seen, was particularly thorny and ultimately counterproductive; after all, the political and ideological utility of the UN is the imprimatur of international society. Despite the fact that all peace interventions are decided upon by the Security Council, or more realistically by the Permanent-5, they are formally conducted on behalf of *all* member-states and are nearly always constituted with troops from some G-77 nations. The UN has always projected the notion of peacekeeping as a multinational and multiracial exercise, deployed for purely conflict-resolution purposes and in the service of international society. The scenes of UN-initiated violence and the rationalisation of this violence in Somalia temporarily undid this impartial image to reveal an action much more analogous with the colonial experience. One consequence of UNOSOM II, therefore, was the widespread consensus among policymakers that the UN should temporarily concentrate its expansion in peace activities on conventional 'second-generation' peacekeeping—that is, interventions that are formally deployed with the consent of local parties within Southern states and that are part of wider peace deals, nearly always defined in terms of political liberalisation. Of course, the necessity of 'local consent' does not mean that UN operations are apolitical; on the contrary, the acceptance by a government of UN peacekeepers invariably indicates the military weakness of its armed forces, the political pressure of external patrons, and the international acceptance of its adversary as legitimate negotiating partner. In the extreme it indicates a form of internationally negotiated and managed 'regime change'. It also does not mean that the UN is a passive administrator of peacekeeping operations. Rather, UN officials are powerful political interlocutors able to coax and, when necessary, compel 'the parties' down the path of liberalisation or 'power-sharing'. On more than one occasion since Somalia, UN envoys have reminded beleaguered presidents that unless they carry through their externally imposed commitments to liberalise then the 'international community' may be forced to review the continued 'service' of peacekeeping in the country; in other words, let often militarily superior rebel groups resort to the armed option against encircled government forces.

In the wider context, what all this goes to show is just how much the political activities of the UN have changed since the collapse of the Second and Third World in the late 1980s. Today, the UN Security Council and relevant UN departments routinely plan, authorise and deploy peace operations, which despite their politically invasive nature are very rarely brought into question. If anything, the fiercest critique of peace operations is a liberal internationalist one of the UN not intervening nearly forcefully or robustly enough—most notably in the DRC, Darfur and Rwanda. Yet conducting such an intrusive set of peace operations would have been politically unthinkable in the past, for example in the 1960s and 1970s, and marks a fundamental transformation of the UN's ideological orientation. In the workshop of peace operations, sub-Saharan Africa, the UN has forged a technocratic, military, and political role in crafting modern liberal states and societies, and is for the time being a major vehicle for effecting social and political change in the southern hemisphere.

16 The Liberal Peace Is Neither: Peacebuilding, State Building, and the Reproduction of Conflict in the Democratic Republic of Congo

STEIN SUNDSTØL ERIKSEN

THE STATE, LIBERAL PEACE, AND THE POLICIES OF STATE-BUILDING

The modern state may be defined as an institution that successfully claims a monopoly on the means of violence, control over a territory and a population and the responsibility to provide services, and is recognised by other states. This is the model of statehood on which all contemporary states are based. It is also the conception that underlies the practices of international institutions, including those involved in state-building and peace building.

At a minimum, state-building involves establishing the state's monopoly over the means of violence with control over the country's entire territory and with an effective administration. Thus, a strengthening of the state's security sector (police, army) and administration are central elements of state-building. To achieve such a strengthening, state-building includes programmes for integration of all armed groups into a national army, strengthening of police and military capacity and general capacity-building of the public sector.

However, existing programmes of state-building do not simply aim to build a state in this minimal sense. They seek to establish a particular kind of state, a liberal one. Liberal in this context means a state that (a) upholds the rule of law, (b) is democratic and (c) is based on a market economy. Given the universal acceptance of this notion of 'stateness', all states are compelled to struggle to approach this ideal, or at least to pretend to be striving to establish it. The idea of the state, therefore, has become what Gopal Balakrishnan calls 'an objectively operative fiction'—an idea that forms the basis for the design of formal institutions, even if the states in question are far from corresponding to it. This is clearly revealed by the type of activities that are undertaken. In addition to capacity-building in the security sector, projects of state-building typically include support of 'good governance', rule of law, democratisation and elections, and protection of human rights.

The number of international missions engaged in state-building has significantly increased over the last 20 years. However, the success of these missions has been limited. While all analysts appear to agree about this, and realise the inherently difficult nature of state-building, they draw different conclusions. Some argue that the lack of success is related to a lack of resources or insufficient attention and adaptation to local contexts, and that the fundamental objective is sound and valuable. Others argue that the problem is more fundamental and that the entire project of external state-building is contradictory and doomed to fail. This debate constitutes the backdrop for the following account of the attempts at state-building in the DRC.

In principle, there are several strategies that external actors can adopt towards 'failed states', that is, states that deviate significantly from this idea of statehood. First, they may decide to do nothing and refrain from interfering—at least beyond providing humanitarian relief. Edward Luttwak gave this perspective its most succinct formulation, when he called for the world to 'give war a chance'. This approach can be justified by referring to the principle of non-intervention, or in realist terms: 'our interests are not served by interference'. Second, they may decide that many states are beyond repair, and that the possibility of changing existing boundaries and permitting the creation of new states should be considered.

In most cases, however, these strategies appear too drastic. The first would imply an acceptance of tremendous suffering. Furthermore, there is no guarantee that letting conflicts run their course would lead to the formation of an effective state. As for the second strategy, it may run the risk of only reproducing existing problems at a lower level. There is a danger that, once recognition is given to some new states, there will be an explosion of new groups or regions demanding their own state, leading to 'anarchy and disorder on a planetary scale'. Another problem is to decide who should be given the authority to determine which states should be granted recognition, and be responsible for overseeing the establishment of new borders. The only plausible candidate for this role would be the UN, but, given its political and economic limitations, it is hard to see how it would be able to handle such a task.

If letting wars run their course will not work, and if redrawing boundaries will only be possible in exceptional cases, the obvious alternative is to continue with the strategy that has, by and large, been followed since the former colonies gained their independence, namely to seek to reconstruct existing states. This has also been the basis of external actors' policies in the DRC.

THE EVOLUTION OF THE CONGOLESE STATE

To understand the nature of the current situation in the DRC and the constraints faced by foreign actors engaged in state-building there, it is necessary to place it in an historical context. This section briefly describes the evolution of the state in the DRC from independence.

While many of its neighbouring countries, such as Angola, Congo-Brazzaville, Central African Republic, Uganda, Rwanda and Burundi were engulfed in civil war, mass violence was by and large avoided in the Congo after the resolution of the Congo crisis in the early 1960s. After the failure of the Katanga and Kasai secession movements in the 1960s, political opposition took a new form. Instead of seeking to establish a new state through secession, opposition groups were incorporated into the existing state through Mobutu's policy of divide and rule. Thus, although there were armed rebellions, they were few and quite easily crushed, and the ruling regime was able to (more or less) maintain control over the state for about 30 years, in spite of the deterioration of the state apparatus and of the country's economy.

Mobutu came to power in a military coup in 1965. His regime was one of the most corrupt in the world, 'unsurpassed in its ability to institutionalise cleptocracy at all levels of society'. Thus, in spite of the country's large resource base, per capita income sank continuously during the Mobutu regime. Moreover, the meagre infrastructure that existed in the country at independence gradually eroded, including the state administration. Lower-level officials often went for long periods without pay, and were compelled to support themselves through blackmail, bribery and theft. As a result of its institutional incoherence, the state was unable to implement its policies and to exert real control over society at the local level.

Mobutu's main power base was in the armed forces. During his early years in power, he provided modern equipment and firepower, and improved the level of training and education for officers, made possible by support from the United States and Belgium. However, Mobutu's control over the army was not secure, and in order to prevent the emergence of potential rivals he undertook frequent purges and reorganisations. The regular purges, low pay and recruitment on the basis of loyalty rather than professionalism had the effect of creating a military that was loyal, but inefficient. The army, had, in Young and Turner's phrase, become 'a mirage', totally incapable of fighting an armed enemy.

In later years, Mobutu bought military loyalty by allowing officers to enrich themselves in the gold and diamond business, and, quite simply, by letting soldiers resort to crime.

We see here a clear example of a weak state being forced to pursue policies that weaken it even further, in order to prevent the emergence of alternative power centres within the state apparatus. This had the additional advantage of freeing Mobutu from the need to strengthen the capacity of the armed forces. The imperatives of capacity and control were incompatible, but because foreign support was available he could maintain control without such capacity.

State control was also limited by the continued influence of traditional leaders. While their influence varied significantly between regions, they remained important figures in many parts of the country, with, among other things, control over land. Mobutu's policies toward traditional leaders wavered between attempts at incorporating them into the state and attempts at disempowering them. However, Mobutu depended on alliances with local leaders, who supported him in return for political control at the local level.

After the cold war, Mobutu could no longer rely on foreign support. As a response to foreign pressure, he tried to liberalise his regime. The military was divided about this process, and in 1993 rival military factions battled in Kinshasa, killing at least 1,200 people. By this time, Mobutu's control over the army had evaporated.

When a coalition led by Laurent Kabila marched towards Kinshasa in late 1996, they met little resistance. Instead of fighting, the army fled, plundering local villages on the way. It soon became clear that the rebels received major support from Rwanda and Uganda. From the fall of Mobutu until 2003, half the territory was outside state control altogether. These areas were nominally under some sort of control by foreign forces, together with their local allies. However, the real control exercised by these groups was quite limited. Ongoing fighting, the continued existence of local militias, and the weak administrative capacity of the concerned parties seriously limited their control. The same applied to those parts of the country nominally under the control of the Kinshasa government.

Within a year of coming to power, Kabila fell out with his erstwhile backers, the governments in Rwanda and Uganda. The foreign forces had become hugely unpopular. Thus, either Kabila could stick with his foreign allies, and risk further undermining domestic support, or he could distance himself from these allies, and face the consequences. After first trying to balance these conflicting imperatives, he ordered all foreign troops out of the country in August 1998. This decision triggered the war that lasted until 2003. Uganda and Rwanda turned against Kabila and, together with their Congolese allies, established new rebel movements in the eastern part of the country. If Angola had not intervened and forced the Rwandans to retreat to the east, the regime would almost certainly have been toppled. Subsequently, Angola was joined by Zimbabwe and Namibia in fighting on the side of the government.

However, the loose alliance that had fought Mobutu soon split, first into one faction supported by Rwanda—Congolese Rally for Democracy (RCD-Goma)—and one supported by Uganda—Movement for the Liberation of Congo (MLC)—and then into several smaller groups. Subsequently, the various factions fought both against the Kinshasa government and against each other. In practice, therefore, the country was divided in three. The western half of the country was under the—at least nominal—control of the central government. The eastern half was divided between Uganda and Rwanda, with their respective Congolese allies.

In January 2001, Laurent Kabila was assassinated. He was replaced by his son Joseph, who appeared to be more willing to negotiate with the rebels and cooperate with international organisations. Peace negotiations were resumed in South Africa, and led to the Pretoria agreement of June 2002, wherein a plan for the establishment of a new government was agreed. Eventually a government of national unity was set up in August 2003. This government remained in power until 2006, when the transitional period ended, and elections were held. Joseph Kabila was elected as president, with 58 per cent of the votes in the second round of the election and a clear majority in parliament.

Western states did not react when Rwanda and Uganda invaded the DRC, and continued to support these countries' ruling regimes, although the invasion constituted a blatant breach of the principle of non-intervention. The professed reason for the initial lack of military intervention by Western states was that the conflict was defined as an internal conflict. But perhaps they defined it as an internal conflict because they did not want to intervene. Once the cold war ended, Uganda and Rwanda had replaced the Congo as the West's main allies in the region, and the West no longer had any interest in supporting Mobutu. In addition, guilt for not intervening to prevent the Rwanda genocide may have made them reluctant to react against Rwanda, whose justification for the intervention in the Congo (Hutu extremists operating from bases there) could not easily be dismissed. As for Uganda, it has become the World Bank and International Monetary Fund's 'success story' and donors were reluctant to criticise its policies.

Neither Western states nor the foreign forces engaged in warfare inside the Congo have demanded a break-up of the Congolese state, or a redrawing of existing formal boundaries. They strongly supported the inter-Congolese dialogue, which aimed at restoring sovereignty through the establishment of a government of national unity and the withdrawal of all foreign troops. They also continued to channel aid funds through the national government. Just as during the cold war, the policies of both Western countries and the DRC's neighbours have consistently contributed to the reproduction of the existing state.

MONUC

MONUC was officially created by the Security Council in November 1999. Its initial task was to monitor the implementation of the peace process (cessation of hostilities, retreat of foreign forces, ensuring the flow of aid). The first task for MONUC was to establish a minimum of security in the country. Large parts of the territory, especially in the east, were outside the control of the central government. Even after the signing of the peace agreement and the official withdrawal of foreign forces, various militias fought for control over different parts of the territory, some with assistance from or close links to governments in neighbouring countries.

Over the following years, the Security Council made a number of resolutions that further expanded both the size and the mandate of the mission. In February 2000, the mission was expanded, and the number of troops was increased to more than 5,500. At that time, the mandate of the mission was expanded as well, from monitoring of the peace process to protection of civilians. Further, in December 2002, another increase in troops was accompanied by the establishment of a military task force. In 2003 and 2004, continued violence in different parts of the country led to further increases in troops and to a new security resolution in October 2004, which redefined the mission's mandate. As a result, the mission expanded to 16,700 troops, making it the largest UN peace operation in the world with an annual budget of more than US$1 billion. This stepwise expansion was a response to criticism for inaction, powerlessness and insufficient deployment of troops.

At the outset, the mission's focus was on monitoring and observation. From 2000, it was expanded to include security-related issues such as monitoring compliance with the Ceasefire Agreement and facilitation of humanitarian assistance.

The deteriorating security situation in the east led to an expansion of MONUC and a new Chapter VII mandate. Subsequently, more UN troops were stationed in the east. This was accompanied by the EU's involvement through the Artemis mission in Ituri in 2003. While these efforts to stem the violence in Ituri succeeded in the short term, violence has periodically resumed in the east, particularly in the Kivus.

In 2003, the Security Council mandated MONUC to 'provide assistance . . . for the re-establishment of a State based on the rule of law'. In 2004, the mission's mandate was expanded again, to include support for the disarmament of foreign combatants and the national disarmament, demobilisation and reintegration (DDR) programme. Importantly, this resolution also committed MONUC to support the electoral process, legislative reform and security sector reform, as well as the promotion and protection of human rights. Thus, although there was still no direct reference to state-building at this point, MONUC had become involved in most parts of the state-building agenda. However, the reference to promotion and protection of human rights was qualified by the fact that this area was not listed among those in which MONUC was authorised to use 'all necessary means within its capacity' (although support of the electoral process was on this list).

The current scope of MONUC's operations is clearly expressed in the Security Council Resolution 1751 of April 2007:

> the Secretary-General proposes, the principal elements of the Mission's mandate would be to assist the Government in building a stable security environment; consolidating democracy; planning security sector reform and participating in its early stages; protecting human rights and strengthening the rule of law; the protection of civilians; and the conduct of local elections. In all areas of its work, MONUC would emphasise the role of civil society in political dialogue and decision-making, ensuring a rights-based approach and the implementation of Security Council resolutions.

The adoption of resolution 1756 in 2007 constituted a further expansion of the mandate, to include not only support of elections, but also strengthening of democratic institutions, support of civil society and promotion of good governance.

As of September 2009, MONUC deployed 18,691 persons, including 1,078 police officers and 3,456 civilians. Troops are stationed in all parts of the country. The civilian parts of the mission are responsible for protection of human rights, organisation of elections, promoting the rule of law, DDR and public relations (including running the radio station Radio Okapi). Clearly, MONUC has become a mission that engages in most parts of the liberal peace-building agenda. In addition to the prevention of violent conflict and provision of security, it is engaged, inter alia, in security sector reform (SSR), DDR, organising elections, and promotion of the rule of law and human rights. Thus, in describing the activities of the MONUC Political Affairs Division (PAD), the MONUC website states that 'PAD monitors and supports democratisation in the DRC. This entails practical support to national and provincial institutions, as well as civil society organisations, to create conditions conducive to the establishment of democracy and the rule of law'. In practice, this means that state-building has become a key task for MONUC, as reflected in its mission: 'to assist a country ruined by war and civil strife to become once again a functioning State able to protect its citizens from war, hunger and abuse, and to give them opportunity for a better life'.

In some areas, international actors have achieved some modest success. First, the elections were held as planned, and took place without large-scale violence. Second, MONUC, other UN agencies and other donors have been able to provide significant humanitarian assistance to suffering civilians. And, third, while peace remains fragile and violent clashes have continued to erupt in the east, the coalition government and the peace process have not broken down.

Yet, in spite of these achievements, when the results are assessed in relation to the liberal peace agenda in general and the aim of state-building in particular, one cannot avoid the conclusion that the mission has failed. In spite of MONUC's efforts and the continued expansion of its size and mandate, it has not succeeded in strengthening the state, which continues to struggle to establish a monopoly of violence and control over territory—let alone to create a stable democracy with 'good governance'. Although return to civil war has been avoided and the government of national unity remains in place, the process of creating a truly integrated national army is still far from completed, the army's capacity to fight rebel groups is severely limited and local militias continue to challenge the state's control over parts of the country.

In terms of state-building, MONUC (and other international actors) has not succeeded. Arthur Kepel sums up the situation: 'against [the] backdrop of the rising anarchy, the UN mission in DRC, or Monuc, today stands thoroughly discredited'. Although optimists may argue that it is too early to draw such a conclusion, the evidence supports Kepel's contention. The question for the remaining parts of this article is why MONUC and other international actors have been unable to move decisively in the direction of building a liberal state.

WHY HAS MONUC FAILED?

We may identify four reasons why MONUC's attempts at state-building in the DRC have failed. First, the resources made available have been insufficient. Second, the policies of MONUC have been hampered by a lack of knowledge of local conditions and unwillingness to adapt policies to local context. Third, the attempts at state-building have run counter to the interests of key domestic actors. And, fourth, the model of state-building on which the effort has been based has been flawed and contradictory.

Resources

The first and probably least important explanation for this failure could be that MONUC has not had sufficient resources. Indeed, compared with other UN peacekeeping missions, this is certainly the case. For instance, in terms of aid per capita, the missions in East Timor, Afghanistan, Bosnia, Sierra Leone and other places have had budgets many times larger than MONUC. Considering the country's vast size and virtually non-existent infrastructure, it is clear that MONUC's resources have been insufficient. Thus, according to UNDPKO there are 15 times as many peacekeepers in Liberia as in the DRC, relative to population size.

However, there was never a realistic chance of obtaining sufficient resources. For political reasons, it would seem extremely unlikely that the peacekeepers would be given anything like the resources needed. It is one thing for donors to find adequate funding for peace-building missions in mini-states like Kosovo or East Timor, quite another to expect them to allocate comparable amounts per capita to a vast country like DRC. This is especially so when the fate of the country has no direct bearing on what is seen as the donor countries' own national interests. While donors may have a genuine wish to help recipient countries, it is a fact that donor policies and actions are always to some extent shaped by other considerations as well. These may include economic or geopolitical interests as well as a wish to enhance their own international standing by being seen as generous or compassionate. Thus, while policies of development, including state-building policies, are always justified with reference to moral concerns and the best interests of recipient countries, donors may be equally motivated by a wish to promote their own national interests. To expect DRC to receive funding comparable to that given to the missions in Kosovo or East Timor is therefore wishful thinking.

More importantly, the idea that MONUC has failed because of a lack of resources implies that it could have succeeded if it had been given more resources. Whether this is the case depends on what one means by 'success'. Had MONUC been given, say five times as much funding as it has had so far, it could probably have prevented some of the violence that has occurred in different parts of the country. Thus, if success means prevention of violent conflict, an increase in resources could probably have led to success. But if success is to be measured by the standards of the liberal peace-building model, it is highly doubtful that more resources would have led to a successful outcome. While some violent conflict could have been prevented by stationing a large number of soldiers in different parts of the country, this would not have enabled MONUC to build an effective state. The latter not only requires resources. It also depends on the will, interests and power of domestic actors.

One Size Fits All

The second reason for failure is that external actors tend to rely on standardised approaches to state-building across countries. Thus, it is assumed that the same model of state-building can be applied everywhere, regardless of local circumstances. This is the assumption underlying the liberal peace model as well as donor programmes of capacity-building, good governance and the like. Such a standardised approach tends to lead to the neglect of the specific conditions found in each state. In the DRC, one consequence of this assumption has been that donors have paid insufficient attention to the variation in local dynamics found in different parts of the country. Thus, as shown by Séverine Autesserre, donors did not adapt their policies to the specific local dimension of the DRC conflict. In particular, they did not address the intricate and complex dynamics of conflict in the eastern parts of the country. The problems of the continued presence of Hutu militias from Rwanda and the local conflicts in Ituri and Kivu were not addressed, leading to the eruption of new violence in late 2008.

However, while this critique is valid enough, one should not draw the conclusion that the main problem with external state-building is that it has relied on standardised strategies. This would imply that the problem could be overcome if donors were more knowledgeable of local conditions and adapted their strategies accordingly. Such adaptation is fundamentally compatible with the liberal peace model and the depoliticising approach to state-building associated with it. The only difference is that it requires more sensitivity to context in the choice of means to be employed. It does not suggest that there is anything wrong with the basic model itself. However, taking context seriously implies that it is not just the means (policies, strategies) that must be adapted to context, but the ends as well. Context not only determines how donors seek to help build liberal-democratic states, but also determines what type of state one can reasonably expect to help build.

Domestic Interests

The third reason for failure is related to power and political economy. For state-building to succeed, key domestic actors must share the goal of creating the type of state that state-builders want. Successful state-building depends on the existence of a domestic social base that makes it possible to maintain stability without using state resources to buy support through patronage. The possibility of succeeding in such a project will depend mainly on internal power relations, and on the creation of a political alliance consisting of social forces with both an interest in strengthening the state and sufficient power to do so. If we assume that regime survival will be a, if not the, primary concern of rulers, it follows that state formation depends on the compatibility of regime interests and power on the one hand, and state formation on the other. Thus, if regime interests are best served by strengthening state institutions, it is likely that such a policy will be attempted.

Conversely, if there is a real or perceived contradiction between regime interests and state-building, it will not. If regime survival does not depend on strengthening the state (and may even be threatened by it) and regimes have alternative strategies for political survival, then state-building is not likely to be pursued. In many countries, ruling regimes have maintained control by incorporating existing elite groups into the patronage networks inherited from the colonial era, laying the groundwork for the emergence of a weak neo-patrimonial state. In a neo-patrimonial system, there is no clear separation between the private and the public, or between the personal interests of officials and the interests of the institution to which they belong. Regimes of neo-patrimonial states secure the support they need, not through the pursuit of state policies, but by using state resources to offer material rewards to clients in return for political support.

In the DRC as well as in most other cases, the programme of state-building started with seeking to establish a peace agreement and create a government of national unity. International recognition and access to aid was made on the condition that all key actors accepted the establishment of a new national coalition government. Members of the coalition government have strong interests in simultaneously preserving the government of national unity and preserving its weakness. The preservation of the government gives them access to state resources and donor funds and maintains their formal political power. At the same time, the state's very weakness is a resource, both because it makes it possible for elite politicians to get access to economic resources, and because it enables them to maintain their own armed groups (sometimes even within the formally integrated national army). This has clearly been the case in the DRC. It is well known that many actors (states, companies, warlords) profit from dealing in (and with) weak, conflict-ridden states. Certain types of activities do not depend on general stability and a well-functioning state. Many groups therefore see continued conflict as being in their interest, since it enables them to continue their business. Given the weakness of the state and the strength of such actors in the DRC, it is doubtful that anyone will be able to rein in all the warlords.

Thus, official donor policies contradict the interests of key actors. In such situations, the prospects of donor success in promoting state-building are bleak. Merely establishing a government of national unity will not remove the underlying causes of conflict. The outcome of power-sharing in the DRC was that the different factions simply divided the state and its resources between them, thus reproducing the patrimonial system, which caused the state's weakness in the first place. This means that the price one may have to pay for peace, at least in the short to medium term, could be the reproduction of state weakness. In other words, the state of Congo will persist, but so will its weakness.

A Flawed Model

The fourth explanation of failure is that the model of state-building on which donor policies have been based is flawed and contradictory. In these policies, the end state is taken for granted, as are the means to be applied to achieve that end. The end is to create a liberal state (with rule of law, protection of human rights, good governance, market economy), and the means employed are: establishing a government of national unity, capacity-building, training of officials, financial support and human resources. This support to the government is to be provided on conditions determined by the donors.

In liberal peace theory, both the possibility and the desirability of the establishment of a liberal-democratic state are taken for granted. This starting point has several implications, both theoretical and political. At the analytical level, it follows that states that deviate from the ideal tend to be described in terms of what they lack rather than in terms of their actual properties. It is the absence of the specified criteria (service provision, a monopoly of violence, control over territory, accountability, participation, rule of law) that defines these states, and not their actual properties. 'Weak states', 'failed states' and 'quasi-states' can then only appear as 'a flawed imitation of a mature Western form'.

Politically, this implies that the absence of anything like a modern state in many countries is seen as a problem to be addressed, in order to enable a 'normal' state to emerge. What is never questioned is the aim of creating a liberal-democratic state. Instead, this aim is treated as a given, determined prior to and independently of the political process. This means that the task of state-builders is to devise policies and strategies that make the creation of such a state possible, without questioning the possibility of creating a state of this kind. If it turns out that governments and citizens in the countries concerned do not want such a state, it is seen as a problem of local 'perceptions' that need to be changed. The question then becomes how local perceptions can be changed, and how domestic actors can be brought to support the aims of the state-builders. The state will then be seen as an external imposition, since it is not allowed to emerge through a political process that involves key domestic actors and to take root in domestic social relations. Following Akeel Bilgrami, we may call this 'Archimedean liberalism'.

This reveals an internal contradiction in liberal peace theory, between national ownership and self-determination on the one hand and liberal universalism on the other. By operating with a fixed, non-negotiable conception of what the state eventually should look like, and by refusing to let the domestic political process determine the nature of the state, donors in practice undermine the self-determination of the states they seek to strengthen. Moreover, by taking the end state as given and by refusing to let the domestic political process determine the nature of the state that should be built, they undermine the prospects for building domestic support for their project. And, without such support, the project cannot succeed. Recognising that there is neither a standardised recipe for state-building nor a standard model of statehood that can be applied across all cases means that the universality of the liberal model of statehood on which donor policies are based must be questioned.

This is not to argue that the liberal state model is to be rejected as a universal normative ideal. This is a separate issue, not discussed here. The point, rather, is that even if one accepts this model as normatively valid, the prospects of succeeding in creating such a state will be undermined if the nature of the state that is to be built is taken as given, prior to any dialogue between the external state-builders and those whose state is to be built. Such an approach implies that the relationship between donors and recipients becomes one between subject and object, where all key decisions are made by one party and applied to the other. In this restricted view of politics, the domestic political arena is hollowed out, and what is left to determine for domestic actors is—at the most—the means they should employ to create such a state.

Attempts at state-building by foreign actors in the DRC have not had much success. Four reasons have been pointed out for this. First, insufficient resources have been provided. Second, donors have used a standardised approach that does not take local context sufficiently into account. Third, domestic power relations have been such that state-building has not served the interests of key domestic actors. Finally, the policy has been based on a fixed, non-negotiable conception of what the state eventually should look like. Although all these factors have contributed to the failure to create a liberal state in the DRC, the last two appear to be more fundamental than the first and the second.

The DRC experience reveals the paradoxical effects of external involvement in state-building. On the one hand, the policies of external actors (other states, international organisations) have contributed to reaffirming the existence of the state in the DRC. Further, the policies of Western countries have been based on the premise that this state should be based on something like the liberal idea of the state described earlier. Their practices have been aimed at facilitating the emergence of a state that corresponds to this idea, by supporting institution-building, good governance, elections, and so on, and by setting up formal institutions based on the liberal model.

On the other hand, these practices have, in the absence of credible local allies with both an interest in and ability to pursue the creation of an effective state, contributed to the reproduction of state weakness. Thus, while the idea that the state in the DRC should persist and be built on liberal principles has been reinforced, an effect of external engagement has been to contribute to the reproduction of weakness and undermine the possibility for creating the type of state that donors seek to establish.

This points to the need to question two of the basic assumptions underlying the liberal peace agenda. First, the idea that a liberal state can be created anywhere, regardless of the specific social and political conditions found in a given country must be rejected. In conflict-ridden societies where many groups benefit from the reproduction of conflict and of state weakness, and where there are no strong groups with an interest in the establishment of such a state, this may simply be impossible. In other words, the model of a liberal-democratic state may not be as universally applicable as assumed. Second, and related, the possibility of externally driven state-building may have been seriously overestimated. While it is clearly possible for donors to alleviate suffering and to prevent (or at least contain) violent conflict, the possibility of building a liberal-democratic state from the outside is far from clear.

Part Six

Globalization and a New World Order?

INTRODUCTION

Demands for intervention in African conflicts were almost immediately followed by demands for engagement in virtually all aspects of African societies to help remove the conditions of conflict and, ultimately, to bring about social change. How can we make sense of such demands? Why do states try to change other states? Young makes an early attempt to understand this, seeking to connect the idea of intervention to deeper theoretical themes. As with conflict and intervention, the mainstream debate has been rather slow to catch up with these issues, but now analytical commentary tends to divide into friendly critics, such as Stamnes, who accept such notions as governance but are very critical as to its implementation, and more hostile ones, who discern a subordinating project in such notions. The Bradleys usefully explain much of the jargon in this area as well as offering a sympathetic yet critical assessment of their own. More critically, Oba shows how dilemmas and controversies about social change are to be found in even the most intimate areas of human life, and that practices and beliefs that seem self-evidently "wrong," often, if not always, need not only more analysis but more humility and less cultural arrogance. One of the most dramatic forms of post–Cold War "global governance" is the project of an international criminal law, a project for which Africa has been a major experimental laboratory. Kelsall presents a fascinating discussion of this tendency, combined with a detailed and critical case study.

17

'A Project to be Realized': Global Liberalism and Contemporary Africa

TOM YOUNG

Liberalism is the 'political theory of modernity'. From the beginning it has always been about globalization. The reasons for this as well as the reasons why it remains obscured are inscribed in its discursive logic. What is different about the current phase of that globalization is the more rapid erosion of obstacles that have hitherto confronted it. Some of these developments have already been examined from this perspective but connecting discursive logics to political action remains notoriously difficult. For many of course even to start with 'ideas' may seem like heresy. Traditionally international relations has conceived of relations between states as driven by 'interests' and though the precise scope of this notion has always remained rather opaque it clearly forms part of a family of positions and standpoints in the social sciences which construe political activity as in practice reducible to such 'interests'. In these views political discourse becomes a kind of froth resting on action inspired by interests. To quote more or less at random but I hope not unfairly, 'national interests overpower morality'. It tends to follow that where states do articulate their positions in terms other than interest (as for example currently with reference to governance, democracy and human rights) then we are witness to some form of higher deception and the analytical trick is to decipher these deceptions and see what interests *really are* in play.

It goes without saying that none of this is of course wholly implausible. However the position taken here is that one cannot make any sense of either domestic politics or relations between states without taking account of 'ideas' though that term has to be understood more broadly than as the texts conventionally constituted by political theory. If I accentuate the element of ideas in the following discussion the least that can be said is that there is no shortage of other approaches. What is required to better explore the connection between political ideas and political action is not the ignoring of political ideas but a more detailed analysis, in this case, of how liberal ideology 'works', the role of state functionaries and professionals in its production and dissemination and the effects of this on relations between states. I suggest that contemporary Africa offers a relatively privileged arena to examine how the liberal project 'works'.

LIBERALISM AND THE LIBERAL PROJECT

There are many excellent accounts of political liberalism considered as ideas in the rather narrow, essentially textual sense. There are far fewer accounts of its thrust, its yearnings, its intense desire to dominate people and communities, in brief its 'project'. It is the connection between the two which is central to understanding contemporary liberalism and its place in the world. What has always lain at the heart of the liberal endeavor is the claim to be able to uncover a 'universal standpoint', the 'view from nowhere', in abstraction from the concrete characteristics of human communities and societies, by reference to a natural level of human existence which is accessible to logical and quasi-scientific modes of reasoning. The actual facts of social and communal life in particular places and at particular times, considered in themselves, are both epistemologically obfuscatory and ontologically oppressive. Thus all liberal theoretical strategies from Hobbes onwards have involved devices (state of nature; veil of ignorance; spaceships) which 'strip out' such features. The crucial strategic move has always been to go behind the apparent social realities to a 'deeper' reality. This theoretical strategy generates, as is well known, the core assumptions of liberal political thought. Thus societies consist of individuals characterized by reason and freedom, engaging in projects the value of which only they can judge. The task of social and political institution-building is to ensure that such individuals cooperate to mutual advantage. The essential institutions to do this are the state and civil society. The *sovereign state* has two important features. Firstly it requires that no other center of political power may legitimately exist and secondly that there is nothing in principle outside the scope of the state and its power. There is of course considerable tension in the liberal tradition on this latter point because in some views states may be constrained by a certain class of supposed universals called human rights but there is considerable difference about how these constraints work in practice. *Civil society* consists of that sphere of social interactions (especially but not only economic ones) that free individuals engage in. These transactions are regulated by the state externally as it were (by law). The state does not concern itself with the content of citizens' activities and since the state is neutral as to competing theories of the good it is able to protect this realm as a realm of freedom and tolerance.

But to halt there is to halt at the point that allows liberalism to obscure its own historical role. Two further issues need to be considered. One concerns the nature of liberal belief. This is a complex matter and my suggestions are tentative. The main one is that Liberalism, in its claims to universal social and political truths, is not *an* ideology it is *the* ideology. Other so-called ideologies are derivative from it (socialism) or parasitic on it ('conservatism'). What is distinctive about this ideology (what arguably makes it ideology) is that, in the way it works, it does not require formal assent to particular propositions or faith—it is in this sense that it is true that the liberal state is neutral as between for example different forms of religious belief (though not of course their consequences). In their historical development liberal states did not, by and large, try and replace religious belief with some other sets of beliefs. Generally speaking individuals within liberal societies are free to hold virtually any opinions however bizarre or eccentric. In a sense the whole purpose of liberal ideology is to present itself as above the level of (necessarily partial) beliefs. Other *mere* beliefs/ideologies are then reducible to interests, a characteristic to which liberalism is apparently immune.

But if liberalism is not about beliefs it must have believers. Historically liberalism is peculiarly associated with the modern 'middle class'. That term leant and lends a false air of familiarity to what was a fundamentally new phenomenon, a stratum of functionaries and intellectuals (often of course the same person was both) who had neither social standing apart from their association with the state (hence their hatred of hierarchy and custom) nor interests (in the social sense), and were peculiarly defined by the possession of 'expertise' and (later) democratic ratification. The salience of this stratum has increased as liberal states have pulverized established social norms and practices as part of a process of 'emancipation' and replaced these with various forms of state-engineered social technique. Thus in large areas of its operation the modern liberal state is beholden to specialized functionaries and associated strata who effectively determine the scope and purposes of its actions and policies. This is the context for the second point about liberalism's historical development, namely its association with modern social science. In a sense liberalism constitutes itself in the form of social science claims to knowledge, closely linked to forms of expertise which insinuate themselves into all aspects of social life. Thus liberalism not only uncovers universal truths but in its social science form it also understands how societies and communities *really* work, better than their members. But the form of this understanding is always shaped by the 'universal standpoint'. If we already know how Man is by Nature what is there to say about how he is in fact except how his nature may be restored to him? This is why so much of Western thought and social science has characterized existing social forms in negatives, categories of what is *not there,* from 'history-less' peoples to 'undeveloped' societies.

These practices of 'stripping out' and of expertise/social engineering have generated an unease with the world, an incurable restlessness, a profound need to impose the deliriums of liberation on everyone else. The balm for this ailment has been new forms and means of domination. Liberalism's political project has not been to inculcate new beliefs but, 'to deconstruct old customary ways of life and to produce new ones'. To use a modern idiom it is about programming not propositions. Liberal social practice is about those disciplines that interiorize new forms of social behavior characteristic of the 'free' 'individual'. As Taylor puts it, 'radical disengagement opens the prospect of self-remaking'. Such emancipated individuals are of course much easier to weld into collectivities and to subject to various kinds of social discipline. Indeed what accounts for much of its 'practical' success is the new forms of power made possible by such disciplines. Part of this is clearly, as Marxists have long stressed, about producing the conditions for industrial capitalism but it is not only about that. As students of war have often noted, 'by revolutionizing society, the state was able as never before to exploit the energies of society for war'.

Yet in unconscious recognition perhaps that the compulsion of moral beliefs comes from their being inscribed in the practices and imperatives of communities, liberalism constructs pseudo-communities of moral compulsion which are not part of the give and take of real communal life but are rather rooted in ideological abstractions. In addition sociologically it was and is faced with real resistance and as often as not, is forced to rework 'customary ways' or to an extent remain dependent on or in tension with them. Thus until recently the armed forces in modern liberal states for example have remained to an important degree pre-modern institutions emphasizing values of heroism and combat almost entirely at odds with liberal ideology. Only recently have they been subject to 'liberalization' not only of the obvious kinds, the abolition of special units for women, tolerance of homosexuality and so on but in the individualization of the soldier's role. Likewise with the family an institution which for radicals has long been an institution of 'oppression'. Again only relatively recently have liberal states moved to 'emancipate' people from the family by individualizing and contractualizing it and still with considerable misgivings as to the impact of such interference on the role of the family as an agent of moral socialization. As these examples show liberalism remains endlessly dynamic, a moving though cumulative agenda. Thus currently part of the function of liberal academia is to explore the as yet 'politically unrealistic' options which may later become part of such an agenda whether this be world government, the destruction of the nation state or the elimination of the differences between men and women.

It is thus both its own discursive logic and endlessly recalcitrant social realities that make liberalism, (*contra* those conservatives who really believe that liberalism is some sort of civic order) a form of permanent revolution, indeed permanent terror, constantly seeking new objects of 'emancipatory' purification. This emancipatory terror generates a logic of modernization that is (and has always been) both domestic and transnational. Indeed it might be suggested that some of the most important features of the modern liberal state are best exhibited in its colonial form, where the non-West is seen as essentially empty. In such circumstances the state is quite clearly the instrument of an enlightened group imposing 'progress' from above on an essentially subject population irrespective of the nature of the 'natives', with at most minor adjustments for local variations. Thus British colonial rule in India, 'represented the great conquering discourse of Enlightenment rationalism, entering into India precisely at the moment of its greatest unchecked arrogance'. Note that the natives are not required to change their overt beliefs, indeed these may even be protected on the model of metropolitan norms. They are however required to changes their practices and behaviors. 'Modernization' involved the extirpation of 'barbarous' practices as much by the manufacture of a local 'middle class' as by direct legal proscription. But 'modernization' was something done to Western societies before it was done to others. The imposition of 'enlightened' practices on colonial populations precisely paralleled their earlier imposition on domestic populations.

CIVIL SOCIETY AND NATION STATE

The examples of the colonial state and domestic enlightenment, while they illuminate aspects of the liberal project, omit perhaps the most central feature of political modernity, the mobilization of consent. Colonial forms proved historically transitory. Indeed liberal colonialism could be said to have dug its own grave. Within a liberal order the very real power of state functionaries cannot simply be a power of subjection and compliance but must be grounded in some 'rational' instruments (public purpose and legal regulation) not least for their own reassurance—'it is psychologically important that representatives and officials think of themselves as dependent on the grass-roots'. The transition to modern political orders *is* a genuine shift. The objects of 'emancipation' cannot simply be coerced, they must also be brought to 'consent' to the changes being visited upon them. All citizens are to be included within a single political space based on feelings of consent not mere compliance.

This new political space was subject to two principles of organization. The first, as already noted, is civil society, a concept which forms an important part of liberal theorizing, sustaining such notions as autonomy and pluralism. The picture as presented by liberal orthodoxy tends however to ignore central features of the historical experience which created civil society. Firstly, that those groups and organizations which did not fit the emerging liberal order (guilds, communal groups, clans etc.) were marginalized or coerced out of existence. Secondly those new forms of association that did flourish in this new order, far from being 'autonomous', were heavily shaped or regulated by legal norms buttressed by state power. It is not accidental that the constitution of civil society is historically concomitant with the final construction of state sovereignty. Thirdly, this emerging civil society was actively formed by state-driven techniques of cultural homogenization (mass compulsory education being perhaps the greatest cultural disaster of modern times) and the promotion of individualism. Finally it is worth noting that historically all this in turn occurred in a context of incessant war-making which fuelled increasing taxation, surveillance and standardization.

Contemporary liberal and social science understandings of 'democracy', 'civil society' and related terms are massively shaped by this historical experience. 'Democracy' has never meant people ruling themselves, or societies electing representatives which actually represent that society. Nor can representative democracy be seen as simply a device for overcoming the problems of size in the democratic polity but is rather rooted in a fear that 'the people' would not necessarily respect liberal notions of 'reason' and 'justice'. The 'representative' was not to represent the views of 'society', but rather that part of it that guaranteed the protection of the liberal constraints on the democratic process. Once the rest of society had become 'educated' to the point it no longer posed a threat to these liberal constraints then access to the democratic process might follow. Virtually all contemporary liberal theory takes as its *starting point* various 'rights' which are not amenable to democratic change.

But there was a second principle of reorganization of modern political space that is almost entirely ignored in the official canon of liberal 'political thought' though not its political practice, namely nationalism. The transition to modern political forms involved more than the imposition of a new kind of political machinery, the state, a new form of social order and a new kind of individualism but took place within the framework of something called nation. It seems implausible to imagine that before 'modernity' people did not form groups which had identities but, following Kaviraj, these were 'fuzzy' rather than 'enumerated'. Political identities have always existed but there is much about modern nationalism as a political practice that was fundamentally new. Modernizing elites and modern nationalism claimed of course to emancipate individuals but this remained and remains an extremely abstract and, as it were, cold business. Thus, and to put it rather crudely, the project of liberal modernity draped itself in reworked particular (group) identities. As a matter of political practicalities and in order to give some emotional warmth to the process the 'nation' had to draw on particular attachments such as kin, people and place (or at least the language of such attachments) but to mobilize them in a different way around a different broader identity. The long historical connection between liberalism and nationalism reflected the importance of nationalism in assisting in the break up of older political communities and ensured that, at least until the second half of the twentieth century, most liberals regarded nationalism as a 'progressive' force.

A LIBERAL INTERNATIONAL ORDER, THE COLD WAR AND INDEPENDENT AFRICA

The emergence of nation-states generated finally a system of such states which itself embodied tensions between the universal and the particular. The concepts and assumptions of the new order required and assumed a language of equality of nations and states, namely national 'self-determination'. But these characteristics in fact only belonged, in the language of an age not unhinged by political correctness, to 'civilized' nations. Until they had proved their capacity for civilization 'uncivilized' nations remained outside the magic circle, though they could aspire to join. Conceptually this of course precisely paralleled domestic developments; just as citizens must be educated to see themselves and act as individuals before they could participate in civil society so states also must be brought to enlightenment before they could be considered equals.

African states came to independence in a period when this liberal international order was being reshaped by the dynamics of the

Cold War which paradoxically strengthened the elements of pluralism within the system. Universalism was constrained by Great Power rivalry. The 'standard of civilization' was abandoned. States were equal and sovereign and could choose their own economic and political systems. Yet in practice the post-independence elites appropriated all the assumptions of Western modernity in both their national and international forms. The newly independent African states were run by people who looked to essentially Western visions of modernity and progress. The need to catch-up often legitimated socialist versions of modernization but everywhere the new state was seen as central to bringing about rapid progress. African elites took to heart the imperatives of modernization and mobilization and were arguably rather more sociologically realistic than their later self-appointed mentors in realizing that these processes, involving such massive transformations of their societies, were incompatible with liberal democracy. Mobilization, both economic and political, by overtly authoritarian means, became the order of the day.

But, 'alien in origin, these [states] possessed neither symbolic depth, nor a common language of deep accountability, nor any indigenous conventions of high-political restraint'. Two processes clearly constrained the implementation of these visions. Firstly African states had to function within specific social settings often deeply antagonistic to the modernizing project. 'A massive obstacle to the rampant doctrinaire state is the great pluralism of African societies'. The African state, to be minimally effective, found itself having to deal with social forces which were not congruent with Western state models which in turn led to various forms of patron clientalism and ethnic coalition-building. In many cases the accumulating difficulties and the shortage of material resources eroded the modernizing impulses of elites and reduced their politics to little more than group aggrandizement. Secondly society, as it were, seeped into the state. Lower level functionaries upon whom elites relied to implement the visions of progress had often only very imperfectly internalized the relevant conceptual vocabulary. Their political 'operational code' could in practice be quite different. In large parts of Africa it has proved impossible to sustain the central institutions of the state, armies and bureaucracies. Rather armies have split along ethnic lines and bureaucracies have failed to administer. Domestic sovereignty has proved highly elusive. Some states threaten to disappear altogether and many are sustained by little more than the imperatives of the contemporary world order.

NEW WORLD ORDER?

The intellectual and political collapse of colonialism and the dynamics of super-power rivalry had sustained a shaky but genuine political pluralism at the international level. The demise of the Soviet bloc removed that shelter. We can now see the post-war period as a deviant phase. Since the end of the Cold War the universal elements of the liberal project have come to the fore. The scope and forms of intervention remain unclear and disputed and shaped by all sorts of 'pragmatic' considerations, including traditional state rivalries and the logistical problems thrown up by new kinds of 'humanitarian' intervention. It is shaped also by the structural forms of particular political systems. But the outlines of an agenda are clear even if to placate certain political forces this is dressed up in the language of 'interests'. Western liberal discourse of course has its cynical and duplicitous side in the context of Cold War and/or Great Power politics (though this is often exaggerated) but the various authors of this discourse (the World Bank and Amnesty International etc. as much as 'theorists') have a great deal in common and genuinely think they stand for a better world. *Because* liberalism is a massive historical forgetting and because it is caught up in its own notions and language of equality (of individuals and states), the liberal social order being offered to African countries has to be the current model in which the state must be restrained, the economy allowed to operate 'freely' and citizens to relate to each other through contract and rights. That is the only form of liberal state and civil society that we (now) know. Thus the dilemma facing such positions is clear: historical amnesia, cultural arrogance and assumptions of equality (about both individuals and states) preclude the overt recommendation to Third World countries of a Hobbesian Leviathan that will do the grim business of 'deconstructing' old ways of life and creating the social preconditions for a liberal state. The only alternative then is to find functional equivalents of Leviathan which can bring about those social transformations.

It is within this space that 'governance' and 'civil society' have come to be central operational concepts in the policies of both Western governments and multilateral bodies. Such considerations are clearly at work in a variety of initiatives from the World Bank's capacity enhancement program to the funding of political parties. World Bank analysts have long moved beyond a crude 'markets-solve-everything' sort of view. 'Private enterprise needs an enabling environment and only government can provide this. So the problems of governance must be faced; they cannot simply be willed away by privatization, economic liberalization and reliance on market processes'. But there is also an emphasis that goes beyond the restructuring of governance (in the narrower sense of technical capabilities and so on) to the restructuring of civil society. There is an implicit recognition that there will be no liberal states until there are liberal persons. This is clear as much in the 'economic' sphere (which in the liberal sense is still largely to be constructed) as in the political. Comparing the management of public enterprises in Eastern Europe with those in Africa Landell-Mills, a leading World Bank expert on Africa, argues: 'African managers cannot easily set aside their loyalties to their community . . . African managers cannot easily escape the heavy social obligations that take up a large proportion of their time'. It is this and other obstacles that outside agencies whose concern is to promote 'governance' and 'development' must somehow remove. 'Setting aside' loyalty to communities is what the liberal project is all about.

Not surprisingly the 'civil society' aspect of this project has been colonized by so-called NGOs. Despite a surface hostility towards the international financial institutions and Western interests and power, NGOs loudly proclaimed emphasis on 'grass roots' participation in the development process is to be understood entirely within Western preconceptions about the state and the person. The bizarre contradictions of this discourse notwithstanding (demanding the protection of cultures in one breath and the elimination of 'cultural bias' in the next) the agenda is known in advance—'progressive', 'grass roots' organizations are simply to be 'mobilized' around it. For their part financial institutions, though in a formal sense controlled by Western states, have a vision of economic order which is rooted in standard liberal conceptions and is not simply the plaything of particular Western interests. Both forces are inclined to deny the sovereignty of African governments, both increasingly stress the creation of 'civil society' and both make no secret of their contempt for and disinterest in cultural traditions that do not square with Western notions of 'rights' and 'justice'.

THE REORDERING OF MOZAMBIQUE

Although in many ways an extreme case (possibly the poorest country in the world) much of this agenda can be seen at work in a country like Mozambique. The logic of liberalism goes well beyond a demand for changes in particular policies (the routine stuff of relations between states) and calls for the restructuring of the state and related matters such as property relationships. That Mozambique was pressured to adopt liberal democracy, despite official propaganda that it was a 'natural' development, has been said as much by President Chissano himself. To change constitutions and at least the form of institutional structures is relatively easy and the pressures to do so became more and more overt. The preamble to the new (1990) constitution was completely rewritten replacing Frelimo's exclusive claim to power and its commitment to build a socialist society with a shorter, less florid and rather different mythic place for Frelimo in the historical process presenting the 'deepening of democracy' as the natural development of Frelimo's achievements. Different icons, essentially those of the Western liberal tradition, were rapidly enumerated—Law, Rights, Equality, Will of the Citizens, even 'pluralism of opinion'. Frelimo's once leading role was shifted into the past tense. The General Principles referred back to its conquest of Independence as 'national heritage', eliding the entire intervening period of socialist endeavor.

Below the formal constitutional level, in a variety of new statutes and regulations, Mozambique has been required to restructure the state in ways which give certain rights to citizens against the state, withdraw the state from many activities and create new forms of representation within the state. There are of course possibilities for certain kinds of resistance to these pressures of the 'foot-dragging' type but what is important is that pressure to design new (Western) institutional structures is intense and unrelenting. Such new structures require of course new kinds of people to man them—especially those able at least to reproduce liberal dogma, primarily though not exclusively in economic matters. On its own account, 'partly by design, partly by default, the Bank today has a near-monopoly on development strategy dialogue with the [Mozambican] Government'. Put more bluntly the Bank has, 'in effect [taken] over the economic policy implementation functions of the Mozambican government'. The economic changes forced on the country have been centrally concerned with reforming the role of the state and the creation of markets/private economic forces, both of these to be carried out in line with 'international standards'. The first has involved increasingly calibrated interference in the detail of economic policy-making as well as the deployment of senior personnel. The second has involved such policies as privatization of state assets and the removal of price controls. Thus by 1994, though the Great Powers continued to be generous with aid, the detail of their shaping of economic policy included insistence on the introduction of VAT, the decontrolling of all prices, direct constraints on subsidies to public enterprises, the complete restructuring of the banking system including detailed instructions as to staff reductions, and the compulsory sale of state companies according to a strict timetable. Behind the scenes, and not easily documented, there has been massive interference at a detailed level, up to and including the forced redeployment of named officials.

Despite the Bank's emphasis on the 'technical' nature of many of these economic reforms there are strong parallels between these changes and those in the political realm, in particular the relationship between the state and the 'market' on the one hand and the state and 'civil society' on the other. Western powers and interests are of course aiding in this, some channeling their aid through NGOs in order to avoid working through the Mozambican government, an orientation that dovetails with the ideological proclivities of many NGOs themselves. Many Western NGOs, often encouraged by their home governments, have set up Mozambican equivalents to deal with (a sort of 'civil society' strategy but which parallels the interlocutor strategy at the state level). Aid is being deliberately directed to assist in the construction of new social groups committed to the market economy. The Commonwealth Secretariat talks of the need 'to break the logic and patterns of thought associated with a command economy and explain how markets work'.

The loss of overall macro-economic control undoubtedly caused the Frelimo government and Mozambican society severe difficulties. Real wages have decreased while prices of basic necessities have sharply increased. Increased charges for medical services combined with ill-understood systems of means-testing meant that many people lost access to even rudimentary health care. Infant mortality remains stubbornly high. Strikes occurred throughout the economy in 1990 and were reflected in open demonstrations of protest at the May Day rally, both that year and the following year. While the official trade union movement the OTM, delinked from Frelimo as a result of the constitutional changes, has struggled to constrain protest within official structures, increasingly desperate people have resorted to individual solutions including moonlighting and crime. There has been a coarsening of urban life with soaring crime rates, rioting, 'necklacing' of criminals by angry crowds, and rural vigilantism. Related phenomena are mutinies and thefts and outright looting by soldiers. It is not wholly far-fetched to suppose that, 'the broader social fabric has deteriorated to one of individual survival at all costs'.

Whatever the surface plausibility of the model of market capitalism in a country like Mozambique the form of transition has created many possibilities for personal enrichment for the political elite and the well-connected. Corruption on a small scale had doubtless always existed but had been kept in check by the Frelimo leadership's moral integrity and socialist ideology. From the late eighties however corruption became rife within the state sector of the economy and notoriously within the armed forces—as one government minister put it, 'There was a moral constraint that was lifted with PRE. Now to be honest means to be stupid'. The main beneficiaries of the disposal of state farms for example have been either foreigners or government and army officials.

But corruption of the crude kind is merely one of the most obvious effects of a transition to a market economy in circumstances of acute deprivation. The huge presence of foreign organizations of all kinds has had a severe impact on the state's capacity to deploy its own personnel as large numbers of the more highly qualified have taken up employment with non-state organizations, often foreign NGOs. Much the same applies to the public sector more generally. Beyond the fairly obvious difficulty of holding onto qualified personnel in the state sector much of the effects of this foreign presence are of course unconscious. Standards of living, notions of status, the trappings and assumptions of Western lifestyles are communicated by example as NGOs take on more local staff. Western norms ('international standards') become those to which people, especially people with any training, aspire.

The common feature of all these aspects of a transition to liberal capitalism has been an increasing dependence on foreign aid of all kinds. Relative to its size Mozambique is now the most heavily indebted country in the world, with foreign debt in 1992 totaling some US$5 billion (about five times GDP). The interest on this debt has had to be constantly rescheduled in order for the fiction of repayment to be maintained at all. The country's exports are negligible and until 1992, 'foreign grants continued to cover half of all Mozambique's merchandise imports'. Most development projects are carried out with foreign aid and even the current budget relies on donor contributions. A whole culture has grown up of appealing for foreign aid for any and every expenditure or 'project'. None of this is likely to change in the foreseeable future. But this extreme material dependence must induce other kinds of dependence, a debilitating loss of self-esteem and sense of self-capacity. This has inevitably had its most profound effects at the political level. There has been a general political fragmentation and loss of political authority at every level which goes well beyond issues of corruption and dependence. It includes the abandonment of an ideological cohesion that, whatever its difficulties, gave the ruling group a certain coherence. And the vacuum has not been replaced by any public discussion but by the unquestioning acceptance that IMF/World Bank strategies are the only possibilities there are. Thus the strategies of the Mozambican state have been reduced to little more than mediating the demands of donors and its domestic constituencies.

All of these features of the contemporary Mozambican situation were cast in a very sharp light by the operations of ONUMOZ in the country during the two-year period from the General Peace Agreement to the elections which took place in 1994. Beyond its extensive formal powers and rights the UN operation in Mozambique was run by its special representative, Aldo Ajello, in a very 'political' way, pressuring and cajoling the various actors involved. The elections formed a central part of the peace process and were largely engineered, paid for and monitored from outside. The creation of 'democratic politics' before the elections was also largely orchestrated by outside interests. Renamo itself received huge amounts of money legitimately to transform itself into a political party (as did other wholly fanciful organizations). The elections were 'run' by the Mozambican National Electoral Commission (the CNE) but in fact by the UNDP.

As to the significance of the elections themselves much remains unclear. In a country as profoundly exposed to Western influence as Mozambique it would be strange if liberal democracy did not represent the aspirations of some or at least constitute their notion of progress. But the significance of other features of the situation remain less obvious. Virtually all those involved in the elections were being paid, by Mozambican standards quite well. This did not prevent strikes and riots by polling staff extending in some cases to hostage taking. That many of the electors had little understanding of the electoral process was evidenced by empirical observation and the large number of spoilt papers and some accidental effects of the shape of the ballot papers themselves. Voter apathy was widely observed by commentators of all persuasions—'most people say they are registering because they have been told they must'. The election campaigns were lackluster. Few parties exploited the radio and TV time they had been given despite the funds allocated for such purposes. Campaigning in the form of rallies and open air meetings was lifeless and rather formalistic. One observer called them the 'elections of silence'.

The UN and the Western Great Powers and the growing group of international bureaucrats who stand for the 'new world order' desperately needed a success in Africa and can be forgiven their triumphalism, Mr Ajello in his last major speech before terminating the mission suggesting that the elections constituted 'proof of the highest order of democratic maturity'. It would be as foolish to suggest that a liberal capitalist transformation is impossible in Mozambique as to suggest that the previously attempted socialist one was. We can take refuge in the cliché that it is too early to say. Yet much of Frelimo's Marxism was of a mimetic kind that bore little relation to the society on which it was being imposed. It is not yet entirely clear that Frelimo's recently adopted liberalism will be so different. As a seasoned participant in the old Mozambican politics commented, 'now that the elections are over, people expect democracy to bring prosperity, just as they believed Marxism would bring development after independence. It may be just another unrealistic dream'. What is clear in practice, is that despite equipping itself with all the trappings of a democratic state, the sheer leverage of outside powers and in particular the coordinating role of the IMF/World Bank, with the full support of the Great Powers, has subjected Mozambique to an extraordinary degree of foreign tutelage, indeed made it a virtual laboratory for new forms of Western domination.

OR DISORDER?

These strategies are not of course without their contradictions. The larger of these concerns globalization itself. While there is no consensus about these processes it seems clear that contemporary states, even strong well-established ones, now face unprecedented pressures from agencies and developments increasingly outside their control. In the historical past nation-state building included the construction of a largely national economy which could deliver at least some material benefits to citizens as well as a national identity that could monopolize their communal and emotional loyalties. These capacities (and possibly these identities) are now being eroded in long established states. In countries barely formed historically speaking, it is hard to see how they can ever be acquired. In any case for many liberals the national state and nationalism have long since ceased to be progressive and globalization is welcomed as an alternative. As the 'development business' constitutes an ideological pseudo-community *par excellence* these ideas, even if at the moment on a rather rarified theoretical plane, are bound to have effects.

More concretely in the African case there is a contradiction at the heart of the current strategy. Liberal society and liberal democracy are forms of social and political order which require citizens who think of themselves as individuals, characterized by material interests amongst which there can be trade-offs. Markets and civil society constitute spheres of interaction for such individuals. Yet far from 'the' market and civil society being 'spontaneous' social developments, as liberal myth requires, to be effective they must be penetrated and shaped by a modernizing state, a modernizing state moreover which is driven by a ruling elite armed with new forms of expertise and motivated by more than just a desire for self-aggrandizement and self-enrichment but also with a vision of how 'to deconstruct old customary ways of life and to produce new ones'. It is arguable that even now the World Bank and others are hobbled by an inability to see that 'free individuals' and the rest of the liberal agenda do not emerge 'naturally' but are the result of political and social processes, often coercive and violent ones. The governance/civil society strategy in many ways undermines the capacities of African states while in fact continuing to need a strong state in the historical sense. Liberal discourse in its more applied forms, notably with regard to development, to some extent reflects these contradictions.

What finally are the prospects for these strategies? It should be noted first that it is widely argued that the recent wave of democratization in Africa (from about 1989) is to be ascribed to an indigenous explosion of civil society. Space prevents a fuller discussion but it is possible to be skeptical about this. The crasser versions of this argument are clearly little more than smokescreens for Western meddling or reflect intra-European or national political dynamics. Generally it is important to bear in mind that there are voices and ventriloquized voices and the latter rarely provide any challenge to the standard Western prescriptions for development and governance. Western triumphalism notwithstanding there would seem to be a range of possible outcomes from the encounter between non-Western social and political practices and the liberal project. Certainly some African elites in countries endowed with certain advantages of wealth and/or location will continue a carefully managed but temporary coexistence of the two aiming in the medium term at the erosion of traditional understandings by liberal democratic norms. As I have already suggested the more astute amongst them may emphasize the traditional elements in their societies in order to kick-start this process. Gradual improvements in the democratic 'performance' of African states will then ensure that democracy becomes a permanent feature of African political systems. The great apparatus of both public and 'private' monitoring institutions that has now been set up in the West (and is busily finding local allies for itself within African countries) is of course part of a common effort to sustain this process, whose essential component, as is recognized by the more candid Western analysts, is a 'civil society' which will marginalize and if necessary pulverize groups whose modes of existence and values are not compatible with liberal democracy. Certainly it is clear that the West is prepared to pay dear for the theatre of democracy. Putting on elections may come to rival converting to Christianity as a way of securing material aid.

But it would be premature to write off other possibilities, including possibilities of resistance. Although a facade of agreement has hitherto been maintained at international gatherings about the supposed universality of Western values some mutterings of dissent were to be heard at the Vienna conference on human rights and at subsequent United Nations junkets. The dissenters were Asian states whose economic weight is growing whereas African states remain supplicants. Yet if the successful Asian states feel their societies being corroded by Western individualism such dissent may amplify and legitimate dissent amongst others. There remain possibilities of resistance in polities where Islam is a potent force. We cannot assume that forms of political living-together which are not premised on Western egalitarian and other assumptions will necessarily disappear.

More likely, though also more complex, and more difficult to make sense of, are what might be called the effects of the 'unbundling' of the liberal project. That is to say that various features of political modernity may be adopted (elections, parties, a language of majoritarianism, etc.) but in a context of refusal to be bound by the liberal agenda and its understandings of civil society and democracy (individualism, secularism and so on). Far from being marginalized by civil society communal groups may in fact find certain institutional features of liberal democracy useful as a means to reinforce or indeed develop their identities. Elections for example make people aware of numbers, their numbers, in a way they often were not before. The venomous hatred now evinced for nationalism and communalism by large sections of the Western intelligentsia bears witness to these possibilities. Finally we cannot ignore the possibilities that the refusal of the liberal agenda may enable some African countries/communities to extend notions of democracy into spheres from which liberal understanding excludes it. As my argument suggests it is only superficially paradoxical that those who are most vehement in foisting the liberal project on Africans are also most insistent that they be subjected to the rigors of the international economy, a set of institutions and practices which has not done great good in Africa. You are free to choose provided you make the right choice. Yet when the current illusions about the 'free market' wear off democracy may well incline people to think again about the distribution of and accountability for economic as well as political power, indeed the very notion of the 'economic' itself. This of course must fly in the face of current forms of globalization in which the international economy is the mailed fist of the liberal project.

It is a moot point as to how secure that project is in some of its heartlands but it is clear that African societies have shown considerable resistance to it and that liberal orders (no less than socialist ones) cannot function without a much greater degree of transformation of those societies. Simply to suggest this invites condemnation from some quarters and we are warned incessantly of the dangers of 'Merrie Africa' fantasies. These dangers, though not false, are greatly exaggerated or at least they must be balanced against other dangers which invariably come with smaller health warnings. As Hobbes found asocial man in the state of nature so liberal academics have found nationalists or entrepreneurs or classes or states in African history (which ones of course has varied with fashion) because those things are universal and thus a true index of humanity. This in itself is a symptom of the difficulties Western liberal thought has with difference, rooted in a fanatical refusal to recognize that the liberal way of life is one among others. Yet that dogma abandoned, it is no more difficult to suggest that African societies may be different from ours than to say that 'we' were once different from 'us'. As the shadowy nightmare of global liberalism takes ever more definite form, armed and emboldened by more malign yokes than Sir John Sinclair could imagine, might it not be that some of us, at least, will have to remember who we once were?

18

Values, Context, and Hybridity: How Can the Insights from the Liberal Peace Critique Literature Be Brought to Bear on the Practices of the UN Peacebuilding Architecture?

ELI STAMNES

CENTRAL TENETS OF THE LIBERAL PEACE CRITIQUE LITERATURE

Values

The common denominator in the liberal peace critique literature is, as the name suggests, that its different contributions demonstrate that contemporary peacebuilding efforts are underpinned by liberal values. The end of the Cold War and its implicit discrediting of an alternative ideology, meant that the promoters of liberal values got free reins, which in turn put its mark on peace operations conducted by the United Nations and other multinational organisations. Whereas their previous engagement had almost without exception been limited to peacekeeping operations guided by the respect for the host states' sovereignty, war-torn societies now became the stage for complex operations aimed at political and economic liberalisation in the name of building peace.

This approach to peacebuilding is based on the assumption that such liberalisation will create stable and peaceful societies: by introducing multi-party democracy, conflicts will play out through party politics instead of through violent means, and the economic growth resulting from marketisation will put an end to conflicts that are due to poverty and struggle for resources. It is also believed that liberalisation will lead to peace at the international stage. This assumption is closely associated with the work of Michael Doyle. Drawing on Kant's ideas of how to achieve *perpetual peace,* he demonstrates that liberal democracies do not go to war with each other. Thus, systems of global governance should, in his opinion, aim to include more states into the 'Liberal Pacific Union'. 'This liberal peace thesis has been critiqued on several grounds. One regards its assumed universality. Critics take issue with the fact that the promotion of what are essentially Western values is treated as having universal validity. In other words, these are values that are historically and spatially specific but are portrayed as being timeless and spaceless truths. Moreover, derived from these values are particular forms of state, economy and social structure. By insisting on their universality there is little room for alternative interpretations. So, not only does this approach presume that it is possible to establish a set of universal 'root causes' to conflict, and an ever valid recipe to address them, it also allows for 'the pre-representation of the political interest of war-torn societies'. Politics and context are thus taken out of the equation.

The universal presentation and apparently altruistic and benign motivations behind these prescriptions make them very persuasive. The same goes for their association with the United Nations and 'international community'. 'The inherent 'goodness' and desirability created by the rhetoric of peacebuilding serves to appease fears of Western hegemony'. Indeed, as Roger Mac Ginty argues, 'one of the features of the liberal peace has been its success in convincing countries and communities that there is no alternative to it'. Liberal peacebuilding is not just seen as the best way to create peace and stability—it is considered to be the only way.

Another ground for critique is the way in which the liberal peace thesis and liberal peacebuilding construct conceptions of war and peace as well as of the actors and recipients of peacebuilding. Underpinning the discourse of liberal peacebuilding is a dichotomous ontology. Binaries such as liberal–non-liberal, peace–war, modern–traditional, developed–underdeveloped, civilised–barbaric are implicit or explicit in discussion of causes, solutions, problems and remedies. Moreover, the 'negatives' such as war, underdevelopment, barbarism etc. are located in the global South. The states that are objects for peacebuilding are thus 'pathologised'. They are seen as 'fragile' or 'failed', in need of external help in order to install the cure of liberal governance. Moreover, individuals or groups inside the recipient states who are resisting liberal reforms are often criminalised or simply considered to be 'spoilers'. Alternative ways of organising society are thus seen as morally inferior. This in turn justifies the intervention of outsiders, the assumption being that they know 'better than the people concerned what peace needs to be built' and how.

Peace is thus constructed as 'obtainable . . . propagated through an epistemic peacebuilding community, involving political, social, economic, and even cultural intervention through external governance'. By locating war in the global South and peace, and its building, in the hands of liberal outsiders, conceptions of war and peace are constructed in such a way that violence becomes an acceptable part of peacebuilding, but is illegitimate when it is conducted by its 'objects'. Hence, illiberal practices can be justified as means towards a liberal peace.

Similar mechanisms also serve to justify the large-scale social engineering project that liberal peacebuilding entails. Whereas Security Council resolutions or invitations from the host states serve to appease sovereignty-related worries, there is no question that this represents challenges to the recipient societies' autonomy. In liberal peacebuilding, peace is equated with conflict management and the construction of strong states through a package of reforms and programmes. These include *inter alia* security sector reform (SSR); disarmament, demobilisation and reintegration (DDR); rule of law programming (RoL); human rights promotion and monitoring; electoral reforms; and measures aimed at creating a market economy. Although these elements are emphasised to different degrees in different contexts, their inclusion in peacebuilding has become commonsensical. They constitute, however, a particular interpretation of the implications of the liberal peace thesis, in which Western models and politico-cultural and economic norms underpin the solutions arrived at. Their assumed universality serves to cloud the possibility for alternative interpretations of the liberal peace, based more solidly in the culture and conditions of the recipient societies.

Other reservations to this particular interpretation and operationalization of the liberal peace thesis include warnings that these different components may be incoherent and work at cross-purposes with each other. It is also argued that the implementation of the various reforms and programmes become ends in themselves rather than means to an end, or that the objective of implementing them as quickly as possible may become a primary concern overshadowing their ultimate objective.

Several liberal peace critics argue that the building of liberal democracies by external actors is actually counter-productive to the goals sought through such interventions. In the words of Roger Mac Ginty, it 'often results in a poor quality peace in which the civil war has ended but inter-group antagonisms remain undimmed, political participation rates are low and any peace dividend is unevenly shared'. On the basis of a study of eleven peacebuilding operations conducted in the period of 1989–98, Roland Paris argues that the liberalisation of the economic and/or political sphere actually had a destabilising effect rather than contributing to peace. 'In some countries, liberalisation exacerbated societal tensions, and in others it reproduced traditional sources of violence'. In his view this is because proponents of the liberal peace 'have tended to blur the distinction between liberalism and liberalisation' and that little is known about the relationship between the latter and violence. In an article on the political economy of peacebuilding, Michael Pugh argues that the socio-economic problems of war-torn societies are aggravated by market liberalisation. This is because it increases the populations' vulnerability to poverty, deprives them from having a say in economic reconstruction, and does little to reduce engagement in and reliance upon shadow economies. It is also argued that the international presence only contributes to a 'negative peace', despite its transformative intentions. It seeks to control conflicts, not transforming them and results merely in the absence of war in the host societies. This is due to its failure to seriously address the question of what would constitute a just social order ('positive peace'). Oliver Richmond takes issue with contemporary peacebuilding's lack of focus on and engagement with society. By being concerned with the 'creation of the hard shell of the state and rather less so on establishing a working society, complete with a viable economy which has an immediately beneficial effect on the labour force or provides a welfare system', only a virtual peace is established. This, he claims, has similarities with former colonial dependencies.

The intrusive and 'educational' nature of the liberal peacebuilding enterprise has also made other authors compare it to imperial modes of governance. Paris describes it as a benign form of the *mission civilisatrice* ('civilising mission'). The internationally sanctioned model for governance serves as a 'standard of civilisation' which must be adhered to in order to be fully accepted as a member of international community. He argues it is benign in that its promotion is not conducted primarily to advance economic interest. It also lacks the racial connotations often underpinning colonialism. Mark Duffield emphasises the difference between the liberal peace and the imperial peace. Whereas the latter was based upon direct territorial control, which would include violence, the former is a non-territorial form of governance in which its objects—people in the South—are not forced but expected to adhere willingly. David Chandler asserts that international actors' peacebuilding and state-building activities constitutes an 'empire in denial', in which the inherent power in such activities works under the guise of terms such as 'ownership', 'assistance' and 'facilitation'. Similarly, Bruno Charbonneau argues that peacebuilding is a hegemonic practice primarily aimed at governing and managing, not helping, its recipients.

A related critique regards this peacebuilding model's effect on world order. Several of the authors contributing to this body of literature point out liberal peacebuilding's bias to the status quo. It is argued that the emphasis on the liberalisation of the economy and the construction of liberal democracies and stable states contributes to the smooth functioning of the current world order, thereby maintaining its particular distribution of power and wealth. By prioritising the state as the frame for intervention, liberal peacebuilding contributes to maintaining the existing system of states, thus serving the interests of those benefiting from it and ignoring those who are marginalised or threatened by its very existence. In connection to the Balkan wars Susan Woodward argues that international involvement has consisted of 'a policy of containment . . . aimed at protecting . . . prosperous democracies against the effects of the region's instability'. This kind of 'riot control' has been conducted by the use of both coercion and rewards. In the case of the Balkans, aspirations to EU and NATO membership have made the latter very tangible. Focusing on France–Europe–Africa security relations, Charbonneau states that 'the promotion of peace and security in Africa has meant the stability of modes of governance that benefit specific governing elites, and that uphold and/or defend a kind of economic development more favourable to France and Europe'.

So, despite the transformative intention of liberal peacebuilding, it has conservative consequences. And, by portraying the creation of liberal regimes as inevitable if peace is to be built, these consequences are camouflaged. This is not to say that Western peacebuilding actors are consciously—or hypocritically, as Mark Duffield argues—working to maintain the status quo, thus acting purely in their own self-interest. Such is the commonsensical nature of the liberal peace thesis that their motivations may indeed be progressive and altruistic. The structural effects are nevertheless the same.

Context

Another main theme in this body of literature is the failure of liberal peacebuilding practices to adequately address the different local contexts in which they take place. Even though the importance of 'local ownership' is emphasised in documents and oral communication connected to contemporary peacebuilding efforts, there is widespread agreement that this is one of the areas most in need of improvement. Whereas proponents and critics of the liberal peace seem to agree on this, the latter demonstrate that there are important differences in conception of local ownership between the two. Liberal peacebuilders, such as the UN, tend to view ownership as a means to 'reinforce the perceived legitimacy of the [peace] operation and support mandate implementation' to 'avoid the appearance of paternalism or neo-colonialism'. Efforts to achieve local ownership in connection to such operations focus on creating local support for the already defined mandate of the operations. Local ownership is thus not seen 'as an ultimate goal or vision [. . .] but as a practical strategy for action'. What is to be owned is, in other words, an externally defined agenda. That agenda includes certain methodologies, objectives and norms. For the critics of liberal peacebuilding, on the other hand, local ownership means building peace from the bottom up, basing strategies on goals and activities defined by a broad constituency in the host society. It should be associated with experienced, not idealised, versions of peace.

The assumed universality of the liberal peace thesis and its derived peacebuilding measures constitutes an obstacle to taking local conditions and resources into account, and for understanding the particular problems of the societies in question. Since the problem is pre-defined as a lack of liberal institutions, local preferences, culture and practices are devalued, often seen as part of the problem, and knowledge about these factors is considered to be relevant insofar as it will help implementing the liberal peacebuilding model. The universality assumption means that the gathering of 'lessons learned' from previous engagements are seen as a useful way to better fine-tune future peacebuilding practices. This in turn, serves to reaffirm liberal peacebuilding's 'significance for everyone, everywhere'. The fine-tuning is therefore merely a repackaging of hegemonic practices. This resonates with what Cox has dubbed 'problem-solving' theory. This 'takes the world as it finds it, with the prevailing social and power relationships and the institutions into which they are organised, as the given framework for action'. Its aim is to make the current system function as smoothly as possible. Failure to take the local context into account can thus be seen to have consequences beyond the concern for the legitimacy and efficiency of particular peacebuilding operations.

There are also organisational reasons for downplaying the importance of context-specific knowledge. Due to the relatively fast rotation of personnel and limited bureaucratic and financial resources, there is a tendency towards standardisation and the generation and use of templates. As a result, similarities are sought out and emphasised at the expense of context awareness. 'For many intervening parties Bosnia becomes Bougainville and the same policy prescriptions (good governance, marketisation, elections, security sector reform, etc.) are introduced regardless of context and local need'. Moreover, contemporary management models with their emphasis on measuring output, outcomes, and impact leave little room for uniqueness and favour standardisation. They also tend to be self-referential, as achievements are measured according to their own standards. Peacebuilding is thus in danger of becoming formulaic and a 'technocratic exercise of ticking boxes'.

The implications of the critiques presented above are manifold, and different solutions are suggested by different contributors. These range from the withdrawal from peacebuilding activities via limiting international involvement to 'security keeping', to revising or fine-tuning the liberal model. The following section will take a closer look at some other suggested solutions. By utilising ideas from post-colonial theory and critical International Relations theory these authors seek to reconceptualise liberal peace-keeping while addressing concerns of the critique presented above.

Hybridity

Authors such as Charbonneau and Kristoffer Lidén seek to nuance the claims that liberal peacebuilding simply imposes liberal values in the recipient societies. Drawing on post-colonial theory, they argue that values imposed by external actors are received, interpreted, challenged, and resisted in a variety of ways. In other words, it is not just a one-way street.

Post-colonial theory provides good insight into the challenges facing liberal peacebuilding because it shows that the relations between colonisers and colonised were complex. It was not just a relationship reducible to violence, although this played a significant role. Neither was it a relationship in which influence and material gains moved in only one direction. The relationship between liberal peacebuilders and its recipients can, according to these authors, be seen in the same light. Although peacebuilding may be described as a hegemonic practice, influence and 'assistance' can work both ways. For example, the recipients may enable peacebuilding actors to build their image as significant actors. It is thus an asymmetric relationship that transforms both.

Moreover, post-colonial theory helps deconstruct the binaries underpinning liberal peacebuilding, such as liberal–non-liberal, peace–war, developed–underdeveloped, civilised–barbarian. It points out that post-colonial societies cannot be described as pre-modern, but hybrid societies, which have experienced and adapted to outside intervention. The post-colonial condition is 'an irreversible state of hybridity'. Since contemporary peacebuilding to a large extent takes place in post-colonial societies, it is not simply the case that external actors impose modern or liberal values on to traditional and non-liberal societies.

Peacebuilding practices based on these insights would, it is argued, involve awareness that measures aimed at liberalisation would cause reactions of acceptance, adaptation and resistance simultaneously. 'The interaction and dynamics between international peacebuilders and national recipients, "spoilers," combatants, and non-combatants' would thus constitute possibilities for change. It is from these possibilities a hybrid, non-hegemonic form of peace can be built. Hence, external involvement is not excluded, but their actions would be guided by the 'affected parties' conceptions of the substantial meaning of peacebuilding', the political objective being 'to create spaces for peaceful self-governance at all levels of society'.

By focusing on the interplay between international and local normative agendas and practices, the assumption that 'one size fits all' is left behind. At the same time it allows for local interpretations of liberal peace. This may well consist of some of the main ingredients of contemporary peacebuilding, but it will be 'better rooted in the social conditions and political processes of the host countries'.

The same emphasis on local interpretations of peace can be found in Oliver Richmond's emancipatory model of peacebuilding. This is not presented as an alternative to the liberal peace project, but rather as a gradation of it. It is not a model that has an empirical equivalent. Rather it exists as an expressed aspiration by certain peacebuilding actors, as well as in critical International Relations literature. It is characterised by a bottom-up approach to peacebuilding, mainly involving private actors and social movements. Compared to contemporary practices of peacebuilding, it is more needs-based in focus and emphasises social welfare and justice to a much larger extent.

Richmond argues that the liberalisation processes of current peacebuilding have created weak states and institutions, with a resulting lack of confidence in the new polity, the economy and the external actors involved in the peacebuilding efforts. Their preoccupation with the reconstruction of the state 'raises serious questions about the sustainability of the peace that is being created.' Hence, if the building of a sustainable peace is the main objective, there must be a stronger focus on redistribution and social welfare. A stronger grounding in the host society is also envisaged achieved by broad consultations as to the meaning of peace and the concrete contents of peacebuilding. The emphasis on peace as opposed to conflict is an important point here. In contemporary peacebuilding, conceptions of threats play a central role—threats that are identified against the liberal peace project. By focusing on concrete understandings of peace, the universalism of liberal peace and its resulting justification for coercive intervention is avoided.

Discursive practices and negotiations are central to this peacebuilding model. Conditionality, which will always be a factor when external actors are involved in peacebuilding, is to be subjected to bottom-up negotiations. Moreover, the conditionality is expected to work both ways, in that the local actors will hold the external actors accountable for observing the terms of the conditionality. The interchange between local actors and the internationals is in this way seen as an integral part of the whole peacebuilding process. This even includes the decision to withdraw external assistance. There can be no exit until both locals and internationals have agreed that a sustainable peace has actually been achieved.

These suggestions do not imply that post-conflict societies are to be left alone. Recognising that peacebuilding is an expression of 'external concern and responsibility', they argue for an engagement that is more on the terms of the recipients. They emphasise that post-conflict societies are complex, so also is the relationship between the external and internal actors. The case is thus made for interventions that do not arrive with preconceptions of what is best for the people concerned, neither in terms of contents, operationalization or process. Instead they should entail broad consultations around the question of what peace would mean in the particular setting, and focus on building on immanent possibilities for change in the host societies.

CURRENT IPBS DEVELOPMENT

As a relatively new addition to the United Nations landscape, the PBA face many challenges and its conduct may be scrutinised from many angles. This section will discuss one aspect of the PBA's current practices from the perspective of the liberal peace critique presented above, namely the development of IPBSs in the two initial countries on the PBC's agenda, Burundi and Sierra Leone. The development of such 'integrated strategies for post-conflict peacebuilding and recovery' is listed as a main objective in the PBC's founding Security

Council and General Assembly resolutions. This work is conducted in the country-specific configurations of the PBC, with the assistance of the Peacebuilding Support Office (PBSO). In general terms IPBSs are supposed to set out the commitments of a host government and the international community, with the ambitious goal to build 'inclusive national capacities to tackle the root causes of conflict that impede sustainable peace.' Seen from a liberal peace critique perspective, this goal formulation poses as many questions as it answers. Let us now try to unpack some of them in the context of IPBS development processes in Burundi and Sierra Leone.

Values

Thomas J. Biersteker states that the 'theoretical underpinnings of the Peacebuilding Commission are profoundly liberal, although they are not explicitly articulated as such'. The Secretary-General's address at the PBC's inaugural session seems to confirm this assertion. Without outright acknowledging the Commission's liberal underpinnings, he stated that a 'core task is to build effective public institutions, within constitutional frameworks and the rule of law'. This reverberates with the particular operationalization of the liberal peace thesis that we saw has underpinned the recent years' peacebuilding efforts. The PBC was thus—in Kofi Annan's mind at least—envisaged to contribute to liberal peacebuilding.

The IPBSs for the first two PBC cases fit this image. The Strategic Framework for Peacebuilding in Burundi, finalised in June 2007, lists the following priority areas: promotion of good governance; comprehensive ceasefire agreement between the Government of Burundi and PALIPEHUTU-FNL; security sector; justice, promotion of human rights and action to combat impunity; the land issue and socio-economic recovery; mobilisation and coordination of international assistance; sub-regional dimension; gender dimension. And the Sierra Leone Peacebuilding Cooperation Framework, finalised in December 2007, sets out the following priorities: youth employment and empowerment; justice and security sector reform; consolidation of democracy and good governance; capacity-building; energy sector; sub-regional dimensions of peacebuilding. Although some of these priorities are specific to the particular cases, a majority of them contains the buzzwords of contemporary liberal peacebuilding.

It is also interesting to note the similarities of the IPBSs in both Burundi and Sierra Leone with the countries' respective Poverty Reduction Strategy Papers (PRSP). Given the coordination mandate of the PBC, this, of course, makes perfect sense. In Sierra Leone's case the overlap is an explicit intention: 'the need to build on existing achievements, strategies and commitments for peace and development and to continue their implementation' is stressed in the framework's Principles of Co-operation. Nevertheless, what is interesting for this discussion is that the PRSPs of the Bretton Woods institutions have been described as 'an exceptionally useful tool for the promotion of the liberal project'.

The formulation of an IPBS is highly political. By providing an 'analysis of priorities, challenges and risks for peacebuilding', it passes judgement on what is important in the society in question and what peacebuilding should entail. The IPBSs of Burundi and Sierra Leone reflect understandings in line with the liberal peacebuilding model, and as we saw in the first section, this can be critiqued from several angles.

Context

In connection to local ownership, the Secretary-General expressed good intentions in his speech at the opening session of the PBC. He emphasised that 'Peacebuilding requires national ownership, and must be home-grown'. In the context of the PBC, local ownership cannot be conceptualised the way it is in connection to peace operations, as discussed above. Since the PBC is not an operational body, but works at the strategic level, there is no operational mandate as such to 'sell' to the host society. So instead of creating local support for an externally defined agenda, the aim of the IPBS development process is to formulate one. However, this does not necessarily mean that the conception of local ownership underpinning the work of the PBC is identical to that promoted by the liberal peace critique authors. The founding resolutions of the PBC affirms:

> the primary responsibility of national and transitional Governments and authorities of countries emerging from conflict or at risk of relapsing into conflict, where they are established, in identifying their priorities and strategies for post-conflict peacebuilding, with a view to ensuring national ownership.

In other words, local ownership is placed in the hands of the government of the countries on the PBC agenda. It is also important to note that the notion of ownership expressed here entails responsibility. A current buzzword in peacebuilding is 'mutual accountability' between the recipient and the international community. However, there are limits to how accountable an advisory body like the PBC can be. The Monitoring and Tracking Mechanism of the Strategic Framework for Peacebuilding in Burundi, for example, confirms this. Here, much more substantial responsibility rests on the government than on the international community.

Both the Strategic Framework for Peacebuilding in Burundi and the Sierra Leone Peacebuilding Cooperation Framework emphasise that their development has been based upon the principles of national ownership and partnership between the countries and the international actors. In practice this meant that the texts of the IPBSs were drafted in the capitals, giving the host governments a central role in developing the contents of the IPBSs. However, the texts were then negotiated, almost word by word, in New York, and were thus affected by the usual intergovernmental dynamics of the UN. This of course may be seen to constitute a limitation to national ownership. In addition, one should not forget the asymmetric power relationship between the donor states that are members of the PBC and Burundi and Sierra Leone. A major motivation for inviting the international community to take part in discussions of their internal affairs is arguably the expectation that this will lead to financial benefits. This was very clear during the inaugural meetings of the country-specific configurations, which 'was perceived as equating to a pledging conference'. One could therefore wonder to what extent the Burundi and Sierra Leone governments were implicitly 'disciplined' to take part in the liberal peace project.

Given the intergovernmental character of the PBC, much emphasis is put on the ownership of the countries' governments. But are there other local actors that count as 'relevant actors' in addition to the government and the different international peacebuilding actors? The PBC's founding resolutions 'Notes the importance of participation of regional and local actors' and 'Encourages the Commission to consult with civil society, non-governmental organisations, including women's organisations, and the private sector engaged in peacebuilding activities, as appropriate'. This opens up for the participation of regional and local actors, but the 'as appropriate' condition implies that they are not seen as central actors.

In light of the arguments presented in the first section, the participation of local civil society is of particular interest here. Initially, such participation in PBC meetings in New York took place as a result of the successful lobby efforts from the Global Partnership for the Prevention of Armed Conflict (GPPAC), the World Federalist Movement–Institute for Global Policy (WFM–IGP) and like-minded members of the Commission. Provisional guidelines for the participation of civil society were then agreed upon in June 2007. These guidelines established that civil society representatives actively involved in peacebuilding may be invited to make oral statements or provide information in the formal meetings of the Organisational Committee and the country-specific configurations, if there is a perceived need and a consensus for this among the members. Civil society representatives may also interact and provide input in the informal country-specific meetings. In addition there may be held public meetings for civil society actors prior to and after the formal meetings of the country-specific meetings, to exchange views and disperse information. Civil society actors may also provide written statements, which the coordinator of the country-specific configuration and the PBSO will 'make every effort to ensure' are 'made available to the members of the respective country-specific configuration.'

In the context of the development of the IPBSs in Burundi and Sierra Leone, this has meant that representatives of civil society have been able to make their views heard in PBC meetings in New York. In addition civil society organisations have engaged in national consultations on the peacebuilding process and frameworks in both countries, bringing together a host of civil society actors, government officials and international actors in-country. In this way they have been able to raise awareness of the PBC's role in the countries, while at the same time creating fora for the articulation of civil society perspectives on the peacebuilding processes in the two countries. Civil society organisations have hence been enabled to give 'timely and informed recommendations to the Commission'. These consultations are believed to have had a real impact on the contents of the IPBSs, as well as having contributed to national dialogues and wider ownership of the peacebuilding process. In this context it is important to note that the civil society consultations did not take place on the initiative of the PBC, but of the civil society actors themselves and, partly, the governments.

With regard to the claim that liberal peace-keeping prioritises general knowledge, standardisation and template use at the expense of local knowledge, the Secretary-General's opening speech reflected a degree of self-reflexivity: 'We must also remember that peacebuilding is inherently political. At times, the international community has approached peacebuilding as a largely technical exercise, involving knowledge and resources. The international community must not only understand local power dynamics, but also recognise that it is itself a political actor entering a political environment'. However, the resolutions establishing the PBC clearly prioritise this kind of knowledge, when stating that one of its main purposes is 'to develop best practices'. This work is to be conducted partly by the PBSO by 'gathering and analysing information relating to [. . .] best practices with respect to cross-cutting peacebuilding issues' and partly by the PBC's Working Group on Lessons Learned (WGLL). The latter systematises insights from past peacebuilding experiences and seek to raise awareness among its members, other member states and UN registered organisations. According to Christian Büger 'it has been used as a tool for identifying and deliberating knowledge that should inform the peacebuilding approach of the PBC'. He also cites PBSO staff describing the WGLL's role as 'training the diplomats'. Underlying such statements is an assumption of the existence of universally applicable peacebuilding knowledge. However, Büger also identifies groups of individuals within the PBC and PBSO who reject such a universality assumption.

The accompanying assumption of a need to educate the recipients of peacebuilding can also be found during the IPBS development process. The description of the situation and peacebuilding challenges in the Strategic Framework for Peacebuilding in Burundi seemed to stem from a local understanding of the issues since it was built upon points made by the Burundi government at the first country-specific meeting. However, preceding this presentation was a trip to Burundi conducted by PBSO staff, during which individuals connected to the government had been told which issues constituted peacebuilding issues and which did not. Similar attitudes could also be observed throughout the drafting period of the Strategic Framework, in that PBSO staff expressed opinions about the appropriate design of a strategy and concerns that the Burundian version fell short of this. It is important to note here that this is not a criticism of the staff of the PBSO. Their mandate is to serve as a knowledge base for peacebuilding and to offer advice and secretarial services. In other words, they were just doing their job. The point is rather to point out that these are examples of the prioritisation of general, assumed universal peacebuilding knowledge at the expense of local understandings as well as illustrations of the technocratic character of the peacebuilding enterprise.

An example that demonstrates the tension between the assumption of universally applicable peacebuilding measures and the need to take the local context into account, took place during the Sierra Leone IPBS development process. During the energy crisis in Sierra Leone in 2007, the government argued for the need to include the energy sector in Sierra Leone's IPBS. Since it was seen as rather controversial to include something that was 'normally considered a medium–long-term development concern' in a peacebuilding strategy, an informal thematic discussion within the country-specific configuration was dedicated to this issue. The meeting concluded, however, that it could be included as an overarching priority issue, and the IPBS was completed the following month.

Hybridity

The example of the inclusion of the energy sector in Sierra Leone's IPBS may hint at the interplay between international and local normative agendas, which the liberal peace critique authors argue should be central to a conceptualisation of peacebuilding. Moreover, the fact that Sierra Leone's IPBS is based upon already existing strategies and commitments, such as Sierra Leone Vision 2025, the Sierra Leone Poverty Reduction Strategy Paper, the Peace Consolidation Strategy, the Improved Governance and Accountability Pact and the report of the Truth and Reconciliation Commission, emphasises the point drawn from post-colonial theory that peacebuilding often takes place in societies that have already received and adapted to foreign interventions of various kinds. However, it is doubtful that the authors presented in the first section would describe the framework as a hybrid, non-hegemonic peacebuilding strategy, or its political objective as creating 'spaces for peaceful self-governance at all levels of society'.

The two IPBSs focus to a certain extent on social welfare and justice issues as advocated by Richmond and others. The economic argument underpinning the inclusion of the energy sector in Sierra Leone's is one example. So also is its inclusion of youth employment and empowerment, which can be seen as a redistribution issue. The prioritisation of the land issue and socio-economic recovery in Burundi's IPBS can also be said to reflect social welfare and justice concerns. Likewise, the inclusion of the gender dimension as a separate priority area there, demonstrates the intention of redistributing power and making women's social welfare a public—and no longer private—matter.

Although the development of the two IPBSs involved a degree of consultation with civil society actors, the processes cannot be said to constitute a bottom-up approach to peacebuilding. Nor did they mainly involve private actors and social movements. National governments, both in the PBC and in Burundi and Sierra Leone, were the main actors when developing the strategies, although they cooperated and consulted with other international and national actors. By UN staff's own admission, the civil society consultations conducted in the countries were insufficient. Several obstacles to participation have been identified in both Burundi and Sierra Leone, such as poor information flows, lack of adequate preparation time, language barriers and lack of financial and logistical resources. The latter were particularly important in limiting civil society organisations in taking part in meetings in New York. It has also been pointed out that there was an over-representation of Western-style, capital-based NGOs. Whereas these are more skilled in communicating with the international actors, and fit the participation requirements set out in the provisional guidelines for participation better, they did not represent the rural grassroots communities most affected by conflict. This meant that rural people's conception of problems and solutions were not taken into account, while at the same time they also lost out on information about the PBC and the development of the IPBSs.

To sum up the arguments made in this section, one could say that the practices of the PBC in connection to developing the IPBSs for Burundi and Sierra Leone fit well into Richmond's *orthodox* model of the liberal peace. Here 'actors are wary and sensitive about local ownership and culture, but still also determined to transfer their methodologies, objectives and norms into the new governance framework . . . This equates to a balanced and multilateral, and still state-centric peace'.

FUTURE IPBS DEVELOPMENT—IMPLICATIONS OF THE LIBERAL PEACE CRITIQUE

Let us now turn to the implications that the insights from the liberal peace critique may have for the PBC's practices of developing IPBSs in the future. This discussion will first be structured around the same headings—values, context, hybridity. Then, some of the main points will be summarised in the form of critical questions to be posed during the current configuration of the IPBS process.

Values

One of the messages from the liberal peace critique literature is that contemporary peacebuilding is based on the assumption of the universal validity of the liberal peace thesis. This entails an acceptance of the proposition that the creation of liberal market democracies is the best, and indeed, only way of achieving stable, peaceful states. Moreover, the universality assumption also includes the tools derived from the liberal peace thesis, making the implementation of these particular reforms and programmes appear as common sense and thus excluding the possibility of alternative operationalisations.

So, how can these insights be brought to bear on the PBC's work of developing IPBSs? Essentially it means that there is a need for increasing the self-reflexivity of all the parties involved in the PBC's different configurations with regard to the values underpinning their discourses and activities. It does not necessarily mean a rejection of the current liberal peacebuilding model, but it entails an awareness of the fact that it is actually a chosen approach, not just common sense or a necessity. Especially, there should be increased awareness of the effects of assuming its universality, with regard to approaching situations with a pre-defined understanding of what the problems are and how to approach them. This is not to say that actors involved are conscious of these dynamics, or approach the issue with arrogance. It is rather to point out that their frames of reference when discussing peacebuilding are coloured by liberal understandings of conflict, war and threats, for example when identifying key concerns in the recipient countries. Hence, there might be an element of 'we know what is best for them' even in the best-intentioned practices.

Another message from the liberal peace critique literature is that contemporary peacebuilding contains a status quo bias. The privileging of a market economy and the maintenance of the stability of the current system of states means that it serves the interests of those benefiting from this particular world order. The involvement in the PBC of the World Bank and other donors favouring this particular economic system seems to suggest that this may be hard to do something about. A mitigating factor, though, is the strong representation of developing countries in the PBC. This may mean a stronger presence of alternative perspectives than is the case with other peacebuilding initiatives. Nevertheless, self-reflexivity is of essence also in this context.

Given that the UN is made up of member states, does that mean that the Organisation is too much 'the servant of the present state system, responsive to the existing configuration of power' or can the PBC become one of the 'interlocutors for the new forces that, in the long run, can change forms of states and the very nature of the state system?' It is in my opinion too early to say, but the PBC can seek to mitigate the inherent statism by choosing to relate to other actors in the host countries in addition to their governments. In order to address this concern, it is crucial that the PBC allow for widespread consultations with civil society when developing IPBSs. Here, it is important to keep in mind Béatrice Pouligny's reminder regarding the large diversity in local civil society. Another relevant question in this context is how to deal with minority-related conflicts when one of the key partners in the PBC is the host government. These are sensitive issues that can easily taint or destroy good working relationships, and the concern for this can constitute an obstacle to dealing with issues that are central to the society in question.

Context

Discussion of the liberal peace critique literature underlined the importance of local ownership in peacebuilding, and the need to reconceptualise it. Local ownership, it was argued, should not just be an efficiency concern and be taken to mean how to secure local support for externally defined mandates. Rather it should mean taking the recipient countries' understanding of the problems and visions of solutions as the starting point of peacebuilding initiatives. In the context of developing IPBSs, this would have wide-reaching implications for the PBC's *modus operandi* as well as resources and time spent on these processes. In line with what was argued above, the development of the IPBSs should be based on much broader consultations in the host society. It would mean a rejection of the assumption that governments, by virtue of being representatives of the states' citizens, have a privileged position in IPBS development. For a solid grounding of the peacebuilding efforts in the host society, people with a variety of experiences must be allowed to have a say, not only the political elites and a few chosen representatives of civil society. This does not just mean that it will be a more time-consuming process. It would also mean increased costs for organising consultations, translating documents and oral presentations, and other ways of facilitating participation. Perhaps enabling different segments of society to have a say would prove such an immense task that it would become the Commission's primary role?

The tendency to privilege general knowledge, standardisation and template use, is also an obstacle to addressing adequately the concerns and conditions of the society in which peacebuilding takes place. This also means a preoccupation with the gathering of 'lessons learned', which in turn serves to reinforce this tendency. Moreover, the resulting prioritisation of generic peacebuilding expertise over local knowledge means that there is a tendency to assume that the recipients of peacebuilding must be taught what peacebuilding is about, and hence what they need. If the PBC were to take these insights seriously, it would mean letting the countries in question set their own agenda, without offering any advice on what are relevant peacebuilding issues. It would also mean privileging a different kind of knowledge. For the PBC and the PBSO, the focus should not be on lessons learned with the purpose of drawing out general knowledge, applicable in all contexts. Rather, a priority should be to generate country-specific knowledge. This would of course have huge implications with regard to financial and bureaucratic resources.

Hybridity

The first section of the paper introduced two related suggestions as to how to address the insights from the liberal peace critique while at the same time not rejecting outside involvement in peacebuilding, or the possibility that elements of the liberal peacebuilding model could be desirable in the recipient societies. Emphasising the complexity—or hybridity—

of post-conflict societies, arguments can be made for basing peacebuilding efforts on local visions of peace stemming from the meeting of external and internal normative agendas. It is suggested that the focus should be more on redistribution and social justice, rather than building of 'the hard shell of the state'. Consultations and negotiations with broad sections of the society are an integral part of peacebuilding, alongside the involvement of civil society actors in the building of a sustainable peace.

The implications of these arguments for the IPBS development process are similar: self-reflexivity with regard to the asymmetrical power relationship inherent in peacebuilding, an emphasis on broad local participation and the prioritisation of the local perspective. One additional implication is that the main focus should not be on conflicts and threats, thus easily reproducing the contemporary liberal peacebuilding agenda. Rather, it should be on visions of peace. Richmond's recommendation in this regard deserves to be quoted in full:

> When internationals engage in conflict zones, one of the first questions they might ask of disputants at the many different levels of the polity might be what type of peace could be envisaged? Working towards such an explicit end goal would be of great benefit to both internationals and recipients of intervention.

He emphasises, however, that these visions must have their basis in the specific context in which peacebuilding occurs.

Another implication is the emphasis on negotiations between the external and internal actors throughout the peacebuilding process and until there is agreement that a sustainable peace has been reached. This might have radical implications for how the tracking and monitoring element of the IPBS is carried out. Since both the process and success criteria are up for continuous debate, there would be little room for generalised benchmarks. This might be a bitter pill for donors to swallow. A third, and perhaps the most difficult implication, is the fact that the PBC would have to be prepared to accept locally based peacebuilding strategies that are not in line with what is considered to be desirable values and outcomes, nor 'the proper way of doing things' at its headquarters in New York.

CRITICAL QUESTIONS

The implications of the insights from the liberal peace critique literature can also take the form of critical questions posed throughout the process of IPBS development as it is today.

These critical questions are intended to increase self-reflexivity with regard to the values, conception of relevant knowledge and relevant actors, and the conception of problems/threats/peacebuilding that are underpinning the IPBS process. They represent thus one way of making some of the insights presented above integral to the process. However, a more wholesale embrace of the liberal peace critique would mean that the processes in different countries would not easily be fitted into a table intended to fit all. In this context—and as a concluding remark—it could be useful to remind ourselves of a lesson from post-colonial theory: the practises of the interveners are also shaped by the recipients, by their challenge, resistance and exploitation. Hence, the future of the PBA and its IPBS practices is not only dependent upon the outcome of the 2010 review process. It depends to a large extent upon the members of the societies in which the PBC chooses to become involved in the years to come.

19
Is the EU's Governance 'Good'?: An Assessment of EU Governance in Its Partnership with ACP States

NIKKI SLOCUM-BRADLEY
AND ANDREW BRADLEY

AFRICAN, CARIBBEAN AND PACIFIC (ACP) GROUP

The ACP Group of States is constituted by 79 developing countries, all but one (Cuba) of which have signed the Cotonou Agreement (CA), which officiates the relationship between the ACP Group and the EU. The Group's founding statute is the Georgetown Agreement, and it has a permanent Secretariat, based in Brussels, Belgium. The Group is structured into six regions: the Caribbean, the Pacific, West Africa, Central Africa, East Africa and Southern Africa.

RELEVANT EU BODIES

The EU currently consists of 27 Member States. Common governing bodies of the EU include the European Council and the European Commission. The European Commission comprises a number of services that have a direct influence on ACP–EC relations, including 'DG Development and Relations with African, Caribbean and Pacific States', responsible for development policy; 'DG External Cooperation Programmes' (EuropeAid), responsible for the implementation of development programmes and projects; 'DG Relex', responsible for external relations; 'DG Trade'; and 'ECHO', responsible for humanitarian aid. These services operate in a semi-autonomous fashion and have different interpretations of the objectives enshrined in the EU Development Consensus. In addition, most of the 27 EU Member States possess national development policies and instruments.

Governance

The word 'governance' derives from a Greek word that means 'to steer'. Academics from diverse disciplinary backgrounds have elaborated upon the 'steering' concept.

Within a policy context, in a Communication in 2003, the EC describes governance as 'the rules, processes, and behaviour by which interests are articulated, resources are managed, and power is exercised in society'. It further specifies that 'the way public functions are carried out, public resources are managed and public regulatory powers are exercised is the major issue to be addressed in that context', and that 'governance concerns the state's ability to serve the citizens'.

The above definitions all focus on governance as a process, leaving the goals and outcomes of these processes unspecified. In contrast, a definition of governance emanating from the World Bank directly incorporates development as a goal of governance and thereby stipulates not only what governance is as a process, but also what the *outcome* of such a process *should* be. In defining governance as 'the manner in which power is exercised in the management of a country's economic and social resources for development', the World Bank explicitly makes a normative statement. However, even when not made explicit, assertions about governance often carry a covert idea about what the ends of governance processes should be.

Good Governance

The 'good' in 'good governance' has been employed sometimes as an adverb, to evaluate the process of governance (which would more correctly be put as 'well governed'); in other instances it is used as an adjective, to evaluate the outcomes of this process. For example, the United Nations Commission on Human Rights identifies the key attributes of 'good governance' as: transparency, responsibility, accountability, participation, and responsiveness (to the needs of the people). Thus, in this conception the normative evaluation 'good' addresses the *processes* of governance, not its outcomes. Orienting more toward the *outcomes* of governance, UN Resolution 2000/64 expressly links good governance to 'prompting growth and sustainable human development'. Kofi Annan, Secretary-General of the United Nations, stated in 1997 that, 'Good governance and sustainable development are indivisible'.

Poor or Malign Governance

A lack of good governance might be called 'poor' or 'bad' governance. As with its counterpart, an unfavourable evaluation of governance can either describe the process or the outcomes of governance. Bad governance—or more adeptly: 'poorly governed'—can describe opaque (as opposed to transparent) management, a lack of clearly defined rules and procedures, or a failure to implement such rules and procedures (e.g. not being accountable to the defined rules and procedures).

Partnership and Power

In studying governance, Yanakopoulos argues the importance of studying the actors, their relationships and the quality of these relationships, emphasizing the role of power asymmetries in relationships between actors. The partnership principle has been introduced in the context of contemporary development cooperation to suggest an evolution from the traditional vertical relation between the donor and recipient to a relationship characterized by cooperation between equals. Thus, in describing 'good governance', UN Resolution 2000/64 recognizes 'the value of partnership approaches to development cooperation and the inappropriateness of prescriptive approaches'.

The nature of a 'partnership' is inherently defined in part by the balance of power between the 'partners'. The power asymmetries between the 'North' and 'South' have been underscored by many writers. The power differential between donor and developing countries and its manifestation in control over access to resources has been noted by Birdsall who writes that ' . . . the powerful make and implement the rules, as the limited access of developing countries to certain rich-country markets suggest[s].' Similarly, a BOND briefing paper argues that although 'donors prefer to focus the governance lens more narrowly within the confines of recipient countries, this distorts understanding of the ways in which global power structures impact on national politics'. Global power structures have an important impact on ACP national and regional politics, and on development. Therefore an understanding of governance processes and outcomes can only be gained by considering these structures. We consider a part of these power structures: those inherent in the relationship between the ACP States and the EU.

Power asymmetries infiltrate all aspects of the ACP–EU partnership, including provisions designed to govern the relationship. The use of one of the provisions for political dialogue between the ACP and the EU illuminates the actual—in contrast to the rhetorical—distribution of power. In its Communication on Governance and Development, the European Commission discusses the modalities in the CA that provide for 'consultation procedures' within the context of 'policy dialogue', which is seen as a key element of good governance. The Communication refers to Article 9 of the CA, which specifies that respect for human rights, democratic principles and the rule of law constitute 'essential elements' of the partnership and that good governance is its 'fundamental element'.

Although this provision is phrased to allow either party to invoke it, only the EU has ever done so, reflecting the division of power within the relationship.

The imbalance of power between the partners trickles down to many other manifestations, including the extent to which joint 'fact finding missions' are deployed to political 'hot spots' by the ACP–EU Joint Parliamentary Assembly (JPA). The EU can use development aid, trade preferences and other 'carrots' to push its agenda and interests, and the (threat of) withdrawal of these as 'sticks'. The ability to distribute these resources affords the EU with a considerable degree of 'power', and the exercise of that power is governance, in accordance with the definition by the EC cited above. While access to resources gives the possessor *potential* power, it can also be argued that aid recipient countries grant the EU this power by allowing the resources that the EU has at its disposal to be used as leverage. If aid recipients were to decline the aid, either categorically or under specific circumstances, these elements of 'power' would dissipate. In other words, it is the recipients' desire for these resources, and inability to eschew manipulation in order to access them, that turns the potential power into real power.

As the specified overarching objective of the 'partnership' between the ACP Group and the EU is the sustainable development of the ACP States, it is worthwhile to examine more carefully what is meant by 'development'.

Development

Ideas about what constitutes development have evolved significantly amongst contemporary development economics scholars, and this definitional evolution has been paralleled by changes in development theory and strategies. Various scholars have traced the evolution of thinking about development in modern times. While development economists, as epitomised by Dudley Seers, over the last quarter century have seen the purpose of development as the reduction of poverty, inequality and unemployment, contemporary scholars, such as Amartya Sen employ the broader concept of 'human development', which includes reducing 'deprivation' as well as broadening choice. For Sen, 'deprivation' encompasses hunger, illiteracy, illness, poor health, powerlessness, voicelessness, insecurity, humiliation and a lack of access to basic infrastructure, while 'choice' includes, *inter alia,* access to information, education, participation, and degree of democracy and liberty. Despite this conceptual expansion, Nafziger argues that the integration of economic development, human rights and conflict reduction into a more holistic understanding of the meaning of development remains an important challenge.

The EU's theoretical understanding of the concept 'development' is captured in the European Consensus on Development that was adopted in 2006. It outlines a new framework for the implementation of the EU's development policy, with particular focus on the attainment of the Millennium Development Goals (MDGs), and provides a common vision designed to guide the development cooperation of the EU, both at its Member States' and Community levels. The Consensus is grounded on the principle of sustainable, equitable and participatory human and social development, and it emphasises the promotion of human rights, democracy, rule of law and good governance. Similarly, the CA underscores economic, social and cultural facets of development, which clearly concurs with a broad conception of human development that encompasses reducing 'deprivation' as well as broadening choice.

Governance is a concept that has come to play a very present role in discussions about sustainable development. In this context, it has been used as an explanation for why development strategies and aid have failed (e.g. due to bad governance), as well as the key to making development (assistance) work (e.g. by implementing good governance). Montagner discusses three ways in which the term governance has been used in the context of the EU's development politics. These include governance applied to the European space and to Community politics, (good) governance within partner countries of the EU, and governance at the heart of the 'organisational field' of civil society. More recently some attention has been given to 'aid governance', whereby donors have been under pressure to apply governance principles in their management of their aid to developing counties. The present study is interested not only in the governance of aid, but all aspects of governance within the context of the ACP–EU 'partnership', with particular regard for their consequences for sustainable development in ACP countries.

GOVERNANCE MECHANISMS AND GOVERNANCE ASSESSMENTS

Distinguishing governance as a purposive activity from governance as an explanatory tool (for example to explain development policy failures), Yanakopoulos investigates the mechanisms through which governance as a purposive activity occurs. She examines the ways in which NGOs influence two processes of governance in particular: norm setting and framing issue areas. Here we will examine governance mechanisms used by the EU in the context of its relationship with the ACP Group. According to the CA and other policy papers, in its relations with ACP States the EU employs, *inter alia,* the following instruments to promote good governance in development cooperation: conditionalities, 'additional support' for results-oriented reforms, incentives, and 'appropriate measures' (sanctions) as specified in Articles 96 and 97 of the CA. However, it can be argued that EU governance is manifested through additional practices, which include: the determination of priority areas and recipients to benefit from financial assistance; negotiation strategies, such as stipulations for the configuration of negotiation partners and linking financial perspectives with certain policy orientations; the identification of interlocutors as development partners; trade and commercial practices within development cooperation, such as Economic Partnership Agreements (EPAs); Fisheries Partnership Agreements (FPAs) and subsidies; and the design of other policies that influence the EU–ACP relationship.

Wielding the 'Governance' Concept

The first mechanism we examine is use of the concept of '(good) governance'. Adding adjectives such as 'bad' or 'good' to governance, and specifying a desired outcome of governance processes, such as sustainable development, makes more explicit the normative aspect inherent to the concept's use. However, whether or not certain outcomes of governance processes are included explicitly or only presumed implicitly when the concept is employed, it has been argued that mere use of the concept has been an act of governance.

Various authors have argued that the EU has imposed its own models for governing and other priorities under the rubric of promoting 'good governance'. This is evident in the EU's Governance Initiative for ACP States and the associated 'governance incentive tranche', developed in 2007. The governance incentive tranche is an instrument for providing supplementary funding to states who credibly commit themselves to satisfactory governance reforms. To this end, the 'governance profile' is an analytical tool that provides an overview of nine areas of governance and assists in identifying main weaknesses and reform priorities. It is not jointly developed with the country in question, nor are its contents fully shared. Rather, based upon the EU's assessment of the country's 'governance profile', the country is encouraged to provide 'relevant, ambitious and credible commitments to reform' in its 'Governance Action Plan' (GAP). The amount of the 'incentive tranche' is unilaterally determined by the EC, and this 'additional support' is utilised to effectuate the reforms stipulated in the GAP. Thus, the introduction of the 'governance incentive tranche' and the procedure through which it is allocated manifest a kind of ex-ante rather than ex-post conditionality.

The EU's use of the concept 'good governance' is exemplified in its failure to distinguish between 'good' and 'democratic' governance and by the elements subsumed under these rubrics. In various EC documents the phrases '*good* governance' and '*democratic* governance' are used interchangeably. For example, the European Commission states that '*good* governance, though a complementary objective, is basically a means towards the ends represented by poverty reduction and the other MDGs'.

The failure to distinguish between 'good' and 'democratic' allows one issue to be guised in the rubric of another. For example, it can be argued that 'access to basic social services' and 'management of migration flows' have nothing to do with '*democratic* governance' but have a lot to do with '*good* governance'. Ironically, an earlier EC Communication on Governance and Development clearly makes this distinction in stating 'Governance concerns the state's ability to serve the citizens. Such a broad approach allows conceptually to disaggregate governance and other topics such as human rights, democracy or corruption.'

By framing a laundry list of its own priorities as aspects of 'good governance', and designing mechanisms purportedly to evaluate countries' achievements at attaining this 'goodness', the EU attempts to establish a particular set of social norms and conventions to guide the decisions and actions of its developing partners.

Hidden under the guise of the rubrics 'good governance' and 'incentives', the EU continues to coerce development partners to follow EU positions and policies. Contrary to the criteria of good governance as a process, this process lacks transparency and results in a lack of ownership on behalf of the countries targeted by the policies. Furthermore, the outcome of this governance may also be less than 'good', since priorities are set that are not necessarily in the best interest of the developing country.

Economic Partnership Agreements (EPAs)

The CA stipulates that EPAs would be negotiated in order to better integrate the ACP States into the global economy, promote sustainable development and eradicate poverty in these countries. Both the content of these agreements as well as the process of negotiations can be seen as mechanisms of governance.

The EPA negotiation process was to a great extent stipulated by the EU, by some accounts, against the will—and interests—of the ACP States. First, the EU stipulated that EPAs were to be concluded not with the ACP Group as a whole, but with six regions within the ACP Group. Furthermore, no country could negotiate within more than one region. Since some countries in Africa are members of more than one regional organisation, they were forced to choose between these groupings. The resulting negotiating groups coincide neither with the six regions of the ACP Group, nor with the membership patterns of the regional organisations. In other words, new regional groupings were formed on the basis of countries' interests for the purpose of negotiating EPAs with the EU. The ACP Group has expressed concern that the pre-existing regional integration processes have been stalled due to the focus placed upon the new alignments for EPAs negotiations—in spite of the fact that supporting *existing* regional integration efforts is allegedly a main goal of these agreements.

Thus, the EU's stipulations for negotiations and the content of interim EPAs have impacted the geopolitical structure of African regions of the ACP Group and threatened the existing regional integration processes.

By insisting on moving negotiations to the regional level, the EU finessed the possibility of more concerted action on behalf of the Group as an entity. The regional negotiating groups are smaller and thus have less power to negotiate an agreement that favours the interest of the developing countries. Due to the EU's relative power and ability to assert its will, the developmental consequences of the still incomplete results of the regional negotiations have been a matter of great concern. In its 2009 Resolution, the ACP Council of Ministers underscored 'the absence of a comprehensive development oriented EPA'. We now turn to examine the potential of the EPAs for promoting sustainable development and reducing poverty in ACP countries.

The reciprocal nature of EPAs, whereby the EU and ACP regions are supposed to open their markets to each other in a reciprocal fashion, has been underscored as problematic by various development-oriented committees and organizations. NGOs and the European Parliament's development committee have underscored the need for additional funds to assist developing countries to adjust to the competition induced through market openness. Even European Commissioner for Trade, Peter Mandelson, has stated that 'Trade will not promote development without parallel investment in the supply side'. Mandelson's acknowledgement is sustained and elaborated by scholars such as Birdsall who claims that many of the world's poorest countries, including most of the poor countries of sub-Saharan Africa have been 'open' for more than two decades. However, many of these countries are commodity dependent, and the value of their exports has stagnated during the same period. As a result, they have not been able to increase their imports relative to their GDP. In addition to lower overall growth, developing countries have had higher volatility of growth rates compared to advanced economies in every decade since the 1960s. This volatility, which can be associated with open markets and especially open capital markets, is most dangerous for the poor *within* countries. This concurs with extensive empirical evidence that openness contributes to within-country inequality.

In spite of widespread recognition that developing countries must first make various adjustments before they stand the potential to benefit from opening their markets, in the content of the interim EPAs, no clear pattern can be identified that the poorer countries have longer to adjust than the richer ones or of the EPAs being tailored to development needs.

Furthermore, the EC has refused requests for additional funding for adjustment programmes that would allow the developing countries to take advantage of opportunities created through EPAs.

In its EPA negotiating strategies and content proposals, the EU is not displaying the key attributes that it uses to characterize good governance. Both the negotiating processes and outcomes may be detrimental to regional integration in the ACP regions, which could have far-reaching political and security consequences. The faltering of intra-regional integration as well as the agendas that the EU is attempting to impose on the ACP regions in the context of EPAs could impact negatively on the sustainable development and alleviation of poverty in ACP States.

Partner Preferences

While the EU is attempting to consolidate itself as a unified actor on the global stage, some of its actions have contributed to the fragmentation and de-construction of the ACP Group. In its dealings with ACP countries, the EC has in recent years shown various signs of withdrawing from the ACP Group as an interlocutor. It has designed separate strategy papers for its relations with the Caribbean, the Pacific, South Africa and 'Africa' and it later elaborated a 'joint strategy' with the latter seemingly in contradiction to the EC's rationale for the latter strategy—that is, to have one common strategy for Africa, the EC has separate strategies for South Africa and for several northern African countries, which are addressed in the EC's European Neighbourhood Policy (ENP). In a further manifestation of disfavour for the ACP Group, the former European Commissioner for Development and Humanitarian Aid, Louis Michel, publicly expressed a preference for working with the regions. The EC has granted high levels of support, financial and otherwise, to the African Union, often with only the reluctant and post-hoc approval of the ACP Group. These actions undermine the ACP Group and empower the actors favoured by the EC. This form of EU governance has a direct impact on the kinds of actors that are empowered to act on behalf of ACP interests and on development. One possibility is that this process will result in dissolution of the ACP Group as such. If this is the case, the full weight of the Group will be lost and only smaller groupings of developing countries will defend their interests in negotiations with the EU. This could result in less advantageous outcomes for sustainable development and poverty reduction in developing countries.

European Development Fund (EDF)

The EDF is the main instrument for providing EU aid for development cooperation in ACP States. The 10th EDF, dispersed during the period 2008–2013, amounts to €22,682 million. This fund is divided between national and regional indicative programmes, intra-ACP programmes and projects, investment facilities, EU Overseas Countries and Territories (OCTs) and the European Commission itself (to cover expenditures for programming and implementation, such as its offices and staff in developing countries). In accordance with the CA, 'ACP States and Regions shall determine the development strategies for their economies and societies in all sovereignty'. In practice, negotiations over the setting of development priorities in ACP countries and regions take place in an environment of 'trade-offs' between the aid recipients and the EU. The result of these negotiations is that the EU's external priorities and commitments are pursued, whilst the ACP Group plays a minor role in the programming of EU financial resources. The EU's *ability* to impose its agenda on ACP states and regions reflects the inequality of the partnership and the imbalance of power; the fact that it *does* so contradicts the CA stipulation that development strategies shall be determined 'in all sovereignty' by the regions and countries concerned. This contradiction reflects not only a lack of *transparency* in the agenda-setting process but also means that the EU is left entirely un*accountable* for the consequences thereof. Both transparency and accountability are key aspects of good governance, as characterized by the EU itself. Furthermore, contrary to the *ownership* criterion of good governance, EU donors' procedures and practices are not conducive to full ownership.

Revision of the Cotonou Agreement (CA)

The EU's imposition of its agenda, and the inequality and power imbalance in the ACP–EU partnership, were also made glaringly evident during the negotiations for the 2005 revision of the CA. The negotiations reached an impasse on the EU's insistence to include an article on 'cooperation in countering the proliferation of weapons of mass destruction', and the EU's reluctance to provide details on the next multi-annual financial framework for the period 2008–2013. To unblock the impasse, the EU negotiators offered the ACP Council of Ministers a so-called 'package deal', whereby a multi-annual financial framework would be provided on condition that the ACP group accept the inclusion of the proposed article. Thus, ACP Ministers were confronted with the choice to accept €22,682 million in development aid and include the article on weapons of mass destruction, or to renounce the financial framework by not accepting the EU imposition. Due to the consequent inclusion of the article, ACP countries are now further burdened with border-control responsibilities, in order to prevent weapons trafficking, but they have been allocated no additional resources to cover the high cost of these imposed duties. Consequently, in order to cover the costs of this EU priority, funds must be diverted from other 'development' priorities. Neither the negotiation process, nor the foreseeable outcomes for sustainable development bear the marks of good governance.

Fisheries Partnership Agreements (FPAs)

ACP–EU relations on fishing are currently governed by 'bilateral' agreements between the EC and individual ACP States. During a fact finding mission by an ACP–EU Joint Parliamentary Assembly (JPA) delegation to the Seychelles during the period 25–27 April 2008 certain problems were raised in relation to the FPA between the Seychelles and the EU. Non-State Actors complained of little EU involvement in the implementation of this Agreement. In particular, they claimed that Seychellois seamen serving on EU registered vessels did not receive the full wage they were entitled to under the FPA, and they pointed out that the EU has been paying the same licensing fee for tuna for some 30 years, despite much higher market prices. Furthermore, contrary to the principle of ownership, Seychelles authorities stated that the FPA dictates how the Government is to utilise the remuneration the EU pays under the FPA. They also claimed that EU Sanitary and Phyto-Sanitary (SPS) rules were inconsistent or applied in an arbitrary manner. For example it was pointed out that different maximum levels of cadmium were set for EU OCTs, such as Réunion and the Seychelles, and that all Seychelles vessels are required to have non-wooden deck, whilst the majority of EC vessels still use wooden decks. Finally, there is evidence that indicates that EU fishing vessels have vastly under-reported, and thus under-paid, their catches. The EU's failure to implement consistent standards and rules as well as its dictation of how remuneration is to be spent, are characteristic of poor governance processes. Its failure to pay fair wages to citizens of developing countries, to pay fair licensing fees, and to enforce honest reporting and payments by its vessels starkly detract from the good governance goal of poverty reduction.

Furthermore, the report of the fact finding mission states that the Seychelles and surrounding countries requested the EC to consider a regional fisheries agreement, to replace the bilateral agreements currently in place. However, according to the report, this was turned down by the European Commission. As with the Seychelles, the EC also rejected repeated requests from the Pacific for a regional fisheries agreement.

The regional contention resulting from the bilateral agreements poses a threat not only to cooperation, integration and political stability in the region but also to long-term, sustainable economic development. Failure to solidify a regional approach to manage such important finite resources could easily lead to every country grabbing—or selling the rights to grab—as much as they can while the supply lasts. This would quickly result in a complete depletion of the fish population, which would have a devastating effect on the Pacific economy, way of life, and the health of its people. Already, as a result of the FPAs, the strong presence of EU fishing boats has rendered local fishing companies unable to compete. Labourers from ACP countries have lost their jobs in the local fishing industries and have thus been forced to migrate—often without legal documentation—to look for other work.

DISCUSSION AND RECOMMENDATIONS

The EU has considerable resources at its disposal that contribute to a significant power differential between it and the ACP Group. It wields a variety of mechanisms to govern these resources in its relationship with ACP States. By illuminating a few of these mechanisms, this paper has endeavoured to shed some light on these governance processes and their outcomes. There is considerable evidence that some policies pursued by the EU are not conducive to the promotion of sustainable development, the alleviation of poverty, and the gradual integration of ACP States into the world economy. The EU has abused its power advantage to impose its political will and economic agenda. The processes by which these impositions occur are far from transparent. We have illuminated various mechanisms that the EU, and especially the EC, has used to steer the members of the ACP Group toward compliance with its own interests and agendas. The opaque nature of these processes, and the fact that they leave the EU entirely unaccountable for their consequences, are trademarks of processes of bad governance. We have further analysed actual and potential outcomes of these governance processes and have found that many of them have resulted, or are likely to result, in consequences that bode ill for sustainable development and the alleviation of poverty in the developing countries. The mark of bad governance as an outcome results from the EU's failure to adhere to policies that it rhetorically endorses. The EU is not managing its relations with the ACP Group in accordance with its vows to respect ACP sovereignty and promote ownership of adopted policies.

In reaction to critiques of how the EU has wielded power in its relationship with developing countries, as well as suggestions that the EU should be held accountable for its actions in this regard, the EC affirmed a commitment to 'dialogue with due regard for principles of partnership' (rather than conditionality) and 'ownership' as well as to 'focusing on both the responsibilities of donors and partner countries in improving governance (mutual accountability)'. Unfortunately, the foregoing analyses have illustrated that this stated commitment has still left much to be desired regarding its manifestation in practice. The EC has also failed to ensure synergies and coherence between the different EC and EU policies and instruments, a declared aim of its Communication on Governance and Development.

Due to some of the current realities of political and social power dynamics in some African countries one cannot advocate simply writing a blank check to developing country governments. On the other hand, the EU's 'paternalistic' claims that it should stipulate how aid is used because it knows what is best for the aid recipients must be grounded in evidence. Evidence provided in this paper demonstrates that the governance outcomes do not justify the governance means employed by the EU. While the EU governance processes discussed have been marked by coercion, the outcomes bode ill for sustainable development in ACP countries. Policies that support sustainable development include paying fair wages and fees for services rendered, applying standards fairly, and resisting the temptation to exploit resources that sustain ACP economies and ways of life. Contrarily, on various accounts the EU has promoted policies and engaged in practices that have contributed to further deprivation in ACP States and regions.

Interference in ACP development agendas is only justified when it can be shown that their implementation would not serve the ACP peoples. When this is the case, or if ACP countries fall short of expectations, rather than imposing duties upon the ACP Group that it is ill-suited to fulfil, the EU should first provide the Group with means for capacity building and institutional support that will allow for the development of a capable, credible, and respected partner.

In order to support the integration of ACP countries into the global economy in a way that promotes sustainable development and poverty reduction, the EU should first ensure that global governance structures are in place that can competently manage the integration process. To support the creation of, and provide resources for, competent, transparent and accountable global structures would be acts of good governance.

Finally, to a certain extent, the ACP Group elevates the EC to its relatively powerful position by failing to act in a collective fashion in order to condense and wield potential power of its own. The ACP Group does have potential carrots and sticks at its disposal. For example, collectively ACP States have attractive natural resources and vast markets, access to which is desired not only by the EU but also others (such as China and the USA). Furthermore, the collective voice of 79 developing countries, plus the support of development-friendly NGOs and other benefactors, could exert a considerable amount of normative pressure. They might begin with a critique of the EC's wielding of governance mechanisms. A partner that manifests the criteria of good governance in its relationships, especially in those with weaker counterparts, will also be better positioned to advocate good governance.

20

Female Circumcision as Female Genital Mutilation: Human Rights or Cultural Imperialism?

ABDULMUMINI A. OBA

The charge of cultural imperialism in relation to human rights generally and women rights in particular is often made against the West. There are three major reasons for this. Firstly, the West is quick to condemn practices in other cultures that it considers unacceptable. This condemnation is sometimes without any real justification. Secondly, the West is guilty of double standard in relation to some of its own practices and practices in other cultures. Western practices are considered as 'civilised' while the non-Western practices are condemned as 'primitive' or 'savage'. Thirdly, whenever the West attempts to eradicate a non-Western practice it considers undesirable or wrong, its actions too often come in the form of external impositions rather than as encouragement of internal critique within the local culture. This chapter examines why the female circumcision discourse in the West fits into the paradigm of cultural imperialism.

INTERROGATING THE DEFINITIONS AND CLASSIFICATIONS OF FEMALE GENITAL MUTILATION

The World Health Organisation (WHO) lumped together all forms of female circumcision under the category of 'female genital mutilation' and takes both terms as synonyms. According to the organisation:

> 'Female genital mutilation' (FGM), often referred to as 'female circumcision', comprises all procedures involving partial or total removal of the external female genitalia or other injury to the female genital organs whether for cultural, religious or other non-therapeutic reasons.

The organisation enumerated the categories of the different types of 'female genital mutilation' as follows:

- Type I—excision of the prepuce, with or without excision of part or all of the clitoris;

- Type II—excision of the clitoris with partial or total excision of the labia minora;
- Type III—excision of part or all of the external genitalia and stitching/narrowing of the vaginal opening (infibulation);
- Type IV—pricking, piercing or incising of the clitoris and/or labia; stretching of the clitoris and/or labia; cauterisation by burning of the clitoris and surrounding tissue; scraping of tissue surrounding the vaginal orifice (*angurya* cuts) or cutting of the vagina (*gishiri* cuts); and introduction of corrosive substances or herbs into the vagina to cause bleeding or for the purpose of tightening or narrowing it; and any other procedure that falls under the definition given above.

The WHO says that the most common type of FGM is excision of the clitoris and the labia minora, accounting for up to 80 per cent of all cases and that the most extreme form is infibulation, which constitutes about 15 per cent of all procedures. The above classification covers a wide spectrum of practices that are now referred to erroneously as 'female genital mutilation'. However, the differences between these practices can be very wide. The least under Type I is 'excision of the prepuce' which involves the removal of the tip of the clitoris. Type III which is also referred to as infibulation is a very extreme practice which cannot be described as female circumcision in the sense that it goes beyond circumcision in concept and form. This is meant to preserve virginity and it is a practice restricted to parts of Sudan and Somalia.

There are two immediate criticisms of the WHO classification. Firstly, the classifications in Types I and IV are unduly wide. The 'excision of the prepuce without excision of part or all of the clitoris', 'excision of the prepuce with part or all of the clitoris;' and the 'excision of the prepuce with all of the clitoris' grouped together under Type I are clearly three different procedures that should have different classification. Again, what do all the procedures listed as Type IV have in common? The lumping of them together was deliberate. Extreme forms are classified together with mild types so that every type becomes *ipso facto* condemnable. The second criticism relates to the classification of all the four types as mutilation. How can the least excision in Type I be classified together with infibulation in Type III and branded as 'genital mutilation'? The classification as a whole and into specific types is therefore inaccurate and misleading. In spite of its glaring inaccuracy, the classification has become the typology of the intellectual, medical and human rights discourses on female circumcision and FGM.

More appropriately, one should speak of partial clitoridectomy, complete clitoridectomy, excision, and infibulation. In Nigeria, the customary form of female circumcision practiced in most communities is partial clitoridectomy, that is, the removal of the tip of the clitoris which is among the least form of Type I. This is also the maximum type permitted in Islam. Within this context, it is difficult to agree with WHO that excision (removal of the clitoris and the labia minora), and infibulation constitute respectively 80 and 15 per cent (total 95 per cent) of all cases of female circumcision.

EVALUATING THE CASE AGAINST FEMALE CIRCUMCISION

The arguments against female circumcision advanced by human rights proponents are examined hereunder.

Male Domination

Radical feminists argue that female circumcision is an expression of male domination of the female by men who want to keep their women sexually controlled while using them to satisfy their (men's) own sexual desires. These feminists who are based mostly in the Western world, and have no idea of what the non-Western woman is or feels, proffer such views. Such views are based on the stereotyping of gender relations based on Western models. Female circumcisions are approved and done at the instance of parents and not husbands and this knocks the bottom off the argument of feminists. Of course, women in cultures that practice female circumcision are often the strongest proponents of the practice which is carried out mostly by women and not men. Another version of the sex domination argument is that the 'male factor' encourages female circumcision. This is because in some cultures, men prefer circumcised girls because these men believe that circumcised girls would avoid immorality and extra-marital infidelity.

Right to Culture and Religion

Human rights values are often at war with each other. Female circumcision can arise out of religious and cultural factors. Those who practice it can argue that they have the right to practice their religion or culture. This raises two issues. First, if female circumcision is a religious practice, then there is a prima facie case of right to religion. Human rights proponents retort quite rightly that harmful cultural or religious practices cannot be permitted under the guise of right to religion or right to culture. However as we shall see below, the case has not been made out that the mild forms of female circumcision particularly the 'sunnatic' type common in Africa which is radically different from infibulation have any harmful effect.

Secondly, is female circumcision really a religious practice? Some have tried to dismiss the link between female circumcision and religion generally and Islam in particular. They say that the female circumcision predated Islam and therefore is not part of Islam. Of course, this is not correct in relation to Islam. The view totally ignores the most elementary aspects of *Usul al-Fiqh* (Islamic jurisprudence) generally and the methodology of deducing legal rules under Islamic law in particular. Many Islamic scholars find support for female circumcision in the Qur'an and other hadith.

Some Muslim scholars and non-Muslim critics of female circumcision argue that the hadith is technically unsound (*da'if*) being weak in transmission. Others have tried to infer an Islamic prohibition of the practice'. This approach is not consistent with Islamic law. A *sunna taqriyyah* is a hadith that relates the Prophet's comment and attitude to practices brought to the notice of the Prophet. In the hadith relating to female circumcision, the Prophet (SAW) did not forbid the practice but only indicated the limits. Islamic scholars have always been careful to point out this. A Muslim medical doctor defined the *sunna* circumcision as being no more than 'cutting-off the prepuce to the clitoris, which is about, in most cases, 1/3 of a centimetre (sometimes less)'. According to some Muslim scholars, *Khifaad* is particularly desirable when the clitoris protrudes beyond the labia. This is because of the stimulation that occurs every time the clothes rub against the clitoris. This constant and unwanted sexual stimulation can create serious psychological and behavioral problems for the girl or woman.

All extreme types of circumcision that go beyond the removal of the prepuce or at most, part of the clitoris should be considered *haram* (unlawful) for Muslims. The practice of 'sunna circumcision' should at least be considered *mustahab* (recommended) or at least *mubah* (permitted). This is why some Muslims insist that they should be allowed without any form of coercion—legal or otherwise—to choose whether or not to perform female circumcision.

Although, a majority of Islamic scholars recognise female circumcision as permissible, opponents of female circumcision have overblown the minority opinion of some 'modern' Islamic scholars who have expressed opposition or reservations about the practice. It is however clear that the scholars who oppose female circumcision are under the erroneous impression that *sunna* female circumcision has been proved to be harmful and that is the sole basis of their objection. No doubt, there are many direct and unequivocal verses in the Qur'an and traditions in the hadith that prohibit self-harm and self-destruction. What is at stake for many Muslims in the hadiths cited in support of female circumcision goes beyond mere verification of authenticity of hadith. The problem is that these scholars did not take the precaution of verifying the health allegations against the 'sunnatic' circumcision before acting upon the allegations. Their approach is contrary to the clear Qur'anic injunction that mandates verification of facts in such circumstances. If these scholars had known that there are no serious medical objections to the 'sunnatic' circumcision, probably, they would not have voiced any objection to the practice.

Another curious distortion associates infibulation with Islam. This approach is no more than a desperate attempt to discredit Islam by associating infibulation with the religion.

Right to Sexual and Corporeal Integrity

Some have argued that female circumcision violates women's rights to sexual fulfilment and corporeal integrity because of the tampering with the clitoris involved in the procedure. It is said that circumcision leads to frigidity in women but this is not an established medical fact. The truth is that our current very limited scientific knowledge of the dynamics of women's sexual satisfaction does not justify the claim that female circumcision leads to frigidity. Many studies have proved that circumcision does not impair the libido and that circumcised women do experience orgasm.

In informal discussions with some of this author's female colleagues who had undergone circumcision, virtually all of them admitted to achieving orgasm and thus see nothing wrong with female circumcision. This may be the reason why the movement to have female circumcision banned does not enjoy the popular support of women in many non-Western countries. The removal of the clitoris does not necessarily make it impossible for a woman to achieve orgasm.

Right to Health

The strongest 'case' against female circumcision is from the medical perspective. The allegation that female circumcision is harmful has been the most potent weapon against the practice. Medical and human rights literature often carry long lists of frightening 'possible' complications that can arise out of FGM. More recently, concern has arisen about possible transmission of the HIV virus due to the use of one instrument in multiple operations. Long-term consequences include cysts and abscesses, keloid scar formation, damage to the urethra resulting in urinary incontinence, dyspareunia (painful sexual intercourse) and sexual dysfunction and difficulties with childbirth.

Genital mutilation may leave a lasting mark on the life and mind of the woman who has undergone it. In the longer term, women may suffer feelings of incompleteness, anxiety and depression.

However, the most misleading aspect of the campaign against FGM is that lists of purported harmful effects do not differentiate between the various types of female circumcision and female genital mutilation but usually lump them together. By this generalisation, the harmful effects of infibulation are transferred to all the various forms of circumcision. This less than scientific approach is found even in the highest quarters.

Contrary to the assertion that female circumcision is harmful, some medical opinions in the West see benefits in female circumcision. Wheeler, citing articles in medical journals published in the West, discusses extensive research that points to improved sexual satisfaction as a benefit of surgical removal of the prepuce. Until recently, medical doctors in the West arguing along the same lines as Islamic jurists who argue in favour of *khifaad* routinely performed surgery in the case of *ambiguous genitalia* where the clitoris was abnormally or excessively large. This has now been condemned. It is easy to argue against these 'old' medical opinions but then such arguments also cast a shadow of doubt on the validity of the so-called new positions.

Opponents of female circumcision often press the health argument too far. Some of them have argued as if HIV comes from female circumcision. This argument is premised on the use of the same cutting instruments on many girls during puberty rites in some African communities. It has also been argued that circumcision leads to drug abuse.

It is an intellectual fraud to link female circumcision (other than infibulation) to maternal and child mortality. Another similar 'scientific' conclusion is that circumcised women 'are much more likely to become sterile'. According to the research, this is due to possible damage to the reproductive organs by infections traced to female circumcision. Although there is clearly no scientific basis for saying that female circumcision causes sterility, some have identified the value of the sterility argument as an ideological weapon against female circumcision.

One very serious negative health-related consequence of the categorisation of female circumcision as FGM is that circumcised women have become objects of curio in Western hospitals. Unnecessary caesarean operations are often performed in the West on circumcised women by doctors who would not care to make any distinction between the categories of female circumcision. This is due to their fears of the health risks generally associated with infibulation. It may also equally be a continuation of the propaganda against female circumcision.

These women experience afresh the indignities and humiliations suffered by Saartjie Baartman the young Khoisan woman who in the 19th century became a medical curiosity in Europe and was exhibited like an animal to a paying public for her steatopygia-enlarged buttocks and her unusually elongated labia. The analogy between these two experiences spanning centuries is clear. There is a clear need to protect circumcised women from this sort of intrusion and medico-voyeurism.

CRITICISM OF THE METHOD

The crude procedure under unhygienic conditions and the absence of analgesic wherein female circumcisions are allegedly performed are emphasised by critics of female circumcision.

The catalogue of crude tools said to be used in carrying out the procedure can be very frightening. Amnesty International listed them as including 'blunt penknife', 'broken glass, a tin lid, scissors, a razor blade or some other cutting instrument' and in the case of infibulation, the use of 'thorns and stitches' to hold together the two sides of the labia majora together. Of course, infibulation is not practiced anywhere outside the Middle Nile region and there is no report of the use of the listed instruments in most African communities. The crude instruments listed are the rare exceptions rather than the rule. Amnesty International also says that 'antiseptic powder may be applied, or, more unusually, pastes—containing herbs, milk, eggs, ashes or dung'. This again, is a list calculated to discredit. Certainly, medical knowledge is not the exclusive preserve of the West. Many overlook or are oblivious of the fact that many African communities in the pre-colonial era had fairly competent surgeons and other medical experts. As a United States–based Nigerian medical doctor rightly cautioned, some communities use analgesics; which types, and their medicinal properties are still unknown to the West.

Opponents of female circumcision also question the competence of the persons performing the operation. For example, Amnesty

International published a testimony of a female circumcision performed by 'half-drunk' women. It is well documented that in African communities, locally trained experts carried out circumcision. For example among the Yoruba, circumcision is a highly technical procedure carried out only by those who have acquired the skill. The practitioners who could be male or female were usually members of families that have specialised in carrying out surgical procedures particularly those concerning circumcision and facial marks. These families have acquired the skill and experience that come from literally centuries of doing these things.

If modern doctors perform the operation, the criticism of lack of expertise would be eliminated. However, the medical world in the West would not countenance the 'medicalisation' of female circumcision. Its practitioners would not allow medical doctors to perform the operation. The procedure does not form part of the medical curriculum. Doctors are now liable to incur severe penalties if they carry out female circumcision. Some have even asserted without advancing any reason, that the 'negative effects' of female circumcision 'are only slightly mitigated when the procedure is performed in a health facility by health professional'. The non-medicalisation of female circumcision has many negative effects. It drives female circumcision underground to the world of quacks and the fear of criminal sanctions prevent parents from bringing their damaged children to hospital when things go wrong with the circumcision. The attitude of the opponents of female circumcision is not formulated by health concerns but an unreasoning blind opposition based on political and other extraneous factors. The argument regarding the unhygienic methods of carrying out female circumcision is merely incidental to their opposition. Otherwise, the female circumcision impasse could be resolved easily with medical doctors performing the mild forms of circumcision within the controlled and sanitary atmosphere of clinical settings.

CRISIS OF TERMINOLOGY

The West has turned the use of language in the human rights discourse as a major weapon in the cross-cultural human rights dialogue. This has given rise to a crisis as to the appropriate terminologies for female circumcision.

Initially, there was talk only of 'female circumcision', then 'female genital mutilation' and sometimes, 'female genital surgery'. These were used interchangeably. The last term is not popular in the West because it 'tends to trivialise the horrors of female procedures' and appears 'to imply that the practice is somehow medical in nature'. The singularly misleading and alarmist term 'female sexual castration' was suggested but it never caught on. This is not surprising. Even the most extreme forms of female circumcision and FGM cannot be described as castration. Most Western opponents of female circumcision prefer the term FGM which some justify with the dubious analogy that in its 'mildest form, clitoridectomy . . . is anatomically equivalent to amputation of the penis'.

Many have pointed out and rightly too, that not all types of female circumcision fall within the categories of female genital mutilation properly so called. The wide gulf between the *sunna* female circumcision and the Pharaohic genital mutilation is so wide that it has been described as 'inaccurate', 'intellectually lazy and misleading' and 'intolerant' to lump all the different practices in the WHO list under the single and derogatory terminology of Female Genital Mutilation. It is apparent that 'not all categories of female circumcision amount to mutilation in a real sense'. Even some opposed to all types of female circumcision find the term 'mutilation' objectionable. It is offensive because it is 'disrespectful of African women who have been circumcised' and to all persons whose culture allows female circumcision.

The objections to the term 'female genital mutilation' have led to the use of the alternative term 'female genital cutting' which is considered a 'straightforward' term devoid of moral judgement. For some, the term FGM is not negotiable. This is so even in the academic context where respect for other views is the norm. The terminology 'female genital mutilation' is still very much in use and defended by African-based scholars and NGOs.

ANTI-FEMALE CIRCUMCISION LEGISLATION AT INTERNATIONAL AND DOMESTIC LEVELS

International human rights laws have been invoked against female circumcision and FGM.

There is also an African regional treaty prohibition of FGM. Under the Protocol to the African Charter on Human and Peoples' Rights on the Rights of Women in Africa, state parties are obligated to campaign against all forms of female genital mutilation in order to eradicate the practice. In addition, state parties are to criminalise the practice of all forms of female genital mutilation, medicalisation and para-medicalisation of female genital mutilation.

Pursuant to the developments on the international human rights scene, many countries have taken legislative action against female circumcision and FGM. In Africa, at least fourteen countries including Egypt, Ghana, Kenya, Sudan and Tanzania have officially banned female circumcision. In Nigeria, the Child Rights Act which was enacted in 2003 was directed towards consolidating all federal laws relating to children and towards giving legal effect to the country's international human rights obligations in respect of the rights of children. This fairly long legislation omitted any reference to female circumcision and FGM because a majority of the legislators could not be persuaded to prohibit the practice. However, some states have legislated against 'female circumcision' and 'genital mutilation'. The disconcerting aspect of these state laws is the definition of 'female circumcision' and 'female genital mutilation'. The Edo State law and other state laws in the country define 'circumcision', as 'the act of cutting off of the clitoris of a female' while 'mutilation' is defined as 'any cutting, incision, damage, removal, of any or all of the female sex organs'.

Persons who can be guilty of an offence under these Nigerian laws include not only those who perform, aid and abet the performance of female circumcision or female genital mutilation, but also 'any person who offers herself' for circumcision or genital mutilation. As regards punishments for a conviction under the law, the Edo law stipulates a fine of one thousand naira or imprisonment for not less than six months or both.

The negative atmosphere created against female circumcision by WHO has become so pervasive that even where there is no domestic legislation against female circumcision, many doctors run away from anything concerning female circumcision for fear of losing their practising licenses.

Many have pointed out that even if female circumcision is as harmful as its opponents claim, criminalisation of female circumcision is not really the answer as it merely causes the practice to be performed secretly underground. This is because those practising it do not accept that it is harmful. There are other adverse effects of criminalisation of female circumcision. For example, the negative effects conviction has on the mother where she is an immigrant. Rather, dialogue, discussion, and the devising of contextualised solutions have been suggested as the proper methods.

Given the deep-rooted cultural practice and the social approval of female circumcision in some areas, most legislations criminalising female circumcision may perhaps belong to what has been described as 'empty gestures calculated to gain approval from the Western community'. But, why a government should criminalise female circumcision merely to win Western approval tells a lot about the interplay involved between human rights and cultural imperialism.

FEMALE CIRCUMCISION, CULTURAL IMPERIALISM AND DOUBLE STANDARDS

Some have pointed out that the campaign against female circumcision is expressive of the cultural imperialism of the West. This position has often been argued from the anthropological perspective, and from the perspective of Western feminist discourse on the African woman. The charge of cultural imperialism against the West in the matter of female circumcision is evident in many respects. Some of these are examined hereunder.

The Scuttled Seattle Compromise

The 'Seattle Compromise' arose in the Harbourview Medical Center, Seattle, Washington. This centre is located in an area which has a large number of Somali immigrants who demand that infibulations be performed on their baby girls. The hospital would not permit infibulations and the immigrants threatened that they would rather pay the large sums of money required to transport their girls back to Somali where infibulations would be done rather than leave their girls without infibulation. In this circumstance in 1996, in order to prevent the threatened infibulations, the hospital's authorities proposed what they perceived as 'a largely symbolic compromise'. This involved 'a small cut to the prepuce, the hood above the clitoris, with no tissue excised, and this would be conducted under local anaesthetic for children old enough to understand the procedure and give consent in combination with informed consent of the parents.'

The hospital was of the view that this mere bloodletting would not violate the anti-FGM laws in the United States. The suggested compromise however provoked a barrage of vehement criticisms that the hospital authorities had to shelve it. The Attorney General swiftly declared that the compromise violated American anti-FGM laws even though those laws talk of removal of tissue. Coleman identified the three main arguments advanced by the objectors to the compromise. The first is that performing this procedure would have sanctioned medically-unnecessary physical injury to children. The second is that 'even talking about cutting female genitals legitimises a barbaric practice, one that disempowers women and serves to keep them out of the American mainstream'. The third is that the compromise interfered with the process of 'Americanisation'.

It is really significant that the basis of the rejection of the compromise was its being 'non-American'. This creates the impression that unless one conforms to America's vision of the world, America will never be pleased with one.

A compromise similar to the Seattle one was also proposed and rejected in Italy where the practice remains a criminal offence. Significantly, it has been adopted in Somalia where *sunna* circumcision and pricking are performed under sanitary and medical conditions in order to protect the girls from infibulation done in unhygienic conditions.

Legalised Female Genital Mutilations in the West

In spite of the vehement Western opposition to female circumcision and 'female genital mutilation', medical doctors in the West routinely carry out other various forms of female genital 'cutting'. The Western woman is the alpha and omega regarding her vagina. She can 'redesign' or 'restructure' her vagina for no other reason than to 'enhance sexual gratification' and to 'aesthetically modify' her labia. The surprising thing is that these operations are perfectly legal and are performed by medical doctors in hospitals at the mere request of the women. The procedures variously and collectively referred to as 'cosmetic genitoplasty', or 'female genital "cosmetic" surgery' often entails serious surgical risks and are not free from grievous side effects. For these reasons, some in the medical world have condemned the practices as FGM. Others have justified the practices on the ground of the 'psychological' advantages the practices offer to women. But then, female circumcision and even infibulation produces similar psychological benefits for women in societies where the practices are acceptable.

FGM in the West is not related or traceable to religion. Rather, it has a cultural basis. Over the years, the West has evolved an individual-centred narcissistic and hedonistic culture. The individual is allowed the fullest avenue for maximum 'enjoyment' particularly in sexual matters with only very minimal interference of the law. There are virtually no bars to the quest for 'sexual fulfilment'. Western women are being pressured to conform to and acquire the beauty models prescribed by fashion houses and the mass media. The 'designer vagina' is just another new fad in the catalogue of female bodily mutilations in the West.

There are other countless ways in which women in the West can legitimately fiddle with their genitals. In the early 1980s, thousands underwent genital piercing procedures whereby their genitals were pierced so that special metal rings and bars could be inserted. The reasons were mainly for 'decoration and sexual enhancement'. Others had plastic surgery performed on their clitoris and vulva to 'change its appearance and sometimes to expose their clitoris to direct stimulation'. Some women desiring a larger clitoris use steroids creams and other forms of steroids to cause the same result. It is interesting to note that the WHO did not deem it fit to include these non-therapeutic genital operations in its list of FGM practices. Logically, these procedures ought to come within the 'scraping of tissue surrounding the vaginal orifice' or 'cutting of the vagina' within the ambit of Type IV of the WHO classifications of FGM (quoted above) but these description were immediately limited by WHO to *angurya* cuts and *gishiri* cuts respectively. This is a clear case of definition-gerrymandering. So complete is this strategy that even some of those who defend female circumcision assume that Type IV 'includes all other unclassified practices involving female genitalia'. But does it? Making a discriminatory distinction between Western practices and non-Western practices in relation to non-therapeutic cuttings in the vagina is nothing but double standards.

The Right to Informed Consent

If women in the West have a choice in what they can do with or to their body including their vaginas, why should non-Western women not have the same choice? Why should non-Western women as adults not be allowed to make an informed choice as to whether or not they want to be circumcised? As we have seen above, the law in many countries denies this choice on pain of stiff punishment. This view considers non-Western women as being incapable of thinking for themselves and therefore needing to be protected from themselves.

Western Feminism

Many articulate African scholars have consistently opposed the Western depiction of Africa and its peoples. To these intellectuals, the Western depictions are in most cases far from the realities in the continent. This is because they see Africa through their own cultural lens. The Western feminist is thus often disappointed when she encounters African women questioning her alien concern and sympathy.

Perhaps the worst example of Western feminism in this context is the African American writer Alice Walker. Walker's works centre around infibulation which for her is the 'standard' female circumcision in Africa. By this less than factual approach, she ignores the crucial differences between infibulation and circumcision and thereby grossly misrepresented Africa. She is also too fictional in her analysis of the effects of infibulation and her presentation of this parody as a social and quasi-medical fact really harmed her credibility. There is no way female circumcision can be described as 'sexual blinding of women' as she did. It is not surprising that she has been criticised vehemently by articulate and enlightened female African intellectuals. While Alice Walker may help distort the popular understanding of the African women generally and female circumcision in particular in the West, she remains an obscure figure in Africa itself. As with many well-known Western specialists on Africa, she remains largely unknown in Africa itself. Her impact in Africa is at best, marginal.

The Western feminist concern has also had a diversionary effect on the problems of women in Africa. Oyeronke Oyewumi rightly pointed out that Walker's 'incessant wailing over the blameless vulva' is distracting most of us from the work we need to do. This is the consensus of articulate Africans.

Donor Driven Research

Another important point often made against the West is that the West manipulates discussions about Africa by determining the topics for research and discussion. Since African researchers are virtually dependent on grants from foreign donors and the United Nations agencies (which are also controlled by the same foreign countries), their research tends to be donor-driven.

Gender studies in Africa are perhaps the most obvious victims of this research pattern and female circumcision more particularly so. Many African scholars are falling over themselves in a rush to partake of the largesse that comes with denigrating African cultures generally and female circumcision in particular. The result is that there is a disconnection between the works of these scholars and reality and also between their theories and their practices in private life. That the West too readily encouraged non-Westerns and minorities who renegade their own peoples does no good for global peaceful co-existence.

Visas and Asylum Incentives

Many in the third world will do anything to be able to obtain visas to Western countries. Refugees and peoples fleeing from poverty, diseases, oppressive governments, and other threatened calamities or atrocities are in the high priority category for visas into these countries. Female circumcision has been advanced as one of the atrocities. It therefore makes sense for asylum seekers and applicants to demonise female circumcision and for others to use the bait of visas as propaganda against female circumcision.

The use of the term 'Female Genital Mutilation' is an insult to the cultures whose practices regarding female circumcision do not logically or medically amount to genital mutilation. Opponents of female circumcision must show clear-cut scientific proofs of the dangers which this type of circumcision (which is very different from infibulation) constitute to the life and health of women before legislation prohibiting these practices is passed. The baseless cataloguing of harmful effects of female circumcision conjured by opponents of female circumcision does no credit to intellectual honesty or scientific integrity.

The various risks associated with the traditional methods of carrying out female circumcision would be eliminated if circumcision is carried out by properly-trained medical personnel. There is a case for medicalisation of female circumcision so that the procedure can be carried out by medical doctors in the proper environment. The Seattle compromise offered an easy way out in the case of infibulation yet it was rejected. The reasons advanced for the rejection of the Seattle compromise paints the West as being more of an intolerant society than a society genuinely interested in ending harmful practices.

Criminalisation of female circumcision exposes many women to penal sanctions. Many of these women are in the poor and vulnerable bracket. This would no doubt add to rather than alleviate the problems of these women. In Africa, where governmental presence is mostly felt in the rural areas through taxation and coercive legislation rather than through social services and economic infrastructures, the concern of foreigners about female circumcision would be hard to understand. Therefore, even if female circumcision is harmful as argued by its opponents, criminalisation is not the answer. Education and enlightenment would be the appropriate weapons; but here perhaps lies the central problem in the struggle against female circumcision. While infibulation is easily discredited, being manifestly harmful, female circumcision is not. No amount of propaganda would convince millions of circumcised women if it contradicts their own experience. More factual reasons must be found to dissuade women from the practice—the 'sexual blinding' or 'sexual castration' argument would sound hollow to these women who in spite of being circumcised live and enjoy what they consider to be a normal and satisfied sexual life.

The world has a duty to strive towards universal human rights. The deep silence on the various non-therapeutic female genital cuttings legally available on demand in the West points to an unacceptable double standard. This Orwellian approach to human rights ('all animals are equal but some are more equal than others') is nothing but sheer cultural imperialism, which creates doubts, aversion, and dissension in the minds of non-Western peoples who are otherwise committed to human rights. It could discredit the idea of universality of human rights and destroy the very roots of human rights.

21
Politics, Anti-politics, International Justice: Language and Power in the Special Court for Sierra Leone

TIM KELSALL

GLOBAL GOVERNANCE, LIBERAL PEACE, INTERNATIONAL LAW

The background to this article is provided by four interrelated processes. The first is the attenuation of national state capacities in the developing world under the influence of processes commonly referred to as 'globalisation'. The second is a transformation of the way in which Africa, and other peripheral areas integrate into the world economy, namely through increasingly informal or illegal forms of economic activity that have led some commentators to speak of a 'criminalisation' of the state. The third is an increase in civil unconventional warfare, also known as 'new war', conditioned in part, though only in part, by struggles over resources. In the 'complex political emergencies' characteristic of new wars, 'emergent political complexes' accumulate force and resources by engaging with transnational corporations, international criminal networks, arms dealers, private security companies, humanitarian NGOs and peacekeeping missions. The fourth process is the international response, namely, a merging of development, security, and 'transitional justice' apparatuses in an attempt to rebuild societies in a liberal mould: what some commentators have called 'post-Westphalian peace building'. Western governments have become increasingly concerned not only by the appalling human costs of new wars, but also by the potential they hold to destabilise the global North. According to Tony Blair, 'We cannot turn our backs on conflicts and the violation of human rights in other countries if we still want to be secure.'

The international response has been both discursive and practical. At the discursive level, political acts and actors have been 'depoliticised', reallocated into criminal categories, for example through terminology such as 'warlords', 'gangs', 'thugs', 'bandits', or just plain 'criminals'; war has been explained by World Bank analysts as an activity driven by desires for criminal economic gain. And practically, the international community has sent peacekeeping missions to areas such as the former Yugoslavia, Rwanda, Sierra Leone, East Timor, Democratic Republic of Congo, and Liberia, and created international courts and issued indictments for the first three. As a result scores of political and military leaders of violent social movements have been arrested, arraigned, and charged as criminals. A clutch of international organisations broadly supports these developments, ranging from the United Nations Office of Legal Affairs, the US State Department (which has a War Crimes Ambassador), and the British Foreign and Commonwealth Office (which has appointed a War Crimes Coordinator), to non-governmental organisations such as Human Rights Watch, the International Centre for Transitional Justice (ICTJ), 'No Peace Without Justice' (NPWJ), the International Coalition of NGOs for the International Criminal Court, Lawyers without Borders, and others.

International criminal justice is instantiated in what Michel Foucault has called a 'discursive regime', namely an institutional edifice with specific precepts, rules and conventions of behaviour. The discourse of international law, which includes its enforceable statutes, the international tribunals with their rules of procedure and evidence and the concrete practices of the courtroom work in combination to produce particular historical 'truths' (events happened this way not that; these considerations are relevant, those are not). These truths underwrite the criminalisation of violent forms of political leadership and empower a punitive penal machinery. Here, discursive practices create truth which issues in power: 'It's the characteristic of our Western societies that the language of power is law, not magic, religion, or anything else'.

Under this regime violent struggles for territory, resources, or allegiance, which lay people, political scientists or sociologists might deem to be 'political' or 'sociological', come to be reclassified as 'criminal'. By being removed from the political sphere, these strategies, acts and modes of behaviour are extracted from the arena of popular debate and struggle (or indeed expert analysis), and rendered susceptible to the intervention of policing, juridical and penal agencies. To borrow a concept from James Ferguson, the apparatus of international justice can be construed as an 'anti-politics machine', part of a larger developmental complex that depoliticises new political formations rendering them amenable to technical solutions.

SIERRA LEONE: WAR, PEACE AND THE CREATION OF THE SPECIAL COURT

The war in Sierra Leone is estimated to have cost some 75,000 lives, with thousands of others suffering atrocities 'unique in their grotesquery'. Among its root causes, social scientists have pointed to a history of corrupt and unaccountable governance; a deep-rooted political culture of violence; a crisis in youth employment and opportunities; a rural social and legal order that dealt unfairly with youth, especially allochtons; and an unstable regional context, in particular the war in neighbouring Liberia. The conflict was fuelled by an economy of plunder and predation, along with the organised exploitation of diamond resources.

The war began in 1991 when a group of one to two hundred fighters calling themselves the Revolutionary United Front (RUF) crossed the Liberian border into Eastern Sierra Leone. Thirteen months later a group of disgruntled government soldiers displaced the ruling All People's Congress regime in a coup that established a military dictatorship: the National Provisional Ruling Council. The war continued in spite of increased army recruitment, the intervention of a West African peacekeeping force (ECOMOG), the hiring of South African mercenaries (Executive Outcomes), and the popular mushrooming of civilian militia, later to be coordinated by one Chief Sam Hinga Norman into a national, Civil Defence Force (CDF). A palace coup in 1996 paved the way to democratic elections in which Ahmad Tejan Kabbah of the Sierra Leone People's Party (SLPP) was elected president, only to be overthrown in 1997 in another coup. The coup-makers invited the rebels to join the government, giving birth to the Armed Forces Revolutionary Council (AFRC)–RUF junta. The junta was itself chased from Freetown in 1998 and the SLPP government restored. Rebel forces continued to control parts of the country, however, and invaded Freetown in January 1999. Though the government survived it remained critically weak and signed a peace treaty and power-sharing agreement in Lomé in 1999. In 2000 UN peacekeepers were kidnapped by rebels and the agreement broke down. The RUF leader, Foday Sankoh, then Chairman of the Strategic Minerals Resources Commission with protocol status of Vice President, was besieged in his house by a mob and later captured and paraded through the streets of Freetown.

Following these events, on 12 June 2000 Tejan Kabbah invited the UN to 'set up a court powerful enough to bring justice to his country'. Five days later, in resolution 1315, the Security Council declared that, 'a credible system of justice and accountability for the very serious crimes committed [in Sierra Leone] would end impunity and would contribute to the process of national reconciliation and to the restoration and maintenance of peace'. In March 2002 Sierra Leone's parliament ratified the treaty between the Government and the UN, providing for a Court that would, 'prosecute persons who bear the greatest responsibility' for war crimes and crimes against humanity committed after the Abidjan Peace Accord of 1996. The first staff to work at the Court arrived in Freetown in July 2002, the first indictments were approved in March 2003 and arrests took place in the weeks that followed. To date thirteen persons have been indicted for crimes that include murder, rape, enslavement, looting and burning, sexual slavery, extermination, acts of terror, conscription of children into an armed force, forced marriage, and attacks on UNAMSIL peacekeepers.

THE TRIALS OF GLOBAL GOVERNANCE

The nine indictees currently in the custody of the Court are being tried in three trials, each dedicated to one of the main factions in the conflict: the RUF, CDF and AFRC.

The trial of the three RUF indictees opened in Freetown on 5 July 2004. In its opening statement, the Prosecution alleged that in 1991 a group of some 200 rebels assisted by Liberian warlord Charles Taylor invaded Sierra Leone, constituting a joint criminal enterprise, the aim of which was to take control of the country's territory and resources, in particular the diamond mining areas, by any means necessary. 'Their motive: power, riches, and control in furtherance of a joint criminal enterprise that extended from West Africa north into the Mediterranean Region, Europe, and the Middle East'. Then, in 1997, a group of disaffected soldiers staged a military coup and took power in Freetown, calling themselves the AFRC. They formed a pact, or junta, with the RUF, and thereafter the two groups were, according to the Prosecution, indistinguishable. Of the three RUF indictees, Issa Sesay occupied a number of senior positions, including RUF Area Commander, Battle Group Commander and Battle Field Commander, and, after Sankoh's imprisonment directed RUF activities countrywide; Morris Kallon was a senior officer and member of the Junta governing body; Augustine Gbao was, among other positions, Commander of the RUF Internal Defence Unit and in charge of its Security Units. Together, these three were accused of 18 counts of war crimes and crimes against humanity.

At the opening of the CDF trial on 3 June, the prosecution alleged that in the aftermath of the 1997 coup, Chief Samuel Hinga Norman—then exiled deputy minister for defence—assumed leadership of a poorly organised band of traditional hunters—the *kamajors*—and, together with Allieu Kondewa, who became the movement's High Priest, and Moinina Fofana, its Commander of War, conscripted civilians into a transformed *kamajor* movement, preparing them for battle 'by means of cultish rituals' intended to make them impregnable to bullets. In this way they 'schemed to take a traditional belief system and manipulated (sic) it to their own ends'. By employing the *kamajors,* and other civilian militias, they began a 'joint criminal enterprise', hatching a 'common plan' to use 'every means, including illegal and forbidden means, to defeat the RUF and AFRC forces and to gain and exercise control over the territory of Sierra Leone'. In the course of carrying out this plan the three committed, planned, instigated and ordered criminal acts in a widespread and systematic fashion; in other cases, they let criminal acts by their subordinates—which were a foreseeable consequence of the plan—go unpunished. According to the prosecution, this rendered the indictees guilty of war crimes—namely violations of Article 3 common to the Geneva Conventions and Additional Protocol II—as well as other serious violations of international humanitarian law. The opening statements gave a graphic foretaste of testimony to come, offering up stories of rape, immolation, decapitation and cannibalism.

The rhetoric of these opening statements is deserving of a paper in its own right. In the case of the RUF the Prosecutor, David Crane, emphasised the greed of the indictees and evoked a deviant criminal organisation whose tentacles penetrated even Western Europe. Each of his opening statements was pervaded by tropes of light and darkness, civilisation and barbarism, and the law was accorded an almost religious status. In the trials proper, these evocative rhetorical strategies were superseded by more prosaic ones. But though the language was more mundane, it was just as strategic and just as important in expanding the law's domain.

The chapter turns now to an analysis of the courtroom's linguistic mini-dramas, pointing to the exercise of power through language, the attempts at resistance, or a counter-discourse, on the part of the indictees, and the efforts of the bench and prosecution to suppress this.

LANGUAGE AND POWER

In the trials of the CDF and RUF indictees, language has been used to exercise power in at least two distinct ways. To begin with, it has been used to redefine history, carving a set of criminal acts from the continuous flow of political events. Second, it has been used to set boundaries to the types of statement that are permissible or sayable in the courtroom. Both depend on what Foucault might call, 'dividing practices', demarcating the social world into a domain appropriate to 'politics' and a space suitable to the intervention of 'the law'.

The first strategy is illustrated by a recurring theme in the Prosecutor's opening statements: the claim to a distinction between political and criminal acts, 'Despite the obvious political dimensions of this conflict', he said, 'these trials—this trial is about crimes . . . war crimes and crimes against humanity'. Going on to say:

> The issues before you are not—cannot be political. We have not charged political crimes. The court of law—this Chamber must focus on the alleged acts of these jointly charged indictees; politics must remain barred from these proceedings.

Crane alleged that, 'the Accused committed international crimes, their actions were criminal, their mindset criminal, not political'. And instructed the court to keep in mind that, 'they are charged with crimes as individuals, jointly and severally, not with political acts'. Crimes, he declaimed, 'are committed by men, not by abstract entities', continuing, 'only by punishing individuals who commit such crimes can the provisions of international law be enforced'.

In an interview with the Prosecutor I asked him what he meant by 'politics':

> TK: you draw a clear distinction, in your opening statement, between 'crime' and 'politics'. Can you give me a definition of 'crime' and a definition of 'politics', as you understand them?
>
> DC: sometimes they merge don't they? And there are political crimes, such as corruption is a political crime, I think . . . but these are international crimes that the world has said that

> all men are not absolved from . . . things such as war crimes and crimes against humanity . . . there's a real issue about injecting politics into a court of law. That's why you have balances of power, not balance of power, but the separation of power, you have an independent judiciary, you have a legislature and you have an executive, or some variation on that theme . . . and the judicial system is always removed from the political process because the tradition and culture have always said that politics and diplomacy have to be removed from the law which is blind, equal and I'm talking in the pure sense now . . . the concept of justice is a fair dealing with an issue void of outside influence, er, to include politics. If you inject politics into justice, you have, you don't have a just result, because again they don't mix.

Two themes emerge here: Firstly, the Prosecutor is suggesting that any act that infringes an international law is by definition criminal, not political. Secondly, any attempt to exert undue influence in the courtroom, for example through popular pressure, is also 'political'. Taken together, the two readings imply that acts that transgress international law and the perpetrators of those acts are criminal, no matter how locally popular they might be. In the RUF trial, Crane made clear that:

> We are not going to question whatever initial politics surrounded the RUF. We are going to show, however, that this abuse of a political process and the discontent of the citizens of Sierra Leone was a mask for these actors' own criminal purposes. This trial is not, cannot be, about this subterfuge of frustrated political aspirations, but about war crimes, the crimes against humanitarian (sic).

Moving to the second exercise of power through language, we find that statements of a political nature, such as those that might take issue with the Prosecutor's attempt to define the ground on which the trial would operate, are rendered unsayable by the Court's rules of procedure. During his introductory remarks to the RUF trial, Presiding Judge Benjamin Itoe stressed that:

> The occasion to make opening statements is not an occasion to make political declarations. We are in a court of law and we will only tolerate matters to be raised here which are strictly acceptable within our judicial practices and that any statement that tends to be political will be called to order and would, of course, not feature in our records.

He warned the Prosecutor himself that the content of his statement must be, 'bereft of anything political' and warned Augustine Gbao that the Court, 'will resist all attempts to transform what should be a proper adjudication of charges before the Court into a political melodrama'. In an exchange with the latter (see below), Judge Thompson made clear, 'our determination to resist any move by anyone, high or low, to allow politics to intrude into the domain of the impartial and dispassionate administration of justice'. This stance was supposedly empowered by Rule 84 of the Rules of Procedure and Evidence, which states that, 'each party may make an opening statement *confined to the evidence* he intends to present in support of his case' (my emphasis).

The attempt to preserve the courtroom as an apolitical sphere was a constant struggle, since the Court as an institution was conditioned by 'politics' on at least three different levels: international, national and local. Internationally, the Court was born out of wrangles between the UN Security Council and the Secretariat. Its mandate—to prosecute those who 'bear the greatest responsibility' was inscrutable to some and rested on the shakiest of philosophical foundations. The Prosecutor himself described it to me as, 'a piece of pure political compromise', claiming however that 'once you actually create the justice ship or boat, once you actually put it in the water and it begins to float away, it literally floats away and leaves the political process and becomes a justice system in the purest sense, and that is equality before the law'. Certainly, the decision to use the Abidjan Peace Accord of 1996 as the start date for the Court's remit was controversial. Arguably this protected certain private military companies from scrutiny, while the decision to circumvent the general amnesty provided at Lomé in 1999 doubtless left the defendants feeling double-crossed (see the testimony from Gbao below).

From an early stage the US was one of the Court's biggest backers. A popular belief in the international community and civil society in Freetown in 2003–4 was that this was a result of America's desire to find an alternative international justice model to the ICC in the Hague, though academic evidence provides little support for this. It was also common to hear Court staff themselves say that the appointment by the UN of David Crane, a former Pentagon lawyer, as Prosecutor reflected the US's disproportionate influence. Meanwhile UN patronage politics was said to have been reflected in the judicial appointments process: none of the judges had relevant experience at international level, and the Registrar of the Court was reportedly denied access to the deliberations surrounding their appointment.

Turning to the national political scene, the trials were arguably convenient for President Kabbah since they neutralised his key opponents and rivals, in particular Hinga Norman. Conspiracy theorists in Freetown suggested that the split between Kabbah and Norman mapped onto a historical intra-SLPP divide. The fact that Kabbah, Norman's former boss, had himself escaped indictment was a source of perplexity to most of the Sierra Leoneans with whom I spoke. The plot was thickened by the fact that defence counsel for Norman's co-defendant, Allieu Kondewa, was Charles Margai. Margai, the son of former Prime Minister Albert Margai, had lost to Kabbah in the competition to lead the SLPP. In 2005 he declared his intention to contest the SLPP presidential nomination again. Court *cognoscenti* speculated about the import of this for his relation to Bankole Thompson, a trial chamber judge from Sierra Leone.

The Court was also home to a local organisational politics expressed through numerous personal rivalries. For example, some at the Court raised eyebrows at the fact that Deputy Prosecutor, Desmond da Silva, who had vastly more courtroom experience than Crane, did not appear in the first two months of trial. Personal and political rivalries between the Judges were also apparent. For instance, a ferocious and ridiculous disagreement occurred between Judges Geoffrey Robertson and Renate Winter surrounding the ruling on the criminality of the recruitment of child soldiers, a dispute that spilled over into Chief Hinga Norman's defence team, and just one example of friction between Robertson and the other judges. In August 2004 an employee of the Court was charged with having sexual relations with a thirteen-year-old girl; rumours were rife about the political machinations that might lie behind this murky affair. These examples, it should be said, were just the tip of an iceberg that threatened to tear a hole in Crane's pure justice ship.

RESISTANCE

The difficulty of keeping politics and justice apart was highlighted during the RUF trial when, at the close of the Prosecution's opening statements, Augustine Gbao was given the opportunity to make an opening statement in his defence. He declared that the indictees were 'against the manner in which the Special Court for Sierra Leone was established' but was immediately cut short by the Bench, which informed him that these questions had already been adjudicated upon.

These were not the only tactics of resistance the defendants deployed. On the opening day of the CDF trial, First Accused Sam Hinga Norman—a man regarded by many Sierra Leoneans as a hero and saviour of the nation—followed the Prosecution's powerful opening statement with a dramatic intervention of his own. During the lunch break he passed a letter to the judges expressing his desire to dismiss his entire legal team and represent himself. Ensuing days witnessed a number of exchanges between Norman and the bench, in which they haggled over the nature and composition of Norman's representation. Norman manipulated these occasions to considerable public effect, requesting at one point to be tried *in absentia.* Indeed, some months into the trial Norman was successful in persuading all the defendants to boycott proceedings. This, however, was a short-lived victory.

On 15 June the trial resumed and Norman made a brief opening statement in which he refused to recognise the legitimacy of the court, claiming, *inter alia,* that it lacked constitutional authority. His supporters, who took up more than half of the public gallery, cheered and waved their arms jubilantly at the close of his speech, earning a reprimand from the presiding judge.

Norman's statement, making a challenge which had already been ruled upon, would not have impressed the judges. But the chief was playing to a different audience. He hoped to be tried in the court of public opinion, not of international law.

Subsequently the first witness was called. Led by Charles Caruso, counsel for the prosecution, he narrated the tale of an attack by *kamajors* on his home town of Koribundo (part of Norman's chiefdom) on 13 February 1998, in which civilians were killed and houses burned. He told of how he had fled to the neighbouring town of Bo, where he was subsequently captured by *kamajors,* who tortured him and killed his brother, telling him they intended to eat the latter. At a later date, after returning to Koribundo, he attended a public meeting in which Hinga Norman told the people of Koribundo not to blame *kamajors* for the attack, but to blame Norman himself.

Norman was later given an opportunity to cross-examine this witness. He began by calling him by a joking, or nick-nickname, 'Kotoba', which means 'short rice' in the *Mende* language. He assured him that, 'You and I know each other very well'. By using this diminutive term, Norman was reminding the witness that he was socially junior to him. He was trying to insert local social hierarchies into the courtroom, upsetting the 'equality of arms' demanded by courtroom procedure. He was implying that there was something improper in a subject telling public tales about his chief. The bench later barred Norman from using familiar names such as this.

The tactic seemed to work, since the witness was unwilling to say that Norman was a bad chief. Having confirmed his virtuosity as a leader, Norman then used his cross-examination to widen the field of debate: to go beyond a narrow description of events to the broader context of war, and, by implication, to shift moral responsibility from individuals to larger social forces; or, to put it in the language of moral philosophy, to have the testimony evaluated on consequentialist rather than deontological grounds.

Norman's counsel, Dr. Bu-Buakie Jabbi, subsequently took up the reins, continuing to try to paint a favourable portrait of Norman, and to elicit exculpatory evidence: 'Did you ever hear that Chief Norman saved the people of Jaima Bongor chiefdom?', 'Did you hear or did you see the *kamajors* repel RUF attacks?', 'Can you tell the court why you gave the prosecution no record of Chief Norman protecting lives and property in Koribundo?'. With a subsequent witness TF2-157, Dr Jabbi cross-examined on the nature of the APC government in power when the rebel invasion began in 1991: 'Can you say how that government came into being?', he asked the witness, and 'Can you say whether it was a legitimate government or not?' The point he was presumably trying to make was that Hinga Norman and the *kamajors* had been fighting a rebel group that from its inception had sought to overthrow an elected government. 'And would you agree that they were therefore—the *kamajors*, they were therefore defending both the local people and the government of the country?'

If the previous section provided examples of the way in which the law seeks to delegitimise non-liberal leaders of the poor by means of discursive operations that firstly define the actions of the former as criminal and secondly prevent the questioning of that definition, this section has shown some of the modalities by which these leaders fight back. The attempt to confine the accused within a grid of power is met by a microscopic tactic of resistance. As de Certeau says, 'The space of a tactic is the space of the other. Thus it must play on and with a terrain imposed on it and imposed by the law of a foreign power'. The weaker party in a relation of domination typically resorts to ruses, *métis*, and strategies to 'navigate among the rules'. The defendants were trying to exonerate themselves, using whatever means lay at their disposal, but principally by challenging the way in which the Prosecution's case and court procedures screened out political context. The larger objective was to call into question not so much 'the facts' of the Prosecution's case, as the labelling of those facts as criminal acts, their significance within the context of Sierra Leonean history, and the right of the Court itself to adjudicate on these matters.

SUPPRESSION

But just as the defendants used language to try and stand up to the power of the Court, so the Court used language to suppress them. Defence tactics often ran aground on the rules of cross-examination and the conventions of courtroom discourse, together with the judges' preconceptions of the kind of evidence 'material' to the case.

On other occasions, Norman's tactics were thwarted by the bench's insistence that he frame his cross-examination as a series of questions: 'Please try to ask short questions, so the witness can answer'. In addition, the Defence was frequently interrupted by the Prosecution objecting to the 'irrelevance' of their questions. Sometimes these objections were overruled, but they were frequently sustained.

Witnesses, it should be noted, were far from being passive objects of manipulation. Well prepared by the OTP, they often as not resisted the Defence's attempts to manoeuvre them into making statements that went beyond the forensic 'facts' of the case to the wider context of war.

Later, Jabbi attempted to portray the *kamajors* as a voluntary, community organisation, but the witness qualified this by saying that civilians joined on orders of the chief: 'What I told you about is what you should know. Know that before you ask a question. If a chief gives an order and says that is—this is what should happen in this land, everybody would have to abide by that'.

As previous examples show, trial procedures typically worked to screen out discussions of the macro-political scene. It should also be noted that witness protection policies tended to obfuscate micro-political context. The identity of witnesses was concealed from the gaze of the public gallery by a screen. Lawyers were instructed not to call them by name, nor to reveal intimate details of their residences or families. In the case of the first witness in the CDF case, Norman's supporters in the public gallery speculated from the witness's ethnic identity that he was part of a rival chiefdom faction that had opposed Norman's accession to the regent chieftancy of Jaima Bongor. He would therefore have an ulterior motive, they presumed, to testify against the Chief. I was unable to verify whether or not this was true. However, it is worth noting that the inability of the Defence to name the witness made it difficult, though perhaps not impossible, to discredit testimony by this route. It should also be mentioned that some witnesses spoke of atrocities committed against them by individuals whom they knew. But the local quarrels that might have motivated these acts of violence, and which might theoretically have mitigated the case against the defendants, were never properly opened up for discussion.

In the struggle to instantiate itself, international criminal law pursues a dual strategy. In the first place, it surrounds itself with instruments of security and violence. As Foucault notices, 'Humanity does not gradually progress from combat to combat until it arrives at universal reciprocity, where the rule of law finally replaces warfare; humanity installs each of its violences in a system of rules and thus proceeds from domination to domination'. Surveying the security of the Court compound, one is reminded of the eighteenth century spectacle of robed English judges accompanied by military squads.

But having secured a space in which to operate, discursive strategies become preeminent. As its second technique, the project to institutionalise international law depends upon the production of historical truths that are narrowly confined to forensic 'facts'. As often as not, the historical and political context in which facts occurred is not of 'materiality' to the case. The effect of this narrow aperture is to cast the facts in a particular light, depoliticising certain modes of action by calling them criminal, motivated, where motivations are spoken of, by pure greed, and providing a point of leverage for the penal apparatus. This facilitates the separation of leaders of violent political movements from the rest of the population, and, in the view of international jurists, sends a powerful message about impunity to other aspiring leaders. As this article has shown, an entire discursive regime comprising rules, procedures and micro-discursive practices is dedicated to this task. De-politicisation has its original inscription in the articles of international law themselves and is reiterated in the courtroom day upon day.

Verbal reiteration is crucial to the law's project. In the first place it is necessary in order to police the boundaries within which court discourse must take place. In the second place, it is a form of ideological manipulation, in which the criminal nature of erstwhile political acts is drip-fed into the minds of the general population. The Court is assisted in this respect by a dedicated outreach programme with fourteen district officers daily disseminating the court's moral message.

Nevertheless, as we have seen, the defendants are fighting back. They take issue with the attempt to depoliticise their actions by striving to reinsert questions of political context into the courtroom. In addition they attempt a variety of other tactics which range from intimidating witnesses to playing to the public gallery. These tactics redound upon the way the Court is viewed publicly. If the defendants can convince the public that the acts they committed were politically justified, even where technically illegal, then the normative force of the law will be considerably weakened. Indeed the ambition of the court to institutionalise the rule of law in Sierra Leone may crumble away.

The wider implication is that the extension of global governance depends not just on the high politics of international organisations and nation-states, with their ability to sign treaties, create institutions and stage dramatic quasi-military interventions. It depends also on the success of microscopic strategies that embed a regime of truth and change the way people in the South think and act. In locations such as the Special Court for Sierra Leone, these strategies are encountering an equally microscopic resistance. To understand global governance, I suggest, scholars must increasingly take such micro-arenas into account.

Part Seven

African Renaissance? The African Union and NEPAD

INTRODUCTION

With the end of the Cold War, the world changed quite dramatically, including in terms of attitudes toward Africa. African states and leaders felt they had to respond, at least in terms of rhetoric and organization and to some extent in reality. Tieku provides a very full account of the various factors in play that prompted a number of African leaders to come together and construct a new organizational architecture for the continent to replace the old Organisation of African Unity. One important feature of that architecture was a concern with issues of economic growth and development, generally known by the acronym NEPAD (New Partnership for Africa's Development). Taylor complements Tieku's account of the politics of the African Union with a detailed look at the background of the development debate in Africa and its shift toward a different understanding of the conditions for the continent's development. His assessment provides some grounds for being skeptical as to whether much has changed. How the new African institutions will develop is still unclear, but more theoretically minded analysts have already attempted to capture in various ways what has been occurring. A particularly interesting example is Abrahamsen, who draws on, but also clearly explains, some important theoretical insights from the French thinker Michel Foucault and points to an explanation of these developments that goes beyond some of the rather crude generalizations about power that are pervasive in the mainstream literature.

22 Explaining the Clash and Accommodation of Interests of Major Actors in the Creation of the African Union

THOMAS KWASI TIEKU

BACKGROUND CONDITIONS

The normative framework that made the creation of the AU possible can be traced back to Pan-African ideals. These ideals, which motivated the formation of the OAU in 1963, failed to lead to the establishment of strong continental institutional structures primarily because of the influence of ideas of modernisation, the effects of the Cold War, and the self-seeking interests of some of the ruling elites in Africa. Although some half-hearted attempts were made to create a common African policy framework, such as the Lagos Plan of Action (LPA) that committed African leaders to the establishment of an African Economic Community by the year 2000, no serious continental institution-building process occurred before 1990. The decisive break occurred in 1991, when the OAU summit in Abuja adopted a draft treaty on economic integration. This treaty, which entered into force in May 1994, provided a 34-year timeframe and a six-stage process for the creation of an African Economic Community (AEC).

However, by 1993 it had become acutely clear that the institutional structure of the OAU could not handle the functional tasks set out in the AEC.

It therefore became imperative for African leaders to consider the possibility of designing a new continental institutional mechanism to pursue their international relations. While these factors created a normative framework for African leaders to be receptive to the idea of a new continental institution, they were not themselves sufficient for setting up the AU. The processes that eventually led to the creation of the AU were triggered by Obasanjo and Mbeki at the OAU summit in Algeria in 1999, and more specifically, their introduction of two separate reform packages. Understanding the formation of the AU therefore requires a good insight into the foreign policy interests of Mbeki and Obasanjo.

MBEKI'S COMMERCIAL INTERESTS AND THE CREATION OF THE AU

The move to create the AU was not initiated only by Mbeki; the very idea of the AU is at the core of the attempts of South Africa's ruling

African National Congress (ANC) to improve the image of Africa in order to attract foreign investment and make the new South Africa an important global trading nation. Understanding the formation of the AU therefore requires some knowledge of the development of the ANC's policy towards Africa.

The eminent statesman Nelson Mandela assumed office clearly aware not only that the end of the Cold War and the spread of neo-liberal ideas had rendered the radical populist and socialist ideology of his ANC unattractive, but also that the leadership role South Africa was expected to play in Africa's concerted response to the challenges of globalisation meant that a new image had to be created. His first major attempt to carve out a worldview for South Africa was to move the ANC away from its traditional populist and socialist ideas through a series of in-house party discussions.

While the internal reorientation of the ANC was ongoing, Mandela's government, mostly through public speeches and policy documents, signalled that the foreign policy of the new South Africa would be guided by liberal internationalism. For instance, in 1996, it made public that its policies would be informed by 'Growth, Employment and Redistribution' (GEAR), a neo-liberal strategy designed to make South Africa a destination for foreign investment and a competitive global trading state. However, since South Africa is located in a continent whose international image as a protector of rights, including property rights, is tainted, the immediate challenge that the ANC faced in its attempt to pursue these twin objectives was finding the appropriate means to improve the image of Africa. Unsurprisingly, the first major foreign policy document, 'Foreign Policy Perspectives in a Democratic South Africa', indicated that human rights and the promotion of democracy would be at the core of its foreign policy.

The neo-liberal stance of the Mandela government, however, created divisions within the ANC, and undermined Mandela's efforts to chart a coherent foreign policy. At least three broad cleavages with distinct positions on South Africa's worldview could be discerned at the time Mbeki took power in 1999. These were: the populist remnants of the ANC, who wanted South Africa to maintain its ties even with rogue states; the liberal internationalists, who believed in the re-invention of South Africa as a global trading state with strong regional and continental interests; and the pragmatists, who held the view that foreign policy should be driven by state interests rather than by ethical values or ideological principles. The inability of the Mandela government to assert its views on all these groups prompted some commentators to suggest that the new South Africa has 'no foreign policy at all'.

Upon assuming office, Thabo Mbeki gave priority to the development of a coherent foreign policy that revolved around the liberal internationalism initiated by his predecessor. Mbeki's prioritisation of foreign policy in the early days of his leadership was intended to cow the opposition to the liberal doctrine within the ANC, and also to signal to the business community that he was committed to the idea of making South Africa a destination for investment and international commerce. Consistent with the ANC's efforts to reshape Africa's image, Mbeki made the promotion of democracy a key aspect of South Africa's foreign policy goals in Africa. This explains why he frequently attacked one-party and personal rule in the continent, and also encouraged African peoples to govern themselves by resisting all tyranny.

Mbeki's vigorous defence of liberal norms and his open condemnation of undemocratic governments in Africa angered some African leaders, many of whom had supported the ANC and given it sanctuary during the liberation struggle. The anger that Mbeki's stance generated, and the resulting accusation that South Africa was 'little more than the West's lackey on the southern tip of Africa', compelled the Mbeki government to adopt a new approach to the promotion of neo-liberalism in Africa. The new strategy entailed placing the neo-liberal message within a broader transformationalist agenda. Instead of open condemnation of illiberal governments in Africa, Mbeki called for the reconstruction of African identity in order, first, to conclude the work of the earlier Pan-Africanist movements and, second, to re-invent the African state to play its effective and rightful role on the global terrain. Mbeki cleverly reintroduced the phrase 'African Renaissance' to serve as the conceptual framework for the new approach. According to the South African government, the African Renaissance is a 'holistic vision . . . aimed at promoting peace, prosperity, democracy, sustainable development, progressive leadership and good governance'.

It was within this context that Mbeki decided to reform the OAU, which had been referred to in the international media as a 'dictators' club', on his first appearance as president of South Africa at the OAU summit in Algiers in July 1999. As well as the image of the OAU, which Mbeki felt was not reflective of the democratic wave in Africa, he considered that the OAU could be strengthened 'so that in its work, it focuses on the strategic objective of the realisation of the African Renaissance'. With the support of Obasanjo, Mbeki managed to influence the African Heads of States and Governments (AHSG) of the OAU to take a number of important pro-democracy decisions. The first sought to reorient the OAU towards the promotion of 'strong and democratic institutions'. The second excluded from the OAU states 'whose Governments came to power through unconstitutional means', and the third called upon the OAU to assist military regimes that may exist on the African continent to move towards a democratic system of government. But why, one may ask, did Obasanjo, a former military leader, support Mbeki in making these pro-democratic changes to the OAU? Obasanjo's support for Mbeki was based on the understanding that it would make the latter receptive to his own OAU reform agenda.

OBASANJO'S AFRICAN VISION AND THE CREATION OF THE AU

The reform package of Obasanjo sought to provide guidelines for the conduct of governance in Africa and to reposition the OAU at the centre of Africa's developmental issues. The essential elements of the reform package are well articulated in the Memorandum of Understanding on the 'Conference on Security, Stability, Development, and Co-operation in Africa' (CSSDCA), which was adopted at the Durban summit in July 2002. In specific terms, the reforms provided benchmarks for judging the behaviour of African leaders in four issue areas—security, stability, development, and co-operation. These principles were meant to redefine security and sovereignty, and to demand certain 'standards of behaviour . . . from every government [in Africa] in the interest of common humanity'.

On security, the reform package aimed at influencing African leaders to treat security as both a human security issue and an interdependent phenomenon. As a human security issue, it proposed that African leaders should redefine their states' security as a multi-dimensional phenomenon going beyond military considerations to include economic, political and social aspects of the individual, the family and the society. In the words of the document, '[t]he concept of security must embrace all aspects of society . . . [and that the] security of a nation must be based on the security of the life of the individual citizens to live in peace and to satisfy basic needs'.

As an interdependent phenomenon, it urged African leaders to see the security of their states 'as inseparably linked to that of other African countries'. This not only implies that the maintenance of security anywhere in Africa is a collective responsibility of all African states, but also suggests that sovereignty no longer offers the protection behind which African leaders can conceal abuse of their citizens.

On stability, it suggested that the criteria for judging the stability of African states should be grounded in liberal principles, such as respect for the rule of law, human rights, good governance, and the participation of African citizens in public affairs. On co-operation and development, the package did not contain anything distinctly different from previous proposals submitted to the OAU. The majority of issues discussed under the co-operation and development sections essentially reiterated the traditional rhetorical Pan-African ideals, such as African solutions for African problems and the importance of integration for Africa's development, among others.

However, the emphasis the reforms laid on the effective participation of civil society in co-operation and development programmes brings to Pan-Africanism an essential missing link. Indeed, the guidelines urged African leaders not only to involve regional and grassroots civil society organisations in the continental decision-making process, but also to allow non-governmental groups to act as the main engine for dealing with security, stability, development and co-operation issues. In addition, they established a clear relationship between development and co-operation and also declared that the 'security, stability and development of every African country is [*sic*] inseparably linked' to that of other African states. This meant that successful management of security, stability and development requires a continental approach.

Not surprisingly, the reform document suggested that African leaders should develop 'a common African agenda based on a unity of purpose' to confront Africa's security, stability and development challenges. Since the OAU did not have the institutional mechanism necessary to provide the common Africa agenda, it was imperative for Obasanjo to demand a restructuring of the Pan-African organisation. In particular, he wanted to reposition the OAU so that it would become the central institution for dealing with Africa's security, stability and development challenges.

These ideas of Obasanjo manifest themselves clearly in both the institutional design and the legal underpinnings of the African Union. For instance, the Peace and Security Council and its protocol, as well as Article 4(h), which gives the AU the right to intervene in domestic affairs on humanitarian grounds, draw heavily on the CSSDCA. In addition, the normative values of the CSSDCA inform much of the principles of the Constitutive Act (CA). Furthermore, Article 22 of the CA, which provides for an Economic, Social and Cultural Council (ECOSOCC), an advisory organ composed of 150 civil society organisations selected from different social and professional groups of the member states of the Union, draws on the civil society dimension of the CSSDCA.

The genesis of Obasanjo's reform package can be traced back to the early 1990s, when he organised non-governmental organisations to develop what Zartman and Deng call 'a strategic vision for Africa'. The idea came from an expert consultative meeting that his own organisation, the African Leadership Forum (ALF), in collaboration with the Organisation for Economic Co-operation and Development (OECD), held in Paris in 1990 to explore the implications of the end of the Cold War for Africa. Among other things, the meeting suggested that it might be useful for Africa to develop an institutional mechanism similar to that of the Organisation for Security and Co-operation in Europe (OSCE) to deal with the post-Cold War challenges. The ALF, led by Obasanjo, took up this initiative.

In November 1990, the ALF, in partnership with the secretariat of the OAU and the Economic Commission for Africa, brought together academics, civil society groups, and business elites to discuss the relevance of the OSCE for Africa. The recommendations of this meeting were put together as a blueprint for an African version of the OSCE. The ALF subsequently held a series of meetings with civil society groups, African intellectuals and business elites to refine the ideas in the blueprint. The revised version of the document which was labelled the CSSDCA was then introduced to African leaders for integration into the OAU framework.

The first official OAU meeting on the CSSDCA took place in May 1991 in Kampala, Uganda when Obasanjo successfully lobbied President Yoweri Museveni, then chairperson of the OAU, to convene an African Heads of State meeting on the document. The meeting, which agreed that Africa needed a common strategy to deal with security, stability and development, led to the Kampala declaration. This declaration was intended for adoption by the AHSG during the OAU Summit in Abuja, Nigeria in June 1991. But due primarily to opposition from Libya's Muammar Gaddafi, Sudan's Omar Hassan Ahmed el-Bashir and Kenya's Daniel arap Moi, the Heads of State and Government were not able to adopt the Kampala declaration. Subsequent efforts by Obasanjo to persuade African leaders to adopt the document not only failed, but his imprisonment in 1995 led to the disappearance of the document from the agenda of the OAU. According to Obasanjo, his attempt failed because 'it threatened the status quo and especially the power positions of a few governments whose domestic hold on unscrupulous power rendered them vulnerable and insecure'. The election of Obasanjo in 1999, therefore, provided him with the opportunity to revive the CSSDCA process.

The need to do so, and, indeed, the urgency for Obasanjo to develop a new foreign policy towards Africa, were quickened by domestic political pressures. Obasanjo's People's Democratic Party (PDP) government came to power at a time when domestic opposition to Nigeria's peacekeeping missions in Liberia and Sierra Leone was at its zenith. In particular, the revelation during the presidential election campaign that Nigeria was spending US$1 million a day on the peace mission of the Economic Community of West Africa Monitoring Group (ECOMOG) in Sierra Leone provoked so much public displeasure that a drastic reduction in Nigeria's involvement in Sierra Leone had become imperative for the new government. Indeed, the ruling PDP was not simply aware that many voters favoured the complete withdrawal of Nigerian troops from Sierra Leone, its leaders also knew that their presidential candidate had suggested, in the heat of the campaign, that it was 'unacceptable for Nigeria to waste money in Sierra Leone when those funds could be used to develop Nigeria'. Of immediate concern to the new government, therefore, was finding a way to reduce Nigeria's peacekeeping burden in Sierra Leone. Any decision to the contrary, as Ogaba Oche of Nigeria's Institute of International Affairs noted, would have generated unfavourable public reaction.

However, since the supposedly internationalist Obasanjo was not prepared to abandon Nigeria's 'vanguard role in West Africa and at the continental level', it became imperative to seek external support. Senior policymakers within the new government also recognised that a long-term policy was needed to prevent the recurrence of such a high burden of peacekeeping on Nigeria. In response, the Obasanjo government created a new Ministry of Co-operation and Integration in Africa within the presidency to help the government deal with foreign policy challenges. This ministry, whose work is supported by a new Peace and Conflict Resolution Institute, was then mandated to develop a policy that would help to institutionalise the ideas of the CSSDCA within the OAU. From the point of view of the Obasanjo government, the integration of the CSSDCA into the OAU would enable the continental institution to take centre-stage in the resolution and management of domestic conflicts in Africa.

According to the reasoning of the PDP government, such involvement of the OAU was necessary so that the costs of future African peacekeeping missions could also be borne by other relatively well-endowed African countries. This explains why the new ministry, unlike the Federal Ministry of National Planning, which traditionally handles 'Nigeria's multilateral international relations in the West Africa sub-region', is primarily in charge of continental integration and co-operation issues. It was against this background that Obasanjo went to the OAU summit in Algiers in July 1999, seeking not only to set 'in motion the process of re-launching the CSSDCA', but also to persuade his colleagues to make the OAU the primary institution for resolving conflicts in Africa.

GADDAFI'S POLITICAL CALCULATIONS

Sensing that the two most powerful African leaders were teaming up to reform the OAU for the advancement of their own interests, Gaddafi intervened during the discussion on 'the item on collective security and conflicts' on the African continent, and invited African leaders to convene an extraordinary summit in Sirte, Libya from 6 to 9 September 1999 in order to 'discuss ways and means of making the OAU effective'. Without any hesitation, the OAU Assembly accepted Gaddafi's invitation. Given Gaddafi's long-standing opposition to most of the issues on which Mbeki and Obasanjo sought to refocus the attention of the OAU, why did the two leaders agree to this extraordinary summit? This question needs an answer because, as the chief executives of two of the most dominant African states, either of them could have influenced the Assembly to turn down the invitation.

Mbeki and Obasanjo welcomed Gaddafi's decision to host the summit because they saw his offer as a good opportunity to reform the OAU to reflect their foreign policy goals without having to meet the huge cost involved in hosting an extraordinary summit. For Mbeki, the Summit was a good opportunity to strengthen the OAU to pursue the goal of the African Renaissance. In the case of Obasanjo, the summit was a good place to persuade African leaders to accept his reforms in order to further Nigeria's historic role 'as a "big brother" and "Giant of Africa," providing security and attempting to spread prosperity as a public good of a benevolent hegemon'.

As indicated earlier, Gaddafi also had his own reasons for convening the summit. Besides the obvious fact that he wanted to take the credit for the re-launch of continental integration initiatives in Africa, his decision to host the summit was also influenced by much broader strategic and geopolitical imperatives. The Libyan leader wanted to use the platform of the summit to cement his full return to the geopolitics of black Africa, and to demonstrate his renewed commitment to the Pan-Africanism project. It was within this context that Gaddafi's announcement to the media, after the meeting of the Assembly, that he had invited African leaders for an extraordinary summit in Sirte in order to create a 'United States of Africa', acquires analytical meaning. Since Gaddafi had not, until this announcement, mentioned any 'United States of Africa' project, and more importantly, to the extent that his invitation did not create any impression that the extraordinary summit had been planned before the Algiers Summit, many observers and African leaders interpreted the media announcement as the usual Gaddafi 'public display'.

It therefore came as a surprise to the 33 African leaders attending the Sirte summit when Gaddafi opened the summit with a presentation of the 'United States of Africa' plan. Equally shocking was his insistence that the plan, which entailed the creation of a continental presidency with a five-year term of office, a single military force, and a common African currency, be approved 'then and there'. Prior to the Sirte summit, meanwhile, the Executive Council had discussed two other proposals and made recommendations on them for the consideration of the Assembly. The first was a proposal, supported by South Africa, asking the summit to mandate the Council of Ministers to study and make recommendations on the best ways to overhaul the OAU. The second was a proposal from Nigeria requesting the

Summit to recognise the CSSDCA as part of the official work of the OAU and to convene a ministerial summit to look at ways of integrating it into the OAU.

Gaddafi's introduction of the 'United States of Africa' proposal meant that the African leaders had three main competing requests and interests to consider. In order to accommodate the three rival demands and interests, the 33 leaders decided to replace the OAU altogether. The Council of Ministers of the OAU was accordingly asked 'to take the necessary measures to prepare the constitutive legal text [for a new continental institution for Africa and] submit its report to the Thirty-sixth Ordinary Session of our Assembly in Lomé in 2000'. In addition, the summit agreed, in line with Obasanjo's proposal, to '[c]onvene an African Ministerial Conference on Security, Stability, Development and Co-operation in the Continent, as soon as possible' in order to integrate the CSSDCA into the institutional structure of the new organisation.

The majority of the African leaders adopted this position because they saw it as the best possible way of avoiding a division among them. Gaddafi and his few supporters, however, presented the Sirte decision to the media as a victory for them. In actual fact, careful reading of the Sirte Declaration shows that the position adopted by the summit favoured South Africa and Nigeria tactically more than any other countries. As subsequent events showed, the victory declared by Gaddafi and his sympathisers was somewhat premature. While many of the leaders who spoke during the Sirte summit cautiously welcomed Gaddafi's proposal, it was clear from their speeches that most of them saw it as too radical and excessively ambitious. It therefore did not take long for those who disagreed with the whole idea to voice their opposition publicly. South Africa, for instance, which 'had a firm hand in the drafting of the Constitutive Act', indicated that 'it will not be part of any united Africa', and consequently opposed the inclusion of Gaddafi's plan in the recommendation of the Council of Ministers. Not surprisingly, the constitutive legal text which was approved at the Lomé summit in June 2000 contained none of the ideas of the 'United States of Africa'. South Africa's dominance in the drafting of the Constitutive Act shed light on the AU's strong focus on the advancement of human rights, democracy and good governance and also underscored the similarities between the objectives of the AU and that of the African Renaissance.

The total rejection of the 'United States of Africa' project and the strong emphasis the constitutive legal text placed on liberal norms were a big blow to the project of the Libyan leader. Gaddafi's disappointment with the whole process was evident in his pronouncements. In response to a question posed by a journalist trying to solicit his opinion on the Assembly's approval of the Constitutive Act during the Lomé summit, Gaddafi quipped: 'It's a victory for Africa. I am proud because I still have a grand ambition for the African continent and I have fixed a date with the heads of state in Syrte [*sic*] in March 2001.'

Gaddafi's dissatisfaction with the turn of events explains why he came to the inaugural ceremony of the African Union in Durban in 2002 'with a range of proposed amendments to the Constitutive Act, including a single army for Africa, an AU Chairman [*sic*] with presidential status and greater powers of intervention in [m]ember [s]tates'. However, the chairperson of the summit, who incidentally happened to be Mbeki, exploited Rule eight of the new rules of procedure of the AHSG, which stipulates that items proposed by a member state must be presented 60 days prior to a meeting, and supporting documents and draft decisions sent to the Chairperson of the commission 30 days ahead of the session, to prevent Libya from tabling the proposal.

The launching of the AU went ahead therefore on 9 July 2002 without consideration of Libya's proposal. Immediately after the inaugural ceremony, however, Gaddafi tabled a motion at the AHSG requesting the African leaders to convene another extraordinary summit as soon as possible to amend the Constitutive Act. The Assembly accepted Libya's invitation and, as the rules of procedure of the AHSG require, referred the proposal accompanying the request for the consideration of the Executive Council.

While the Assembly's acceptance of Libya's invitation seems to indicate Gaddafi's influence over the African leaders, the support for the extraordinary summit from the great majority of them had nothing to do with Gaddafi's proposal. There were certainly few African leaders who genuinely felt that Libya had a case, and there were those who caved in to Libya's request in order to keep 'a potentially troublesome Member State' within the AU.

However, an important and much overlooked factor in convening the summit was the pressure that women's rights activists brought to bear on African leaders. Prior to the Durban summit, representatives of civil society working on gender and development had mounted a spirited campaign aimed at increasing the participation of women in the AU. Having successfully lobbied the Council of Ministers in February 2001 to agree to promote their participation, the women's groups appeared at the Durban Summit demanding further reforms.

Central to the demands of the gender groups was a request for the AHSG to amend the Constitutive Act (CA) so that the promotion of gender equality could be added to the objectives of the AU. They also wanted the AHSG to delete all the gender-insensitive phrases in the constitutive legal text. Interviews with diplomats accredited to the AU indicate that many of the leaders, such as Yoweri Museveni of Uganda, John Kufuor of Ghana, Thabo Mbeki of South Africa, and Olusegun Obasanjo of Nigeria, who consider themselves progressive, became embarrassed when their attention was drawn to some of the gender-insensitive phrases in the CA. In fact, diplomatic sources indicate that, had it not been for the concerns of the women's groups, South Africa would have objected to the extraordinary summit. Thus, just like many other AU members, South Africa's support for convening the Extraordinary Summit was primarily motivated by the issues the gender groups raised. The influence of the gender groups in part explains why South Africa enthusiastically supported an amendment to the CA that replaced the phrase 'founding fathers' with 'founders', and in part accounts for South Africa's support for the inclusion of a clause in the CA that made 'effective participation of women in decision-making' one of the central objectives of the AU.

Nigeria, which also thought Gaddafi was pushing through utopian ideas in defiance of reality, had other reasons for supporting the extraordinary summit. Its supportive stand was predicated on the idea that the Summit would provide an opportunity to influence African leaders to make the Peace and Security Council, which was developed after the drafting of the CA, an organ of the AU. In addition, it was widely felt in official circles that it was strategically unnecessary to oppose Libya's proposal openly at the AHSG level; the Nigerian officials were, of course, aware that the proposal had few sympathisers in the Executive Council.

As with the AHSG, only a handful of Executive Council members, composed primarily of the same people who had rejected similar ideas during the drafting of the CA, were interested in Libya's proposal. Many of them did not even find it appealing enough to require a full ministerial summit. The Executive Council therefore decided to refer Libya's amendment proposal to an ad hoc ministerial committee. While this committee was considering a date for its meetings, the Executive Council further agreed to convene an Extraordinary Ministerial summit in Tripoli in December 2002 in response to Libya's invitation. It is interesting that Libya's proposal, the basis for requesting the extraordinary summit, was not put on the agenda of the Executive Council meeting in Tripoli. However, it decided to consider the report of the ad hoc Committee prior to the meeting of the AHSG in February 2003 in Addis Ababa.

The ad hoc committee, whose work was dominated by South Africa and Nigeria, held its meetings in Sun City in South Africa in

January 2003. As expected, it rejected almost all the ideas contained in Libya's amendment proposal. Also, those elements of the proposal that were accepted were revised extensively. The report submitted for the consideration of the Executive Council and subsequent approval of the AHSG as the amendment to the CA had little commonality with the original proposal. Indeed, with the exception of two clauses that drew their insights from Libya's proposal, the amendment that was adopted by the African leaders at the extraordinary summit in Addis Ababa on 3 February 2003 conceded little to Gaddafi's United Africa project. The two clauses that can be credited to Gaddafi are that concerning the extension of grounds for intervention to include serious threats to legitimate order to restore peace and stability, and that concerning preventing members of the Union from renouncing their membership. Nigeria also got what it wanted, because the amendment contained a clause that made the Peace and Security Council an organ of the AU.

23
'Partnership' through Accommodation?: African Development Initiatives and Universal Policy Prescriptions

IAN TAYLOR

THE NEW PARTNERSHIP FOR AFRICA'S DEVELOPMENT (NEPAD): GOALS AND PRESCRIPTIONS

One of the most eye-catching aspects of Nepad is its stated position that if Africa is to begin to emerge from poverty, the continent requires a GDP growth rate of seven per cent per annum and that given Africa's present low saving and investment ratio, the continent would need US$64 billion of resource inflows *every* year, about thirteen per cent of Africa's gross national income per year. As part of this, Nepad proposes that African leaders will hold each other accountable and will practise good governance and in return, the West will commit itself to aiding Africa's renaissance and development through increased disbursals of aid and capital flows.

Nepad openly links development, security, governance and democracy together and reflects a nascent pan-Africanism that has been part of Africa's identity and hopes for decades. Having said that, it would be an exaggeration to claim, as the Executive Secretary of the UNECA did that Nepad is the most important advance in development thinking for Africa in the past forty years. Rather, Nepad might be seen as a reaction to and stemming from, an environment in which the West has seemingly disengaged from the continent and from a globalising world that appears to be leaving Africa behind.

Though we should be most cautious in advancing the idea that Africa is marginalised from the rest of the world, Nepad operates from the essential premise that the countries of the industrialised world, many of them former colonialists, have dodged their historical responsibility towards Africa. Problematically, this position then grants outsiders the role of 'rescuing' the continent, with internal actors (very much restricted to local elites) playing a supporting role, at best. Noting this, critics including Patrick Chabal have cast Nepad as an elaborate attempt to guarantee the continuation of resources to Africa in order to maintain the personal rulerships on the continent, rather than as a genuine project to reconfigure Africa's place in the world.

At the same time, Nepad has cast itself the role of reversing the largely negative perceptions of the continent that currently prevail and which dominate, to varying degrees, the media in the West. Whilst promoting Africa is an admirable enterprise, it does however spring from a questionable understanding of Africa's 'image' in the rest of the world.

Indeed, the impression that there is some sort of cabal or conspiracy among those 'who do not want Africa to succeed' is based on particular assumptions vis-à-vis global politics. Curiously, such sentiments are a return to the sort of attitudes that characterised much of the 1960s–1980s when the initial African recovery plans were first formulated. Thus whilst on the one hand we can trace an evolution in development thinking in Africa, crystallised in Nepad, on the other we have come full circle.

FROM THE LAGOS PLAN TO THE NEW PARTNERSHIP

Nepad has not, obviously, sprung from a vacuum and indeed there are a host of predecessors to the Partnership that allows observers to place this latest African renewal programme within its broader historical and intellectual context. Any evaluation of this wider milieu must recognise that since the early 1980s a philosophical approach to economics and development, one that is broadly in alignment with the orthodox strictures of liberalisation, privatisation and the 'free market', has progressively become dominant and that this has gradually but profoundly influenced pan-African strategies for development, ending in Nepad. In short, the values and norms associated with liberal prescriptions have become the starting point from which African (elite) dialogue with their Western counterparts bases its broad foundations. That understandings of Africa's developmental options based on liberalisation are grafted onto highly dysfunctional political and economic systems, is rarely commented upon by the promoters of such 'solutions'.

At the same time, 'alternative' visions for Africa have largely lost credence, particularly outside of Africa but also from within. This, after all, is implicit in Nepad. Yet though Nepad has abandoned the stance popular in the 1970s of seeking to blame all of Africa's predicament on the colonial legacy, the baby has been thrown out with the bathwater—there is now little appreciation of the manner by which the continent has been inserted into the global economy and in particular, how and why this has stimulated and perpetuated neo-patrimonial systems of governance.

The Nepad project itself acknowledges that previous plans have largely failed. But, in stating this, the document shows little appreciation or understanding of the true nature of post-colonial politics on the continent. Indeed as Patrick Chabal has pointed out, Nepad raises two important questions. The first is whether African leaders, and those who advise them, are willing to study the 'variety of reasons' that have hitherto prevented development. The second is whether there really is today a new 'set of circumstances' when it comes to the exercise of power on the continent'. As Chabal notes, 'Unless the lessons of the past are learnt, there is very little reason to believe that the nature of politics in Africa will change simply because of the (admittedly) admirable ambition displayed by Nepad'.

THE BEST LAID PLANS . . .

Although debate regarding Africa's development emerged before, during and immediately after the decolonisation process, it was really in the 1970s that questions pertaining to how and where Africa would 'fit' into the wider international political economy became prominent. Most resolutions adopted by African leaders through the Organisation of African Unity (OAU) in the early years of independence had been aimed at the notion that the economic integration of Africa was a prerequisite for real independence and development. This was the main theme of the declarations from Algiers (1968), Addis Ababa (1970 and 1973), Kinshasa (1976) and Libreville (1977). But from the late 1970s onwards, Africa became progressively inundated with various plans, frameworks, agendas and declarations all aimed (to varying degrees) at promoting development and, later, democracy.

In brief, Africa has never been short of plans and programmes. However, what arguably has united such declarations has been the fact that the vast majority have been elitist programmes drawn up with very little popular consultation. Even a widespread knowledge of their existence on the continent has often been lacking.

Early post-colonial economic proposals were generally motivated by the desire (at least rhetorically) to surmount what were regarded as problems emanating from the legacy bequeathed by colonialism. Thus stress was laid on accelerated projects to develop infrastructure and education whilst import-substitution, encouraged at the time by development agencies and international financial institutions (IFIs), was meant to stimulate industrialisation. This strategy fell apart before the twin problems of the collapse in the price of primary commodities and the debilitating effect of malgovernance eroded the resources and capacity of a great many African states to pursue such policies.

By the late 1970s, African development had begun to manifestly stall on a continental level and solutions and explanations for the emerging crisis of development were required and necessary. Crucially, reflections on how and why this disastrous situation had arisen came at the tail-end of the push for a New International Economic Order (NIEO). This in itself was influenced by Dependency Theory which broadly argued that the South's relationship to the North was historically contingent and that its status of impoverishment and dependence was rooted in the process by which it had been integrated into the capitalist world economy during the colonial period, a theme that drew its intellectual heritage from Lenin. Although originally drawn up by Latin Americanists, African scholars (or scholars working on Africa) notably Walter Rodney soon applied the theory to the continent, arguing that Africa had been integrated into the world economy at a subordinate position in the emerging global division of labour. Much of the intellectual oeuvre within Africanist academia at the time broadly supported the Dependency position.

The NIEO as applied to Africa was supposed to address the various issues surrounding the ongoing global trade and investment regimes that were felt to hinder the continent's development. Promoting an ideological mix of global Keynesianism heavily influenced by Dependency Theory, the NIEO called for a restructuring of the perceived external and structural constraints on development. One of the most forceful African advocates at the time of both the NIEO and the broadly *dependencia* position was Adebayo Adedeji, then Director-General of the UN Economic Commission for Africa (UNECA). Adedeji was to become a leading figure behind the push for both the Monrovia meeting and the later Lagos Plan of Action.

THE LAGOS PLAN OF ACTION

Initially meeting in Monrovia, Liberia, in July 1979, African leaders advanced the idea that the continent's development could not be contingent on simply waiting for benefits to accrue from the types of special relationships crafted with Europe through the Yaoundé and Lomé agreements, nor could Africa progress without actively tackling the legacy of under-development left by Africa's insertion into the global capitalist economy by colonisation. Autocentricity and the continued demand for a NIEO were intrinsically wrapped up in this thrust. The Monrovia meeting determined that a number of strategic tasks were necessary in order for Africa to develop and overcome the impasse that the continent was experiencing by the mid-1970s. Amongst other resolutions, Monrovia pronounced that the creation of national and regional bodies was necessary to pursue autocentricity and that Africa had to develop self-reliance in food production whilst engaging in developmental-oriented planning. The lofty aim at the time was to create modern and developed, or at least discernibly developing—if economic growth rates are measured—economies by the year 2000. Borrowing from the Europeans, a Common Market was deemed necessary to be in place by 2025. The Monrovia Declaration closed with the decision to direct the OAU's Secretary General and the Executive Secretary of the UNECA to formulate a programme to stimulate such development.

This process continued in July 1980 with the Second Extraordinary Session of the Heads of States and Governments, which was held in Nigeria and produced the much-vaunted Lagos Plan of Action (LPA) and the Final Act. Essentially, the Lagos Plan of Action was a clarification of the broad philosophy that Monrovia had indicated and was a document that sought to arrive at strategies that might promote growth on a continent that was disengaged and less influenced by the vagaries of the global market. An emphasis on inter-African trade and investment through regional co-operation was central to the LPA, in spite, or perhaps because of the fact that, by 1980—when the LPA was adopted—almost all the economic co-operation schemes optimistically launched in the 1960s—the halcyon days of African integration—had become largely moribund. The reduction in external debt, import-substitution policies and a general goal of autocentric development further underpinned the Lagos Plan.

Perhaps unsurprisingly given both the Dependency approach that provided the framework for its analysis and (and this is perhaps the most important) the fact that it was African elites themselves conducting the exercise, the LPA's conclusions were a classic dependency interpretation of the African condition. It exonerated African leaders and blamed the historical injustices suffered by the continent and the continued dependence on external forces for the crisis. Certainly, the LPA went out of its way to absolve the post-colonial elites of any responsibility for Africa's predicament. In other words, and this seems rather remarkable from the vantage point of today, the LPA failed to generally consider the broad issues of malgovernance and accountability but rather focused on the external as the source of all of Africa's woes, a situation that had frustrated 'all efforts'.

That the LPA failed is incontrovertible. Based on faulty assumptions about Africa's economic condition, and ignoring systematic malgovernance, its prescriptions were described as 'economically illiterate' by Christopher Clapham. Primarily, the LPA strategy was based on a continuation of import substitution and hinged on three conditions that Africa simply did not possess.

THE ERA OF STRUCTURAL ADJUSTMENT

A year later, in 1981, the World Bank responded to the LPA with its own analysis. The Bank's Berg Report came out strongly against most of the LPA's positions, in particular the notion that the state should be the main engine of growth and the absolution by the LPA of the malevolent role played by African elites in their continent's demise. Meddling by the state in the supposed free running of the market was particularly criticised and was seen as a main reason for Africa's declining growth record, coupled with malgovernance. The perceived over-ambitious targets of the LPA, such as a pan-continental Common Market *à la* European Community, were also critiqued.

In essence, the Berg Report was a rebuttal of the Dependency-tinged, NIEO-informed LPA. The Monrovia Declaration and the LPA were launched on the eve of the election to government of conservative neo-liberals in

Britain and the United States, and the Plan of Action in particular advanced a vision at sharp variance with the gathering thrust of global capitalism and the views of key elites in the developed world. Indeed, separate from the failure of African elites to really do anything about Africa's declining situation, the demise of the Plan's vision played itself out as an integral part of the reassertion of Western-centred hegemony. This was coupled with the steady demise, though not outright extinction—as the initial position of the ANC in the early 1990s in South Africa demonstrated—of a protesting voice in Africa's relations with the developed world.

Although various adjustment packages had been implemented in Africa before the 1980s, the Berg Report was to usher in a new era in African politics and development, the era of Structural Adjustment Programmes (SAPs). Just as the LPA had skated over the behaviour of African elites, the Berg Report remained relatively uncritical of donor activities. The Report advanced a dual strategy for the continent: privatisation and liberalisation. Reform packages that were rolled out in the 1980s by all the main creditors as well as donors contained these two basic elements as essential conditionalities for disbursements.

These elements staked out both an economic and political project and came at a historical juncture when financial indebtedness and economic mismanagement were acting to drastically undermine the continent's development trajectory. At the same time, leaders within Africa began to realise that agreeing to the ongoing restructuring process as promoted through SAPs, even if their commitment was only rhetorical, was necessary for political survival.

The means to overcome Africa's crisis were identified (even if unconsciously) as a return to two old theoretical approaches: neo-classical economics, and Modernisation Theory. Within SAPs was an implicit echoing of the modernisers' argument that the 'fundamentals' had to be in place to assure economic development. Not bringing such 'fundamentals' into place was blamed for the lack of success of SAPs in many African countries. Indeed, the failure to implement SAPs has been held to be a contributing factor in explaining Africa's continued demise even after SAPs were introduced. In other words, there was a considerable disparity between rhetorical and practical commitment to economic and political reform. In fact, new loans disbursed by the IFIs as part of a SAP were often seen simply as new sources of largesse to distribute to supporters and clients, with minimal intention to fulfil signed commitments. Yet, the pretence that both donor and recipient were engaged in serious reform was often played out for public consumption.

However, the supposed 'one-size-fits-all' approach which characterised much of the SAPs generated a counter-reaction in the form of the UNECA's Priority Programme for Economic Recovery 1986–1990 (APPER). Later transformed and repackaged as the United Nations Programme of Action for Africa's Economic Recovery and Development (UN-PAAERD), the aim of both initiatives was to ostensibly attempt to work with SAPs through projects that might allow African states to connect with the global market through 'shared commitments' and joint efforts. Essentially, the debt issue and the scant levels of domestic investment were seen as major stumbling blocks to any successful implementation of the SAPs (rather than elite resistance and obstruction) and thus, echoing Nepad's prescriptions some twenty years later, an injection of capital was deemed necessary if the continent was to be developmentally kick-started and if the SAP-affected countries were to be cushioned from the more negative effects of the programmes. Thus assisting African states to put into practice policy reforms in line with the SAPs was deemed essential to the whole recovery project.

The impact of SAPs on Africa and African elites' positions, particularly as *glasnost* and *perestroika* made Africa's strategic position less and less clear, resurfaced in July 1989 with the UNECA's African Alternative Framework to Structural Adjustment Programmes for Socio-Economic Recovery and Transformation.

The Framework sprang from studies by Adebayo Adedeji and other African economists, frustrated at the perceived sidelining—by both African elites and their industrialised partners—of their LPA. Thus the AAF–SAP maintained that huge capital investment in Africa was necessary to spur economic growth whilst questioning the insistence by donors that Africa should increase its exports as a means of escaping the crisis of development. Rather, the AAF–SAP asserted that a change in consumption patterns to favour locally- or regionally-produced goods over imported products was required whilst internationally, the Framework demanded that the donors should support programmes designed and implemented by African governments themselves and aimed at tackling specific national problems, rather than seeking to impose the perceived blanket programmes associated with SAPs. In other words, the AAF–SAP in effect demanded increased flows of aid but with little control by the donors on how this was to be spent, arguing that African leadership was best placed in deciding how to spend such resources.

Yet, the assertion that there should be some sudden change in consumption patterns, without addressing the fundamental problem of rapacious elites was bound to fail as was the idea that capital resources should be simply handed over to African leaders to spend as they saw fit. This suggests that the AAF–SAP was perhaps little more than a nationalist counter-reaction against SAPs.

Indeed, the AAF-SAP's understanding of the African crisis was limited in scope, dangerously simplistic. The AAF–SAP of 1989 was however adopted by the UN General Assembly, which voted in favour of it. However, like almost all previous plans in Africa, the AAF–SAP never got off the ground, primarily due to the lack of commitment by both those African leaders who had signed the Framework (thus echoing the fate of the LPA) and the IFIs and Western governments.

Interestingly, just as the Lagos Plan had been followed by the Berg Report, the AAF–SAP was rapidly followed by a new World Bank document in 1989, *Sub Saharan Africa: From Crisis to Sustainable Growth*. This report argued that sound incentives and a decent infrastructure were required to construct an enabling environment for African growth to develop. The Report also touched on malgovernance as a major cause of Africa's impasse. But, somewhat signalling a shift from its previous hard-nosed stance towards the role of the state, the report asserted that human resource development was required (a role that the state could perform) and that a social safety net was also needed. Broadly, an acceptance of the normative principles of neo-liberalism, whilst advocating ameliorating policies to cope with the effects that such policies have on vulnerable groups, at the same time as sharing the blame between endogenous and exogenous factors, now emerged as defining principles, something which has been maintained to date and which informs to varying degrees Nepad's own prescriptions.

Such broad tendencies were not simply confined to the discussion around Africa's specific problems, but also played themselves out on a wider level. The UNECA convened the Arusha conference on Popular Participation for Democracy in Africa, subsequently issuing The African Charter for Popular Participation for Development (1990). The African Charter demanded that African governments respect 'freedom of association, especially political association' and the 'presence of democratic institutions', whilst it called for the 'rule of law and social and economic justice' and 'political accountability of leadership at all levels'. In other words, contra to Nepad promoters' claims to its uniqueness and path-breaking vision, the African Charter was demanding much the same elements for African renewal as Nepad, but over ten years earlier and with a particular emphasis on elite accountability. Ordinary Africans, through their grassroots involvement in the African Charter, had for the first time expressed the notion that democracy and accountability was central and that the blame for Africa's demise could be sourced to a large degree (but not, obviously, exclusively) from within Africa—or rather, from within the palaces of African presidents.

In this context, the UN moved to bring into being its New Agenda for Development of Africa (NADAF).

The UN-NADAF asserted that a basic precondition for economic development was political and social stability. No longer was there a pretence that governance had nothing to do with poor economic performance or that Africa's woes were all exogenous, as the much-vaunted LPA had tried to assert. Essentially, the rapid evaporation of the optimism associated with the end of the Cold War and its supposed implications for an Africa now free of East-West rivalry meant that a new analysis of Africa's predicament was deemed necessary, building on the African Charter. But again, the UN-NADAF included ingredients that were to re-emerge with Nepad.

This last element is now replicated in the notion of Nepad's peer review and the US$64 billion in new investment and assistance to 'good' African polities. At the same time, market access for African economies, in particular the ability to export to the developed world, was identified as crucial. Measures to enable this should be implemented as a matter of urgency within the framework of the World Trade Organisation (WTO). In this understanding, the UN-NADAF saw the WTO as having strengthened a rules-based trading system and that furthering liberalisation opened up opportunities for sustainable development and growth if African countries seized the occasion *and* if they reformed themselves.

AFRICAN ECONOMIC COMMUNITY

As the growing consensus on what was wrong with Africa—namely a lack of democracy and excessive state interference in the economy—emerged, confrontation with the developed world over the evils of a dependency generated by the global capitalist system gave way to 'dialogue'. This actuality was confirmed with the formulation of the African Economic Community (AEC) in 1991. The AEC was established by the Abuja Treaty at an OAU Summit in June 1991, but only came into force in May 1994 after the requisite numbers signed up for ratification. Its main aim was to establish a pan-continental economic community by 2025, predicated on the by now standard fare of the gradual removal, among Member States, of obstacles to the free movement of persons, goods, services and capital.

So far, like many other African plans and declarations, the Abuja Treaty has failed to meet its stated objectives. Even taking 1994 and not 1991 as its starting point, the Treaty has thus far failed in meeting the target of its First Stage (1994–1999) which was to be the strengthening of existing regional economic communities within a period not exceeding five years. It is unlikely, judging on the evidence so far, that its Second Stage (1999–2007), of stabilising tariff barriers and non-tariff barriers, customs duties and internal taxes within a period not exceeding eight years will be met. Time will tell whether all its other Stages will follow the same fate. Many of the ideals of the AEC are now replicated by Nepad.

TOWARDS THE AFRICAN RENAISSANCE

All of the above plans, declarations, frameworks and programmes provide the broader context of what was to develop in the late 1990s—a concerted attempt by a select few African presidents to re-package and exclusively define the question of Africa's development to the wider world. It is important to provide the above-detailed context to demonstrate that not only did Nepad not emerge from a vacuum, but also to show that Africa's history is replete with previous initiatives and in this light there is a danger that Nepad might simply be another one added to the list. The failure of the previous plans is largely due to the lack of capacity and resources *and* a systematic lack of political will on behalf of African leaders to seriously attempt to implement what they have signed up to. This is not to arbitrarily dismiss the very real exogenous constraints placed upon African manoeuvrability nor overlook the debilitating effect the debt burden has placed on African budgets. Certainly, African agency has been inhibited to an unusual degree. It remains true then that slavery and colonialism exacted an extremely heavy toll in sub-Saharan Africa and that the international exchange system does not always function to the benefit of developing countries; but African governments did have some room to manoeuvre, to bring about more development; and they have, in the final analysis, proven to be notoriously deficient in that respect.

It is that context that the 'African Renaissance' sought to address. Certainly, the genesis of Nepad, aside from the plethora of above-mentioned projects, can be sourced to Thabo Mbeki's 'vision' of an African Renaissance. Since late 1996 when Mbeki started to play a more active role in the formulation of South Africa's foreign policy, the idea of a continental renewal has developed momentum within Mbeki's thinking. Mbeki formally introduced the idea of a Renaissance in an address to an American audience in April 1997. Also in 1997, a document entitled *The African Renaissance: A Workable Dream* was released by the Office of South Africa's then Deputy President. It suggested five areas of engagement with the African continent: the encouragement of cultural exchange; the 'emancipation of the African woman from patriarchy'; the mobilisation of youth; the broadening, deepening and sustenance of democracy; the initiation of sustainable economic development. As part of this, Mbeki asserted that 'political organisations and governments in all African countries should be mobilised to act in furtherance of the objectives of the African Renaissance'.

Thus Mbeki sought to place South Africa at the forefront of solving Africa's problems through his advocacy of the renaissance concept and active diplomacy. This culminated in the birth of Nepad.

In an address at the United Nations University in April 1998, Mbeki expanded on some of the core elements that formed the substance of his vision. Amongst these were included the need to establish and maintain systems of good governance; to introduce new economic policies which seek to create conditions that are attractive for the private sector; to reduce the participation of the state in the ownership of the economy and to build modern economies; to establish regional economic arrangements to lessen the disadvantages created by small markets; to introduce policies that would ensure access to good education, adequate health care, decent houses, clean water and modern sanitation. In spite of the impassioned rhetoric, the essential features of the African Renaissance and how to encourage its development remained vague: high on sentiment, low on substance. Furthermore, in light of the various plans previously advanced on the continent, they were not particularly original.

Whilst their advocacy by the President of the most developed country in Africa was of note, it must be said that Mbeki's pronouncements constituted little more than an endorsement of the existing prescriptions vis-à-vis development, albeit presented in Africanist terms. Indeed, much of Mbeki's pronouncements was couched as contemporary commonsense and broadly fitting with Mbeki's own domestic economic programme. In fact, it was admitted that Mbeki's version of the African Renaissance acceded to orthodox notions of what constitutes 'best practice' and 'good' economic policy.

Mbeki's definition of the African Renaissance was thus based upon the expressed desire to promote the liberalisation of markets, free trade and liberal democratic institutions across the continent. In this sense, the latest version(s) of Africa's recovery plans have settled quite comfortably into a post-Cold War era where the hegemony of the market has been reasserted. Mbeki's prescriptions reflect the orthodox view in both contemporary development discourse and international relations.

THE STRATEGIC JUNCTURE

The debacle at the WTO meeting in Seattle in December 1999 meant that a new realisation dawned on the world's elites: concerns over the direction that globalisation was taking threatened to overturn the global trading regime as defined by the WTO. Seattle had demonstrated quite clearly that without the concerns and interests of the (elites of the) developing world being consented, the WTO process could be quite effectively—and very publicly—stopped in its tracks. The later meltdown at Cancun in 2003 proved this to be the case, particularly when it was combined with the concerns of domestic constituencies in the West who could vote in elections. It was thus seen as strategically preferable by the West's elites to engage with reformers of Mbeki's and Obasanjo's credentials, who are essentially relatively 'moderate', than risk allowing a process to develop whereby all sorts of 'unreasonable' demands reminiscent of the NIEO might be put on the table.

In the light of this opening, South Africa exerted a great deal of energy in constructing a nascent bloc of initially developing but later specifically African countries from which a broadly orthodox but reformist agenda could be launched to reinvigorate Africa and which could place on the table concerns about the global trading regime and Africa's stalled development. In Cairo in March 2000 South Africa met with Brazil, India, Nigeria and Egypt to launch a developing nations trade bloc to challenge the G-7 in the post-Seattle round of WTO negotiations and it was at that time that it became apparent that a troika of reform-minded African leaders, namely Thabo Mbeki, Egyptian President Hosni Mubarak and Nigerian President Olusegun Obasanjo were joining together in a variety of multilateral initiatives to push their agenda at every opportunity.

South Africa, enervated by the idea of an African Renaissance, emerged as the pivotal state in trying to forge a common strategy and approach to global trade and development. Also, the profile of Mbeki was raised at international fora.

Mbeki's profile received a boost at the G-77 meeting in Havana in April 2000 when the body adopted a resolution that agreed with Mbeki's vision of a united South within global trading bodies such as the WTO. At the same meeting, it was clear that Mbeki's approach was shared by key African leaders, such as Obasanjo and Algeria's Abdelaziz Bouteflika, who reiterated the position that the developing world was being excluded from global decision-making mechanisms and processes, resulting in the perpetuation of inequitable relations. Indeed, the G-77 summit was cast as the starting point of a collective process, which would come to reconfigure the future of the global system. The G-77 agreed to form a Directorate to drive this process and Mbeki was included, along with Obasanjo and Mahathir Mohamed of Malaysia.

Within Africa, the three most active Presidents in the calls for renewal and reform (Bouteflika, Mbeki and Obasanjo) requested from the OAU the mandate to draw up a new plan for the continent's development. This was granted in 1999. The three leaders then engaged in a flurry of diplomacy, with the mandate for drawing up a recovery programme being extended by the G77 at the summit in Havana in April 2000. These trips, dominated by Mbeki, included flying visits to the United States, Britain, Germany and Denmark. During the visit to Washington in late May 2000, Mbeki won the backing of President Clinton for a supposed far-reaching package of measures to address Africa's problems, including proposals on debt relief, world trade rules, the restructuring of international financial institutions and investment promotion for Africa. The proposed plan or programme of action was the first specific elaboration of Mbeki's call at the EU–Africa summit in Cairo in April 2000 for a new global system. At this time it seemed that Pretoria was emerging as the de facto acknowledged 'leader' of Africa. This position was seemingly recognised when the EU invited Mbeki as the sole 'special guest' to a two-day EU summit in Feira in northern Portugal in June 2000. The EU regarded Mbeki's presence as 'a mark of the warm and growing relations between the EU and South Africa', and saw it as reaffirming the commitments given at the first-ever summit between Africa and the European Union, held April 2000 in Cairo.

A month after Feira, the OAU Summit (in Togo, July 2000) mandated the three leaders (Bouteflika, Mbeki and Obasanjo) to enter into discussion with the North on behalf of Africa in order to develop more details regarding the proposed 'partnership' for the continent's rebirth.

Following the raising of the issue of a 'partnership' with the leaders of the G-7 at their summit in Japan, work on developing the Millennium Africa Recovery Plan (MAP) began in earnest and a process of engagement on a bilateral and multilateral level was pursued. The MAP sought to be the 'declaration of a firm commitment by African leaders to take ownership and responsibility for the sustainable economic development of the continent. The starting point is a critical examination of Africa's post-independence experience and an acceptance that things have to be done differently to achieve meaningful socio-economic progress'. In return for this critical introspection and a pledge for better governance, the Plan demanded wealthier countries commit themselves to substantially increase aid and investment to Africa. The MAP introduced the idea of 'a constructive partnership between Africa and the developed world', later the cornerstone of Nepad.

The whole programme was predicated upon an 'important prerequisite', namely 'a partnership with the rest of the world, especially the developed countries, multilateral institutions and (global and national) private sector players'. In this, 'the focus of the MAP is not increased aid but increased investments in viable infrastructure and business opportunities'. This new initiative was said to 'offer a historic opportunity for the advanced countries of the world to enter into a genuine partnership with Africa, based on mutual interests and benefit, shared commitment and binding agreement, under African leadership'.

A presentation on MAP was made by Mbeki to the World Economic Forum in Davos, Switzerland in January 2001. At this Forum, Mbeki went to greater lengths to explain the degree of consultation that he and his colleagues had gone to. Indeed, Mbeki went out of his way to claim legitimacy and support from the developed world. Yet, all of these meetings took place without any feedback to African civil society and no interaction or debate with actors outside of the narrow confines of the MAP initiators and ministerial meeting rooms. It is thus barely credible that Mbeki should later boldly state that Nepad was 'the outcome of [an] independent African process to confront the particular challenges of our day' or that the Executive Secretary of the UN's Economic Commission for Africa should claim that Nepad is an agenda 'with plans prepared through participatory processes, giving voice to [the] people'. Indeed, the lack of dialogue within Africa, contrasted with the activist approach to getting Western approval, provoked President Jammeh of The Gambia, to remark:

> If it is an African project, why take it to the Westerners to approve it? Was it necessary to take it to the G-8 Summit? That is why I am sceptical about it . . . If the problem is an African one, what I believe is that before talking to the G-8 . . . we should have brought it to Africa, and each country should have gathered its intellectuals and allowed them to debate it—as we did with the African Union project.

The contents of both the MAP and Nepad (which effectively replaced it) can be seen as recycled elements from previous plans and statements that have marked out Africa's post-independence experience at regular intervals. This conundrum is an obstacle facing Nepad's credibility. In other words, given the large number of initiatives, and their rapid consignment to the history books, why should Nepad be different?

Meanwhile, the so-called 'Omega Plan' was being touted by Senegal's President Abdoulaye Wade as another recovery plan. The Omega Plan was first presented at the Franco-Africa Summit in Yaoundé, Cameroon in January 2001 and was then showcased at the OAU's Extraordinary Summit in Sirte in March 2001. The MAP was 'designed to present a common front when Africa deals with the developed world, seek aid and investment in return for good governance, and unite African countries against social and economic problems like AIDS. On the other hand, the Omega Plan, drawn up by the Senegalese president, set goals and define[d] financial means to narrow infrastructural gaps'.

Yet, Wade's plan was highly problematic. It involved obtaining repayable treasury bonds from the developed world to finance what was essentially a pan-continental infrastructure scheme which, Wade readily admitted and advertised, would advantage Western contractors and businesses. In 2001, it was agreed to combine the two projects (Omega and MAP). This meeting, attended by the five core MAP Steering Committee countries (South Africa, Nigeria, Algeria, Senegal and Egypt) and also involving the UNECA Executive Secretary and representatives from the OAU, developed what was known as MAP Final Draft 3 (b).

THE NEW AFRICA INITIATIVE

The MAP Final Draft 3 was presented to the OAU Summit in Lusaka, Zambia (9–11 July 2001) as A New African Initiative: Merger of the Millennium Partnership for the African Recovery Programme and the Omega Plan (NAI). This gave the NAI indispensable political legitimacy and—at least in principle—pan-African buy-in. At the same time, the endorsement made the NAI (what is now known as Nepad), at least on paper, a subsidiary of the pan-continental body, though the selectivity that must necessarily go with Nepad's strictures on good governance and democracy means that Nepad will be (or rather, should be) more discerning. This is because, as various commentators have noted, any plan dependent on or subjected to the whims of the diverse membership of the African Union will likely die a very quick death indeed. Progress from such a body will, undoubtedly, be excruciatingly slow. The paradox, of being officially a pan-continental initiative but one that is by its nature bound to be discriminatory if it is to be taken seriously, is a weakness of Nepad that will remain ever-present.

Returning to the naissance of Nepad, after endorsement by the pan-African body, the NAI promoters went about garnering international support. Tellingly, and in a perhaps unintentional—but still damning—indictment of the G-8's track record on priorities, Italian foreign minister Renato Ruggiero claimed that 'the G-8 is, *for the first time in its history* [emphasis added] dealing with the questions of poverty [and] access of the commodities from the developing south to international markets'. But equally, as one commentator put it, 'it was inevitable that [the NAI] would be well received by the G-8 since it was spot on in terms of timing and political correctness. When you have rioters trashing Genoa in the name of kinder Third World treatment, no politician is going to say it is a bad idea'.

The first meeting of the Heads of State and Government Implementation Committee (HSIC) of the NAI met in Abuja, Nigeria on 23 October 2001. This HSIC was made up of Algeria, Botswana, Cameroon, Egypt, Gabon, Mali, Mauritius, Mozambique, Nigeria, Senegal, South Africa, Tunisia, Ethiopia, Rwanda and São Tomé and Principe. One of the key achievements was to change the name from the NAI to the New Partnership for Africa's Development or Nepad. Maintaining the momentum, the Nepad HSIC endorsed at its March 2002 summit in Abuja the Draft Report on Good Governance and Democracy as well as the African Peer Review Mechanism (APRM). The Democracy and Political Governance Initiative (DPGI) as it has subsequently become was planned to be the basis for settling which states could take part in, and at what level, in Nepad. The DPGI ostensibly established a set of norms, values and standards by which African leaders taking part in Nepad would hold each other accountable to. The APRM on the other hand stressed the need to spawn the essential will by political leaders to maintain the key commitments and obligations of Nepad.

This then is the origin and context of Nepad. Unlike the LPA and many other plans and frameworks, Nepad—at least on paper—addresses what it sees as an issue in Africa's developmental malaise, namely the poor levels of governance and the role of African leaders, whilst at the same time calling for globalisation to benefit Africa. But what really sets Nepad apart from similar previous endeavours is the fact that it contains the African Peer Review Mechanism, which seeks to monitor and advise governance issues. This is a considerable move forward for the continent, particularly as any attempt to apportion 'blame'—or even suggest that malgovernance might be a problem—manages to generate considerable debate and controversy. Even today, well into Africa's fourth decade of independence, there are those who still cast Africa's problems as an exogenous problem against which African leaders battle hard to implement real reforms and development, only to be frustrated by hostile (nameless) external forces.

Like virtually all other previous plans and programmes, with the exception of the African Charter on Human and People's Rights, Nepad is fundamentally a project initiated and drawn up by state leaders. This perhaps is one of the main weaknesses facing the successful implementation of Nepad—the divorce between rhetoric and action. Problematically, the democracy advanced as a solution to Africa's problems refers to a system by which elites that promise 'reform' and 'liberalisation' are largely entrenched and where popular involvement in decision-making is limited to periodic leadership choices via carefully managed elections, organised by contending elites. In other words, the formulaic type of democracy which is practised has served somewhat to soothe social and political pressures created by SAPs, but amounted to little more than 'low intensity democracy'. By its very nature, such democracy dissipates much of the energies of the marginalised into parliamentary procedures that in themselves are acted out by political fractions whose power and prestige, not to mention access to resources and patronage, rapidly have become dependent on participation in parliamentary politics, however 'really' democratic such exercises have turned out to be. Indeed, the promotion of such democracy has been instrumental in some cases in disempowering the poor by introducing the multiparty mantra as a new political panacea, while entrenched a new rather exclusive elite in reality.

The call to end corruption and mismanagement (a welcome call by any standards) and the push for democratic accountability (again, something which can be fully subscribed to) have become linked to a rather narrow understanding of democracy. Thus whilst many African states have undergone 'democratisation', such projects have largely been short-lived and/or contained what can only be regarded as a democratic façade. One need only think of the type of transitions that have occurred in states such as Malawi, Mozambique and Zambia to acknowledge that there has been scant concrete progress for the average person.

Indeed, the very logic of personal rule and neo-patrimonial politics on the continent has meant that whilst there have been 'democratic transitions', there has been only a limited change in the political structures in most of Africa. Because political power grants one access to resources (customs revenues, foreign aid, possibly taxation and often, parastatals), elections on the continent are about much more than simply the chance to be the head of state and are almost life-and-death struggles for the ability to maintain oneself as a Big Man. Political slogans for 'democracy' and an end to corruption are useful mobilising devices and may even be believed by many ordinary people, but having captured political power, the new incumbent's clients will invariably anticipate and demand material benefits for their support.

Problematically, as Patrick Chabal and Jean-Pascal Daloz have noted, neither the voters nor the political competitors appear to be intrinsically opposed to such patronage systems. Rather, the aim is to be on the winning side and even if the profits from such a system are unevenly circulated, those inside the loop and who gain from such arrangements do not complain—it is only when they slip out of the charmed circle that grievances and criticism against corruption generally emerge. Structural, rather than simply agential, explanations as to the persistence of patrimonial regimes are thus necessary. The 'democratic transitions' of the late 1980s, rather than entrenching democracy on the continent, have instead amplified the pressure on political actors to disperse patronage. Elections are an opportunity for the Big Man to show that he is more munificent, more of a father figure, than his opponent and once elected, he must reward his supporters. As Ahmadou Kourouma wryly notes in his remarkable fictitious treatment of an African president: 'the president must appear to be the wealthiest man in the land. There is no future, no influence to be had in independent Africa for he who wields supreme executive power if he does not parade the fact that he is the richest and most generous man in his country. A true, great African leader gives gifts, ceaselessly, every day'.

But, even after political changes, the entrenchment of democratic values remains relatively shallow and compromised, even if such transitions have allowed a greater space for different voices to be heard these days, compared to the one-party era of the 1960s and '70s. As such, Nepad's fixation on a US$64 billion 'reward' in return for practising 'democracy' cannot be seen as a serious attempt to 'fix' Africa's problems. Rather, it is actually a recognition by Africa's leaders that orthodox liberal prescriptions are *de rigueur* and that rhetorical pronouncements on matters pertaining to development must fit accordingly. But, given that many (perhaps most?) African leaders are a source of the continent's problems rather than the solution, can Nepad gain legitimacy by advancing these same elites as the source of the way out? Whilst a move away from the Dependency idea of the 1970s is certainly apposite, the failure to confront the realities of Africa's deep-rooted problems means that Nepad is unlikely to be the answer to the continent's malaise—even if it does receive the North's seal of approval.

24

The Power of Partnerships in Global Governance

RITA ABRAHAMSEN

In the last few years 'partnership' has become a ubiquitous term in descriptions of North–South relations, indicating that the power differential frequently perceived to obtain in the various structures, institutions and practices of global governance are being reversed in favour of the South. In particular, aid relationships have been recast as partnerships between donor and recipient countries, with donors attesting that they no longer seek to impose their vision of development on poor countries but instead wish to be partners in strategies determined and 'owned' by recipients themselves. Thus, the World Bank and the International Monetary Fund (IMF) have ostensibly abandoned their heavily criticised structural adjustment programmes and aid conditionality in favour of partnerships with developing countries. Debt forgiveness under the Heavily Indebted Poor Countries Initiative (HIPC) now engages poor countries as partners responsible for developing their own poverty reduction strategies in consultation with the Bretton Woods institutions. By the same token, the majority of bilateral donors and multilateral organisations like the OECD and the EU have enthusiastically endorsed partnerships as a new basis for North–South relations, as epitomised by the OECD's slogan 'building partnerships for progress'. In this way, multilateral and bilateral donors alike argue that the over-prescriptive and interventionist development models of the past did not work, and that they are no longer in the business of telling poor countries what to do. By contrast, in the words of World Bank President James Wolfensohn, current development orthodoxy holds that recipient countries must be 'in the driver's seat—exercising choice and setting their own objectives for themselves'.

The extent to which partnerships represent a transformation in North–South relations is both deeply contested and crucially important. Even commentators supportive of the general thrust of partnerships frequently draw attention to the difficulties in achieving 'genuine' partnership based on equality and mutual respect in a context where one party is in possession of the purse and the other the begging bowl, while more critical voices maintain that partnerships are simply a disguise for continued donor dominance of developing countries. The New Partnership for Africa's Development (NEPAD) has, for example, been dismissed by one analyst as a 'western wolf in African sheepskin', suggesting that behind the claim to African ownership there is a persistent subservience to western power and western values.

This paper suggests that understanding the transformations currently taking place under the rubric of partnership demands a novel analysis of power relations. Thus far most assessments of partnerships have tended to analyse power as the capacity of certain actors to control (more or less) directly the actions of others. In this way, despite the important differences that exist between critics and supporters of partnerships, the analytical parameters of the debate have been set by a shared conceptualisation of power and have revolved around the extent to which power is being transferred from donors to recipients. This is undoubtedly an important issue, but the transfer of power from the North to the South is only one of the ways in which transformations in global governance can take place and in which the power of partnerships can operate. Indeed, I argue that too narrow a focus on the transfer of power between partners prevents contemporary analyses from capturing the full significance of these transformations, as the power of partnerships does not lie primarily in relations of domination, but in techniques of cooperation and inclusion. Analysing these relationships and their role in global governance hence requires a broader conceptualisation that takes account of how strategies of partnership can themselves act as forms of power through the production of specific forms of legitimate action and agency.

Drawing on analyses of governmentality in modern liberal societies, I argue that partnerships invoke specific technologies of global liberal governance which help produce modern, self-disciplined citizens and states that can be trusted to govern themselves according to liberal democratic norms. Focusing primarily on relations between Africa and the donor community, I show that by enlisting recipient states as partners or agents in their own self-management, partnerships govern through the production and consent of responsible African states. Power is certainly present in these partnerships, but its forms, structures and technologies cannot be encapsulated solely in terms of domination or coercion. Instead, the power of partnerships is voluntary and coercive at the same time, producing both new forms of agency and new forms of discipline.

WHO GOVERNS IN PARTNERSHIPS?

Since the dawn of independence, the question 'who governs?' has informed and underpinned analyses of Africa's relations with the west, and fear and accusations of imperialism and neo-colonialism abound in discussions of the aid relationship. The emergence of partnerships as a new framework for North–South relations can be explained in large part as a response to such persistent and longstanding charges of undue intervention, and donors self-consciously present partnerships as a way of returning power and influence to African states. By the late 1990s, there was also a growing recognition among the donor community that conditionality-based lending had failed to generate the desired results in terms of economic growth and good governance, and 'ownership' accordingly emerged as a key term in development discourse. Thus, the World Bank's Comprehensive Development Framework, launched in 1999, argues that policy reform and institutional development should not be imported or imposed, but must be homegrown. The UK government similarly maintains that over-prescriptive aid conditionality has a poor track record in persuading governments to reform their policies, while the IMF presents its new policies as intended to 'bring about substantive changes in the way countries' programs are formulated . . . and embody a greater degree of national ownership'. Ownership is expected to make development aid more efficient and effective.

According to the World Bank, the 'single most important theme running through the dialogue on development effectiveness is the need to put committed developing country governments and their people, at the center of their development process'. The Bank continues: 'Our vision is that the developing country defines its national development strategy. Official development institutions determine their assistance strategies in support of this national strategy, and in consultation with each other'. The 1996 report of the OECD's Development Assistance Committee (DAC) also calls for 'a compact' for effective partnerships, where recipient countries are ultimately responsible for their own development. In this way, partnerships emerge as a way of overcoming the weaknesses of previous development models, while at the same time returning power and decision-making to recipient countries.

Taking their clue from donors' presentation of partnerships, academic debates have been preoccupied precisely with questions of whether, and to what extent, the new partnerships have returned power to developing countries. At the risk of some simplification, two main positions can be identified in the literature. The first regards partnerships as a positive initiative, seeking to increase recipients' leadership in the design and implementation of development strategies. At the same time, the intrinsic difficulties of achieving a relationship of equality between rich and poor countries are often acknowledged. Because the term is open to multiple interpretations, these analyses frequently note, there is ample room for differential practices and varying *degrees* of partnership. Genuine partnerships are seen to imply mutual respect and equality of power and influence, but this is difficult to realise due to the nature of the aid relationship. Moreover, it is recognised that genuine partnerships are not necessarily in the interest of donors, who in most cases would resent losing influence over how development resources are utilised. Maxwell and Riddell accordingly suggest that there are weak and strong forms of partnerships. The former is confined to information sharing and policy dialogue, whereas the latter is characterised by jointly agreed country programmes and multi-annual financial agreements. In practice, they argue, donors have been more keen on the former, resulting in a situation that is often not all that different from the conditionalities of the past, especially as the absence of multi-annual financial agreements means that recipients are constantly under the review of donors and the IFIs. From this perspective, the road to 'genuine partnerships' may well be paved with good intentions, but it is also 'littered with potential pitfalls' as transferring power to the aid recipient is easier said than done.

The second position dismisses partnerships as little more than rhetoric, a disguise for the continued domination of the South by the North. Partnerships, in this interpretation, are not 'for real', nor are they intended to transfer power to poor countries. Instead partnerships are primarily rhetorical innovations, a re-branding of old-style practices and policies, or quite simply 'spin' of the kind we have come to associate with contemporary politics. For Gordon Crawford, for example, partnerships are a 'myth', 'part of a trend by international agencies by which their intervention in political and economic reforms in sovereign states is disguised and simultaneously accorded greater legitimacy, free of the criticism that conditionality has attracted'. Partnerships are used for 'instrumental reasons' to conceal 'the continued exercise of power by international agencies'. Fowler similarly regards partnerships as a 'mystification of power asymmetry' and a 'more subtle form of external power imposition'. According to such interpretations then, nothing much has changed with the introduction of partnerships, and despite claims to the contrary, western countries and agencies retain the power to impose their values and solutions on poor countries.

Empirically these two positions are reflected in analyses of the Poverty Reduction Strategy Papers (PRSPs) and NEPAD. The extent to which partnerships are actually 'genuine' and developing countries can be said to 'own' their development strategies have been at the centre of debates over the PRSPs, one of the most pervasive forms of partnerships between donors and developing countries. Under the Heavily Indebted Poor Country Initiative (HIPC), countries are required to prepare a PRSP in order to qualify for debt forgiveness, and these poverty reduction plans also form the basis for many bilateral donors' relationship with poor countries. The PRSPs are to be developed in partnership and consultation not only with donors, but also with representatives of domestic civil society and poor people themselves in order to ensure both national ownership and that development resources benefit the poor. But as critics are quick to point out, despite all the emphasis on the need for home-grown development plans, the Boards of the IMF and the World Bank retain the power to veto a country's PRSP, placing the notion of 'ownership' under serious strain. As noted by the Reality of Aid project, 'If the IMF and the World Bank reject a government's PRS, the government would lose access to trade credits, aid and finance and probably default on its debt obligations. Ultimately, its domestic economy could collapse'. The claims to ownership and consultation are also challenged by the fact that the current poverty reduction strategy remains firmly within the neo-liberal economic policies of the structural adjustment period, and critics argue that the macro-economic framework of the PRSPs is non-negotiable. In addition, consultations with civil society have often been limited, and poor people and critical voices have been sidelined or marginalised in the process. From this perspective, the extent to which conditionality has been abandoned is highly questionable, and while disagreeing about donors' intentions and the exact extent of their power, there is general agreement that they continue to govern in development partnerships. Local empowerment, to the extent that it has taken place through the consultation processes, has been highly selective, tending to favour certain state ministries and well-resourced, often foreign, NGOs.

Similar concerns about influence and ownership have surfaced in debates about NEPAD, in large part because of its overt commitment to neo-liberal norms and values. When NEPAD was launched in 2001, it was championed as Africa's own development plan. Its chief architects are prominent leaders like South Africa's Thabo Mbeki and Nigeria's Olusegun Obasanjo, and much was made of its 'Africanness' and apparent break with the structural adjustment era. While the initiative is widely regarded as a welcomed sign of the continent's renewed commitment to peace, democracy and good governance, the financial resources required to implement the programme have raised doubts about the extent to which NEPAD can be a partnership of equality. An additional capital flow of US$64 billion a year is required for the programme's success, and while NEPAD maintains that Africa is not appealing 'for further entrenchment of dependency through aid', it is clear that the bulk of the resources would have to come from development assistance, especially given the continent's low level of foreign direct investment. Critics regard this dependency on foreign assistance as an indication that NEPAD is not actually 'owned' by Africans at all.

CODESRIA's (previous) Executive Secretary Adebayo Olukoshi, for example, characterises it as 'an uncritical, even opportunistic pandering to an external donor community that is as cynical as it is self-serving'. In other words, because NEPAD so adamantly endorses the neo-liberal values and policies of donors, the balance of power between Africa and the west within the partnership is questioned. For critics, NEPAD represents at best a few elite Africans who have internalised western values and dressed them up in an African garb; a 'western wolf in African sheepskin'. At worst, it is 'a neo-colonial project through which the western world would like to not only promote their strategic and national security interests, but also ensure perpetuation of Africa's dependent development under globalisation'.

CONCEPTUALIZING POWER

The literature on partnership contains numerous insights and raises important issues in global governance. It is certainly the case that these are unequal partnerships, and that their neo-liberal economic framework is largely non-negotiable for countries wishing to remain recipients of aid or achieve debt restructuring or forgiveness. Undoubtedly, donors still hold considerable power over poor countries, as illustrated time and time again by the economic uncertainties encountered by African states when aid is withheld or withdrawn. Yet despite these insights, there are significant and inherent analytical limitations to the conventional literature, arising primarily from its conceptualization of power.

In common with much political science and international relations scholarship, discussions of partnerships tend to draw on a conception of power as domination. The classic formulation of this view comes from Robert Dahl, who defined power as the ability of A to get B to do what B would not otherwise do. Power, in this definition, is coercive and intentional, leading to observable behavioral change in its target population. In a later dialogue with Dahl's work, Lukes identified three dimensions of power. The first refers to Dahl's pluralist view, where power is employed deliberately by one actor over another. This requirement of intent and overt conflict of interest was later challenged by Bachrach and Baratz, who drew attention to non-decision as a form of power. The ability to shape political agendas and prevent issues from entering public debate, they argued, is also a way of exercising power. In Lukes' formulation this is the second dimension of power, which takes account of how prevailing political values and institutional arrangements can both limit opportunities and bias the directions of political choices. To these, Lukes famously added a third dimension, focusing on the ability to form the very interests and values that determine action in the first place. In his words, 'A may exercise power over B by getting him to do what he does not want to do, but he also exercises power over him by influencing, shaping or determining his very wants'. For Lukes this is the 'most insidious exercise of power' as it works to shape people's 'perceptions, cognitions and preferences' in ways that may be contrary to their own interests, making people accept the existing order of things, including their own domination.

The literature on partnership can be readily mapped along these three dimensions of power, although the first two tend to predominate. Power in partnerships is conceived primarily as domination, a capacity clearly visible in the ability of A (donor) to get B (recipient) to do what B would otherwise not do. Specifically, this translates into the adoption of neo-liberal economic policies and practices of good governance that is perceived to benefit western interests, frequently at the expense of African governments and/or their poor populations. Similarly, power as non-decision, the ability to shape political agendas and keep issues off the negotiating table figures prominently in critiques of partnerships, particularly in terms of the non-negotiable character of economic liberalism. Rich countries are perceived to be able set the terms of the partnerships due to their superior economic resources and Africa's aid dependency. Moreover, international institutions and decision-making structurally favor rich countries, and in a discussion drawing explicitly on Lukes, Crawford argues that decisionmaking bodies in the partnership for governance reform in Indonesia are constructed so as to ensure that the reform agenda of international agencies remains relatively unchallenged. Issues of crucial importance to Indonesian civil society, including constitutional reform and civil–military relations, have, according to Crawford, been kept off the agenda because such reform would not benefit international agencies.

The third dimension of power is less explicitly addressed in the literature. There are, however, frequent references to partnerships as a more insidious and subtle form of power.

Because they appear to rest on consent and legitimacy, such accounts argue, partnerships are a way of influencing a country's development choices more effectively, or in 'a far more all-encompassing way'. In an insightful analysis, Harrison argues that through contemporary aid practices certain sections of the African elite and bureaucracy come to internalize the neo-liberal values of global governance. While not explicitly stated or theorized, these interpretations derive actors' interests from their structural position in the world economy and the global capitalist system is seen to shape actors' ideology in ways that ultimately serve the interests of capitalists rather than the poor. Thus, in keeping with Lukes' third dimension of power poor countries are prevented from realizing their 'real' interests due to the hegemonic ideology of neo-liberalism.

While not wishing to dismiss the insights of the partnership literature as either insignificant or erroneous, my argument is that important aspects of the power of partnerships in global governance cannot be captured within Lukes' three dimensions. Instead, an expanded conceptualization that incorporates governmentality as a form of power is required. The term governmentality refers to the 'the conduct of conduct', a particular modern form of power that is characterized by an increasing reliance on pastoral care and techniques of normalization and consensus, as opposed to more overtly coercive forms of power. An important point to note in this context is that power is not the antithesis of freedom; instead governmentality is based around and works through the exercise of freedom. Governmentality can be seen as the contact point between technologies of dominating others and those of constituting the self, or in the words of Foucault, governmentality is 'where technologies of domination of individuals over one another have recourse to processes by which the individual acts upon himself and, conversely . . . where techniques of the self are integrated into structures of domination'. Power in this understanding is not purely instrumentalist, but works through systems of knowledge and discursive practices to provide the meanings, norms, values and identities that not only constrain actors, but also constitute them. In this sense, human beings, or the subject, are not only power's intended target, but also its effect. The modern self is both the object of improvement and the subject that does the improving.

The use of freedom as a formula for rule is particularly evident in contemporary neo-liberal forms of governance. One characteristic of this mode of governance is an increasing decentralization and pluralization of power and decision-making centers, away from the state and towards various quasi-autonomous non-governmental organizations and institutions, so that today the 'conduct of conduct' increasingly obtains in sites 'at a distance' from the state itself. In what is frequently described as the 'new managerialism', the move towards decentralization is accompanied by a vast array of new mechanisms and techniques of auditing, accounting, monitoring and evaluation which link these various and disparate entities to political strategies at the state level. While such networks and techniques are the condition of existence for rule 'at a distance', they simultaneously accord actors a degree of autonomy and responsibility for decisions and actions. Power is in significant ways decentered, and as Rose observes, this is a form of rule that governs through 'the instrumentalization of a regulated autonomy'.

PARTNERSHIPS AND TECHNOLOGIES OF AGENCY

My suggestion is that partnerships can be seen as part of a similar neo-liberal political rationality and employ similar technologies at the global level. Put simply, using freedom as a formula of rule, partnerships help produce modern, self-disciplined citizens and states by enlisting them as responsible agents in their own development. From this perspective, partnerships are part of a particular way of thinking about and acting upon the world that goes beyond mere ideology or rhetoric. The rationality of neo-liberalism holds that to govern less is to govern better, and in the same way as neo-liberal forms of rule in western liberal democracies are bound up with critiques of welfarism, corporatism, and excessive interventionism, the emergence of partnerships is intimately linked to a view of development aid as overly interventionist and stifling of initiatives and 'developmental energies' in recipient countries. Thus, by governing less, development assistance is to be made more efficient and effective.

The reinterpretation of how to govern better is accompanied by a new conceptualization of the subjects to be governed, and one of the notable changes in the discourse on partnerships is the inscription of developing countries as agents. While this has clearly been a gradual move, evident long before recent talk of partnerships, it is only with the introduction of partnerships that developing countries are primarily *partners* rather than *recipients;* the active creators of their own future and development rather than the objects of external benevolence. This reconceptualization of the subject of government is in turn linked to new technologies of power, and in particular what Dean in a different context has termed technologies of agency. Such technologies of agency engage its target population as active and free subjects, as informed and responsible actors capable of taking control of their own lives and futures. Thus, target populations of 'unemployed', 'drug users', 'underdeveloped countries', etc, are no longer simply victims, but subjects to be empowered. Frequently this involves the deployment of contracts through which subjects are committed to a range of 'normalizing, therapeutic and training mechanisms' designed to empower them, optimize their skills, their entrepreneurship, and so on. Modern liberal rule in this sense governs through the management of freedom, and the retreat from state interventionism is simultaneously a positive technology of government through various strategies of 'responsibilisation' and empowerment.

In the case of development partnerships, technologies of agency and responsibilisation are clearly evident. The discourse of partnerships places developing countries 'in the driver's seat', assigning them prime responsibility for their own development strategies. This reconfiguration of the subject of government confers obligation and duties, at the same time as it opens up new possibilities for decision and action. To a significant extent, development aid as a principle of international solidarity gives way to an obligation on the part of the developing country to manage its own underdevelopment wisely. Only then will development assistance be forthcoming, as the language of partnership emphasizes again and again. The World Bank, for example, stresses that partnerships will only be entered into with 'committed developing country governments' that meet 'a minimum level of performance', while the OECD argues that developing countries must 'commit to basic objectives of social development and increased participation' and 'carry out sound financial management'. Bilateral donors make similar statements. The UK government emphasizes that partner governments must 'have a commitment to the principles of the agreed international development targets and . . . [pursue] policies designed to achieve these', while the US *National Security Strategy* is unambiguous in its declaration that 'Nations that seek international aid must govern themselves wisely . . . For freedom to thrive, accountability must be expected and required. Through partnership contracts, or Memorandums of Understanding as they are frequently called, recipients are enlisted as the active agents of their own reform according to accepted and agreed standards.

One of the key effects of the technology of agency is that self-government or self-discipline takes on a particular significance. In principle, donors are willing to enter into partnerships with all developing countries—the onus is on them to prove that they are committed, responsible and willing to govern themselves wisely. In current partnerships this is perhaps seen most starkly in the African Peer Review Mechanism of NEPAD. The

Peer Review Mechanism (PRM) is voluntarily acceded to by the member states of the African Union and acts as a 'mutually agreed instrument for self-monitoring'. The mandate of the mechanism is to ensure that the policies and practices of participating states conform to the values and standards of the 'Declaration on democracy, political, economic and corporate governance', and countries that join have to submit to periodic peer reviews to ascertain progress and compliance. The rationale of the PRM is to make donor-imposed conditionalities superfluous, hoping that donors will eventually abandon their own monitoring processes and accept the outcomes of the African peer review. So far 19 out of 53 countries in the African Union (AU) have agreed to be assessed under the PRM, and the first review started in Ghana in May 2004.

In the broader context of liberal governmentality, the PRM can be seen as an institutionalized form of self-discipline. African countries are asked to subject themselves to detailed reviews and although entirely voluntary, the result is likely to be used by donors to decide whether or not they qualify for development partnerships. The policies and standards they are asked to live up to are those contained in the NEPAD document, which conform by and large to the liberal development goals of international donors, stressing the need for good governance, economic liberalism, peace and security. Interestingly, the PRM has no sanctions to impose on governments that fail to meet its governance criteria, a concern that has been raised by donors. On the other hand, the AU Chairman Joaquim Chissano stresses that no sanctions are needed to make the review effective: 'Punishment', he says, 'will come by itself because investors will shy away'. NEPAD thus becomes a self-disciplining device embedded in deeper structures of governance. It is not that power has disappeared from the aid relationship, and indeed power may well have been transferred to the PRM and African states as agents responsible for their own future. Power is in significant ways decentered and works through the freedom of African states, in the sense that they are expected to exercise their agency responsibly and in ways consistent with international norms and values. Countries that do can expect to be rewarded with material support from donors. Countries that for whatever reason do not are likely to see assistance being redirected towards more responsible partners. In this way, it is in the self-interest of African states to act in a disciplined manner.

The emphasis on self-discipline aside, the donor community recognizes that many poor countries lack the necessary bureaucratic and technological resources to prepare their own poverty reduction and development plans, and partnerships are generally combined with various programs for capacity and institution building. Countries that are willing to enter into partnerships, but do not have the capacity to formulate their own strategies are offered various forms of assistance and training. The UN Economic Commission for Africa (UNECA), for example, runs a Poverty Reduction Strategies Learning Group and there are numerous other training opportunities. The World Bank President is worth quoting at some length on this point:

> We should offer our assistance to all countries in need. But we must be selective in how we use our resources . . . where aid cannot be effective because of bad policy or corruption, we need to think of new ways to help people. Not the old technical assistance approaches of the past that relied too heavily on foreign consultants. But helping countries to design and implement their own development . . . *Our goal is to support the fit and help make the unfit fit. This is all about inclusion.*

The quotation is instructive in that it draws attention to the power of partnerships as a form of inclusion. While capacity building initiatives are presented by donors as technical transfers of knowledge and procedures, and as such as a crucial part of development, it is important to recognize that they are also political interventions designed to produce particular modern subjects. Through such initiatives governments have the opportunity to learn to practice their freedom responsibly and in this way capacity building is simultaneously empowering and disciplinary, in that it both constitutes and regulates the identities, behavior, and choices of their target countries. A similar observation is made by Gould and Ojanen, who argue that development represents 'an attempt to build the capacity of "weak" Southern states to attain more responsible "citizenship" in the international community of liberal democracies'. Craig and Porter also observe that poverty reduction is a mode of liberalism that has the disciplined inclusion of the poor and their places as a central task. In common with advanced liberal rule more generally, partnerships can thus be seen as strategies that seek to govern 'the very subjects whose problems they seek to redress'. This argument has important implications for recent analyses of why African governments go along with what Mercer has termed the 'performance of partnership' and what Harrison calls the 'pantomime of ownership'. As Mercer perceptively argues, different actors in development partnerships employ different strategies to achieve particular outcomes, depending on where they are positioned within an asymmetrical framework of power relations. Even for some of the weaker partners there may be good reasons for 'performing their role in the partnership'. In the case of NEPAD, for example, various African countries may have different motivations for their involvement and endorsement of the partnership. Importantly, though, this does not reduce partnerships wholly to a 'myth', or a performance in any simple sense. The reconceptualization of recipient countries as partners in their own development is not simply a trick of deception, or a rhetorical device, but has very real productive power. In partnerships technologies of governing others are inseparable from technologies of self-government. Understood as a form of 'conduct of conduct', partnerships invest countries with a set of goals and self-understanding and give them an incentive to participate voluntarily in various programs to improve, educate and help themselves. In addition to NEPAD's Peer Review Mechanism and the various capacity building initiatives, partnerships come with a multitude of new mechanisms for monitoring, evaluating, and auditing the behavior and choices of recipient countries. As many critics have observed, through such mechanisms donors become ever more intimately involved in the affairs of recipient governments, to the extent that Harrison has suggested that it is more useful to conceive of donors 'as part of the state itself. As technologies of governance, however, it is also important to appreciate the productive power of such auditing mechanisms. As Power has observed, to be audited an organization must actively transform itself into an auditable commodity; one structured to conform to the need to be monitored *ex-post*. Audits thus reshape in their own image that which it is to monitor. In contemporary partnerships, various types of auditing technologies are instruments of a new form of governance and power, designed to engender new forms of conduct. They become technologies for the creation of new kinds of subjectivities, of self-managed individuals and states who render themselves auditable. The 'performance' involved in partnership is thus not simply in terms of 'pretending', but in the sense of being performative and constitutive of the subject, its practices and procedures.

The power of partnerships is not therefore to be found only, or even primarily, in instances of domination or imposition, and this in turn places the opposition of power and partnership in many conventional analyses in an importantly different light. By defining power primarily as domination, and as the antithesis of freedom, the existing literature tends to perceive partnerships either as a way of abolishing, reducing or 'taming' power by subjecting it to contract, or conversely as a continuation of domination. Thus, for Maxwell and Riddell the polarization is between 'conditionality or contract', whereas for Crawford the question is 'partnership or power?'. The implication of such oppositions is either that the partnership contract is a way of moving away from power and imposition, or more idealistically, that partnerships should be totally free of power relations. From the perspective of governmentality, however, partnerships derive their power precisely from the production and regulation of freedom, and their contracts of accountability and empowerment are simultaneously vehicles for relations of domination and for polymorphous techniques of subjugation.

The purpose of this article has not been to evaluate partnerships as a new approach to development, nor to analyze their effects in any empirical detail, but rather to contribute towards a fuller analytical account of recent transformations in North–South relations. I have argued that partnerships can be regarded as a form of advanced liberal governmentality that increasingly governs through the explicit commitment to the self-government and agency of African states. Lest I should be misunderstood, this is not to say that power as domination has disappeared; to be sure, western countries and the institutions of global governance still hold considerable sway over African states due primarily to their aid dependency and general economic weakness. Nevertheless, the power of partnerships in global governance cannot be captured through a conceptualization of power as domination alone, but requires attention to the manner in which power produces its effect, its technologies and rationalities.

Partnerships, as a form of advanced liberal power, work not primarily as direct domination and imposition, but through promises of incorporation and inclusion. They derive their power through simultaneously excluding *and* incorporating, in a manner that shapes the behavior and interests of states and state actors. Drawing on liberal principles that hold that everyone is equal and entitled to their freedom and autonomy, this principled equality acts as a powerful form of disciplinary power. Failure to meet the agreed criteria for inclusion in partnerships (sound social and economic policies) can be cast as the ill-discipline of particular countries. It is no longer the donor community that withholds development assistance, but instead the onus is placed on Africa to live up to the principles that merit co-operation. Using freedom as a formula of rule, partnerships help produce modern, self-disciplined citizens and states by enlisting them as responsible agents in their own development. The freedom required by contemporary development governmentalities is certainly not to be understood as a simple liberation from aid conditionality and undue donor interventions. But neither is it to be understood as a mere ideological fiction or a rhetorical device, nor an iron cage of discipline binding African states even more tightly within structures of western power. The rationality of partnership constitutes developing countries as capable agents, responsible for their own future and in this way it does open up room for agency and maneuver. However, it is essential to recognize how this freedom is inextricable from the imposition and exercise of constraints. Indeed, the two are mutually related in an emerging structure of aid governmentality.

Part Eight

The Return of Geopolitics?

INTRODUCTION

It is far too soon to tell whether Africa's relations with the rest of the world are going through a major change, but some scholars think so, and some facts are certainly suggestive. It is undeniable that the resurgence of economic interest in the continent is profound and probably unprecedented. The texts in this section all make efforts to clarify some of those basic facts. Volman suggests that, though it may bring benefits, the renewed interest in African oil on the part of a number of powers also tends to produce a militarization of relations on the continent, which may have very negative effects. It may be possible in certain areas to move in a more analytical direction. Power and Mohan, while reviewing a great deal of empirical material, suggest some useful ways to look at the new China–Africa relationship. Finally, as with the Congo, we should not forget how destructive politics can be. Keenan shows the effects of the "war on terror"; his article is impassioned and partisan, is based on a lifetime of study of the area, and is scrupulously documented. All of these cases suggest the possibility that Africa's relations with the rest of the world may be becoming more "normal," less concerned with changing Africa and more concerned with living with it.

25

China, India, Russia, and the United States: The Scramble for African Oil and the Militarization of the Continent

DANIEL VOLMAN

Since the end of the Cold War—and particularly over the past decade—Africa's status in the international geopolitical order has risen dramatically. The continent was once treated as a convenient battlefield in the global rivalry between the United States and the Soviet Union precisely because neither superpower had any vital interests at stake on the continent. Now, a number of developments—especially the continent's increasing importance as a source of energy supplies and other raw materials—have radically altered the picture. They have led to the growing economic and military involvement of China, India, and other emerging industrial powers in Africa and to the re-emergence of Russia as an economic and military power on the continent. In response the United States has dramatically increased its military presence in Africa and created a new military command—the Africa Command or Africom—to protect what it has defined as its 'strategic national interests' in Africa. This has ignited what has come to be known as the 'new scramble for Africa' and is transforming the security architecture of Africa.

SECURITISATION AND THE NEW SCRAMBLE FOR AFRICA

The desire of China, India, Russia, the United States and other emerging powers to gain and expand their access to supplies of oil, natural gas, uranium, copper, cobalt, coltan, gold, platinum, diamonds, and other strategic resources is well known, so it is not necessary to repeat it here. What is needed is some perspective on the significance of this in the broader context of Africa's economic relations with the rest of the world. For example, China's growing role in oil production in Africa is often cited as the most important example of how these new powers are usurping the place of the United States and European countries and threatening to 'expel' the West from Africa. But China still only gets less than 9 per cent of sub-Saharan Africa's total oil exports; 32 per cent of Africa's oil still goes to the United States and 33 per cent still goes to Europe. China does obtain significant amounts of oil from African countries—some 30 per cent of its total imports, primarily from Sudan, Angola, and Nigeria—but it actually gets more of its imported oil from the Middle East, specifically from Saudi Arabia where oil production is dominated by American firms. So the situation is a little more complicated than the picture that is often presented.

One of China's smaller, but most noteworthy, endeavours is in Ethiopia, where the Chinese firm Zhongyuan Petroleum Exploration Bureau (part of the China Petroleum and Chemical Company [SINOPEC]) is conducting a seismic survey to explore for oil and gas deposits in the Ogaden region—which is populated mostly by Somalis—under a contract from the Malaysian firm Petronas and South-West Energy, an Ethiopian company licensed in Hong Kong. In April 2007, hundreds of members of the Ogaden National Liberation Front (the ONLF, which is fighting to make the region a part of Somalia) attacked the company's premises in Abole, overpowering 50 Ethiopian Army troops who were guarding the facility and killing 65 Ethiopians—mostly labourers—and nine Chinese technicians. Seven Chinese oil workers were kidnapped and then released to the Red Cross five days after the attack. The Ethiopian government launched a major military offensive against the ONLA in June 2007, but in November 2007, Zhongyuan announced that it would not return to resume work in the Ogaden. Petronas is now expecting to hire an Iranian firm named Oil Exploration Operation Company to continue exploration work in Ogaden. Pexco, another Malaysian firm, is also expected to begin gravity survey work in January 2008 on two exploration blocks in the Ogaden. American companies are also active in this volatile region. In August 2008, Titan Resources Corporation (owned by Nelson Bunker Hunt) announced that it had signed a twenty-five year production-sharing agreement with Ethiopia for the right to explore for oil and gas in two blocks in the Ogaden basin and the Blue Nile basin in the north of the country and that it expected to invest as much as US$60 million in the project.

China and India are also interested in acquiring access to uranium, copper, and other minerals. For example, Chinese and Indian firms are now exploring for uranium in Niger. In July 2007, Tuareg rebels kidnapped a Chinese executive of the China Nuclear International Uranium Corporation to protest Chinese operations in Niger and alleged Chinese arms sales to the government; he was later released unharmed. And in September 2008, China signed a deal with the Democratic Republic of Congo for a loan of US$5 billion to rehabilitate the mining industry, construct railways and roads, and build hospitals and other infrastructure projects. In exchange, China will receive copper, cobalt, nickel, gold, and timber.

It is important to recognise that China, India, and other countries have other reasons for expanding their involvement in Africa besides economic self-interest. China and India have long-standing historic ties to Africa. They both have an ideological and political interest in contesting Western dominance of the global economic and political order and in countering American claims to hegemony based on its assertion that it is the 'world's only remaining superpower.' They both have a genuine interest in promoting economic development and social progress on the continent. They both hope to use their relationships with Africa to enhance their global status as great powers in their own right. And they both seek to reduce internal economic, political, and social conflicts by providing new opportunities in Africa for their corporations and their citizens.

It is also important to recognise that China and India do invest in projects besides resource extraction and that many of these projects can or may contribute significantly to the economic development of African countries. The Chinese investment plan for DR Congo, for instance, includes the rehabilitation of the mining industry and the construction of major infrastructure projects including transportation and power production projects. China's increasing willingness to fund these projects demonstrates that China has been sensitive to criticism of its initial focus on resource extraction and that China does respond to pressure for the reform of its investment practices in Africa.

THE GROWING MILITARY INVOLVEMENT OF CHINA, INDIA, AND OTHER EMERGING POWERS IN AFRICA

In order to enhance their global status as great powers in their own right, both China and India have used military programmes—arms sales, military training programmes, other security assistance programmes, and a growing military presence in Africa—to bolster their ties with African countries and help them achieve their economic and political objectives in Africa.

China has used military programmes to strengthen the military capacities of key African allies and to expand its influence in Africa, particularly in major oil-producing countries. Sudan has received F-6 and F-7 fighter aircraft, T-62 light tanks, anti-aircraft systems, trucks, and other weapons. Zimbabwe has received at least nine J-7 fighter aircraft, six K-8 trainer aircraft, ten T-69 tanks, 30 T-59 tanks, and as many as 100 T-63 armoured transport vehicles. Angola has ordered eight Su-77 fighter aircraft. China sold over US$1 billion-worth of sophisticated weaponry to Ethiopia and Eritrea between 1998 and 2000—including Su-77 fighter aircraft for Ethiopia—in violation of the UN arms embargo imposed during the bloody border war between the two countries. China has also supplied military equipment to Algeria, Zambia, Namibia, and Mauritania, including C-802 ship-to-ship missiles for Algeria as well as K-8 trainer aircraft for Zambia (which received eight) and Namibia (which received four).

Nigeria, another oil-exporting country facing massive resistance in the oil-rich Niger Delta, has significantly expanded its arms purchase from China, including 15 F-7 fighter aircraft from China in 2005 for a reported US$251 million. In addition, Chinese military ties with the Nigerian Government were significantly expanded in September 2004 when the Chinese arms producer Poly Technology announced that it would enter into a partnership with the government-owned Defense Industries Corporation of Nigeria (DICON) to modernise Nigeria's domestic arms industry. After years of neglect, the Nigerian government wants to revive DICON and expects to resume production of small arms, grenades, ammunition, and other light weapons for the Nigerian military.

These actions have led to criticism of China's role in Africa, particularly from 'alarmists' in the United States who emphasise China's ties with repressive regimes and its willingness to invest without imposing the types of conditions imposed by the World Bank and other international financial institutions or by Western governments. While these critiques are valid, China's practices are not unique. The United States has used the same means to build ties with repressive African regimes—particularly in oil producing countries like Algeria, Nigeria, Angola, Chad, and Equatorial Guinea—and has noticeably reduced its pressures for democratisation, respect for human rights, and financial transparency in recent years.

India has also begun to dramatically expand its military presence in Africa (particularly its naval presence) and also in the Indian Ocean, through which the oil tankers that carry nearly all of India's oil imports—along with those of China, Japan, Malaysia, Korea, and other developed and developing industrial powers in Asia—must travel. India has announced that it intends to build up its naval forces in the Indian Ocean in order to protect the flow of oil and expects to acquire a fleet of modern aircraft carriers and nuclear submarines over the next decade. In addition to the purchase of a refurbished Russian aircraft carrier in 2008, India also bought a refurbished American warship, the 17,000-ton amphibious transport dock USS Trenton.

In October 2008, Indian warships began conducting patrols off the Somali coast to protect ships from pirate attacks. On 11 November, helicopter-borne Indian marine commandos prevented pirates from hijacking an Indian merchant vessel in the Gulf of Aden. On 19 November, an Indian warship sank what was described as a 'pirate mother ship' after the pirates fired on it. And on 20 November, Indian naval sources told the BBC that India had been given formal approval by the United Nations to enter Somali waters in 'hot pursuit' of pirate ships.

India established a listening post in northern Madagascar in July 2007, which consists of a radar surveillance station equipped with a high-tech digital communications system and which is intended, at least in part, to monitor Chinese activities. In 2003, India signed a defence cooperation agreement with Seychelles; and, in 2006, it signed a defence agreement with Mozambique to provide arms and to conduct regular naval patrols off Mozambique's coast. According to a recent report by Chatham House, India's new military policy toward Africa is motivated, to a certain extent, by 'concerns about Chinese expansionism' and 'this shift in policy comes in part because of India's desire to compete with China's growing influence in the region.'

THE RE-EMERGENCE OF RUSSIA AS AN ECONOMIC AND MILITARY POWER IN AFRICA

While considerable attention has been paid to the emerging role of China, India, and other new powers in Africa, far less notice has been taken of the re-emergence of Russia as a significant power in Africa and the implications that this has with regard to both energy supplies and security. Russia essentially withdrew from Africa at the end of the Cold War, but under President Putin and the administration headed by President Medvedev, Russia has undertaken major new initiatives in Africa. Russia, as a major producer and exporter of oil and natural gas, does not need new supplies of energy from Africa. Instead, it is trying to increase its control over energy sources throughout the world to strengthen its own economic and political power. Russia is particularly interested in gaining control over the supply of oil and natural gas from Africa to European countries.

In September 2008, Russia's state natural gas company, Gazprom, signed a memorandum of understanding with the state-owned Nigeria National Petroleum Corporation for oil and gas exploration, production, and transportation, processing of gas, and construction of power plants in Nigeria; Gazprom expects to spend between US$1 billion and US$2.5 billion on these projects in the coming years. In addition, Russia held preliminary talks with Nigeria about a multi-million dollar pipeline that will run for 2,850 miles (4,128 km) across the Sahara and will be used to transport Nigerian gas across Niger and Algeria to Algerian export terminals for delivery to Europe by way of Spain. The proposed deal is expected to cost US$10 billion for the pipeline and US$3 billion for other installations, and will be capable of delivering up to 30 billion cubic meters of gas to Europe annually. In September 2008, however, the energy commissioner of the European Union (EU) Andris Piebalgs visited Nigeria and presented a counter-offer to the Nigerian Government; he proposed that the EU develop the pipeline instead, thus preventing Russia from gaining control over what Europe hopes will become an alternative to Russian supplies of natural gas.

During President Putin's visit to Libya in April 2008, the two countries signed deals on energy cooperation, military assistance, and construction of a 310-mile (500-km) railway line between Sirte and Benghazi. The railway line is expected to cost US$3.8 billion. Gazprom plans large-scale exploration and production projects in cooperation with Libya's national energy company, including the construction of liquefied natural gas installations and gas-fired electricity plants in Libya. Russia has also cancelled Libya's US$4.5 billion debt for arms purchases from the Soviet Union and announced plans to sell Libya US$3 billion worth of new weaponry, including fighter aircraft, attack helicopters, and submarines.

In March 2006, Russia signed a US$8 billion deal with Algeria to cancel that country's debt for past arms sales in exchange for a commitment to buy Russian military equipment, including 32 MiG-29 SMT fighter aircraft, 28 Su-30MK fighter aircraft, 16 Yak-130 trainer aircraft, four S-300PMU2 anti-aircraft systems, 38 Pantsir-S1 air defence missile-and-gun systems, 185 T-90S tanks, and 216 Komet-E anti-tank missiles. In March 2008, Algeria announced that it intended to return the 12 MiG-29s delivered the previous year to Russia because they did not meet Algeria's technical expectations and it is still unclear exactly what aircraft Russia will deliver in the future to complete the contract. Deliveries of the Yak-130 trainer aircraft to Algeria are expected to begin in January 2009. And in November 2008, Sudan announced that Russia had sold it 12 MiG-29 fighter aircraft.

THE RESPONSE OF THE UNITED STATES: THE NEW US MILITARY COMMAND FOR AFRICA (AFRICOM)

US foreign policymakers view the activities of these new and re-emerging powers in Africa as a serious challenge to American interests on the continent. The United States currently gets about 20 per cent of its imported oil from Africa—more than it gets from the Middle East—and this figure is expected to rise to about 25 per cent of US imports in the next few years. And in 2002, American officials announced that African oil would now be defined as a 'strategic national interest' of the United States. This means that—just as in the case of oil supplies from the Persian Gulf—the United States is now committed to the use of all necessary means, including military force, to ensure the free flow of oil from Africa on to world markets.

Most foreign policymakers in Washington—including leading members of the Bush administration—remained convinced that China's actions in Africa do not threaten vital US national security interests and that the United States and China can cooperate in developing the continent's natural resources in a way that is mutually beneficial. But a growing and increasingly vocal group of legislators, and influential think tanks insist that China has become a strategic global rival to the United States and that its actions—especially in Africa—represent a direct challenge to the United States.

These 'alarmists' point to the considerable resources that China is devoting to Africa and to the engagement of Chinese officials at the highest level—including President Hu Jintao and Premier Wen Jiabao, both of whom have made tours of the continent and have hosted high-level meetings in Beijing with African heads of state—as evidence of a 'grand strategy' on the part of China that jeopardises vital US national security interests and that is aimed, ultimately, at usurping the West's position on the continent. 'Amidst all of this hoopla over China's rapidly growing economy, there is a dark side to [that] country's economic expansion,' Congressman Christopher Smith (Republican of New Jersey) told the House International Relations Committee hearing on 'China's Influence in Africa' in July 2005. 'China is playing an increasingly influential role on the continent of Africa, and there is concern that the Chinese intend to aid and abet African dictators, gain a stranglehold on precious African natural resources, and undo much of the progress that has been made on democracy and governance in the last 15 years in African nations.'

Although the 'non-alarmist' view of China continues to guide US policy toward Africa, the Bush administration had pursued a strategy in Africa that relied on the use of military force to protect US interests on the continent—particularly its interest in the free flow of African oil to world markets—and to counter the growing involvement of potential global competitors—and in particular the one country that could realistically become a rival global peer in Africa. Based on this strategy, the Bush administration radically increased

US military activities in Africa and, in February 2006, announced that it would create a new US military command for Africa—Command or Africom—to oversee America's growing military presence on the continent. While the principal missions of Africom will be to protect access to strategic raw materials in Africa and to make the continent a major front in the Global War on Terrorism, the creation of Africom should also be seen in part as one element of a broad effort by the Bush administration to develop a 'grand strategy' of its own that will contain China's efforts. It should also be understood as a measure that is intended to demonstrate to Beijing that Washington will match China's actions, thus serving as a warning to the Chinese leadership that they should restrain themselves or face possible consequences to their relationship with America as well as to their interests in Africa.

So, what will Africom actually do when it becomes fully operational? Basically, it will take over the implementation of a host of military, security cooperation, and security assistance programmes, which are funded through either the State Department or the Defense Department. In the following section, we present a list of US military training and surplus military equipment sales programmes that are designed to strengthen the African military as part of an American global war on terror.

Bilateral and multilateral joint training programmes and military exercises

The United States provides military training to African military personnel through a wide variety of training and education programmes. In addition, it conducts military exercises in Africa jointly with African troops and also with the troops of its European allies to provide training to others and also to train its own forces for possible deployment to Africa in the future. These include the following:

FLINTLOCK 2005 AND 2007 These are Joint Combined Exchange Training (JCET) exercises conducted by units of the US Army Special Forces and the US Army Rangers, along with contingents from other units, to provide training experience both for American troops and for the troops of African countries (small numbers of European troops are also involved in these exercises). Flintlock 2005 was held in June 2005, when more than one thousand US personnel were sent to North and West Africa for counter-terrorism exercises in Algeria, Senegal, Mauritania, Mali, Niger, and Chad that involved more than three thousand local service members. In April 2007, US Army Special Forces went to Niger for the first part of Flintlock 2007 and in late August 2007, some 350 American troops arrived in Mali for three weeks of Flintlock 2007 exercises with forces from Algeria, Chad, Mali, Mauritania, Morocco, Niger, Nigeria, Senegal, Tunisia, Burkina Faso, France, the Netherlands, and the United Kingdom.

TRANS-SAHARAN COUNTER-TERRORISM PARTNERSHIP (TSCTP) The Flintlock exercises were conducted as part of Operation Enduring Freedom—Trans-Saharan Counter-Terrorism Partnership (TSCTP) which now links the United States with eight African countries: Mali, Chad, Niger, Mauritania, Nigeria, Tunisia, Morocco, and Algeria. In 2004, the TSCTP was created to replace the Pan-Sahel Counter-Terrorism Initiative, which was initiated in 2002. The TSCTP also involves smaller, regular training exercises conducted by US Army Special Forces throughout the region. Although changing budgetary methodology makes it difficult to be certain, it appears that the TSCTP received some US$31 million in FY 2006, nearly US$82 million in FY 2007, and US$10 million in FY 2008.

EAST AFRICA COUNTER-TERRORISM INITIATIVE (EACTI) The East Africa Counter-Terrorism Initiative is a training programme similar to the TSCTP. Established in 2003 as a multi-year programme with US$100 million in funding, the EACTI has provided training to Kenya, Uganda, Tanzania, Djibouti, Eritrea, and Ethiopia.

AFRICA CONTINGENCY OPERATIONS TRAINING AND ASSISTANCE PROGRAM (ACOTA) This programme, which began operating in 2002, replaces the African Crisis Response Initiative launched in 1997 by the Clinton administration. In 2004, it became part of the Global Peace Operations Initiative. ACOTA is officially designed to provide training to African military forces to improve their ability to conduct peacekeeping operations, even if they take place in hostile environments. But since the training includes both defensive and offensive military operations, it also enhances the ability of participating forces to engage in police operations against unarmed civilians, counter-insurgency operations, and even conventional military operations against the military forces of other countries.

By FY 2007, nineteen African countries were participating in the ACOTA programme (Benin, Botswana, Burkina Faso Ethiopia, Gabon, Ghana, Kenya, Malawi, Mali, Mozambique, Namibia, Niger, Nigeria, Rwanda, Senegal, South Africa, Tanzania, Uganda, and Zambia). In 2004, ACOTA became a part of the Global Peace Operations Initiative (GPOI) and the Bush Administration's FY 2008 budget included a request for a little more than US$40 million for ACOTA activities. The GPOI itself, a multilateral, five-year programme that aims to train 75,000 troops—mostly from African countries—by 2010, will receive more than US$92 million under the president's FY 2008 budget, which also provides US$5 million to reorganise the armed forces of the Democratic Republic of Congo, US$16 million to reorganise the Liberian military, and US$41 million to help integrate the Sudan People's Liberation Army into the national army as part of the peace process for southern Sudan.

INTERNATIONAL MILITARY EDUCATION AND TRAINING PROGRAM (IMET) The IMET programme brings African military officers to military academies and other military educational institutions in the United States for professional training. Nearly all African countries participate in the programme—including Libya for the first time in FY 2008—and in FY 2006 (the last year for which country figures are available) it trained 14,731 students from the African continent (excluding Egypt) at a cost of US$14.7 million.

In addition, the United States supports capacity development of the African military through the transfer of needed equipment under its foreign military sales programme as well as direct commercial sales programme. The *Foreign Military Sales Program (FMS)*, which is conducted by the Defense Security Co-operation Agency of the Defense Department, provides loans to finance the purchase of virtually all of this equipment through the Foreign Military Financing Program (FMF), but repayment of these loans by African governments is almost always waived, so that they amount to free grants. In FY 2006, sub-Saharan African countries received a total of nearly US$14 million in FMF funding, and the Maghrebi countries of Morocco and Tunisia received almost another US$21 million; for FY 2007, the Bush administration requested nearly US$15 million for sub-Saharan Africa and US$21 million for the Morocco and Tunisia; and for FY 2008, the administration requested nearly US$8 million for sub-Saharan Africa and nearly US$6 million for the Maghreb.

In recent years, US private military contractors, such as DynCorp and Pacific Architects and Engineers, have been awarded contracts to train and equip the Southern Sudanese military as part of the implementation of the peace agreement for Southern Sudan as well as the training of African troops all over the continent on peacekeeping operations. In February 2008, the State Department announced that it would be awarding more than US$1 billion-worth of contracts in Africa for the next five-year period (2009–2013) to as many as four private military contractors.

Under the *Direct Commercial Sales Program (DCS)*, the Office of Defense Trade Controls of the Department of State licenses the sale of police equipment (including pistols, revolvers, shotguns, rifles, and crowd control chemicals) by private US companies to foreign military forces, paramilitary units, police, and other government agencies. In FY 2008, American firms are expected to deliver more than US$175 million worth of this kind of hardware to Algeria through the DCS programme, along with US$2 million worth for Botswana, US$3 million worth for Kenya, US$19 million worth for Morocco, US$17 million worth for Nigeria, and US$61 million worth for South Africa. In addition, ad hoc transfers of surplus US military equipment are made under the Excessive Defense Articles Program (EDA). Transfers to African recipients have included the transfer of C-130 transport planes to South Africa and Botswana, trucks to Uganda, M-16 rifles to Senegal, and coastal patrol vessels to Nigeria. Citing the commercial nature of these sales, the State Department refuses to release any further information on these transactions to the public on the grounds that this is 'proprietary information,' i.e. this information is the private property of the companies involved.

ANTI-TERRORISM ASSISTANCE (ATA) PROGRAMME Since September 11, 2001, however, the overwhelming majority of US military-related programmes with African nations have primarily been focused on providing training, equipment, and technology to support their participation in America's global war on terrorism. The largest ATA programme in Africa is targeted at countries of the Horn of Africa. The *East Africa Counter-Terrorism Initiative (EACTI)* helped Kenya to create the Kenyan Anti-terrorism Police Unit (KAPU) in 2004 and to conduct anti-terrorism operations by East African armed forces. The programme is now training and equipping members of a multi-agency, coastguard-type unit to patrol Kenya's coastal waters. Between 2003 and 2005, ATA provided training both in Kenya and in the United States to 454 Kenyan police, internal security, and military officers in courses on 'Preventing, Interdicting, and Investigating Acts of Terrorism,' 'Crisis Response,' 'Post-Blast Investigation,' 'Rural Border Operations,' and 'Terrorist Crime Scene Investigation.' The creation of the KAPU was financed with US$10 million from the FY 2003 Peacekeeping Operations Appropriation for Kenya, along with US$622,000 from ATA; the ATA spent US$21 million on training for Kenya in FY 2004 US$3.5 in FY 2005, and another US$3.2 in FY 2006. The administration requested US$2.9 for FY 2007 and an additional US$5.5 in FY 2008.

The second largest ATA programme in Africa at present is one used to help fund the *Trans-Saharan Counter-Terrorism Partnership (TSCTP)*. For FY 2007, the administration requested US$7.2 million in ATA funding for the TSCTP and for FY 2008 requested another US$6 million in ATA funding for FY 2008 for Africa Regional activities, most of which may be used to fund the TSCTP. ATA programmes are also being used to train and equip police, internal security, and military forces in a number of other African countries, including Tanzania (US$2.1 million in FY 2006), Mauritius (US$903,000 in FY 2006), Niger (US$905,000 in FY 2006), Chad (US$625,000 in FY 2006), Senegal (US$800,000 in FY 2006), Mali (US$564,000 in FY 2006), Liberia (US$220,000 in FY 2006), Ethiopia (US$170,000 in FY 2006). Training courses provided to these countries include topics like 'Investigation of Terrorist Organisations', 'Rural Border Operations', 'Antiterrorism Instructor Training', 'Terrorist Crime Scene Investigation', and 'Explosive Incident Countermeasures'. In Djibouti, this training helped to create the country's National Crisis Management Unit, within the Ministry of the Interior, to respond to major national emergencies.

ATA utilises training facilities at three International Law Enforcement Academy (ILEA) centres, one located in Botswana. In 2003, students from Botswana, Ethiopia, and Tanzania attended a course on 'Terrorist Investigations' at the Botswana ILEA centre. In 2004, students from Djibouti, Malawi, Uganda, and Zambia took the same course there. In 2005, students from Botswana, Ethiopia, Kenya, and Tanzania attended a course on 'Combating Domestic and Transnational Terrorism' at the Botswana ILEA centre and students from Angola, Mozambique, Uganda, and Zambia took a course on the 'Police Executive Role in Combating Terrorism.'

Other programmes that complement America's war on terror are the *Combined Joint Task Force–Horn of Africa* (CJTF–HOA) and the *Joint Task Force Aztec Silence* (JTFAS). In October 2002, the US Central Command played the leading role in the creation of this joint task force that was designed to conduct naval and aerial patrols in the Red Sea, the Gulf of Aden, and the eastern Indian Ocean as part of the effort to detect and counter the activities of terrorist groups in the region. Based at Camp Lemonier in Djibouti, long the site of a major French military base, the CJTF–HOA is made up of approximately 1,400 US military personnel—primarily sailors, Marines, and Special Forces troops—that work with a multinational naval force composed of American naval vessels along with ships from the navies of France, Italy, and Germany, and other NATO allies.

The CJTF–FOA provided intelligence to Ethiopia in support of its invasion of Somalia in January 2007 and used military facilities in Djibouti, Ethiopia, and Kenya to launch air raids and missile strikes in January and June of 2007 and May of 2008 against alleged al-Qaeda members involved in the Council of Islamic Courts in Somalia. The command authority for CJTF–HOA, under the US Central Command, was expected to be transferred to Africom by 2008. Under the initial five-year agreement with Djibouti, the CJTF–HOA base occupied less than a hundred acres, but under a new five-year agreement signed in 2007, the base has expanded to some five hundred acres.

In addition, the CJTF–HOA has established three permanent contingency operating locations that have been used to mount attacks on Somalia, one at the Kenyan naval base at Manda Bay and two others at Hurso and Bilate in Ethiopia. A US Navy Special Warfare Task Unit is currently based at Manda Bay, where it is providing training in anti-terrorism operations and coastal patrol missions.

The Joint Task Force Aztec Silence (JTFAS) was created in December 2003 by the US European Command to carry out counter-terrorism operations in North and West Africa and to co-ordinate US operations with those of countries in those regions. Specifically, JTFAS was charged with conducting surveillance operations using the assets of the US Sixth Fleet and to share information, along with intelligence collected by US intelligence agencies, with local military forces. The primary assets employed in this effort are a squadron of US Navy P-3 'Orion' based in Sigonella, Sicily. In March 2004, P-3 aircraft from this squadron and reportedly operating from the southern Algerian base at Tamanrasset were deployed to monitor and gather intelligence on the movements of Algerian Salafist guerrillas operating in Chad and to provide this intelligence to Chadian forces engaged in combat against the guerrillas.

And, in a particularly ominous incident, in September 2007, an American C-130 'Hercules' cargo plane stationed in Bamako, Mali, as part of the Flintlock 2007 exercises was deployed to resupply Malian counter-insurgency units engaged in fighting with Tuareg forces and was hit by Tuareg ground fire. No US personnel were injured and the plane returned safely to the capital, but the incident constitutes a major extension of the US role in counter-insurgency warfare and highlights the dangers of America's deepening involvement in the internal conflicts that persist in so many African countries.

NAVAL OPERATIONS IN THE GULF OF GUINEA Although American naval forces operating in the oil-rich Gulf of Guinea and other areas along Africa's shores are formally under the command of the US Sixth Fleet, based in the Mediterranean, and other US Navy commands, Africom will also help co-ordinate naval operations along the African coastline. As US Navy Admiral Henry G. Ulrich III, the commander of US Naval Forces (Europe) put it to reporters at Fort McNair in Washington, DC, in June 2007, 'we hope, as they [Africom] stand up, to fold into their intentions and their planning', and his command 'will adjust, as necessary' as Africom becomes operational.

The US Navy has been steadily increasing the level and pace of its operations in African waters in recent years, including the deployment of two aircraft carrier battle groups off the coast of West Africa as part of the 'Summer Pulse' exercise in June 2004, when identical battle groups were sent to every ocean around the globe to demonstrate that the United States was still capable of bringing its military power to bear simultaneously in every part of the world despite its commitment to the wars in Iraq and Afghanistan.

More recently, American naval forces led an unprecedented voyage by a NATO fleet that circumnavigated the African continent from August to September 2007. Under the command of its flagship, the guided missile cruiser USS Normandy, the ships of Standing NATO Maritime Group One—composed of warships from Denmark, Portugal, the Netherlands, Canada, Germany, and the United States—conducted what were described as 'presence operations' in the Gulf of Guinea, then proceeded to South Africa, where they participated in the Amazolo exercises being held by the South African Navy, and then sailed to the waters off the coast of Somalia to conduct more 'presence operations' in a region which has experienced an upsurge in piracy. Later that same month, the guided missile destroyer USS Forrest Sherman arrived off South Africa to engage in a separate joint training exercise with the South African Navy frigate SAS Amatola.

And in another significant expansion of US Navy operations in Africa, the USS Fort McHenry amphibious assault ship began a six-month deployment to the Gulf of Guinea in November 2007, the first phase of the Africa Partnership Station Initiative. The USS Fort McHenry was accompanied by the High Speed Vessel HSV-2 'Swift' (the prototype for a new fast assault ship capable of operating in shallow, coastal waters) and two maritime prepositioning ships—the USNS 2nd Lieutenant. John P. Bobo and USNS Lance Corporal Roy M. Wheat—from Maritime Prepositioning Ship Squadron 1, one of three prepositioning squadrons used to stockpile equipment at strategic locations around the world. The ships made ports of call in Senegal, Liberia, Ghana, Cameroon, São Tomé and Principe, Gabon, and Angola, and trained more than 1,200 sailors and other military personnel from these countries.

During their deployment, the ships conducted three weeks of amphibious assault exercises off Monrovia, Liberia, (known as Western Africa Training Cruise 2008) in March 2008 and conducted similar exercises off Dakar, Senegal, in April 2008 before returning to Norfolk, Virginia. Its mission was to serve as a 'floating schoolhouse' to train local forces in port and oil-platform security, search and rescue missions, and medical and humanitarian assistance. According to Admiral Ulrich, the deployment matched up perfectly with the work of the new Africa Command. 'If you look at the direction that the Africa Command has been given and the purpose of starting up the Africom, you'll see that the (Gulf of Guinea) mission is closely aligned', he told reporters in June 2007.

In February 2008, the US 6th Fleet conducted seven days of joint maritime exercises (known as Exercise Maritime Safari 2008) at Nigeria's Ikeja Air Force Base with the Nigerian Navy and Air Force as part of the African Partnership Station Initiative. The American forces involved included P-3 'Orion' aerial surveillance aircraft from the squadron based in Sigonella, Sicily, and elements of the 6th Fleet's Maritime Patrol Operations Command Center. The highlight of the exercises was a search and rescue exercise off Lagos.

The USS Forrest Sherman and the USS Normandy, as part of the 6th Fleet's Southeast Africa Task Force, made the first tour by American warships of the waters off East Africa in 2007 with visit to eight countries. The Southeast Africa Task Force made its second voyage in April 2008, when the landing-ship dock USS Ashland visited Madagascar, Mauritius, and Reunion.

In addition to direct naval operations in African waters, the Bush administration also negotiated *Base Access Agreements for Cooperative Security Locations* with the governments of Botswana, Gabon, Ghana, Kenya, Mali, Morocco, Namibia, São Tomé and Principe, Senegal, Sierre Leone, Tunisia, Uganda, and Zambia. Under these agreements, the United States gains access to local military bases and other facilities so that they can be used by American forces as transit bases or as forward operating bases for combat, surveillance, and other military operations. They remain the property of the host African government and are not American bases in a legal sense, so that US government officials are telling the truth—at least technically—when they deny that the United States has bases in these countries.

In addition to these publicly acknowledged base access agreements, the Pentagon was granted permission to deploy P-3 'Orion' aerial surveillance aircraft at the airfield at Tamanrasset in southern Algeria under an agreement reportedly signed during Algerian President Abdelaziz Bouteflika's visit to Washington in July 2003. Brown and Root-Condor, a joint venture between a subsidiary of the American company, Halliburton, and the Algerian state-owned oil company, Sonatrach, is currently under contract to enlarge the military air bases at Tamanrasset and at Bou Saada. In December 2006, Salafist forces used an improvised mine and small arms to attack a convoy of Brown and Root-Condor employees who were returning to their hotel in the Algerian town of Bouchaaoui, killing an Algerian driver and wounding nine workers, including four Britons and one American.

Over the coming year, there is one major issue related to the new command that remains to be resolved: whether and where in Africa will Africom establish a regional headquarters. A series of consultations with the governments of a number of African countries—including Morocco, Algeria, Libya, Egypt, Djibouti, Nigeria, and Kenya—following the announcement of Africom found than none of them were willing to commit to hosting the new command. The public response throughout Africa was so unanimously hostile to the idea of a permanent and highly visible American military presence on the continent that no African government—except that of Liberia—was willing to take the political risk of agreeing to host the new command.

This constitutes a signal victory for civil society all across the continent and an important demonstration that the dynamics of global relations and political relations within states have changed radically since the end of the Cold War. Even in Africa—once treated as a convenient arena for manipulation and intervention by both superpowers—the United States can no longer rely on compliant regimes to do its bidding and faces growing opposition from popular political organisations and civic institutions (political parties; newspapers and other independent media; churches, mosques, and other religious institutions; trade unions; community associations; human rights organisations; environmental groups; and private business interests) that are gaining more and more power to challenge US policy. Privately, however, many African rulers have assured the United States that they are still eager to collaborate with the Pentagon in less visible ways, including participating in US security assistance programmes and agreeing to allow US forces to use local military bases in times of crisis.

Africom became fully operational as a unified combatant command on 1 October 2008, just a month before the election to select President Bush's successor. For the time being, Africom's headquarters will remain in Stuttgart, Germany. In its FY 2009 budget request, the Bush administration requested US$398 million to create and staff the new command. This will cover the cost of creating an Africom intelligence capacity, including a Joint Intelligence Operations Center; launching a stand-alone Theater Special Operations Command for Africom; deploying support aircraft to Africa; building a limited presence on the African continent that is expected to include the establishment of two of five regional offices projected by Africom; and conducting training, exercises, and theatre security cooperation activities over the coming year.

It will be up to President Barack Obama to decide whether or not to follow the path marked out by the Bush administration—a strategy based on its determination to depend upon the use of military force in Africa and elsewhere to satisfy America's continuing addiction to oil—or to chart a new path based on an international and multilateral partnership with African nations and with other countries that have a stake in the continent (including China and India) to promote sustainable economic development and democracy in Africa and a new global energy order based on the use of clean, safe, and renewable resources.

Six months into his presidency, it is hard to tell whether President Obama will opt out for the latter option or not. If anything, given the political forces lined up, he is more likely to follow the policies of his predecessor. The President is genuinely convinced of the necessity and legitimacy of the Global War on Terrorism and the administration has come under unprecedented pressure from business interests and lobbyists (especially from the oil companies); certain think tanks and NGOs; and the Pentagon; and from some African governments to pursue the plan for Africom initiated by the Bush administration. Secretary of State Hillary Clinton's visit to seven strategic African countries clearly demonstrated that the Obama administration will continue the militarisation of US policy toward Africa to secure its energy security unless it comes under pressure to change direction. However, members of the US Congress are now beginning to give Africom the critical scrutiny it deserves and to express serious scepticism about its mission and operations. Moreover, a number of concerned organisations and individuals in the United States and in Africa—the Resist Africom Campaign—came together in August 2006 to educate the American people about Africom and to mobilise public and congressional opposition to the creation of the new command. And the Resist Africom Campaign will continue to press the Obama administration to abandon the Bush plan for Africom and pursue a policy toward Africa based on a genuine partnership with the people of Africa, multilateralism, democracy, human rights, and grass roots development.

THE IMPACT OF THE 'NEW SCRAMBLE FOR AFRICA' ON AFRICAN SECURITY, POLITICAL REFORM, AND ECONOMIC DEVELOPMENT

The effects of the growing economic, political, and military competition in Africa between China, India, Russia, the United States, and other external powers on the policy space for African nations have been contradictory and ambiguous. It has allowed African governments to manipulate their external partners and to use their growing leverage to play different foreign powers off against each other. It has provided African governments and private businesses with access to new sources of loans, credits, and other financial assistance as well as to new sources of development assistance. It has increased the market for African energy supplies and other resources. These can be seen as developments that have expanded the policy space for African nations in ways that are generally beneficial for Africans. In some cases, however, it is clear that African governments have used their growing leverage over their external partners in ways that have harmed their citizens. For example, a number of repressive and undemocratic governments in Africa have used their increased revenues to buy arms to be used to keep themselves in power or when they pursue development projects that are environmentally dangerous or destroy existing communities.

At the same time, this competition has undermined African producers of raw materials, textiles, and other commodities. It has exacerbated internal political conflict in a number of African countries as external powers compete for political influence by providing support to different political groups within African countries and as these groups seek to use their ties to external powers to strengthen their position against their domestic political rivals. As noted above, it can enhance the internal security capabilities of repressive and undemocratic governments that violate human rights and encourage them to rely on the use of force to stay in power and block political reform. In some cases, it has encouraged these governments to use their military forces to invade neighbouring countries, as in central Africa, where six countries sent their troops into the Democratic Republic of Congo or in the Horn of Africa, where Ethiopia and Eritrea fought a bloody border war and where Ethiopia invaded and occupied Somalia. These can be seen as developments that have limited the policy space for African nations in ways that are generally harmful for Africans.

The 'new scramble for Africa' has had an enormous impact—both beneficial and harmful—on Africa and is transforming Africa's security architecture. As this competition continues to evolve, there is a clear need for future research on several topics. First of all, we need to know more about what China, India, Russia, the United States, and other external powers are doing in Africa. Second, we need to learn more about what impact this is having on particular African countries. And third, we need to determine what can be done to help shape these developments and what can be done to avoid or mitigate its negative effects in the future.

26
Towards a Critical Geopolitics of China's Engagement with African Development

MARCUS POWER AND
GILES MOHAN

China's growth has required a concerted economic internationalisation and with it changing foreign policy discourses, that bring China closer binationally and multilaterally to other countries. As a result the orientation of China's vision of 'development' both nationally and internationally is shifting. Although still premised on long-standing claims of 'peaceful' and 'harmonious' co-operation part of China's recent internationalisation is the extension of a 'new', 'pragmatic' vision of development. This 'new' vision of interaction around development co-operation is growth-oriented and market-based leading some observers to characterise it as 'market extremism', even a form of neoliberalism, though one with 'Chinese characteristics' in recognition of the traces of Maoism and the continuing importance of the state.

In its pursuit of this growth-oriented strategy, a number of African countries (particularly those with significant natural resource endowments) have come to occupy centre stage in Chinese foreign policy, as potential sources of raw materials to fuel China's growth. In this way China's foreign policy is understood by some to be shifting from a concern with 'ideology' to a preoccupation with 'business', using what Joseph Nye terms 'soft power' to cajole client states into accepting Chinese contracts. For observers like Chris Alden and Ian Taylor soft power is part of China's 'oil diplomacy' in which notionally unconditional aid, low interest loans and technical co-operation agreements are used to cement bilateral deals over oil supply, engineering contracts, and trade agreements.

The rapid resurgence of China in recent years is thus beginning to radically alter the global geopolitical ecology of investment, production, and trade. China's greatly expanded scale of operations has generated massive demand for capital, goods, raw materials and energy that have pushed up commodity prices with important implications for the economies of many African countries. It is the effects on governance of China's overseas aid and investment packages that have particularly vexed most commentators in the West. In some policy circles, mainly those inhabited by what Nye terms the 'China hawks', China's new aid offensive has been greeted with scepticism and concern, captured in the idea that China is some kind of 'rogue creditor' practising opportunistic lending and proliferating problematic forms of 'rogue aid'. One of the biggest criticisms of Chinese aid is the lack of political conditionalities, which some argue will lead to deepened debt and governance crises in Africa. Many observers and commentators have taken this focus on aid and conditionality further to argue that China is potentially a neo-colonial power, where African resources are 'plundered' by Beijing and sent back in the form of Chinese goods thereby cementing the long standing uneven division of labour between Africa and the rest of the world.

Despite these negative and possibly justifiable warnings about a 'new' imperialism China's emergence as a global development actor raises short-term political questions about alternative policy approaches in countries of the global South as well as longer-term ideological questions around the very meaning of development itself. Many African leaders have heralded the relevance of a Chinese 'model' of development even though Deng Xiaoping once told an African head of state that *there was no Chinese model to emulate.* Others see this 'model' as an alternative 'to the American model' or as 'defying the conditionalities of the Bretton Woods institutions' even though Chinese lending does come with its own conditions. Joseph Stiglitz even touts China as a 'model' for how developing nations should rise and escape the prescriptions of Anglo-American neoliberalism. Further, many commentators have been quick to note the 'lessons' that Africa can learn from this 'model' and even to suggest that China can be Africa's 'economic role model'. Yet Deng was right, there is no single, coherent 'Chinese model'. Many observers seem to conflate the various possible and often overlapping meanings of this term in problematic and contradictory ways. It is thus often used simultaneously to refer to a Chinese model of development in China, a Chinese development model enacted in Africa to steer the continent's development and as a global model of interaction around development co-operation. Thus the singularity and coherence of a Chinese 'model' has often been considerably overstated, despite the internal variation within China and the growing difficulties the Chinese state is facing in managing the complex range of corporate agents now active overseas. We might also question the supposed 'Chinese' nature of this 'model' given the extent to which China has looked to and drawn from East Asian examples of state practice in pursuing 'development'. China's government officially denies the existence of a 'Beijing Consensus' but an official version of the Chinese path to development is known as 'Xiaokang', the creation of a moderately prosperous and harmonious socialist society. Deng reintroduced the term Xiaokang (which was initially used in early Chinese poetry) in 1979 as a goal of Chinese modernisation.

In this chapter we explore the relationships between China's development, its foreign policy and Africa's political economy and more broadly assess whether current theories in IR, political geography and development studies can adequately address these evolving relationships. While we are by no means apologists for China we pursue an international political economy perspective informed by post-colonial theory which sees China's interests in Africa as not substantially different from those of other industrialised countries vying for the continent's resources, either now or in the past. The tendency to demonise and over-determine China's role by Western critics perhaps reveals more about their fears and concerns about competition from China than it does about the shape of contemporary China–Africa relations. Our first question then is what theoretical tools are available in IR, political geography and development studies to begin the analysis of contemporary China–Africa relations? Within this we argue for a broad political economy perspective, which is not deterministic but instead regards the unrolling of 'neoliberalism with Chinese characteristics' as a political *process.* As such we need to focus on the mechanisms, networks and discourses through which it is disseminated. For IR this means deconstructing numerous discourses, particularly Chinese geopolitical discourses, with a view to understanding how they have come to inform policy and practice. It also requires us to understand the mechanisms linking foreign policy discourses and events on the ground. For this we propose a state-centred political economy informed by post-colonial theory that examines how 'markets' are engendered and legitimated through seemingly non-market processes.

Our second focus is essentially empirical in terms of drawing upon these theoretical insights in order to analyse contemporary China–Africa relations. We ask how 'new' is China's aid offensive in Africa and to what extent does China re-work older discourses of geopolitics and development to legitimise its current engagement with Africa? Additionally we seek to assess how China's vision of development 'travels' and how its local manifestations differ through interaction with African institutions. This approach recognises the differences between African polities, the agency of African political actors, the flexibility of the apparently rigid 'Beijing Consensus', and the extent to which China's insistence on 'non-interference' really allows for locally relevant and 'nationally owned' development policy.

IR, POLITICAL GEOGRAPHY AND DEVELOPMENT: BEYOND REDUCTIONISM

We begin by addressing our first question that if China's growth is changing its relationship with African states what theoretical tools are available to analyse contemporary China–Africa relations? We examine how IR and development studies have comprehended African politics and development, arguing that they have tended to treat knowledge as culturally siloed rather than hybrid, and mistreated the state to implicitly re-centre Western political norms. As a result we challenge the idea that knowledge about international relations and countries is so culturally determined that only concepts derived from scholars embedded in the context in question can adequately interrogate that context. Instead we see knowledge as labile so that rather than reify and/or exoticise theories 'with Chinese characteristics' or 'Western rationality' we need a more hybrid and emergent view of how theories of international relations evolve. This opens up a space to analyse Chinese IR theories, albeit tentatively, and the ways they shape international engagements in general and with Africa in particular. From there we move to understanding the mechanisms for analysing how these normative policy concerns coming from China are made real in Africa and how we can explain differences between African states. Here we take a broadly structural approach that relies on a Marxian political economy, which examines the interests of different fractions of international capital and their entwining with state interests. But rather than treat the unfolding of these interests under the current conjuncture of neoliberalism as somehow automatic we prefer the idea of neoliberalisation as a political *process* that relies on a range of market and non-market discourses and practices to become embedded in particular contexts. In this way our framework ties together questions of structure, agency and discourse as part of a totality.

IR, Africa and the Virtue of Hybrid Theories

The linkages between development discourses and theories of international relations are often implicit rather than explicit. However, both share something of a Eurocentrism and reductionism, which places Africa as the subject of history and modernity. In turn this forecloses a wide range of different African forms of political agency, agency which is actually completely necessary to any understanding of the dynamics of international relations. That said there have been a number of attempts in recent years at thinking past 'Western' IR which has increasingly been seen as 'ethnocentric, masculinised, northern and top-down' with many critics arguing that it has consistently ignored or misrepresented Africa in particular. International relations remains configured, as it was in Stanley Hoffman's designation over thirty years ago, as 'An American Social Science'. There have been some parallel debates about 'critical geopolitics' and its neglect of the periphery of the world system (particularly Africa) in focusing on European or North American geopolitical discourses. Writing a few years after the establishment of the journal *Political Geography,* Peter Perry claimed that: 'Anglo-American political geography poses and pursues a limited and impoverished version of the discipline, largely ignoring the political concerns of four fifths of humankind'. Eleanore Kofman reiterated this in the mid-1990s, noting 'the heavily Anglocentric, let alone Eurocentric, bias of political geography writing'. In this, political geography is not alone; the same critique has periodically been levelled at 'Anglo-American' human geography more widely. In this Orientalist-inspired sense knowledge *about* international relations serves to define and delimit the material practices of international diplomacy in which Africa is marginalised and managed.

Tim Dunne argues that Western IR ignores Africa, because of its neorealist insistence on placing the state at the centre of explanations. Dunne goes on to argue that for Africa the state as conventionally understood is largely absent and so IR is incapable of comprehending the 'real' political dynamics of the continent. This is in contrast, he argues, to the clearly delimited and coherent states of Europe which makes IR relevant to them. Dunne argues that Africa '*does* generate meaningful politics' and so we need 'better' IR, which problematises questions of sovereignty, power and the 'nation'. While Chris Brown is sympathetic to the broad project of a meaningful analysis of Africa in the world, he criticises Dunne and others for conflating IR with neorealism. Brown's argument is that neorealism suffers from serious limitations that are evident even before one transplants it to Africa. In particular the normalisation of the European state as the benchmark for analysis creates certain teleological arguments in which Africa, and some other regions, can only be found wanting. The effect of arguing that Africa underlines the limits to theory and is so different that it requires an, as yet, unspecified 'new' theory only serves to marginalise Africa from core debates of IR. We wholeheartedly concur with Brown when he cites various examples of where IR has focused on global structures rather than states which has been fruitful for both IR and an analysis of Africa. Yet we cannot understand Africa in international relations without an analysis of the state which recognises its structural determinations as well as its local uniqueness, something we deal with below.

So, critiques of certain IR theories mirror those of development for an implicit and Eurocentric statism thereby constructing knowledge in hegemonic ways. We would however argue that there are other ways of approaching the development/international politics nexus and that China–Africa relations offer the opportunity for de-centring the West from accounts of global politics and looking more closely at the 'entwining' of knowledges (as many post-colonial theorists have urged). In developing the critique of the likes of Dunn, Pinar Bilgin argues that these laudable attempts to insert the periphery into IR are based on a reversal of 'Western' theorising. Bilgin argues that such attempts should not limit their task to looking beyond the spatial confines of the 'West' in search for insight understood as 'difference', but also ask awkward questions about the 'Westernness' of ostensibly 'Western' approaches to world politics and the 'non-Westernness' of others. The same may also be said about the 'Westernness' of ostensibly 'Western' approaches to development and the 'non-Westernness' of others. For there may be elements of 'non-Western' experiences and ideas built in to 'Western' ways of thinking about and practising development and world politics. The reverse may also be true. What we think of as 'non-Western' approaches to world politics or 'development', in other words, may be suffused with 'Western' concepts and theories. Bilgin argues that this requires becoming curious about the effects of the historical relationship between the 'West' and the 'non-West' in the emergence of ways of thinking and doing that are in Homi K. Bhabha's words 'almost the same but not quite'. Rather than becoming fixated with China's or Africa's exceptionalism it is possible that a process of 'mimicry' may emerge, in other words, as a way of 'doing' world politics or development in a seemingly 'similar' yet unexpectedly 'different' way. In this hybridity and mimicry we can accommodate the pressing ontological and epistemological point that neither 'China' nor 'Africa' is homogenous and that outcomes will inevitably be complex and differentiated as opposed to singular and similar as our earlier discussion of the Chinese 'model' of development suggests.

Here then we have been trying to comprehend contemporary approaches to IR coming from China as a way of understanding how they influence and condition the country's multiple modes of engagement with Africa. An important point about theory and policy in China is that 'the significance of a scientific theory lies in its ability to guide human behaviour' so that there has been, and still are, strong links between the outputs of Chinese foreign policy research centres and the Chinese Communist Party (CCP). In reviewing the state of Chinese IR Zhang identified three contrasting schools. One argues that 'Chinese scholars needed to 'catch up' by 'importing Western IR theories'. By contrast there is another seeking to re-work Marxism–Leninism in order to develop an IR 'with Chinese characteristics', what Leonard refers to as the 'neocomms' (neo-communists). While potentially interesting this is still mired in what Zhang sees as an 'increasingly anachronistic' Maoist orthodoxy based on Lenin's reading of imperialism tempered with world-systems theory, which he believes fails to produce any new insights. The third approach also seeks to capture the specificity of China's development trajectory and argues that most IR theory has been developed in particular geopolitical contexts which serve to extend the hegemony of the dominant powers. Although not explicit and still in what Zhang terms a 'primary stage' this mutual engagement may lead to a more 'international' IR theory.

An example of the growing confidence of China's IR theorising is the question of *tianxia*, based on a nationalistic use of history. Drawing on two millennia of thinking, some public intellectuals see it as a normative ideal that could guide foreign policy. Meaning literally 'all under heaven' it has different inflections that can mean 'we, the Chinese', all people, or a world institution. A key element is transformation, which is about transforming 'enemies' into 'friends', but can also be interpreted as a more thoroughgoing cultural conversion to be more 'like us', namely enlightened Chinese, which smacks of earlier European colonial discourses. Although a piece of populist thinking, and in no way universally accepted, it shows a growing intellectual confidence among an increasingly nationalistic Chinese, keen to develop Chinese theory for a Chinese century. It is not our intention to analyse the logical consistency of *tianxia*, but to follow William A. Callahan's argument that 'each imperial system that he (Zhao Tingyang, the leading exponent of *tianxia*) criticises . . . has had its own utopian ideal to inspire its governance regime'. This then urges us to critically examine the changing range of theoretical models informing Chinese foreign policy.

China's integration into the liberal world order we would argue has produced hybrid results that require us to think carefully about 'non-Western' similarity/difference. Further, much of the critical literature on development has focused on the US as holding a dominant and centralising position in the international development business and has explored the continuation of imperial power relations through the contemporary pursuit of 'development'. Yet as Michael Hardt and Antonio Negri have argued, in today's world 'imperial geopolitics has no centre and no outside', which opens up an analysis of China as a potential 'imperialist' power, although we would argue that such analysis must be rooted in actually existing effects and not read off a priori from a set of ideological and strategic prejudices. However, in valorising 'non-Western' perspectives we are not advocating an uncritical relativism, which treats, for example, the proclamations of the Chinese government as any more legitimate than claims by rival governments vying for African resources. This necessarily has to be historicised in order to analyse continuities and identify traces of the past that influence (or are manipulated by) contemporary actors. This avoids *de novo* accounts that suggest what China is doing is, first, out of the blue in terms of Chinese foreign policy and, second, a significant departure from past practices of other external interests on the continent.

Political Economy and an Emergent Chinese Neoliberalism in Africa

While the first theoretical intervention is essentially deconstructive in making a case for examining the relationality and hybridity of international relations theory our second attempts to develop a framework for analysing how China–Africa interactions actually play out. This is vitally important since too many mainstream accounts of this interaction take a universalising stance arguing that 'China' acts uniformly across 'Africa' and that the impacts on economies, polities and environments are essentially the same. Here we set out briefly our political economy framework for analysing China–Africa relations.

We start from a structural analysis of the changing global economy and its implications for development. Philip McMichael's characterisation of a move from 'developmentalism' to 'globalism' is instructive here, as is his observation that such moves have been a response to the crises of a previous regime. He argues that developmentalism, essentially a social-democratic welfarism, was a response to the crisis of nineteenth-century monetary control via the gold standard and the destablising effects of the World Wars. This Keynesian developmentalism came during the period of formal decolonisation and underpinned state-led, protectionist and redistributive development policy. Globalism, by contrast, is the ideology of neoliberalism and is a countermobilisation to the constraints of social protectionism, which seeks to engender market rule through institutional coercion which has weakened the power of some states. Neoliberal capitalism is a project of reinstating or cementing class privileges which works through what some have termed 'accumulation by dispossession'. Far from being a temporary feature of capitalism, primitive accumulation is an incomplete and recurring phenomenon, given new legitimacy under neoliberalism in which displacement of people from their land and a violent proletarianisation are the norm for many in the developing world.

The idea of China being 'neoliberal' is often queried given the traditional understanding of 'neoliberalism' as entailing strict market features unimpeded by state planning which is seen to be irreconcilable with the reality of the Chinese experience. To what extent however is a discussion of neoliberalism useful in analysing China's development trajectory and internationalisation strategy? Giovanni Arrighi, for example, argues that China has refused to follow neoliberal prescriptions, implementing reforms gradually rather than by 'shock therapy' and emphasising a national interest in stability. Rather than doctrinaire neoliberalism Chinese policies emerge from a 'pragmatic approach to problems of governance'. Arrighi thus almost idealises the 'Chinese model' as ecologically aware, labour-friendly, egalitarian and decentred; a model of accumulation *without* dispossession. China's hybridised 'market society' is depicted here as offering a new development path that is attractive to other nations and as opening up the possibility of a 'new Bandung', one that 'can do what the old one could not' and creating a 'commonwealth of civilisations on an economic basis'. Arrighi's analysis implies that the Chinese development path provides a useful exemplar for the rest of the world and that the rise of China may therefore help to reduce global inequalities and to move toward a more sustainable and just form of political economy. Arrighi contends that contemporary China is pursuing a model of market society that is similar in many ways to the paternalistic commodifying 'natural' path that Adam Smith saw in earlier centuries. Arrighi's contention that China has not yet developed full-blown capitalism is largely based on Samir Amin's observation that the rural peasantry has not yet been dispossessed of land and so full proletarianisation has not emerged.

It could even be argued that Chinese economic policies are arguably neo-mercantilist in nature rather than being completely 'neoliberal'. They are of course fundamentally capitalist and as such, the post-Mao Chinese leadership is doing precisely what the West wants it to do yet is, on occasion, castigated if and when processes unleashed by this liberalisation play themselves out on the global stage and in areas formerly held to be within the West's spheres of influence (e.g., 'Africa'). David Harvey rightly emphasises that China is a 'strange case' as the outcome has been a particular kind of neoliberalism interdigitated with 'authoritarian centralised control'. Aihwa Ong detects however that Harvey has trouble fitting China into his 'neoliberal template', proposing instead to understand neoliberalism as a technology for governing 'free subjects'. Nonetheless, we would concur that neoliberalisation does capture some basic features of market re-orientation in China. The Chinese state remains officially critical of neoliberal ideology, even as it encourages the forces of neoliberalism, whilst the state also counters neoliberalism with nationalism. Our characterisation of China's economic vision as 'neoliberal' is necessarily tentative and provisional, however, and our research aims to understand further the applicability and appropriateness of this classification. In this process we can look to and seek to learn from the experiences of other 'post-socialist' states undergoing transformation (particularly the USSR).

For Harvey, the economic liberalisation in China started by Deng Xiaoping was initially intended as an attempt to empower China in relation to what was going on in Taiwan, Hong Kong, and Singapore as the Chinese sought to compete with those economies. Initially, Harvey argues, the Chinese did not want to develop an export-led economy, but what their reforms led to was the opening up of industrial capacity in many parts of China, resulting in China's ability to market commodities on the world stage, due to good technology, a reasonably educated and certainly very cheap labour force. The Chinese quickly found themselves moving into the global economy and in doing so they gained much more in terms of FDI, leading to greater interest in the neoliberalisation process. Whether it was by accident or design, is not clear, but it certainly has had far-reaching consequences. The post-1978 structural transformations under Deng followed a time when China had been economically devastated by the cultural revolution of 1966–76 under Mao Zedong. Deng believed that neoliberalisation was compatible with China's political regime in which the state–party forms the political arena for civil society and for Chinese economic actors. Indeed it was, as the market had become a potential solution and a means to 'fix' and resolve the impasse in the accumulation of capital under state socialism. Neoliberalisation could be repackaged as 'modernisation' allowing the state to legitimise itself in the process and to increase its presence as a result. In this formulation, authoritarian control is not some strange oddity adding 'Chinese characteristics' to neoliberalism but is rather a reaction to the process of marketisation itself. The aim was to achieve economic liberalisation that would contribute to the preservation of the power of the state, of the party and of the political regime of the state–party. Arguably this is also an objective that provides part of the common ground between China and some of its new African partners.

In countering the tendency to misrepresent the (African) state in IR and avoiding a determinism that simply treats (Chinese) neoliberal involvement in Africa as some *deus ex machina* which robs African actors of any agency we focus on the state and its relations to capital. Here we are persuaded to a degree by James Ferguson's broad-brush thesis that far from Africa being marginalised by globalisation it is selectively incorporated into it through enclaved investments of the type that major Chinese SOEs engage in. Like Harvey's accumulation by dispossession this is based on exclusion and alienation of peasant producers. These tend to be in the minerals sector and draw inspiration from oil extraction with its gated compounds protected by private security forces and limited linkages with the local economy. In contrast to a colonial and post-colonial developmentalist model that promoted 'thick' sociality through company towns these contemporary projects create much thinner social investments. Ferguson goes on to argue that allied to this mode of insertion into Africa is a bifurcated governance model in which the increasingly *unusable* formal state structures are 'hollowed out' fiscally and in terms of authority and personnel, while the *usable* enclaves are governed efficiently as private entities in a similar vein to pre-colonial mercantilist exploitation. For the marginalised, according to Ferguson, all that remains is a transnational humanitarian form of governance orchestrated by international NGOs and implemented by the more able, former state employees now lured by higher salaries.

Ferguson's analysis chimes with much of what we see in China's engagement with Africa, but we argue that the relationships between state and capital are more complex, especially given that Chinese capital is, at minimum, split between the large, state-influenced TNCs and a myriad smaller, independent entrepreneurs. Whereas in the past Chinese firms and the state were coincidental, now there is some relative autonomy of Chinese firms from state agendas, although the ties between the CCP and the large Chinese multinationals remain quite strong. However, smaller private Chinese firms, which have proliferated in Africa, are independent of Chinese state agendas to a degree even though they are encouraged. The outcomes of China's involvement in Africa will primarily be shaped by state–capital dynamics, particularly how Chinese capital and parts of the Chinese state intertwines with fractions of capital and political blocs within Africa. As Ferguson notes the internationalisation of capital makes the relationships between capital and the state more complex, and breaks away from a rigid territorialisation of the political and economic which assumes capital has a nationality. We then have to examine different fractions of capital—some of which may be enclaved—and what role states play in enabling these to succeed or how capital itself exploits (unintended) differences in state policies. This is more complex than Ferguson's bifurcated model of un/usable Africa and it is a profoundly political process as different classes seek to transform the state in pursuit of their interests. This is also important as Chinese policy responds to local political conditions while the Chinese doctrine of respecting sovereignty and non-interference is implicitly based on an assumption that a state exists in the first place. While we saw earlier that Dunn explains away IR per se, because of an assumed lack of adequate state-ness in Africa, we would argue that state forms exist but that they are different from the liberal ideal recognised by most political theory.

HISTORIES OF THE PRESENT: CHINA'S GEOPOLITICS AND THE INVENTION OF HISTORY

China's engagement with Africa has changed and expanded significantly in the last decade or so but it also builds on longer geopolitical traditions and histories of co-operation and interaction with the continent. While this history of China–Africa linkages is important for shaping contemporary development it is also used ideologically by China to legitimise its recent commercially centred activities. It is the sense of historical mutuality around shared experiences of colonialism that is used to defend China's current interventions in Africa against accusations of imperialism and to situate China discursively as part of both the 'developing' and 'developed' world. Beijing has also argued that both China and Africa are 'cradles of civilisation', that both face common challenges and even 'enemies' and that as a result they have common strategic interests and a shared perspective on major international issues. Further, the belief that the West's historical experiences in achieving 'development' are distant from African experiences and offer few transferable lessons has been popular both in China and in many parts of Africa.

The particular shape of current China–Africa relations can be traced back to the connections forged during the anti-colonial struggles for independence during the revolutionary period of Chinese foreign policy from 1950 to the early 1970s. At this time China's foreign policy was fiercely critical of the bipolar Cold War world and was seeking to wrest the leadership of the non-aligned nations away from Moscow. The clients of Chinese policy in Africa have been various liberation movements, which it used to foster an alliance across the continent preaching nationalism as the guiding principle. There have been many partners in Chinese foreign policy that have received less support in terms of concessional aid than these client states and who had an uneasy relationship with China during the Maoist period. Two key historical moments stand out here—the Asian–African Conference that met in Bandung, Indonesia in April 1955 and the establishment of the Afro-Asian People's Solidarity Organisation (AAPSO), which held its first conference in 1957. More broadly, the roots of this engagement are to be found in the wider climate of 'third worldism' and in the movement towards non-alignment.

Afro-Asian solidarity in particular, forged in the crucible of independence struggles, would go on to provide an important political foundation for the evolving China–Africa relationship. Given China's colonial history and struggle against poverty, the Chinese claimed that their unique understanding of Africa's economic dilemma lies at the root of Sino-African solidarity and could serve as a strong foundation for cordial relations. Bandung thus became 'a symbol of Afro-Asia as a viable political concept' and China invoked the Bandung spirit to gain support for initiatives that China favoured. It does not appear that Africa was important to China at Bandung however and although it marked the beginning of significant Chinese initiatives in the continent there is little evidence that China foresaw this with clarity.

We can however trace the emergence of key guiding principles of China–Africa co-operation to the Bandung gathering. The 'five principles' of *pancheela* (alternately *panchsheel* or *panchshila*), agreed upon by India's Jawaharlal Nehru and China's Zhou Enlai at the conference, were meant to serve as a model for intra-Asian relations. These were as follows: 'respect for territorial integrity; nonaggression; non-interference in each other's internal affairs; equality and mutual benefit in relations; and peaceful coexistence'. In 1964, following a tour of ten African countries, Chinese Premier Zhou Enlai confirmed Beijing's support for African struggles against imperialism (which he called 'the poor helping the poor') setting the stage for Africa to become an ideological battleground with both Washington and Moscow. When in Ghana and Mali Zhou Enlai announced eight guiding principles for Chinese aid to foreign countries that were a development of *pancheela* including talk of equality, mutual benefit, non-interference and respect for sovereignty. The principles for aid and co-operation also reflected China's own experience as an aid recipient itself over the preceding sixty years where the Chinese had not appreciated their 'client' status and were partly calculated to 'show up the North'.

However, Peking's failures in Africa during the late 1960s may partly be attributed to the ignorance of PRC leaders and their failure to grasp the significance of regional antagonisms and cultural and historical differences between the various countries while trying to apply a general model of revolution to all African 'liberation movements'. During this time China tried to provide support to liberation movements in Angola, Mozambique and South Africa, for example, but 'backed the wrong horse in all three cases'. Similarly the Chinese were not especially interested in domestic developments in African countries let alone in actively propagating Communism there. China's relations with its 'third world partners' and 'poor friends' were 'either thin or troubled through much of the Maoist period' as it refused to join key organisations like the G77 or the Non-Aligned Movement.

China's emphasis on South–South co-operation has long been seen as a key element in its efforts to oppose unilateral global dominance and an important way of building a relationship that will support Beijing's diplomatic offensive against 'hegemonism'. For Ian Taylor the link connecting all Chinese foreign policy over the past fifty years is a desire to diminish and contain the influence of hegemonic powers and also to carve out a rightful place for China in the world, born from a sense that China has been 'muscled out' of international relations. Some authors are sceptical about China's interest in Africa as a form of South–South co-operation while development in China itself remains immensely uneven and the domestic basis for Chinese prosperity is in fact politically volatile. So does China represent a new form of development 'partnership' extending across the South? In what follows we argue that China has always engaged strategically with Africa and used the continent to bolster its national and geopolitical interests, which marks it out as similar to other superpowers. Therefore, perhaps this is not a new form of South–South development co-operation, but rather something quite similar to what other countries have done (and do) with respect to Africa.

THE GEOPOLITICS OF CHINA'S AFRICA POLICY

While China's engagement with Africa is premised upon this long-standing 'solidarity' it is but one way in which its development strategy is exported and embedded. As we have argued there are multiple ways in which development is governed and the mediation of China's strategy through individual African states is the key to the development outcomes of this engagement. Hence, we shift focus to China's recent involvement in Africa that emerged in the post-Cold War period and to examine Chinese discourses around aid and governance in particular. Chinese practices seem to be changing, largely as a result of its experiences in Sudan. We may be seeing a growing multilateralism by the Chinese and one where its non-interference dogma is breaking down.

Liberal Internationalism and China's Foreign Policy

Over the past decade China's stance on foreign relations has shifted. China's transformation from a revolutionary power to a post-revolutionary state is reflected in the apparent shift in national priorities since the birth of the PRC in 1949 between the two major periods of PRC history: the era of 'revolution' under Mao Zedong (1949–76) and the era of 'modernisation' under Deng Xiaoping (since 1978). Chinese foreign policy discourses are shifting as multilateralism is prioritised over concerns with multipolarity, which underpinned much of the Mao era.

Beijing's advancement of the concept of multipolarity, defined as the construction of more or less flexible alliances to contain every form of hegemony and to build a new and just international order, has often motivated increasing China's engagement in Africa. In the second phase Leonard sees a broad left–right schism within the PRC, with old guard communists being much more belligerent towards other international powers and seeing the need to enhance domestic military capability. The 'new right' are a small but influential group who want complete liberalisation and a market-oriented foreign policy. The current leadership are variously described as 'populist' and 'new left', because they espouse a belief in markets but tempered by the need to reduce inequality. Within them is a liberal internationalist group that wants engagement with the norms of the international community based on the idea of 'peaceful ascendance'.

Since late 2003, top-level Chinese officials have used the term 'peaceful ascendance' to describe an ideal growth plan for Chinese economic, political, and military expansion but the implications of this policy remain ambiguous. The populist concept of 'scientific development' currently guides the socio-economic ideology of the CCP, seen as the latest version of 'socialism with Chinese characteristics' and an extension of the ideas of Mao and Deng. It is dominated by egalitarian concepts such as the creation of a 'harmonious' and 'person-based' society, sustainable development, increased democracy and social welfare. Very much associated with Hu Jintao, it seeks to shift the focus of the official government agenda from 'economic growth' to 'social harmony'. What does 'pursuing development in a scientific way' mean? Could it be modernisation discourse dressed up as something different, something Chinese?

China's Africa Policy

These general principles are reiterated in the more focused polices towards Africa a key driver of which has been demand for energy supplies and natural resources. By the mid-1990s this had become the mainstay of China's foreign policy. China began importing oil in 1993 and what has followed is a deepening reliance and dependency on imported oil and gas so that China has increasingly been looking at ways of obtaining supplies and securing transport routes. This need to increase and diversify sources of oil is clearly not unique to China and has seen a renewed interest in Africa as a source of oil and other strategic minerals such as copper and cobalt.

The China–Africa summit of November 2006 was by far the biggest diplomatic event that China had hosted to date. In addition to a package of debt cancellation and technical co-operation they launched a US$5-billion China–Africa Development Fund to encourage Chinese companies to invest in Africa, and the Chinese also published the equivalent of a white paper entitled *China's Africa Strategy*. The policy is premised on respect for sovereignty and 'non-interference' in national political processes, which marks it out as different from Western approaches that inevitably come with conditions. Indeed, non-interference has been claimed to be a long-standing principle of China's engagement with Africa but has this ever been more than just rhetoric used to conceal/camouflage deeper interests? Western donors increasingly promote development 'partnerships' and the local 'ownership' of development agendas, articulating an equalising rhetoric that attempts to disavow and displace European paternalism and remove the emphasis on external accountability for policy and its outcomes. It is not yet clear whether Chinese discourses around South–South co-operation and partnership are different to this but there is clearly a much longer history of thinking about co-operation across the South within China.

Clearly China's growing economic strength means that it is unlikely to have a partnership of equals with its new African friends but we need to know much more about how China understands 'co-operation' and more about the oft-invoked 'win–win' claims made for this. That said, China's involvement in Africa does permit the 'revival of triangulation', which means African states can pursue relations with more than one external state and play donors and investors off against one another.

The Softening of Non-interference

Chinese discourses of partnership also relate to its role in multilateral organisations, to its contestation of hegemony and to its desire to become a major centre of influence in a multipolar world. Along with an additional tool of Chinese foreign policy, the provision of preferential trade access to African 'partners', these discourses and initiatives construct China as a viable alternative to the West whilst simultaneously signalling China's role as a generous global power. As part of its liberal internationalism and its ascension to the WTO, China recognises it needs to court votes to protect and promote its interests. Respect for sovereignty and non-interference represent two key phrases that have been repeated in China's rhetoric surrounding its aid disbursements to Africa. This rhetoric encourages the impression that China is not imposing its political views, ideals or principles onto recipient countries.

This forms the core of its non-interference policy and the perception that China is now 'non-ideological' and pragmatic, since its concerns are for securing resources rather than transforming hearts and minds. At the same time there is a discourse of mutual interdependence, which fits with China's foreign policy doctrine of peaceful ascendance. At the core is an acknowledgement that 'although Africa might need China, China definitely needs Africa more for her development process'. This reveals the essentially commercial and transparent nature of China's engagement with Africa. It is less about a managed process of 'catching up' with more developed nations, but an even-handed recognition that Africa's resources are vital for China's growth and that this is a 'win–win' situation for both parties. This commercialism over aid strategy infuses much policy, but it remains to be seen if the dividends from this growth reach the poorer sections of African societies.

We would argue that non-interference has always been a flexible practice, depending on the circumstances, and also that such a principle necessarily cannot be permanent. Where deals are signed with unpopular dictatorial regimes that could later be revised by a new government, it becomes necessary for the Chinese to protect such regimes. The Chinese are themselves well aware that their non-interference stance is untenable in Africa. Given that the economic relationship matters to China, its government has a vested interest in long-term stability, and its current rhetoric suggests an understanding that this is best procured by 'harmony' and the careful balancing of interests, not by force. Non-interference is a principle that is certainly breaking down as shown by China's involvement in Sudan. This goes against some of the 'rogue aid' discourses since China is now acting more 'responsibly' in seeking to resolve internal governance issues.

Sudan is a case in point for how China's stance has changed. China's stance on human rights was framed in its anti-imperialist rhetoric, which has two elements. One is historical, which argues that Western powers are hypocritical given the colonial abuses.

The second rebuttal is related in that any conditionality around human rights is seen by the Chinese as necessarily an abuse of human rights. It is this defence of sovereignty that has characterised China's Sudanese engagement. Over the past ten years China's 'blind-eye' support for various Khartoum governments in return for uninterrupted running of the oil industry by the Chinese National Petroleum Corporation (CNPC) has had massive political impacts. Sudan's oil-rich regions generate considerable revenue, but there have been negligible improvements in service delivery for affected civilian populations. Moreover China has supplied arms to Sudan and helped develop northern Sudan's arms manufacturing industry. China's diplomacy on Darfur became more public from 2006 to the point where it cannot be said to be not 'interfering'. Beijing has however underestimated the political risk posed by Darfur to its interests in Sudan, as well as its standing in Africa and on the international stage. The appointment of a new special ambassador in May 2007 was part of China's efforts to bolster its image and contribute to solutions. For example, more aid has been given to Darfur. Such moves also enabled China to promote its own interests through more vocal diplomacy and participation in multilateral forums and initiatives on Darfur. Yet China's more proactive diplomacy was accompanied by continuity in defending the sovereignty of Sudan and arguing against further sanctions, as well as deepening economic links. Thus for this 'pariah state' the impact of oil has been to further concentrate wealth rather than achieve broader development, and this seems likely to worsen even if, as a result of diplomacy, it may lose some of its 'pariah' status. The Sudan case is pivotal for not only showing how China is changing, but also for the ways that Western donors are seeking to co-operate with China in finding solutions to African development.

Hence, there are questions about the delivery of Chinese 'aid' and possibilities of development co-operation between donors. The view that China is not imposing its political views, ideals or principles onto recipient countries is further cemented by the complexity of disassociating Chinese aid and investment and the lack of transparency in China's overseas aid allocation and disbursement. There is clearly no official definition of 'aid' in China and some considerable ambiguity about what constitutes 'aid'. The realities which are selected for critique are the lack of transparency on how Chinese aid is allocated, its amount and level, and effectiveness. Compounding the perception of China as a 'rogue creditor' is the lack of details about the level and terms of its own aid to other countries—so data and information in that regard are sketchy. The volume of Chinese aid is often regarded as a state secret and data on this is not collected in the same way as it is by Western aid donors. It seems entirely possible that while it may seem appropriate for Westerners to pick out the education and health sectors as obvious categories to be treated as 'aid', China's own preference has been to think of its relations with individual countries in a much more holistic way. Chinese practice is unfamiliar (or at least uncomfortable) with the notion of 'development' policy as an independent policy field of the kind that emerged among the Western nations in the course of the 1950s. China has thus generally not been offering integrated development projects for Africa. Instead, it frequently offers a series of infrastructural and one-off development projects formulated bilaterally. Moreover, meta-narratives about aid, or references to the establishment of Xiaokang societies elsewhere in the world, do not appear to exist.

Aid is also often tied up with other forms of assistance and economic co-operation and neither is it given by a single Ministry. The Ministry of Commerce provides most bilateral aid through its Department of Foreign Aid but it also comes from the Ministries of Health and Education whilst the Ministry of Finance provides multilateral aid. Additionally, aid and development assistance do not just come from central government sources but also from provincial governments and urban administrations.

In concrete terms the blurring of aid, investment and development is realised through the mechanisms for funding projects. Sautman and Hairong contend that in contrast to Western aid, which increasingly goes directly to national budgets as 'sectoral support', Chinese aid is usually assigned to designated projects (usually infrastructure related) and is therefore harder to siphon off. The Chinese also usually part-pay for their oil and other resources in infrastructure which means there is less free-floating cash for unscrupulous diversion. There is limited evidence however that the move to direct budget support and sector-wide approaches by Western donors is any better than the bilateral, project-based approach of the Chinese. One argument for project-led development approaches is that they are bounded and one can more easily see if they are not completed, whereas the other approaches potentially put money into a rather opaque pot where it can be siphoned off at every stage of implementation. Budget and sectoral support may increase 'ownership' by recipient governments but it might also be seen as introducing Western donors more deeply into the heart of government. There has thus been a blurring of 'outside' and 'inside' in this era of 'post-conditionality' as the institutions and mechanisms of governance become increasingly inseparable from the international mechanisms of governance with which they are engaged. In some ways it could be argued that China (with its emphasis on non-interference) has not sought to blur inside and outside in quite the same way as Western donors and by its insistence on bilateral relations has actually done something rather different.

A not dissimilar issue around the politics of aid concerns China's relations with the African Union and NEPAD, both of which China actively supports and are 'test-beds' for its changing stance on multilateral politics. Whatever the efficacy of NEPAD, it posits a multilateralist approach to solving Africa's development problems. While the Chinese state-backed investors are relatively lax about transparency, accountability and sustainability of investments, NEPAD has been developing the African Peer Review Mechanism in an effort to encourage African countries to set standards and put in place procedures for vetting and monitoring investments. Again, there are potential tensions and it seems likely that in the rush to attract and maintain Chinese investments, African countries may be tempted into a race for the bottom in terms of labour and environmental standards.

'CRITICAL GEOPOLITICS', GEOECONOMICS AND CHINA–AFRICA RELATIONS

The rapid economic growth registered by 'rising powers' like China, Brazil and India in recent years and the growing evidence of cooperation around a broad spectrum of issues among states of the global South have revived the hope (or spectre) of a new 'Bandung'. For commentators like Arrighi, China holds up the possibility of a 'new Bandung' and a 'commonwealth of civilisations on an economic basis'. The notion that China may be an exemplar of contemporary egalitarianism in relations with the periphery would seem to be contradicted however by the evidence currently emerging from Africa. Further, there *is* evidence of rising social unrest in China, despite this being held up as a model of accumulation *without* dispossession. The more convincing power of Arrighi's argument lies however in his conception of geopolitics as the endless process by which political cultures and institutional complexes are constructed and in the way he clearly links international events (like the rise of China) to their economic context in a world system characterised by global flows and relations. In a similar vein Neil Smith and Deborah Cowen have argued that there has been a recent recasting of traditional geopolitical logics and practices in the context of (amongst other things) globalisation and that these may better be captured today by a 'geoeconomic' conception of space, power and security, which sees geopolitical forms 'recalibrated by market logics'. Thus it could be argued that geoeconomics is crucial to any interpretation of contemporary China–Africa engagement and to our understanding of the spatial reconfiguration of contemporary political geographies that results from this engagement.

From the case of China in Africa we call for an intensification of the dialogue between critical geopolitics and critical development theory. Geopolitics and development theory are conventionally kept apart by a well-established social scientific division of labour which assumes that the domain of the (geo) political is discrete and separable from the supposedly economic and technical domain of development. Picking up on our earlier discussion of development and IR it is impossible to understand the contemporary making of development theory and practice *without* reference to geopolitics and the geopolitical imagination of non-Western societies. Power and knowledge cannot be adequately grasped if abstracted from the gravity of imperial encounters and the geopolitical history of West/non-West relations. This is not to say that development is little more than the continuation of politics by another means since we cannot dismiss aid as simply part of some past and therefore 'outdated sideshow in the repertoire of geopolitics'. Yet all conceptualisations of development contain and express a geopolitical imagination which condition and enframe its meanings and relations. China's contemporary vision of development does not envisage a domain completely separate from foreign policy concerns and actively mobilises historical discourses of geopolitics (respect for sovereignty, non-interference in political affairs, anti-hegemonism) and the language of commonality and mutuality (solidarity, friendship, anti-imperialism) in order to justify and legitimate its contemporary Africa policy.

Rather than separating out the (geo)political from the economic and technical aspects of development theories and practices we have critically explored *the geopolitics of China's relations with African development* in a more open and inclusive way rather than to speak only of 'aid' or 'development assistance' in isolation. This required unravelling the complexity of China's aid disbursement and disentangling the blurring of aid, trade and overseas investment (which themselves have complex routes to Africa). Martyn Davies *et al.* make a distinction between 'aid' and development assistance, but it is not always as easy as they suggest to differentiate between the two. 'Aid' was historically used as an important geopolitical tool for the Chinese in the contest with Taiwan (also an aid giver) and the USSR (where the Chinese aimed to shame the Kremlin by stepping up their charity and economic aid and by providing fewer arms). 'Aid' thus became an important way of exposing the limitations of China's opponents, both Western and Soviet. A critical geopolitics must therefore examine how China's historical imagination of geopolitics has enframed the meanings attached to 'development' and the relations forged with African 'partners' as a result. This historical imagination of geopolitics remains crucial since it forms a discursive field through which current foreign policy is legitimised. Further engagement with Chinese (and African) approaches to IR is an important first step in this regard.

Whilst Chinese 'aid' is used to further geopolitical claims it has been different from Western approaches. A continuing point of distinction is the bilateral disbursement of aid, the absence of grand, moralising meta-narratives and the emphasis on South–South 'co-operation'. China's strategy is 'one of humanitarian and development aid plus influence without interference, in contrast to the West's coercive approach of sanctions plus military intervention'. A critical geopolitics of China–Africa relations must acknowledge the orientalisms at work in Western characterisations of China as an exception and acknowledge that there may be aspects of China's vision of development that are 'almost the same' as those of Western donors 'but not quite'. One point of similarity is China's desire to align with aspects of the Western economic-growth paradigm based on science and knowledge.

China has seemed hesitant however about challenging the contemporary world order (or the widening income and wealth inequalities within its borders) and thus to a certain extent a process of 'mimicry' is at work in China's ('neoliberalised') vision of successful economic development which may be producing seemingly 'similar' yet unexpectedly 'different' outcomes. Further, China is not the only show in town and Chinese engagement with Africa needs to be understood in the context of the wider contemporary 'scramble for Africa' of which it is a part. This includes the efforts of the EU, of the US Africa Command (AFRICOM), the India–Africa Forum, the Turkey–Africa Summit and the Tokyo International Conference on African Development (TICAD). Allied to this is the need to disaggregate 'China' and 'Africa' since neither represents a coherent and uniform set of motivations and opportunities. The supposed 'Beijing Consensus' that many commentators have often (prematurely) proclaimed has proven to be remarkably flexible and malleable in the way it has been adapted to different political contexts in Africa. In order to understand why, it is necessary to foreground questions of political economy and in particular state–capital dynamics in exploring how Chinese capital and parts of the Chinese state intertwine with fractions of capital and political formations within Africa. We also need to know much more about the range of impacts China is having on forms of African governance, the role China takes in situations of conflict and about the relations China has with local, regional and global institutions. A critical geopolitics must also engage with the media discourses on China's engagement with Africa which draw on a range of orientalist assumptions that essentialise China and over-simplify its motivations whilst remaining deeply uncritical of Western interactions with the continent. This requires a 'post-colonial' analysis of the constructed imaginaries of 'China' and 'Africa', and the geopolitical images and representations of Chinese and African ideologies, foreign policies and cultures that circulate and sediment in popular culture. Allied to this is a concern for the dynamics of 'class' and 'race' in particular African countries.

Finally, a critical geopolitics of China's engagement with African development involves a nuanced understanding of China's search for new sources of energy and raw materials. Whilst China's presence in Africa is frequently described as an imperialist 'scramble', a 'mad dash', a resource 'grab', even a 'rape' the image of a defenceless African populace passively submitting to the will of external powers is depressingly all too familiar. How is China's 'soft power' and oil diplomacy mediated by African agency and more generally what are the specific discourses, processes and mechanisms that are involved in the rolling out and reception of 'neoliberalism with Chinese characteristics'? Ultimately, it is up to African leaders to manage their relations with China for the benefit of their own economies and citizens. It is not China's responsibility to 'look out' for African self-interest. China's abandonment of ideology in favour of a focus on economic growth arguably affords Africa a greater degree of space in its connection with China but only if this manoeuvrability is used wisely by Africa's elites. In some countries this should not be a problem as adept and proficient governments are more than able to manage the relationship to mutual benefit. In others however there is a concern that predatory elites at the apex of neo-patrimonial regimes and not especially bothered by the impulse to promote development will make a mess of the chance to make the most of a renewed Chinese interest in Africa.

27

A New Phase in the War on Terror: The Implications of Proxy Intelligence and Western Complicity with State Terrorist Agencies

JEREMY KEENAN

THE IN AMENAS TERRORIST ATTACK

The Tiguentourine (GPF) is located in the Algerian province (*wilaya*) of Illizi, deep in the Algerian Sahara. Operated by BP, Statoil and Sonatrach (Algeria's national oil company), it is Algeria's third largest gas field, producing, before the attack, about 11.5 percent of the country's natural gas. Prior to the attack, some 800 people, mostly Algerians, were employed at the facility. In the early morning of 16 January 2013, it came under attack from terrorists.

The details of the attack, have been recorded in considerable detail elsewhere. The main points were that two buses, taking employees to the In Amenas airport, came under attack at around 5:40 am as they left the plant. The terrorists, estimated to number about 40, but later put at 32 by the Algerian authorities, were unable to reach the buses and take the passengers (mostly foreign nationals) hostage, as they were too well defended by gendarmes. Repulsed by the gendarmes protecting the bus, the terrorists then entered and took over the Tiguentourine facility. Over 800 people, some 685 Algerians and 146 foreign nationals were taken hostage.

Local army and gendarmerie forces were soon on the scene, with DRS Special Intervention Forces, under the command of General Athman Tartag, head of the DRS's internal security and counter-terrorism directorate, arriving and taking over command later in the day. The Algerian nationals were freed, while some 107 foreign nationals were also freed or escaped. The siege was ended on the morning of the fourth day when the Algerian forces, on General Tartag's orders, launched a final assault on the facility. The objective was to wipe out the terrorists, with little or no concern given to saving the lives of the hostages. The result was that 38 or 39 foreign nationals, along with 29 terrorists were killed. The number of Algerian nationals and military killed was not given but believed to be around 10.

SUSPICIONS OF ALGERIAN COMPLICITY

Algeria claimed that the gas facility had been the subject of an Al Qaeda terrorist attack.

To be more specific, it claimed that the attack had been organised by Mokhtar ben Mokhtar (MBM), who, according to the Algerian authorities, was formerly a commander of Al Qaeda in the Islamic Maghreb (AQIM) who broke away to form his own terrorist group, the al-Mulathameen (Masked) Brigade, or al-Mua'qi'oon Biddam (Those who Sign with Blood), and, since In Amenas, the Al-Mourabitoun, a merger between the al-Mulathameen and the predominantly African jihadist group of the Movement for Oneness and Jihad in West Africa (MUJAO), all of whom were or are reputedly affiliated to Al Qaeda. However, there were several reasons to be suspicious of Algerian complicity in the attack.

Intelligence-Security Failure

Algeria's DRS is probably one of the world's most ruthlessly efficient intelligence services. There is little that happens or moves in Algeria, its Saharan regions, or in neighbouring countries, that is not known to the DRS. Its informants and operatives are "everywhere". In an interview published on October 19, 2012, former Algerian Prime Minister Sid Ahmed Ghozali described the DRS, including all its paid and other informers, as an organisation of 2 million people.

Moreover, security in the Algerian Sahara, especially in its border regions and around its oil and gas facilities, is rigorous. There has never been a substantive attack on an Algerian oil or gas facility, even in the civil war ("Dirty War") of the 1990s. Since 2011, Algeria has claimed to have at least 7,000 gendarmes of the GGF (Gendarmerie garde-frontières) in defensive position along the Algerian-Libyan border, as well as over 20,000 troops in the 4th and 6th military regions, namely Ouargla and Tamanrasset. The fourth region is responsible for guarding the Hassi Messaoud and In Amenas oil and gas fields and the Libya border region. The sixth region covers Algeria's southern border regions adjoining Mali and Niger. Both commands contain several military bases with air facilities designed to undertake helicopter and fixed-wing aerial attacks, air transportation and surveillance.

Uncertainty of Terrorists' Route

The Algerian authorities have given five different versions of the route taken by the terrorists; a demonstration of "confusion" which merely adds to the impression that the Algerian authorities were involved in a cover-up designed to mask a complete failure of their security system, complicity or both.

The first statement came from the Interior Minister, Dahou Ould Kablia in the early stages of the incident. He stated that the attack did not come from Libya.

Then, on January 19th, an article in *Liberté* written by the newspaper's deputy editor Mounir B (Boudjemaa), a leading mouthpiece of the DRS, confirmed that the attack had come from Libya. This then seems to have been confirmed by Ould Kablia.

On January 21st, following an official denial from the Libyan government, Ould Kablia attempted to clarify the situation by saying that the attackers had come from Aguelhok in northern Mali, crossing the Algerian-Malian border and then the Algeria-Niger frontiers (a geographical contortion) before getting to Tiguentourine via places the Minister named as "Abid" and "Ijil". The trip was said to have taken two months.

If the attackers had come from Mali, whether via Niger or not, they would have had to cross well over 1,000 km of Algerian territory. Security in those parts of Algeria is so tight that such a journey would have been virtually impossible without the collusion of the security services.

When the Algerian authorities realised the implausibility of this version of events, they reverted to the Libya option, which became the fourth official version of events. The government said that it was now certain the terrorists had come through Libya, as they had been able to access satellite positioning of the calls made on their phones.

However, if the attackers had crossed from Libya, as the Algerian authorities claimed, it raises a number of awkward questions. For instance, how had the attackers been able to cross a border which was not only closed, at least "officially", but allegedly heavily guarded by several thousand border guards who the government claimed to have posted there to control the post-Gadhafi arms trafficking from Libya?

Then, on February 23rd, according to an article in the *Wall Street Journal:* "Algiers-based antiterrorism investigators claim to have retraced part of a 1,200-mile itinerary followed by the militants from the small hamlet of Aguelhok, in Mali, along Algeria's borders with Niger and through southern Libya, by harnessing the logbooks of the satellite phones they carried."

This story may be true. But, it suffers from a number of problems. Firstly, Aguelhok is not a likely starting point for the reason that the Malian Islamists were known to have been gathering at that time in other parts of Mali. Also, since the massacre of Mali army soldiers by Islamists at Aguelhok on January 24th, 2012, Islamists have tended to keep away from Aguelhok. Indeed, it is probably the last village or town in Mali from which they would have set out on such an operation.

Secondly, travelling along "Algeria's borders with Niger" does not seem a wise route to have chosen because that region is heavily secured on both sides of the border.

Thirdly, how do these satellite phone positions marry up with those claimed to have been obtained by the Algerians when they said that the terrorists came through Libya? Terrorists avoid the use of satellite phones in such operations for the simple reason that their positions can be tracked. If, however, they had been assured a safe passage, then revealing their location would not matter.

Case "Solved" and the Terrorists Reportedly Killed

Another reason for suspicion was the speed with which the Algerian authorities "solved" the case, at least in terms of who did it and why, and then proceeded to pronounce the death of the two main culprits.

Within a couple of days of the end of the siege, the Algerian authorities asserted that MBM had masterminded the attack, while the actual leader of the attack was a certain Mohamed Lamine Bouchneb. Even though the Algerian authorities offered no firm or verifiable evidence as to how this information was obtained, it appears to have been accepted readily and unquestioningly by Western intelligence agencies, their governments, and the corporate media.

As for the motive, it was quickly accepted, again with little or no verifiable evidence, that the attack was revenge by Islamist terrorists for France's military intervention in Mali and Algeria's provision of overfly rights to France's military aircraft.

In what might be seen as an attempt to give the incident official closure, on 23 April an Algeria court passed the death sentence on MBM *in absentia* and on Bouchneb posthumously. Bouchneb was said by the Algerians to have been killed in the bloodbath at In Amenas. MBM was actually reportedly killed in Northern Mali a few weeks later.

The court hearing itself appears to have been something of a farce, at least in so far as no verifiable evidence of either MBM's or Bouchneb's involvement in the In Amenas attack appears to have been presented, apart from the say-so of the Algerian authorities. Nor was there any sign of any such evidence, or lack of it, being subjected to cross-examination by any semblance of a defence counsel. That is not surprising as Algeria's judicial system is firmly under the control of the regime and its DRS. Indeed, few outside the British government, a stalwart ally of the Algerian regime, its Foreign and Commonwealth Office (FCO) and its Special Immigration Appeals Commission are now prepared to give much credibility to Algeria's judicial system.

The British government has developed an increasingly close relationship with Algeria since the mid-1990s, firstly in the wake of BP's major investment into Algeria in 1995 and then, since the launch of the global war on terror (GWOT), through arms sales, further energy deals and, since 2010, close support for the DRS and its alleged counter-terrorist operations.

Algeria's Failure to Collaborate in Investigations

As one of the most ardently vociferous countries in the forefront of the war on terror, it must be regarded as extraordinary that Algeria has not only failed to cooperate at almost every level with the countries of those killed at In Amenas, but has done almost everything possible to block their investigations into the incident. For instance, key forensic evidence, which would have gone a long way to explaining the cause of death of some of the foreign nationals, notably Paul Morgan, has been either withheld or destroyed.

One is left with the conclusion that Algeria has much to hide. This became even more apparent around the anniversary of In Amenas. Indeed, Algeria's attempts to block any external investigation were seen very clearly on the anniversary of the attack. Algeria felt it had the sole—"sovereign"—right to investigate the In Amenas attack. Indeed, when France opened its own judicial investigation into the January 2013 attack on 30 December 2013, Algeria's reaction was not merely uncooperative, but thoroughly hostile. The Justice Minister Tayeb Louh, in a remarkable demonstration of ignorance of international law, said that Algeria had the sole right to investigate the attack. Louh even went so far as to say that a special judge was conducting an investigation. The fact that a year had gone by without anyone being aware of this fact is typical of the way in which Algeria has tried to prevent any foreign or international body from delving into what actually happened at In Amenas and what led up to it.

ALGERIA'S CREATION OF ITS OWN TERRORISTS

The fifth area of suspicion is that Algeria has a long record of creating its own terrorists. Any analyst who knows Algeria would immediately suspect 'collusion' because probably the majority of 'terrorist' incidents within Algeria since 2002/3 (as in the 1990s) have involved some degree of collusion between the DRS and the 'terrorists' involved in the operation.

Indeed, this is the problem that John Schindler—a senior US intelligence officer, 10-year member of the US National Security Council and the current head of Security Studies at the US Naval War College—tried to bring to the attention of Western governments and intelligence services in July 2012 and again in the wake of the In Amenas incident. On July 10, 2012, Schindler published an article entitled "The Ugly Truth about Algeria" which described how Algeria's DRS, over a period of two decades, has created its own terrorists and used them for their own "state terrorism."

His article blew the whistle on counterterrorism in Algeria and the inadequacies of the US intelligence community in regard to its understanding of the Algerian regime, or *junta* as he called it, and its DRS when he pointed out that the armed Islamic groups—the "terrorist" groups—were, in fact, the creation of the DRS. The GIA (Armed Islamic Group) of the 1990s was the predecessor of the Groupe Salafist pour le prédication et le combat (GSPC), which changed its name to Al Qaeda in the Islamic Maghreb (AQIM) in 2006–2007.

After In Amenas, Schindler spoke of "Algeria's hidden hand," drawing attention to the parallel between Algeria's DRS and Pakistan's Inter-Services Intelligence and the problems that the ISI's relationship with the Taliban has caused for the US and the West in general.

This 'collusion' to which Schindler is referring, and which I have documented in depth in my two volumes on terrorism in the Sahara (*The Dark Sahara,* 2009; *The Dying Sa-*

hara 2013), has involved the creation of DRS-run "terrorist" groups; the DRS infiltration of genuine terrorist groups; DRS units masquerading as terrorists and the fabrication of false-flag terrorist incidents.

THE DRS'S MOTIVES FOR THE IN AMENAS ATTACK

I believe that the In Amenas attack was intended to be a "false flag" hostage-taking operation that went wrong. The DRS has undertaken similar operations at least twice before. Reason for suspicion is one thing, motive and evidence another. The DRS had two motives for what, I believe, was intended to be a "false flag" hostage-taking operation, which, like Tibhirine, "went wrong."

One is that the DRS was angry with Algeria's President, Abdelaziz Bouteflika, and wanted to embarrass him for granting France overfly rights to attack the Islamists in Mali on January 11, 2013. Apart from a "post-colonial" agreement between the French and Algerian secret services that "terrorism" in North Africa would be left to the DRS to handle, the militant Islamist extremist groups in Mali that were attacked by the French were all being led, as explained below, by DRS agents or associates. It is debatable, however, whether the In Amenas attack could have been arranged at such short notice, five days after the start of French military operations in Mali.

The second motive, although more complex, is more plausible and, I believe, what actually happened. In the year or two before the Libyan Revolt of 2011, relations between Algeria and its Western allies became increasingly tense. The reason for that is a long and complex story. The story began in 2003 when Algeria, as the US's new ally in the GWOT, undertook the above-mentioned kidnapping of 32 European tourists, in order to legitimise Washington's launch of a new African or "trans-Sahara" front in the GWOT.

While the 2003 and subsequent "false flag" operations enhanced the Al Qaeda brand in the region (through its regional franchise of AQIM) and thus helped the US legitimise its GWOT, it placed the US and its allies, notably the UK, on the increasingly slippery slope of countenancing Algerian "state" terrorism. By around 2010, the US and UK, who by then had both developed close "counter-terrorism" alliances with the DRS, were becoming increasingly anxious at the extent to which the DRS had so thoroughly infiltrated AQIM that many local people in the region actually spoke of AQIM and the DRS as one and the same organisation. The West was also becoming increasingly anxious about the nature and scale of its new ally's involvement in an array of criminal activities, notably drug trafficking and hostage-taking, that were leading some analysts to talk of Algeria as a "mafia state."

The problem of allowing such a dangerous relationship to develop and continue was not simply that it raised the question of US and UK complicity in terrorism, but that both countries had become so dependent on Algeria's DRS for their regional intelligence that they were unable to distinguish between disinformation and "truth" and so discern what was really going on in the region. For Western intelligence services, truth and fiction became conflated in a sea of disinformation, with the result that by around 2010, and probably much earlier, the tail was wagging the dog.

By mid-2011, the relationship between Algeria and the "West"—notably the US and UK, but also France—became particularly fraught, as the NATO allies came to learn that Algeria, its supposed ally in the GWOT, was covertly supplying the Gadhafi regime with substantial support. Then, in the following year, these same countries could do little more than read reports of how the DRS, their partner in counter-terrorism, was supporting the Islamist incursion in Mali.

By the latter part of 2012, the DRS knew that its relationship with these Western countries was coming under review. It therefore sent a warning to the West, in the form of an article in the *El Khabar* newspaper. The article reminded the West that Algeria was the only country in the region that could really counter terrorism. The main story of the article described how the Algerian security forces had captured a terrorist network, led by none other than Mohamed Lamine Bouchneb, that was threatening oil/gas installations, stating that Algeria was the only country in the region that had the means and the preparedness to fight such terrorism. In short, the DRS sought to remind the West that it was the West's appointed gendarme in the region and that it should not abandon it lightly.

If this interpretation is correct, then it was a warning that the West either ignored, or, because of its own inadequate intelligence, failed to see and understand. The result was that Bouchneb, a DRS agent, was ordered to take foreign nationals hostage from the two buses leaving Tiguentourine and that they would subsequently be released, as in the successful 2003 operation, by a fabricated army operation. However, the plan went wrong because the attackers encountered unexpected resistance from the gendarmes guarding the two buses, at which point the plan began to unravel. Bouchneb's men entered the complex to find hostages, but soon became trapped there by surrounding security forces.

The Identity of the Terrorists: Mokhtar ben Mokhtar and Mohamed Lamine Bouchneb

The strongest evidence of the involvement of Algeria's DRS in the In Amenas attack concerns the identity of Mohamed Lamine Bouchneb as a DRS agent. However, before turning to Bouchneb, let us deal first with Mokhtar ben Mokhtar (MBM), or Belmokhtar as he is frequently known, as it was MBM, according to the Algerian authorities who allegedly masterminded the attack, with Bouchneb being his key lieutenant on the ground.

Whilst MBM may have been the mastermind, or at least one of the masterminds of the In Amenas attack, although he was not present in person, it should not be taken as a simple fact.

There are several reasons for this. The first is the small matter of whether he was actually alive. Since MBM became an outlaw in the mid-1990s, the Algerian authorities have reported his death on seven occasions prior to the In Amenas attack. An eighth occasion was in March 2013 when he was allegedly, but seemingly falsely, identified as being killed by French military forces in northern Mali. This is why he is sometimes also known as "*le phantôme.*" The penultimate report of his death was on 26 June 2012 when he was reportedly hit in the chest by a rocket-propelled grenade during fighting between the MNLA (Mouvement National de libération de l'Azawad) and Islamist forces in Gao (Mali). A few weeks later, he was reported to be forming a new terrorist group, the Al-Mourabitoun. The most interesting thing about his seventh death was that it was reported by *Liberté*'s "Mounir B" (Boudjemaa), a known DRS "scribe." If MBM was not killed on June 26, as now appears to be the case, why did the DRS want him reported dead?

A second reason is that during the six months between MBM's June 26th "death" and the In Amenas attack, he appeared to change his modus operandi. In his nearly 20 years of outlaw activity prior to his Gao "death", he rarely, if ever, issued statements in any medium; was rarely, if ever, photographed or even seen. He was an enigma. However, since his Gao "reincarnation", he has been "singing like a canary", with regular epistles of one sort or another being issued on websites, video-recordings, interviews etc. He has become an open book. Indeed, his video recording that accompanied the In Amenas attack and which shows him full-face (unveiled) is so unusual that it is actually difficult to know whether it is MBM or not. However, Rocque Pascual, who spent nine months as a hostage of MBM in 2009–10, confirmed in an interview to *El Païs* shortly after the In Amenas attack that the video is indeed of MBM.

This seeming transformation in his character and modus operandi since mid-2012 coincides with a range of publicity, mostly emanating from DRS-related sources, about his outlaw operations and relations with AQIM. The question is: How much of it is true? We do know that much of what has been written about MBM in the international media since he came on the scene some 20 years ago is incorrect or exaggerated. For example, although the Algerian authorities named MBM as the hostage-taker for most of the 6-month long duration of the kidnapping of 32 European tourists in the Sahara in 2003, he played no part at all in the operation. That false-flag operation was led by the DRS agent El Para, with Abdelhamid Abou Zaïd (deceased 2013), AQIM's leader in the Sahara-Sahel, as second-in-command. The operation provided the US with the justification for launching a second or Saharan front in the GWOT.

Similar confusion and ambiguity surrounds MBM's alleged membership of and relations with AQIM and its leaders. He has worked with AQIM cells and leaders on many operations. But he has also 'broken' from them on occasion and "done his own thing". More importantly, he has also "worked" for Algeria's DRS. Many local people in the Sahara, especially those who understand how security and terrorism in Algeria are manipulated by the DRS, regard MBM as a DRS agent. He is perhaps best described as a "freelance".

A further reason for questioning MBM's alleged role as the mastermind of the In Amenas attack was the highly suspicious and very public series of announcements in the one-two months before the attack saying that he had broken with AQIM to set up his own terrorist (jihadist) operation that would span the Sahara from Mauritania, through the Sahel and Algeria to Libya and even Chad. Again, it is difficult to distinguish between DRS propaganda and what may be the truth. By early December, there was firm evidence that the Islamist/terrorist groupings of AQIM, MUJAO and Ansar al-Din in Mali were fragmenting. Even so, the huge coverage given to this fragmentation by the predominantly Algerian media, especially MBM's role, raises suspicions about the role the DRS may have been playing in it.

Irrespective of DRS "disinformation", there is sufficient evidence to believe that a "new" jihadist grouping may have been coming into play during the two-three months prior to the In Amenas attack. This new grouping, comprising many of the Islamists that had been operating in northern Mali, but also possibly others from Mauritania, Libya and elsewhere, was called "Those who Sign with Blood," with its nominal leader, real or fictive, being MBM.

The fact that this grouping was so closely associated with MBM raises the question of the extent to which it may actually have been linked to the DRS. This question is at the core of our understanding of who was behind the In Amenas attack.

As mentioned earlier, there is substantial evidence of MBM having "worked for" the DRS on several occasions since he turned 'outlaw' almost 20 years ago. The most recent has been in Mali, where there is abundant evidence that the insurgent Islamist groups, or rather their leaders (which includes MBM), who succeeded in taking over northern Mali during 2012, were supported by Algeria's DRS.

Mohamed Lamine Bouchneb: DRS Agent

Although MBM was the alleged mastermind of the In Amenas attack, it was led by Mohamed Lamine Bouchneb, who was reportedly killed in the second day of the siege. Two days after his reported death, "Mounir B," the DRS scribe, wrote a detailed *resumé* of Bouchneb that portrayed him as one of the Sahara's leading jihadists. The article identified Bouchneb as MBM's right-hand man and the key man in the In Amenas attack.

"Mounir B" gave Bouchneb a glowing jihadist CV, stating that he was responsible for the terrorist attack on Djanet airport in 2008 (the attack was actually in 2007) and the kidnapping on February 2, 2011, of an Italian tourist, 53 year old Maria Sandra Mariani. However, like his report of MBM's death at Gao, "Mounir B's" account of Bouchneb was almost entirely false. While Bouchneb did lead the attack on Djanet airport and kidnapped Ms Mariani, both were DRS "false flag" operations.

BOUCHNEB'S ROLE IN DRS-MANAGED TERRORIST TRAINING CAMPS

Even stronger evidence of Bouchneb's (and MBM's) relationship with the DRS comes from the testimonies of three independent witnesses who had been held captive and trained in terrorists techniques (killing and indoctrination) in an "Al Qaeda" (GSPC/AQIM) training camp in the Algerian Sahara.

The existence of such camps has been suspected for several years. However, I was unable to obtain hard evidence of the existence of any such camp or camps until after 2009, since when I have been able, with the help of colleagues, to conduct wide-ranging interviews with three former occupants of one such camp. In *The Dying Sahara,* I referred to the location of this camp by the pseudonym of Tamouret.

All three witnesses have provided detailed accounts, now corroborated by photographic evidence and further witness reports, of how Tamouret was run by the DRS under the management, surveillance and control of the Algerian army. Tamouret is believed to have been opened in 2005, although the above-mentioned witnesses believe that similar camps existed before then. The witnesses believed Tamouret to have been closed down on the order of President Bouteflika in 2009—at a time when Bouteflika is believed to have felt he had secured sufficient power over the DRS. Most of the occupants are known to have moved subsequently to northern Mali.

The camp's purpose was to press-gang, indoctrinate and train marginalised youths, in various degrees of alienation from their communities across North Africa (and even further afield), to commit atrocities in Algerian communities with whom they had no connection. They were generally executed after they had performed their tasks, or before, if they gave any hint of dissent. These youths, often mere teenagers, were seen as disposable, much as the Iranians regarded the peasant children they sent across Iraqi minefields in the 1980s.

Those who remained in the camp (i.e. not killed) numbered, at any one time, about 270. They were trained specifically in snipping and throat-slitting (*égorgement*). The camp was visited by senior army officers (believed by witnesses to be both regular army and DRS) almost every evening. The ordnance used in the camp was Algerian army issue. Prisoners, to be killed as part of the training process, were delivered to the camp by the Algerian army/DRS in a more or less continual flow. One witness claims to have seen some 180 murders undertaken in this way during his seven-month stay in the camp.

The dead bodies were disposed of by burial details. The witnesses have provided details of the burial locations that they know. With the help of colleagues, some of these graves have now been located and investigated, with the dead bodies and skeletal remains (along with accompanying data and evidence) being recorded photographically.

Two of the three witnesses to these crimes, who I have been able to re-interview since the In Amenas attack, re-confirmed the main organiser of the camp as being AQIM leader Abdelhamid abou Zaïd, and that they saw him in the company of senior army/DRS officers almost every evening. MBM was also identified as visiting the camp and was perceived by the witnesses as being a "logistics officer" for the DRS. Bouchneb was identified as being one of the most frequent visitors to the camp. He was seen regularly in the company of the camp organiser, Abou Zaïd, MBM whom he also visited, and the army/DRS officers.

This witness evidence has revealed that both MBM and Bouchneb worked closely with the DRS in the running of Tamouret. It is noteworthy that the main witness, when notified that Bouchneb was killed at In Amenas, expressed the view that Bouchneb was too seasoned a DRS/AQIM operative to be risked in such an operation.

WAS GENERAL RACHID LAALALI BOUCHNEB'S DRS "HANDLER"?

If Bouchneb was the leader of the In Amenas attack, as the Algerian authorities have stated, the key question, knowing that he was a DRS agent/operative, is whether he undertook the operation on his own initiative, as a rogue DRS operative, or on the instructions of the DRS. Given Bouchneb's track record as a DRS operative and the Algerian government's confused and contradictory accounts of the terrorists' route to In Amenas, along with "Mounir B's" disinformation, the latter would seem the more likely. If that was indeed the case, the question becomes: who was his DRS handler?

In the two years prior to the In Amenas attack, the above-mentioned witnesses from Tamouret had made frequent reference in their testimonies to "The Great One" as being some sort of dignitary, perhaps a religious personage, whose 'word' superseded all others. However, during that period, I had never managed to identify "The Great One." Then, a few weeks after the In Amenas attack, I was able, with the assistance of a close colleague, to re-access the testimonies and witnesses from Tamouret about the activities of Bouchneb at the camp. During the course of these new interviews, it was revealed that "The Great One" was a nick-name, a play on words, as is customary amongst AQIM networks.

The DRS, under the command of General Mohamed Mediène, known as "Tewfik/Toufik," contains three directorates: the Directorate for Internal security (DSI), under the command of General Athmane ("Bachir") Tartag; the Directorate for Documentation and External Security (DDSE), under the command of General Rachid Laalali, and the Directorate for Central Security (which oversees the security of the army) under General M'henna Djebbar.

According to the Tamouret witnesses, Bouchneb was said to have had a close and "privileged relationship" with General Laalali. This identification of General Laalali as Bouchneb's likely handler "makes sense" in terms of General Laalali's external responsibilities and the fact that much of the DRS's fabricated terrorism and related activities, such as drug smuggling and the establishment of AQIM in the Sahara-Sahel, are either outside Algeria's borders or, as demonstrated in the DRS' support for both Mali's Islamist insurgency during 2012 and the Gadhafi regime during Libya's revolution in 2011, almost perpetually crossing them.

Perhaps the greatest corroborating evidence of General Laalali's role in 'managing' operatives in these sectors was, as mentioned above, his sudden flight to Bamako on December 9, 2010 to rescue Sultan Ould Badi from the hands of the Malian police authorities. If Laalali had responsibility for the DRS's shady operations relating to fabricated terrorism and drug smuggling in Algeria's southwest border regions, it is logical that he would have the same responsibilities for Algeria's southeastern borderlands: Bouchneb's sector.

This new information about the relationship between Bouchneb and General Laalali raises the critical question of whether Generals Tartag and Lallali were working together in planning some sort of false-flag terrorist operation at In Amenas, similar, as has been suggested by French intelligence sources, to that at Tibhirine in 1996, or whether they were following their own individuals strategies, perhaps seeing each other as rivals in the succession to General Mediène's overall command of the DRS. Habib Souaïdia's evidence throws some light on this.

HABIB SOUAÏDIA'S EVIDENCE: RIFTS BETWEEN THE DRS AND ARMY

Habib Souaïdia was a former Algerian army officer (1989–95) and author of *La Sale Guerre* (2001) who blew the whistle on the DRS's role in Algeria's Dirty War of the 1990s. His analysis of the In Amenas attack was published four weeks after the attack.

In *La Sale Guerre,* Souaïdia revealed how the DRS had not only infiltrated and manipulated the armed Islamic groups in Algeria but also masqueraded as Islamists, thus succeeding in portraying them as responsible for a large proportion of the estimated 200,000 killed in the Dirty War. Victory in the libel case brought against him in Paris by Algeria's former defence minister, Khaled Nezzar, rubber-stamped Souaïdia's book as the authoritative account of the criminality of the Algerian regime and its secret service.

Thanks to his contacts in the DRS and the Algerian army, Souaïdia, has again been able to throw light on what happened amongst the Algerian security forces at Tiguentourine.

In most countries, there is one special service dedicated to managing such crises as Tiguentourine. However, in Algeria's case, three units/commands were involved, totaling 450 men: a recipe for disaster.

According to Souaïdia, fighting broke out between the commanders of these units almost immediately. The DRS's General Tartag, who had taken overall command, set the ball rolling by calling Colonel Abdelhafid Abdaoui, commandant of the regional gendarmerie, an *uled el-qahba* (son of a whore). The reason for Tartag's loss of control, according to Souaïdia, was because Abdaoui, on the orders of his commanding officer, had begun discussions with the hostage-takers and local notables. This was followed by a clash between the army commander, Major-General Abderrezak El-Chérif, commander of the 4th military region (Ouargla), and his officers, and Tartag's DRS Officers, who wanted to take over control of the operation. Souaïdia says that the tension between the groups was so high that one could hear the click of the safety catches on their weapons.

This unseemly clash between senior DRS officers on the one hand and those of the gendarmerie and army on the other led to the entire operation spiraling out of control and to the resulting bloodbath. Although the DRS, the country's intelligence service, is technically only a unit of the army, it had become the most powerful force in the country. Its boss, General Mohamed Mediène ("Toufik"), regarded by many as the most powerful man in the country, had referred to himself as "The God of Algeria." Not surprisingly, Mediène, his DRS and top Generals such as Tartag, were not popular amongst most senior army officers who felt, with good reason, that they were under the thumb of the DRS. The Algerian prime minister's reports of his country's 'united command' of the situation at In Amenas could not have been further from the truth.

By January 17, the second day of the siege, the situation had become very tense. After entering the site, the assailants searched for the expatriates. Some had already been killed the previous day in the attack on the bus heading to the airport, but 30 were being held by 11 terrorists in the living quarters. According to Souaïdia, Tartag took "the brutal decision" to bombard them from a distance. Tartag ordered three M24 helicopters to fire laser-guided missiles into the group, killing the 11 terrorists along with the 30 hostages. General El-Chérif was reportedly angered by and wholly opposed to such brutality.

The security forces then set about tracking down the remaining terrorists. On January 19, four terrorists who were holding three Japanese and two others (possibly Americans) were encircled by a group of parachutists and members of the SSI. Information released by the Algerian authorities claimed that "the hostage-takers tried to leave the base with their hostages in their vehicles." According to Souaïdia, this statement was untrue. Instead, Tartag, in defiance of General El-Chérif, ordered an M24 helicopter to fire three missiles into the vehicle. In addition to killing the terrorists and their hostages, nine parachutists and two gendarmes were killed, with 17 others severely wounded.

FURTHER EVIDENCE AND DEVELOPMENTS

Two further significant developments occurred in August and September 2013. The first was my discovery in August of an article published in the Arab-language version of the daily newspaper *El Khabar* on November 12, 2012, two months before the In Amenas attack, which appeared to be giving a fairly unambiguous warning of the likelihood of an imminent terrorist attack on an oil/gas installation in the region. Detailed investigations into the article confirmed it was not a forgery.

The article raises a number of questions, namely:

If the article was true, at least in as much as the security forces had actually dismantled such a terrorist network and arrested its members, why did the DRS and/or Sonatrach (the Algerian state oil company) not warn their IOC (international oil companies) partners in the country, especially BP and Statoil, the operators of the Tiguentourine plant near In Amenas, that a terrorist gang was planning to attack an installation in the region?

If Bouchneb was amongst the terrorist network's members captured, why was he not in detention at the time of the In Amenas attack? If he was not captured, why were the oil companies not warned of his plan, which should have been seen as an on-going and real threat, with security being increased at all oil/gas installations in the country?

If the article was fabricated, as the evidence indicates, why did the DRS write it? The answer, I believe, is that it was intended as a warning (that was either not seen or ignored) to Western countries, especially the US and UK, who by 2012 were seriously questioning their support for the Algerian regime and more especially its DRS.

THE DISMANTLEMENT OF THE DRS

The second development was the dismantlement of the DRS. In September 2013, nine months after In Amenas, Algeria began the dismantlement of its DRS and the re-organisation of its intelligence services. The main outcome of the DRS's dismantlement was that most of the top DRS Generals involved with In Amenas were dismissed/"retired." Most explanations attribute this purge of the DRS to the longstanding tension within the regime between the presidency and the DRS. However, there are many who believe that the real reason was to do with In Amenas. Several well-informed sources are of the view that both Algeria's Western allies, notably the US and UK, as well as the Algerian army, believe that the DRS overstepped the mark at In Amenas. But what mark was overstepped? Two explanations are likely to be given. One, which is more widely known, is that General Tartag's decision to destroy the terrorists, irrespective of the cost in terms of the death toll amongst the hostages, resulted in a bloodbath that might well have been averted had he accepted advice and adopted internationally recognized procedures for handling such a situation. The second explanation, which is less widely known and is arguably the main reason for the "cover-up" that is taking place over In Amenas, is because it was the DRS that actually instigated the entire operation.

The evidence for this allegation rests largely on the relationship, outlined above, between Bouchneb and General Rachad Lallali, namely that Bouchneb, the leader of the terrorist attack, was a DRS agent. If this relationship was unknown by either Algeria's allies or even Algeria's top army commanders, the ISCI articles brought it to their attention. This has been confirmed to me by intelligences services involved in the case.

However, while I might well be correct in my claim that Bouchneb was once a DRS agent, what evidence is there that he had not turned against his DRS minders at some point before the In Amenas attack? That is, of course, quite possible. Such patterns of behavior are characteristic of people in his position. In this case, however, it seems unlikely, for two reasons. I was in close contact with local people in the region both shortly before and immediately after the In Amenas attack. These local people knew Bouchneb well and were adamant that he was still (until his death at In Amenas) "the DRS's man in the [Djanet-Illizi-SE] region." The second reason is that if he had turned against the DRS, he would almost certainly have suffered the fate of others who had turned against the DRS. He would have been killed before the attack. Indeed, Bouchneb, more than most, because of his association with the killing in the Tamouret training camp, was familiar with what happened to those who contravened, double-crossed or fell out with the DRS.

Thus, on both of these arguments, the DRS has been adjudged to have overstepped the mark: both in its disastrous handling of the siege and its botching of its "false-flag" operation that lead to the siege. The outcome has been enormously damaging to both Algeria's international reputation and its economy: the security situation at In Amenas is such that foreign workers have still by April 2014 not returned to the facility.

From the West's perspective, it has always been understood that the DRS's relationship with "terrorist" groups, such as the GIA, GSPC and now AQIM, has involved Algeria's oil and gas facilities being "off limits." That is probably the reason why there has never been an attack on these facilities, even during the course of the "Civil War" of the 1990s. The fact that that "agreement" broke down at In Amenas, albeit possibly through a botched false-flag operation, has led the West, especially the US (with the UK stepping into line), to reach the conclusion that the DRS had "passed its sell-by date." Hence, the backing of the US, UK and also France, for Bouteflika's extraordinarily bold moves in dismantling it.

The Algerian army had an additional reason for wanting the DRS dismantled. This is because the DRS, while just a branch of the army, had become its controller. The army was sick and tired of being under the DRS's thumb. It may also have felt that the Tamouret operation had gone too far. The main line of DRS control over the army had been through General M'henna Djebbar's DCSA, which may explain why it was the first of the "big three" directorates (army, internal and external security) to be taken away from the DRS in the September 2013 purge and placed directly under the control of General Gaïd Salah, the army Chief of Staff, with both M'henna Djebbar and seven of his top colonels being dismissed.

EL WATAN'S "ALTERNATIVE NARRATIVE"

Apart from the Algerian government's expressions of indignation and anger at the French judicial enquiry, Algeria's most significant response to these criticisms and allegations came through an article published in Algeria's daily *El Watan* (French language) newspaper. The article does more than sow confusion and muddy the waters. It is the beginning of what would appear to be an attempt by the Algerian government and its "new" DRS to construct an "alternative narrative" of what happened at In Amenas.

The most significant item in the *El Watan* article is that it states, quite specifically, that more than 30 terrorists were killed (32 to 38, depending on the source), and not 29, as hitherto stated by the Algerian authorities and cited in almost all reports and articles on the subject. It also states that seven others were captured, not three as has always been stated by the Algerian authorities, while two others, "in addition to Mokhtar Belmokhtar," directly involved in the attack, of whom there has hitherto been no mention, escaped.

These numbers contradict the data hitherto provided by Algeria. If they are true, then the Algerian authorities have been lying to all interested parties. If it is false, as seems more likely, then I believe it is part of an attempt, resonant of DRS practice, to create confusion and, in this case, an alternative narrative.

Either way, it is clear that Algeria, quite apart from the many allegations that have already been made about DRS complicity in the attack, cannot be trusted to manage anything resembling the sort of international and transparent investigation that sooner or later must be held into this affair.

IN AMENAS AND THE WESTERN POWERS

In my third ISCI article, I alleged that the In Amenas attack has been the subject of a "cover up" by almost all official bodies in the countries involved in or affected by what went on at In Amenas, especially in terms of the key questions of who might have been the behind the attacks and why. Within the Western countries most affected by the In Amenas attack, especially the UK, enquiries at all official levels are being met with near silence. It is as if a sense of "omertà"—a code of silence—has engulfed all government agencies involved, with the establishment media falling dutifully into line

The reason for this is that these Western powers are all deeply incriminated in Algeria's terrorism. The US, UK and France, for instance, backed the Algerian military's effective coup d'état of 1992 when it annulled the general election that was on the brink of being won by the Front Islamique du Salut (FIS). In 1995, BP signed its first major investment contract in Algeria. Three years later, three senior British government ministers, Geoffrey Hoon (Defence), Jack Straw (Home Secretary) and Robin Cook (Foreign Affairs), ordered the Foreign and Commonwealth Office (FCO) to commit perjury in order to prevent the revelation in court of the Algerian regime's atrocities against its own innocent citizens. At that time, the reason for Britain's support for Algeria was to access Algeria's oil and gas resources. It also backed the Algerian military regime as a bulwark against Islamism. The UK, with its own domestic Muslim population, was, and still is, particularly fearful of the emergence and spread of "Islamist" tendencies within the UK. In Algeria, however, both in the 1990s and today, there are no simple demarcations between "Islamists", so-called "jihadists", DRS agents, "associates" and criminal operatives. Washington's support was similar, but took on a new and more radical slant after 9/11 when it entered into a global war on terror alliance with the Algerian regime, a key dimension of which was to fabricate terrorism and false-flag incidents in order to justify the launch of the GWOT into Africa and so promote US strategic interests on the continent.

There has been a deepening of relations between the UK government and Algeria over the last decade. The main change followed the restructuring of the British intelligence services by Prime Minister Tony Blair in 2004, when Sir Richard Dearlove resigned as head of the Secret Intelligence Service MI6 and was replaced by John Scarlett. Regarded by many as a "Blair crony" and overly subservient to "requests" from Washington, Scarlett was chairman of the Joint Intelligence Committee and, as such, responsible for what became known as the "dodgy dossier," which made a number of allegations about Iraq's WMD that, while convenient for Blair's agenda on Iraq, were all subsequently proven to be false.

From 2006 onwards, following Washington's request that London assist in its "development-security" programme in "southern Algeria," the British government, taking its cue from Washington, developed closer and very accommodating relations with the Algerian regime. I was briefed on this by the US State Department in Washington in August 2006. The FCO asked my views on the matter. I advised, in the strongest possible terms, that it desist from any such assistance to or relations with Algeria's DRS. In 2006, it lifted its embargo on arms sales to Algeria. In early

2009, Patrick Tobin was appointed the FCO's regional counter-terrorism security advisor. He went to Timbuktu in early April and then on to Algiers where he worked in close association with the DRS, being instrumental in setting up the joint UK-Algerian committee on counter-terrorism which first met in March 2010. On May 31, 2009, a British hostage, Edwin Dwyer was murdered by AQIM leader Abdelhamid abou Zaïd. The British government failed to intervene on his behalf, even though it had been informed that Abou Zaïd was a DRS agent.

The UK-Algerian joint committee on counter-terrorism has become a more or less permanent forum for secret dealings between the two countries. In November 2009, Alistair Burt MP, the UK's Parliamentary Under-Secretary of State at the FCO with responsibility for the Middle East and North Africa and counter-terrorism, while in Algiers to finalise arrangements for the second meeting of the committee, told the Algerian media that "London is ready to provide Algiers with military equipment required in its war on terror." At the meeting, Britain made it clear that it would not only work increasingly closely with Algeria's DRS, but that it would be providing it with material, intelligence, training and other such co-operative needs. The fact that Algeria's neighbours were expressing their concerns about Algeria's role in regional terrorism, and that British intelligence services had received several briefings, not least from US intelligence sources, that Algeria's DRS was behind most of the terrorist groups operating in North Africa, were ignored by the FCO.

Burt was dismissed from this post on October 7, 2013, precisely three days before he was scheduled to meet and answer previously submitted questions from relatives of the In Amenas deceased.

The UK, along with most other Western powers, is guilty of prioritizing its access to Algeria's hydrocarbons over any concerns for the regime's serious abuses of human rights. More serious for the UK government (along with the US) is that its support for the regime, especially its DRS, makes it complicit in state terrorism.

The extent of Western, especially UK and US, complicity in Algerian state terrorism is a potentially explosive issue for these Western countries. If it transpired that they had knowledge of the Tamouret terrorist training camp or, were complicit in the camp's operations, such as through the provision of certain identification technologies, then the ethical basis and raison d'être of the GWOT would be called into question.

It is therefore important for the British government, as well as other Western governments and interests, that the In Amenas inquest is limited in its scope and not allowed to explore such critical questions as who was behind the attack, and why. Indeed, as the British government prioritises the expansion of its arms sales and energy sourcing contracts with Algeria, the "cover-up" of the In Amenas case becomes an imperative.

LIST OF ORIGINAL SOURCES

1. INDEPENDENCE BY RIGHT

Jackson, R. H. "Independence by Right." In *Quasi-states: Sovereignty, International Relations & the Third World*, 82–106. Cambridge: Cambridge University Press, 1990. Permission by Cambridge University Press.

2. REGIMES OF SOVEREIGNTY

Grovogui, S. "Regimes of Sovereignty: International Morality and the African Condition." *European Journal of International Relations* 8, no. 3 (2002): 315–38. Permission courtesy of Sage.

3. THE RISE OF THE STATE SYSTEM IN AFRICA

Warner, C. M. "The Rise of the State System in Africa." *Review of International Studies* 27, no. 5 (2001): 65–89. Permission granted by Cambridge University Press.

4. POLICY AUTONOMY AND THE HISTORY OF BRITISH AID TO AFRICA

Adapted from: Killick, T. "Policy Autonomy and the History of British Aid to Africa." *Development Policy Review* 23, no. 6 (2005): 665–81. Permission courtesy of the Overseas Development Institute.

5. "DEVELOPMENT IS VERY POLITICAL IN TANZANIA"

Jennnings, M. "Development Is Very Political in Tanzania." In *The Charitable Impulse*, edited by O. Barrow and M. Jennings, 109–32. Oxford: Currey, 2001. Permission granted by Boydell & Brewer.

6. EVOLUTION OF THE UNITED NATIONS ANTI-APARTHEID REGIME

Stultz, N. M. "The Evolution of the UN Anti-apartheid Regime." *Human Rights Quarterly* 13, no. 1 (1991): 1–23. Permission by Johns Hopkins University Press.

7. WHAT NEXT? SELECTIVE GENOCIDE IN BURUNDI

Lemarchand, R. "Selective Genocide in Burundi." In Minority Rights Group report no. 20, 19–22. London: Minority Rights Group, 1974. Permission courtesy of Minority Rights Group.

8. THE SCRAMBLE FOR AFRICA

Griffiths, I. "The Scramble for Africa: Inherited Political Boundaries." *Geographical Journal* 151, no. 2 (1986): 204–16. Permission granted by Wiley and the Royal Geographical Society.

9. THE OAU INTERVENTIONS IN CHAD

May, R., and S. Massey. "The OAU Interventions in Chad: Mission Impossible or Mission Evaded?" *International Peacekeeping* 5, no. 1 (1998): 46–65. Permission courtesy of Taylor & Francis.

10. FRENCH AFRICAN POLICY IN HISTORICAL PERSPECTIVE

Adapted from: Chafer, T. "French African Policy in Historical Perspective." *Journal of Contemporary African Studies* 19, no. 2 (2001): 165–82. © The Institute of Social and Economic Research, reprinted by permission of Taylor & Francis on behalf of The Institute of Social and Economic Research.

11. PROPAGANDA AND POLITICS

Stockwell, J. "Propaganda and Politics." In *In Search of Enemies: A CIA Story,* 191–202. London: Deutsch, 1978. Permission untraceable.

12. "FLEE! THE WHITE GIANTS ARE COMING!"

Gleijeses, P. "'Flee! The White Giants Are Coming!' The United States, the Mercenaries, and the Congo 1964–65." *Diplomatic History* 18, no. 2 (1994): 207–37. Permission granted by Oxford University Press.

13. THE PROSPECTS OF SOCIALISM

Westad, O. "The Prospects of Socialism: Ethiopia and the Horn." Chap. 7 in *The Global Cold War.* Cambridge: Cambridge University Press, 2005. Permission granted by Cambridge University Press.

14. REBEL MOVEMENTS AND PROXY WARFARE

Prunier, G. "Rebel Movements and Proxy Warfare: Uganda, Sudan and the Congo." *African Affairs* 103 (2004): 359–83. Permission courtesy of Oxford University Press.

15. THE UNITED NATIONS IN AFRICA

Al-Qaq, R. K. "United Nations Peace Operations and the Management of World Order." Unpublished paper, 2006. Published courtesy of the author.

16. THE LIBERAL PEACE IS NEITHER

Eriksen, S. S. "The Liberal Peace Is Neither: Peacebuilding, State Building and the Reproduction of Conflict in the Democratic Republic of Congo." *International Peacekeeping* 16, no. 5 (2009): 652–66. Permission granted by Taylor & Francis.

17. "A PROJECT TO BE REALIZED"

Young, T. "'A Project to be Realised': Global Liberalism and Contemporary Africa." *Millennium* 24 (1995): 527–46. Permission granted by Sage.

18. VALUES, CONTEXT, AND HYBRIDITY

Stamnes, E. "Values, Context and Hybridity: How Can the Insights from the Liberal Peace Critique Literature Be Brought To Bear on the Practices of the UN Peacebuilding Architecture?" Working paper written for The Future of the UN Peacebuilding Architecture Project. Washington, DC: Center for International Policy Studies; Ottawa, Ontario: University of Ottawa; Oslo: Norwegian Institute of International Affairs, 2010. The project was led by Professor Roland Paris and supported by the Carnegie Cooperation of New York, the Norwegian Peacebuilding Centre, and the Canadian Department of Foreign Affairs and International Trade. Permission granted by the author and sponsoring centers.

19. IS THE EU'S GOVERNANCE "GOOD"?

Slocum-Bradley, N., and A. Bradley. "Is the EU's Governance 'Good'?: An Assessment of EU Governance in Its Partnership with ACP States." UNU-CRIS Working Paper W-2010/1. Bruges, Belgium: United Nations University Institute on Comparative Regional Integration Studies, 2011. Permission courtesy of the authors.

20. FEMALE CIRCUMCISION AS FEMALE GENITAL MUTILATION

Oba, A. A. "Female Circumcision as Female Genital Mutilation: Human Rights or Cultural Imperialism?" *Global Jurist* 8, no. 3 (Frontiers) (2008): article 8. Permission courtesy of Berkeley Electronic Press.

21. POLITICS, ANTI-POLITICS, INTERNATIONAL JUSTICE

Kelsall, T. "Politics, Anti-politics, International Justice." *Review of International Studies* 32, no. 4 (2006): 587–603. Permission granted by Cambridge University Press.

22. EXPLAINING THE CLASH AND ACCOMMODATION OF INTERESTS OF MAJOR ACTORS IN THE CREATION OF THE AFRICAN UNION

Tieku, T. K. "Explaining the Clash and Accommodation of Interests of Major Actors in the Creation of the African Union." *African Affairs* 103 (2004): 249–67. Permission courtesy of Oxford University Press.

23. "PARTNERSHIP" THROUGH ACCOMMODATION?

Taylor, I. "'Partnership' through Accommodation? African Development Initiatives and Universal Policy Prescriptions." In *Africa, Regional Cooperation and the World Market,* edited by H. Melber, 9–39. Uppsala: Nordiska Afrikainstitutet, 2006. Permission courtesy of the Nordic Africa Institute.

24. THE POWER OF PARTNERSHIPS IN GLOBAL GOVERNANCE

Abrahamsen, R. "The Power of Partnerships in Global Governance." *Third World Quarterly* 25, no. 8 (2004): 1453–67. Permission granted by Taylor & Francis.

25. CHINA, INDIA, RUSSIA, AND THE UNITED STATES

Volman, D. "China, India, Russia and the United States: The Scramble for African Oil and the Militarization of the Continent." *Current African Issues* 43. Uppsala: Nordiska Afrikainstitutet, 2009. Permission courtesy of the Nordic Africa Institute.

26. TOWARDS A CRITICAL GEOPOLITICS OF CHINA'S ENGAGEMENT WITH AFRICAN DEVELOPMENT

Power, M., and G. Mohan. "Towards a Critical Geopolitics of China's Engagement with African Development." *Geopolitics* 15, no. 3 (2010): 462–95. Permission courtesy of Taylor & Francis.

27. A NEW PHASE IN THE WAR ON TERROR

Keenan, J. "A New Phase in the War on Terror." London International State Crime Initiative, 2014. Earlier parts of this paper were previously published by the ISCI. Permission granted by ISCI and the author.

LIST OF CONTRIBUTORS

RITA ABRAHAMSEN is Professor in the Graduate School of Public and International Affairs, University of Ottawa. She is the author (with M. C. Williams) of *Security beyond the State: Private Security in International Politics* (Cambridge University Press, 2011) and *Disciplining Democracy: Development Discourse and the Good Governance Agenda in Africa* (Zed Books, 2000).

RICHARD K. AL-QAQ is Research Associate at the Centre for International Studies and Diplomacy at the School of Oriental and African Studies, University of London. His main research interests are the United Nations, particularly the organization's political activities in the Southern hemisphere, theories and practices of international conflict resolution, and emerging powers in world politics. He is author of *Managing World Order: United Nations Peace Operations and the Security Agenda* (I. B. Tauris, 2009).

ANDREW BRADLEY is Assistant Secretary-General for Political Affairs and Human Development of the African, Caribbean and Pacific Group of States. His responsibilities include the maintenance of African, Caribbean and Pacific Group–European Union relations, migration, human and social development, conflict prevention and resolution, and the promotion of democracy and human rights. Previously, he was a career diplomat serving in South African embassies and missions in Canada, Switzerland, and Belgium.

TONY CHAFER is Professor of Contemporary French Area Studies at the University of Portsmouth. He has authored two books, *From Rivalry to Partnership? New Approaches to the Challenges of Africa* (Ashgate, 2011) and *The End of Empire in French West Africa: France's Successful Decolonisation* (Berg, 2002). His recently co-edited volume is *Francophone Africa at Fifty* (Manchester University Press, 2013). Professor Chafer is an expert on Francophone African countries and French relations with sub-Saharan Africa.

STEIN SUNDSTØL ERIKSEN is at the Department of Development Studies at the Norwegian Institute of International Affairs. He has published several reports on international development and analysis of governance. Recent publications include "Regimes, Constituencies and the Politics of State Formation: Zimbabwe and Botswana Compared," *International Political Science Review,* 2012, 33 (3), and "Possibility of State Formation: The Experience of Botswana in a Theoretical Perspective," *European Journal of Developmental Research,* 2011, 23 (3).

PIERO GLEIJESES is Professor of United States foreign policy at Johns Hopkins University. Professor Gleijeses's research primarily concerns the historical relationship between Latin American and the United States as well as their foreign policy experiences. He authored the celebrated *Conflicting Missions: Havana, Washington and Africa 1959–76* (University of North Carolina Press, 2002), which looks at Cuban engagement with Africa in contrast to American approaches to the continent, among several other works.

IEUAN GRIFFITHS is Professor Emeritus of Geography at the School of African and Asian

Studies, University of Sussex. He is author of *The African Inheritance* (Routledge, 1995) and *An Atlas of African Affairs* (Methuen, 1984). The article reproduced in this volume was based on an Eva Taylor Lecture given at a meeting in the Royal Geographical Society's House on November 4, 1985.

SIBA N. GROVOGUI is Professor of Political Science at Johns Hopkins University. His main areas of interest are International Relations theory and political theory. Professor Grovogui has published numerous articles concerning the nature of colonial encounters, contested experiences, and the hermeneutics of race. His recent work includes "Counterpoints and the Imaginaries behind Them: Thinking beyond North American and European Traditions," *International Political Sociology,* 2009, 3 (3), as well as "No Bridges to Swamps: A Postcolonial Perspective on Disciplinary Dialogue," *International Relations,* 2009, 23 (1).

ROBERT H. JACKSON is Professor of International Relations and Political Science at Boston University. His areas of specialization are international ethics, international law, and regional expertise on postcolonial Africa. Jackson has written extensively on International Relations and has authored several books including *Classical and Modern Thought on International Relations* (Palgrave Macmillan, 2005), *The Global Covenant* (Oxford University Press, 2000), and an introductory textbook to International Relations which he co-authored with Georg Sorensen (Oxford University Press, 1999).

MICHAEL JENNINGS is Senior Lecturer in the Department of Development Studies at the School of Oriental and African Studies, University of London. Jennings's research expertise centers on the various development narratives that have emerged over the last century as well as security issues in East Africa. He also contributes to briefing documents on a wide range of issues concerning sub-Saharan Africa. Publications include *Surrogates of the State: Non-Governmental Organisations, Development and Ujamaa in Tanzania* (Kumarian Press, 2008).

JEREMY KEENAN is Research Associate in the Department of Anthropology and Sociology at the School of Oriental and African Studies, University of London. His research interests include issues of security and globalization, the anthropology of development, and the militarization of Africa. He advises several international organizations on security and political risk in the North African region. Author of six books on the Sahara, his recent work centers on U.S. relations with Africa, including *The Dying Sahara: US Imperialism and Terror in Africa* (Pluto Press, 2012) and *The Dark Sahara: America's War on Terror in Africa* (Pluto Press, 2009).

TIM KELSALL is a social scientist with interests in Africa, Southeast Asia, and Development Studies. He holds a PhD from the School of Oriental and African Studies, University of London, and has taught politics at the University of Oxford and Newcastle University. He was a former editor of *African Affairs,* one of the foremost journals covering African studies.

TONY KILLICK is Senior Research Associate of the Overseas Development Institute, London, and a consultant on development policy issues. He was Director of ODI from 1982 to 1987, Senior Research Fellow there from 1987 to 1999, Visiting Professor at the University of Surrey from 1988 to 2003, and President of the Development Studies Association from 1986 to 1988.

RENE LEMARCHAND is Professor Emeritus of Political Science at the University of Florida. Professor Lemarchand has developed wide research interests over a long career that has seen him teach a wide variety of courses related to Africa, with particular attention paid to the role of ethnic conflict. He worked at the University of Florida for his entire academic career after joining the Political Science Faculty in 1971. Recent work includes *The Dynamics of Violence in Central Africa* (University of Pennsylvania Press, 2009).

SIMON MASSEY is Senior Lecturer in the Faculty of Business, Environment and Society, Coventry University. He has a diverse range of research interests including international security as well as border and territorial disputes in Africa. He has published for numerous think tanks, policy institutes, and academic journals, including recent work such as *The Constitutional Crisis in Madagascar* (with Bruce Baker), a Chatham House Briefing Paper, and "Ties that Bind and Ties that Don't: France's Role in Bringing Together and Pulling Apart the People of the Comoros Archipelago," in *France in Africa* (Chester University Press, 2012).

ROY MAY is Professor Emeritus of African Politics at Coventry University. He has taught both undergraduate and postgraduate courses in African politics, development, aid, and Third World politics, and he founded the African Studies Centre at the university in 1995. Selected publications include "Commentary: The Crisis in Chad," *African Affairs,* 2006, 105 (420) and editing (with Oliver Furley) *Ending Africa's Wars* (Ashgate, 2006).

GILES MOHAN is Professor of International Development at the Open University. His research interests primarily concern the politics of development and the relationship between transnational networks and state development. He is currently focusing on China–Africa relations. His previous work includes "Chinese Migrants in Africa as New Agents of Development? An Analytical Framework," *European Journal of Development Research,* 2009, 21 (4) (with Tan-Mullins).

ABDULMUMINI A. OBA is a member of the Department of Jurisprudence and International Law at the University of Ilorin, Nigeria. He previously worked in legal practice and at the Law Office of the Ministry of Justice. He also writes on legal and social issues.

MARCUS POWER is Professor in the Department of Geography at Durham University. His research interests include development in a critical-theoretical context and postcolonialism with reference to Portugal and Lusophone Africa. He has authored *Rethinking Development Geographies* (Routledge, 2003) and published several articles in leading geographical journals including "Anti-racism, Deconstruction and Over-development," *Progress in Development Studies,* 2006, 6 (1) and "The Short Cut to International Development: Representing Africa in 'New Britain,'" *Area,* 2000, 31 (1).

GÉRARD PRUNIER is a social scientist who specialises in African affairs. His publications include *The Rwanda Crisis: History of a Genocide* (Columbia University Press, 1995) and *From Genocide to Continental War* (Hurst, 2009). His subsequent work focuses on his statelessness in Somalia since the fall of the Siad Barre regime.

NIKKI SLOCUM-BRADLEY is Research Fellow of the Institute for European Studies and Associate Research Fellow at the United Nations University Centre for Comparative Regional Integration Studies in Belgium. Her research encompasses a broad range of issues at the nexus of psychology, sociology, politics, and international relations. She has published in a variety of journals and books across disciplines and edited *Promoting Conflict or Peace through Identity* (Ashgate, 2008). She has also authored a variety of background papers for policy forums.

ELI STAMNES is Senior Researcher at the Norwegian Institute of International Affairs. She is working on the role of gender and the Global Responsibility to Protect. Recent work includes "'Speaking R2P' and the Prevention of Mass Atrocities," *Global Responsibility To Protect,* 2009, 1 (1) and 'The Responsibility To Protect: Integrating Gender Perspectives into Policies and Practices," *Global Responsibility To Protect,* 2012, 4 (2).

JOHN STOCKWELL was educated at the Presbyterian school in Lubondai before attending the University of Texas. After graduating, he joined the U.S. Marine Corps and later joined the Central Intelligence Agency. Stockwell spent several years working for the CIA in Africa before publishing *In Search of Enemies* (W. W. Norton, 1979), revealing much about the nature of U.S. clandestine operations in Africa at the height of the Cold War. Other work includes *The Praetorian Guard: The US Role in the New World Order* (South End Press, 1990).

NEWELL M. STULTZ is Professor Emeritus of Political Science at Brown University. His work centers on comparative politics with regionalist expertise on South Africa. Beyond his position at Brown University, Professor Stultz has also held positions at Northwestern University, Rhodes University (South Africa), and the University of South Africa. He has taught a wide variety of courses related to Africa over his career, with his more recent work including "Political Inclusion and Parliamentary Changes among Thirteen States in Former British Africa," *Africa Insight,* June 2006, 36 (2).

IAN TAYLOR is Professor in International Relations and African Politics in the School of International Relations, University of St. Andrews. He has authored and edited several books and published over sixty academic articles. Professor Taylor has presented his work in six continents and holds the position of Chair Professor in the School of International Studies, Renmin University of China, the highest rank a non-Chinese academic can hold at a Chinese university. His most recent work has been *The Forum on China-Africa Cooperation (FOCAC)* (Routledge, 2011).

THOMAS KWASI TIEKU is Assistant Professor of International Relations at the University of Toronto. His most recent work examines the changing nature of relations between the United States and the African continent, *U.S.-Africa Relations in the Age of Obama* (Cornell University Press, 2012). Other research interests include the African peace process and evaluating governance.

DANIEL VOLMAN is a scholar and activist who has published extensively on a diverse range of issues including U.S.–Africa relations, military involvement in Africa and Barack Obama's security policies with references to the region. He is Director of the African Security Research Project in Washington, DC, as well as being a member of the Association of Concerned Africa Scholars.

CAROLYN M. WARNER is Professor of Political Science, Arizona State University. She has taught a wide range of both undergraduate and postgraduate courses including Comparative Politics, Politics of the European Union, as well as Religion and Politics. A recent book was *The Best System Money Can Buy: Corruption in the European Union* (Cornell University Press, 2007).

ODD ARNE WESTAD is a historian in Norway. Professor Westad gained his PhD from the University of North Carolina at Chapel Hill and has held Visiting Fellowships at Cambridge University, Hong Kong University, and New York University. His book, *The Global Cold War: Third World Interventions and the Making of Our Times* (Cambridge University Press, 2006), won the 2006 Bancroft Prize and the Michael Harrington Prize of the American Political Science Association.

TOM YOUNG teaches politics and international relations at the School of Oriental and African Studies, University of London. He is the co-author (with Margaret Hall) of *Confronting Leviathan: Mozambique since Independence* (Hurst, 1997) and *Africa: A Beginner's Guide* (Oneworld Publications, 2010). He previously edited the companion volume to this, *Readings in African Politics* (James Currey and Indiana University Press, 2003).

INDEX

Note: Page numbers in *italics* refer to maps

CPSIA information can be obtained
at www.ICGtesting.com
Printed in the USA
JSHW031417260123
36790JS00003B/92